MAGILL'S QUOTATIONS
IN CONTEXT

LON-Z

Magill's
QUOTATIONS
in Context

Edited by
FRANK N. MAGILL

Associate Editor
TENCH FRANCIS TILGHMAN

VOLUME TWO—LON-Z

SALEM PRESS
INCORPORATED
ENGLEWOOD CLIFFS, N.J.

FIRST EDITION

Third Printing

LIBRARY OF CONGRESS CATALOG CARD NUMBER: 65-21011

PRINTED IN THE UNITED STATES OF AMERICA

ISBN 0-89356-132-0

A London particular

Source: BLEAK HOUSE (Chapter 3)
Author: Charles Dickens (1812-1870)
First published: 1853
Type of work: Novel

Context: Esther Summerson has been reared by a woman, Miss Barbary, who calls herself the girl's godmother, but who is really her aunt. Esther is an illegitimate child, the issue of a love affair between Miss Barbary's sister and a Captain Hawdon. Ashamed of her sister's sin and of the child's existence, her guardian never tells her of her parents and forces her to live a cheerless life. Miss Barbary's death frees Esther from fourteen years of close confinement, and she spends the next six years leading a more normal life at a private school. When she is twenty, her benefactor, John Jarndyce, brings her to London to serve as companion to his young cousin, Ada Clare. Esther, who has never known anything but the quiet life of the counties, is overwhelmed at her first sight of London, and especially by the dense, dirty fog which fills the streets. The man who had come to welcome her tells her that it is a peculiar characteristic of the city.

> . . . I asked him whether there was a great fire anywhere? For the streets were so full of dense brown smoke that scarcely anything was to be seen.
> "O dear no, miss," he said. "This is **a London particular.**"
> I had never heard of such a thing.
> "A fog, miss," said the young gentleman.

The lonely of heart is withered away

Source: THE LAND OF HEART'S DESIRE
Author: William Butler Yeats (1865-1939)
First published: 1894
Type of work: Dramatic fantasy

Context: Mary Bruin, wife of Shawn Bruin, spends her time reading "an old book" written by the Bruin Grandfather and in day-dreaming. She hears and sees a Faery Child who has come to try to steal her soul. Despite the advice of the older and "wiser" people, Mary invites the Child into the house and feeds her. Then begins a conflict between this world and that of the Faeries. Mary wants to go to Faery-land, where all is peaceful and beautiful, but she loves Shawn and wants to stay with him. Running through the play is the motif of the beauties of the land of heart's desire. It is stated by The Voice before it becomes recognizable

587

as The Child's, by The Child, and by "many voices singing." The beauty and tone of the poem can be illus- trated by quoting some of the lines sung by these "many voices":

> The wind blows out of the gates of the day,
> The wind blows over the lonely of heart,
> And **the lonely of heart is withered away;**
> While the faeries dance in a place apart,
> Shaking their milk-white feet in a ring,
> Tossing their milk-white arms in the air;
> For they hear the wind laugh, and murmur and sing
> Of a land where even the old are fair,
> And even the wise are merry of tongue . . .

The long arm of the law

Source: HISTORY OF THE PERSIAN WARS (Book VIII, "Urania," chapter 140)
Author: Herodotus (c.484-425 B.C.)
First transcribed: c. 430 B.C.
Type of work: Historical commentary on the Persian Wars

Context: In Book VIII of his *History of the Persian Wars,* Herodotus gives an account of Xerxes' march into Athens and the destroying by fire of the Acropolis. Too, he gives a vivid account of the Athenian victory a Sal- amis, and the confusion occasioned by Artemis' sinking of Xerxes' ship. After Xerxes' retreat to the Asian mainland, the Great King sent a famous letter to the Greeks.

> "I forgive the Athenians all the injuries committed by them against me. . . . And now I say this: Why are you so mad to levy war against the king? . . . For the power of the king is more than human, and **his arm is exceeding long.** . . . Be persuaded, then; for this is a high honor to you, that the great king, forgiving your offenses alone among all Greeks, is willing to become your friend."

A long farewell to all my greatness

Source: KING HENRY THE EIGHTH (Act III, sc. ii, l. 351)
Author: William Shakespeare (1564-1616)
First published: 1623
Type of work: Historical drama

Context: Cardinal Wolsey is an arrogant, overbearing, ambitious, and un- scrupulous adviser to King Henry the Eighth of England. He is conniving secretly for an alliance with France, and urges the king to divorce his wife of twenty years, Katharine of Aragon. Wolsey hopes the king will then marry the Duchess of Alençon, but the king falls in love with a Protestant, Anne Bullen, instead. In alarm, Wolsey writes the pope to delay the divorce. A copy of this letter and an inventory of the great wealth which Wolsey has amassed fall into the king's hands. Confronted with these evidences of his double-dealing and grasping ambition, and deprived of his offices by an irate king and jealous courtiers, Wolsey sadly contemplates the precarious nature of worldly greatness.

WOLSEY

• • •

Farewell? **A long farewell to all my greatness.**
This is the state of man: to-day he puts forth
The tender leaves of hope; to-morrow blossoms,
And bears his blushing honours thick upon him;
The third day comes a frost, a killing frost,
And when he thinks, good easy man, full surely
His greatness is a-ripening, nips his root,
And then he falls as I do.

• • •

And when he falls, he falls like Lucifer,
Never to hope again.

Long is the way and hard, that out of hell leads up to light

Source: PARADISE LOST (Book II, ll. 432-433)
Author: John Milton (1608-1674)
First published: 1667
Type of work: Epic poem

Context: At the end of the grand council at Pandemonium, in Hell, the rebel angels vote to try to spite the Divine Will by seducing the new creation, man, to their party, as Beelzebub has advised. None of the fallen angels is willing, however, to risk the journey to find out if the prophecy of Heaven has been fulfilled: that a new universe with man as its famed inhabitant has been brought into existence. Satan alone dares the task, and he arises to take it upon himself to try to escape Hell in order to investigate the matter for his followers. He knows that what he will attempt will not be easy, and he says:

"O progeny of heaven, empyreal thrones,
With reason hath deep silence and demur
Seized us, though undismayed: **long is the way
And hard, that out of hell leads up to light;**

589

Our prison strong, this huge convex of fire,
Outrageous to devour, immures us round
Ninefold, and gates of burning adamant
Barred over us prohibit all egress."

Look a gift horse in the mouth

Source: GARGANTUA AND PANTAGRUEL (Book I, chapter 2)
Author: François Rabelais (1495-1553)
First published: 1532-1564
Type of work: Mock heroic chronicle

Context: Gargantua, the gigantic son of Grangosier and Gargamelle, was physically precocious as a youth, although his actions differed more in degree than in kind from those of other youngsters. "He was continually wallowing and rolling up and down in the mire." Rabelais also has him experiment with and apparently believe in all the superstitions of his day. He also literally breathes the clichés and commonplaces. The one about the gift horse was used by John Heywood in *Proverbes,* (1546), Part I, chapter 5, by Cervantes in *Don Quixote,* Part II (1615), Book IV, chapter 62, and widely later on. Rabelais says:

He took the cranes at the first leap, and would have the mail-coats to be made link after link. He always **looked a gift horse in the mouth**, . . .

Look before you leap

Source: THE PROVERBS OF JOHN HEYWOOD (Part I, chapter 2)
Author: John Heywood (1497?-1580?)
First published: 1546
Type of work: Gnomic poem

Context: In the Preface, the author says that proverbs are useful to "both old and young." He is including as many in his work as he can remember, not to teach anybody but merely to remind people of these "plain pithy proverbs old." In Chapter 2 he is talking with a friend, a "certain young man," who asks whom he should marry, a "maid of flowering age, a goodly one," or a "widow, who so many years bears,/ That all her whiteness lieth in her white hairs." The author tells his friend that he does indeed do well to seek advice before marrying, for this particular act demands caution. In a bit of proverbial wisdom common in England and America. the author rounds off his advice to his young friend:

590

And though they seem wives for you never so fit,
Yet let not harmful haste so far outrun your wit
But that ye hark to hear all the whole sum
That may please or displease you in time to come.
Thus, by these lessons, ye may learn good cheap
In wedding and all thing to **look or ye leap.**

Look for me in the nurseries of Heaven

Source: TO MY GODCHILD (Stanza 3)
Author: Francis Thompson (1859-1907)
First published: 1891
Type of work: Lyric poem

Context: The Catholic poet Francis Thompson knew both abject poverty and almost complete isolation from society. He was found destitute by the editor Wilfrid Meynell into whose hands some of Thompson's poetry had come. Meynell took the poet in and, together with his wife Alice Meynell, gave him friendship and encouragement. "To My Godchild" is written to the Meynell's son Francis. In the poem the poet expresses the warmth that the birth of the child has brought to him. He hopes that his name will give his godson "a poet's power"; yet he wishes the child to take his legacy from others far greater. The poet says: "My song I do but hold for you in trust,/ I ask you but to blossom from my dust." Even after death the poet will still watch over his godchild through "a golden crevice in the sky,/ Which I have pierced but to behold you by!" When the godchild dies, the poet says that he should not look for his godfather among the "bearded counsellors of God," nor among the younger poets, but among the "nurseries of Heaven." The final lines of the poem read:

. . .

Pass by where wait, young poet-wayfarer,
Your cousined clusters, emulous to share
With you the roseal lightnings burning 'mid their hair;
Pass the crystalline sea, the Lampads seven:—
Look for me in the nurseries of Heaven.

Look homeward, Angel!

Source: LYCIDAS (Line 163)
Author: John Milton (1608-1674)
First published: 1637
Type of work: Elegiac pastoral poem

Context: John Milton, in mourning the death of Lycidas—Edward King —tells the river god Alpheus to bid all the flowers of the fields to wilt and

591

die in sympathy. He then speculates where the body of King may be—in the waters of the stormy Hebrides off the western coast of Scotland or in the seas off Land's End in Cornwall. Near Land's End is St. Michael's Mount, a rock off the south coast of England markedly similar to Mont St. Michel in France; the English mount looks toward the coast of Spain. The reference to St. Michael's Mount brings up the idea of the archangel Michael, the guardian angel who spoke to Moses on the mount. Milton tells him to look homeward, toward England, away from possible foreign threats, to the disaster at home; he conjures him to melt in pity for the death of Lycidas. Thomas Wolfe (1900-1938) uses the phrase ironically as the title for his novel (1929). Finally in accordance with an old superstition still current among sailors to the effect that dolphins, or porpoises, push drowned people to shore with their noses, Milton asks them to bring home the hapless Lycidas. He says:

Look homeward, Angel! now, and melt with ruth:
And, O ye Dolphins, waft the hapless youth.

Look within

Source: MEDITATIONES (Book VI, 3)
Author: Marcus Aurelius Antoninus (121-180)
First transcribed: Second century
Type of work: Private meditations

Context: Marcus Aurelius wrote down his inner thoughts in seemingly private meditations. They are direct, bare, and at times disconnected. In Book VI, he begins by saying, "The Universal Substance is docile and ductile; and the Reason that controls it has no motive in itself to do wrong." He then counsels that one should do his duty in all acts of life, even dying. "So it is enough in this also to get the work in hand done well." He then urges close and perceptive observation:

Look within. Let not the special quality or worth of anything escape thee.

The Lord gave, and the Lord hath taken away

Source: JOB 1:21
Author: Unknown
First transcribed: c.900-500 B.C.
Type of work: Religious saga

Context: Job, of the land of Uz, a man who is "perfect and upright" and who fears God and eschews evil, is the father of seven sons and three daughters and the owner of seven thousand sheep, three thousand camels, five hundred yoke of oxen, and five hundred she asses. In a dialogue with God, Satan argues that Job has always been protected and blessed by the Almighty and that adversity would cause Job to curse Him. God grants Satan permission to test Job with the single restriction that he not harm Job himself. Job then receives the information from four messengers that all of his animals and his sons and daughters have either been taken by his enemies or destroyed by natural causes. On receipt of the information, Job grieves and says that he will return to the earth as he had come:

Then Job arose, and rent his mantle, and shaved his head, and fell down upon the ground, and worshipped,
And said, Naked came I out of my mother's womb, and naked shall I return thither: **the Lord gave, and the Lord hath taken away;** blessed be the name of the Lord.
In all this Job sinned not, nor charged God foolishly.

Lord, how long?

Source: ISAIAH 6:11
Author: Isaiah
First transcribed: c.800-200 B.C.
Type of work: Religious prophecy and exhortation

Context: Prophet of the Almighty, Isaiah declares the vision of "Judah and Jerusalem in the days of Uzziah, Jotham, Ahaz, and Hezekiah, kings of Judah." Proclaiming the Lord's awareness of the wickedness of the Israelites and warning them of the coming destruction, he relates his vision of the Almighty in the year that King Uzziah dies. God is on His throne, surrounded by seraphim who praise His name. Although Isaiah feels himself unworthy to look upon such magnificence, one of the seraphim purifies him with a coal from the altar. When the Lord asks, "Whom shall I send?," Isaiah answers that he will willingly serve the Creator. The Lord then tells Isaiah to speak to the Israelites although they will refuse to hear or understand. Isaiah asks the duration of his role as spokesman of the Lord:

Then said I, **Lord, how long?** And he answered, Until the cities be wasted without inhabitant, and the houses without man, and the land be utterly desolate,
 And the Lord have removed men far away, and there be a great forsaking in the midst of the land.

Lord of himself

Source: THE CHARACTER OF A HAPPY LIFE (Stanza 6)
Author: Sir Henry Wotton (1568-1639)
First published: 1657
Type of work: Lyric poem

Context: In "The Character of a Happy Life" Sir Henry Wotton presents the idea that the truly happy man is the one who has manifold virtues instead of great possessions. He does not serve another person's will, but lives in accordance with his honest thoughts and follows simple truth. His reason is never overmastered by passion; he so lives that he is always spiritually prepared for death. He never envies those who rise in the world, especially if their rise is the result of chance or vice; praise of another does not sadden him. He pays no attention to common rumors; his conscience is free, and neither flatterers nor accusers can cause him pain. When he prays to God, he asks rather for grace than for possessions; he spends his innocent days in the company of friends or in reading good books. He is unambitious, neither hoping to rise in the world nor fearing that fortune will cast him down. By being his own man he has far more than does he who has only material possessions. The concluding stanza of the poem is:

> This man is free from servile bands
> Of hope to rise or fear to fall,
> **Lord of himself,** though not of lands,
> And having nothing, yet hath all.

Lost Angel of a ruined Paradise!

Source: ADONAIS (Stanza 10)
Author: Percy Bysshe Shelley (1792-1822)
First published: 1821
Type of work: Elegy

Context: Adonais is "An Elegy on the Death of John Keats." Shelley's thesis is that Keats was killed by the critics who wrote scathing reviews of *Endymion.* The title of the elegy suggests a parallel with Adonis, the beautiful young man (Keats) who was slaughtered by a boar (the critics). Like the classical elegies, *Adonais* contains pastoral elements. "Oh, weep for Adonais—he is dead!" Shelley moans. He calls on Urania, the Mother of poets, to mourn the death of her son. Shelley describes the beauties of Rome, where Keats died. Then he calls on Keats's "quick Dreams,/ The passion-wingéd Ministers of thought," to mourn the loss of the genius that gave birth to them. These fertile thoughts, which could have kindled many minds, will die along with their author. One of the beautiful thoughts comes and grieves:

> And one with trembling hands clasps his cold head,
> And fans him with her moonlight wings, and cries;
> "Our love, our hope, our sorrow, is not dead;
> See, on the silken fringe of his faint eyes,
> Like dew upon a sleeping flower, there lies
> A tear some Dream has loosened from his brain."
> **Lost Angel of a ruined Paradise!**
> She knew not 'twas her own; as with no stain
> She faded, like a cloud which had outwept its rain.

The loud laugh that spoke the vacant mind

Source: THE DESERTED VILLAGE (Line 122)
Author: Oliver Goldsmith (1728-1774)
First published: 1770
Type of work: Didactic and descriptive poem

Context: In the happier days of Auburn, the village of the poem, the people lived wholesomely, gaining from their labor only what life required. The countryman's best companions were "innocence and health; / And his best riches, ignorance of wealth. / But times are alter'd; trade's unfeeling train/ Usurp the land and dispossess the swain." The poet then moves on to a recollection of the happy sounds of evening in those earlier days:

> The mingling notes came soften'd from below;
> The swain responsive as the milk-maid sung,
> The sober herd that low'd to meet their young;
> The noisy geese that gabbled o'er the pool,
> The playful children just let loose from school;
> The watchdog's voice that bay'd the whisp'ring wind,
> And **the loud laugh that spoke the vacant mind;**
> These all in sweet confusion sought the shade,
> And fill'd each pause the nightingale had made.

Love all, trust a few

Source: ALL'S WELL THAT ENDS WELL (Act I, sc. i, l. 73)
Author: William Shakespeare (1564-1616)
First published: 1623
Type of work: Dramatic comedy

Context: Bertram, Count of Rousillon, is about to depart for service at the Court of France. His mother, recently widowed, gives him advice and her blessing. (It is interesting to compare the countess' brief speech of advice and farewell here with Polonius' lengthy discourse as he says goodbye to his son Laertes in *Hamlet*. Inasmuch as the plays' dates of composition are close together, and Shakespeare was near the apex of his career, the difference between the speeches is a clear example of how the bard gave the stamp of individuality to his characters.)

COUNTESS

Be thou blessed, Bertram, and succeed thy father
In manners, as in shape. Thy blood and virtue
Contend for empire in thee, and thy goodness
Share with thy birthright. **Love all, trust a few,**
Do wrong to none.

• • •

Be checked for silence,
But never taxed for speech.

• • •

Farewell my lord.

• • •

Love bade me welcome

Source: THE TEMPLE ("Love," II, stanza 1)
Author: George Herbert (1593-1633)
First published: 1633
Type of work: Religious poem

Context: In "Love" the speaker says that when he appears at a gathering he is welcomed by Love, but his soul draws back from entering because his soul is begrimed by sin. Love, seeing that he is abashed, asks him if there is anything he wants. He replies that he wants to be a worthy guest, and Love assures him that he will be. The speaker says that he has been so unkind and ungrateful that he is not worthy even to look upon Love; when, however, Love says that he made the eyes, the speaker confesses to having marred them by looking upon the wrong things. In his misery he says that he should go where he belongs, but Love says that someone else took upon himself all the blame for the speaker's wrongdoing and invites him to sit down at the table, where he is fed. The poem means that Christ's love, which assumes man's sins, welcomes the soul, even though sinful, to the spiritual feast in Heaven. The poem begins thus:

Love bade me welcome; yet my soul drew back,
    Guilty of dust and sin;
But quick-eyed Love, observing me grow slack
    From my first entrance in,
Drew nearer to me, sweetly questioning,
    If I lacked anything.

596

Love conquers all

Source: ECLOGUES (X, l. 69)
Author: Virgil (70-19 B.C.)
First transcribed: c.40-37 B.C.
Type of work: Pastoral poem

Context: In this poem, Virgil calls upon the muse to help him write about a friend, Gallus, whose mistress has deserted him. Virgil tells how the mountains, the plants, the animals, the shepherds and swineherds, even the pastoral gods, mourn for the unhappy lover. Gallus is compelled to recognize the tyranny of the god of love. He knows he can find no solace in activities that once brought him joy. He says:

"As if this could heal my frenzy, or as if that god could learn pity for human sorrows! Now once more, nor Hamadryads nor even songs have charms for me; once more adieu, even ye woods! No toils of ours can change that god. . . . **Love conquers all** (*omnia amor vincit*); let us, too, yield to Love!"

Love is blind

Source: THE CANTERBURY TALES ("The Merchant's Tale," Line 1598)
Author: Geoffrey Chaucer (1343?-1400)
First transcribed: c.1393-1400
Type of work: Collection of tales

Context: The old Italian knight named January has determined to get married to a young girl, not over twenty. Against the advice of some of his friends, but with that of others, he worries about whom he should marry. "Many fair shap and many a fair visage/ Ther passeth thurgh his herte nyght by nyght." Finally he chooses one. And having chosen her, he naturally thinks she is the best in the world.

For **love is blynd** alday, and may nat see.
And whan that he was in his bed ybroght,
He purtreyed in his herte and in his thoght
Hir fresshe beautee and hir age tendre,
Hir myddel smal, hire armes longe and selendre,
Hir wise governaunce, hir gentillesse,
Hir wommanly berynge, and hire sadnesse.

Love is blind

Source: THE MERCHANT OF VENICE (Act II, sc. vi, 1. 36)
Author: William Shakespeare (1564-1616)
First published: 1600
Type of work: Dramatic comedy

Context: Lorenzo, a Venetian Christian, is in love with Jessica, daughter of the Jew usurer Shylock. They plan to elope. To assist them, two friends, Gratiano and Salerio, meet before Shylock's house. Lorenzo is late in arriving, but he finally comes. Jessica appears above, in boy's clothes. She then descends, bearing a chest of her father's wealth. Then she speaks to her lover:

JESSICA
Here, catch this casket, it is worth the pains.
I am glad 'tis night, you do not look on me,
For I am much ashamed of my exchange.
But **love is blind,** and lovers cannot see
The pretty follies that themselves commit;
. . .

Love is noght old as whan that it is newe

Source: THE CANTERBURY TALES ("The Clerk's Tale," Line 858)
Author: Geoffrey Chaucer (1343?-1400)
First transcribed: c.1393-1400
Type of work: Collection of tales

Context: This is the ancient folk tale, drawn from a number of medieval sources, of Patient Griselde, or Grisildis as Chaucer recounts it. At the end of the story concerning the trials the noble husband set for his peasant wife, Chaucer has his clerk say, "No wedded man so hardy be t'assaille/ His wyves pacience, in hope to fynde/ Grisildis, for in certain he shall faille!" In the episode from which the quotation is taken, this "flour of wyfly pacience" is most sorely tried when her lord and master announces that he will send her home to the humble cottage without even the dress on her back, and finally threatens to replace her with a new wife. She meekly accepts his commands and replies to him:

But sooth is seyde, algate I find it trewe—
For in effect it preved is on me—
Love is noght old as whan that it is newe.
But, certes, lord, for noon adversitee,
To dyen in the cas it shal not be
. . .

Love me, love my dog

Source: THE PROVERBS OF JOHN HEYWOOD (Part II, chapter 9)
Author: John Heywood (1497?-1580?)
First published: 1546
Type of work: Gnomic poetry

Context: The author is telling, while quoting as many proverbs as possible, the story of a young man who married for money instead of for love, and thereby fell upon thorns, for almost immediately he discovered that he could not satisfy his old ex-widow wife, and as a consequence she nagged him so much that he was forced to seek solace away from home. In seeking this solace he spent her money so freely that within three years he had run through it all. He was forced therefore to come home to her and to try to arrange a reconciliation. The wife, however, reminds him of his former ill treatment of her:

> And sure one of my great griefs, among many,
> Is that ye have been so very a hog
> To my friends. What, man? love me, love my dog!
> But you, to cast precious stones before hogs,
> Cast my good before a sort of cur dogs
> And salt bitches. . . .

The love of money is the root of all evil

Source: I TIMOTHY 6:10
Author: Unknown
First transcribed: 61-180
Type of work: Pastoral epistle

Context: The writer, perhaps Paul, but probably a pseudonymous writer using Paul's name, sends this pastoral letter to Timothy, perhaps Paul's friend in Christ, but probably another church official. Admonishing his fellow preacher to preserve the true doctrine, he declares that the Christian is redeemed by Christ, not the law, which, however, is still valuable for the unrighteous. Proclaiming Christianity as the faith for all men, he describes the good bishop, the good deacon, the role of the Church, and the place of the elder. The false teachers having been condemned, the writer urges his friend to remain apart from them and to place no emphasis on worldly possessions, which bring only sorrow:

> For we brought nothing into this world, and it is certain we can carry nothing out.
> And having food and raiment, let us be therewith content.

• • •

For **the love of money is the root of all evil:** which while some covet after, they have erred from the faith, and pierced themselves through with many sorrows.

Love seeketh only Self to please

Source: SONGS OF EXPERIENCE ("The Clod and the Pebble," Stanza 3)
Author: William Blake (1757-1827)
First published: 1794
Type of work: Lyric poem

Context: When Blake published *Songs of Experience* in the same volume with *Songs of Innocence,* he added the significant subtitle: *Shewing the Two Contrary States of the Human Soul.* Professor Ernest Bernbaum remarks: "In this second state, Man and his World have fallen away from their original innocence and joy. Materialism is a barrier against their return. To childhood, experience often proves dark, cruel, sinister, or tyrannous"—*Anthology of Romanticism* (1948), p. 1088. In this lyric the idealistic state of innocence concerning love is voiced by the Clod, with the cynical, cold, and realistic reply of experience spoken by the Pebble. To the Clod's assertion that love is selfless and self-sacrificing, the Pebble replies that, in reality, love is selfish and sadistic:

"Love seeketh not itself to please,
Nor for itself has any care,
But for another gives its ease,
And builds a Heaven in Hell's despair."

So sung a little Clod of Clay,
Trodden with the cattle's feet,
But a Pebble of the brook
Warbled out these metres meet:

"Love seeketh only Self to please,
To bind another to its delight,
Joys in another's loss of ease,
And builds a Hell in Heaven's despite."

Love sought is good, but given unsought is better

Source: TWELFTH NIGHT (Act III, sc. i, 1. 168)
Author: William Shakespeare (1564-1616)
First published: 1623
Type of work: Dramatic comedy

Context: Viola, on a sea voyage with her twin brother, Sebastian, is shipwrecked on the seacoast of Illyria. Convinced that her brother has been drowned, she determines to serve temporarily the ruler of Illyria, Duke Orsino, in the guise of a eunuch and under the name of Cesario. The duke employs her thus to press his suit for the hand of the Countess Olivia, who does not love him and who has put him off by pleading mourning for a dead brother. Viola-Cesario, with an entourage, calls at Olivia's home, gains admittance, and attempts to persuade Olivia of the duke's devotion. Olivia rejects the duke but realizes that she has fallen in love with the messenger, believing Viola to be a man. Now, on Viola-Cesario's second visit, Olivia confesses her love, and in an attempt to persuade an angry and perplexed Viola she argues:

OLIVIA
. . .

Cesario, by the roses of the spring,
By maidhood, honour, truth, and every thing,
I love thee so, that, maugre all thy pride,
Nor wit, nor reason, can my passion hide.
Do not extort thy reasons from this clause,
For that I woo, thou therefore hast no cause.
But rather reason thus with reason fetter;
Love sought is good, but given unsought is better.

Love, that in gentle heart is quickly learnt

Source: THE DIVINE COMEDY, INFERNO (Canto V, 1. 100, as translated by H. F. Cary)
Author: Dante Alighieri (1265-1321)
First transcribed: c.1314
Type of work: Christian allegory

Context: After passing over the Acheron into Hell proper, Dante observes those who love not God and must perforce traverse the river. The poet faints at the sights and sounds which greet him, and he is aroused by thunder and urged by Virgil, to move downward ring by ring. The first circle is Limbo, where all the ancient, virtuous pre-christian souls must stay forever. The second is for carnal sinners, who are tossed forever by furious winds. Here Dante talks to Francesca of Rimini: "O gracious creature and benign! . . . will we hear of that?" He asks her for the story of her fatal love for her brother-in-law, Paolo Malatesta. She replies:

Love, that in gentle heart is quickly learnt,
Entangle him by that fair form, from me
Ta'en in such cruel sort, as grieves me still:
Love, that denial takes from none belovéd,
Caught me with pleasing him so passing well
That, as thou seest, he yet deserts me not.

• • •

Love that moves the sun

Source: THE DIVINE COMEDY, PARADISO (Canto XXXIII, l. 145, as translated by H. F. Cary)
Author: Dante Alighieri (1265-1321)
First transcribed: c.1320
Type of work: Christian allegory

Context: In these, the final lines of one of the world's supreme works of beauty, power, and wisdom, Dante focuses his belief on the central tenet of the Christian faith: *L'amor che move il sole e l'altre stelle.* The occasion is the contemplation of the brightness of the Divine Majesty, the glimpse of the great mystery of the Trinity, the union of man with God.

Here vigour fail'd the towering fantasy:
But yet the will roll'd onward, like a wheel
In even motion, by the **Love** impell'd,
That moves the sun in Heaven and all the stars.

The lover rooted stays

Source: FRIENDSHIP
Author: Ralph Waldo Emerson (1803-1882)
First published: 1841
Type of work: Lyric poem

Context: Emerson glorifies the value of friendship in this poem, which was originally published as the motto of the essay "Friendship." True friendship is more stable than anything else in the world. A good friend gives meaning to life and makes the world seem beautiful: "Through thee alone the sky is arched,/ Through thee the rose is red;/ All things through thee take nobler form . . . The mill-round of our fate appears/ A sun-path in thy worth." The friend has inspired the poet: "Me too thy nobleness has taught/ To master my despair;/ The fountains of my hidden life/ Are through thy friendship fair." The poet learns that true friendship is magnificently constant:

> A ruddy drop of manly blood
> The surging sea outweighs,
> The world uncertain comes and goes;
> **The lover rooted stays.**
> I fancied he was fled,—
> And, after many a year,
> Glowed unexhausted kindliness,
> Like daily sunrise there.

Love's the ambassador of loss

Source: TO OLIVIA (Line 2)
Author: Francis Thompson (1859-1907)
First published: 1908
Type of work: Lyric poem

Context: Francis Thompson spent a number of years of his life solitary, friendless, and poverty-stricken. When he was taken in by Wilfrid Meynell, an editor, and the editor's wife Alice, he experienced genuine friendship and family warmth. Some of his poems were written to the Meynell children. "To Olivia" reflects not only the poet's destitute past, devoid of love, but also his fear of allowing love to enter his heart again. The poet's metaphorical presentation of love as "shy snow" expresses this apprehension. Yet it is the snow-like quality of the child's affection that appeals to the poet. "My heart," he says, ". . . would fear thee not at all,/ Wert thou not so harmless-small." The naturalness of the child, which the poet calls "thy arrows . . . still unbarbed with destined fire," does more to draw his love than if he had before him the same person "Full-panoplied in womanhood." The opening lines of the poem read:

> I fear to love thee, Sweet, because
> **Love's the ambassador of loss;**
> White flake of childhood, clinging so
> To my soiled raiment, thy shy snow
> At tenderest touch will shrink and go.

Love's young dream

Source: LOVE'S YOUNG DREAM
Author: Thomas Moore (1779-1852)
First published: 1811
Type of work: Song

Context: Moore's *Irish Melodies* were written to be sung, not read as poetry. In fact, Moore was very reluctant to have them printed without the music, and consented only because a pirated edition, replete with errors, was already on the market. Like most songs, the *Irish Melodies* are more notable for the sweetness of the language and the harmony of the rhythm than for any depth of thought. Moore said of them: "I am better able to vouch for the sound than for the sense." The line quoted is from a lament for the time when the poet was young and could give his whole life to love. The tone is nostalgic rather than sad. The song begins:

> Oh! the days are gone, when Beauty bright
>   My heart's chain wove;
> When my dream of life, from morn till night,
>   Was love, still love.
> New hope may bloom,
> And days may come,
> Of milder, calmer beam,
> But there's nothing half so sweet in life
> As **love's young dream.**

Luxurious lobster-nights, farewell

Source: A FAREWELL TO LONDON (Stanza 12)
Author: Alexander Pope (1688-1744)
First published: 1715
Type of work: Satire

Context: Though he satirizes bluntly, even crudely, in this poem, it would appear that Pope, upon contemplating retirement into the country to work on his translations of Homer, had mixed emotions. He loved the London life, though he could see the weaknesses and the sins of his friends and acquaintances. Though some persons, like Earl Warwick, are treated harshly, the poet speaks fondly of others: "Farewell Arbuthnot's raillery/ On every learned sot;/ And Garth, the best good Christian he,/ Although he knows it not." And though he could satirize town life and its endless round of activities, Pope knew the pleasures of city tables, both public and private, including the table of Richard Boyle, Earl of Burlington, known for his tastes:

Luxurious lobster-nights, farewell,
For sober, studious days!
And Burlington's delicious meal,
For salads, tarts, and pease!

Mad March hare

Source: REPLICATION AGAINST CERTAIN YOUNG SCHOLARS (Line 35)
Author: John Skelton (c.1460-1529)
First published: Original edition undated, c.1528
Type of work: Satiric poem

Context: In this Replication (reply) to the Cambridge heretics, Skelton reviles the Lutheran Protestants for, among other things, preaching that it is "idolatry to offer to images of our Blessed Lady." The reference to the mad March hare is also in John Heywood's *Proverbes* (1546), Part II, Chapter 5. Skelton addresses the Protestants with anger:

I say, thou **mad March hare,**
I wonder how ye dare
Open your jingling jaws
To preach in any clause,
Like prating popping daws,
Against her excellence

• • •

That never did offence.

Majestic though in ruin

Source: PARADISE LOST (Book II, l. 305)
Author: John Milton (1608-1674)
First published: 1667
Type of work: Epic poem

Context: At the grand council of the rebel angels in Hell, following their expulsion from Heaven, Satan calls for discussion of the future course of action. Moloch pleads for guerrilla warfare; Belial suggests mere endurance of Hell; Mammon calls for peace. Then Beelzebub, the Lord of the Flies, as his name means in Hebrew, rises to address the assembled leaders of the rebels and their followers. He is next to Satan himself in importance and has been earlier in Heaven an angel of great rank; he still retains much of his majesty, even in Hell, and so Milton describes him as he rises to address the hellish crew:

. . . in his rising seemed
A pillar of state; deep on his front engraven
Deliberation sat and public care;
And princely counsel in his face yet shone,
Majestic though in ruin: sage he stood
With Atlantean shoulders fit to bear
The weight of mightiest monarchies; his look
Drew audience and attention . . .

Make a virtue of necessity

Source: INSTITUTIO ORATORIA (Book I, VIII, 14)
Author: Quintilian (c.35-c.95)
First transcribed: c.85
Type of work: Handbook of Oratory

Context: Quintilian expresses his views on teaching literature, rhetoric and oratory. In Book I he discusses elementary education and the necessity of teaching such great poets as Homer and Virgil early, even if the pupils are not able to understand fully; the boys will reread these authors "for the love of letters and the value of reading are not confined to one's schooldays but end only with life." In teaching literature, the teacher should analyze the parts of speech, the poetic meter of prose as well as of poetry. "To make virtue of necessity," is proverbial. It is used by Chaucer: *Troilus and Criseyde* (1372-1386), Book IV, 1. 1586; by Rabelais: *Works*, Book V, chapter 23 (1552); by Robert Burton: *Anatomy of Melancholy*, Part III, Sec. 3, Memb. 4, Subsect. I (1621-1651). Quintilian uses the proverb in this context: In studying the works of the poets, the teacher

. . . will point out what words are barbarous, what improperly used, and what are contrary to the laws of language. He will not do this by way of censuring the poets for such peculiarities, for poets are usually the servants of their metres and are allowed such license that faults are given other names when they occur in poetry: for we style them *metaplasms, schematisms* and *schemata,* as I have said, and **make a virtue of necessity.**

Make hay while the sun shines

Source: THE PROVERBS OF JOHN HEYWOOD (Part I, chapter 3)
Author: John Heywood (1497?-1580?)
First published: 1546
Type of work: Gnomic poetry

Context: A young friend has asked the author if he should marry "a maid of flowering age, a goodly one," or a "widow, who so many years bears, /

That all her whiteness lieth in her white hairs." The author has answered by bringing to mind all the "plain pithy proverbs" which have served "both old and young" to caution them to approach marriage on leaden feet. The friend admits the wisdom of these proverbs, but he urges that against these sayings he can advance "other parables, of like weighty weight, / Which haste me to wedding, as ye shall hear straight." He then provides some examples:

> . . . a thousandfold would it grieve me more
> That she, in my fault, should die one hour before
> Than one minute after; then haste must provoke,
> When the pig is proffered to hold up the poke.
> **When the sun shineth make hay;** which is to say,
> Take time when time cometh, lest time steal away.

Malefactors of great wealth

Source: THERE WILL BE NO CHANGE IN POLICY (Speech at Provincetown, Massachusetts)
Author: Theodore Roosevelt (1858-1919)
First published: 1907
Type of work: Speech

Context: In his address in Provincetown, Massachusetts, at the laying of the cornerstone of the Pilgrim Memorial Monument, on August 20, 1907, President Theodore Roosevelt reaffirms the government's determination to bring civil and criminal action against corporations and the wealthy men directing them when the corporations and their directors violate the Sherman laws dealing with monopolies and combinations. The President agrees that possibly the government action is in part responsible for the trouble with the stock market but only because certain men have combined to create financial stress so as to discredit the Government's policy and bring about its reversal. Concerning the matter, Roosevelt says:

> . . . On the New York Stock Exchange the disturbance has been peculiarly severe. Most of it I believe to be due to matters not peculiar to the United States, and most of the remainder to matters wholly unconnected with any governmental action; but it may well be that the determination of the Government (in which, gentlemen, it will not waver) to punish certain **malefactors of great wealth** has been responsible for something of the trouble; . . .

Malt does more than Milton can

Source: A SHROPSHIRE LAD (LXII, stanza 2)
Author: A(lfred) E(dward) Housman (1859-1936)
First published: 1896
Type of work: Lyric poem

Context: A. E. Housman's original title for *A Shropshire Lad* was *Poems by Terence Hearsay,* Terence being an imaginary farm lad who supposedly lived in the county of Shropshire. Housman develops the poem beginning " 'Terence, this is stupid stuff:' " by means of a dialog between Terence and his friend. The friend finds Terence drinking his beer rapidly, and, commenting on Terence's poetry, says, "Come, pipe a tune to dance to, lad." Terence's response is that there are better things to dance to than poetry. He first asks, "Say, for what were hop-yards meant?"; then in answer to his question he praises the power that beer has to make a man see a different kind of world. But Terence knows that the world of alcoholic spirits is an illusory one and that "The mischief is that 'twill not last." He explains that after a drinking bout, he sobers up to find that it is "the old world yet" and that he must "begin the game anew." In showing the advantage of alcohol over poetry, Terence says:

> Oh many a peer of England brews
> Livelier liquor than the Muse,
> And **malt does more than Milton can**
> To justify God's ways to man.
> Ale, man, ale's the stuff to drink
> For fellows whom it hurts to think: . . .

Mammon wins his way where Seraphs might despair

Source: CHILDE HAROLD'S PILGRIMAGE (Canto I, stanza 9)
Author: George Gordon, Lord Byron (1788-1824)
First published: 1812 (Cantos I and II)
Type of work: Narrative poem in Spenserian stanzas

Context: Even as a youth, Byron formed strong emotional attachments which frequently ended in disillusionment. The Cambridge friends he gathered about him at Newstead Abbey showed no sorrow at the imminence of his departure, in 1809, for two years of travel. His dearest friend, Lord Delawarr, declined to see him off on the last day because he had some shopping to do. Worst of all, his childhood sweetheart, Mary Ann Chaworth, had called him "that lame boy," and had subsequently married a prosperous country squire. As the Childe (young man of noble birth) of the poem, Byron expresses his cynicism. He refers to his erstwhile friends as "flatt'rers of the festal hour;/The heartless parasites of present cheer. . . ." His "lemans" (sweethearts) care only for "pomp and power."

> Maidens, like moths, are ever caught by glare,
> And **Mammon wins his way where Seraphs might despair.**

A man after his own heart

Source: I SAMUEL 13:14
Author: Unknown
First transcribed: 1100-400 B.C.
Type of work: Religious history

Context: When the high priest Samuel becomes old, the Israelites seek to be like other nations by having a king. Although God warns the people that trouble will come if they have a king, He finds them determined; He therefore leads Samuel to select Saul, a tall, handsome, and promising young man. After anointing Saul, Samuel tells him to wait seven days in Gilgal until he comes to offer a sacrifice and show him what to do. A tremendous Philistine army gathers, the frightened Israelites are left in disorder, and still Saul waits for Samuel. After waiting seven days, Saul assembles the people and offers a sacrifice. Samuel comes immediately and says to Saul that, since he has not kept the Lord's commandment:

> . . . thy kingdom shall not continue: the Lord hath sought him **a man after his own heart,** and the Lord hath commanded him to be captain over his people, because thou hast not kept that which the Lord commanded thee.

Man as a social animal

Source: ETHICS (Part IV, Proposition XXXV, note)
Author: Benedictus de Spinoza (1632-1677)
First published: 1677
Type of work: Philosophic essay

Context: Spinoza presents his philosophy in the form of mathematical problems, proceeding from definitions and axioms to propositions and corollaries. He believes, "Man is to man a God." In order to obtain that which is most useful to him, man should live in obedience to reason. By living in obedience to reason, he will be most useful to himself when he is useful to others. In spite of satirists who scorn, theologians who censure, and misanthropes who advocate a life of solitary simplicity, man's life is infinitely easier when he co-operates with other men. One difficulty is that man is not entirely reasonable; he does not live peaceably with his fellows. As Spinoza remarks of him:

> . . . they are scarcely able to lead a solitary life, so that the definition of **man as a social animal** has met with general assent; in fact, men do derive from social life much more convenience than injury.

Man is a reasoning animal

Source: EPISTLES TO LUCILIUM (XLI, "On the God within us")
Author: Seneca (c.4 B.C.-A.D. 65)
First transcribed: 63-65
Type of work: Moral essay in the form of a letter

Context: Seneca, a Stoic, believes in the god within oneself, the god one can feel while contemplating the wonders of nature. He maintains that man should cultivate the goodness in himself and not its external aspects. As he says:

> Suppose that he [a man] has a retinue of comely slaves and a beautiful house, that his farm is large and large his income; none of these things is in the man himself; they are all on the outside. Praise the quality in him which cannot be given or snatched away, that which is the peculiar property of the man. Do you ask what this is? It is soul, and reason brought to perfection in the soul. For **man is a reasoning animal.** Therefore man's highest good is attained, if he has fulfilled the good for which nature designed him at birth.

Man is a rope stretched between the animal and the Superman

Source: THUS SPAKE ZARATHUSTRA (Prologue, part IV, as translated by Thomas Common)
Author: Friedrich Wilhelm Nietzsche (1844-1900)
First published: 1883
Type of work: Philosophy

Context: In the "Prologue" to *Thus Spake Zarathustra,* Nietzsche gives his interpretation of the life of Zarathustra, or Zoroaster, as a young man. At the age of thirty Zarathustra goes into the mountains where he lives for ten years, learning all he can. At the end of that time, having made up his mind to teach to mankind what he has learned, he descends into the

610

village. There everyone has gathered at the market-place to see a rope-dancer perform. Zarathustra begins teaching the people about the Superman who will surpass man. He delivers a sermon, attempting to show that adoring the soul to the detriment of the body will keep man in a servile state. He cries out against self-satisfaction and says:

> Lo, I teach you the Superman: he is that lightning, he is that frenzy!—
> When Zarathustra had thus spoken, one of the people called out: "We have now heard enough of the rope-dancer; it is time now for us to see him!" And all the people laughed at Zarathustra. But the rope-dancer, who thought the words applied to him, began his performance.

IV

> Zarathustra, however, looked at the people and wondered. Then he spake thus:
> **Man is a rope stretched between the animal and the Superman**—a rope over an abyss.

Man is a thinking reed

Source: PENSÉES (Section VI, number 347, as translated by W. F. Trotter)
Author: Blaise Pascal (1623-1662)
First published: 1670
Type of work: Philosophic commentary

Context: Blaise Pascal, as a seventeenth century scientist and mathematician, accepted the discoveries of Copernicus, Galileo, and Newton. He was challenged intellectually by the scientific advancement, but at the same time he found the brave new world which was being brought into being disturbing, too. The dignity of man was still of primary importance to Pascal, and he believed man should find dignity as a human being from commanding his own thoughts, not from space and time. He believed man could command the world by his thought, and that such command would be worth more than mere ownership or possession of the world. He said, "Thought constitutes the greatness of man." It is, he believed, the power of thought that sets man apart from animals; without thought man is but a "stone or a brute":

> **Man is** but a reed, the most feeble thing in nature; but he is **a thinking reed.** The entire universe need not arm itself to crush him. A vapour, a drop of water suffices to kill him. But, if the universe were to crush him, man would still be more noble than that which killed him, because he knows that he dies and the advantages which the universe has over him; the universe knows nothing of this.

611

Man is born free, and everywhere he is in chains

Source: THE SOCIAL CONTRACT (Book I, chapter 1)
Author: Jean Jacques Rousseau (1712-1778)
First published: 1762
Type of work: Political treatise

Context: In *The Social Contract,* Rousseau's best known and most influential work, an effort is made to establish the thesis that the authority of the people of a state or nation is absolute and should reside in them rather than in a sovereign. The people make up a body politic composed of members all of whom are equal. That such a situation does not exist, says Rousseau, is attributable to man's having exchanged natural liberty for civil liberty and natural law for manmade law. Consequently, he now finds himself, as Rousseau writes in the opening sentence of the first chapter, no longer free:

> **Man is born free, and everywhere he is in chains.** Many a one believes himself the master of others, and yet he is a greater slave than they. How has this change come about? I do not know. What can render it legitimate? I believe that I can settle this question.
>
> If I considered only force and the results that proceed from it, I should say that so long as a people is compelled to obey and does obey, it does well; but that, so soon as it can shake off the yoke and does shake it off, it does better; for, if men recover their freedom by virtue of the same right by which it was taken away, either they are justified in resuming it, or there was no justification for depriving them of it.

Man is by nature a political animal

Source: POLITICS (III, chapter 6)
Author: Aristotle (384-322 B.C.)
First transcribed: Third century B.C.
Type of work: Political and philosophical treatise

Context: This statement, used often by Aristotle, best sums up his discourse on politics, in which he holds that men band together for mutual protection and gregariousness. He defines the need to organize, the rights and definition of citizenship, then comes to a conclusion:

> . . . Now it has been said in our first discourse, in which we determined the principles concerning household management and the control of slaves, that **man is by nature a political animal;** and so even when men have no need of assistance from each other they none the less desire to live together. . . .

612

Man proposes, but God disposes

Source: THE IMITATION OF CHRIST (Book I, chapter 19)
Author: Thomas à Kempis (1380-1471)
First transcribed: c.1418
Type of work: Devotional poetry

Context: This is a book of advice to Christians on how to improve their souls and their relationship to God. This particular expression had been used earlier and widely, in the *Chronicle of Battel Abbey* (p. 27, Lower's translation), and in *The Vision of Piers Plowman* (Line 13994, edition of 1550). In *Don Quixote,* Part II (1615), Book IV, chapter 55, Cervantes said: "Man appoints, and God disappoints." In Proverbs 16:9, the reading is, "A man's heart deviseth his way; but the Lord directeth his steps." Thomas à Kempis says:

> The purpose of righteous men hangeth
>   rather in the grace of God than
>   in man's own wisdom; in him
>   they trust always in all things they do.
> For **man purposeth and God disposeth;**
>   and man's way is not in man (to carry out).

Man shall not live by bread alone

Source: MATTHEW 4:4
Author: Unknown (traditionally Matthew the Apostle)
First transcribed: c.75-100
Type of work: Gospel

Context: After Jesus is baptized in the Jordan by John the Baptist, the Spirit of God descends upon Him like a dove. A voice from heaven declares, "This is my beloved Son, in whom I am well pleased." Then Jesus, led by the Spirit into the wilderness, fasts for forty days and forty nights. The devil comes to Him with three temptations. In the first two, he dares Jesus, if He be the Son of God, to command stones to turn to bread and to throw Himself from the top of the temple in Jerusalem. The third temptation, that Jesus fall down and worship the devil, will bring a reward of all the kingdoms of the world. When Jesus declines, the devil departs, and angels minister to the pure Son. Of the first temptation, Matthew writes:

> And when the tempter came to him, he said, If thou be the Son of God, command that these stones be made bread.
> But he answered and said, It is written, **Man shall not live by bread alone,** but by every word that proceedeth out of the mouth of God.

A man, Sir, should keep his friendship in constant repair

Source: THE LIFE OF SAMUEL JOHNSON, LL.D.
Author: James Boswell (1740-1795)
First published: 1791
Type of work: Biography

Context: In 1755, having completed the work of compiling his famous dictionary, Samuel Johnson (1709-1784) went about the task of writing the "Preface" to it. Near the end, he tells of his despondence at having protracted his work so long that most of those whom he has hoped to please "have sunk into the grave. . . ." Years later, James Boswell, Johnson's biographer, reflects on the strangeness of such depression in a man then only forty-five years old. Johnson actually, however, lived thirty years longer and once admitted that he had more friends in later life than in his youth. Boswell's reflections, however, lead him to a principle he has long believed in: that since men like to live as long as they can, it is wise to "be continually adding to the number of our friends, that the loss of some may be supplied by others." Boswell explains that Johnson himself, late in life, was of the same opinion. Expressing this idea,

. . . He said to Sir Joshua Reynolds, "If a man does not make new acquaintance as he advances through life, he will soon find himself left alone. **A man, Sir, should keep his friendship in constant repair."**

Man that is born of a woman is of few days, and full of trouble

Source: JOB 14:1
Author: Unknown
First transcribed: c.900-500 B.C.
Type of work: Religious saga

Context: The Book of Job is the story of an upright and pious man whom God allows Satan to afflict in order to test his faithfulness since Satan has claimed that Job is upright only because God has "made an hedge about him." Satan is certain that if Job's possessions be taken from him, "he will curse thee [God] to thy face." The trial is made: Job's family is killed, his belongings are swept away and he is afflicted with boils. Then three of his friends ("Job's comforters") come to him to prove that he must have sinned, else God would not have punished him, for God is always just. In the course of a long lamentation, in which he maintains that he has not sinned and that God owes him justice, Job touches upon the brevity of human life:

Man that is born of a woman is of few days, and full of trouble.
He cometh forth like a flower, and is cut down: he fleeth also
as a shadow, and continueth not.

Man to command and woman to obey

Source: THE PRINCESS (Part V, l. 440)
Author: Alfred, Lord Tennyson (1809-1892)
First published: 1847
Type of work: Narrative poem

Context: The conflict between Princess Ida's determination to assert female integrity and independence, and the prince's determination to win her as his bride threatens to develop into battle, with his father's forces assembled at the gate of Ida's palace. Presented with an ultimatum, Ida sends back a scornful answer: she rejects the prince forever, and all men, for their age-old treatment of women as inferior; their qualities, she says, are really finer and purer than men's. To this statement the prince's father responds that it is the law of nature that men are made to manage the world, and women only to keep the home; if women are allowed to govern, chaos will result.

> . . . This is fixt
> As are the roots of earth and base of all,—
> Man for the field and woman for the hearth;
> Man for the sword, and for the needle she;
> Man with the head, and woman with the heart;
> **Man to command, and woman to obey;**
> All else confusion.

Man wants but little here below

Source: THE VICAR OF WAKEFIELD (Chapter 8)
Author: Oliver Goldsmith (1728-1774)
First published: 1766
Type of work: Ballad

Context: Goldsmith's *The Vicar of Wakefield* has long been one of the most popular English novels. The plot, recounting the misfortunes which beset the family of the Reverend Dr. Primrose, is inconsistent and highly improbable, but the story is nonetheless delightful; happily, everything works out well in the end. On one occasion, the family goes on a picnic, during which the conversation turns to poetry. Mr. Burchell, a family friend, remarks that English poetry "is nothing at present but a com-

615

bination of luxuriant images, without plot or connexion; a string of epithets that improve the sound, without carrying on the sense." As an example of true poetry, he offers the company a ballad about a lovelorn lass disguised as a man who comes upon a hermit's cottage in the forest. Her blushes disclose her sex, and she tells the hermit of her distress in love. The hermit in the end turns out to be her lost lover, and all ends well. Early in the poem, the hermit offers to share his meager fare with the disguished lady. Goldsmith may have unconsciously rephrased a line from *The Complaint* by Edward Young (1683-1765): "Man wants but little, nor that little long."

> "Then, pilgrim, turn, thy cares forego,
> All earth-born cares are wrong;
> **Man wants but little here below,**
> Nor wants that little long."

The manner of giving is worth more than the gift

Source: LE MENTEUR (Act I, sc. i, l. 90)
Author: Pierre Corneille (1606-1684)
First published: 1643
Type of work: Dramatic comedy

Context: Volumes of Corneille's "best" plays in translation seem to omit "Le Menteur," so to get an English version of the speech of the servant Cliton to his master Dorante: "La façon de donner vaut mieux que ce qu'on donne," it is necessary to consult one of the adaptations popular in seventeenth and eighteenth century England, though the minister whose parishioner sent him a jar of peaches in brandy phrased the idea thus when he wrote her: "I don't care much for peaches, but I do appreciate the spirit in which they were sent." Sir Richard Steele (1672-1729), in his *The Lying Lover, or The Ladies' Friendship* (London, 1704), gives the speech to Latine in his dialogue, with Bookwit:

> Be free to Women, they'll be free to you. Not every open-handed Fellow hits it neither. Some give by Lapfulls, and yet ne'er oblige. **The Manner, you know, of doing a thing is worth more than the thing itself.** Some drop a Jewel, which had been refus'd if bluntly offer'd.

Manners are the happy ways of doing things

Source: BEHAVIOR
Author: Ralph Waldo Emerson (1803-1882)
First published: 1860
Type of work: Moral essay

Context: Emerson analyzes that aspect of human conduct known as "manners." "The power of manners is incessant"; they give us "the mastery of palaces and fortunes." Manners "make us . . . endurable to each other," and they "grow out of circumstances as well as character." Our true manners are expressed not by our speech but by our "look and gait and behavior." No matter whether in a court or a drawing-room, "the basis of good manners is self-reliance. . . . Those who are not self-possessed, obtrude, and pain us. . . . The hero should find himself at home, wherever he is; should impart comfort by his own security and good-nature to all beholders. The hero is suffered to be himself. . . . Manners impress as they indicate real power." "Superior people" are truthful and direct, and they inspire confidence and respect. The essence of good manners is "the wish to scatter joy and not pain around us." Manners are a "silent and subtile language . . . the visible carriage or action of the individual, as resulting from his organization and his will combined":

> There is always a best way of doing everything, if it be to boil an egg. **Manners are the happy ways of doing things;** each once a stroke of genius or of love,—now repeated and hardened into usage. They form at last a rich varnish, with which the routine of life is washed, and its details adorned. If they are superficial, so are the dew-drops which give such a depth to the morning meadows. Manners are very communicable: men catch them from each other . . .

Man's inhumanity to man

Source: MAN WAS MADE TO MOURN (Stanza 7)
Author: Robert Burns (1759-1796)
First published: 1786
Type of work: Dirge

Context: Robert Burns was born in a rural Scotland still crushed under the heel of feudalism. His tenant-farmer father had no means of rising or of lifting the yoke of grinding labor from the shoulders of his gifted son. And though Burns became a published poet accepted by Edinburgh society, he died still oppressed by want. It is not surprising that he wrote poems of such deep personal despondency and social rebellion as "Man Was Made to Mourn"; the wonder is that he wrote so much that has true humor and mirth. In this poem, based on a folk song his mother sang, the poet is stopped on a cold evening's walk by an aged mourner of human miseries. Man, says the old stranger, is beset in youth by folly and in age by want. He must labor by the hundreds to support one haughty lord who may even deny him the privilege to earn bread. If, asks the old man, I was born this lord's slave, why was I given the idea of freedom? If I was not, why am I helpless against his cruelty? Finally the old man consoles the youth with the thought that death is the recompense for want, for while it is dreaded by the rich, it comes as welcome to the poor. In one stanza the white-haired sage declares:

> Many and sharp the num'rous ills
> Inwoven with our frame!
> More pointed still we make ourselves,
> Regret, remorse, and shame!
> And man, whose Heaven-erected face
> The smiles of love adorn,
> **Man's inhumanity to man**
> Makes countless thousands mourn!

A man's reach should exceed his grasp

Source: ANDREA DEL SARTO (Line 97)
Author: Robert Browning (1812-1889)
First published: 1855
Type of work: Dramatic monologue

Context: Browning imagined this speech as being spoken by the Italian painter, Andrea del Sarto, who gained fame in the early sixteenth century. Andrea is speaking to his wife and reflects upon his stature as a painter. So perfect had his technical skill become, that he was called "the faultless painter." But he lacked the depth of conviction and intensity of feeling that a great artist must have. He has technical perfection, but lacks feeling; other painters he knows of have greatness of soul, but lack the skill that Andrea possesses. He sees in this situation a comment upon life: there is always something missing in human effort so that perfection is never attainable. Yet a man must strive for perfection.

> Ah, but **a man's reach should exceed his grasp,**
> Or what's a heaven for?
> . . .
> I know both what I want and what might gain,
> And yet how profitless to know, to sigh
> "Had I been two, another and myself. . . ."

Many a man has fought because he feared to run away

Source: THE MARRIAGE OF GUENEVERE (Act IV, sc. iii)
Author: Richard Hovey (1864-1900)
First published: 1891
Type of work: Dramatic tragedy

Context: The day after his marriage to Guenevere, Arthur, King of Britain, goes away to war. While the king is away, Launcelot arrives at Camelot and discovers that Guenevere is the mysterious Lady of the Hills whom he had met in the forest and with whom he had fallen in love. At court he and Guenevere express their mutual love. They have a tryst one night, but unfortunately an agent of the wicked Morgause, sister to Arthur, spies on them. Queen Guenevere is then accused of high treason for her affair with Launcelot. Guenevere's brother Peredure, who is in love with Morgause, cannot believe the accusation against his sister. The court jester, Dagonet, arrives to tell Peredure that the accusation is a plot by Morgause. Knowing Peredure's feeling toward Morgause, Dagonet first asks: "Are you brave, my lord?" "Brave?" Peredure questions.

DAGONET
"I know you are as quick in a quarrel as a Spaniard, and will whip out your rapier on less provocation than any man at the court. But are you brave?
(*Sings*)   For there are worser ills to face
        Than foeman in the fray;
    And **many a man has fought because—**
        He feared to run away.
        Ri fol de riddle rol.
Are you brave, sir?"

Many are called, but few are chosen

Source: MATTHEW 22:14
Author: Unknown (traditionally Matthew the Apostle)
First transcribed: c.75-100
Type of work: Gospel

Context: Jesus, confronted in Jerusalem by the chief priests and Pharisees, who are alarmed at His entry into the city and who question His authority as a teacher or prophet, speaks to them of the Kingdom of Heaven. Fearful of the multitude, which holds Jesus to be a prophet of God, the Pharisees can only hear His pointed words. Teaching in His customary parables, Jesus compares the Kingdom of Heaven with a wedding feast made ready by a king for his son. When the invited wedding guests refuse to attend, the king denounces them and sends his servants into the streets to invite the good and the bad. At the feast, on seeing that one guest has not come in a wedding garment, the king casts him out. Jesus concludes the parable with the words:

For **many are called, but few are chosen.**

Many hands make light work

Source: THE PROVERBS OF JOHN HEYWOOD (Part II, chapter 5)
Author: John Heywood (1497?-1580?)
First published: 1546
Type of work: Gnomic poetry

Context: The author is telling a young man the dangers of marrying while young, and of marrying either a young maid for love or an old widow for riches. In telling these dangers, he is using as many proverbs as possible. He is now telling an illustrative story about what happened when a young man married an old widow for her riches. They started off well, but soon fell into disagreement. The young man then began to seek and find new interests. The neglected widow-wife started to complain that he did not love her any more and that he was wasting her money. The proverb that she uses means exactly the opposite of what it means to us today. In the following passage it is the widow-wife talking:

Flattering knaves and flearing queans being the mark,
Hang on his sleeve: **many hands make light wark.**
He hath his hawks in the mew; but make ye sure,
With empty hands men may no hawks allure.

The many-splendored thing

Source: THE KINGDOM OF GOD ("In No Strange Land," Stanza 4)
Author: Francis Thompson (1859-1907)
First published: 1913
Type of work: Religious poem

Context: In many of his poems the Catholic poet Francis Thompson treats profound religious themes. Much of the beauty of the poem entitled "The Kingdom of God" ("In No Strange Land") comes from the simplicity of the treatment of the subject. The theme is first developed through analogy. The poet asks: "Does the fish soar to find the ocean,/ The eagle plunge to end the air— . . . ?" Then discarding the ideas of the Kingdom of God lying "where the wheeling systems darken,/ And our benumbed

620

conceiving soars!," the poet says the beating of the wings of angels is at "our own clay-shuttered doors," if we would only listen. Man has become estranged from Heaven; Heaven is in the same place it has always been. The poet gives the theme of his poem in the following lines:

> The angels keep their ancient places;—
> Turn but a stone, and start a wing!
> 'Tis ye, 'tis your estrangèd faces,
> That miss **the many-splendoured thing.**

Many things fall out between the cup and the lip

Source: PERIMEDES THE BLACKE-SMITH
Author: Robert Greene (1558-1592)
First published: 1588
Type of work: Pastoral in prose

Context: Many aphorisms affirm the difference between aims and accomplishments. One that comes to mind declares "Man proposes and God disposes." Another common proverb deals with a slip between pouring the liquid and swallowing it. Earliest seems to be Homer's account of Antinous and Odysseus in *Odyssey,* Book 22, Lines 8-18, written about 850 B.C. As Antinous was about to drink wine from the golden goblet, Odysseus loosed a "bitter arrow" at him that struck him in the throat, and the cup fell from his hands before it reached his lips. Palladas, a fifth century teacher in Alexandria, summed up the story in Epigram 32 in the *Greek Anthology,* Book X. The earliest statement of the phrase in English is found in the writing of Robert Greene. A writer of pot-boilers in his early days, Greene composed a number of pastorals, following the popularity of *Arcadia* (1580) by Sir Philip Sidney (1554-1586). To Robert Burton, (1577-1640) in his *Anatomy of Melancholy* (1621) is also attributed the form: "Many things happen between the cup and the lip." Our current version comes from *The Ingoldsby Legends: Lady Rohesia* (1840) by R. H. Barham: "There's many a slip/ 'Twixt the cup and the lip." Many other slips come to mind: between the egg and the bird, between the hand and the mouth, and between the offer and the check. However the most often used is some variant of the one by Greene:

> Though men determine, the gods dispose, and oft times **many things fall out between the cup and the lip.**

621

Mark but this flea

Source: POEMS ("The Flea," Line 1)
Author: John Donne (c.1572-1631)
First published: 1633
Type of work: Metaphysical love poem

Context: This poem is "metaphysical" as the term was first used in the eighteenth century in that the poet works by means of dissimilar images which his ingenuity or "wit" has almost violently yoked together. The image here is grotesque, as was often true in such poetry, and is developed to great length. The flea has bitten both the poet and his mistress; in the insect's body their blood mingles, thus making a third blood. Three lives are therefore merged in the insect. If the mistress kills it, she will kill three beings. The flea, by containing their mingled blood, becomes a kind of marriage bed. The lady claims that she has not been weakened by the loss of blood, and the poet replies that she will lose no more when she yields to him than she lost through killing the flea. The opening lines of the poem are,

> **Mark but this flea,** and mark in this,
> How little that which thou deniest me is;
> It sucked me first, and now sucks thee,
> And in this flea, our two bloods mingled be;
> Thou know'st that this cannot be said
> A sin, nor shame, nor loss of maidenhead. . . .

Marlowe's mighty line

Source: TO THE MEMORY OF SHAKESPEARE (Line 30)
Author: Ben Jonson (1573?-1637)
First published: 1623
Type of work: Poetic panegyric

Context: Had Shakespeare never existed, the plays of the short-lived Christopher Marlowe (1564-1593) might be judged today to contain the greatest of Elizabethan dramatic poetry. Some of Marlowe's verse is as lofty as anything written by the Bard of Avon. Consider these lines from Scene 14 of his greatest play, *The Tragedy of Dr. Faustus* (1592; pub. 1604): "Was this the face that launched a thousand ships, / and burnt the topless towers of Ilium?/ Sweet Helen, make me immortal with a kiss." Only because in his few plays Marlowe did not reach the peaks as often as Shakespeare, and descended more frequently into banality, is he rated below Shakespeare. Ben Jonson, greater than Marlowe as a dramatist because of his larger body of plays, gives him credit for great poetry though conceding that Shakespeare surpassed not only him, but John Lyly (1554?-1606), who demonstrated in *Campaspe* (1584) how drama can also be literature, and Thomas Kyd (1558-1594), author of *The Spanish Tragedy* (c. 1595).

> For, if I thought my judgment were of years,
> I should commit thee surely to thy peers,
> And tell how far thou didst our Lyly outshine,
> Or sporting Kyd or **Marlowe's mighty line.**

The mass of men lead lives of quiet desperation

Source: WALDEN (Chapter I, "Economy")
Author: Henry David Thoreau (1817-1862)
First published: 1854
Type of work: Literary journal

Context: Thoreau placed himself in partial isolation in a hermitage at Walden Pond, Concord, Massachusetts, for the period 1845-1847, and during this time reflected deeply on the conditions and circumstances of humanity. In this first part of his journal he pictures the majority of men as slaves and drudges to daily labor. A man's true situation is what he believes it to be, says Thoreau, and most men are so downtrodden with the unrelieved task of earning their living and serving their masters that they soon collapse into a leaden resignation, unable to believe that life holds any real happiness or reward for them.

> **The mass of men lead lives of quiet desperation.** What is called resignation is confirmed desperation. . . .
> When we consider what, to use the words of the catechism, is the chief end of man, and what are the true necessaries and means of life, it appears as if men had deliberately chosen the common mode of living because they preferred it to any other. Yet they honestly think there is no choice left . . .

May there be no moaning of the bar, when I put out to sea

Source: CROSSING THE BAR (Stanza 1)
Author: Alfred, Lord Tennyson (1809-1892)
First published: 1889
Type of work: Lyric poem

Context: Tennyson asked that this poem be placed at the end of all editions of his poetry, for this simple, muted lyric is his final thought on death. The tone is one of quiet acceptance and of faith undisturbed. He compares his journey into death with the passage of a ship away from the land and beyond the bar of sand at the entrance to the harbor, and hopes that his end will come quietly and without turmoil, his soul returning to eternity as a tide returns to the depths of the ocean, silently, with no turbulence and strife where the water flows by the bar.

> Sunset and evening star,
>   And one clear call for me!
> And **may there be no moaning of the bar,**
>   **When I put out to sea,**
>
> But such a tide as moving seems asleep,
>   Too full for sound and foam,
> When that which drew from out the boundless deep
>   Turns again home.

The meek shall inherit the earth

Source: PSALMS 37:11
Author: Unknown
First transcribed: c.400-200 B.C.
Type of work: Religious poetry

Context: The righteous man is cautioned not to be envious if the wicked prosper, because in time evildoers will fade as the grass after its season. The poet points out that the land is promised to those who trust in God. The godly man is to take delight in the Lord and He will grant him his desires. When the psalmist urges that the faithful rest in the Lord, he implies that there is relief from worry and bother and that relaxation follows when one trusts in God. Even though the wicked man succeeds, the righteous man is not to become angry and depressed for in the end those who serve God will inherit the earth. (In his Sermon on the Mount, Matthew 5:5, Christ says "Blessed are the meek: for they shall inherit the earth.")

> For yet a little while, and the wicked shall not be: yea, thou shalt diligently consider his place, and it shall not be.
>   But **the meek shall inherit the earth;** and shall delight themselves in the abundance of peace.

The melancholy days are come

Source: THE DEATH OF THE FLOWERS (Stanza 1)
Author: William Cullen Bryant (1794-1878)
First published: 1825
Type of work: Lyric poem

Context: This romantic, lamenting poem is an experiment in verse form and sound effects. Bryant evokes the melancholy deadness of autumn and laments the death of "the fair young flowers," the "beauteous sisterhood." These lovely flowers are now in their graves and can never be brought to life again. Bryant gives a list of all the flowers that were killed by the plague-like frost. Even a "calm mild day" of autumn is unable to revive them. The poem ends with a comparison.

The dead flowers remind Bryant of his sister, "one who in her youthful beauty died, / The fair meek blossom that grew up and faded by my side." It seemed sad "that one so lovely should have a life so brief," and yet the poet is reconciled by the fact that it was appropriate that his sister, "So gentle and so beautiful, should perish with the flowers." The first stanza of the poem evokes the gloom of the autumn scene:

> **The melancholy days are come,** the saddest of the year,
> Of wailing winds and naked woods, and meadows brown and sere.
> Heaped in the hollows of the grove, the autumn leaves lie dead;
> They rustle to the eddying gust, and to the rabbit's tread;
> The robin and the wren are flown, and from the shrubs the jay,
> And from the wood-top calls the crow through all the gloomy day.

The memory be green

Source: HAMLET (Act I, sc. ii, l. 2)
Author: William Shakespeare (1564-1616)
First published: 1603
Type of work: Dramatic tragedy

Context: The sense of this saying, more often conveyed as "fresh in memory" or "the memory is fresh," is quite current. Thomas Moore, the famous Irish poet, used a similar phrase in Stanza 2 of his poem *Oh Breathe Not His Name* (published in *Irish Melodies,* 1807-1834):

> And the tear that we shed, though in secret it rolls,
> Shall long keep his memory green in our souls.

In *Hamlet,* the newly crowned King Claudius of Denmark, brother and secret murderer of the dead King Hamlet, announces to the court his marriage to the late king's widow, Gertrude. By using this phrase, Claudius is acknowledging the brevity of the mourning period for the dead king, and then tries to explain it away.

CLAUDIUS
Though yet of Hamlet our dear brother's death
The memory be green, and that it us befitted
To bear our hearts in grief, and our whole kingdom
To be contracted in one brow of woe,
Yet so far hath discretion fought with nature
That we with wisest sorrow think on him,
Together with remembrance of ourselves.

• • •

Men are most apt to believe what they least understand

Source: ESSAYS ("Of Cripples," Book III, chapter 11, as translated by Charles Cotton)
Author: Michel de Montaigne (1533-1592)
First published: 1588
Type of work: Philosophical essay

Context: In the essay "Of Cripples," Michel de Montaigne discusses human reason. He believes man is more concerned with discovering causes than he is with discovering truths. Rather than ask how a thing is done, man should ask if a thing is done. But if man does not understand, he fabricates an explanation; a world is created without foundation. Many so-called truths are drawn from "idle beginnings and frivolous causes," and Montaigne believes that many of the world's ills are brought about because men are afraid to profess their ignorance. They merely accept all things they cannot disprove. Men should believe God, not other men. Of himself, he says:

I am plain and heavy, and stick to the solid and the probable, avoiding those ancient reproaches, *Majorem fidem homines adhibent iis, quae non intelligunt* (**Men are most apt to believe what they least understand.**)—*Cupidine humani ingenii, libentius obscura creduntur* (Through the lust of human wit, obscure things are most easily credited.)

626

Men have died from time to time but not for love

Source: AS YOU LIKE IT (Act IV, sc. i, ll. 106-8)
Author: William Shakespeare (1564-1616)
First published: 1623
Type of work: Dramatic comedy

Context: Rosalind, banished by her uncle Duke Frederick, is in Arden Forest, but disguised as a boy named Ganymede. She meets her love, Orlando, who does not recognize her. But she urges Orlando, who says that he is in love with Rosalind, to court her as though she were Rosalind. Clever, saucy Rosalind teases Orlando in her own person though disguised as the rustic boy. She tells Orlando that Rosalind will not have him. Orlando responds that if she will not have him, then he will die. Rosalind tells him that men have died for various reasons but never for love. She then asks him how long he will love Rosalind, and he replies "for ever, and a day." To this she chidingly responds that men and women are warmer in wooing than in staying married:

ROSALIND

. . . The poor world is almost six thousand years old, and in all this time there was not any man died in his own person, videlicet, in a love-cause. . . . **Men have died from time to time,** and worms have eaten them, **but not for love.**

• • •

. . . Orlando, men are April when they woo, December when they wed. Maids are May when they are maids, but the sky changes when they are wives.

Men indeed splendidly wicked

Source: RAMBLER, No. 4, March 31, 1750
Author: Samuel Johnson (1709-1784)
First published: 1750
Type of work: Essay

Context: Johnson's *Rambler* essays were published from March 20, 1750, until March 14, 1752, appearing on Tuesdays and Saturdays for a total of 208 numbers. The essays made up the sole contents of a six-page, single-column paper, and usually dealt with a serious moral, philosophical, or literary topic. In No. 4 Johnson praises the currently popular realistic novels of such writers as Richardson and Fielding as being, for the young, excellent guides to good conduct and sound morality. Since novelists are free to select from reality the details and "to cull from the mass of mankind those individuals upon which the attention ought most

627

to be employed," they are also obligated so to balance a character's good and evil characteristics as not to make him appear admirable. We should not "lose the abhorrence of their faults . . . or, perhaps, regard them with some kindness for being united with so much merit." Of such characters, Johnson says,

> There have been **men indeed splendidly wicked,** whose endowments threw a brightness on their crimes, and whom scarce any villany made perfectly detestable, because they never could be wholly divested of their excellences; but . . . their resemblance ought no more to be preserved than the art of murdering without pain.

Men lied to them, and so they went to die

Source: THERMOPYLAE (First line)
Author: Robert Hillyer (1895-   )
First published: 1919
Type of work: Sonnet

Context: This sonnet deals with both the tragedy and the triumph of man's noble sacrifice in deceived and unavailing efforts to champion truth and goodness. For man's destiny is to lose himself in an unfortunate, unappreciated cause or to endure the long misery of disillusionment and purposelessness. "For life deals thus with Man;/ To die alone deceived or with the mass,/ Or disillusioned to complete his span." Those who die in battle united in a common cause, though they are exhorted and commanded by the lies of others, are fortunate to have their purposeful visions. Those who are not fortunate enough to die for their concept of truth are likely to live to see their truth for what it is—a lie. Even the sceptics offer themselves through natural inclination and trust that somehow they will not have died in vain. Since self-sacrifice is natural to man, even necessary to him, all great incidents of such sacrifice are similar; the participants are equally victimized, the tragic consequences are equally unavoidable. Thermopylae and Golgotha are one, "the young dead legions in the narrow pass;/ The stark black cross against the setting sun." The poem begins:

> **Men lied to them, and so they went to die.**
> Some fell, unknowing that they were deceived,
> And some escaped, and bitterly bereaved,
> Beheld the truth they loved shrink to a lie. . . .

Men may come and men may go, but I go on for ever

Source: THE BROOK (Refrain)
Author: Alfred, Lord Tennyson (1809-1892)
First published: 1855
Type of work: Lyric poem

Context: A man, Lawrence Aylmer, "in middle age forlorn," sits by a brook sadly recalling the time twenty years before when he said goodbye to his brother Edmund, who was leaving for Italy, where he hoped to regain his failing health. The trip was in vain, for Edmund died in Italy shortly after. He was a poet, a sensitive and perceptive person, and of frail health. Before leaving England, Edmund had written a poem about this brook, tracing its origin in the wild hills and its progress down to the level farmlands. The continuous and everlasting flow of the waters is contrasted with the brevity and irregularity of human life and, in particular, of the life of Edmund Aylmer. The brook sings:

> And out again I curve and flow
> To join the brimming river,
> For **men may come and men may go,**
> **But I go on for ever.**

Men may rise on stepping-stones of their dead selves to higher things

Source: IN MEMORIAM (Part I, stanza 1)
Author: Alfred, Lord Tennyson (1809-1892)
First published: 1850
Type of work: Elegy

Context: The poet faces the fact of death: his friend Arthur Hallam is gone from him forever. In his grief he despairingly toys with the word "death," referring to the saying that men may change, assuming new and better characters and personalities, and, in a sense, allowing their old selves to die; there is a kind of resurrection, as if men emerge from the corpses of their former beings and tread upon them as they leave the level of their past lives to climb to a higher one. The poet accepts this survival of "death," but asks how one is to rise above the real death of a loved one. And he can find no answer: this death is absolute loss.

> I held it truth, with him who sings
> To one clear harp in divers tones,
> That **men may rise on stepping-stones**
> **Of their dead selves to higher things.**

629

> But who shall so forecast the years
> And find in loss a gain to match?
> Or reach a hand thro' time to catch
> The far-off interest of tears?

Men should be what they seem

Source: OTHELLO (Act III, sc. iii, l. 126)
Author: William Shakespeare (1564-1616)
First published: 1622
Type of work: Dramatic tragedy

Context: Iago, ancient (or ensign) to Othello, a Moorish military commander in the service of Venice, is angry at Othello for preferring Michael Cassio, a Florentine, as his lieutenant instead of himself. He determines to bring about the downfall of both the Moor and Cassio. Othello, appointed governor of Cyprus, moves his troops to the island. A storm delays their arrival but also drives off a threatening Turkish fleet, and Othello orders a general rejoicing, which Cassio is to keep within bounds. Iago gets him drunk, pricks him on to a quarrel with a henchman, arouses Othello, and has the satisfaction of seeing Cassio reduced to the ranks. Shamed, Cassio acts upon Iago's crafty suggestion that he seek the aid of Othello's wife Desdemona to regain his position. Cassio talks to Desdemona. Then, seeing Othello and Iago approaching, he, still shamefaced, steals off. Iago then insinuates to Othello that Cassio is behaving guiltily as if there were something illicit between Desdemona and Cassio. Othello shakes off the suggestion, but Iago skillfully and subtly persists.

IAGO
   For Michael Cassio,
I dare be sworn, I think that he is honest.

OTHELLO
I think so too.

IAGO
Men should be what they seem;
Or those that be not, would they might seem none.

OTHELLO
Certain, men should be what they seem.

Men shut their doors against a setting sun

Source: TIMON OF ATHENS (Act I, sc. ii, l. 150)
Author: William Shakespeare (1564-1616)
First published: 1623
Type of work: Dramatic tragedy

Context: Timon is a generous and considerate patron of the arts and an extravagant, even lavish entertainer. He repays a kindness sevenfold and is well on his way to bankrupting himself. A Cynic philosopher named Apemantus, a plain-spoken fellow hated by everyone for his perceptive chiding, ridicules Timon's openhandedness and tries to warn him against his friends during a banquet and masque at Timon's house.

APEMANTUS
. . .
We make ourselves fools, to disport ourselves,
And spend our flatteries, to drink those men,
Upon whose age we void it up again
With poisonous spite and envy.
Who lives, that's not depraved, or depraves?
Who dies, that hears not one spurn to their graves
Of their friends' gift?
I should fear those that dance before me now
Would one day stamp upon me. 'T has been done.
Men shut their doors against a setting sun.

Men who hunt perpetually for their personal Northwest Passage

Source: NORTHWEST PASSAGE (Foreword)
Author: Kenneth Roberts (1885-1957)
First published: 1936
Type of work: Novel

Context: This quotation, serving as the foreword to the first book of *Northwest Passage,* a novel of exploration and adventure during the latter half of the eighteenth century, fittingly reflects the theme and subject-matter of the book as a whole. It is the story of two men, one with a dream, the other with a talent, who, hunting "perpetually for their personal Northwest Passage," endure discouragement, physical hazards, and repeated failure without relenting their obsessive efforts or altering their determined courses. Major Rogers, a courageous, untiring soldier, dreams of finding a northwest passage across America to the East. He proves himself well qualified for such an exploration only to be thwarted by an ambitious political machinery. However, neither reversals, physical suffering,

631

nor disfavor deadens his determination or blurs his vision of the Northwest Passage. A talented artist named Langdon Towne, hoping to paint Indians in the natural state, risks social disgrace, physical dangers, and the loss of his beloved in order to pursue his financially unrewarding occupation. Both men exhibit the unextinguishable spark that compels them onward, one toward the realization of a dream, the other toward the fulfillment of a talent.

> . . . On every side of us are **men who hunt perpetually for their personal Northwest Passage,** too often sacrificing health, strength and life itself to the search; and who shall say they are not happier in their vain but hopeful quest than wiser, duller folk who sit at home, venturing nothing. . . .

Mene, Mene, Tekel, Upharsin

Source: DANIEL 5:25
Author: Unknown
First transcribed: c.300-150 B.C.
Type of work: Religious prophecy or apocalyptic writing

Context: King Belshazar of Babylonia, during a tremendous feast for his court, demands the gold and silver drinking vessels, confiscated from the temple in Jerusalem by his father, King Nebuchadnezzar. When the feasting court starts drinking from the vessels and praising idols, the fingers of a man's hand appear and write some unintelligible words on the wall. After the wise men of the nation fail to explain the writing, the queen suggests that Daniel, an exile of Judah who had interpreted dreams for Nebuchadnezzar, be called. Daniel reminds Belshazar that God struck his father with madness, removing his power, until he humbled himself before Him. Adding that Belshazar, too, has been arrogant and has followed other gods, Daniel states that God sent the mysterious hand:

> And this is the writing that was written, **MENE, MENE, TEKEL, UPHARSIN.**
> This is the interpretation of the thing: MENE; God hath numbered thy kingdom, and finished it.
> TEKEL; Thou art weighed in the balances, and art found wanting.
> PERES; Thy kingdom is divided, and given to the Medes and Persians. . . .
> In that night was Belshazar the king of the Chaldeans slain.

Merry as crickets

Source: GARGANTUA AND PANTAGRUEL (Book I, chapter 29, as translated by Sir Thomas Urquhart)
Author: François Rabelais (1495-1552)
First published: 1532-1564
Type of work: Satire

Context: The shepherds of the country of Grangousier, father of Gargantua, one day stop some bakers from Lerne and ask if they can buy some of their cakes at regular market prices. The bakers refuse, instead hurling outrageous insults, even striking one friendly shepherd with a whip. He in turn throws his cudgel, and a general battle starts, in which the bakers of Lerne are bested. The shepherds are honest people and pay for the cakes they then take. The bakers hurry home to Lerne, where they tell the king, Picrochole, of the battle. Picrochole gets together his army and enters the country of Grangousier. Grangousier, who is a peace-loving man, wants to avoid a fight and sends for his son, Gargantua, who is away at school. In his letter to Gargantua, Grangousier says:

> . . . The exploit shall be done with as little effusion of blood as may be. And, if possible, by means far more expedient, such as military policy, devices and stratagems of war, we shall save all the souls, and send them home as **merry as crickets** unto their own houses. . . .

A method in his madness

Source: HAMLET (Act II, sc. ii, l. 206)
Author: William Shakespeare (1564-1616)
First published: 1603
Type of work: Dramatic tragedy

Context: This phrase is often used, in the misquoted form given above, when anyone obtains sensible results by means not readily understood, or by means which strike the viewer as odd, strange, or eccentric. In the play, Prince Hamlet learns that his father was murdered by his father's brother, the present King Claudius of Denmark. In order to screen his own thoughts and actions and to disarm his well-guarded uncle, Hamlet pretends to be demented. Polonius, the king's chief councilor, believes him to be so and tries to get further confirmation of his belief. Hamlet, aware of Polonius' intentions, and, under cover of his pretended madness, makes game of the tedious old fool. Hamlet is reading as he walks. Polonius asks him what he is reading.

633

Words, words, words.

• • •

POLONIUS
I mean the matter that you read, my lord.

HAMLET
Slanders sir, for the satirical rogue says here, that old men have
grey beards [and] that their faces are wrinkled, . . . I hold it not
honesty to have it thus set down; for yourself sir shall grow old as
I am, if like a crab you could go backward.

POLONIUS [*aside*]
Though this be madness, yet there is method in't.

• • •

Methoughts I heard one calling, "Child"; and
I replied, "My Lord."

Source: THE TEMPLE ("The Collar," Lines 35-36)
Author: George Herbert (1593-1633)
First published: 1633
Type of work: Religious poem

Context: Divines used the words "the collar" to symbolize discipline, the restraint imposed upon one by conscience; "slipping the collar" was to free oneself from discipline. In the poem the poet says that he is free and will do whatever he pleases. Why should he always be subject to another's will? The world is full of good things that he has been denying himself; he will cast away his self-imposed restraint, burst out of the cage of virtue in which he has enclosed himself, and begin to live a life of pleasure, because he that willingly forbears to do what he wants to do deserves his fate. As the poet raves on about the life of indulgence he will lead, he seems to hear a voice calling, "Child," and he answers, "My Lord." The presumption is that the thought of Christ makes him see the folly of the wicked course he had thought to embark upon. The last stanza of the poem follows:

But as I raved, and grew more fierce and wild
    At every word,
Methoughts I heard one calling, "Child";
And I replied, "My Lord."

634

Midsummer madness

Source: TWELFTH NIGHT (Act III, sc. iv, l. 59)
Author: William Shakespeare (1564-1616)
First published: 1623
Type of work: Dramatic comedy

Context: A self-loving steward, Malvolio, nurses ridiculous aspirations for the affections of his mistress, Countess Olivia. He is greatly disliked by Sir Toby Belch, Olivia's bibulous uncle, and Maria, the countess' waiting woman. They, together with Sir Andrew Aguecheek, a ridiculous and hopeless suitor to Olivia and tool of Sir Toby, seek revenge on Malvolio because he has interfered in their affairs. They accomplish their aim by dropping a love note for him to discover in the garden. He finds it and, completely duped into believing it to be from Olivia and meant for him, obeys its injunctions to appear before her in yellow stockings, cross-gartered, smiling idiotically and kissing his hand. Olivia, in mourning for a dead brother, is amazed by the sober and civil steward's appearance and behavior, and thinks he is mad.

MALVOLIO
Remember who commended thy yellow stockings—

OLIVIA
Thy yellow stockings?

MALVOLIO
And wished to see thee cross-gartered.

OLIVIA
Cross-gartered?

MALVOLIO
Go to, thou art made, if thou desirest to be so— . . . If not, let me see thee a servant still.

OLIVIA
Why this is very **midsummer madness**. . . . Good Maria, let this fellow be looked to. . . . Let some of my people have a special care of him, . . .

The mighty have no theory of technique

Source: PH. D'S. ("Sophia Trenton," Stanza 28)
Author: Leonard Bacon (1887-1954)
First published: 1925
Type of work: Satirical poem

Context: This poem is a whimsical satire aimed at pedantry and sham in the academic world. When only a freshman, Sophia Trenton becomes enchanted by her English professor's inspired lecture on Shelley. She is so thoroughly carried away that she persists enthusiastically in her studies until she has completed work for the Ph.D., having done a flimsy dissertation on "Shelley in his musical relations." In time, however, she exhausts the fires of her dream world and finds reality only through involvements with real human demands. Finally she leaves Columbia University, completely disillusioned but with the prospects of redeeming herself in another environment. Early in the story, while she is still a freshman, her enthusiasm for the romanticists motivates her to try her hand at writing poetry and to join a group of campus poets, a rather odd group who are ready to distinguish themselves, if only by strange habits. These talented youths meet once a week in a downtown tavern to talk about poetry. On technique in writing they all agree:

> It is the idiot name
> Given to effort by those who are too weak,
> Too weary, or too dull to play the game.
> **The mighty have no theory of technique,**
> But leave it to
> Second-story men of letters and small critics.

The mighty hunter before the Lord

Source: GENESIS 10:9
Author: Unknown
First transcribed: c.1000-300 B.C.
Type of work: Religious history and law

Context: Nimrod, "the mighty hunter before the Lord," is referred to in the genealogy of Ham, one of Noah's sons. He was the son of Cush, whose settlement extended from Babylonia to Ethiopia. As a descendant of Noah, Nimrod's role in the story of mankind was a peculiar one. The descendants of Noah had the obligation of repeopling and of settling the earth, and of reestablishing the various cultures, all mankind except Noah and his sons having been destroyed by a great flood because of wickedness. The descendants of Ham suffered a curse from God which

636

made them subservient to the descendants of Noah's other sons, Ham at one time having foolishly shown disrespect to his father. In the genealogical account are these words concerning Nimrod:

And Cush begat Nimrod: he began to be a mighty one in the earth.
He was a mighty hunter before the Lord: wherefore it is said,
Even as Nimrod **the mighty hunter before the Lord.**

The milk of human kindness

Source: MACBETH (Act I, sc. v, 1. 18)
Author: William Shakespeare (1564-1616)
First published: 1623
Type of work: Dramatic tragedy

Context: Lady Macbeth, in her castle at Inverness, has received a letter from her husband, with the story of his encounter with three witches who hailed him as Thane of Cawdor and as "King hereafter." While still overcome with astonishment at their prophecy, he receives word that, for his valor in battle, he had indeed been created Thane of Cawdor in place of the rebel thane who had conspired with Norway against Scotland. The sudden fulfilment of part of the witches' prophecy has fired Macbeth's ambition: he may yet be king. But his wife, more clear-sighted and more ruthless than he, knows that her husband may well lack the strength of mind needed to achieve the goal he seeks. In her soliloquy she analyzes her husband's character and resolves to bolster his weakness with her greater strength.

LADY MACBETH
Glamis thou art, and Cawdor, and shalt be
What thou art promised: yet do I fear thy nature;
It is too full o' **the milk of human kindness**
To catch the nearest way. . . .

Millions for defense, but not one cent for tribute

Source: A HISTORY OF THE UNITED STATES (Edward Channing, Volume IV)
Author: Charles Cotesworth Pinckney (1746-1825)
First spoken: 1797
Type of work: Diplomatic comment

Context: The occasion for this famous quotation was the "X Y Z Affair." American vessels were being stopped on the high seas by order of

637

the French Directory, and President Adams sent three commissioners to Paris to negotiate. Pinckney was one of the commissioners, the other two being John Marshall and Elbridge Gerry. Talleyrand would not receive the Americans directly, but sought to deal with them through three agents, designated X Y Z in the American dispatches. The agents demanded a large bribe for receiving the commissioners and also stipulated that the United States should make a loan to France. The commissioners indignantly refused these demands, Pinckney's words being variously reported as "No, no. Not a sixpence"; "not *a damned penny* for tribute"; and the version quoted above. The phrase has also been attributed to Robert Goodloe Harper (1765-1825), but inscribed on a cenotaph in memory of Charles Cotesworth Pinckney, St. Michael's Church, Charleston, S. C., appears the best-known version:

Millions for defence, but not one cent for tribute.

Millions of spiritual creatures walk the earth

Source: PARADISE LOST (Book IV, l. 677)
Author: John Milton (1608-1674)
First published: 1667
Type of work: Epic poem

Context: Eve asks Adam why the moon and stars shine all night long. Adam tells her that the heavenly bodies must pass around the earth each day. Milton is here using the Ptolemaic cosmology, which is earth-centered. The poet also has Adam say that the light of the moon and stars prevent chaos from coming again to reclaim the created universe. He suggests, too, that there are astrological influences, although he seems cautious in this regard; whether because of growing disbelief in astrology in seventeenth century England or because of religious reasons, one cannot tell. Milton also has Adam say that human beings are not the only creatures on earth, that heavenly spirits walk the night under starlight to sing God's praises when all mundane creatures are fast asleep:

". . . nor think, though men were none,
That heaven would want spectators, God want praise;
Millions of spiritual creatures walk the earth
Unseen, both when we wake, and when we sleep:
All these with ceaseless praise his works behold
Both day and night. . . ."

Millions ready saddled and bridled to be ridden

Source: LAST REMARKS WHILE ON THE SCAFFOLD, 1685 (quoted by Macaulay in *History of England,* Chapter V)
Author: Richard Rumbold (1622-1685)
First published: 1848
Type of work: Harangue

Context: After the Stuarts had been restored to England's throne and the old despotism resumed, the country still seethed with rebellion; and in 1683 the Rye House Plot was hatched. The plan was to waylay and assassinate Charles II and his brother (later James II) at Rye House Farm, as they returned from the Newmarket races. The royal party returned early, however, and the plot was frustrated. When word of the conspiracy leaked out, it served as an excuse to execute not only the plotters but a number of prominent members of their party. Among those brought to the scaffold was a brave and sincere man named Richard Rumbold, who owned Rye House Farm. He fought his captors gallantly, and was mortally wounded; but his conquerors could not forego the pleasure of seeing him hanged and quartered, so his trial was brief. Macaulay describes his courage:

. . . Though unable to stand without the support of two men, he maintained his fortitude to the last, and under the gibbet raised his feeble voice against Popery and tyranny with such vehemence that the officers ordered the drums to strike up, lest the people should hear him. He was a friend, he said, to limited monarchy. But he never would believe that Providence had sent a few men into the world ready booted and spurred to ride, and **millions ready saddled and bridled to be ridden.**

The mills of God grind slowly, yet they grind exceeding small

Source: SINNGEDICHTE: "Retribution"
Author: Friedrich von Logau (1604-1655); translated by Henry Wadsworth Longfellow (1807-1882)
First published: 1654
Type of work: Poetical aphorism

Context: Friedrich von Logau was the principal poet of the Silesian school of poetry in the seventeenth century and the leading epigrammatist. A series of twelve of his epigrams on such subjects as money, sin, creeds, and truth were translated by Henry Wadsworth Longfellow. The aphorism on retribution, or divine vengeance, is given below in its entirety. A number of parallels exist, one of the earliest being from Euripides' *Medea:* "Slowly but surely withal moveth the might of the gods."

An early English version is in George Herbert's *Jacula Prudentum* (1640): "God's mill grinds slow, but sure"; a version from the Italian is from Giovanni Torriano's *A Common Place of Italian Proverbs* (1666): "God's mill grinds slowly, but bitter is the bran." The meaning of the saying is that although God's justice may not be inflicted upon a wrongdoer for some time after he does an evil deed, yet justice will eventually be done, and when it is done, it will be exceedingly thorough. Von Logau's complete epigram is:

> Though **the mills of God grind slowly, yet they grind exceeding small;**
> Though with patience he stands waiting, with exactness grinds he all.

The mind is its own place

Source: PARADISE LOST (Book I, l. 254)
Author: John Milton (1608-1674)
First published: 1667
Type of work: Epic poem

Context: These lines appear in one of Satan's first speeches, just after he and the other rebel angels have been hurled into Hell. Satan is temporarily defeated, but still unrepentant of his pride in opposing himself to God and His will. Satan's words here are reminiscent of a statement by Sir Thomas Browne in *Religio Medici* (1642), "The heart of man is the place the devils dwell in: I feel sometimes a hell within myself." In Book IV, line 75, of *Paradise Lost,* Milton also has Satan say, in similar vein, "Which way I fly is Hell; myself am Hell." Satan is made to recognize his own nature, despite his vaunt:

> Hail, horrors, hail,
> Infernal world, and thou, profoundest hell,
> Receive thy new possessor: One who brings
> A mind not to be changed by place or time.
> **The mind is its own place,** and in itself
> Can make a Heaven of Hell, a Hell of Heaven.
> What matter where, if I be still the same. . . .

Minds that have nothing to confer find little to perceive

Source: YES, THOU ART FAIR
Author: William Wordsworth (1770-1850)
First published: 1845
Type of work: Lyric poem

Context: Throughout his life, Wordsworth, as an exponent of romantic poetry, proclaimed the power and value of the imaginative faculty.

640

There is no finer expression of his belief in the creative power of the imagination than this lyric in which he describes the attractiveness of a maiden as the result of both natural beauty and the impetus to "feed my heart's devotion." A similar concept is noted in "Lines Composed a Few Miles above Tintern Abbey," in which the poet proclaims himself a lover of nature, the meadows, mountains, woods, "of all the mighty world/ Of eye, and ear,—both what they half create,/ And what perceive." In the present poem the function of the imagination is the same, but the object of contemplation is the beauty of woman. He writes:

> Yes! thou art fair, yet be not moved
>> To scorn the declaration,
> That sometimes I in thee have loved
>> My fancy's own creation.

> Imagination needs must stir;
>> Dear Maid, this truth I believe,
> **Minds that have nothing to confer**
> **Find little to perceive.**

Miniver coughed and called it fate, and kept on drinking

Source: MINIVER CHEEVY (Stanza 8)
Author: Edwin Arlington Robinson (1869-1935)
First published: 1907
Type of work: Poetic character sketch

Context: In "Miniver Cheevy" Robinson attempts to portray a man who, being unable to accept the reality of the age in which he lives, turns to the imagined romance of the past. Poor Miniver is set dancing when he sees "The vision of a warrior bold." Miniver dreams of "Thebes and Camelot,/ And Priam's neighbors." Although he has never seen a Medici, "He would have sinned incessantly/ Could he have been one." And so, unable to bear the brutality and lack of grace of the present day, he takes to drink and to dreams of days passed. This is the classic portrait of the romantic escapist who cannot face life as he finds it.

> Miniver Cheevy, born too late,
>> Scratched his head and kept on thinking;
> **Miniver coughed, and called it fate,**
> **And kept on drinking.**

641

The mirror of all courtesy

Source: KING HENRY THE EIGHTH (Act II, sc. i, 1. 53)
Author: William Shakespeare (1564-1616)
First published: 1623
Type of work: Historical drama

Context: The Duke of Buckingham suspects Cardinal Wolsey of being ready to stir up trouble between England and France—even of plotting with the French King. He remarks to friends upon the growing power and influence of the ambitious Cardinal. On the point of exposing Wolsey to the king, Buckingham is arrested on trumped-up charges of high treason. Now, tried, convicted, and condemned, he appears on the street, guarded. As he does so, bystanders discuss the pernicious cardinal and the beloved duke.

SECOND GENTLEMAN
Certainly
The Cardinal is the end of this.

. . .

FIRST GENTLEMAN
And generally, whoever the King favours,
The Cardinal instantly will find employment,
And far enough from Court too.

SECOND GENTLEMAN
All the commons
Hate him perniciously, and o' my conscience
Wish him ten fathom deep. This duke as much
They love and dote on, call him bounteous Buckingham,
The mirror of all courtesy.

Miserable comforters are ye all

Source: JOB 16:2
Author: Unknown
First transcribed: c.900-500 B.C.
Type of work: Religious saga

Context: Job, of the land of Uz, a righteous man who is blessed in the eyes of the Lord, is a wealthy patriarch with seven sons and three daughters. Satan challenges God to let Job be tested to discover whether the good man will curse God. Job's possessions and his children are taken away from him, and he himself is tortured by boils covering his body, but he still refuses to forsake the Almighty. Lamenting the day of his birth and his life of travail, Job listens to his friends Eliphaz the Temanite, Bildad and Shuhite, and Zophar the Naamathite, who argue that God does not punish the innocent and that His ways are inscrutable. When they strongly suggest that their friend is suffering for his sins, Job insists that he is innocent and reproves them by saying (thus giving rise to the expression "Job's comforters"):

> I have heard many such things: **miserable comforters are ye all.**
> . . . if your soul were in my soul's stead. . . .
> . . . I would strengthen you with my mouth, and the moving of my lips should assuage your grief.

Mithridates, he died old

Source: A SHROPSHIRE LAD (LXII, stanza 4)
Author: A(lfred) E(dward) Housman (1859-1936)
First published: 1896
Type of work: Lyric poem

Context: One of A. E. Housman's recurring themes is the dreariness and bleakness of life and man's life-long burden to endure it. In the poem beginning " 'Terence, this is stupid stuff:' " a friend asks the country lad Terence to give some of his poetry. Terence tells his friend that beer is better than poetry to make life pleasant, and help one forget the terrible reality of living. Beer and ale, though, can give only temporary relief, Terence says, so he must adjust to the world somehow. As there is more ill fortune than good fortune, he adjusts to the ill. He illustrates his method of facing the world by relating the tale of Mithridates VI, King of Pontus, who supposedly made himself immune to poison by taking it in larger and larger quantities. The result was that all attempts to poison the king were unsuccessful. The efficacy of the method is ironically expressed in the last line of the concluding verses of the poem:

> They put arsenic in his meat
> And stared aghast to watch him eat;
> They poured strychnine in his cup
> And shook to see him drink it up:
> They shook, they stared as white's their shirt:
> Them it was their poison hurt.
> —I tell the tale that I heard told.
> **Mithridates, he died old.**

Moderation in all things

Source: THE LADY OF ANDROS (Act I, sc. i, l. 34)
Author: Terence (Publius Terentius Afer, c.190-159 B.C.)
First transcribed: Second century B.C.
Type of work: Dramatic comedy

Context: This is the first play adapted by Terence from the Greek of Menander. A critic some four hundred years later gave as the argument, a kind of plot summary, the following: "Glycerium, erroneously supposed to be the sister of a courtesan from Andros, was seduced by Pamphilus and being with child received his promise to marry her. His father had already arranged a match for him with a daughter of Chremes, and on discovering his intrigue made as if the marriage were still to take place, hoping in this way to discover his son's real sentiments. Acting on the advice of Davus, Pamphilus raised no objection. When, however, Chremes found that Glycerium had given birth to a child, he broke off the match between his daughter and Pamphilus. Afterwards he discovers to his surprise that Glycerium is a daughter of his own and marries her to Pamphilus." With such an excess of emotions, it seems strange that one of the opening speeches should give us the proverb.

SIMO

. . . As for the usual doings of young men, such as interesting themselves in keeping horses or hounds, or in philosophical lectures, he didn't pick out one of these above the rest, but still followed 'em all with moderation. I was delighted.

SOSIA

And quite rightly, Sir: I think the golden rule in life is **moderation in all things.**

Moderation is best in all things

Source: THE ELEGIES OF THEOGNIS
Author: Theognis (c.570-490 B.C.)
First transcribed: c.500 B.C.
Type of work: Gnomic poetry

Context: Sententious poetry has a long tradition, with its golden age at the time of Hesiod. Theognis, a nobleman in perilous times who supported the gentry rather than the rising democrats, wrote a series of poems of advice to a young friend, Cyrnus. Unfortunately, during the last centuries much of the sense and most of the poetry were spoiled by systematizing Theognis' writing as autobiography, whereas the fragments speak eloquently without crutches of emendation. *Sententiae,* number 220, begins the discussion of how a young man should comport himself: "Keep to the middle of the path without swerving to either side." Later, in number 335 he repeats the admonition as follows:

Be not too zealous; **moderation is best in all things.**

Monarch of all I survey

Source: VERSES SUPPOSED TO BE WRITTEN BY ALEXANDER SELKIRK, DURING HIS SOLITARY ABODE IN THE ISLAND OF JUAN FERNANDEZ
Author: William Cowper (1731-1800)
First published: 1782
Type of work: Poetic monologue

Context: The real Alexander Selkirk, or Selcraig (1676-1721), was a Scottish sailor who was marooned on Juan Fernandez, an island off Valparaiso, Chile, in 1704. For four years and five months he remained alone on the island, being finally rescued by a privateer in 1709. Selkirk's adventure created great interest in eighteenth century England and was the subject of a great deal of writing, both historical and fictitious. The best-known account is the novel *Robinson Crusoe,* by Daniel Defoe (1660-1731). Both Defoe and Cowper describe Selkirk as a very pious man, though he is said to have left Scotland to evade appearing before a kirk-session, in 1695, to face the charge of indecent behavior in church. Cowper, being of a deeply religious nature himself, pictures Selkirk as missing "Society, friendship, and love" (Stanza 3), but, most of all, "the sound of the church-going bell" (Stanza 4). The poem begins:

I am **monarch of all I survey,**
My right there is none to dispute;
From the centre all round to the sea,
I am lord of the fowl and the brute.

The moon was made of green cheese

Source: GARGANTUA AND PANTAGRUEL (Book I, chapter 2)
Author: Francois Rabelais (1495-1553)
First published: 1532-1564
Type of work: Mock heroic chronicle

Context: Gargantua, the gigantic son of Grangosier and Gargamelle, as a small boy behaves with the same vulgarities of other boys, although his actions are exaggerated. "He was continually wallowing and rolling up

645

and down in the mire." He believes in many of the superstitions that one hears laughingly quoted today, and Rabelais is poking fun at them. The belief about the moon and cheese was used by John Heywood in *Proverbes* (1546), Part II, chapter 7. It is of course a common reference today. Rabelais says about Gargantua's childhood:

> He would pull at the kid's leather, or vomit up his dinner, then reckon without his host. He would beat the bushes without catching the birds, thought **the moon was made of green cheese,** and that bladders are lanterns.

Morality, thou deadly bane

Source: A DEDICATION TO GAVIN HAMILTON (Stanza 5)
Author: Robert Burns (1759-1796)
First published: 1786
Type of work: Satiric poem

Context: Burns dedicated his first book of poetry to his friend, lawyer Gavin Hamilton. Amusingly, however, the poet placed the dedication poem in the volume in the twenty-fifth place, perhaps surmising that an ecclesiastical satire, one of many that Burns wrote, might not make a popular opening. The poem was written when Hamilton, along with Burns, one of the New Lichts who held to a liberalized interpretation of Calvinistic doctrine, was persecuted by an Auld Licht minister and charged among other things with two absences from church in December and three in January. Hamilton was exonerated by the church councils. Burns was bitter against the kind of religion that brought such charges. A religion like this, he felt, degrades man by its doctrines and masked sanctimoniousness and lack of compassion. In the middle of this poem, which is marked in general by jesting and jovial charm, Burns's bitterness flashes out in lines such as,

> **Morality, thou deadly bane,**
> Thy tens o' thousands thou hast slain.
> Vain is his hope, whose stay and trust is
> In mortal mercy, truth, and justice.

The more fool I

Source: AS YOU LIKE IT (Act II, sc. iv, l. 16)
Author: William Shakespeare (1564-1616)
First published: 1623
Type of work: Dramatic comedy

Context: The scene is the Forest of Arden, whither has fled Duke Senior, whose throne has been usurped by his younger brother, Frederick. With him

646

have come several attendant lords. Rosalind, Duke Senior's daughter, had remained at the court of her usurping uncle because of her affection for the latter's daughter, Celia. But when Duke Frederick discovers that his niece has fallen in love with Orlando, the son of a supporter of his elder brother, he banishes her from his court. Rosalind decides to join her father. Dressed in boy's clothes and accompanied by her faithful cousin Celia and Touchstone, a clown, she enters the Forest of Arden in search of the deposed Duke. The three are exhausted after their long journey and dejected in spirits. The following conversation ensues:

CELIA

I pray you bear with me, I cannot go no further.

TOUCHSTONE

For my part, I had rather bear with you than bear you; yet I should bear no cross if I did bear you, for I think you have no money in your purse.

ROSALIND

Well, this is the forest of Arden.

TOUCHSTONE

Ay, now I am in Arden, **the more fool I;** when I was at home I was in a better place, but travellers must be content.

More in sorrow than in anger

Source: HAMLET (Act I, sc. ii, l. 232)
Author: William Shakespeare (1564-1616)
First published: 1603
Type of work: Dramatic tragedy

Context: This line is usually heard in the contracted form given, but its meaning is precisely the same as Shakespeare meant it in *Hamlet.* In the play, Horatio, a school friend of Prince Hamlet of Denmark, and two officers of the watch, Bernardo and Marcellus, have seen the ghost of the recently dead King Hamlet on the battlements of the castle. They come to tell the prince their news. Hamlet has been brooding on his father's death and is thus receptive to their words. He questions them closely about the apparition:

HAMLET
. . .
Hold you the watch tonight?

MARCELLUS AND BERNARDO
We do my lord.

HAMLET
Armed say you?

. . .

MARCELLUS AND BERNARDO
My lord, from head to foot.

. . .

HAMLET
What, looked he frowningly?

HORATIO
A countenance **more in sorrow than in anger.**

More knave than fool

Source: DON QUIXOTE (Part I, Book IV, chapter 4)
Author: Miguel de Cervantes Saavedra (1547-1616)
First published: 1605
Type of work: Satirical novel

Context: The question of whether a person is acting through craft or stupidity has been a puzzle with many fictional characters. One, in *The Jew of Malta* (1633) by Christopher Marlowe (1564-1593), declared: "Now will I show myself to have more of the serpent than the dove, that is, more knave than fool." Andrew's master spoke similarly in Don Quixote's first knightly adventure. Riding home after having been dubbed knight, the Don hears cries. Hurrying to the rescue, he finds a fifteen-year-old boy tied to an oak tree, being flogged by his master. This is in Part I, Book I, Chapter IV. Later, in Book IV, Chapter 4, he tells Sancho about the episode and how he:

. . . demanded the cause of his severe chastisement? The rude fellow answered, that he had liberty to punish his own servant, whom he thus used for some faults that argued him **more knave than fool.**

More matter with less art

Source: HAMLET (Act II, sc. ii, l. 96)
Author: William Shakespeare (1564-1616)
First published: 1603
Type of work: Dramatic tragedy

Context: Hamlet, Prince of Denmark, is informed by his dead father's ghost that he was murdered in his sleep by his brother Claudius, the present Danish King, and that Hamlet's mother, Gertrude, was adulterous with Claudius. Hamlet swears to avenge his father by murdering the well-guarded king. As a start, and hoping to relax the king's guard, Hamlet pretends to be mad by behaving oddly in the presence of Ophelia, daughter of the king's chief councilor, Polonius. Ophelia tells her father, and Polonius concludes that the prince is insane. He hurries to report Hamlet's strange behavior to the royal couple. But he talks around the subject, is foolish, and longwinded.

POLONIUS
• • •
Mad call I it, for to define true madness,
What is't but to be nothing else but mad?
But let that go.

GERTRUDE
More matter with less art.

POLONIUS
Madam, I swear I use no art at all.
That he's mad 'tis true; 'tis true, 'tis pity,
And pity 'tis 'tis true—a foolish figure,
But farewell it, for I will use no art.
• • •

More sinned against, than sinning

Source: KING LEAR (Act III, sc. ii, l. 60)
Author: William Shakespeare (1564-1616)
First published: 1608
Type of work: Dramatic tragedy

Context: This saying has become a proverb in the English language. In the play, Lear, King of Britain, an old, irascible man divides his kingdom between his two eldest daughters, Goneril and Regan, and cuts off his youngest, Cordelia, with nothing. When he does so, a faithful follower,

649

Kent, questions the decision and is banished for his pains. Soon, however, Kent's warning comes true: Lear is stripped of his bodyguard of one hundred knights and turned out by Goneril and Regan to wander on the heath accompanied only by his jester. Reduced to impotent fury, he curses his offspring and hurls defiance at the raging storm that swirls about him. Cold, miserable deserted by all except his fool, he is found by his friend, Kent, who, at peril of his life, did not leave the country. Lear, on the verge of madness, does not recognize his old follower, but continues his raving.

LEAR
Let the great gods
That keep this dreadful pother o'er our heads
Find out their enemies now. . . .
         Close pent-up guilts,
Rive your concealing continents, and cry
These dreadful summoners grace. I am a man
More sinned against, than sinning.

The more the merrier

Source: THE PROVERBS OF JOHN HEYWOOD (Part II, chapter 7)
Author: John Heywood (1497?-1580?)
First published: 1546
Type of work: Gnomic poetry

Context: The author is telling stories to a young man who asked if he should marry for love or money, and is proving by his stories that either way the youth will likely regret his decision. Now the story is about a young man who married a rich widow. The marriage did not prosper, because soon husband and wife found more grounds for disagreement than for concord. The husband is now talking to the author and reporting on his wife's deficiencies. He says that, "Every man can rule a shrew, save he that hath her," and, "She will lie as fast as a dog will lick a dish." She nags him for spending too much time away from home, yet drives him away with her nagging. Then in discussing the advantages of eating alone or with others, the author quotes a proverb that is widespread, and the young husband responds with another:

The mo the merrier, we all day hear and see.
Yea, but the fewer the better fare, (said he).

650

More things are wrought by prayer than this world dreams of

Source: MORTE D'ARTHUR (Lines 247-248)
Author: Alfred, Lord Tennyson (1809-1892)
First published: 1842
Type of work: Narrative poem

Context: Tennyson later incorporated this poem into "The Passing of Arthur" in the *Idylls of the King.* As in his other poems on classical and medieval themes, Tennyson invests "Morte D'Arthur" with modern philosophy and Christian morality. Lying in the barge which is about to carry him away to death, Arthur gives Bedivere a sermon on prayer as he contemplates his own fate:

> ". . . but thou,
> If thou shouldst never see my face again,
> Pray for my soul. **More things are wrought by prayer**
> **Than this world dreams of.** Wherefore, let thy voice
> Rise like a fountain for me night and day.
> For what are men better than sheep or goats
> That nourish a blind life within the brain,
> If, knowing God, they lift not hands of prayer
> Both for themselves and those who call them friend?
> For so the whole round earth is every way
> Bound by gold chains about the feet of God. . . ."

The morn in russet mantle clad

Source: HAMLET (Act I, sc. i, l. 166)
Author: William Shakespeare (1564-1616)
First published: 1603
Type of work: Dramatic tragedy

Context: The opening scene of *Hamlet* occurs on the ramparts of the Danish castle of Elsinore. The guard is changed at midnight and, by prearrangement, the relieving officer, Bernardo, is joined by fellow officer Marcellus and Horatio, a friend of young Prince Hamlet. Horatio is present to confirm a report of a ghost which has appeared twice previously on the battlements. Horatio is skeptical of the reports, but soon the apparition appears and is recognized as the ghost of the dead King Hamlet. It will not stay or speak at Horatio's demand but disappears. The three men discuss the unsettled conditions in the kingdom since King Hamlet died and decide the appearance of his ghost is an omen of evil. The ghost reappears, is about to speak, when, at the crow of a cock, he once more vanishes. Following a subdued discussion of it, the worried Horatio realizes day is dawning.

• • •

But look **the morn in russet mantle clad**
Walks o'er the dew of yon high eastward hill.
Break we our watch up, and by my advice
Let us impart what we have seen to-night
Unto young Hamlet, for upon my life
This spirit dumb to us will speak to him.

• • •

The morning stars sang together

Source: JOB 38:7
Author: Unknown
First transcribed: c.900-500 B.C.
Type of work: Religious saga

Context: Job, a righteous man in the land of Uz, has lost his wealth and children and felt the torture of sores on his body as a result of a challenge that Satan has put to God. Refusing to curse God, but lamenting his condition and maintaining his innocence, Job hears out the arguments of Eliphaz the Temanite, Bildad the Shuhite, and Zophar the Naamathite, concerning his guilt, but rejects their condemnation of him. Elihu, dismissing the three men as incapable of convincing the sufferer, argues that pain serves to warn the sinner, that Job has sinned by judging God, that God cannot commit evil, and that man cannot understand the magnitude of the Almighty. Finally, from the whirlwind, God speaks to Job, reminding him of his insignificance and asking:

> Where wast thou when I laid the foundations of the earth? . . .
> Whereupon are the foundations thereof fastened? or who laid the corner stone thereof;
> When **the morning stars sang together,** and all the sons of God shouted for joy?

The most potent thing in life is habit

Source: THE ART OF LOVE (Book II, l. 345)
Author: Ovid (43 B.C.?-A.D. 18)
First transcribed: First century
Type of work: A satiric poem on seduction

Context: Ovid is giving advice on how to be successful in wooing a lover. He says that the lover should be kind, considerate and willing to suffer some frustrations before expecting to win his object. Women are

652

given to flightiness, Ovid says, and must be suffered in this their nature. He counsels, further, that one cannot expect success immediately. Love's growth is fragile and often tenuous. He says:

> Love is frail at birth, but it grows stronger with age if it is properly fed. The roaring bull that frightens you today was the tender calf you stroked not long ago. . . . Let your mistress become accustomed to you and your curious ways, for **the most potent thing in life is habit.** Be with her on all occasions until you notice that she is used to you and needs your presence.

Mother o' mine, O mother o' mine!

Source: MOTHER O' MINE (Refrain)
Author: Rudyard Kipling (1865-1936)
First published: 1902
Type of work: Lyric poem

Context: In this short poem Kipling extols the virtue of a mother's love, the deep love that knows no end no matter what the son does. If he were hanged for murder, his mother's love would follow him. If he were "drowned in the deepest sea," his mother's tears would come down to him. And if he were "damned of body and soul," still his mother's prayers would make him whole.

> If I were damned of body and soul,
> I know whose prayers would make me whole,
> **Mother o' mine, O mother o' mine!**

A motley fool

Source: AS YOU LIKE IT (Act II, sc. vii, l. 13)
Author: William Shakespeare (1564-1616)
First published: 1623
Type of work: Dramatic comedy

Context: This play is generally felt to be Shakespeare's most nearly perfect romantic comedy. Duke Senior and his followers are living in Arden forest because Frederick, the Duke's brother, has usurped the throne. Now the Duke, with Amiens, a lord attending on him, and other lords are searching in the forest for Jaques, a melancholic lord who also attends on Duke Senior. The character of Jaques is revealed in the following dialogue between himself and Duke Senior, when the former appears in the forest.

653

DUKE SENIOR
Why how now monsieur, what a life is this,
That your poor friends must woo your company.
What, you look merrily.

JAQUES
A fool, a fool! I met a fool i' th' forest,
A motley fool—a miserable world—
As I do live by food, I met a fool,
Who laid him down and basked him in the sun,
And railed on Lady Fortune in good terms,
In good set terms, and yet a motley fool.

• • •

Mouths without hands; maintained at vast expense

Source: FABLES ANCIENT AND MODERN ("Cymon and Iphigenia," Line 401)
Author: John Dryden (1631-1700)
First published: 1700
Type of work: Narrative poem

Context: Some of the fables, or stories, retold in this work are modernizations of Chaucer; others Dryden translated from Boccaccio, as he did the story of Cymon and Iphigenia. At this point in the tale Cymon, with his fellow Cyprians, is driven ashore by a gale and captured by the people of Rhodes. The victors in the skirmish are modeled by Dryden after the militia, or train-bands, he saw in seventeenth century London, men who trained infrequently and were little able to command any respect as soldiers, much less fight a real enemy:

The County rings around with loud Alarms,
And raw in Fields the rude Militia swarms;
Mouths without Hands; maintain'd at vast Expense,
In Peace a Charge, in War a weak Defence:
Stout once a Month they march a blust'ring Band,
And ever, but in times of Need, at hand:
This was the Morn when issuing on the Guard,
Drawn up in Rank and File they stood prepar'd
Of seeming Arms to make a short Essay,
Then hasten to be Drunk, the Business of the Day.

Much learning doth make thee mad

Source: ACTS 26:24
Author: Unknown (traditionally Luke)
First transcribed: 60-150 (probably c.80-90)
Type of work: Religious history and tradition

Context: The author tells of Paul's arrest and trial in Jerusalem after the completion of his third missionary journey. The people, stirred up by some Asian Jews, seize Paul in the temple. The mob is prevented from killing him in the street by the intervention of some Roman soldiers. Paul is brought to trial before the high court of the Jews, the Sanhedrin. Paul throws the session into chaos by declaring that he is a Pharisee and believes in the Resurrection; the Pharisees and Sadducees begin arguing so violently that Paul has to be transferred to prison in Caesarea, where he is tried first by Felix and then by Festus, Roman rulers. Paul finally appeals his case to Caesar. In the meantime King Agrippa comes to salute Festus on his ascending to power in Caesarea. Paul repeats his testimony of defense before Agrippa and Festus:

And as he thus spake for himself, Festus said with a loud voice,
Paul, thou art beside thyself; **much learning doth make thee mad.**

Much might be said on both sides

Source: THE SPECTATOR (Volume I, number 122)
Author: Joseph Addison (1672-1719)
First published: July 20, 1711
Type of work: Essay

Context: Joseph Addison, who with Richard Steele is credited by many with returning the English public of the eighteenth century to a concern for sound moral and social attitudes following the riotous living that followed the restoration of Charles II, created the figure of Sir Roger de Coverley in the pages of the famous *Spectator* magazine. The urbane but gossipy narrator of many of the magazine's essays, Mr. Spectator, is also an important creation of Addison and Steele; not only is he amusing, but also highly informative as to the conditions and thinking of the period in England. Sir Roger is, in the imaginative scheme of the periodical, a friend of Mr. Spectator and a member of the Spectator Club. Sir Roger, over a period of time, evolves from the position of an irresponsible rake, to that of a lovable, politically fuddled Tory squire. In this passage, Sir Roger de Coverley, en route to visit court with his acquaintances Tom Touchy and Will Wimble, refuses to participate in an exchange of snap judgments, and, the narrator advises us:

. . . after having paused some time, told them, with the air of a man who would not give his judgment rashly, that **much might be said on both sides.** They were neither of them dissatisfied with the knight's determination, because neither of them found him in the wrong by it. . . .

Much of a muchness

Source: ALICE'S ADVENTURES IN WONDERLAND (Chapter 7)
Author: Lewis Carroll (Charles Lutwidge Dodgson, 1832-1898)
First published: 1865
Type of work: Imaginative tale for children

Context: The lasting fame of the Oxford lecturer in mathematics, Charles Lutwidge Dodgson, rests with his imaginative stories for children, centering around a young friend, Alice Liddell, and written under the pen name, Lewis Carroll. In *Alice's Adventures in Wonderland,* Alice becomes bored while her sister reads a book and runs after a White Rabbit, tripping and falling a great distance down into the rabbit hole. When she stops falling, Alice finds herself in a queer land in which many strange things happen. She attends a tea with the Mad Hatter, the March Hare, and a sleepy Dormouse, at which the Dormouse tells a disjointed tale about three little sisters who live at the bottom of a well and draw treacle from it. The Dormouse, becoming sleepy, abruptly changes the thought and has the sisters drawing pictures of "all manner of things":

> The Dormouse had closed its eyes by this time, and was going off into a doze; but, on being pinched by the Hatter, it woke up again with a little shriek, and went on: "—that begins with an M, such as mouse-traps, and the moon, and memory, and muchness—you know you say things are **'much of a muchness'**—did you ever see such a thing as a drawing of a muchness!"

Mum's the word

Source: DON QUIXOTE (Part II, Book IV, chatper 44)
Author: Miguel de Cervantes Saavedra (1547-1616)
First published: 1615
Type of work: Satirical novel

Context: The use of "mum" to signify silence is widespread. Starting as an inarticulate sound, as we say "mumble," the word then became "momme" in Middle English, and meant "soundless." A "mummer" is an actor in a dumb show. In *Merry Wives of Windsor* (Act V, sc. ii, l.

656

6) Slender tells Mr. Page how he recognizes his daughter: "I come to her in white and cry 'Mum.' " Sancho, suspecting that it was the Duke's servant who impersonated the Countess in the Duke's practical joke on Don Quixote, tells his master:

> . . . Adad, sir, . . . you may think I'm in jest, but I heard him open just now, and I thought the very voice of Madam Trifaldi sounded in my ears. But **mum's the word.** I say nothing. . . .

Murder will out

Source: THE CANTERBURY TALES ("The Prioress's Tale," Line 576)
Author: Geoffrey Chaucer (1343?-1400)
First transcribed: 1387-1392
Type of work: Legend of the "miracle of our Lady"

Context: The Prioress tells of a city in Asia which had a Jewish section, through which a Christian lad, aged seven, passed daily. The lad was a widow's son, and was accompanied by an older boy. The story stretches its tone of tenderness somewhat close to the satiric, but probably Chaucer was not intending to be satiric. The Jews in the section of the street resent the piety of the lad and his constant praising of the Virgin. They are therefore susceptible when "the serpent Satan" plants in their minds hatred of this boy and suggests that the lad should be done away with. The belief that murder cannot be concealed is widespread. Chaucer uses it elsewhere ("The Nun's Priest's Tale," lines 4242 and 4247), and Shakespeare uses it (*Hamlet,* Act II, scene ii, line (622). In "The Prioress's Tale," Chaucer tells how the Jews disemboweled the lad and threw him into a privy; then he concludes:

> **Mordre wol out,** certyn, it wol nat faille,
> And namely ther th'onour of God shal sprede;
> The blood out crieth on youre cursed dede.

Music has charms to soothe a savage breast

Source: THE MOURNING BRIDE (Act I, sc. i)
Author: William Congreve (1670-1729)
First published: 1697
Type of work: Dramatic tragedy

Context: The scene of Congreve's tragedy is Granada, one of the kingdoms of Old Spain. Almeria, a princess of Granada, dressed in mourn-

657

ing, bewails the fate of Anselmo, late king of Valencia, who has recently died and been buried in Granada as a captive. Almeria's sorrow and that of her chief attendant seem overly great, even though we learn that Anselmo had once had Almeria as his captive and had treated her as well as his own child, before losing a war to Granada and himself becoming a captive. In a dialogue between Almeria and Le-onora, her chief attendant, we learn a little later the real cause of the intense sorrow: King Anselmo, her father's prisoner, was Almeria's father-in-law; Almeria and Alphonso, the Prince of Valencia, were secretly married. Alphonso is now presumed dead, drowned at sea. The quotation is the opening lines of the play, spoken by Almeria when music accompanying the opening curtain ceases.

> **Musick has Charms to sooth a savage Breast,**
> To soften Rocks, or bend a knotted Oak.
> I've read, that things inanimate have mov'd,
> And, as with living Souls, have been inform'd,
> By Magick Numbers and persuasive Sound.
> What then am I? Am I more senseless grown
> Than Trees, or Flint? O force of constant Woe!

My baby at my breast, that sucks the nurse asleep

Source: ANTONY AND CLEOPATRA (Act V, sc. ii, ll. 312-313)
Author: William Shakespeare (1564-1616)
First published: 1623
Type of work: Dramatic tragedy

Context: Cleopatra, beautiful Queen of Egypt, is in the act of killing herself. Alone with her attendants in her tomb, a captive of Octavius Caesar, she prefers to die rather than to allow herself to be exhibited to the populace of Rome as his prisoner. There is nothing left to live for since her lover Mark Antony is dead, and with him, her imperial dreams. Charmian, an attendant, is with her.

CLEOPATRA
• • •

Come thou mortal wretch,
[*Applies an asp to her breast.*]
With thy sharp teeth this knot intrinsicate
Of life at once untie. Poor venomous fool,
Be angry, and dispatch. O couldst thou speak,
That I might hear thee call great Caesar ass,
Unpolicied.

CHARMIAN
O eastern star!

658

Peace, peace.

Dost thou not see **my baby at my breast,
That sucks the nurse asleep?**

CHARMIAN
O break! O break!

My candle burns at both ends

Source: FIGS FROM THISTLES (First Fig)
Author: Edna St. Vincent Millay (1892-1950)
First published: 1922
Type of work: Lyric poem

Context: In a sense this brief poem is a flash autobiographical image of the poetess. The daring, independent, playful effervescence of the lines reflects the charm and energy of this famous young lady. The same qualities of personality and attitude toward life can be found in her letters of this period. They reflect an optimistic outlook, a whimsical imagination, aggressiveness, and a genial spirit. To live fully, alertly, and originally seems to have been her desire, and her life in many ways realized this desire. She lived for several years after finishing at Vassar as a Bohemian in Greenwich Village. She was a powerful spokesman for the spirit of revolt and emancipation in the 1920's. Her brief poem makes vivid the intensity of her living:

My candle burns at both ends;
　　It will not last the night;
　　But ah, my foes, and oh, my friends—
　　It gives a lovely light!

My center is giving way, my right is pushed back, situation excellent, I am attacking

Source: MESSAGE TO GENERAL JOSEPH JOFFRE
Author: Ferdinand Foch (1851-1929)
First published: Unknown (1914 or 1918)
Type of work: Military message

Context: Although sometimes attributed to Marshal Foch during the Second Battle of the Marne, the communiqué is generally conceded to have been sent by him during the First Battle of the Marne in 1914 to the chief

659

of the general staff of France, General Joseph Joffre, who, before the German troops crossed the Marne and advanced on Paris, ordered Foch to maintain the line at all costs. On September 9, Foch secured from General d'Esperey a corps, which he placed on his left, moved one of his own corps opposite the German center, then struck, routing the troops of General von Hausen, and finally ordered a general attack. Before the strike, General Foch is supposed to have written:

My center is giving way, my right is pushed back, situation excellent, I am attacking.

My child-wife

Source: DAVID COPPERFIELD (Chapter 44)
Author: Charles Dickens (1812-1870)
First published: 1849-1850
Type of work: Novel

Context: Dickens was at his best when he was creating the unforgettable characters of his novels. One of the most enchanting and pathetic of all is Dora, the young and soon-dead wife of David Copperfield. When he first meets his eventual bride, he says of her, "She had the most delightful little voice, the gayest little laugh, the pleasantest and most fascinating little ways, that ever led a lost youth into hopeless slavery." When, however, later on, he attempts to impress upon Dora that, because of his reduced circumstances, they will have to live very frugally, she faints dead away. "A thing of light, and airiness, and joy," she has not grown up at all. After the marriage and after a particularly bad dinner at which Copperfield has been embarrassed for his guest, Dora comes to him, asks him to call her his "child-wife," and says,

"I don't mean, you silly fellow, that you should use the name instead of Dora. I only mean that you should think of me that way. When you are going to be angry with me, say to yourself, 'it's only **my child-wife!**' When I am very disappointing, say, 'I knew, a long time ago, that she would make but a child-wife!' When you miss what I should like to be, and I think can never be, say, 'still my foolish child-wife loves me!' For indeed I do."

My days are swifter than a weaver's shuttle

Source: JOB 7:6
Author: Unknown
First transcribed: c.900-500 B.C.
Type of work: Religious saga

Context: Job, of the land of Uz, "perfect and upright" before the Lord, is a wealthy man with seven sons and three daughters. Challenging God, Satan says that if Job were to lose his possessions and family he would surely curse God. Job, however, after hearing of the loss of his wealth and children, remains humble before the Lord. When Satan receives God's permission to torture the body of Job with boils, the upright man still refuses to curse the Almighty. Confronted by his friends Eliphaz the Temanite, Bildad the Shuhite, and Zophar the Naamathite, Job laments the day of his birth and the agony of his life, and to Eliphaz's argument that God does not punish the innocent, Job begs to be shown how he has erred. In his suffering, he wishes for death, but complains of his condition and of the brevity of life:

> My flesh is clothed with worms and clods of dust; my skin is broken, and becomes loathsome.
> **My days are swifter than a weaver's shuttle,** and are spent without hope.

My God, my God, why hast thou forsaken me?

Source: PSALMS 22:1
Author: Unknown
First transcribed: c.400-200 B.C.
Type of work: Religious poetry

Context: Imploringly the psalmist asks why God has forsaken him and has not helped him when he has moaned day and night without rest. He remembers that God heard the groans of his ancestors and delivered them. His friends have laughed him to scorn because he continues to trust in God, Who sustained him in his youth. His evil enemies with the strength of many bulls have encompassed him, piercing his hands and feet, gloating over him, and casting lots for his garments. He then begs God not to let these events occur and ends the psalm with a vow to praise the Lord in the congregation. The final lines of the poem are in stark contrast with the opening words:

> **My God, my God, why hast thou forsaken me?** why art thou so far from helping me, and from the words of my roaring?

O my god, I cry in the daytime, but thou hearest not; and in the night season, and am not silent.

Jesus, hanging on the cross, his hands and his feet pierced, taunted by the crowds, his garments divided by lots among thieves, appropriately re- calls the beginning words of this psalm of lament (Matthew 27:46 and Mark 15:34).

My heart is a lonely hunter

Source: THE LONELY HUNTER (Stanza 6)
Author: Fiona Macleod (William Sharp, 1855-1905)
First published: 1896
Type of work: Lyric poem

Context: The identity of the actual writer of the poems and tales that appeared under the name Fiona Macleod remained a carefully guarded secret until William Sharp's death in 1905. Using his pseudonym, Sharp published several volumes that combined Celtic paganism and a deep worship of nature. The Fiona Macleod poem "The Lonely Hunter" appeared in the volume entitled *From the Hills of Dream* under the general heading "From the Heart of a Woman." The poem presents a maiden lamenting for her lover who "lies in the darkness, under the frail white flowers" in the "rowan-tree hollow." Nature aids the maiden in guarding the place where the lover lies, but not even the objects of nature can echo the whispers of the deceased lover. The poem ends with the following stanza:

O never a green leaf whispers, where the green-gold branches
    swing:
O never a song I hear now, where one was wont to sing.
Here in the heart of Summer, sweet is life to me still,
But **my heart is a lonely hunter** that hunts on a lonely hill.

My heart is like a singing bird

Source: A BIRTHDAY (Stanza 1)
Author: Christina Rossetti (1830-1894)
First published: 1861
Type of work: Lyric poem

Context: Christina Rossetti, the pale, beautiful sister of Dante Gabriel Rossetti and a follower of the artistic the- ories of the Pre-Raphaelite group of poets and painters, observed the nat- ural surroundings about London and

662

became closely acquainted with God's creations, which she often used symbolically for moral teachings. Her love of nature and her careful attention to detail are shown, for example, in "A Birthday." She sings with joy of the birthday or the beginning of her life, the day on which her love comes to her:

> My heart is like a singing bird
>> Whose nest is in a watered shoot;
> My heart is like an apple-tree
>> Whose boughs are bent with thickset fruit;
> My heart is like a rainbow shell
>> That paddles in a halcyon sea;
> My heart is gladder than all these
>> Because my love is come to me.

My heart is turned to stone

Source: OTHELLO (Act IV, sc. i, ll. 193-194)
Author: William Shakespeare (1564-1616)
First published: 1622
Type of work: Dramatic tragedy

Context: Othello, Moorish military governor of Cyprus in the service of Venice, chose Michael Cassio as his lieutenant in preference to Iago, whom he made his ancient (or ensign), a lower ranking officer. As a result, Iago determines to destroy them both. By means of clever and evil machinations and luck he convinces Othello that his bride, Desdemona, is unfaithful to him with Cassio. To clinch his case, Iago places the Moor where he overhears Cassio discussing and deriding Bianca, his mistress, but Othello believes he is talking about Desdemona. Now, thoroughly persuaded that his wife is false with Cassio, Othello is torn between hate for them both and love for her. Iago's plot is working well.

OTHELLO
I would have him nine years a-killing. A fine woman! A fair woman! A sweet woman!

IAGO
Nay, you must forget that.

OTHELLO
Ay, let her rot and perish, and be damned tonight; for she shall not live. No, **my heart is turned to stone;** I strike it, and it hurts my hand. O the world hath not a sweeter creature; she might be by an emperor's side, and command him tasks.

663

My heart was in my mouth

Source: SATYRICON (Section 62)
Author: Petronius (died c.66)
First transcribed: c.60
Type of work: Prose satirical romance

Context: At the home of Trimalchio a great feast has ended, and the people are sitting around amusing themselves. Niceros, friend of Trimalchio, tells about a friend of his who was a werewolf. One night Niceros persuaded this friend to go out with him. They came to a cemetery. Niceros recounts the events. (The literal translation of the phrase is: "My soul was in my nose.")

> Then when I looked round at my friend, he stripped himself and put all his clothes by the roadside. **My heart was in my mouth,** but I stood like a dead man. He made a ring of water round his clothes and suddenly turned into a wolf. . . . after he had turned into a wolf, he began to howl, and ran off into the woods.

My kingdom for a horse!

Source: KING RICHARD THE THIRD (Act V, sc. iv, l. 7)
Author: William Shakespeare (1564-1616)
First published: 1597
Type of work: Historical drama

Context: Having won his way to the throne of England by means of a series of murders (among them the murders of his brother, the Duke of Clarence; Edward, Prince of Wales, son of Henry VI; Lord Rivers; Lord Grey; Lord Hastings; and Edward and Richard, sons of Edward IV) Richard III finds himself brought to bay on Bosworth Field by Henry, Earl of Richmond, the future Henry VII. In the battle, Richard's horse is killed; he desperately seeks for another, so that he can meet Richmond in hand-to-hand combat. In his anguish, shortly before his death at the hands of Richmond, he cries:

KING RICHARD
A horse, a horse, **my kingdom for a horse!**

CATESBY
Withdraw my lord, I'll help you to a horse.

KING RICHARD
Slave, I have set my life upon a cast,
And I will stand the hazard of the die.

I think there be six Richmonds in the field;
Five have I slain to-day instead of him.
A horse, a horse, **my kingdom for a horse!**

My large kingdom for a little grave

Source: KING RICHARD THE SECOND (Act III, sc. iii, l. 153)
Author: William Shakespeare (1564-1616)
First published: 1597
Type of work: Historical drama

Context: Bolingbroke, in revolt against King Richard II, has sent Northumberland to speak to the king and tell him that Bolingbroke does not want the crown. All he wants is that his banishment be lifted and all the lands that the crown took from his father be returned. In his weakness, Richard does as Bolingbroke requires. But he bitterly denounces himself for having had to grant these demands. When Northumberland returns to Richard after all of Bolingbroke's demands have been met, Richard asks what else he must do, and bitterly itemizes the things he will do.

RICHARD
I'll give my jewels for a set of beads;
My gorgeous palace for a hermitage;
My gay apparel for an almsman's gown;
My figured goblets for a dish of wood;
My sceptre for a palmer's walking staff;
My subjects for a pair of carved saints,
And **my large kingdom for a little grave,**
A little, little grave, an obscure grave. . . .

My library was dukedom large enough

Source: THE TEMPEST (Act I, sc. ii, ll. 109-110)
Author: William Shakespeare (1564-1616)
First published: 1623
Type of work: Tragi-comedy

Context: Prospero, a magician, lives on an island with his daughter Miranda. The girl is now fifteen years old, and her father thinks it is time she is told about his earlier life. He relates to her how he, who was the Duke of Milan, allowed the affairs of government to drift into the hands of his unscrupulous brother, Antonio. Prospero describes his own absorption while his power was slipping away. His mind was on the study of liberal arts.

· · ·

> Me, poor man, **my library**
> **Was dukedom large enough:** of temporal royalties
> He thinks me now incapable.

· · ·

My life closed twice before its close

Source: MY LIFE CLOSED TWICE BEFORE ITS CLOSE (Stanza 1)
Author: Emily Dickinson (1830-1886)
First published: 1896
Type of work: Lyric poem

Context: This brief poem has as its subject the intense grief caused by the necessity of being parted from those dear to us, a subject as old as poetry. Twice has this sad necessity befallen the poet, and she wonders if even life-after-death will reveal to her any third event that will be as impossible to comprehend as were these two, which, in the magnitude of her grief, were like death itself. It is difficult to conceive of our own death and equally difficult to conceive of the death of another dear to us. The parting from such a one is all the hell to which a human should be subjected.

> **My life closed twice before its close;**
> It yet remains to see
> If Immortality unveil
> A third event to me,
>
> So huge, so hopeless to conceive
> As these that twice befell.
> Parting is all we know of heaven,
> And all we need of hell.

My love's more ponderous than my tongue

Source: KING LEAR (Act I, sc. i, ll. 78-79)
Author: William Shakespeare (1564-1616)
First published: 1608
Type of work: Dramatic tragedy

Context: Lear, King of Britain, makes a foolhardy decision: to divide his kingdom among his three daughters Goneril, Regan, and Cordelia, while he still lives. As he rashly parcels it out, he requires each of them to tell him how much she loves him. First Goneril, then Regan flatter him and get their thirds. Before Lear turns to Cordelia, his youngest and only honest daughter, she speaks her thoughts, contrasting herself to Regan's protestation of love.

CORDELIA [*aside*]
Then poor Cordelia—
And yet not so, since I am sure **my love's
More ponderous than my tongue.**

My man Friday

Source: ROBINSON CRUSOE
Author: Daniel Defoe (1660-1731)
First published: 1719
Type of work: Novel

Context: Daniel Defoe's novel of adventure was inspired by the actual experiences of Alexander Selkirk, who was a castaway on Juan Fernandez Island off Chile, in 1704. Defoe's narrative is written in what the author termed "easy, plain, and familiar language," in the first person. Critics have noted for many years that the title-hero is a middle-class person who expounds and exemplifies the middle-class virtues in a way that was uncommon in fiction at the time. In the novel Robinson Crusoe sets sail for Africa to buy a cargo of slaves. When the ship is wrecked on the rocks off an island, he is the sole survivor and manages to live in reasonable comfort on the island for thirty-five years. After living alone for twenty-four years, Crusoe finds his little island "invaded" by cannibals from another island. Crusoe rescues a native held prisoner by the cannibals and names his new companion Friday, the day of the week of the native's rescue. Friday becomes a loyal and devoted servant for his rescuer as the weeks and months pass. After rescuing Friday and giving the poor fellow food and drink, Crusoe becomes more curious about the strangers who have come to his island. The next morning, accompanied by his new companion, Crusoe sets out:

. . . having now more courage, and consequently more curiosity, I took **my man Friday** with me, giving him the sword in his hand, with the bows and arrows at his back . . . and away we marched to the place where these creatures had been. . . .

My master thou, and guide

Source: THE DIVINE COMEDY, INFERNO (Canto I, as translated by H. F. Cary)
Author: Dante Alighieri (1265-1321)
First transcribed: 1329
Type of work: Christian allegory

Context: Dante, in his thirty-fifth year ("midway this life we're bound upon") finds himself lost in a dark wood representing the troubled state of Italy at that time and—on another level—the alienation of the soul from God. Here he encounters three beasts, images of the sins of Youth, Manhood and Age, the leopard representing incontinence, the lion, bestiality, the she-wolf, fraud. Bewildered and terrified, Dante sees the form of a man who speaks to him with a "voice faint through long disuse of speech." The form is the shade of Virgil, appointed to be Dante's guide and representing Human Philosophy which leads man from "moral unworthiness to temporal felicity." Claiming the long-dead Roman poet as the inspirer of his own work, Dante greets him:

> "Glory and light of all the tuneful train!
> May it avail me, that I long with zeal
> Have sought thy volume, and with love immense
> Have conn'd it o'er. **My master thou, and guide!**
> Thou he from whom alone I have derived
> That style, which for its beauty into fame
> Exalts me.

My name is Ozymandias

Source: OZYMANDIAS
Author: Percy Bysshe Shelley (1792-1822)
First published: 1818
Type of work: Sonnet

Context: Ozymandias, an ancient Egyptian king, had a huge statue of himself erected in the desert. He proudly felt that this monument would glorify his name forever. But now, several thousand years later, the statue inspires only pity and ironic humor, for the gigantic head has fallen from the "vast and trunkless legs of stone" and lies half buried in the sand. On this ridiculously bodiless face one still reads the arrogant "frown,/ And wrinkled lip, and sneer of cold command." With somber irony, Shelley praises the clever sculptor who gave immortality not to Ozymandias's glory but to the king's presumptuous conceit. In the sestet of the sonnet, the poet emphasizes the tragically vain ineffectuality of all human attempts to achieve immortality through earthly glory:

And on the pedestal these words appear:
"My name is Ozymandias, king of kings:
Look on my works, ye Mighty, and despair!"
Nothing beside remains. Round the decay
Of that colossal wreck, boundless and bare
The lone and level sands stretch far away.

My only books were woman's looks, and folly's all they've taught me

Source: THE TIME I'VE LOST IN WOOING
Author: Thomas Moore (1779-1852)
First published: 1815
Type of work: Song

Context: Moore wrote his *Irish Melodies* to be sung, and he sang them himself in some of the most aristocratic drawing rooms in London, where he was welcomed like a minstrel of old. Of his many songs which were popular when he was alive to sing them, "The Time I've Lost in Wooing" is one of the few that have survived to grace twentieth century anthologies and song books. The theme and style of the song are reminiscent of the Cavalier Poets of the seventeenth century, to whom nothing seemed more important than wooing a lady fair. The poet confesses, with obviously not very sincere regret, that though he has lost a great deal of time in wooing, he has become none the wiser, and "Against a glance/ Is now as weak as ever." The song begins:

The time I've lost in wooing,
In watching and pursuing
　　The light that lies
　　In woman's eyes,
Has been my heart's undoing.
Though Wisdom oft has sought me,
I scorn'd the lore she brought me,
　　My only books
　　Were woman's looks,
And folly's all they've taught me.

My punishment is greater than I can bear

Source: GENESIS 4:13
Author: Unknown
First transcribed: 1000-300 B.C.
Type of work: Religious history and law

Context: The sons of Adam and Eve, Cain, a farmer, and Abel, a shepherd, make separate offerings to God from the fruit of their labor. Cain, angry

669

that God should find the sacrifice of Able acceptable, while his own offering is rejected, slays his brother. As punishment, God puts a curse upon Cain's efforts to till the soil and condemns him to the life of a vagabond and fugitive. In response:

And Cain said unto the Lord, **My punishment is greater than I can bear.**
Behold, thou hast driven me out this day from the face of the earth; and from thy face shall I be hid; and I shall be a fugitive and a vagabond in the earth; and it shall come to pass, that every one that findeth me shall slay me.

My salad days, when I was green in judgment

Source: ANTONY AND CLEOPATRA (Act I, sc. v, ll. 73-74)
Author: William Shakespeare (1564-1616)
First published: 1623
Type of work: Dramatic tragedy

Context: Usually shortened to "my salad days" or "the salad days," this saying is still current, and refers to the fresh, green, early years of life. In the play, Cleopatra, Queen of Egypt, is separated from Mark Antony, her lover and a ruler of Rome, who is at home on urgent affairs of state. She has him constantly in her thoughts, writes him every day, and is hungry for news of him. Cleopatra asks her attendant Charmian if ever she loved Julius Caesar so, and Charmian teases her about that earlier affair. She finally admits she is but echoing words Cleopatra once used about Caesar.

CHARMIAN
　　By your most gracious pardon,
I sing but after you.

CLEOPATRA
　　My salad days,
When I was green in judgement, cold in blood,
To say as I said then. But come, away;
Get me ink and paper.
He shall have every day a several greeting,
　　　　　• • •

My soul still flies above me for the quarry it shall find!

Source: THE FALCONER OF GOD (Stanza 4)
Author: William Rose Benét (1886-1950)
First published: 1914
Type of work: Lyric poem

Context: The poet, speaking metaphorically, pictures his soul as a high-flying falcon ready to swoop upon the "bird of . . . [his] desire," the "white heron . . . with silver on its wings," which the poet, that part of him which is physical, has alarmed from its hiding in the marshes. The poem, then, is one of aspiration, wherein the power and promise of the soul determine a wonderful and expectant hunt that seeks in the marshes of life the glorious and treasured prize. But this hunt carries with it failure and disappointment as well as hope, and finally is sustained in the face of inevitable failure only by the persistence of the hunter. The poem begins at the anticipatory moment of the hunt: "I flung my soul to the air like a falcon flying." The hunter moves through the "reedy fens" thrashing the cover until the bird he seeks rises to the stars, "flashing silver fire." When the falcon kills it, suddenly the bird becomes only "a dark and heavy weight/ Despoiled of silver plumage. . . ,—/ All of the wonder/ Gone that ever filled/ Its guise with glory." But the hunter flings his "soul on high with new endeavor," and pledges to find the heron of his desire:

> The pledge is still the same—for all disastrous pledges,
> All hope resigned!
> **My soul still flies above me for the quarry it shall find!**

My strength is as the strength of ten

Source: SIR GALAHAD (Stanza 1)
Author: Alfred, Lord Tennyson (1809-1892)
First published: 1842
Type of work: Lyric poem

Context: Sir Galahad, purest of the knights of King Arthur's court, reveals that, although he enjoys the triumphs of the combat field, his heart has not ties on earth, and his whole allegiance is to his religious faith: "My knees are bow'd in crypt and shrine;/ I never felt the kiss of love. . . ." Galahad is a religious mystic as much as a knight, one who is given not only heavenly visions and experiences, but miraculous strength as well. Because he has no desires of his own and lives in a perfect faith, thoroughly dependent on God, he is without fear.

My good blade carves the casques of men,
My tough lance thrusteth sure,
My strength is as the strength of ten,
Because my heart is pure.

My times are in thy hand

Source: PSALMS 31:15
Author: Unknown
First transcribed: c.400-200 B.C.
Type of work: Religious poetry

Context: The poet, feeling that danger is imminent, expresses his confidence in God, his "rock and fortress" to "pull me out of the net that they have laid privily for me." He is weak and wasted with sorrow; both his enemies and his neighbors avoid him because of his grief; he is forgotten as though he were already dead. The object of slander, he petitions God to make his enemies, not him, ashamed. God will, he says, hide the innocent believers in His presence, as in a tent, so that they will be protected from gossipers. All "saints" should praise God because He rewards the faithful and punishes the wicked. The psalmist's lament and his faith are illustrated in the following lines (See also Browning: "Rabbi Ben Ezra," l. 4):

For I have heard the slander of many: fear was on every side: while they took counsel together against me, they devised to take away my life.
But I trusted in thee, O Lord: I said, Thou art my God.
My times are in thy hand: deliver me from the hand of mine enemies, and from them that persecute me.

Mystery of mysteries!

Source: THE MONASTERY (Chapter 12)
Author: Sir Walter Scott (1771-1832)
First published: 1820
Type of work: Novel

Context: Two Scottish brothers, Halbert Glendenning, a Protestant, and Edward, a Catholic, are vying for the hand of Mary Avenel in the religiously troubled year 1559. A family spirit of Mary's house (such spirits, Scott wrote in his introduction to the novel, being a Highland tradition), the White Lady of Avenel, has twice snatched from the hands of the monks of Melrose a Bible confiscated by them from Mary's dying mother. This episode took place at a time when possession of a Bible by a lay

672

Catholic was taken as equivalent to heresy, and when such a possession by Protestants was extremely rare. Halbert invokes the White Lady and begs her to let him see and read the sacred book. With "an air sad and solemn," she begins her reply:

"Within that awful volume lies
The **mystery of mysteries!**
Happiest they of human race,
To whom God has granted grace
To read, to fear, to hope, to pray,
To lift the latch, and force the way;
And better had they ne'er been born,
Who read to doubt, or read to scorn."

A mystic bond of brotherhood makes all men one

Source: ESSAYS ("Goethe's Works")
Author: Thomas Carlyle (1795-1881)
First published: 1832
Type of work: Essay

Context: After having reviewed the Collected Works of Johann Wolfgang von Goethe (in 1828), Carlyle was moved by the death of the great German on March 22, 1832, to take a further look, in one of his longest essays, at the man and his writing. He begins with thoughts on the greatness of great men. Among the other eulogies of Goethe, he is determined to "set down what he partially has seen into." To explain his interest in someone not of his own land or language, the essayist quotes Herr Teufelsdröckh, the central figure of his earlier *Sartor Resartus:*

"Deny it as he will," says Teufelsdröckh, "man reverently loves man, and daily by action evidences his belief in the divineness of man. What a more than regal mystery encircles the poorest of living souls for us! . . . Of a truth, men are mystically united; **a mystic bond of brotherhood makes all men one.**"

Nailed her colors to the mast!

Source: MARMION (Introduction to Canto I, paragraph 10)
Author: Sir Walter Scott (1771-1832)
First published: 1808
Type of work: Narrative poem

Context: Scott introduced each of the six cantos of his poem *Marmion,* a semi-historical tale of false and true love on the Scottish Border in the early 16th century, with a verse epistle to a friend. The introduction to the first canto, written to scholar and poet William Stewart Rose, is a eulogy of Britain's naval hero of the Napoleonic wars, Lord Nelson, and the rival statesmen Sir William Pitt and Charles James Fox. Speaking of Fox's firm, patriotic stand at the opening of the war against France, Scott wrote:

> When Europe crouch'd to France's yoke,
> And Austria bent, and Prussia broke,
> And the firm Russian's purpose brave
> Was barter'd by a timorous slave,
> Even then dishonour's peace he spurn'd,
> The sullied olive-branch return'd,
> Stood for his country's glory fast,
> **And nail'd her colours to the mast!**

The name died before the man

Source: A SHROPSHIRE LAD ("To an Athlete Dying Young," XIX, stanza 5)
Author: A(lfred) E(dward) Housman (1859-1936)
First published: 1896
Type of work: Lyric poem

Context: The theme of this poem is the tragedy of those men who outlive their own fame. To give this theme concrete form, Housman describes an athlete who once won a race for his town and was carried home in triumph. Now he is dead, in the flower of his youth, and is being borne in his coffin to become a "Townsman of a stiller town." Yet this apparent tragedy of an early death is in reality a supreme gift: the young athlete will not have the experience of seeing his record broken by others; his fame will endure. Fortunate is the man who can die at the height of his glory and take that glory with him. Once he is safely dead, cheers or silence will make no difference to him.

> Eyes the shady night has shut
> Cannot see the record cut,
> And silence sounds no worse than cheers
> After earth has stopped the ears:
>
> Now you will not swell the rout
> Of lads that wore their honours out,
> Runners whom renown outran
> **And the name died before the man.**

Natural selection

Source: ON THE ORIGIN OF SPECIES (Chapter 3)
Author: Charles Robert Darwin (1809-1882)
First published: 1859
Type of work: Scientific treatise

Context: In *On the Origin of Species* Darwin puts forth the theory of evolution and says that evolution is caused by natural selection. Nature cannot "take a sudden leap from structure to structure . . . for natural selection acts only by taking advantage of slight successive variations. . . ." In chapter 3 Darwin considers the question of "how species arise in nature. How have all those exquisite adaptations of one part of the organization to another part, and to the conditions of life, and of one organic being to another being, been perfected? . . . we see beautiful adaptations everywhere and in every part of the organic world." How do varieties, Darwin asks, "become ultimately converted into good and distinct species . . . ?" The formation of species and of genera results from "the struggle for life":

. . . Owing to this struggle, variations, however slight and from whatever cause proceeding, if they be in any degree profitable to the individuals of a species, in their infinitely complex relations to other organic beings and to their physical conditions of life, will tend to the preservation of such individuals, and will generally be inherited by the offspring. The offspring, also, will thus have a better chance of surviving, for, of the many individuals of any species which are periodically born, but a small number can survive. I have called this principle, by which each slight variation, if useful, is preserved, by the term **Natural Selection,** in order to mark its relation to man's power of selection . . .

Nature, red in tooth and claw

Source: IN MEMORIAM (Part 56, stanza 4)
Author: Alfred, Lord Tennyson (1809-1892)
First published: 1850
Type of work: Elegy

Context: Attempting to analyze the validity of human faith in the final triumph of good, the poet examines the position man occupies on earth and wonders if the natural scheme of which he is a part is somehow in opposition to God. It seems to him that although Nature has created man as her highest achievement, she knows nothing of his spirit and of his spiritual hunger to communicate with God. Nature is without sympathy—she has no consideration for the individual's life and even allows species to die away. The law of Nature is struggle for life, animal killing animal for mere survival; but even in this environment men develop faith in God and in his love.

> Man, her last work, who seem'd so fair,
> Such splendid purpose in his eyes,
> Who roll'd the psalm to wintry skies,
> Who built him fanes of fruitless prayer,

> Who trusted God was love indeed
> And love Creation's final law—
> Tho' **Nature, red in tooth and claw**
> With ravine, shriek'd against his creed. . . .

Nature teaches beasts to know their friends

Source: CORIOLANUS (Act II, sc. i, l. 6)
Author: William Shakespeare (1564-1616)
First published: 1623
Type of work: Dramatic tragedy

Context: Caius Martius, an extremely proud, noble general of Rome, hates the rabble of the city, who are rebelling because of a famine. He has no compassion for them but lashes out at them as a cowardly, fickle, stupid mob. He welcomes the news that the Volcians, old enemies of Rome, are up in arms again, for it is a means of draining off the rebellious segment of the populace. He leads the Romans in battle and defeats the Volcians near Corioles, their capital, and is thenceforth called Coriolanus. During his absence from Rome, the enmity that the people have for this man of overweening pride does not diminish. Sicinius and Brutus, tribunes of the people, side with them, while Menenius, a friend of the general, tries to defend him.

MENENIUS
The augurer tells me we shall have news to-night.

BRUTUS
Good or bad?

MENENIUS
Not according to the prayer of the people, for they love not Martius.

SICINIUS
Nature teaches beasts to know their friends.

676

Nature will out

Source: AESOP'S FABLES ("The Cat-Maiden")
Author: Aesop (fl. sixth century B.C.?)
First transcribed: Fourth century B.C.
Type of work: Moral tales of animals

Context: The original tale is called "The Cat and Aphrodite": the cat falls in love with a handsome young man, and the goddess of love changes her into a beautiful woman out of pity. When the young man falls in love with her, the goddess tests the marriage by letting a mouse loose in the room. The cat-woman jumps out of bed and tries to catch and eat the mouse, at which point Aphrodite restores her to her feline condition. The moral attached is: "So it is with men who are fundamentally evil. Even though they may change their condition, they do not change their character." In the popular version of the fable, Zeus or Jupiter argues that nature can be changed, whereas Aphrodite or Venus says no. Again a wedding is arranged, but at the nuptial feast a startling thing occurs:

> "Wait a minute," replied Venus, and let loose a mouse into the room. No sooner did the bride see this than she jumped up from her seat and tried to pounce upon the mouse. "Ah, you see," said Venus, **"Nature will out."**

Naught shelters thee, who wilt not shelter Me

Source: THE HOUND OF HEAVEN (Stanza 2)
Author: Francis Thompson (1859-1907)
First published: 1893
Type of work: Religious poem

Context: In his poem *The Hound of Heaven,* the Catholic poet Francis Thompson develops the theme of God's love ever in pursuit of man who tries to find consolation elsewhere. In his mad flight "From those strong Feet that followed," the poet seeks refuge everywhere. No longer looking for help "In face of man or maid," he turns to little children, but "just as their young eyes grew sudden fair/ With dawning answers there,/ Their angel plucked them from me by the hair." His hope lies then in Nature, but there he finds no consolation, and the trailing voice speaks: " 'Lo! naught contents thee, who content'st not Me.' " Finally the voice speaks again, telling him that only He can give love to one " 'so little

677

worthy of any love. . . .' " What the poet had lost as a child and what he has been seeking, God has stored up for him. The power and the speed of the persistent pursuit of God's love are suggested in the meter of the following lines:

> Still with unhurrying chase,
> And unperturbèd pace,
> Deliberate speed, majestic instancy,
> Came on the following Feet,
> And a Voice above their beat—
> **'Naught shelters thee, who wilt not shelter Me.'**

Naught so sweet as Melancholy

Source: ANATOMY OF MELANCHOLY (The Author's Abstract)
Author: Robert Burton (1577-1640)
First published: 1621-1651
Type of work: Essays

Context: From his extended reading in obscure and little-known books, an English vicar wrote one of the most influential books in English literature. Dickens read it and modeled his style and thinking upon it. Sterne's *Tristram Shandy* (1759-1767) contains passages taken almost literally from it, and Boswell in his *The Life of Samuel Johnson, LL.D.,* (1791), reports that Burton's *Anatomy of Melancholy* was "the only book that took Johnson out of bed two hours sooner than he meant to rise." A contemporary, William Strode (1602-1645), in his "Song in Praise of Melancholy," declared that "There's naught in life so sweet,/ If man were wise to see't,/ But only Melancholy,/ O sweetest Melancholy." Burton, after a poem in Latin, "Democritus Junior to his Book," presents a dozen octaves, "Abstract of Melancholy," all with the same refrain. Here is the first stanza:

> When I go musing all alone,
> Thinking of divers things fore-known,
> When I build Castles in the air,
> Void of sorrow and void of fear,
> Pleasing myself with phantasms sweet,
> Methinks the time runs very fleet,
> All my joys to this are folly,
> **Naught so sweet as Melancholy.**

A necessary evil

Source: FRAGMENTS OF ATTIC COMEDY (as translated by J. M. Edmonds, Number 651)
Author: Menander (342-291 B.C.)
First transcribed: Third century B.C.
Type of work: Dramatic comedy

Context: The practice of Victorian translators to ignore the context and supply a fanciful translation produces some interesting results in rhyme. This translation probably comes from earlier translations and mottos such as this from *The Spectator* (1711): "Marriage is an evil most men endure." The Greek Menander, taking his cue from Aristophanes and the older writers, no doubt follows a long tradition of laughing at marriage, just as his successors do in Latin. There is no certain way now to find what the situation is in which this fragment appears, but its meaning is clear enough.

> Now you're to wed, remember this, my lad,
> 'T will mean much good if you get little bad.
>
> . . .
>
> Marriage, you'll find, has long been and is still
> An ill, sir, but **a necessary ill.**

Necessity is the mother of invention

Source: THE REPUBLIC (Book II, 369-C)
Author: Plato (427-347 B.C.)
First transcribed: Fourth century B.C.
Type of work: Political philosophy

Context: Homer speaks about his mother wit as solution to his many problems, but perhaps the first statement of necessity fostering invention comes from Socrates, who argues for the perfect state. In the first book of the *Republic* Plato records that his master allows the argument on justice to run an illogical course since no definition is put forth. In the next book he suggests that justice can be administered only through the state, hence the discussion of the ideal state. The phrase in the quotation below is otherwise translated as "its real creator, as it appears, will be our needs," and "apparently it will be the outcome of our necessity." Five centuries later Persius says, "Hunger is the teacher of the arts and the bestower of invention," while two thousand years after Plato, Wycherly shortens the form to *"Necessity, mother of invention."* Franck in 1694 combines this with another pat phrase in "Art imitates Nature, and *necessity is the mother of invention,"* whereas Sheridan in 1779 states "Sheer *neces-*

sity,—the proper *parent of* an art so nearly allied to *invention." A modern addition is *"Necessity is the mother of invention,* and peril is the father."

Then, I said, let us begin and create in idea a state; and yet the true creator is **necessity, who is the mother of** our **invention. . . .**

Neither a borrower nor a lender be

Source: HAMLET (Act I, sc. iii, l. 75)
Author: William Shakespeare (1564-1616)
First published: 1603
Type of work: Dramatic tragedy

Context: Minted by Shakespeare, this saying has, like many of his lines, achieved the status of a proverb. Specifically, Polonius, the chief councilor to King Claudius of Denmark, gives his son Laertes much advice as he bids him farewell just before the young man embarks from Elsinore for France. Polonius is rich in old saws and sage counsel, which the young man patiently hears.

POLONIUS

• • •

Neither a borrower nor a lender be,
For loan oft loses both itself and friend,
And borrowing dulleth edge of husbandry.

• • •

Neither fish nor flesh

Source: THE PROVERBS OF JOHN HEYWOOD (Part I, chapter 10)
Author: John Heywood (1497?-1580?)
First published: 1546
Type of work: Gnomic poetry

Context: The author is informing a young man who comes to him for advice that the waters of marriage are seldom untroubled. To substantiate his point he recounts how a couple came to him for advice, and he advised that each go back home. The man and wife took his advice. Then the wife returned, stating that at the home of her uncle and aunt, she was not well received. Those two people bade her God speed but not welcome, and the rest of the family, taking their cue from those worthies, treated her coldly. The wife especially rebelled against the treatment given her by a kinswoman who could "hold with the hare, and run with the hound," and is otherwise given to expediency:

680

Her promise of friendship for any avail,
Is as sure to hold as an eel by the tail.
She is **nether fish, nor flesh,** nor good red herring.

Neither maid, widow, nor wife?

Source: MEASURE FOR MEASURE (Act V, sc. i, l. 177)
Author: William Shakespeare (1564-1616)
First published: 1623
Type cf work: Tragi-comedy

Context: Duke Vincentio of Vienna, a too-kindly man, realizes that lax law enforcement in the city must be corrected. He turns over the cares of state to his deputy, Angelo, and departs. Angelo revises an old statute which imposes the death penalty for fornication. The first victim, who is to be an example, is a young noble, Claudio, who, engaged to Juliet upon a true contract of marriage, has got his fiancée with child. Claudio's sister, Isabella, a beautiful novice in a convent, pleads with Angelo for Claudio's life. Angelo will spare Claudio if Isabella gives herself to him. The duke, returned, learns of these events. Disguised as Friar Lodowick, he tells Isabella how she may save her brother without sacrificing herself. Five years earlier, he reveals, Angelo had made a similar contract to marry a noble lady, Mariana, but jilted her because she could not produce her dowry. Isabella is to agree to an assignation with Angelo, and then Mariana will, in the dark, take her place. The plan succeeds. Now the duke, to prepare the final exposure of Angelo, questions the veiled Mariana.

DUKE
What, are you married?

MARIANA
No my lord.

DUKE
Are you a maid?

MARIANA
No my lord.

DUKE
A widow then?

MARIANA
Neither, my lord.

681

DUKE
Why you are nothing then—
Neither maid, widow, nor wife?

Never, never, never, never, never

Source: KING LEAR (Act V, sc. iii, l. 308)
Author: William Shakespeare (1564-1616)
First published: 1608
Type of work: Dramatic tragedy

Context: Old King Lear, broken in spirit and power, clasps the dead body of Cordelia, his youngest daughter, in his arms. He realizes too late, that she loved him more than did her sisters, Goneril and Regan. The latter, rewarded with his kingdom for their fulsome, false, and flattering protestations of love, have turned on him, abused him, stripped him of his followers, turned him away from their doors, and have driven him to madness. Now, after his reunion with Cordelia and the downfall of her sisters, she is pointlessly murdered. Lear finally accepts the fact that she is dead, and worn out with suffering, still hoping against hope, he dies of a broken heart.

. . . No, no, no life?
Why should a dog, a horse, a rat, have life,
And thou no breath at all? Thou'lt come no more,
Never, never, never, never, never.
Pray you undo this button. Thank you sir.
Do you see this? Look on her, look her lips—
Look there, look there—   [*Dies.*]

Never speak evil of the dead

Source: LIVES AND OPINIONS OF EMINENT PHILOSOPHERS (Book I, chapter 3)
Author: Diogenes Laertius (fl. 200)
First transcribed: Third century
Type of work: Biographical essays, apocryphal anecdotes

Context: Although not so well known as Plutarch for his biographical works, Laertius has given us choice anecdotes of the ancients, especially the Greeks of the Golden Age. Chilo or Chilon lived at the time of Herodotus, that is about 500 B.C. or earlier, and it is the latter who recalls the wisdom of the phrase maker. The expression is literally translated as "Of the dead nothing but good."

682

As Herodotus relates in his first Book, when Hippocrates was sacrificing at Olympia . . . it was Chilon who advised him not to marry, or if he had a wife, to divorce her and disown his children. . . . Being asked wherein lies the difference between the educated and the uneducated, Chilon answered, "In good hope." . . . These again are some of his precepts: To control the tongue. . . . Not to abuse your neighbors. . . . Do not use threats. . . . Be more ready to visit friends in adversity than in prosperity. Do not make an extravagant marriage. **Never speak evil of the dead.** Honor old age. Consult your own safety. . . . Do not laugh at another's misfortune. . . . Obey the laws. Be restful.

Never the twain shall meet

Source: THE BALLAD OF EAST AND WEST (Stanza 1)
Author: Rudyard Kipling (1865-1936)
First published: 1889
Type of work: Ballad

Context: The Ballad of East and West is essentially a tale of the similarity between two men; on the outside they are diametrically and inevitably at opposition; but the confrontation of two strong men places both on an equal footing. Kamal, a border-raider in India, steals the Colonel's horse to lure the English Colonel's son into his territory in search of the animal. The land through which the Colonel's son rides is Kamal's, and Kamal could have sealed the Colonel's son's doom simply by raising his hand, as Kamal's men are everywhere. When the two meet, however, Kamal sends his own son to return with the Colonel's son because of the latter's courage and nobility.

> Oh, East is East, and West is West, and
> **never the twain shall meet,**
> Till Earth and Sky stand presently at God's
>   great Judgment Seat;
> But there is neither East nor West, Border
>   nor Breed, nor Birth,
> When two strong men stand face to face,
>   though they come from the ends of the earth!

Never was so much owed by so many to so few

Source: THE WAR SITUATION (Speech)
Author: Sir Winston Spencer Churchill (1874-1965)
First spoken: British House of Commons, August 20, 1940
Type of work: Laudatory oration

Context: In a recapitulation to the House of Commons under the title "The War Situation, I," on August 20, 1940, Churchill looks at the events of the first year of fighting and compares them to those of World War I. Fewer Britons have been killed, but the consequence to belligerents has been more deadly. He discusses the possibility of a complete blockade of Hitler and his allies, one that must include food, which has now become essential in the manufacture of war materials, such as fats for explosives and potatoes for alcohol. Optimistically, he sees Britain achieving parity with the enemy and approaching superiority, especially in the air.

> The gratitude of every home in our Island, in our Empire, and indeed throughout the world, except in the abodes of the guilty, goes out to the British airmen who, undaunted by odds, unwearied in their constant challenge and mortal danger, are turning the tide of the World War by their prowess and their devotion. **Never in the field of human conflict was so much owed by so many to so few.** All hearts go out to the fighter pilots . . .

A new broom sweeps clean

Source: THE PROVERBS OF JOHN HEYWOOD (Part II, chapter 1)
Author: John Heywood (1497?-1580?)
First published: 1546
Type of work: Gnomic poetry

Context: The author is advising a young man about whether he should marry a young maid for love or an old widow for money. In advising, he is including all the old proverbs he can think of. He has finished a story about a young couple who married for love and foundered on the rocks of poverty. Now he has turned to the story of a young man who married for money. This rich old widow, whose "age and appetite fell at a strong strife," was "made like a beer port, or a barrel," and was "as coy as a croker's mare." In talking about her, her neighbors finally decided she would do for the young fool, for "every man as he loveth/ Quoth the good man when that he kissed his cow." The author further tells his story:

> It would have made a horse break his halter sure
> All the first fortnight their ticking might have taught
> Any young couple their love ticks to have wrought.
> Some laughed, and said: all thing is gay that is green.
> Some thereto said: **the green new broom sweepeth clean.**
> But since all thing is the worse for the wearing,
> Decay of clean sweeping folk had in fearing.

New philosophy calls all in doubt

Source: AN ANATOMY OF THE WORLD: THE FIRST ANNIVERSARY (Line 205)
Author: John Donne (1572-1631)
First published: 1611
Type of work: Metaphysical poem

Context: In the death of Mistress Elizabeth Drury in 1610, at the age of fifteen years, John Donne sees the frailty and decay of the whole world. When God made man and the world, he made them good, but Eve corrupted them, and since her time, they have steadily deteriorated. Life, which was once long, has become short; mankind has shrunk from his earlier heroic stature to a pigmy size. Animals have degenerated; climate has worsened. And a new philosophy, the Copernican theory of the revolution of the earth around the sun, has completely upset man's conception of his position in the cosmos. Under the Ptolemaic theory of astronomy, the earth was the center of the universe, and man, king of the earth, was by extension king of the universe. But the Copernican theory made the earth an insignificant satellite of an unimportant star, one of millions, and robbed man of his former glory. This theory thoroughly upset nearly all natural philosophy. The only thing men were sure of was that they had to begin afresh their pursuit of knowledge. Donne says:

> And **new philosophy calls all in doubt;**
> The element of fire is quite put out;
> The sun is lost, and th' earth, and no man's wit
> Can well direct him where to look for it.

The night cometh, when no man can work

Source: JOHN 9:4
Author: Unknown (traditionally John the Apostle)
First transcribed: by 130
Type of work: Gospel

Context: As Jesus and His disciples pass by a blind beggar, the disciples question the cause of the man's infirmity; is it his own sinfulness or that of his parents? Jesus says that the man's blindness is not a result of sin, but that this man's handicap will give Him an opportunity to perform another work of God. Jesus, referring to His time on the earth as the day, says that He must hasten to do the works of the Father because soon there will again be the night, or darkness, referring to the time after His death:

> I must work the works of him that sent me, while it is day: **the night cometh when no man can work.**

685

As long as I am in the world, I am the light of the world.

When he had thus spoken, he spat on the ground, and made clay of the spittle, and he anointed the eyes of the blind man with the clay.

The Nightmare Life-in-Death was she

Source: THE RIME OF THE ANCIENT MARINER (Part III, stanza 11)
Author: Samuel Taylor Coleridge (1772-1834)
First published: 1798
Type of work: Literary ballad

Context: The most dramatic section of "The Rime of the Ancient Mariner" is Part III: a ship is becalmed, her men parched for lack of water, but the agony that will lead to the mariner's redemption has only begun. Out of a friend's dream, out of traditional tales of ghost-ships and of spectral characters dicing for men's souls, and out of other romantic narratives and poems, Coleridge compounded a mysterious skeleton ship and two ghostly passengers—Death and Life-in-Death—that decide the fate of the mariner: to live on while his shipmates die:

Her lips were red, her looks were free,
Her locks were yellow as gold:
Her skin was as white as leprosy,
The Night-mare LIFE-IN-DEATH was she,
Who thicks man's blood with cold.

The naked hulk alongside came,
And the twain were casting dice;
"The game is done! I've won! I've won!"
Quoth she, and whistles thrice.

Night with her train of stars

Source: I. M. MARGARITAE SORORI (Stanza 2)
Author: William Ernest Henley (1849-1903)
First published: 1888
Type of work: Lyric poem

Context: Henley's poem, written in memory of Margaret, sister of the poet's wife, is a metaphor comparing death with the setting of the sun over a city. The sun has completed its day's work, and now as it begins to fall, the "old, grey city" takes on another aspect: "smoke ascends/ In a rosy-and-golden haze," "spires shine," and "Shadows rise." The poet relieves death of its sorrow and its finality and makes it assume the serenity of sleep.

The "late lark" that was twittering in the afternoon "sings on" as the sun sinks, and the poet asks that at his own death may there be "Some late lark singing," and that he, like the sun that has ended its labors and has set, "be gathered to the quiet west." Death then becomes "Night with her train of stars." Here the poet gives his metaphoric picture of death:

> The sun,
> Closing his benediction,
> Sinks, and the darkening air
> Thrills with a sense of the triumphing night—
> **Night with her train of stars**
> And her great gift of sleep.

The ninety and nine

Source: MATTHEW 18:12
Author: Unknown (traditionally Matthew the Apostle)
First transcribed: c.75-100
Type of work: Gospel

Context: Jesus, when asked by the disciples who the greatest is in the Kingdom of Heaven, attempts again to explain to them His mission and the way to the heavenly realm. Drawing a child to Him, He says that only those who come with the faith and obedience of the child can enter the Kingdom. Further, He warns that it will be better for whoever causes the child or faithful one to fall to have about his neck a millstone and be thrown into the sea than to face the wrath of God. To show the Almighty's concern for the little ones, He tells the disciples a parable:

> How think ye? if a man have a hundred sheep, and one of them be gone astray, doth he not leave **the ninety and nine,** and goeth into the mountains, and seeketh that which is gone astray?
> And if so be that he find it, verily I say unto you, he rejoiceth more of that sheep, than of the ninety and nine which went not astray.
> Even so it is not the will of your Father which is in heaven, that one of these little ones should perish.

No continuing city

Source: HEBREWS 13:14
Author: Unknown
First transcribed: 60-96
Type of work: Religious argument and exhortation

Context: The writer, expressing his strong belief in the revelation of God through Christ, argues that the new faith of Christianity rises above the faith of the Old Testament. Pointing to the futility of the old sacrificial practices and encouraging the people for their faith in Christ, he defines "faith" as "the substance of things hoped for, the evidence of things not seen" and urges the people to persevere in their belief and to accept suffering as a sign of God's love. In a list of admonitions, he exhorts them to cling to the sacrificed Christ and to follow Him in suffering, for the earthly city and the temporal flesh must pass. Only the eternal city and the immortal flesh are of significance:

> Let us go forth therefore unto him without the camp, bearing his reproach.
> For here have we **no continuing city,** but we seek one to come.

No greater grief than to remember days of joy when misery is at hand

Source: THE DIVINE COMEDY, INFERNO (Canto V, ll. 124-125, as translated by H. F. Cary)
Author: Dante Alighieri (1265-1321)
First transcribed: c.1314
Type of work: Christian allegory

Context: The poet Dante, much distressed by viewing lovers condemned because of carnal sin to the first ring of Hell, asks and is given permission to talk to the shades themselves. Paolo and Francesca of Rimini, speaking of brother and husband Gianciotto who had them put to death for committing adultery, and recalling their tempestuous love, are ever grieved and driven before the winds, never to touch or embrace again. This recollection of things past is an echo of Boethius' "In every adversity of fortune, to have been happy is the most unhappy kind of misfortune," and of Chaucer's "A man to han ben in prosperitee, and it remembren, whan it passed is."

> "Francesca! your sad fate
> Even to tears my grief and pity moves.
> But tell me; in the time of your sweet sighs,
> By what, and how Love granted, that ye knew
> Your yet uncertain wishes?" She replied:
> **"No greater grief than to remember days
> Of joy, when misery is at hand**—that kens
> Thy learn'd instructor."
> • • •

No limit but the sky

Source: DON QUIXOTE (Part I, Book III, chapter 3)
Author: Miguel de Cervantes Saavedra (1547-1616)
First published: 1605
Type of work: Satirical novel

Context: "The sky's the limit," in modern parlance, characterizes something unlimited. Cervantes uses it in its literal sense describing the hazing of Sancho Panza in the inn to which Don Quixote goes, believing it, with his usual gift of being able to see what he wants to, a noble castle. The next morning he leaves, refusing to pay for food and lodging, since none of the Romances of Chivalry speaks of cash transactions. He is able to escape without paying his share, but Sancho is not so lucky. He also refuses to pay. "Doesn't the self-same law that acquitted the knight acquit the squire?" However some of the other lodgers of the inn, "all brisk, gamesome, arch fellows":

> . . . encompassed Sancho and pulled him off his ass, while one of 'em went and got a blanket. Then they put the unfortunate squire into it and observing the roof of the place they were in to be somewhat too low for the purpose, they carried him into the back-yard, which had **no limit but the sky,** and there they tossed him for several times together in the blanket, as they do dogs on Shrove-Tuesday.

No man at all can be living for ever, and we must be satisfied

Source: RIDERS TO THE SEA (Last speech)
Author: John Millington Synge (1871-1909)
First published: 1904
Type of work: Dramatic tragedy

Context: John Millington Synge, product of the Irish Literary Renaissance, took *Riders to the Sea* from an actual account related to him when he visited the Aran Islands. The setting is Inishmaan, the middle and by far the most interesting of the Aran Group. A man's body is washed up on Donegal, and by the nature of his dress he is thought to be a native of Inishmaan. The play is concerned with the burial of this man, who turns out to be Maurya's son. The beautiful tragic irony and noble pity of the play place it at the crest of Celtic Drama. The great question of the play is how Maurya will accept the death of her son. In the end she is resigned and takes the death with cosmic understanding.

MAURYA
Michael has a clean burial in the far north, by the grace of the Almighty God. Bartley will have a fine coffin out of the white

689

boards, and a deep grave surely. What more can we want than that? **No man at all can be living for ever, and we must be satisfied.**

No man but a blockhead ever wrote, except for money

Source: THE LIFE OF SAMUEL JOHNSON, LL.D. (For 1776)
Author: James Boswell (1740-1795)
First published: 1791
Type of work: Biography

Context: During 1776, in one of their many conversations, Boswell and Johnson spoke briefly of a trip to Italy that Johnson was contemplating taking with some friends. Boswell notes that Dr. Johnson spoke of the trip in "a tone of animation" and expressed a wish to visit Rome, Naples, Florence, and Venice, "and as much more as we can." Boswell records that he expressed the hope that Johnson would write an account of his travels for publication. To this Johnson replied, says Boswell:

"I do not see that I could make a book upon Italy; yet I should be glad to get two hundred pounds, or five hundred pounds, by such a work." This shewed both that a journal of his Tour upon the Continent was not wholly out of his contemplation, and that he uniformly adhered to that strange opinion, which his indolent disposition made him utter: **"No man but a blockhead ever wrote, except for money."** Numerous instances to refute this will occur to all who are versed in the history of Literature.

No man can serve two masters

Source: MATTHEW 6:24
Author: Unknown (Traditionally Matthew the Apostle)
First transcribed: c.75-100
Type of work: Gospel

Context: This quotation is from that part of Jesus' teaching traditionally called "the Sermon on the Mount." Jesus first gives expression to the "Beatitudes," then assures His hearers that He has not "come to destroy the law;" he has come "to fulfill." He teaches them to pray, giving as a model "The Lord's Prayer," warns against ostentatious religious observances and against laying up "treasures upon earth." This last injunction leads naturally to the warning against attempting to love both God and material wealth (Mammon), which Jesus puts into the form of a vivid metaphor:

No man can serve two masters: for either he will hate the one, and love the other; or else he will hold to the one, and despise the other. Ye cannot serve God and mammon.

No man is born an angler

Source: THE COMPLEAT ANGLER: TO ALL READERS OF THIS DISCOURSE
Author: Izaak Walton (1593-1683)
First published: 1653
Type of work: Dialogue on fishing

Context: Before taking leave of his readers in the preface to *The Compleat Angler,* Izaak Walton derides the idea that one can catch trout by having a different fly for each month of the year. Such a system would not work because a fly that appears at a certain time in one year may appear, owing to differences in the weather, a month sooner or later the next year. Nevertheless, Walton says that he has described the twelve flies in greatest popular esteem, although there are places where it is impossible to catch trout unless one has a reproduction of a fly peculiar to that locality. To indicate that no one is a natural fisherman, but must learn the techniques of angling, he concludes the preface by saying:

. . . but for the generality, three or four flies neat and rightly made, and not too big, serve for a trout in most rivers all the summer. And for winter fly-fishing, it is as useful as an almanac out of date. And of these, because as no man is born an artist, so **no man is born an angler,** I thought fit to give thee this notice.

No man worth having is true to his wife

Source: THE RELAPSE; OR, VIRTUE IN DANGER (Act III, sc. ii)
Author: Sir John Vanbrugh (1664-1726)
First published: 1697
Type of work: Dramatic comedy

Context: Like so many plays of the period 1660-1700, this one is a comedy about people who find love, and like it, outside of marriage. In this play we find Loveless, a handsome young man of no fortune, who has been reclaimed for respectability by his marriage to a wealthy, beautiful young woman named Amanda. Though he believes he loves his wife, and certainly recognizes the debt he owes her for giving him wealth, he finds himself actively pursuing Berinthia, Amanda's cousin and a widow who enjoys men. Worthy, a gentleman of the town and former lover of Berinthia, wants to make Amanda his prize in love, and he gently blackmails his former mistress into helping him seduce her cousin. Berinthia, at the first opportunity, speaks to Amanda, who is jealous of her husband, whom she has seen ogling other women. Amanda says not loving Loveless would not help her problem, to which she receives this reply:

691

BERINTHIA

No, nor nothing else, when the wind's in the warm corner. Look you, Amanda, you may build castles in the air, and fume, and fret, and grow thin and lean and pale and ugly, if you please. But I tell you, **no man worth having is true to his wife,** or can be true to his wife, or ever was, or ever will be so.

No matter how thin you slice it, it's still boloney

Source: CAMPAIGN SPEECH
Author: Alfred E. Smith (1873-1944)
First spoken: 1936
Type of work: Political oration

Context: Though defeated in his campaign for the presidency of the United States in 1928, Al Smith, the "Happy Warrior," was one of the most popular politicians of his time. Four times governor of New York, he was a leading Democratic figure because he could talk to the people in their own language. His speeches were noted for their sense of the comic and their avoidance of the heavy and the stilted, and he tossed off phrases to be recalled later without association with the occasions that produced them. "Bunk" and "Boloney" were favorite words. Called on one day to help with the laying of the cornerstone of the New York State Office Building, he looked at the trowel handed to him and commented: "Nothing doing. That's just boloney. Everyone knows I can't lay bricks." And asked during a campaign about the New Deal, he implied that he wanted nothing to do with any part of it, in this figurative phrase:

No matter how thin you slice it, it's still boloney

No rule is so general, which admits not some exception

Source: ANATOMY OF MELANCHOLY (Part I, sec. 2, memb. 2, subsec. 3)
Author: Robert Burton (1577-1640)
First published: 1621-1651
Type of work: Essays

Context: To help his readers understand the framework of his study of Melancholy, Burton precedes each Partition by an elaborate topical analysis. Thus, Partition I, Section 1 is a general discussion of the causes of the disease. Section 2 declares that Melancholy is either Supernatural (Member 1) or Natural (Member 2). One natural cause is Diet, and in Subsection 3, the author considers customs in diet. The modern version of his first sentence is "The exception proves the rule," though some who say so do not realize that "proves" means "tests," rather than "con- firms." As Burton puts it in one of his complicated sentences:

> No rule is so general, which admits not some exception; to this therefore which hath been hitherto said (for I shall otherwise put most men out of commons), and those inconveniences which proceed from the substance of meat, and intemperate or unseasonable use of them, custom somewhat detracts and qualifies, according to that of Hippocrates, 'Such things as we have been long accustomed to, though they be evil in their own nature, yet they are less offensive. . . .'

No sooner said than done

Source: ANNALS (Book IX, fragment 315 as quoted by Priscianus)
Author: Quintus Ennius (c.239-169 B.C.)
First transcribed: c.81 B.C.
Type of work: Historical and personal recollections

Context: Ennius was a friend of the great men of his period; and from what fragments are extant, he appears not unlike Boswell. In the ninth book he chronicles the events in Scipio's African campaign; and in fragment 313-314, he states, perhaps in relation to Hannibal's defeat, "Fortune on a sudden casts down the highest mortal from the height of his sway, to become the lowliest thrall." Scholars still ponder why the recorder of this phrase, Priscianus, substituted *frux* for *fruigo: Dictum factumque facit frux.* Much later, in *Hamlet,* this *"proverbium celeritatis"* becomes "suit the word to the action, *the action to the word."* In 315, perhaps Scipio to Hannibal, the conversation is as follows:

> "But to what end do I speak so? 'No sooner said than done'— so acts your man of worth."

No young man believes he shall ever die

Source: TABLE TALK, OR ORIGINAL ESSAYS ON MEN AND WOMEN ("On the Feeling of Immortality in Youth")
Author: William Hazlitt (1778-1830)
First published: 1821-1822
Type of work: Familiar essay

Context: William Hazlitt's personality is revealed in his essays. He felt things keenly, and his writings have a warmth, vividness, and zest which are characteristic of the man. Hazlitt lived during a period of dissent and

693

partisanship. He was a stanch supporter of the French Revolution, and believed even the dictatorship of Napoleon was preferable to royal despotism. It is said that he was so depressed by Napoleon's defeat at Waterloo that for days he wandered the streets of London, gaunt, unkempt, and drinking heavily. In his essay "On the Feeling of Immortality in Youth," Hazlitt confesses that he himself lost the feeling of youth when the French people lost their struggle for liberty. But he feels that young men in general have an "overweening presumption" that while those around them may die, they will live forever. He opens his essay with these words:

No young man believes he shall ever die. It was a saying of my brother's, and a fine one. There is a feeling of Eternity in youth which makes us amends for everything. To be young is to be as one of the Immortals. . . .

A noble mind disdains not to repent

Source: THE ILIAD (Book XV, l. 227, as translated by Alexander Pope)
Author: Homer (c.850 B.C.)
First transcribed: Sixth century B.C.
Type of work: Epic poem

Context: While Achilles continues to sulk, the Trojans make great advances with the inspired Hector, son of King Priam, in command. He drives the Greeks back to their ships while the god Zeus busies himself with other matters. This Trojan success causes Poseidon, Zeus' brother and god of the sea, to defend the Greeks and drive back the Trojans, wounding Hector. Zeus, furious at this interference, orders Iris, rainbow, to visit Poseidon and persuade him to interfere no longer. Poseidon responds angrily, saying that while he rules the deep, the earth is a kind of no-man's land where any god can busy himself. Her reply turns away wrath.

"And must I then (said she), O sire of floods!
Bear this fierce answer to the king of gods?
Correct it yet, and change thy rash intent;
A noble mind disdains not to repent.
To elder brothers guardian fiends are given,
To scourge the wretch insulting them and heaven."

694

Nobody likes the bringer of bad news

Source: ANTIGONE (Line 278)
Author: Sophocles (496-405 B.C.)
First transcribed: Fourth century B.C.
Type of work: Dramatic tragedy

Context: In Thebes there has been a history of bad news, and as one of the few humorous characters in all Greek tragedy remarks, this fact does not make the bearer of such news popular. King Creon has just put down a rebellion and buried a loyal nephew who supported his cause, but he leaves to rot his brother, the antagonist who claimed the throne. The two sisters of these ill-fated warriors are deeply concerned that the soul of the outcast will not find peace, so the more valorous Antigone performs with dirt and libations the symbolic act under the very noses of the guards set to prevent these rites. This treasonous act will be punished by the death of both the perpetrator and the guard. The soldier chosen to bring the news to the King is very reluctant to do so.

> GUARD
> . . . The lot chose poor old me
> to win the prize. So here I am unwilling,
> quite sure you people hardly want to see me.
> **Nobody likes the bringer of bad news.**

Nobody's enemy but his own

Source: DAVID COPPERFIELD (Chapter 25)
Author: Charles Dickens (1812-1870)
First published: 1849-1850
Type of work: Novel

Context: David Copperfield, after finishing his schooling, decides to enter the practice of law and is attached to a law firm for training. A young man about to enter society and a profession, Copperfield is invited to a dinner given by Mr. and Mrs. Waterbrook; Mr. Waterbrook is a gentleman of stuffy dignity and very knowing in the ways of the business world. A minor guest at the dinner is one of Copperfield's former schoolmates, Tommy Traddles. Naturally curious about how his old friend is doing, Copperfield asks Mr. Waterbrook his opinion of the young man. Waterbrook replies that Traddles will never amount to much, for, although he is inoffensive, he lacks ambition and the ability to force himself into the world.

> "Traddles," returned Mr. Waterbrook, "is a young man reading for the bar. Yes; he is quite a good fellow—**nobody's enemy but his own.**"

695

"Is he his own enemy?" said I, sorry to hear this.

"Well," returned Mr. Waterbrook, . . . "I should say he was one of those men who stand in their own light. Yes, I should say he would never, for example, be worth five hundred pound."

None but the brave deserves the fair

Source: ALEXANDER'S FEAST: OR, THE POWER OF MUSIC (Stanza 1)
Author: John Dryden (1631-1700)
First published: 1697
Type of work: Lyric poem

Context: This poem is one of two Dryden wrote in honor of St. Cecilia's Day, for presentation by a musical society in London which was formed to honor the patroness of music. In the poem Dryden shows the power of music on mankind. At a great triumphal feast Alexander the Great is honored for the conquest of Persia; Timotheus provides the music—with lyre, flute, and other instruments— with which, as the feast progresses, he shows his power to sway his listeners. He plays upon the moods and actions of Alexander, to cause the king to think of himself as a god, to boast of his exploits, to laud the pleasures of wine, and to think about love. The "fair" of the poem is Thais, who is seated "like a blooming Eastern bride / In flow'r of youth and beauty's pride," by Alexander the Great, conqueror of his world:

Happy, happy, happy pair!
None but the brave,
None but the brave,
None but the brave deserves the fair.

None of woman born shall harm Macbeth

Source: MACBETH (Act IV, sc. i, ll. 80-81)
Author: William Shakespeare (1564-1616)
First published: 1623
Type of work: Dramatic tragedy

Context: At the play's beginning three witches foretell Macbeth's rise from general to Thane of Cawdor to King of Scotland, and all comes true with some bloody help from Macbeth. He murders King Duncan to usurp his throne, and he has Banquo, a former fellow-general, slain because he fears him and his sons as future usurpers of his own place. Everything the witches told Macbeth has come true. He meets the three weird sisters in a cavern to find out what the future now holds in store for him. They an-

696

swer his demands by a show of apparitions. An armed head first warns him of Macduff, a Scots nobleman.

The second apparition is of a bloody child.

SECOND APPARITION
Macbeth, Macbeth, Macbeth!

MACBETH
Had I three ears, I'd hear thee.

SECOND APPARITION
Be bloody, bold, and resolute; laugh to scorn
The power of man. For **none of woman born
Shall harm Macbeth.**

None so blind as those that will not see

Source: AN EXPOSITION OF THE OLD TESTAMENT (Jeremiah 5:21)
Author: Matthew Henry (1662-1714)
First published: 1708-1710
Type of work: Biblical commentary

Context: Jeremiah, fiery and irrepressible prophet, delivers a sermon in which he catalogs the sins of his people. In it he warns them of the fate which will overtake Jerusalem if God's injunction is ignored: destruction and defeat at the hands of the Babylonian armies, followed by slavery. Reminding them that even in His wrath God will not utterly destroy His people, Jeremiah tells them in effect that while they are worshiping false gods and debauching themselves, their enemy is marching upon them. However, he creates no great impression on his listeners, for all that he begins with the thunderous words of an angry Jehovah: "Hear now this, O foolish people, and without understanding; which have eyes, and see not; which have ears, and hear not: Fear ye not me?" Henry's exposition of these words exemplifies his ability to illustrate his point by the use of unforgettable terms:

. . . Nay, it is the corrupt bias of the will that bribes and befogs the understanding: **none so blind as those that will not see.**

697

Nor Hell a fury, like a woman scorned

Source: THE MOURNING BRIDE (Act III, sc. ii)
Author: William Congreve (1620-1729)
First published: 1697
Type of work: Dramatic tragedy

Context: This quotation bears a resemblance to a line in a slightly earlier play, Colley Cibber's *Love's Last Shift* (1696), "We shall find no fiend in hell can match the fury of a disappointed woman." Here Almeria, Princess of Granada, mourns the death of her secret husband, supposedly lost at sea. Her father, to her distress, intends to marry her off to Garcia, a favorite, not knowing of his daughter's marriage to Alphonso, son of the enemy king of Valencia. Almeria's father has brought home captives from a swift campaign against the Moors: one captive is a warrior named Osmyn, actually Almeria's husband in disguise; another captive is Zara, the Moorish queen, madly in love with Osmyn-Alphonso. Now that her husband is dead, she intends having Osmyn as her own. To complicate matters, King Manuel, Almeria's father, falls in love with Zara, his royal captive. He frees her from her chains, avows his love, gives her his royal signet, and plans to marry her. Zara goes to the dungeons, using the ring as her passport, to free Osmyn-Alphonso. There she discovers Almeria clasped in Osmyn-Alphonso's arms. Not knowing of their marriage, but blinded by jealousy and chagrin, Zara swears vengeance upon the man she loves:

ZARA
Vile and ingrate! too late thou shalt repent
The base Injustice thou hast done my love:
Yes, thou shalt know, spite of thy past Distress,
And all those Ills which thou so long hast mourn'd;
Heav'n has no Rage, like Love to Hatred turn'd,
Nor Hell a Fury, like a Woman scorn'd.

Not a mouse stirring

Source: HAMLET (Act I, sc. i, l. 10)
Author: William Shakespeare (1564-1616)
First published: 1603
Type of work: Dramatic tragedy

Context: These words are perhaps more often remembered from their rearrangement in *A Visit from St. Nicholas* (1823) by Clement Clark Moore: ". . . Not a creature was stirring,—not even a mouse. . . ." There can be little doubt, however, that Moore remembered his Shake-

698

speare. As the opening scene of *Hamlet* begins late on a chilly night, Francisco is standing guard on the ramparts of the Danish castle of Elsinore. Another guard, Bernardo, comes to relieve him. As they identify each other in the murk, they are jumpy and nervous because an apparition resembling the late King Hamlet has appeared on the battlements the last two nights. They expect it to appear again, as they converse quietly.

> BERNARDO
> 'Tis now struck twelve, get thee to bed Francisco.

> FRANCISCO
> For this relief much thanks, 'tis bitter cold,
> And I am sick at heart.

> BERNARDO
> Have you had quiet guard?

> FRANCISCO
> **Not a mouse stirring.**

> BERNARDO
> Well, good night. • • •

Not God! in gardens! when the eve is cool?

Source: MY GARDEN
Author: Thomas Edward Brown (1830-1897)
First published: 1893
Type of work: Lyric poem

Context: Thomas Edward Brown, clergyman and distinguished educator, was born on the Isle of Man, whose disappearing legends he dedicated himself to preserving. Although he was often harsh and sometimes cynical in his writings, he had a gentle personality and love of nature which can best be seen in the simple, but effective answer to the fool of Psalm 14:1, who said in his heart that there is no God. The complete poem reads:

> A garden is a lovesome thing, God wot!
>   Rose plot,
>   Fringed pool,
>   Ferned grot—
>   The veriest school
>   Of peace; and yet the fool

Contends that God is not—
Not God! in gardens! when the eve is cool?
Nay, but I have a sign;
'Tis very sure God walks in mine.

Not much the worse for wear

Source: THE DIVERTING HISTORY OF JOHN GILPIN (Line 183)
Author: William Cowper (1731-1800)
First published: 1782
Type of work: Humorous ballad

Context: For much of his life, Cowper suffered from religious despondency, which on several occasions drove him into madness. Despite this affliction—or rather, because of it—he cultivated a sense of humor or whimsicality which adds charm to much of his poetry. On one occasion he remarked apologetically: "If I trifle, and merely trifle, it is because I am reduced to it by necessity—a melancholy . . . engages me sometimes in the arduous task of being merry by force. And, strange as it may seem, the most ludicrous lines I ever wrote ["John Gilpin"] have been written in the saddest mood, and, but for that saddest mood, perhaps had never been written at all." Cowper's merry hero, John Gilpin, is a London linen-draper whose horse runs away with him on his twentieth wedding anniversary. His mad ride through the English countryside is hilariously described. The horse attains his goal, the home of his owner, who obligingly supplies Gilpin with a spare wig and a hat, his own having been lost on the way. It is this borrowed hat which is described in the famous line:

Whence straight he came with hat and wig;
A wig that flow'd behind,
A hat **not much the worse for wear,**
Each comely in its kind.

Not that I loved Caesar less; but that I loved Rome more

Source: JULIUS CAESAR (Act III, sc. ii, ll. 22-23)
Author: William Shakespeare (1564-1616)
First published: 1623
Type of work: Dramatic tragedy

Context: Marcus Brutus, a respected, noble Roman, is a member of the group of assassins that kill Julius Caesar. He does so because he believes Caesar's dictatorial power and immense popularity to be a danger to Rome's ancient freedoms. To calm the people's fears and confusion after the murder, Brutus speaks to them in the Forum and seemingly succeeds in explaining his reasons for killing Caesar.

BRUTUS
. . .

Romans, countrymen, and lovers, hear me for my cause, and be silent, that you may hear. Believe me for mine honour, and have respect to mine honour, that you may believe. Censure me in your wisdom, and awake your senses, that you may the better judge. If there be any in this assembly, any dear friend of Caesar's, to him I say, that Brutus' love to Caesar was no less than his. If then, that friend demand, why Brutus rose against Caesar, this is my answer—**not that I loved Caesar less; but that I loved Rome more.** Had you rather Caesar were living, and die all slaves, than that Caesar were dead, to live all free men? . . .

Not to be flung aside are the glorious gifts of the gods

Source: THE ILIAD (Book III, ll. 62-63, as translated by A. T. Murray)
Author: Homer (c.850 B.C.)
First transcribed: Sixth century B.C.
Type of work: Epic poem

Context: In this, the tenth year of the seige of Troy, the troops of both armies are reviewed by their commanders before the battle. Paris, who really is the cause of the war inasmuch as he has claimed Helen as his reward for judging Aphrodite as the most beautiful of the goddesses, steps from the ranks and brashly dares any Greek to decide the battle in personal combat. When Menelaus, husband of Helen, accepts with a vengeance, Paris withdraws in terror, only to be chided by his brother Hector. Paris, after this speech, agrees to do battle with the outraged Greek:

"Hector, seeing that thou dost chide me duly, and not beyond what is due—ever is thy heart unyielding, even as an axe that is driven through a beam by the hand of a man that skilfully shapeth a ship's timber, and it maketh the force of his blow to wax; even so is the heart in thy breast undaunted—cast not in my teeth the lovely gifts of golden Aphrodite. **Not to be flung aside,** look you, **are the glorious gifts of the gods,** even all that of themselves they give, whereas by his own will could no man win them. . . ."

701

Not to mince words

Source: DON QUIXOTE (Part I, Preface)
Author: Miguel de Cervantes Saavedra (1547-1616)
First published: 1605
Type of work: Satirical novel

Context: Mincier is Old French and means "to make small," as to mince meat, or "to diminish in importance." The novelist, having completed his book, is tempted to let it go into the world "naked as it was born, without the addition of a preface, or the numberless trumpery of commendatory sonnets, epigrams, and other poems that usually usher in the concepts of authors." However Prefaces are traditional, and Cervantes wants to state his purpose in the novel, "the destruction of that monstrous heap of ill-contrived romances of chivalry." As he continues pondering how to begin:

. . . an ingenious gentleman, and of a merry disposition came in and surprised me. He asked me what I was so very intent and thoughtful upon? I was so free with him as **not to mince the matter,** but told him plainly I had been puzzling my brain for a preface to *Don Quixote.*

Not worth his salt

Source: SATYRICON (Section 57)
Author: Petronius (died c.66)
First transcribed: c.60
Type of work: Prose satirical romance

Context: The author and Ascyltos, two pupils of Agamemnon, a teacher of rhetoric, are at the home of Trimalchio for dinner. They discuss the difficulties of various professions, especially a doctor's and a money-changer's. At this point, "tickets were carried round in a cup, and a boy who was entrusted with this duty read aloud the names of the presents for the guests." That is, each ticket had a riddle on it concealing the name of the present. Ascyltos begins to make fun of everything and to laugh uproariously. One of Trimalchio's men gets angry and berates him:

. . . "What are you laughing at, sheep's head?" he said. "Are our host's good things not good enough for you? I suppose you are richer and used to better living? As I hope to have the spirits of this place on my side, if I had been sitting next him I should have put a stopper on his bleating by now. A nice young shaver to laugh at other people! Some vagabond fly-by-night **not worth his salt."**

Nothing can be said to be certain, except death and taxes

Source: LETTER TO M. LE ROY (November 13, 1789)
Author: Benjamin Franklin (1706-1790)
First published: 1789
Type of work: Personal letter

Context: Benjamin Franklin, probably the most versatile genius of the eighteenth century, carried on a large correspondence with his many friends at home and abroad; in these letters he exchanged ideas and information with the leading scientists, statesmen, and political thinkers of his day. One such friend was Jean Baptiste Le Roy, French physicist; and it is interesting to note that in most of Franklin's letters, regardless of their recipient, there is the same warmth and wisdom associated with him in other matters. His penchant for appropriate sayings and deceptively simple maxims did not desert him in his correspondence. This letter to M. Le Roy, written shortly before Franklin's death, proves that his powers did not fail him in his old age. In it Franklin inquires after his friend's health, jokes about the danger of living in France in 1789, and expresses some concern over Le Roy's safety; he has not heard from the latter in almost a year. Before concluding the letter, he adds a bit of important news and a characteristic comment:

> Our new Constitution is now established, and has an appearance that promises permanency; but in this world **nothing can be said to be certain, except death and taxes.**

Nothing emboldens sin so much as mercy

Source: TIMON OF ATHENS (Act III, sc. v, l. 3)
Author: William Shakespeare (1564-1616)
First published: 1623
Type of work: Dramatic tragedy

Context: Timon of Athens is a tragedy framed around the effects of ingratitude. Timon suffers from it when, having spent his substance lavishly on fair-weather friends, he tries to get loans from them and is repulsed. His true but penniless friend, Alcibiades, an Athenian general, encounters Athenian thanklessness when he goes to the Senate and attempts to plead against the death sentence of a soldier who has served Athens faithfully. Before he can utter a word, three Senators approach, one of whom is speaking about some other case, but in words that reveal their heartlessness.

FIRST SENATOR
My lord, you have my voice to 't, the fault's
Bloody; 'tis necessary he should die.
Nothing emboldens sin so much as mercy.

SECOND SENATOR
Most true; the law shall bruise 'em.

Nothing fats the horse so much as the king's eye

Source: MORALS ("On the Education of Children")
Author: Plutarch (c.45-c.125)
First transcribed: Unknown
Type of work: Ethical essay

Context: In this essay on the training of "free children," Plutarch offers much advice, from the choice of mate, to conception, to early formal education. He stresses the fact that the child must be allowed some holiday from study, just as the grown man allows himself a time for recreation. But a good education is even more valuable than health or beauty, for both of those may pass but a good education will remain. The selection of good teachers is therefore of utmost importance. They should have blameless lives, pure characters, and great experience. This statement about the fatness of the horse is a famous proverb, used by Xenophon and Aristotle.

> We ought also to censure some fathers who, after entrusting their sons to tutors and preceptors, neither see nor hear how the teaching is done. This is a great mistake, for they ought after a few days to test the progress of their sons, and not to base their hopes on the behavior of a hireling; and the preceptors will take all the more pains with the boys, if they have from time to time to give an account of their progress. Hence the propriety of that remark of the groom, that **nothing fats the horse so much as the king's eye.**

Nothing is little to him that feels it with great sensibility

Source: LETTER TO GIUSEPPE BARETTI (July 20, 1762)
Author: Samuel Johnson (1709-1784)
First published: 1791
Type of work: Personal letter

Context: In 1751, Giuseppe Baretti (1719-1789), an Italian language teacher, writer, and lexicographer, came to London and made the

704

acquaintance of Dr. Johnson. Their friendship continued until Johnson's death; and on a number of occasions when Baretti returned to the Continent, Johnson wrote him cordial letters to keep him abreast of the London scene. In this instance Johnson tells Baretti of the activities of some of their mutual friends and devotes a substantial portion of the letter to a melancholy account of his disappointment at changes he discovered when he recently returned to his native Lichfield. He inquires whether Baretti has not also been disappointed upon his return to Milan or "whether time has made any alteration for the better." Men, he writes, borrow happiness from hope, but frequently the hope ends in disappointment. Musing on the effect of everyday things on the meditative mind, Johnson remarks:

> Moral sentences appear ostentatious and tumid, when they have no greater occasions than the journey of a wit to his own town: yet such pleasures and such pains make up the general mass of life; and as **nothing is little to him that feels it with great sensibility,** a mind able to see common incidents in their real state, is disposed by very common incidents to very serious contemplations.

Nothing is so much to be feared as fear

Source: JOURNAL (7 September, 1851)
Author: Henry David Thoreau (1817-1862)
First published: 1906
Type of work: Literary journal

Context: Thoreau's thoughts concerning the recently published book of an acquaintance lead to his entering an observation on the cowardice which dominates the lives of many men. Whatever harmful effect a bad thing may have is not as much to be deplored as the fear men feel for that effect. It is contemptible, he says, to be so afraid of error that one is prevented from doing anything at all, even thinking. There is no error and no wrong great enough to be of permanent consequence. In fact, says Thoreau, God may prefer honest atheism to faith in men who believe only because they are afraid.

> Miss Martineau's last book is not so bad as the timidity which fears its influence. As if the popularity of this or that book would be so fatal, and man would not still be man in the world. **Nothing is so much to be feared as fear.** Atheism may comparatively be popular with God himself.

Nothing is too late till the tired heart shall cease to palpitate

Source: MORITURI SALUTAMUS (Stanza 22)
Author: Henry Wadsworth Longfellow (1807-1882)
First published: 1875
Type of work: Philosophical poem

Context: Longfellow took the title of this poem, written for the fiftieth anniversary reunion of the class of 1825 of Bowdoin College, from the salute of the doomed gladiators to the Roman emperor: "O Caesar, we who are about to die salute you!" He salutes the halls of the school, the deceased teachers who had inspired him and his classmates ("Peace be to them; eternal peace and rest. . . ."), the younger generation ("All possibilities are in its hands. . . ."), and his classmates: "This throng of faces turned to meet my own,/ Friendly and fair, and yet to me unknown. . . . Vanish the rolling mists of fifty years. . . . Hail, my companions, comrades, classmates, friends!" The poet is afraid to open the "volume" of the past, so full of tragedy and comedy. He tells a tale to uplift the spirits of the aged throng, a tale from the *Gesta Romanorum* called "Of Remembering Death and Forgetting Things Temporal." The story concerns a scholar who is tempted to leave his books and seek worldly riches. The poet tells this didactic tale because even an old man can repent, improve, and achieve. "Old age is still old age," but "The night hath not yet come. . . . Even the oldest tree some fruit may bear. . . . And as the evening twilight fades away/ The sky is filled with stars, invisible by day":

> But why, you ask me, should this tale be told
> To men grown old, or who are growing old?
> It is too late! Ah, **nothing is too late**
> **Till the tired heart shall cease to palpitate.**
> Cato learned Greek at eighty; Sophocles
> Wrote his grand Oedipus, and Simonides
> Bore off the prize of verse from his compeers,
> When each had numbered more than four-score years,
> And Theophrastus, at fourscore and ten,
> Had but begun his "Characters of Men."

Nothing spoils a romance so much as a sense of humor in the woman

Source: THE WOMAN OF NO IMPORTANCE (Act I)
Author: Oscar Wilde (1856-1900)
First published: 1894
Type of work: Dramatic comedy

Context: Lady Hunstanton has invited several guests to tea, among whom are Lady Caroline Pontefract and her henpecked husband, Sir

John. Lady Caroline shows constant anxiety over the health of her husband. She reminds him that he should have his muffler; she sends him to put on his overshoes; and she has him sit near her where he will be less exposed. When the guests start to the Yellow Drawing-Room for tea, Sir John offers to carry the cloak of one of the ladies. His wife stops him and suggests, ". . . you might help me with my workbasket." Mrs. Allonby, a witness to the scene, tells Lord Illingworth, another guest, "I should have thought Lady Caroline would have grown tired of conjugal anxiety by this time! Sir John is her fourth!" Illingworth scoffs at so much marriage and says twenty years of it makes a woman "something like a public building." Mrs. Allonby then asks if there is such a thing as twenty years of romance.

LORD ILLINGWORTH
"Not in our day. Women have become too brilliant. **Nothing spoils a romance so much as a sense of humour in the woman.**"

Nothing succeeds like success

Source: ANGE PITOU (Vol. 1, chapter 7)
Author: Alexandre Dumas, *père* (1802-1870)
First published: 1852
Type of work: Historical romance

Context: Ange Pitou, having failed in his studies to become an abbé, has left home and been taken in by the "philosophical farmer" Billot. The time is just before the French Revolution, and the French farmers and peasants are growing restive under the oppressive rule of the nobles. A revolutionary pamphlet stressing independence, liberty, and equality is sent by Billot's landlord, Dr. Gilbert, to Billot. Pitou, who is able to read, is asked to read it to a group of husbandmen, who applaud greatly. The comment about success is an old French proverb. Here is the way Dumas gives the passage:

Pitou had well performed his part; he had read energetically and well. **Nothing succeeds so well as success.** The reader had taken his share of the plaudits which had been addressed to the work, and submitting to the influence of this relative science, Billot himself felt growing within him a certain degree of consideration for the pupil of the Abbé Fortier. Pitou, already a giant in his physical proportions, had morally grown ten inches in the opinion of Billot.

Nothing whatever to wear!

Source: NOTHING TO WEAR (Line 56)
Author: William Allen Butler (1825-1902)
First published: 1857
Type of work: Humorous poem

Context: Butler's attack on feminine vanity tells the story of Miss Flora McFlimsey, a wealthy young woman. She has made three expeditions to the fashion centers of Paris, each time spending six weeks buying clothes. On her last trip, her purchases made up the major part of a steamship's cargo. Yet, only three months after returning, she complains heartbrokenly that she has nothing to wear. The narrator of the poem becomes engaged to her, but their bond is broken when he invites her to a fashionable ball and attempts to convince her that she has many suitable things to wear; she calls him hopelessly insensitive to a woman's needs and sends him away. The poem ends with a picture of the poor in the slums, who truly have nothing to wear.

> And yet, though scarce three months have passed since the day
> This merchandise went, on twelve carts, up Broadway,
> This same Miss McFlimsey, of Madison Square,
> The last time we met was in utter despair,
> Because she had **nothing whatever to wear!**

Now a' is done that men can do, and a' is done in vain

Source: IT WAS A' FOR OUR RIGHTFU' KING (Stanza 2)
Author: Robert Burns (1759-1796)
First published: 1796
Type of work: Song

Context: Like many other of Burns' best songs, written for a five-volume collection of old Scottish airs, this one was meant to be sung to an old tune and was itself modeled on an earlier street ballad. But its concise characterization and skillful blending of the themes of patriotism and love are due to Burns' own genius. Without narrative the poem suggests through two laments the story of lovers parted forever by the defeat of the Jacobite cause, the effort to place the Stuart pretender on the British throne. First speaks the soldier, who has had to flee from Scotland for his life when the man he thinks the rightful king was defeated. Then speaks the girl left behind him: "I think on him that's far awa'/ The lee-lang night, and weep. . . ." Without describing either speaker, Burns achieves a feeling of contrast by the woman's open grief and the soldier's restrained speech:

Now a' is done that men can do,
And a' is done in vain;
My love and native land farewell,
For I maun cross the main,
My dear,
For I maun cross the main.

Now or never was the time

Source: THE LIFE AND OPINIONS OF TRISTRAM SHANDY, GENT. (Book IV, chapter 31)
Author: Laurence Sterne (1713-1768)
First published: 1759-1767
Type of work: Novel

Context: Tristram's father, at one point in the novel, receives a legacy of a thousand pounds from an aunt. This sudden largess places him in the difficult circumstance of deciding how "to lay it out mostly to the honour of his family." After pondering a vast range of projects, he finally narrows to two: either to send his son Bobby abroad for the Grand Tour, or to fence in the Oxmoor, "a fine, large, whinny, undrained, unimproved common, belonging to the Shandy estate." Some fifteen years earlier, Mr. Shandy had become involved in a lawsuit about the land; since then he had been most anxious to develop the property. The legacy, Tristram says, now stimulates anew Mr. Shandy's interest in the Oxmoor and

. . . naturally awakened every other argument in its favour; and upon summing them all up together, he saw, not merely in interest, but in honour, he was bound to do something for it;—and that **now or never was the time.**

Now wherefore stoppest thou me?

Source: THE RIME OF THE ANCIENT MARINER (Part I, stanza 1)
Author: Samuel Taylor Coleridge (1772-1834)
First published: 1798
Type of work: Literary ballad

Context: Contemplating a tale on the Wandering Jew and another on the wanderings of Cain (the first never materialized, the second produced a fragment), Coleridge turned his Ancient Mariner into a wanderer who, as part of his expiation for a crime, must tell his story of sin and redemption to those in need of its lesson: "He prayeth best, who loveth best/ All things both great and small." The Mariner has no difficulty singling out those overly complacent persons to whom he must speak, and at the opening of the poem he has halted a wedding guest:

> It is an ancient Mariner,
> And he stoppeth one of three.
> "By thy long grey beard and glittering eye,
> **Now wherefore stopp'st thou me?**
>
> The Bridegroom's doors are opened wide,
> And I am next of kin;
> The guests are met, the feast is set:
> May'st hear the merry din."
>
> He holds him with his skinny hand;
> "There was a ship," quoth he.

O brave new world that has such people in it!

Source: THE TEMPEST (Act V, sc. i, ll. 183-184)
Author: William Shakespeare (1564-1616)
First published: 1623
Type of work: Tragi-comedy

Context: Prospero, formerly Duke of Milan, and now a skilled magician, rules an enchanted island. With him is his daughter, the beautiful Miranda. Prospero divines that his brother, Antonio, who usurped his dukedom, and King Alonso, who helped Antonio accomplish the theft twelve years before, are passing the island in a ship. He causes a wild tempest which drives the ship ashore. All the ship's passengers survive but are separated. After various adventures, Prospero causes the whole company to come to him. He reveals himself and forgives all. Miranda has seen only one person in addition to her father, and now, when she sees the assembled company, she is delighted with the prospects of a world that has such beautiful inhabitants.

MIRANDA
                    O wonder!
How many goodly creatures are there here.
How beauteous mankind is. **O brave new world
That has such people in't!**

PROSPERO
                    'Tis new to thee.

710

O call back yesterday, bid time return

Source: KING RICHARD THE SECOND (Act III, sc. ii, l. 69)
Author: William Shakespeare (1564-1616)
First published: 1597
Type of work: Historical drama

Context: Richard II has returned from Ireland to find that Bolingbroke, his cousin whom he had banished, has returned from banishment and invaded England. As Richard lands, he reassures his followers that his cause is just and therefore favored and assisted by God. "God for his Richard hath in heavenly pay / A glorious angel: then if angels fight, / Weak men must fall, for heaven still guards the right." But in the midst of Richard's unrealistic speech, Salisbury enters and reports the true state of affairs.

SALISBURY

• • •

Discomfort guides my tongue,
And bids me speak of nothing but despair.
One day too late I fear me, noble lord,
Hath clouded all thy happy days on earth.
O call back yesterday, bid time return,
And thou shalt have twelve thousand fighting men.

• • •

O Captain! my Captain! our fearful trip is done

Source: "O CAPTAIN! MY CAPTAIN!" (Stanza 1)
Author: Walt Whitman (1819-1892)
First published: 1866
Type of work: Elegiac ode

Context: This quotation is from one of several elegiac poems that Whitman composed in commemoration of President Lincoln. In it the poet uses the familiar metaphor of the ship of state with the dead President as its captain. The vessel is described as entering port after a long and dangerous voyage (the Civil War), while around the harbor stand crowds of people "all exulting" in their happiness at the successful conclusion to such a hazardous journey. But just at the moment of triumph the captain, who has steered his ship through so many dangers, falls bleeding and dead upon the deck. For him the joyful welcome is too late. The familiar first stanza follows:

O Captain! my Captain! our fearful trip is done,
The ship has weather'd every rack, the prize we sought is won,
The port is near, the bells I hear, the people all exulting,
While follow eyes the steady keel, the vessel grim and daring;

But O heart! heart! heart!
　　O the bleeding drops of red,
　　　Where on the deck my Captain lies
　　　　Fallen cold and dead.

O clear conscience and upright! How doth a little
failing wound thee sore

Source: THE DIVINE COMEDY, PURGATORIO (Canto III, ll. 8-9, as translated by
　　H. F. Cary)
Author: Dante Alighieri (1265-1321)
First transcribed: c.1320
Type of work: Christian allegory

Context: Dante has met with a friend Casella, who awaits the Jubilee day, and passes into Purgatory, overjoyed when Cato, the guardian, says, "Run to the mountain to cast off those scales,/ That from your eyes the sight of God conceal." The poet follows the spirits, only to lose sight of his guide Virgil. Virgil, himself not a Christian, having been born too soon, "with the bitter pang of self-remorse, seem'd smitten."

O clear conscience and upright!
How doth a little failing wound thee sore.
Soon as his feet desisted (slackening pace)
From haste, that mars all decency of act,
My mind, that in itself before was wrapt,
Its thought expanded, as with joy restored;
And full against the steep ascent I set
My face, where highest to heaven its top o'erflows.

•　•　•

O cuckoo! Shall I call thee bird, or but a wandering voice?

Source: TO THE CUCKOO (Stanza 1)
Author: William Wordsworth (1770-1850)
First published: 1807
Type of work: Lyric poem

Context: In this poem the bird becomes a symbol for gathering the poet's recollections, the "golden time" of schoolboy days when, seeking the cuckoo, he roved "through woods and on the green," the "vision-ary hours" of sunshine and of flowers. The bird represents the hope and the love of youthful emotional response, so vividly experienced and so rarely recaptured. Of the particular lines of the quotation, Words-

712

worth comments: "This concise interrogation characterizes the seeming ubiquity of the voice of the cuckoo, and dispossesses the creature almost of a corporeal existence,—the Imagination being tempted to this exertion of her power by a consciousness in the memory that the cuckoo is almost perpetually heard through the season of spring, but seldom becomes an object of sight."

O blithe New-comer! I have heard,
I hear thee and rejoice.
O Cuckoo! Shall I call thee Bird,
Or but a wandering Voice?

While I am lying on the grass
Thy twofold shout I hear,
From hill to hill it seems to pass
At once far off, and near.

O death, where is thy sting?

Source: I CORINTHIANS 15:55
Author: Paul
First transcribed: c.54-57
Type of work: Religious epistle

Context: The Corinthian believers are told by Paul that the essence of faith is the belief, confirmed by many witnesses, that Christ rose from the dead and that all who trust Him will also be resurrected. The resurrected form of life will be different from the physical form; man will then be immortal and imperishable. The resurrection, says Paul, is the final victory over death:

So when this corruptible shall have put on incorruption, and this mortal shall have put on immortality, then shall be brought to pass the saying that is written, Death is swallowed up in victory.
O death, where is thy sting? O grave, where is thy victory?

O fool, I shall go mad

Source: KING LEAR (Act II, sc. iv, l. 289)
Author: William Shakespeare (1564-1616)
First published: 1608
Type of work: Dramatic tragedy

Context: Lear, King of Britain, foolishly divides his kingdom between his dissembling and flattering daughters Goneril and Regan. He retains one

713

hundred knights, the name of King, and the right to live with each daughter on an alternating monthly basis. Soon, however, Goneril, with whom he first resides, treats the old king with disrespect, reduces his retinue, and criticizes his men. Enraged, Lear curses her and her future offspring and hurries off to live with Regan. Before he and his men arrive, Goneril's steward, Oswald, reaches Regan with a letter relating all that has happened. Regan refuses the old man admittance until he has apologized to Goneril. When Goneril arrives, Lear realizes the daughters are leagued against him, and he cries out in a helpless rage which approaches madness. His fool crouches by his side, huddling from an impending storm.

LEAR

    . . . No, you unnatural hags,
I will have such revenges on you both,
That all the world shall—I shall do such things;
What they are, yet I know not, but they shall be
The terrors of the earth. You think I'll weep.
No, I'll not weep.   *[Storm and tempest.]*
I have full cause of weeping; but this heart
Shall break into a hundred thousand flaws
Or e'er I'll weep. **O fool, I shall go mad.**

O generation of vipers

Source: MATTHEW 3:7
Author: Unknown (traditionally Matthew the Apostle)
First transcribed: c.75-100
Type of work: Gospel

Context: John the Baptist, comparing his voice in the desert and his prophecy of the advent of the Lord with those of Isaiah, is preaching in the wilderness of Judea. He calls on the people to repent, declares that "the kingdom of heaven is at hand," and exhorts his hearers to prepare the road for the Lord. From Jerusalem, Judea, and the area of the Jordan, the people come to him, confess their sins, and are baptized in the river. When John sees among the crowd Pharisees and Sadducees, strict, conservative, and proud followers of the law, he likens them to snakes that flee a burning field and warns them against their false security:

    But when he saw many of the Pharisees and Sadducees come to his baptism, he said unto them, **O generation of vipers,** who hath warned you to flee from the wrath to come?

O God! O Montreal!

Source: A PSALM OF MONTREAL (Refrain)
Author: Samuel Butler (1835-1902)
First published: 1878
Type of work: Narrative poem

Context: A half-humorous dialogue between the poet and a man working in the Montreal Museum of Natural History, this short poem has as its message that a young city in a young country has little time for culture and no real acquaintance with it. A copy of a famous masterpiece of Greek sculpture, the Discobolus, is found abandoned in a side room, where a workman is busy stuffing an owl. When asked why the Discobolus has been neglected in storage, the man reveals his barbarity by saying that the statue is indecent, and that *he* is a person of station. The poet can comment only with a cry of despair, as the stuffer of owls explains:

"The Discobolus is put here because he is vulgar—
He has neither vest nor pants with which to cover his limbs;
I, Sir, am a person of most respectable connections—
My brother-in-law is haberdasher to Mr. Spurgeon."
O God! O Montreal!

O Liberty! Liberty! how many crimes are committed in thy name!

Source: HISTORY OF THE GIRONDISTS, Alphonse de Lamartine (Book LI, chapter 8)
Author: Madame Roland (1754-1793)
First spoken: 1793
Type of work: Biographical anecdote

Context: During the French Revolution (1789-1799) Madame Roland was one of the prominent leaders of the Girondists, the moderate republican party so named because early members were mostly deputies from the Department of Gironde. She was an idealist—a fierce hater of the aristocracy, but a lover of the common man and a worshiper of Liberty, being strongly imbued with the philosophy of Jean-Jacques Rousseau. In 1793 the Girondists were expelled from the Convention by the extremists, the Jacobins and the Cordeliers; and their leaders, Madame Roland among them, were summarily tried and sent to the guillotine. Madame Roland showed great courage both at her trial and at her execution. Upon hearing her sentence, she rose and said, "I thank you for considering me worthy to share the fate of the good and great men you have murdered!" Clad in a white robe to symbolize her innocence, and with her long black hair unbound, she rode in a cart to her execution, accompanied only by a wretched old man. As an act of kindness, she permitted the old man to be executed first, and then, ascending the scaffold, she bowed to the statue of Liberty nearby and exclaimed,

> "O Liberty! Liberty! how many crimes are committed in thy name!"

O mighty Caesar! Dost thou lie so low?

Source: JULIUS CAESAR (Act III, sc. i, l. 148)
Author: William Shakespeare (1564-1616)
First published: 1623
Type of work: Dramatic tragedy

Context: When Caesar is attacked boldly and stabbed to death in the Senate, his close young friend, Mark Antony, flees in amazement and terror, as do many other persons who are present. The conspirators are about to capitalize on their deed by making a bold show of their bloody swords and hands and crying "Peace, freedom, and liberty!" in the streets. But before they do so, a servant, recognized as belonging to Antony's household, comes to Brutus and conveys a message from Antony: though Antony loved and honored Caesar, he is ready to follow the fortune of Brutus. All that he asks is a safe conduct to come and hear from Brutus' lips his reasons for killing Caesar. This request Brutus grants, erroneously convinced that Antony will prove harmless now that his mentor, Caesar, is dead. Antony arrives; and before coming directly to Brutus, he stops at the body of Caesar and says, with breaking heart:

ANTONY
O mighty Caesar! Dost thou lie so low?
Are all thy conquests, glories, triumphs, spoils,
Shrunk to this little measure? Fare thee well.
• • •

O mother of a mighty race

Source: O MOTHER OF A MIGHTY RACE (Stanza 1)
Author: William Cullen Bryant (1794-1878)
First published: 1847
Type of work: Patriotic poem

Context: Bryant praises America, the "mother of a mighty race." The older countries are jealous of the young nation's youthful health and energy, but

716

their taunts are harmless, for "They do not know how loved thou art,/ How many a fond and fearless heart/ Would rise to throw/ Its life between thee and the foe." America is a nation full of "graceful maids" and "generous men." In this land of faith and truth, ". . . man is loved, and God is feared. . . . ." It is a land of freedom, a "shelter for the hunted head." As the years pass, America will increase in riches, virtue, and glory, and her "form shall tower" over all her jealous neighbors. Bryant explains the jealousy of America's sister nations:

> **O mother of a mighty race,**
> Yet lovely in thy youthful grace!
> The elder dames, thy haughty peers,
> Admire and hate thy blooming years.
> > With words of shame
> And taunts of scorn they join thy name.
>
> For on thy cheeks the glow is spread
> That tints thy morning hills with red;
> Thy step—the wild-deer's rustling feet
> Within thy woods are not more fleet;
> > Thy hopeful eye
> Is bright as thine own sunny sky.

O Romeo, Romeo, wherefore art thou Romeo?

Source: ROMEO AND JULIET (Act II, sc. ii, l. 33)
Author: William Shakespeare (1564-1616)
First published: 1597
Type of work: Romantic tragedy

Context: Romeo is in the Capulet garden below Juliet's window. Juliet appears at the window above, unaware that Romeo is below. Romeo then speaks *at* his love but not loud enough to disturb her. Romeo is not so much aware as is Juliet of the danger of their situation in being the children of enemy families. He is, rather, bewitched by her beauty and wants to come close: "O that I were a glove upon that hand, / That I might touch that cheek," he says. Juliet then sighs, and Romeo, enraptured, speaks and listens:

> ROMEO
> • • •
> O speak again bright angel, for thou art
> As glorious to this night being o'er my head,
> As is a winged messenger of heaven
> Unto the white-upturned wond'ring eyes
> Of mortals that fall back to gaze on him,

717

When he bestrides the lazy pacing clouds,
And sails upon the bosom of the air.

JULIET
O Romeo, Romeo, wherefore art thou Romeo?
Deny thy father, and refuse thy name.
Or if thou wilt not, be but sworn my love,
And I'll no longer be a Capulet.

O that this too too solid flesh would melt

Source: HAMLET (Act I, sc. ii, l. 129)
Author: William Shakespeare (1564-1616)
First published: 1603
Type of work: Dramatic tragedy

Context: A combination of factors gives this opening line of Hamlet's first soliloquy great poignancy. His uncle Claudius, new King of Denmark, has just ascended the throne and announced his marriage to Hamlet's mother, Queen Gertrude. Hamlet, a sensitive, introspective person, is shattered by these events. Not only is his mother's hasty marriage unseemly and incestuous, not only does he dislike his uncle Claudius on personal terms, but also he now has even more reason to detest him because Claudius has usurped his rightful inheritance, the throne itself. Now Hamlet is alone. He feels drained, disgusted, miserable, and betrayed. His thoughts are on death. (Most scholars are now agreed that the line should read "sullied flesh," but "solid" is fixed in the popular memory.)

HAMLET
O that this too too solid flesh would melt,
Thaw and resolve itself into a dew,
Or that the Everlasting had not fixed
His canon 'gainst self-slaughter. O God, God,
How weary, stale, flat, and unprofitable
Seem to me all the uses of this world!
• • •

O that way madness lies

Source: KING LEAR (Act III, sc. iv, l. 21)
Author: William Shakespeare (1564-1616)
First published: 1608
Type of work: Dramatic tragedy

Context: Lear, King of Britain, and in his dotage, foolishly divides his kingdom between his two eldest daughters, Goneril and Regan, and

718

cuts off his youngest, Cordelia, with nothing. A faithful friend, Kent, questions the old man's actions and is exiled. Soon, however, the irascible old king is stripped of his bodyguard of one hundred knights and turned out by the daughters to wander on the heath. Reduced to impotent fury, he curses his eldest daughters and hurls defiance at a raging storm that swirls about him on the heath. Cold, miserable, deserted by all but his jester, he is found by Kent, who, at peril of his life, did not leave the country. Lear, on the verge of madness, does not recognize Kent, but allows himself and the fool to be led toward the shelter of a hovel. Before they enter, sanity returns to the distraught old man in fits and starts.

LEAR

　　. . . Filial ingratitude,
Is it not as this mouth should tear this hand
For lifting food to't? But I will punish home.
No, I will weep no more. In such a night
To shut me out! Pour on, I will endure.
In such a night as this! O Regan, Goneril—
Your old kind father, whose frank heart gave all—
O that way madness lies, let me shun that.
No more of that.

O tiger's heart, wrapped in a woman's hide

Source: KING HENRY THE SIXTH: PART THREE (Act I, sc. iv, l. 137)
Author: William Shakespeare (1564-1616)
First published: 1623
Type of work: Historical drama

Context: The Duke of York, rebelling with his sons, especially Richard the "valiant crook-back prodigy" who later is to become King Richard III, has fought against superior numbers led by Queen Margaret. York's forces have been dispersed, and he captured. Margaret taunts him for taking up arms against the king. York curses her for an inhuman monster. Margaret shows York a handkerchief stained with the blood of his son Rutland, and offers it to him to dry his eyes. York responds that Margaret is not beautiful nor virtuous nor self-governed, but a tiger in human form. This quotation, parodied by Robert Greene as "Tygers heart wrapt in a Players hide" (1592), is held to be the first reference, albeit indirect, to Shakespeare as an actor and a reviser of old plays.

YORK
• • •
Thou art as opposite to every good,
As the Antipodes are unto us,
Or as the South to the Septentrion.

719

O tiger's heart, wrapped in a woman's hide,
How couldst thou drain the life-blood of the child,
To bid the father wipe his eyes withal,
And yet be seen to bear a woman's face?
Women are soft, mild, pitiful, and flexible;
Thou stern, obdurate, flinty, rough, remorseless.

· · ·

O what a fall was there

Source: JULIUS CAESAR (Act III, sc. ii, 1. 195)
Author: William Shakespeare (1564-1616)
First published: 1623
Type of work: Dramatic tragedy

Context: Whenever anyone in high place or position dies or loses his place and prestige, we hear the familiar saying "What a fall was there." Specifically, the famous saying occurs during Mark Antony's funeral oration over the body of his fallen friend and mentor, Julius Caesar. Antony has gathered the crowd of Roman citizens around him as he points out Caesar's gaping wounds and skillfully turns the mood of the crowd to one of vengeance on Caesar's murderers, who, led by Brutus, believe they killed Caesar as the only way to preserve ancient and precious Roman freedoms. Now, at the climax of his masterful speech, Antony plays upon their volatile emotions.

ANTONY
· · ·
Then burst his mighty heart,
And in his mantle muffling up his face,
Even at the base of Pompey's statue,
Which all the while ran blood, great Caesar fell.
O what a fall was there, my countrymen!
Then I, and you, and all of us fell down
Whilst bloody treason flourished over us.

· · ·

O what a noble mind is here o'erthrown!

Source: HAMLET (Act III, sc. i, 1. 157)
Author: William Shakespeare (1564-1616)
First published: 1603
Type of work: Dramatic tragedy

Context: Informed by his father's ghost that he, his father, was mur- dered by his brother, Claudius, and that his wife and Hamlet's mother

720

Queen Gertrude, was adulterous with him, Hamlet's mind teeters. Horrified and distracted, he swears to avenge his father's death. But how? Claudius is well guarded. Hamlet pretends madness in Ophelia's presence. She, in love with Hamlet, reports his strange behavior to her father, Polonius, chief councilor of the king. He in turn tells the king that Hamlet has lost his mind over love of Ophelia. The councilor and king determine to test Hamlet by putting Ophelia in his way. Hamlet is aware of the plot. He is angry at Ophelia for lending herself to duplicity, as did his mother, and he rails at her. The phrase "all but one" is for the hidden king's benefit.

HAMLET
 . . . I say we will have no moe marriage. Those that are married already, all but one, shall live, the rest shall keep as they are. To a nunnery go.   [*Exit.*]

OPHELIA
O what a noble mind is here o'erthrown!
The courtier's, soldier's, scholar's, eye, tongue, sword,
. . .
Th' observed of all observers, quite, quite down,
. . .

O, ye race of men, born to soar

Source: THE DIVINE COMEDY, PURGATORIO (Canto XII, l. 88, as translated by H. F. Cary)
Author: Dante Alighieri (1265-1321)
First transcribed: c.1320
Type of work: Christian allegory

Context: The argument for this division follows the poets' admission through the gates of Purgatory, from whence they wind their way upward to the first station of penance. Here proud souls, surrounded by statues illustrating humility, are expiating the sin of pride by carrying heavy stones. The path then passes over illuminated tile or rock whereon is traced the history of the world's proud: "What master of the pencil or the style/ Had traced the shades and lines, that might have made/ The subtlest workman wonder?" Virgil then urges Dante to look up and follow the angel sent to guide them, who now urges them onward.

A scanty few are they, who, when they hear
Such tidings, hasten. **O, ye race of men!**
Though **born to soar,** why suffer ye a wind
So slight to baffle ye? He led us on
Where the rock parted: here, against my front,
Did beat his wings; then promised I should fare
In safety on my way
. . .

721

O, yet we trust that somehow good will be
the final goal of ill

Source: IN MEMORIAM (Part LIV, stanza 1)
Author: Alfred, Lord Tennyson (1809-1892)
First published: 1850
Type of work: Elegy

Context: The poet wants to compose poetry which will express the love he felt for his dead friend, Authur Hallam, but he despairs of doing so for fear that his words are trivial and unworthy of his love and of its object. This fear is called a needless one by the "Spirit of true love," which tells him that spirits live on, unaffected by human failings, and that he must not cast away his love merely because it is not perfect. One must find the good in life and treasure it, ignoring the rest; God has made everything for a purpose, and all, even that which appears evil, will ultimately serve the good that He has designed.

> O, yet we trust that somehow good
> Will be the final goal of ill,
> To pangs of nature, sins of will,
> Defects of doubt, and taints of blood;
>
> That nothing walks with aimless feet;
> That not one life shall be destroy'd,
> Or cast as rubbish to the void,
> When God hath made the pile complete. . . .

Of all sad words of tongue or pen, the saddest are these:
"It might have been!"

Source: MAUD MULLER (Stanza 53)
Author: John Greenleaf Whittier (1807-1892)
First published: 1854
Type of work: Narrative poem

Context: This poem, like "The Barefoot Boy," extols the virtues of simple rural life, and it also reveals certain aspects of human psychology. "Maud Muller, on a summer's day,/ Raked the meadow sweet with hay." She enjoys "simple beauty and rustic health," but she is full of "a nameless longing" for the "far-off town," for "something better than she had known." A Judge rides up on his horse, and Maud shyly gives him a drink of water from the spring. They talk of the weather, the countryside, the haying. The Judge leaves regretfully, and the generous Maud thinks of how she could help her family and the poor if she were the Judge's wife. The Judge would like to marry Maud and be, "Like her, a harvester of hay." But his family is rich and proud, and so he "closes his heart" to Maud and marries a rich wife who lives "for fashion, as he for power." And yet all his life he longs for Maud and the "meadows and clover-blooms." Maud marries "a man un-learned and poor" and ages quickly from childbirth and hard work. She dreams of the manly Judge and the comfortable life he represents, not realizing that the Judge idealizes rural life. But she takes up "her burden of life again,/ Saying only, 'It might have been.'" All humans share the same psychological fate:

Alas for maiden, alas for Judge,
For rich repiner and household drudge!

God pity them both! and pity us all,
Who vainly the dreams of youth recall,

For **of all sad words of tongue or pen,
The saddest are these: "It might have been!"**

Ah, well! for us all some sweet hope lies
Deeply buried from human eyes;

And, in the hereafter, angels may
Roll the stone from its grave away!

Of cabbages—and kings

Source: THROUGH THE LOOKING-GLASS (Chapter 4, "The Walrus and the Car-penter," stanza 11)
Author: Lewis Carroll (Charles Lutwidge Dodgson, 1832-1898)
First published: 1871
Type of work: Imaginative tale for children

Context: Noted Oxford mathematician Charles Lutwidge Dodgson, is better known by his pen-name Lewis Carroll, and for the popular children's fantasies, *Alice's Adventures in Wonderland* and *Through the Looking-Glass,* in which a young friend, Alice Liddell, appears as the central character. In *Through the Looking-Glass,* Alice imagines that she passes through the mirror over the mantle in her home to a reflected room of Looking-Glass House, which is inhabited by chessmen and which is located in a land composed of a large chessboard. Wishing to become a queen in the giant chessgame, Alice is advised by the Red Queen to travel to the eighth square, but she is met by the twin brothers Tweedledum and Tweedledee, who refuse to direct her until Twedeledee has recited for her

723

the longest poem they know, "The Walrus and the Carpenter," which tells of a walrus and carpenter who trick and eat a group of trusting oysters instead of chatting with them:

> "The time has come," the Walrus said,
> "To talk of many things:
> Of shoes—and ships—and sealing-wax—
> **Of cabbages—and kings—**
> And why the sea is boiling hot—
> And whether pigs have wings."

Of making many books there is no end

Source: ECCLESIASTES 12:12
Author: Unknown
First transcribed: c.250-200 B.C.
Type of work: Religious confession

Context: The writer, calling himself "the Preacher" and repeating often his view of life, "vanity of vanities; all is vanity," observes that wealth, pleasure, wisdom, folly, hopes, and labor lead alike to the grave. The wise man, however, can use his wisdom to choose the less vain things of the world. The writer, confronted by stern and fixed laws of nature, the prosperity of the wicked, and the suffering of the righteous, and his own inability to know God's wisdom, laments the certainty of the grave and of the failure of most of man's attempts, and argues that youth should enjoy itself, for old age and death show only vanity. In an epilogue concerning the words of "the Preacher," apparently written by a disciple, admonitions on books and duty are given:

> The words of the wise are as goads. . . .
> And further, by these, my son, be admonished: **of making many books there is no end;** and much study is a weariness of the flesh.
> Let us hear the conclusion of the whole matter: Fear God, and keep his commandments: for this is the whole duty of man.

Of man's first disobedience

Source: PARADISE LOST (Book I, l. 1)
Author: John Milton (1608-1674)
First published: 1667
Type of work: Epic poem

Context: Like many another seventeenth century author, Milton believed the greatest poetic achievement to be an epic poem. Unlike most of his contemporaries, he succeeded in writing a great one. *Paradise Lost* is the supreme epic poem of Protestant Christianity, and it uses the characteristic qualities of the epic which can be traced back many centuries to the Homeric prototypes. In practice the epic poet announces the subject of his poem and then invokes the aid of the gods for his task. Milton announces his subject and then invokes the aid, not of Kalliope, the Greek muse of epic poetry, but the Holy Spirit who inspired the writers of Scripture:

> **Of man's first disobedience,** and the fruit
> Of that forbidden tree, whose mortal taste
> Brought death into the world, and all our woe,
> With loss of Eden, till one greater Man
> Restore us, and regain the blissful seat,
> Sing, Heavenly Muse, that on the secret top
> Of Oreb, or of Sinai, didst inspire
> That shepherd, who first taught the chosen seed,
> In the beginning how the Heavens and Earth
> Rose out of chaos. . . .

Of nothing, nothing, nothing—nothing at all

Source: THE END OF THE WORLD (Last line)
Author: Archibald MacLeish (1892-   )
First published: 1926
Type of work: Sonnet

Context: The poem begins with the words, "quite unexpectedly," but withholds the unexpected while it goes through a descriptive passage deceivingly light and beguilingly amusing. The poet gives a sweeping view of several concurrent spectacles taking place under the big top at a three-ring circus—before the unexpected happened. Performing all at once were the armless ambidextrian, Ralph the lion, the band and the clowns when "quite unexpectedly the top blew off," leaving nothing but the black void of the night sky overhead. The repetition of *there* focuses attention upon the empty night as seen through the open top. The poem suddenly conveys the sense of a terrible awe accompanying the hush and darkness of the scene. The unexpected event becomes a gloomy revelation of the end of the world, and carries with it a deep philosophical significance, naturalistic in implication. The picture is presented vividly and intensely:

> And there, there overhead, there, there, hung over
> Those thousands of white faces, those dazed eyes,
> There in the starless dark the poise, the hover,
> There with vast wings across the cancelled skies,
> There in the sudden blackness the black pall
> **Of nothing, nothing, nothing—nothing at all.**

725

Off with his head

Source: KING RICHARD THE THIRD (Act III, sc. iv, l. 78)
Author: William Shakespeare (1564-1616)
First published: 1597
Type of work: Historical drama

Context: The various lords are talking about the proper day for the Coronation of Edward as King Edward V. Hastings says that he can speak for Richard, Duke of Gloucester and Lord Protector, because he loves Richard and Richard loves him. At this moment, Richard enters and with sugared words declares his affection for Hastings. The announcement of plans for the Coronation upsets him, however, because his own devilish schemes are not quite ripe. Deceptively he asks Hastings the punishment due to anybody who conspires his death. Hastings answers the punishment should be death. Richard then accuses Edward's wife, "that monstrous witch," and his mistress, that "harlot strumpet Shore," of bewitching him and withering up his arm. The following lines reveal Richard's plotting and his uncontrollable temper:

HASTINGS
If they have done this deed, my noble lord—

RICHARD
If? Thou protector of this damned strumpet,
Talk'st thou to me of ifs? Thou art a traitor.
Off with his head. Now by Saint Paul I swear,
I will not dine, until I see the same.

• • •

Offscouring of scoundrels, would ye live forever?

Source: THE FRENCH REVOLUTION (Volume II, Book VIII, chapter 4)
Author: Thomas Carlyle (1795-1881)
First published: 1837
Type of work: History

Context: Considering the role played by journalism in the overthrow of the monarchy, Carlyle mentions the handbills and posters, lasting scarcely a day, but evidence of man's desire to communicate, even though his words are not destined for immortality. Here he first phrases the idea later uttered in World War I and commemorated by Carl Sandburg in his poem "Losers" (1921), about
That sergeant at Belleau Woods

Walking into the drumfire, calling his men,
"Come on, you . . . Do you want to live forever?"

Speaking of the existence of a spirit in the word of man, as in man himself, Carlyle says:

> . . . His immortality, indeed, and whether it shall last half a lifetime or a lifetime and a half; is not that a very considerable thing? Immortality, mortality:—there were certain runaways whom Fritz the Great [Frederick II of Prussia, 1712-1786] bullied back into line with a: "R—, wollt ihr ewig leben." Unprintable **offscouring of scoundrels, would ye live forever?**

Oh, had our simple Eve seen through the make-believe!

Source: EVE (Stanza 5)
Author: Ralph Hodgson (1871-1962)
First published: 1913
Type of work: Narrative poem

Context: In this narrative poem Hodgson laments the folly of Eve. "Mute as a mouse in a/ Corner the cobra lay." The snake attempts to entice Eve to eat of the forbidden fruit, and Eve, simple and unsuspecting, is easily tricked. The animals that witness the Fall of Man give vent to their emotions in their hatred for the dreaded cobra. Hodgson paints a picture of the celebration that will take place "under the hill to-night—", as Satan, having accomplished his purpose, drinks a toast to the "simple Eve."

> **Oh, had our simple Eve**
> **Seen through the make-believe!**
> Had she but known the
> Pretender he was!
> Out of the boughs he came,
> Whispering still her name,
> Tumbling in twenty rings
> Into the grass.

Oh! how many torments lie in the small circle of a wedding-ring

Source: THE DOUBLE GALLANT; OR, THE SICK LADY'S CURE (Act I, sc. ii)
Author: Colley Cibber (1671-1757)
First published: 1707
Type of work: Dramatic comedy

Context: One of the stock characters in dramatic literature through the centuries, and in prose fiction too, is the older man married to a lively

727

young wife; the husband's constant fear is, conventionally, that he may not satisfy his wife in some way and so end up a cuckold, looking foolish in everyone's eyes, including his own. Sir Solomon Sadlife in *The Double Gallant* is such a character, a man who has begun to hate his young wife because she may become dissatisfied with him. Sir Solomon is deeply troubled, for he does not like his wife's activities. He detests her pet Dutch mastiff; he despises the women who come to gossip in the morning and to drink tea in the afternoon; he loathes the fops who congregate in the park across the street from his house; and he disapproves of his wife's extravagance. He sums up his view of women himself: "O fool, to trust thy honoui with a woman! a race of vipers! They were deceivers . . . from the beginning." After speaking with three suitors for his niece's hand in marriage, and dismissing each one, Sir Solomon speaks of his own problems to his servant, Supple:

> SIR SOLOMON SADLIFE
> . . . I'll step into the *Park,* and see if I can meet with my hopeful spouse there! I warrant, engag'd in some innocent freedom, (as she calls it,) as walking in a mask, to laugh at the impertinence of fops that don't know her; but 'tis more likely, I'm afraid, a plot to intrigue with those that do. **Oh! how many torments lie in the small circle of a Wedding-Ring!**

Oh, my America, my Newfoundland

Source: ELEGY XIX: ON HIS MISTRESS GOING TO BED (Line 27)
Author: John Donne (1572-1631)
First published: 1633
Type of work: Metaphysical poem

Context: John Donne begins his poem by telling his lady to disrobe in preparation for going to bed with him. He catalogues her garments as he sees her remove them. Then in bed he discovers her, as one continually discovers the one he loves. She is his America, a country so new that it had probably not yet been colonized at the time Donne wrote his poem. "Newfoundland" is a word play on the region still known by that name and a territory that the lover has just discovered. Donne refers to his love as a mine of precious stones, reflecting the view of most of the population of Europe at that time that America was a vast storehouse of gold and gems of every kind. He says that he is blest in discovering her, because to enter into the bonds or confines of her body is to be set free, and he means both physically and spiritually. This extremely ingenious praise of physical love contains the following passage:

> **Oh, my America, my Newfoundland,**
> My kingdom, safest when with one man manned,

My mine of precious stones, my empery;
How am I blest in thus discovering thee!

Oh sleep! it is a gentle thing

Source: THE RIME OF THE ANCIENT MARINER (Part V, stanza 1)
Author: Samuel Taylor Coleridge (1772-1834)
First published: 1798
Type of work: Literary ballad

Context: For seven days and nights the Ancient Mariner lives in spiritual agony and despair among his dead shipmates—all because he slew an albatross. He envies the dead men, but cannot himself die. He tries to pray, but finds it impossible: "A wicked whisper came, and made/ My heart as dry as dust." Finally, the turning point in the poem is reached as the mariner becomes aware of the beauty and joy of the water snakes, "every track/ . . . a flash of golden fire," and feels a "spring of love" gush from his heart. He blesses the snakes, signifying a change in his attitude toward God's living creatures—an attitude he did not possess when he killed the albatross. At last he finds he can pray, and the albatross, that had been hung around his neck by his shipmates, falls into the sea. The process of healing begins; he sleeps:

> **Oh sleep! it is a gentle thing,**
> Beloved from pole to pole!
> To Mary Queen the praise be given!
> She sent the gentle sleep from Heaven,
> That slid into my soul.

Oh that I had wings like a dove!

Source: PSALMS 55:6
Author: Unknown
First transcribed: c.400-200 B.C.
Type of work: Religious poetry

Context: In anguish the psalmist pleads that God be accessible to him and listen to his petition. He is distraught because of persecution by his wicked enemy. In soreness of heart he trembles with the horror of death. Longing for escape from his bitter lot, he imagines himself flying with the swift, sure flight of the dove far away from the howling storm of conflict to the serenity of the distant wilderness:

> And I said, **Oh that I had wings like a dove!** for then would I
> fly away, and be at rest.

729

Lo, then would I wander far off, and remain in the wilderness. Selah.
I would hasten my escape from the windy storm and tempest.

Oh, the little more, and how much it is!

Source: BY THE FIRESIDE (Stanza 39)
Author: Robert Browning (1812-1889)
First published: 1855
Type of work: Dramatic monologue

Context: The speaker of this poem asks his wife to accompany him in imagination back to the mountain gorge in Italy where they had, years before, realized the moment of deep mutual understanding that began the love between them. He recalls the agony he felt as he struggled to find the words and the courage to confess the depth of his love to her. The words of the excerpt describe the delicate balance of the lover's emotions at this moment of crisis. To render their love concrete with a word of agreement is only accessory; to let the moment pass without expressing its meaning seems to threaten him with the loss of everything.

> Oh, the little more, and how much it is!
> And the little less, and what worlds away!
> How a sound shall quicken content to bliss,
> Or a breath suspend the blood's best play,
> And life be a proof of this!

Oh, to be in England now that April's there

Source: HOME-THOUGHTS, FROM ABROAD
Author: Robert Browning (1812-1889)
First published: 1845
Type of work: Lyric poem

Context: Browning wrote this poem in 1838, during his first trip into Italy. It may be considered the nostalgic recollection of the delicate beauties of the English spring by an Englishman who must spend the season away from his native land. At the time of the writing, the first signs of spring are becoming evident; the poet then looks ahead into May, when the spring in the countryside has become full, but has not lost its fineness and gentleness. The Mediterranean spring in Italy, by contrast, is grosser, a "gaudy melon-flower."

> Oh, to be in England
> Now that April's there,

And whoever wakes in England
Sees, some morning, unaware,
That the lowest boughs and the brushwood sheaf
Round the elm-tree bole are in tiny leaf,
While the chaffinch sings on the orchard bough
In England—now!

Oh wad some Power the giftie gie us to see oursels as ithers see us!

Source: TO A LOUSE (Stanza 8)
Author: Robert Burns (1759-1796)
First published: 1786
Type of work: Satirical poem

Context: "To a Louse" is a winning and merry piece of social criticism. It opens with the poet speaking in mock indignation to a louse crawling on the fine bonnet of a lady who sits in church unconscious of the intruder. First Burns comments on its impudence, then demands in exaggerated anger how dare it crawl upon "sae fine a lady," bidding it go find its meal on "some poor body." Following stanzas develop this contrast between a beggar's squalor, with lice in "thick plantations," and "Miss's" gauze and lace. "How daur ye do't?" asks the poet, still in amusement. Then, as the bonnet's wearer shakes her head, he changes to addressing her, her homely name of Jenny abruptly identifying her as a simple village girl aping the fashionable world and mocked by the louse. Thinking of the foolish girl, the poet begins the final stanza with lines that have grown proverbial:

> Oh wad some Power the giftie gie us
> To see oursels as ithers see us!
> It wad frae monie a blunder free us,
> An' foolish notion:
> What airs in dress an' gait wad lea'e us,
> An' ev'n devotion!

Oh, why should the spirit of mortal be proud?

Source: SONGS OF ISRAEL ("Mortality," Stanza 1)
Author: William Knox (1789-1825)
First published: 1824
Type of work: Lyric poem

Context: William Knox, a Scottish poet born at Firth, attempted farming without success from 1812 to 1817, following his elementary education.

731

The primary factor in his failure, the tragic weakness which was to plague him throughout life, was his addiction to alcohol. In 1820, he settled in Edinburgh and, befriended by Sir Walter Scott, became a journalist. Convivial habits undermined his health, however, and he died in 1825 of paralysis. The author of numerous graceful and thoughtful lyrics, Knox achieved his most effective work in *Songs of Israel,* one of Abraham Lincoln's favorite poems. The first section, "Mortality," is in effect a *memento mori,* or a contemplation of the brevity of life and the inevitability of death. Since all men die, regardless of their earthly station, the poem asserts, man has no claim to pride and self-sufficiency. The first stanza reads:

> **Oh, why should the spirit of mortal be proud?**
> Like a swift-fleeting meteor, a fast-flying cloud,
> A flash of the lightning, a break of the wave,
> Man passeth from life to his rest in the grave.

An old and haughty nation proud in arms

Source: COMUS (Line 33)
Author: John Milton (1608-1674)
First published: 1637
Type of work: Masque

Context: John Milton composed *A Masque,* now commonly known as *Comus,* to celebrate the inauguration of John, Earl of Bridgewater and Viscount Brackley, as President of Wales. It was first presented in the great hall of Ludlow Castle, the Earl's headquarters. The poet says that this region that fronts the setting sun, Wales, an old and haughty nation proud in arms, will now be ruled by a trusted servant of the King. The Welsh are of great antiquity as a people in Britain, having been there for untold centuries before other peoples invaded the island. The valor and pride of the Welsh are traditional. The poet says, speaking in the person of the attendant spirit, that Lord Bridgewater's daughter and two sons are on the way to the castle to witness the inauguration ceremonies, but their way lies through a thick and tangled forest. He says:

> . . . And all this tract that fronts the falling sun
> A noble peer of mickle trust and power
> Has in his charge, with tempered awe to guide
> **An old and haughty nation proud in arms;**
> Where his fair offspring nursed in princely lore,
> Are coming to attend their father's state
> And new-entrusted sceptre, but the way
> Lies through the perplexed paths of this drear wood . . .

Old and stricken in years

Source: JOSHUA 13:1
Author: Unknown
First transcribed: c.625-600 B.C.
Type of work: Religious history

Context: The leadership of the Israelites is passed on to the great warrior, Joshua, after Moses has completed his task of delivering them from Egyptian bondage and leading them to Canaan. Joshua spends the years of his manhood in subduing the inhabitants of Canaan so that the Israelites can claim their inheritance of "the promised land." Although when Joshua becomes old his conquest of the Canannites is still not nearly complete, God tells him that He will conclude the work that Joshua has begun, and that now Joshua is to begin another task of supreme importance, the making of an equitable division of the land among the different tribes of Israel:

> Now Joshua was **old and stricken in years;** and the Lord said unto him, Thou art old and stricken in years, and there remaineth yet very much land to be possessed.
>
> . . .
>
> . . . them will I drive out from before the children of Israel: only divide thou it by lot unto the Israelites for an inheritance, as I have commanded thee.

Old father, old artificer, stand me now and ever in good stead

Source: A PORTRAIT OF THE ARTIST AS A YOUNG MAN (End of Chapter 5)
Author: James Joyce (1882-1941)
First published: 1914-1915 (in *The Egoist*); 1916 (in book form)
Type of work: Novel

Context: James Joyce's *A Portrait of the Artist as a Young Man* utilizes a "stream of consciousness" method to portray a young man's preparation for life as an artist. The events of the novel are not so much dramatic as they are statically revelatory; various critical phases of the young man's development are shown through what Stephen Dedalus, the young Irish hero of the book, calls "epiphanies." By the end of the novel, Stephen has liberated himself from his friends, his family, his nation, and his Church— and from the ideas which would have restrained him as a writer. The novel ends with two entries from the young man's diary. (Stephen is the son of Daedalus, the great Greek artificer, only in a metaphorical sense, of course.)

April 26. . . . Welcome, O life! I go to encounter for the millionth time the reality of experience and to forge in the smithy of my soul the uncreated conscience of my race.

April 27 **Old father, old artificer, stand me now and ever in good stead.**

Old folks at home

Source: OLD FOLKS AT HOME
Author: Stephen C. Foster (1826-1864)
First published: 1851
Type of work: Popular song

Context: The most popular of all of Foster's compositions, this song is the lament of a Negro suffering from homesickness for his family and the scenes of his childhood. His travels have taken him far from the plantation where he grew up, spending many happy days in play with his brother about his parents' farm. He finds nothing to cheer him in any of the places to which he wanders, nothing to ease his heart; and he goes on, consumed with longing for his home and the people who provided him with the only contentment he has ever found in life.

> All up and down de whole creation,
> Sadly I roam,
> Still longing for de old plantation,
> And for de **old folks at home.**

> All de world am sad and dreary,
> Everywhere I roam,
> Oh! Darkies how my heart grows weary,
> Far from de **old folks at home.**

The old—old sophistries of June

Source: THESE ARE THE DAYS WHEN BIRDS COME BACK
Author: Emily Dickinson (1830-1886)
First published: 1890
Type of work: Lyric poem

Context: Emily Dickinson, noted for the often stark economy of her style and for the sharpness of her images, found in a small circle of friends and a circumscribed world a universal note. A careful observer of nature, she viewed the fields and their inhabitants with almost a pagan love. For example, in the lyrical poem "These are the days when Birds come back—," she writes of the beauty, yet deception of Indian summer days.

734

Overwhelmed by the glow of the short reminder of the warm months, she compares the last pleasant days of the season with the Last Supper and pleads that she be allowed to partake of the sacrament of nature. The first three stanzas read:

> These are the days when Birds come back—
> A very few—a Bird or two—
> To take a backward look.

> These are the days when skies resume
> **The old—old sophistries of June—**
> A blue and gold mistake.

> Oh fraud that cannot cheat the Bee—
> Almost thy plausibility
> Induces my belief.

The old order changeth

Source: MORTE D'ARTHUR (Line 240)
Author: Alfred, Lord Tennyson (1809-1892)
First published: 1842
Type of work: Narrative poem

Context: Tennyson takes the story of King Arthur's death from Malory's *Le Mortre d'Arthur.* King Arthur is mortally wounded at Lyonness. Sir Bedivere, the only surviving knight of the Round Table, carries him to a chapel. Arthur gives Bedivere his sword Excalibur and orders him to cast it into the lake. But Bedievere hides the sword, planning to preserve the marvelous weapon as a memento of Arthur. The king is furious at Bedivere's disobedience, but the knight hides the sword again. When Arthur threatens to kill him, Bedivere throws the sword into the mere: "But ere he [the sword] dipt the surface, rose an arm/ Clothed in white samite, mystic, wonderful,/ And caught him by the hilt, and brandished him/ Three times, and drew him under in the mere." It is the same arm that had presented the sword to Arthur many years before. Bedivere carries the dying Arthur to the lake, where three queens in "a dusky barge" receive the king. Bedivere laments that he is now without his companions and his king: "For now I see the true old times are dead. . . ." But Arthur comforts him:

> And slowly answered Arthur from the barge:
> **"The old order changeth,** yielding place to new,
> And God fulfils Himself in many ways,
> Lest one good custom should corrupt the world.
> Comfort thyself: what comfort is in me?
> I have lived my life, and that which I have done
> May He within himself make pure! . . ."

735

The oldest hath borne most

Source: KING LEAR (Act V, sc. iii, l. 325)
Author: William Shakespeare (1564-1616)
First published: 1608
Type of work: Dramatic tragedy

Context: This half-line is part of the final speech in the play, and is spoken over the body of humbled, exhausted, and broken-hearted King Lear, who, at the play's beginning, is headstrong, foolish, and proud. By dividing his kingdom between his evil elder daughters, Goneril and Regan, merely because they profess great love for him, he has hurried himself and his fortunes to this lamentable condition. From the time of the kingdom's division all has been discord: he has been abused, insulted, stripped of his followers, even deprived of shelter. Enraged, miserable, all but deserted, and pushed to the verge of insanity, the old man has gone through personal crises that, in their cruelty and intensity, are out of all proportion to his initial offense: giving up his kingdom while he still lived. Learning too late that his youngest daughter, Cordelia, loved him best, he dies, worn out and disillusioned, when he realizes that she, too, is dead. Edgar, son of a friend of the old king, and one who must help rebuild the kingdom, laments:

EDGAR
The weight of this sad time we must obey,
Speak what we feel, not what we ought to say.
The oldest hath borne most; we that are young
Shall never see so much, nor live so long.

Once more unto the breach

Source: KING HENRY THE FIFTH (Act III, sc. i, l. 1)
Author: William Shakespeare (1564-1616)
First published: 1600
Type of work: Historical drama

Context: King Henry V and his soldiers have departed from England, leaving her "guarded with grandsires, babies, and old women," to conquer France. The English are laying siege to Harfleur. Henry, his noblemen, and soldiers, approach the walls of the city with scaling-ladders. Henry spurs them to battle with the following speech:

HENRY
Once more unto the breach, dear friends, once more;
Or close the wall up with our English dead.

In peace, there's nothing so becomes a man,
As modest stillness, and humility.
But when the blast of war blows in our ears,
Then imitate the action of the tiger;
Stiffen the sinews, summon up the blood,
Disguise fair nature with hard-favoured rage.

. . .

One can acquire everything in solitude—except character

Source: DE L'AMOUR (Fragment I)
Author: Stendhal (Marie-Henri Beyle, 1783-1842)
First published: 1822
Type of work: Philosophic maxims

Context: Stendhal, pen name of Marie-Henri Beyle, has become a figure of increasing importance in French literature, and his appeal to the modern reader is undoubtedly stronger than it was to his contemporaries. Indeed, he disliked France and, after participating in several campaigns of the Napoleonic wars, lived for a number of years in Italy; consequently, his works were not largely read during his lifetime. However, a close analyst of emotions, thoughts, and motives, he was hailed later in the 19th century as a precursor of Balzac, and he influenced Bourget, Taine, and Zola, among others. His fame rests chiefly on two of his four novels, *Le Rouge et le Noir* (1830) and *La Chartreuse de Parme* (1839). The first is a psychological novel dealing with the life of a brilliant, ambitious, and unscrupulous young man, Julian Sorel. The second, with its highly romantic plot and exciting picture of Italian court intrigue, was by far his most popular work. Stendhal's early writings were of a miscellaneous nature, including several biographies and a romantic novel, *Armance*. In 1822 he published *De l'Amour,* a series of notes on the effects of four kinds of love on a variety of temperaments. Appended to the essay was a section entitled "Fragments Divers," in which the author renders a "modest encore" of random afterthoughts with an apology for any repetition. Speaking of the power of love and the effect of companionship upon the personality, Stendhal writes:

One can acquire everything in solitude—except character.

One crowded hour of glorious life is worth an age without a name

Source: OLD MORTALITY (Chapter 33)
Author: Sir Walter Scott (1771-1832)
First published: 1816
Type of work: Novel

Context: Henry Morton is a stanch Covenanter, one of the group of Scotch Presbyterians who banded together to oppose the English Crown's encroachment on their religious liberties. Though he fights well against the English forces under Claverhouse, he is at last accused as a traitor by a fanatic group within the Covenanters themselves and sentenced to death. In the scene following his rescue by his foeman, Claverhouse, Morton watches with interest as the paradoxical characteristics of great cruelty and great courage are illustrated in his enemy, characteristics Scott drew directly from the historical Claverhouse. Claverhouse tells Morton that he hopes to die on some ". . . well-fought and hard-won field of battle . . . with the shout of victory in my ear; *that* would be worth . . . having lived for!" To emphasize these words, Scott prefaced his chapter with lines he marked anonymous, though it is probable he wrote them. He uses almost the same words in another novel, *Count Robert of Paris* (Chapter 25) when the Countess of Paris, Amazonian victress of many jousts and warrior in the First Crusade, refutes a suggestion that true virtue lies in delighting men and bringing up children. Though a loyal wife, she asserts that "One hour of life, crowded to the full with glorious action . . . is worth whole years . . . of paltry decorum."

> Sound, sound the clarion, fill the fife!
> To all the sensual world proclaim,
> **One crowded hour of glorious life**
> **Is worth an age without a name.**

One good turn deserves another

Source: THE PROVERBS OF JOHN HEYWOOD (Part I, chapter 11)
Author: John Heywood (1497?-1580?)
First published: 1546
Type of work: Gnomic poetry

Context: The author is recounting the troubles of a young man who married too soon and against the wishes of his aunt and uncle. When the young husband returned to his foster parents, the uncle said that since the fellow had acted in haste, he could repent in leisure, and so saying chased him away from his former home. Traveling with a companion,

738

the young husband decides to try his luck at the homes of some of his other kinsmen. But when he and his companion come to the home of one of them, the companion is greeted warmly, but the young husband is coolly received. The master of the house says that he has heard of the younger man's "matter," and he wants nothing to do with him:

> And by'r lady, friend! nought lay down, nought take up;
> Ka me, ka thee; **one good turn asketh another;**
> Nought won by the tone, nought won by the tother.
> To put me to cost, thou camest half a score miles
> Out of thine own nest, to seek me in these out isles:
> Where thou wilt not step over a straw, I think,
> To win me the worth of one draught of drink,
> No more than I have won of all thy whole stock.

One good turn deserves another

Source: SATYRICON (Section 45)
Author: Petronius (died c.66)
First transcribed: c.60
Type of work: Prose satirical romance

Context: A great feast at the home of Trimalchio, a newly-rich vulgarian, has been finished, and the host, called "the tyrant" by the author, has retired. The author then begins to "draw the conversation" from his neighbors. One guest discusses how much harder times are now than they used to be, because all the people are skeptics: "as it is, the gods are gouty in the feet because we are sceptics." Echion, an old-clothes dealer, answers, however, that " 'There's ups and there's downs', as the country bumpkin said when he lost his spotted pig." He then discusses the coming "superb spectacle," a gladiatorial combat that is to last three days. In discussing this event, he mentions some "decayed twopenny-halfpenny gladiators" who fought badly. He ends this discourse by saying:

> . . . One man, a Thracian, had some stuffing, but he too fought according to the rule of the schools. In short, they were all flogged afterwards. How the great crowd roared at them, "Lay it on!" They were mere runaways, to be sure. "Still," says Norbanus, "I did give you a treat." Yes, and I clap my hands at you. Reckon it up, and I give you more than I got. **One good turn deserves another.**

One little ewe lamb

Source: II SAMUEL 12:3
Author: Unknown
First transcribed: 1100-400 B.C.
Type of work: Religious history

Context: King David, having an adulterous relationship which leads to the pregnancy of Bathsheba, the beautiful wife of one of his soldiers, orders the husband, Uriah, placed in the front lines of battle, where he would be certain to be killed. When David marries Bathsheba, the prophet Nathan, by telling him a parable of a rich man and a poor man, makes him realize that he is like the rich man who takes away the only little ewe lamb of the poor man:

> . . . There were two men in one city; the one rich, and the other poor.
> The rich man had exceeding many flocks and herds:
> But the poor man had nothing, save **one little ewe lamb,** which he had bought and nourished up: and it grew up together with him, and with his children; it did eat of his own meat, and drank of his own cup, and lay in his bosom, and was unto him as a daughter.
> And there came a traveler unto the rich man, and he spared to take of his own flock and of his own herd, to dress for the wayfaring man that was come unto him; but took the poor man's lamb, and dressed it for the man that was come to him.

One man's meat is another man's poison

Source: DE RERUM NATURA (Book IV, l. 637)
Author: Titus Lucretius Carus (c.98-55 B.C.)
First transcribed: First century B.C.
Type of work: Didactic epic

Context: Lucretius, in Book IV, attempts to explain the senses: sight, sound, smell, taste. In speaking of taste, he explains that flavor is perceived when food is squeezed in the mouth and the juices distributed through the pores of the palate. Smooth juices give a pleasant taste, while rough ones are unpleasant. He further explains that food that might be good for one animal would not be good for another because of the different structure of the food and of the bodies. Similarly when the body structure is altered by sickness, something which is ordinarily sweet will taste bitter. Lucretius' idea about meat and poison was used by Beaumont and Fletcher, in 1647, in *Love's Cure* (Act III, sc. ii) as, What's one man's poison . . ./ Is another's meat or drink." Lucretius says it this way:

740

Next I will explain how different food is sweet and nourishing for different creatures, and why what is sour and bitter for some may yet seem very delicious to others, why there is so great a difference and distinction in these things that what is **one man's meat is another man's** rank **poison**. . . . Besides, hellebore is rank poison to us, but given to goats and quails makes them fat.

One may smile, and smile, and be a villain

Source: HAMLET (Act I, sc. v, l. 108)
Author: William Shakespeare (1564-1616)
First published: 1603
Type of work: Dramatic tragedy

Context: The ghost of Denmark's late King Hamlet for three previous nights has been seen on the battlements of Elsinore Castle. The young Prince Hamlet, accompanied by friends, waits, tonight, to see and talk to the apparition. It appears, and Hamlet shakes off his protesting, fearful companions and follows where it beckons. In a deserted area at the foot of the battlements, the ghost reveals to Hamlet that he, his father, was murdered in his sleep by his brother, the present King Claudius, and that Hamlet's mother was adulterous with Claudius. The ghost demands revenge on his murderer. Hamlet, horrified and distracted, calms himself only after he writes his fearful and damnable discovery in his notebook. He remembers how Claudius smiled at him when he called him his son.

HAMLET
. . .

O villain, villain, smiling damned villain!
My tables—meet it is I set it down
That **one may smile, and smile, and be a villain;**
At least I am sure it may be so in Denmark.
                                        [*Writes.*]
So uncle, there you are. Now to my word;
It is, adieu, adieu, remember me.
I have sworn't.

741

One of those people who would be enormously
improved by death

Source: BEASTS AND SUPER-BEASTS ("The Feast of Nemesis")
Author: Saki (Hector Hugh Munro, 1870-1916)
First published: 1914
Type of work: Short story

Context: In "The Feast of Nemesis" Mrs. Thackenbury complains about remembrances at Christmas, Easter, and birthdays; whereupon Clovis declares, ". . . all these days of intrusive remembrance harp so persistently on one aspect of human nature and entirely ignore the other. . . ." Clovis complains that there is no outlet for demonstrating feelings toward people you simply loathe. Therefore, he suggests that a Nemesis Day be set aside each year during which one could pay off old scores and grudges. Clovis next asserts that one prime target for the celebration would surely be Waldo, whom nearly every person in his acquaintance despises. Clovis plans to lure Waldo into a hammock and then throw a lighted fusee into a near-by wasps' nest. Mrs. Thackenbury protests that poor Waldo might be stung to death.

> "Waldo is **one of those people who would be enormously improved by death**," said Clovis; "but if you didn't want to go as far as that, you could have some wet straw ready to hand, and set it alight under the hammock at the same time that the fusee was thrown into the nest. . . ."

One pearl of great price

Source: MATTHEW 13:46
Author: Unknown (traditionally Matthew the Apostle)
First transcribed: c.75-100
Type of work: Gospel

Context: Jesus, having chosen His twelve disciples, teaches them their mission and tells them to expect persecution. When He upbraids the towns of Galilee and He and His disciples pick corn on the Sabbath, the Pharisees become alarmed. Jesus, however, effectively defends His words and actions and continues His ministry around the Sea of Galilee. As the crowds press upon Him, He gets into a boat and preaches from the sea. Speaking in parables to the people, but interpreting them for the disciples, He explains to them their privilege in understanding His teachings. Later, in another parable, He reenforces His message of the Kingdom of Heaven:

> Again, the kingdom of heaven is like unto a merchant man, seeking goodly pearls:

Who, when he had found **one pearl of great price,** went and sold all that he had, and bought it.

One sad, ungathered rose

Source: MY AUNT (Stanza 6)
Author: Oliver Wendell Holmes (1809-1894)
First published: 1831
Type of work: Satiric poem

Context: In this humorous poem, Holmes describes his aunt, a "dear, unmarried, deluded" old lady who still preserves the mannerisms of her lost youth. She still wears a painful girdle, combs her gray hair in a "spring-like way," and refuses to wear glasses. Holmes's aunt became an eternally eligible maiden as a result of her training in the fashionable "finishing school" to which her father sent her, hoping "she should make the finest girl/ Within a hundred miles." Holmes brilliantly satirizes the ridiculously ineffectual training which these "finishing schools" provided. The object was to make a young girl irresistibly attractive and charming. The poor aunt was "braced against a board," "laced up," and "starved down": "Oh, never mortal suffered more/ In penance for her sins." When she returned home, the girl was so ravishing that her father feared the helpless creature would be abducted and attacked by some "rabid youth." But the father need not have worried about his daughter's safety, for the "finishing school" unfortunately produced a rose which was destined to remain unplucked:

Alas! nor chariot, nor barouche,
　Nor bandit cavalcade,
Tore from the trembling father's arms
　His all-accomplished maid.
For her how happy had it been!
　And Heaven had spared to me
To see **one sad, ungathered rose**
　On my ancestral tree.

One swallow does not make a spring

Source: NICOMACHEAN ETHICS (I, vii, 18)
Author: Aristotle (384-322 B.C.)
First transcribed: Fourth century B.C.
Type of work: Philosophical treatise

Context: Aristotle probes into the nature of happiness in the first part of the *Ethics,* following a discussion of the means to the end of good. He

743

states that of two goods always choose the better; of two kinds of lives always choose the richer, the life of contemplation. That first collector of English proverbs, John Heywood, in 1546 reports "One swallow maketh not summer"; whereas North-brooke in 1577 says "One swallowe prouveth not that summer is neare." Cervantes in Spain in 1605 flatly contends "One swallow never makes a summer." Aristotle frames the quotation thus:

> . . . From these premises it follows that the Good of man is the active exercise of his soul's faculties in conformity with excellence or virtue, or if there be several human excellences or virtues, in conformity with the best and most perfect among them. Moreover this activity must occupy a complete lifetime; for **one swallow does not make a spring,** nor does one fine day; and similarly one day or a brief period of happiness does not make a man supremely blessed and happy.

One that loved not wisely, but too well

Source: OTHELLO (Act V, sc. ii, l. 344)
Author: William Shakespeare (1564-1616)
First published: 1622
Type of work: Dramatic tragedy

Context: This famous line is now usually heard as "He (or she) loves not wisely but too well" but means precisely the same as when penned by Shakespeare: to describe a love affair between obviously unsuitable partners. In the play, Othello, a Moorish military commander in the service of Venice, has been victimized by Iago, his ancient (or ensign). The latter hates the Moor because he has made Michael Cassio his lieutenant and not Iago. The ancient determines to destroy both of them. The evil Iago not only convinces Othello that his sweet bride Desdemona is unfaithful with Cassio but that she must die. Othello smothers her in her bed. No sooner does he do so than Iago's entire plot is unraveled, and the Moor realizes that he has been diabolically duped. About to be removed to Venice for trial, he tries to exculpate himself:

OTHELLO
    . . . I pray you in your letters,
When you shall these unlucky deeds relate,
Speak of me, as I am. Nothing extenuate,
Nor set down aught in malice. Then must you speak
Of **one that loved not wisely, but too well;**
Of one not easily jealous, but being wrought,
Perplexed in the extreme; of one whose hand,
Like the base Indian, threw a pearl away,
Richer than all his tribe; . . .

One that loves his fellow men

Source: ABOU BEN ADHEM
Author: Leigh Hunt (1784-1859)
First published: 1844
Type of work: Lyric poem

Context: James Henry Leigh Hunt— journalist, poet, critic, essayist, and friend of Lamb, Moore, and Byron— is remembered as a writer principally for his *Autobiography* (1850) and for two brief lyrics, "Abou Ben Adhem" and "Rondeau" ("Jenny Kissed Me"). "Abou Ben Adhem" is based on a passage in *Bibliothèque Orientale,* by Barthélemy d'Herbelot. In Hunt's poem Abou wakes from a deep and peaceful dream to see an angel in his room writing in a golden book. "What writest thou?" he asks, and the angel answers,

> "The names of those who love the Lord."
> "And is mine one?" said Abou. "Nay, not so,"
> Replied the angel. Abou spoke more low,
> But cheerly still; and said, "I pray thee then
> Write me as **one that loves his fellow-men.**"
> The angel wrote, and vanished. The next night
> It came again with a great wakening light,
> And showed the names whom love of God had blessed,
> And lo! Ben Adhem's name led all the rest.

One touch of nature makes the whole world kin

Source: TROILUS AND CRESSIDA (Act III, sc. iii, l. 175)
Author: William Shakespeare (1564-1616)
First published: 1609
Type of work: Dramatic tragedy

Context: The Trojan War is in its eighth year. Achilles, champion of the Greeks and drunk with his own fame, is insubordinate and unco-operative, and renders the Greek effort ineffective. He remains in his tent, mocking the efforts of his fellow generals. A challenge to individual combat arrives from Hector, the Trojan champion. Although the generals know it is really intended for Achilles, they decide to send dull-witted Ajax to fight Hector, and thus spite Achilles. Stung, Achilles questions wise Ulysses, one of the Greek princes, as to why he is treated thus. Ulysses gives him a little lecture on the flightiness of fame and reputation.

ULYSSES
. . .

> Perseverance, dear my lord,
> Keeps honour bright; to have done, is to hang
> Quite out of fashion, . . .

745

If you give way,
Or hedge aside from the direct forthright,
Like to an entered tide they all rush by,
And leave you hindmost.

. . .

One touch of nature makes the whole world kin,
That all with one consent praise new born gawds,

. . .

The present eye praises the present object.

. . .

Since things in motion sooner catch the eye,
Than what stirs not.

. . .

One woe doth tread upon another's heel

Source: HAMLET (Act IV, sc. vii, l. 164)
Author: William Shakespeare (1564-1616)
First published: 1603
Type of work: Dramatic tragedy

Context: Ophelia is the daughter of Polonius, chief councilor of King Claudius of Denmark. She has some reason to believe Prince Hamlet loves her, but when she allows herself to be a tool of her father and the king, Hamlet turns on her. Shortly, Hamlet accidentally kills her father and is sent to England as a result. Ophelia loses her mind. Laertes, her brother who has been in France, returns home to avenge his father's death and is talking with the king when Queen Gertrude brings them news of Ophelia's death.

GERTRUDE
One woe doth tread upon another's heel,
So fast they follow; your sister's drowned, Laertes.

. . .

There is a willow grows askant the brook,
There on the pendent boughs her coronet weed
Clamb'ring to hang, an envious sliver broke,
When down her weedy trophies and herself
Fell in the weeping brook.

. . .

The idea of this quotation was expressed somewhat differently nearly half a century after Shakespeare when Robert Herrick wrote: "Thus woe succeeds a woe, as wave a wave" in *Sorrows Succeed* (1648). Edward Young, in *Night Thoughts* (1742-1745), returned to Shakespeare's image:

746

Woes cluster; rare are solitary woes;
They love a train, they tread each other's heel.

Only a sweet and virtuous soul, like seasoned timber, never gives

Source: THE TEMPLE ("VIRTUE," Stanza 4)
Author: George Herbert (1593-1633)
First published: 1633
Type of work: Religious poems

Context: The Temple is a collection of lyric poems on religious subjects. Many of the poems are obscure and difficult, but not the present one. It says that when a beautiful day comes into being, so sweet, "so cool, so calm, so bright," its death is inevitable; the dews of evening mourn for it. And the sweetly perfumed rose, with flushed and beautiful face that dazzles the eyes, must also die, as its root is ever in its grave, the earth. The spring of the year is the same as the day and the rose, destined to end; it is "full of sweet days and roses"— Herbert here effects a neat coupling of the first and second stanzas of the poem—but it must die in the heat of summer. The only thing that is not transitory is a sweet and virtuous soul; it is like well-seasoned timber that does not bend under stress. The whole world can be burned into ashes and charcoal, but the virtuous soul lives on. The day, the rose, the spring, the whole world will end, but not the virtuous soul. The first stanza follows:

> Only a sweet and virtuous soul
> Like seasoned timber, never gives;
> But though the whole world turn to coal,
> Then chiefly lives.

The only gift is a portion of thyself

Source: GIFTS
Author: Ralph Waldo Emerson (1803-1882)
First published: 1844
Type of work: Moral essay

Context: Emerson is quite skeptical about the value of giving gifts. Even though "it is always so pleasant to be generous, . . . the impediment lies in the choosing." The best gifts are the services we render out of neces-sity. But all gifts are in a sense inap-propriate: "It is not the office of a man to receive gifts. How dare you give them? We wish to be self-sustained. We do not quite forgive a giver. . . . For, the expectation of

747

gratitude is mean, and is continually punished by the total insensibility of the obliged person." In a true friendship, mere gifts are unimportant, for friends "cannot be bought and sold." The true gift "must be the flowing of the giver unto me, correspondent to my flowing unto him":

> . . . But our tokens of compliment and love are for the most part barbarous. Rings and other jewels are not gifts, but apologies for gifts. **The only gift is a portion of thyself.** Thou must blee for me. Therefore the poet brings his poem; the shepherd, his lamb; the farmer, corn; the miner, a gem; the sailor, coral and shells; the painter, his picture; the girl, a handkerchief of her own sewing. This is right and pleasing, for it restores society in so far to the primary basis, when a man's biography is conveyed in his gift, and every man's wealth is an index of his merit. . . .

Only the monstrous anger of the guns

Source: ANTHEM FOR DOOMED YOUTH (Stanza 1)
Author: Wilfred Owen (1893-1918)
First published: 1920
Type of work: Elegy

Context: The poetry of Wilfred Owen, one of the poets who found his material in the horrors of World War I, was made known to the world through his posthumous volume, *Poems* (1920). In a poem which serves as the preface, he wrote that his book is not about heroes but about war. Above all, he continued, it is concerned with the poetry inherent in the pity of war. "Anthem for Doomed Youth," an elegy, begins with a question, "What passing-bells for these who die as cattle?" The answer is that only the guns and the reality of war itself offer the anthems for the dead. "No mockeries for them," says the poet. All of the ceremonial respects are to be supplied by the glory of their own sacrifice. No candles can be held "to speed them all;" but "in their eyes/ Shall shine the holy glimmers of goodbys." And their flowers shall be "the tenderness of patient minds." The poem begins:

> What passing-bells for these who die as cattle?
> **Only the monstrous anger of the guns.**
> Only the stuttering rifles' rapid rattle
> Can patter out their hasty orisons.

Only they conquer love that run away

Source: CONQUEST BY FLIGHT: SONG (Lines 15-16)
Author: Thomas Carew (1595?-1639)
First published: 1640
Type of work: Lyric poem

Context: Thomas Carew's "Conquest by Flight" contains advice for both ladies and young men. It tells the ladies to fly from smooth lovers' talk and from oaths mixed with tears; the grief of their lovers is infectious, and the very air, filled full of sighs, will blast them. They are to stop their ears when their lovers protest, lest they themselves fall a-weeping when the love affair is over and done with and they bewail their misspent pity. The young men are to flee when the young ladies dart amorous glances at them, as ladies' looks have power to wound. In their lips, their eyes, their smiles, and their kisses love lies—a play on "residing" and "prevaricating." The only course for the young man to pursue is to flee from the fair ones, because only the ones who run away can conquer love. The conclusion of the poem follows:

> . . . And ladies' looks have power to maim;
> Now 'twixt their lips, now in their eyes,
> Wrapped in a smile, a kiss, love lies,
> Then fly betimes, for **only they**
> **Conquer love that run away.**

Open my heart and you will see graved inside of it, "Italy"

Source: DE GUSTIBUS (Lines 43-44)
Author: Robert Browning (1812-1889)
First published: 1855
Type of work: Lyric poem

Context: This vivid, graphic lyric expresses Browning's love for Italy, for its warmth, informality, and spontaneity—qualities which, he implies in this poem, he does not find in England. He includes a reference to a house he loved and gives the flavor of the Mediterranean scene: before the house stretches ". . . the great opaque/ Blue breadth of sea without a break. . . ." "While, in the house, forever crumbles/ Some fragment of the frescoed walls,/ From blisters where a scorpion sprawls." He emphasizes his love for Italy by quoting a saying attributed to Queen Mary I on the loss of the French city of Calais, which had been in English control for more than two centuries.

749

Queen Mary's saying serves for me—
(When fortune's malice
Lost her—Calais)—
Open my heart and you will see
Graved inside of it, "Italy."

The Oracles are dumb

Source: ON THE MORNING OF CHRIST'S NATIVITY: THE HYMN (Stanza 19)
Author: John Milton (1608-1674)
First published: 1645
Type of work: Religious poem

Context: In "On the Morning of Christ's Nativity" John Milton deals with the effects on the world of Christ's birth. One of them was the return of peace, truth, justice, and mercy to the world. Justice was understood as the pious worship of God, and a re-establishment of this justice was the banishment from their shrines of all the evil spirits or devils which had for ages misled humanity, who took them for gods. It is true that the perfect bliss of humankind will not come into being until Christ has died on the cross, but the evil spirits feel His might even on the day of His birth. Throughout the pagan world the shrines of the gods become silent: Apollo can no more prophesy at his celebrated shrine at Delphi; priests and sibyls no longer fall into trances or spells to deceive the people. From Europe, Palestine, and Egypt the dispossessed false gods desert their shrines and go into banishment, so strong is the power emanating from the Babe in Bethlehem. Of the silencing of the gods Milton says:

The Oracles are dumb;
No voice or hideous hum
Runs through the archéd roof in words deceiving.

Other irons in the fire

Source: THE ACHARNIANS
Author: Aristophanes (448-385 B.C.)
First transcribed: Fourth century B.C.
Type of work: Dramatic comedy

Context: The belief that it is wise to have more than one project working at any given time is firmly seated in proverbial lore. It was widely referred to in Elizabethan times—*Westward Hoe,* a comedy by Webster and Dekker (1607, Act I, sc. ii.) says: "There's other irons in the fire"; John Chapman, in *Widow's Tears* (1612), gives a variant: "I have other irons on the anvil." It has been popular down to today. Its opposite, however, as is often true of proverbs, is widespread: that is, counsel against trying to do too many things at one time, in the proverb: "Many irons in the fire, part must cool," which dates back at least to the middle of the sixteenth century. In America, Thomas C. Haliburton said (*The Clockmaker; or The Sayings and Doings of Samuel Slick of Slickville,* 4th ed. London, 1838, p. 309): "There's a plaguy sight of truth in them are old proverbs. They are distilled facts steamed down to an essence. . . . Now when you come to see all about the country you'll find the truth of that are one—'*A man that has too many irons in the fire is plaguy apt to get some on 'em burnt.'* " Aristophanes' counsel is of the desirability of having more than one project going at one time. The following is a fanciful translation (which literally discusses a merchant in Athens who in time of war creates a peace by ingratiating himself to both sides, especially by frying small fishes in skillets over charcoal) and is similar to "many fish to fry."

> He works and blows the coals
> And has plenty of **other irons in the fire . . .**

Our birth is but a sleep and a forgetting

Source: ODE, INTIMATIONS OF IMMORTALITY (Stanza 5)
Author: William Wordsworth (1770-1850)
First published: 1807
Type of work: Ode

Context: This famous ode is based upon the Platonic doctrine (found in the dialogue called the *Meno*) that all knowledge is merely recollection. The doctrine asserts that the soul has lived elsewhere before it assumed human form, and that it brings knowledge, in the form of recollection, from this other life. Thus the child, closer to this former existence, has a clearer memory of it, a memory that fades as he grows older. Hence, Wordsworth is able to call the child "Thou best Philosopher," because he, clearer in vision and closer to his immortal origins, can see that which the adult has lost the power to understand, most particularly the beauty of nature. The fifth stanza of the ode begins:

> **Our birth is but a sleep and a forgetting:**
> The Soul that rises with us, our life's Star,
> > Hath had elsewhere its setting,
> > And cometh from afar.
> > > • • •
> Heaven lies about us in our infancy!
> Shades of the prison-house begin to close
> Upon the growing Boy. . . .

751

Our fathers and ourselves sowed dragon's teeth

Source: LITANY FOR DICTATORSHIPS (Conclusion)
Author: Stephen Vincent Benét (1898-1943)
First published: 1936
Type of work: Lyric poem

Context: This poem is a dedication to all who have suffered at the hands of dictatorial governments, and an acknowledgment of the failure of the modern century to prevent the oppressions of such governments. Most of the poem constitutes a cataloguing of atrocities done in the name of the "Perfect State." The poem begins: "For all those beaten, for broken heads,/ The fatherless, the simple, the oppressed,/ The ghosts in the burning city of our time. . . ." It then proceeds to name the various agonies—public and private, physical and mental—of people under oppression. After these atrocities are named and partially described, the poet makes an indictment against his own society and age for its failure to achieve a lasting and secure peace. "We thought we were done with these things but we were wrong," he says. Alluding to the myth of Cadmus, who sowed dragon teeth, out of which armed men sprung up and killed each other with the exception of five, he vivifies the impending disaster of the world situation during the thirties:

> Now the boar and the asp have power in our time.
> Now the night rolls back on the West and the night is solid.
> **Our fathers and ourselves sowed dragon's teeth.**
> Our children know and suffer the armed men.

Our little systems have their day

Source: IN MEMORIAM (Prologue, stanza 5)
Author: Alfred, Lord Tennyson (1809-1892)
First published: 1850
Type of work: Elegy

Context: The poet, having recovered much of his balance after suffering extreme shock from the death of his friend, Arthur Hallam, looks back upon his protracted grief and sees that it was excessive. He had fallen into the common human error of trusting too much in the things of the earth and neglecting to maintain faith in God. Those who trust only in people and things are left helpless when friends and possessions are taken from them. Men should look not to earth, but to eternity, and must never forget that everything in human life is made by God, and will last only a short time.

752

Our little systems have their day;
They have their day and cease to be;
They are but broken lights of thee,
And thou, O Lord, art more than they.

Our reason is our law

Source: PARADISE LOST (Book IX, 1. 654)
Author: John Milton (1608-1674)
First published: 1667
Type of work: Epic poem

Context: Satan, in the shape of a beautiful serpent, appears to Eve as she is alone in the Garden, to tell her that he has acquired speech and understanding by eating of the fruit of the tree of knowledge. Eve fails to recognize the serpent as Satan and is deceived by his story and flattery. Satan leads her to the tree to invite her to eat of the fruit also. Eve speaks innocently to the serpent, telling him what he, of course, already knows. She tells him that she and Adam have been given only one command which they must obey, that God has commanded them not to eat of the fruit of the tree of knowledge.

> "Serpent, we might have spared our coming hither,
> Fruitless to me, though fruit be here to excess,
> The credit of whose virtue rest with thee,
> Wondrous indeed, if cause of such effects.
> But of this tree we may not taste nor touch;
> God so commanded, and left that command
> Sole daughter of his voice: the rest, we live
> Law to ourselves, **our reason is our law.**"

Our remedies oft in ourselves do lie, which we ascribe to heaven

Source: ALL'S WELL THAT ENDS WELL (Act I, sc. i, ll. 231-232)
Author: William Shakespeare (1564-1616)
First published: 1623
Type of work: Dramatic comedy

Context: Bertram, young Count of Rousillon, departs from his home for service at the Court of France. Behind him remain his mother and her ward, the lovely and accomplished Helena, daughter of a physician. While living in the countess' home, Helena has fallen in love with Bertram but believes their difference in rank makes her love hopeless. Parolles, a servant and follower of Bertram, tells her, before he follows his

753

master, to pray to Heaven and marry a good husband and use him well. But Helena is not planning to follow his advice.

HELENA

Our remedies oft in ourselves do lie,
Which we ascribe to heaven.

. . .

Impossible be strange attempts to those
That weigh their pains in sense, and do suppose
What hath been, cannot be.

. . .

But my intents are fixed, and will not leave me.

Out damned spot, out I say!

Source: MACBETH (Act V, sc. i, l. 38)
Author: William Shakespeare (1564-1616)
First published: 1623
Type of work: Dramatic tragedy

Context: Macbeth, general in King Duncan of Scotland's army, is to be Thane of Cawdor and later king, according to three witches' prophecies. He is made Thane of Cawdor for meritorious military service, and the king, being in the neighborhood of Macbeth's castle, stays overnight. Impatient and ambitious, Macbeth, with his wife's help, murders the king in his sleep. Macbeth escapes blame, and, the king's son having fled, is elected and crowned king. He becomes a bloody tyrant in the land. Lady Macbeth had not shrunk from the murder of Duncan, and, subsequently, in her waking hours, is superbly in command of herself. But while she sleeps, her suppressed emotions and stifled conscience demand expression. She walks in her sleep, crying out in conscience-tortured anguish, reliving the night of the regicide.

LADY MACBETH

Out damned spot, out I say! One—two—why, then 'tis time to do 't. Hell is murky. Fie my lord, fie! A soldier, and afeard? What need we fear who knows it, when none can call our power to account? Yet who would have thought the old man to have had so much blood in him?

Out of sight, out of mind

Source: THE IMITATION OF CHRIST (Book I, chapter 23)
Author: Thomas à Kempis (c.1380-1471)
First transcribed: c.1420
Type of work: Mystical allegory

Context: In this chapter, "Of Meditation of Death," Thomas à Kempis advises the reader to live always as if he would die tomorrow, to do good while he is well, for he may be unable to do good when he is sick. One should think only of one's soul's health. The proverb has been used by Googe in *Eglogs* (1563), by Fulke Greville (*Sonnet* LVI), by Hendyng in *Proverbs, MS* (c.1320), by Lady Ann Bacon in "Letter to Lady Jane Cornwallis" (1613), and by numerous American authors. Thomas à Kempis begins his discussion of the necessity of doing good by saying:

> This day a man is and tomorrow he appeareth not: full soon shall this be fulfilled of thee; look whether thou canst do otherwise.
> And when man is **out of sight** soon he passeth **out of mind**.

Out of the cradle endlessly rocking

Source: LEAVES OF GRASS ("Out of the Cradle Endlessly Rocking")
Author: Walt Whitman (1819-1892)
First published: 1860 under the title of "A Word Out of the Sea"
Type of work: Narrative poem

Context: The poet begins a reminiscence of a childhood experience that changed him into a poet. Wandering from his bed, the child goes to the seashore near his Long Island home. He hears the song of a male mockingbird lamenting the loss of his mate. In an ecstasy the child's soul says "Now in a moment I know what I am for—I awake." He will be a poet, continuing the bird's song of unsatisfied love. The sea "the savage old mother" has all this time suggested in an undertone another theme for his poetry. After whispering all night, she speaks plainly before daybreak "the low and delicious word DEATH."

> **Out of the cradle endlessly rocking,**
> Out of the mocking bird's throat, the musical shuttle,
> . . .
> From the myriad thence arous'd words,
> From the word stronger and more delicious than any,
> . . .
> I, chanter of pains and joys, uniter of here and hereafter,
> Taking all hints to use them—but swiftly leaping beyond them,
> A reminiscence sing.

755

Out of the depths have I cried

Source: PSALMS 130:1
Author: Unknown
First transcribed: c.400-200 B.C.
Type of work: Religious poetry

Context: The psalmist raises his longing cry of supplication to the Lord from the depths of his soul, which is despairing from sin. All men are guilty of unrighteousness, but God is forgiving: hence, men revere Him. The poet awaits reconciliation with his Lord more eagerly than the night sentry awaits the dawn. He urges Israel have faith in God, for He will freely forgive all her sinfulness. The psalmist commences the poem with an earnest plea that God listen to his prayer:

> **Out of the depths have I cried** unto thee, O Lord.
> Lord, hear my voice: let thine ears be attentive to the voice of my supplications.

Out of the frying pan into the fire

Source: THE PROVERBS OF JOHN HEYWOOD (Part II, chapter 5)
Author: John Heywood (1497?-1580?)
First published: 1546
Type of work: Gnomic poetry

Context: The author is telling a story to a young friend to illustrate that only ill results from a marriage between a young man and an old woman. He tells of such a marriage. Soon after the nuptials, the young man begins to lose interest in his wife. She then begins to complain that he is spending her money on drink and lewdness. She confides these suspicions to the author and asks him to determine if these actions are really occurring. The author responds, however, that it is wiser not to confirm such suspicions, for confirmation would not better the situation:

> . . . if ye took him, what could ye gain?
> From suspicion to knowledge of ill, forsooth!
> Could make ye do but as the flounder doeth—
> Leap **out of the frying pan into the fire;**
> And change from ill pain to worse is worth small hire.

Out of thine own mouth will I judge thee

Source: LUKE 19:22
Author: Unknown (traditionally Luke the Apostle)
First transcribed: c.80-100
Type of work: Gospel

Context: The author, perhaps Luke, Paul's physician friend, or possibly an unknown author, relates the life of Christ. As Jesus journeys from Galilee to Jerusalem, He crosses the Jordan River at Jericho. Zaccheus, a rich publican of small stature, climbs a sycamore tree along the way so he can see Jesus. Jesus notices Zaccheus, who repents immediately in the presence of the Master, and says that salvation is come to his house that day. Since the people following Him mis-understand and expect the Kingdom of Heaven to come at once, Jesus tells them a parable to help them understand His kingdom. A nobleman before leaving on a journey, entrusts each of his servants with a certain amount of money, a pound. On returning he finds that one servant has made ten pounds, another five, and another has hidden his money and earned nothing. The nobleman is angry with the servant:

And he saith unto him, **Out of thine own mouth will I judge thee,** thou wicked servant. Thou knewest that I was an austere man, taking up that I laid not down, and reaping that I did not sow:
Wherefore then gavest not thou my money into the bank, that at my coming I might have required mine own with usury?

Out of this nettle, danger, we pluck this flower, safety

Source: HENRY IV, PART I (Act II, sc. iii, l. 10)
Author: William Shakespeare (1564-1616)
First published: 1598
Type of work: Historical drama

Context: Harry Percy, called Hotspur, in company with Mortimer and Glendower, is in rebellion against Henry IV. Just as the plot is hatching, Percy is at his home in Warkworth Castle with his wife Kate. As the scene opens, Percy is reading a letter, in which the writer offers excuses for not joining the power against the King. Hotspur curses the man's cowardice in passages intermixed with sections of the letter, as this excerpt demonstrates:

HOTSPUR
. . . "But for mine own part my lord I could be well contented to be there, in respect of the love I bear your house." He could

757

be contented; why is he not then? In respect of the love he bears our house; He shows in this, he loves his own barn better than he loves our house. Let me see some more. "The purpose you undertake is dangerous"; why that's certain, 'tis dangerous to take a cold, to sleep, to drink, but I tell you, my lord fool, **out of this nettle, danger, we pluck this flower, safety.** . . .

Out upon it! I have loved three whole days together

Source: THE LAST REMAINS ("Out upon it! I have loved," Stanza 1)
Author: Sir John Suckling (1609-1642)
First published: 1659
Type of work: Lyric poem

Context: Suckling's light-hearted and cynical attitude towards love is apparent in this short poem. The poet proclaims that he has been in love with and constant to one woman for three whole days, an astonishing accomplishment. If the weather does not change, he may even remain true to her for three days more. The greatest tribute that he can pay to the lady who is the object of this amazing fidelity is that she is the only woman who could have kept him faithful so long. The poem begins and ends as follows:

> **Out upon it! I have loved**
> **Three whole days together;**
> And am like to love three more,
> If it prove fair weather.
> . . .
> Had it any been but she,
> And that very face,
> There had been at least ere this
> A dozen dozen in her place.

Oxford street, stony-hearted stepmother!

Source: CONFESSIONS OF AN ENGLISH OPIUM-EATER (Part II)
Author: Thomas De Quincey (1785-1859)
First published: 1822
Type of work: Autobiography

Context: As a youngster De Quincey was a brilliant but erratic person. At the age of fifteen he ran away from school, apparently because of restrictions he disliked and dissatisfaction about himself. He traveled to London, where he hid himself from friends and relatives, living a life of appalling want, wandering up and down the thoroughfares, especially

758

Oxford Street, most of the time excruciatingly hungry. Often he found other young people in circumstances of poverty, hunger, and homelessness. One of them was a girl of fifteen who was, apparently, a prostitute of some experience, but also a friend to the homeless boy. Her only name known to De Quincey was Ann. Following his reconciliation with his guardians, De Quincey left London and his sufferings there, though he later wrote of it emotionally,

> So then, **Oxford-street, stony-hearted stepmother!** thou that listenest to the sighs of orphans, and drinkest the tears of children, at length I was dismissed from thee: the time was come at last that I should no more pace in anguish thy never-ending terraces; no more should dream, and wake in captivity to the pangs of hunger. Successors, too many, to myself and Ann, have, doubtless, since trodden in our footsteps,—inheritors of our calamities. . . .

Paid him in his own coin

Source: DON QUIXOTE (Part I, Book III, chapter 4)
Author: Miguel de Cervantes Saavedra (1547-1616)
First published: 1605
Type of work: Satirical novel

Context: Paying "in kind," "tit for tat," are common expressions for the need for making change in the currency in which one is paid. The expression occurs in one of the most earthy of all of Don Quixote's adventures. Two flocks of sheep are transformed by the knight's feverish imagination into the army of the pagan Emperor Alifanfaron of Taprobana (Ceylon), come to claim the daughter of the leader of the other army, Pentapolin of Garamantas (in Africa). When Don Quixote charges one flock, to help the Christian, shepherds of both flocks rain stones upon him. The wounded champion tries to drink his "magic balsam," but a stone breaks the jar in which he is carrying it, and he chokes on the horrible-tasting concoction. He vomits over Sancho, who has come to help him.

> . . . his master's loathsome drench . . . caused such a sudden rumbling in his maw, that, before he could turn his head, he unladed the whole cargo of his stomach full in his master's face, and put him in so delicate a pickle as he was himself. Sancho having thus **paid him in his own coin,** half blinded as he was, ran to his ass. . . .

Pains of love be sweeter far than all other pleasures are

Source: TYRANNICK LOVE (Act IV, sc. i)
Author: John Dryden (1631-1700)
First published: 1670
Type of work: Song

Context: This quotation comes from one of the lyrics that Dryden wrote to be sung as part of the stage performance of his tragedy. In the lyric the poet warns us that love should be snatched in youth while one can find it and enjoy it to the fullest. "Love and time" should be respected and appreciated, for their "golden gifts" become more complicated and more costly as the years pass by. Dryden reminds us that young love may be a tyrant, that it can hurt; but he also maintains that the pleasures of love more than compensate for the sorrows that one may find attendant upon it:

> Ah how sweet it is to love,
> Ah how gay is young desire!
> And what pleasing pains we prove
> When we first approach Loves fire!
> **Pains of Love be sweeter far**
> **Than all other pleasures are.**

Paint the mortal shame of nature with the living hues of art

Source: LOCKSLEY HALL SIXTY YEARS AFTER (Line 139)
Author: Alfred, Lord Tennyson (1809-1892)
First published: 1886
Type of work: Dramatic monologue

Context: An old man talks to his grandson on the grounds of their ancestral estate. The nearby chapel containing the body of the founder of the family inspires him to compare the present age with former times, when men lived within a moral code and served, in thought and action, the order of goodness they saw in the cosmos. But the present times have decayed, he says, and now men are faithless, self-serving, and corrupt. The writers of the time have decayed with their society and now delight in vividly portraying all the varieties of human vice, all the crimes men commit against nature.

> Authors—essayist, atheist, novelist, realist, rhymester, play your
>   part,
> **Paint the mortal shame of nature with the living hues of art.**

> Rip your brothers' vices open, strip your own foul passions bare;
> Down with Reticence, down with Reverence,—forward—naked—
>   let them stare.

A palace and a prison on each hand

Source: CHILDE HAROLD'S PILGRIMAGE (Canto IV, stanza 1)
Author: George Gordon, Lord Byron (1788-1824)
First published: 1818
Type of work: Narrative poem in Spenserian stanzas

Context: In a letter to his publisher, John Murray, Byron wrote, on July 1, 1817: "The Bridge of Sighs (*i.e., Ponte dei Susperi*) is that which divides, or rather joins the palace of the Doge to the prison of the state. It has two passages: the criminal went by the one to judgment, and returned by the other to death, being strangled in a chamber adjoining, where there was a mechanical process for the purpose." Standing on the Bridge of Sighs, Byron reflects upon the "dying Glory" of Venice, thinking back to a time "when many a subject land/ Looked to the wingéd Lion's marble piles. . . ." Thomas Hood (1799-1845) used the Bridge of Sighs as a title for a pathetic poem on suicide (1846). The first two lines of Byron's Canto IV read:

> I stood in Venice, on the Bridge of Sighs;
> **A palace and a prison on each hand.** . . .

Pale Death with foot impartial

Source: ODES (Book I, Ode IV, "Spring's Lesson," l. 13, as translated by C. E. Bennett)
Author: Horace (65-8 B.C.)
First transcribed: 23-13 B.C.
Type of work: Ode

Context: In the first three stanzas of this ode Horace describes, with delightful imagery, the coming of spring. The last two stanzas change the mood of the ode. Horace implies that death, which comes with winter, will also come one day to each of us.

> Now also is it meet in shady groves to bring sacrifice to Faunus, whether he demand a lamb or prefer a kid.
> **Pale Death with foot impartial** knocks at the poor man's cottage and at princes' palaces. Despite thy fortune, Sestius, life's brief span forbids thy entering on far-reaching hopes.

• • •

Pale hands I loved beside the Shalimar

Source: KASHMIRI SONG (Stanza 1)
Author: Laurence Hope (Adela Florence Cory Nicolson, 1865-1904)
First published: 1901
Type of work: Lyric poem

Context: Adela Florence Cory Nicolson lived in India much of her life. The volume of poems in which "Kashmiri Song" appeared bore the title *The Garden of Kama and Other Love Lyrics from India, arranged in verse by Laurence Hope.* Whether the lyrics are drawn from Indian originals is doubtful, but the poems suggest the intense sensuality of love and romance in the Far East. The pleasures of the sense of touch are evoked repeatedly by the author: "pale dispensers of my Joys and Pains," "pale hands, pink tipped"; and finally, "the hot blood rushed wildly through the veins/ Beneath your touch. . . ." The mood of the poem is tempered with the mention of the "Lotus buds that float/ On those cool waters"; then follows the suggestion that strangulation by these same hands would be better than their giving a sign of farewell. The poem opens with the following stanza:

> **Pale hands I loved beside the Shalimar,**
>   Where are you now? Who lies beneath your spell?
>   Whom do you lead on Rapture's roadway, far,
>   Before you agonise them in farewell?

A pale horse

Source: REVELATION 6:8
Author: St. John the Divine
First transcribed: c.90-96
Type of work: Apocalyptic epistle

Context: John, variously identified as John the apostle, a pseudonymous writer, and John the presbyter, addresses to seven churches in Asia a series of God-inspired letters, in which he speaks of the redemptive power of Christ and the rewards for the persecuted faithful. After receiving the messages from the Almighty, he declares that he saw, through the opened door of Heaven, God on his throne, surrounded by four strange beasts and holding in His hand a scroll of doom, closed with seven seals, which could be opened only by Christ, symbolized by a slain lamb. Praising Father and Son, he describes the plagues to be released against the unrighteous with each broken seal. With the breaking of the first four seals come four different horses, each representing a torture for man. The fourth seal broken, there is revealed the dreaded horseman of war and hunger:

And I looked, and behold **a pale horse:** and his name that sat on him was Death, and Hell followed with him. And power was given unto them over the fourth part of the earth, to kill with sword, and with hunger, and with death, and with the beasts of the earth.

Panting Time toiled after him in vain

Source: PROLOGUE SPOKEN BY MR. GARRICK, AT THE OPENING OF THE THEATRE IN DRURY-LANE, 1747
Author: Samuel Johnson (1709-1784)
First published: 1747
Type of work: Prologue to a drama

Context: David Garrick, the famous English actor, began his long career as manager of Drury Lane Theatre with a revival of *The Merchant of Venice* on September 15, 1747, and asked his close friend Samuel Johnson to write the prologue. Johnson uses the occasion to castigate the public for its poor taste, as evidenced by the kinds of plays recently written, and deplores the deterioration of the stage since the days of Shakespeare and Ben Jonson. Playwrights, catering to the taste of the time, have permitted intrigue and obscenity to replace sound plot and true wit in their dramas, and have lost sight of the true function of tragedy—to improve mankind. Johnson hopes, however, that Garrick's production of *The Merchant of Venice* may mark the beginning of a new era in the drama when truth will again, as it did in Shakespeare's day, "diffuse her radiance from the stage." The prologue opens with Johnson's praise of Shakespeare:

> When Learning's Triumph o'er her barb'rous Foes
> First rear'd the Stage, immortal Shakespear rose;
> Each Change of many-colour'd Life he drew,
> Exhausted Worlds, and then imagin'd new:
> Existence saw him spurn her bounded Reign,
> And **panting Time toil'd after him in vain:**
> His pow'rful Strokes presiding Truth impress'd,
> And unresisted Passion storm'd the Breast.

Parting is such sweet sorrow

Source: ROMEO AND JULIET (Act II, sc. ii, l. 195)
Author: William Shakespeare (1564-1616)
First published: 1597
Type of work: Dramatic tragedy

Context: Juliet cannot force herself to break off her interview with Romeo, who is standing in the orchard beneath her balcony, though she fully

763

realizes the wisdom of her nurse in urging her to come away. She is torn between wisdom and love. She exits, leaving Romeo to comment on her beauty and his love, but then she reappears to urge further that Romeo send for her the next day so that they can be married. Finally, it is agreed that Juliet will send a messenger at nine the next morning, and Romeo can then send her his final plans. Juliet would have Romeo go, but would also have him stay:

JULIET

'Tis almost morning: I would have thee gone.
And yet no farther than a wanton's bird,
That lets it hop a little from her hand,
Like a poor prisoner in his twisted gyves,
And with a silken thread plucks it back again,
So loving-jealous of his liberty.
. . .

Good night, good night. **Parting is such sweet sorrow,**
That I shall say good night till it be morrow.

Pass me the can, lad; there's an end of May

Source: LAST POEMS (IX, stanza 1)
Author: A(lfred) E(dward) Housman (1859-1936)
First published: 1922
Type of work: Lyric poem

Context: In his poem that begins "The chestnut casts his flambeaux," A. E. Housman uses May with all its delights at the height of the spring season to represent the pleasure and happiness that man is ever seeking. But happiness is elusive just as is youth. In the poem two young men look out of the tavern window onto the sudden storm that has spoiled their plans. There will be other spring seasons in the future "but then we shall be twenty-four." The two lads see their plight as that of humanity, because others "Have sat in taverns while the tempest hurled/ Their hopeful plans to emptiness . . ." One of the friends has his solution to existence: "Pass me the can, lad . . ." The opening stanza of the poem describes the sudden wresting away of the delights of spring:

The chestnut casts his flambeaux, and the flowers
Stream from the hawthorn on the wind away,
The doors clap to, the pane is blind with showers.
Pass me the can, lad; there's an end of May.

Passing rich with forty pounds a year

Source: THE DESERTED VILLAGE (Line 142)
Author: Oliver Goldsmith (1728-1774)
First published: 1770
Type of work: Didactic and descriptive poem

Context: The first effects of the Enclosure Act and of the early stages of the Industrial Revolution had been to drive the population of rural England in large numbers into the cities or to America. Goldsmith, who believed that the well-being of the country depended upon a "bold peasantry" permanently settled on the land, gave an idealized picture of rural life in his village of Auburn in earlier days. Among the villagers whom he describes is the clergyman, usually considered to be a portrait of his own father. He is a man quite content to do his duty in his humble surroundings, nor has he any desire for a position with more wealth and power:

> A man he was to all the country dear,
> And **passing rich with forty pounds a year;**
> Remote from towns he ran his godly race,
> Nor e'er had changed, nor wish'd to change his place;
> Unpractic'd he to fawn, or seek for power,
> By doctrines fashioned to the varying hour;
> Far other aims his heart had learned to prize;
> More skill'd to raise the wretched than to rise.

The passive Master lent his hand

Source: THE PROBLEM (Line 47)
Author: Ralph Waldo Emerson (1803-1882)
First published: 1840
Type of work: Philosophical poem

Context: In the second half of "The Problem," Emerson elaborates on his theory of universal inspiration by the Oversoul. The Deity teaches the bird to build its nest, the fish to "outbuild her shell," the pine tree to grow new leaves. The Parthenon, the Pyramids, and "England's abbeys" are all kin: "For out of Thought's interior sphere / These wonders rose to upper air;/ And Nature gladly gave them place,/ Adopted them into her race,/ And granted them an equal date/ With Andes and with Ararat." "The word by seers or sibyls told" exists alongside (and has equal authority with) the "accent of the Holy Ghost." Emerson is uplifted by the works of such great Christian writers as Augustine and Taylor, "And yet, for all his faith could see,/ I would not the good bishop be." Emerson shows that the artist and the architect are only tools in the hands of the Deity:

These temples grew as grows the grass;
Art might obey, but not surpass.
The passive Master lent his hand
To the vast soul that o'er him planned;
And the same power that reared the shrine
Bestrode the tribes that knelt within.
Ever the fiery Pentecost
Girds with one flame the countless host,
Trances the heart through chanting choirs,
And through the priest the mind inspires.

The paths of glory lead but to the grave

Source: ELEGY WRITTEN IN A COUNTRY CHURCHYARD (Line 36)
Author: Thomas Gray (1716-1771)
First published: 1751
Type of work: Didactic elegy

Context: Following the evocation of the twilight atmosphere at the beginning of the "Elegy," Gray imagines that beneath the green grass of the churchyard sleep "The rude forefathers of the hamlet." The everyday sounds of morning "No more shall rouse them from their lowly bed." No more shall they go about their homely tasks of plowing their land or maintaining their homes. Their lives and their work may have been simple and commonplace, but they were nonetheless worth while. The poet cautions against deprecating what these simple people did and reminds us that death comes to all men:

Let not Ambition mock their useful toil,
 Their homely joys, and destiny obscure;
Nor Grandeur hear, with a disdainful smile,
 The short and simple annals of the poor.

The boast of heraldry, the pomp of pow'r,
 And all that beauty, all that wealth, e'er gave
Awaits alike th' inevitable hour.
 The paths of glory lead but to the grave.

A patriot is a fool in every age

Source: SATIRE ("Epilogue," Dialogue I, l. 41)
Author: Alexander Pope (1688-1744)
First published: 1738
Type of work: Satirical poem

Context: The name of patriot in Pope's time was generally given to those persons in opposition to the court, according to the poet's own notes. Some of them, he adds in the note, and implies in the text of the poem, had "views too mean and interested to deserve that name." The "Jekyl" of the context is Sir Joseph Jekyl, Master of the Rolls, who was solid in his political persuasion as a Whig. In a note to the poem, Pope said of him, "He sometimes voted against the Court, which drew upon him the laugh here described of ONE who bestowed it equally upon Religion and Honesty." Pope wrote:

> . . . with Scripture still you may be free;
> A horse-laugh, if you please, at Honesty;
> A joke on Jekyl, or some odd Old Whig,
> Who never changed his principle or wig.
> **A patriot is a fool in ev'ry age,**
> Whom all Lord Chamberlains allow the stage:
> These nothing hurts; they keep their fashion still,
> And wear their strange old virtue as they will.

Patriotism is the last refuge of a scoundrel

Source: THE LIFE OF SAMUEL JOHNSON, LL.D. (For 1775)
Author: James Boswell (1740-1795)
First published: 1791
Type of work: Biography

Context: On April 7, 1775, Boswell and Johnson dined at a tavern in London with a group of friends. During the evening a wide variety of topics was discussed, ranging from classical literature to wolves to politics to the theater. Of the observations about politics, Boswell writes:

> Patriotism having become one of our topicks, Johnson suddenly uttered, in a strong determined tone, an apophthegm, at which many will start: **"Patriotism is the last refuge of a scoundrel."** But let it be considered, that he did not mean a real and generous love of our country, but that pretended patriotism which so many, in all ages and countries, have made a cloak for self interest. I maintained, that certainly all patriots were not scoundrels. Being urged, (not by Johnson) to name one exception, I mentioned an eminent person, whom we all greatly admired.
> JOHNSON. "Sir, I do not say that he is *not* honest; but we have no reason to conclude from his political conduct that he *is* honest. . . ."

767

Pay the piper

Source: LOVE FOR LOVE (Act II, sc. i)
Author: William Congreve (1670-1729)
First published: 1695
Type of work: Dramatic comedy

Context: Sir Sampson Legend has two sons, Valentine and Ben. Valentine, the older, has displeased his father by his expensive living, putting himself in debt. The younger son, Ben, is a sailor; he is expected home at any moment. Sir Sampson wishes to leave his fortune to the younger son and has come to show the necessary document, signed by Valentine, to Foresight. Foresight's interest in the matter stems from the fact that he and Sir Sampson are arranging a marriage between Ben and Miss Prue, Foresight's daughter by an earlier marriage. Sir Sampson enters to interrupt Foresight's worrying about whether his second, and younger, wife may be about to make him a cuckold. As he enters, Sir Sampson flourishes the document which will enable Ben to be his heir:

> SIR SAMPSON LEGEND
> . . . here 'tis, I have it in my Hand, Old Ptolomee; I'll make the ungracious Prodigal know who begat him; I will, Old Nostrodamus. Why, I warrant my Son thought nothing belong'd to a Father, but Forgiveness and Affection; no Authority, no Correction, no Arbitrary Power; nothing to be done, but for him to offend, and me to pardon. I warrant you, if he danc'd till Doomsday, he thought I was to **pay the Piper**. Well, but here it is under Black and White . . . ; that as soon as my Son Benjamin is arriv'd, he is to make over to him his Right of Inheritance.

Pay too much for your whistle

Source: THE WHISTLE
Author: Benjamin Franklin (1706-1790)
First published: 1818
Type of work: Essay

Context: The familiar essay in which this quotation occurs was at one time very popular in the United States, as were so many of Franklin's writings, for its simple, common-sense moral. Franklin tells of an episode that took place when he was seven years old: on a holiday he was given some copper coins which he immediately spent in the purchase of a whistle. When his incessant whistling annoyed his family, he was told that he had paid for his toy four times what it was worth. This lesson remained with him all of his life, and was called to mind whenever he was tempted to sacrifice a greater happiness for a lesser, or saw anyone else doing so. Two character-istic paragraphs from the essay illustrate his point.

> This however was afterwards of use to me, the impression continuing in my mind; so that often, when I was tempted to buy some unnecessary thing, I said to myself, *Don't give too much for the whistle;* and I saved my money.

> . . .

> If I knew a miser, who gave up every kind of comfortable living, all the pleasure of doing good to others, all the esteem of his fellow-citizens, and the joys of benevolent friendship for the sake of accumulating wealth, *Poor man,* said I, *you* **pay too much for your whistle.**

Peace hath her victories

Source: SONNET XVI ("To the Lord General Cromwell, May, 1652," Line 10)
Author: John Milton (1608-1674)
First published: 1694
Type of work: Sonnet

Context: At the time Milton wrote this poem, Oliver Cromwell, the hero of the British Civil War of the 1640's, was not yet Lord Protector of the Commonwealth, although it looked as though he would become the chief executive of the nation. At the time proposals were presented to Parliament to establish an official Church in England, supported by taxes and regulated by the government. Milton's poem asks Cromwell, who had helped rid England of Charles I and estab-lished Anglicanism, to use his power and influence to prevent another official Church from being fastened upon the English. Although the proposals were for a broad Protestant basis and would have admitted clergy from all orthodox Protestant denominations, Milton, like most Englishmen, wanted no established religion, with clergy hired and regulated by the government. After citing Cromwell's victories of the past, Milton writes:

> . . . yet much remains
> To conquer still; **peace hath her victories**
> No less renowned than war, new foes arise
> Threatening to bind our souls with secular chains:
> Help us to save free conscience from the paw
> Of hireling wolves whose gospel is their maw.

769

Pearls before swine

Source: MATTHEW 7:6
Author: Unknown (traditionally Matthew the Apostle)
First transcribed: c.75-100
Type of work: Gospel

Context: Jesus, in the Sermon on the Mount, declares the rewards in Heaven for those faithful to God. Explaining that He has come to fulfill the old law rather than to destroy it, He teaches the virtuous life through the new law, which He compares with the old. He admonishes the people to give alms privately, to pray privately, and to dismiss the material things of the world as unimportant. He also warns them of the danger of judging their fellow men and exhorts them to examine themselves before being critical. Citing two animals considered vile to the Jews, he possibly cautions the people against spreading the word of the Kingdom of God indiscriminately:

Give not that which is holy unto the dogs, neither cast ye your **pearls before swine,** lest they trample them under their feet, and turn again and rend you.

A peck of trouble

Source: DON QUIXOTE (Part I, Book III, chapter 4)
Author: Miguel de Cervantes Saavedra (1547-1616)
First published: 1605
Type of work: Satirical novel

Context: Apologizing for not coming to the help of his squire while Sancho was being tossed in a blanket, Don Quixote explains that he was enchanted and could not get over the wall, and that the inhabitants of the castle were spirits of the other world. Sancho replies that they were as much flesh and blood as he is and that the wise thing would be to "jog home and look after our harvest." He adds:

. . . 'tis as plain as the nose in a man's face, that these same adventures which we hunt for up and down, are like to bring us at last into **a peck of troubles,** and such a plaguy deal of mischief, that we shan't be able to set one foot afore t'other.

The pen is mightier than the sword

Source: RICHELIEU (Act II, sc. ii)
Author: Edward Bulwer-Lytton (1803-1873)
First published: 1839
Type of work: Historical drama

Context: In Act II, Cardinal Richelieu, in his palace, is getting a report about plots against him from the Capuchin monk Joseph, his confidant. In his anger, the Cardinal seizes a long two-handed sword that he had once used against the English, but which is now too heavy for him to swing. His page boy François, reminds him that he now has at his command other weapons. Going to his writing desk, the Cardinal makes the statement that has served as topic for so many school debates:

> RICHELIEU
> Beneath the rule of men entirely great
> **The pen is mightier than the sword.** Behold
> The arch-enchanter's wand!—itself a nothing!
> By taking sorcery from the master hand
> To paralyze the Caesars—and to strike
> The loud earth breathless! Take away the sword;
> States can be saved without it!

A penny for your thoughts

Source: THE PROVERBS OF JOHN HEYWOOD (Part II, chapter 4)
Author: John Heywood (1497?-1580?)
First published: 1546
Type of work: Gnomic poetry

Context: The author is informing a young friend about the dangers of marrying for love or for money, and of marrying young. Having given him the story of a couple who married for love, he has now turned to a tale of a young man who married for wealth. After a short time of marriage, the young man and his old wife began to disagree on nearly everything, and their disagreements seem irreconcilable. To further confound the moral, the author tells about how the attractions of young wife versus worldly goods might be misinterpreted:

> This passed, and he cheered us all, but most cheer
> On his part, to this fair young wife did appear.
> And as he to her cast oft a loving eye,
> So cast her husband like eye to his plate by;
> Wherewith in a great musing he was brought.
> Friend! (quoth the good man), **a penny for your thought.**

For my thought, (quoth he); that is a goodly dish.
But of truth I thought: better to have than wish.
What! a goodly young wife, as you have (quoth he)?
Nay, (quoth he), goodly gilt goblets, as here be.

A penny plain and twopence colored

Source: A PENNY PLAIN AND TWOPENCE COLOURED (Chapter 13)
Author: Robert Louis Stevenson (1850-1894)
First published: 1887 in *Memories and Portraits*
Type of work: Essay

Context: Reminiscing on his youth, Stevenson says that much of the glamour of life as he experiences it as a man is due to his having been exposed to Skelt's juvenile drama in his childhood. As a boy he had often spent hours in his favorite bookshop trying to decide which of the fascinating titles to select, usually to the exasperation of the clerk in the shop. Much of the pleasure of possessing one of the plays was in coloring the illustrations with water colors. Stevenson always bought the plain edition for a penny in order to have that additional pleasure. He adds, ". . . nor can I quite forgive that child who, wilfully foregoing pleasure, stoops to 'twopence coloured.' " The final joy was in cutting out the illustrations and setting them up as scenery of the play. Paying homage to Skelt, Stevenson says: "The world was plain before I knew him, a poor penny world; but soon it was all coloured with romance." The two editions of the plays available to him as a boy, with the price of each, gives Stevenson the title of his essay:

"A Penny Plain and Twopence Coloured."

A penny saved is a penny got

Source: THE CASTLE OF INDOLENCE (Canto I, stanza 50)
Author: James Thomson (1700-1748)
First published: 1748
Type of work: Descriptive poem

Context: Imitating the manner of Edmund Spenser in diction, treatment of subject matter, and stanza pattern, the poet describes a romantic castle in a "pleasing land of drowsyhed." The castle is a retreat for a wizard named Indolence. One of the amuse- ments of the inhabitants of the castle and their visitors is to gaze into a "huge crystal magic globe," named Vanity's Mirror. The crystal ball showed "as you turned, all things that do pass/ Upon this ant-hill earth; where constantly/ Of idly-busy men the restless fry/ Run bustling to and fro with foolish haste/ In search of pleasures vain. . . ." Looking into the magic ball one can see spendthrift, foppish heirs, studious scholars, literary men, politicians, soldiers, and all other kinds of humans. Among them is that race of town-dwellers that follows narrow commercial interests, seeking to lay up wealth, in Thomson's view a labor of vanity:

> "Of Vanity the Mirror" this was called.
> Here you a muckworm of the town might see
> At his dull desk, amid his ledgers stalled,
> Eat up with carking care and penurie,
> Most like to carcase parched on gallow-tree.
> **"A penny savèd is a penny got"—**
> Firm to this scoundrel maxim keepeth he,
> Ne of its rigour will he bate a jot,
> Till it has quenched his fire, and banishèd his pot.

Penny wise, pound foolish

Source: ANATOMY OF MELANCHOLY (Democritus Junior to the Reader)
Author: Robert Burton (1577-1640)
First published: 1621-1651
Type of work: Essays

Context: The *Anatomy of Melancholy* is an analysis of the causes, species, symptoms, and cure of melancholy. First published in 1621, it incorporated new material in subsequent editions up to the posthumous version of 1651. It is a treasure house of quotations from Latin, Greek, French, and Spanish authors, combining irony and noble ideals, wit and learning. In his preliminary "Democritus Junior to the Reader," the author announces that he will tell the "Gentle Reader" about the original Democritus, a fifth century B.C. contemporary of Socrates. Democritus laughed at the follies of his time that he saw about him. How amused he would be today to see current stupidities! The "wittol" of whom the author speaks is a fool or yokel, the name originating from the woodpecker that hatches cuckoo eggs laid in its nest, thus becoming cuckold. The quoted phrase means to save pennies and waste dollars. Democritus Junior mentions the Greek's probable amusement at seeing:

> . . . a wittol wink at his wife's honesty, and too perspicuous in all other affairs; one stumble at a straw, and leap over a block; rob Peter, and pay Paul; scrape unjust sums with one hand, purchase great manors by corruption, fraud, and cozenage, and liberally to distribute to the poor with the other, give a remnant to pious uses, etc.; **penny wise, pound foolish;** blind men judge of colours. . . .

773

Performed to a T

Source: GARGANTUA AND PANTAGRUEL (Book IV, chapter 51, "Table-Talk in Praise of Decretals")
Author: François Rabelais (1495-1553)
First published: 1532-1564
Type of work: Mock Heroic chronicle

Context: The episode on the Island of the Papimaniacs is one of the most satiric in all literature, doubly so coming from a man of the Church. In this diatribe, the decretals and the "extravagants," the extraordinary decrees, are held up to ridicule. Homenas, the bishop who had seen the pope, is the host of Pantegruel and Panurge, who enjoins them to "visit church first, and taverns after."

> Now topers, pray observe that while Homenas was saying his dry mass, three collectors, or licensed beggars of the church, each of them with a large basin, went round among the people, saying, with a loud voice, "Pray remember the blessed men who have seen his face." As we came out of the temple, they brought their basins brim full of papimany chink to Homenas, who told us that it was plentifully to feast with; and that, of this contribution and voluntary tax, one part should be laid out in good drinking, another in good eating, and the remainder in both: according to an admirable exposition hidden in a corner of their holy decretals: which was **performed to a T,** and that at a noted tavern not much unlike that of Will's of Amiens. Believe me, we tickled it off there with copious cramming, and numerous swilling.

Perish the thought!

Source: THE TRAGICAL HISTORY OF KING RICHARD III, ALTER'D FROM SHAKE-SPEARE (Act V)
Author: Colley Cibber (1671-1757)
First published: 1699
Type of work: Historical tragedy

Context: Lovers of Shakespearean plays have almost to a man detested the liberties which Restoration and eighteenth century writers took with the plays of the master dramatist. Colley Cibber's rewritten, or as he called it, "alter'd" version of *Richard III* is often regarded as one of the worst examples of what has been done to a Shakespearean play. As in the original, Cibber has Richard fall asleep the night before the Battle of Bosworth Field, only to have his fitful rest troubled by the appearance of some of his victims: Henry VI; Lady Anne, Richard's wife; and the little princes, his newphews, whom Richard had murdered in the Tower of London. Catesby, Richard's servant, comes to waken his master shortly after one o'clock, so that he will have ample time to don his armor for the next day's battle. Richard tells Catesby of his horrid dream, saying it causes as much terror as an opposing army of ten thousand men. Catesby tries to reassure his master and hearten him:

CATESBY
Be more yourself, my Lord: consider, Sir,
Were it but known a dream had frighted you,
How wou'd your animated foes presume on't?

RICHARD
Perish that thought!—No, never be it said
That Fate itself could awe the soul of *Richard.*

Persuade them to go out of the rain

Source: UTOPIA (Book I, as translated by Ralph Robinson)
Author: Sir Thomas More (1478-1535)
First published: 1516
Type of work: Political essay

Context: Thomas More meets Raphael Hythloday in Antwerp and is told of the marvelous island of Utopia which he has discovered. The people on the island live in true communal friendship under the beneficent rule of King Utopus. More points out that such a system would not be accepted with pleasure by most of the rest of the world. Raphael agrees but also feels that it is useless to attempt to change wrong opinions. The modern phrase for this quotation, used by Raphael, is "not sense enough to come in out of the rain." Raphael tells More:

. . . Wherefore Plato by a goodly similitude declareth, why wise men refrain to meddle in the commonwealth. For when they see the people swarm into the streets, and daily wet to the skin with rain, and yet cannot **persuade them to go out of the rain** and to take their houses, knowing well, that if they should go out to them, they should nothing prevail, nor win ought by it, but be wet also in the rain, they do keep themselves within their houses, being content that they be safe themselves, seeing they cannot remedy the folly of the people. . . .

Petticoat government

Source: KNICKERBOCKER'S HISTORY OF NEW YORK (Book IV, chapter 4)
Author: Washington Irving (1783-1859)
First published: 1809
Type of work: Satire

Context: Washington Irving's humorous and satirical "history" of New York "from the Beginning of the World to the End of the Dutch Dynasty" was first published as written by the fictional Diedrich Knickerbocker. As Irving himself said of this work, it began as a parody of certain kinds of writing and ended by being a comic history. The quotation in question comes from the section of the history dealing with the governorship of New Amsterdam under William Kieft, called William the Testy because of his ill-humor. On an occasion the Dutch lost Fort Goed Hoop to Yankees, who stole upon the little garrison while the latter took their afternoon nap. After storming for several hours, William the Testy prepared New Amsterdam for war by erecting a new flagpole and perching a windmill on each bastion. Though such preparations might seem inadequate, the people were satisfied.

These warlike preparations in some measure allayed the public alarm, especially after additional means of securing the safety of the city had been suggested by the governor's lady. It has already been hinted in this most authentic history, that in the domestic establishment of William the Testy "the gray mare was the better horse"; in other words, that his wife "ruled the roast," and in governing the governor, governed the prinvince, which might be said to be under **petticoat government.**

Philistine

Source: ESSAYS IN CRITICISM, FIRST SERIES ("Heinrich Heine")
Author: Matthew Arnold (1822-1888)
First published: 1863
Type of work: Social, moral, and literary essay

Context: In his essay on Heinrich Heine, poet, critic, and essayist, "the most important German successor and continuator of Goethe," and a Jew whose sympathies lay with France, whose Revolution had given his race its freedom, Arnold first uses his famous description of the middle·· class, "the Philistines." He says that Heine's chief battle was against "Philistinism," an expression which the Germans use, but which neither the French nor the English have. He explains the term:

776

Philistine must have originally meant, in the mind of those who invented the nickname, a strong, dogged, unenlightened opponent of the chosen people, of the children of the light. The party of change, the would-be remodellers of the old traditional European order, the invokers of reason against custom, the representatives of the modern spirit in every sphere where it is applicable, regarded themselves, with the robust self-confidence natural to reformers as a chosen people, as children of light.

Physician, heal thyself

Source: LUKE 4:23
Author: Unknown (traditionally Luke the Apostle)
First transcribed: c.80-100
Type of work: Gospel

Context: Scholarly opinion is divided about the authorship of Luke: some scholars contend that Luke, the physician friend of Paul, wrote the gospel of Luke and part of *Acts;* others believe that one writer, not Luke, wrote all of *Luke* and *Acts.* However, the value of these books is unquestioned. After receiving baptism from John and being tempted in the wilderness, Jesus begins His public ministry in the province of Galilee and then in the town of Nazareth, His boyhood home. It is customary on the Sabbath for a layman to stand in the synagogue and read a passage of his own selection from the prophets. Jesus chooses Isaiah 58:6, stating that now He has come to fulfill this prophecy of preaching with the Spirit to the poor, imprisoned, and handicapped. Sensing that His listeners are scoffing, Jesus adds:

> . . . Ye will surely say unto me this proverb, **Physician, heal thyself:** whatsoever we have heard done in Capernaum, do also here in thy country.
> And he said, Verily I say unto you, No prophet is accepted in his own country.

Pickwickian sense

Source: THE PICKWICK PAPERS (Chapter I)
Author: Charles Dickens (1812-1870)
First published: 1836-1837
Type of work: Novel

Context: Samuel Pickwick, Dickens' most lovable creation, is President of the club that bears his name. At a meeting of the club he has just delivered a learned paper entitled "Speculations on the Source of the Hampstead Ponds with Some Observations on the Theory of Tittle-bats." In his speech, Mr. Pickwick alludes to the dangerous conditions in the contemporary world: stage coaches upsetting, horses bolting, boilers bursting. In the midst of the cheers greeting these remarks, the voice of Mr. Blotton is heard crying "No!" Mr. Pickwick accuses Mr. Blotton of jealousy, to which allegation Mr. Blotton replies by calling Mr. Pickwick a humbug. In the ensuing wrangle, the chairman asks Mr. Blotton if he had used the word "humbug" in a common sense. Mr. Blotton answers that he had used the word in its "Pickwickian sense." The term has come to mean the use of a word in a sense contrary to its real meaning, or with no meaning at all. The exchange follows:

> "The Chairman was quite sure the hon. Pickwickian would withdraw the expression he had just made use of.
> "Mr. Blotton, with all possible respect for the chair, was quite sure he would not.
> "The Chairman felt it his imperative duty to demand of the honourable gentleman, whether he had used the expression which had just escaped him, in a common sense.
> "Mr. Blotton had no hesitation in saying, that he had not—he had used the word in its **Pickwickian sense.** (Hear, hear.) He was bound to acknowledge, that, personally, he entertained the highest regard and esteem for the honourable gentleman; he had merely considered him a humbug in a Pickwickian point of view. (Hear, hear.)"

A pillar of fire

Source: EXODUS 13:21
Author: Unknown
First transcribed: 1000-300 B.C.
Type of work: Religious history and law

Context: The Israelites having been enslaved and persecuted for centuries in Egypt, God tells Moses to lead them to a "promised land," Canaan. Pharaoh refuses to let them leave until God sends plagues and pestilences to afflict the Egyptians. Only after the oldest son in every Egyptian family dies does Pharaoh allow Moses to take the Israelites out of Egypt. God instructs Moses to go through the wilderness of Shur, rather than through the land of the Philistines, a more direct route along the Mediterranean Sea. God's guidance is portrayed in two familiar symbols: the pillar of column of a cloud by day (a long, slender, vertical cloud structure which connects Heaven and Earth) and a pillar or column of fire by night (fire has been associated with divinity from earliest times):

778

And the Lord went before them by day in a pillar of a cloud, to lead them the way; and by night in **a pillar of fire,** to give them light; to go by day and night.

Pitched betwixt Heaven and Charing Cross

Source: THE KINGDOM OF GOD ("In No Strange Land," Stanza 5)
Author: Francis Thompson (1859-1907)
First published: 1913
Type of work: Religious poem

Context: The Catholic poet Francis Thompson, son of a Lancashire doctor, studied medicine for a while at Owens College, Manchester, but abandoned his studies and, destitute, went to London to live. Allusions to London appear as an integral part of the theme of the poem "The Kingdom of God" ("In No Strange Land"). The poet's theme is that the Kingdom of God is not out "where the wheeling systems darken,/ And our benumbed conceiving soars!," but "at our own clay-shuttered doors." Bringing the theme even closer to his British reader, Thompson introduces Charing Cross, a section of London near Trafalgar Square, and the Thames river, which flows through London. His vision shows him "Christ walking on the water/ Not of Gennesareth, but Thames!" Continuing his allusions, the poet depicts the angels that in Jacob's dream were going up and down the ladder between heaven and earth, as descending on Charing Cross:

> But (when so sad thou canst not sadder)
> Cry;—and upon thy so sore loss
> Shall shine the traffic of Jacob's ladder
> **Pitched betwixt Heaven and Charing Cross.**

The place whereon thou standest is holy ground

Source: EXODUS 3:5
Author: Unknown
First transcribed: c.1000-300 B.C.
Type of work: Religious history and law

Context: Because of a famine in their own land, the Hebrews, under the leadership of the patriarch Jacob, settled on the eastern border of Egypt. Kings rose up who did not respect the initial kindness shown to the Hebrews and reduced them to a state of servitude. They set taskmasters over them, "made their lives bitter with hard bondage," and tried to check the spirit and growth of the people. At last to a Hebrew woman of the tribe

779

of Levi was born a son destined to free his people. Because of a decree that all Hebrew male babies be killed, the wise mother hid the infant near the place where Pharaoh's daughter bathed. Pharaoh's daughter found the child, named him Moses, and reared him as her own, securing the child's own mother, unknowingly, as a nurse. Moses grew up as an Egyptian, but his heart was with his own people. Soon his compassion expressed itself in his slaying a cruel Egyptian taskmaster. Forced into self-exile because of this act, he went into the land of Midian, married a Midianite, and settled with his father-in-law, Jethro. When the burden of the Hebrews still in Egypt became unbearable, their cry unto God was heard. Now being the time for the destiny of Moses to be fulfilled, "the angel of the Lord appeared unto him" in a visible manifestation. The place of the appearance was sanctified by the divine presence:

> And he (God) said, Draw not nigh hither: put off thy shoes from off thy feet, for **the place whereon thou standest is holy ground.**

A plague on both your houses

Source: ROMEO AND JULIET (Act III, sc. i, l. 102)
Author: William Shakespeare (1564-1616)
First published: 1597
Type of work: Dramatic tragedy

Context: The time is the day after the masked ball at which Romeo met and fell in love with Juliet. Mercutio and Benvolio, friends of Romeo, have this morning found Romeo, and have teased him about his whereabouts on the night before. Further, Romeo has been sought out by Juliet's nurse and has appointed his meeting place with her. Benvolio is a quiet-tempered and benevolent man. Mercutio is quick tempered and changeable—mercurial. Now they are walking on the street. Benvolio says that the day is hot and they should retire because if they meet the Capulets they "shall not 'scape a brawl." Mercutio, however, will not go away. The Capulets approach. A fight is being provoked. Romeo enters and tries to stop it. But Tybalt, the Capulet who is determined to fight, and Mercutio draw. They fight, and Mercutio is struck down. Three times he curses the houses of Montague and Capulet, in one of Shakespeare's fine condemnations of this feuding. To Romeo's comment that the wound "cannot be much," Mercutio replies:

MERCUTIO
No 'tis not so deep as a well, nor so wide as a church door, but 'tis enough, 'twill serve. Ask for me to-morrow, and you shall find me a grave man. I am peppered, I warrant, for this world. **A plague a both your houses!** . . .

Plain as a nose on a man's face

Source: GARGANTUA AND PANTAGRUEL (Prologue to Book V)
Author: François Rabelais (1495-1553)
First published: 1532-1564
Type of work: Mock heroic chronicle

Context: Rabelais, the author, addresses the "indefatigable topers, and you thrice-precious martyrs of the smock" on the question whether "men are not such sots nowadays as they were in the days of yore," in other words, "that formerly men were fools, and in this generation are grown wise." Shakespeare uses the expression in *The Two Gentlemen of Verona,* as does Robert Burton in *The Anatomy of Melancholy* (1621-1651). Rabelais says that fools "shall go to pot" and "all manner of folly shall have an end." He adds:

Folly having been driven back and hidden towards the centre during the rigour of the winter, 'tis now to be seen on the surface, and buds out like the trees. This is as **plain as a nose in a man's face. . . .**

Plain living and high thinking are no more

Source: WRITTEN IN LONDON, SEPTEMBER, 1802
Author: William Wordsworth (1770-1850)
First published: 1807
Type of work: Sonnet

Context: The early years of the nineteenth century were trying ones for Englishmen. The French Revolution in 1789 set off a wave of reactionary fear in England, and the two nations were at war by 1793. This sonnet is addressed to a nation threatened by the temptations of prosperity. As the poet writes: "This was written immediately after my return from France to London, when I could not but be struck, as here described, with the vanity and parade of our own country, especially in great towns and cities, as contrasted with the quiet, and I may say the desolation, that the revolution had produced in France. This must be borne in mind, or else the reader may think I have exaggerated the mischief engendered and fostered among us by undisturbed wealth." Complaining that neither nature nor book any longer delights us, he declares:

Rapine, avarice, expense,
This is idolatry; and these we adore:
Plain living and high thinking are no more:

The homely beauty of the good old cause
Is gone; our peace, our fearful innocence,
And pure religion breathing household laws.

Play up! play up! and play the game!

Source: VITAÏ LAMPADA (Stanza 1)
Author: Sir Henry Newbolt (1862-1938)
First published: 1892
Type of work: Patriotic poem

Context: The title of Sir Henry Newbolt's poem "Vitaï Lampada" means "the lamp of life." The poem is also called "Play the Game." The repeated refrain "Play up! play up! and play the game!" is at first the cheer at a school cricket match when the team, though trailing, is still determined to win. The important point, the poet says, is the spirit of the game, as "it's not for the sake of a ribboned coat,/ Or the selfish hope of a season's fame." The refrain is repeated next as the rallying cry after the "sand of the desert is sodden red," and the gun is jammed, and the colonel dead. The future looks bleak: "The river of death has brimmed its bank. . . ." But the voice of a schoolboy with his cherished heritage says, "Play up! . . ." The poem opens with the following stanza:

There's a breathless hush in the close to-night—
Ten to make and the match to win—
A bumping pitch and a blinding light,
An hour to play and the last man in.
And it's not for the sake of a ribboned coat,
Or the selfish hope of a season's fame,
But his Captain's hand on his shoulder smote
"Play up! play up! and play the game!"

Played the sedulous ape

Source: A COLLEGE MAGAZINE (Part I)
Author: Robert Louis Stevenson (1850-1894)
First published: 1887 as Chapter IV of *Memories and Portraits*
Type of work: Reminiscent essay

Context: Robert Louis Stevenson describes the manner in which he went about learning to write. As a youth, he was considered an idler, but he was hardworking and persistent in his one great desire—to learn to write. Work toward this one goal absorbed his time completely. Always he took two books around with him, one to read, the other to write in Sometimes

782

during his walks, he carried on dramatic dialogues with himself and wrote down conversations from memory. He also kept diaries, but his best training was in imitating the styles of good writers. Whenever he read a passage that contained a quality he especially liked, he immediately sat down and tried "to ape that quality." He wrote and rewrote without ever achieving his goal. But in his painstaking labor of imitating, he got practice in the elements of composition. Concerning his practice, Stevenson says:

> . . . I have thus **played the sedulous ape** to Hazlitt, to Lamb, to Wordsworth, to Sir Thomas Browne, to Defoe, to Hawthorne, to Montaigne, to Baudelaire and to Obermann.

The play's the thing

Source: HAMLET (Act II, sc. ii, 1. 633)
Author: William Shakespeare (1564-1616)
First published: 1603
Type of work: Dramatic tragedy

Context: The ghost of Hamlet, late King of Denmark, has appeared on the battlements of Elsinore Castle to inform his son, Prince Hamlet, that he was murdered by his brother, Claudius, who has since married the widowed Queen Gertrude and usurped the crown. The ghost makes his son swear to avenge his murder, a vow that young Hamlet willingly takes. But after this emotion-charged scene is over, the Prince is assailed by doubts: is the ghost really that of his father or is it the Devil who has assumed his shape? He must have further evidence before he proceeds with his vengeance. Luckily, a troupe of strolling players stops at the castle. Quickly young Hamlet plans to have them produce a tragedy, the story of which resembles the Ghost's description of the murder. The reaction of Claudius to the play will demonstrate whether he is guilty or innocent, and then Hamlet will know what to do. In his soliloquy the Prince says:

> . . . the devil hath power
> T' assume a pleasing shape; yea, and perhaps
> Out of my weakness and my melancholy,
> As he is very potent with such spirits,
> Abuses me to damn me: I'll have grounds
> More relative than this: **the play's the thing**
> Wherein I'll catch the conscience of the king.

The pleasant land of counterpane

Source: THE LAND OF COUNTERPANE (Stanza 4)
Author: Robert Louis Stevenson (1850-1894)
First published: 1881
Type of work: Poem for children

Context: Robert Louis Stevenson had a gift for writing poems for children. Just as in most of his children's verses, in "The Land of Counterpane" he puts himself into the child's world, viewing the things around him delicately and simply. This poem recalls the poet's sickly childhood and the pastimes of a small boy isolated from the outside world. The memory of the long hours of confinement stand out in the poet's mind as he says "And all my toys beside me lay/ To keep me happy all the day." Then for "an hour or so," with his power of creation, he gives movement to his own world of activity among the bedclothes. Soldiers are put into action, fleets of ships move about, and cities are established. Then the poet concludes:

> I was the giant great and still
> That sits upon the pillow-hill,
> And sees before him, dale and plain,
> **The pleasant land of Counterpane.**

Please do not shoot the pianist. He is doing his best

Source: IMPRESSIONS OF AMERICA
Author: Oscar Wilde (1856-1900)
First published: 1906
Type of work: Travel memoir

Context: In 1882 Oscar Wilde arrived in the United States and began a lecturing tour that carried him across the country. One lecture was delivered in April of that year before an audience of miners at the Tabor Opera House in Leadville, Colorado. According to Wilde's own account of the occasion, his comments on art only succeeded in putting many of the miners to sleep. Wilde was held in high esteem by the miners, however, largely because of a demonstration of his ability to hold his whiskey. Commenting on his lecture Wilde says:

> I read them passages from the autobiography of Benvenuto Cellini and they seemed much delighted. I was reproved by my hearers for not having brought him with me. I explained that he had been dead for some little time which elicited the enquiry "Who shot him"? They afterwards took me to a dancing saloon

where I saw the only rational method of art criticism I have ever
come across. Over the piano was printed a notice:—

**PLEASE DO NOT SHOOT THE
PIANIST.
HE IS DOING HIS BEST.**

Plough the watery deep

Source: THE ILIAD (Book III, l. 357, as translated by Alexander Pope)
Author: Homer (c.850 B.C.)
First transcribed: Sixth century B.C.
Type of work: Epic poem

Context: After nine years of war, the siege of Troy is lifted for a short time as the two champions, Paris and Menelaüs, prepare for a duel to decide in single combat the outcome of the long quarrel. Both sides solemnize the occasion by sacrificial offerings, the opposing kings joining together on the plains to discuss the terms. Agamemnon himself performs the rites, saying

"Hear and be witness. If, by Paris slain,
Great Menelaüs press the fatal plain;
The dame and treasures let the Trojan keep,
And Greece returning **plough the watery deep.**
If by my brother's lance the Trojan bleed,
Be his the wealth and beauteous dame decreed:
The appointed fine let Ilion justly pay,
And every age record the signal day.
This if the Phrygians shall refuse to yield,
Arms must revenge, and Mars decide the field."

A poem should not mean
But be

Source: ARS POETICA (Stanza 12)
Author: Archibald MacLeish (1892-   )
First published: 1926
Type of work: Lyric poem

Context: "Ars Poetica," stating the dictum of the new critics, an organic theory of poetry, through a number of similes leads up to the inevitable statement that a poem should *be,* not *mean.* "A poem should be wordless/ As the flight of birds." It is not merely a speaking agent but a self-contained power, autonomous in nature. The poet compares a poem to

785

the motionless climb of the moon which, slowly, imperceptibly rising, leaves the forest silhouetted against the sky. Comparably, the poem with an imperceptible artistry works its natural effect upon the mind. It calls attention to memory by memory as the moon discovers twig by twig of the silhouetted trees. A poem is an experience which stands on an equal footing with other experiences. "A poem should be equal to:/ Not true." A poem should be

> For all the history of grief
> An empty doorway and a maple leaf,

> For love
> The leaning grasses and two lights above the sea—

> **A poem should not mean**
> **But be.**

Poetic justice

Source: THE DUNCIAD (Book I, l. 52)
Author: Alexander Pope (1688-1744)
First published: 1728-1743
Type of work: Satirical poem

Context: In this satire, at which he worked for many years, Pope roasted many of his contemporaries for their poor poetry and lack of wit. It is an example of wholesale revenge upon people for whom the poet had evolved some enmity or antipathy. In a mock-epic fashion, Pope begins with an extended invocation to "Dulness, Jove, and Fate" and their servants. He notes that in much earlier times the Goddess Dulness ruled all Britain, in the days before learning had reached many people. He adds that, being an immortal, Dulness still, with some success, strives for mastery over the contemporary scene. In the "cave of Poetry and Poverty," Dulness sits upon a throne, with winds from her cave carrying abroad all sorts of poor literature, including "Journals, Medleys, Merceries, Magazines." Four guardian virtues guard the throne of Dulness and support her:

> Fierce champion Fortitude, that knows no fears
> Of hisses, blows, or want, or loss of ears:
> Calm Temperance, whose blessings those partake,
> Who hunger and who thirst for scribbling sake:
> Prudence, whose glass presents th' approaching jail:
> **Poetic Justice,** with her lifted scale,
> Where, in nice balance, truth with gold she weighs,
> And solid pudding against empty praise.

Poetic license

Source: DE ORATORE (Book I, division 16, l. 70)
Author: Marcus Tullius Cicero (106-43 B.C.)
First transcribed: c.55 B.C.
Type of work: Rhetorical dialogue on the art of oratory

Context: Cicero, through a mouthpiece, takes the point of view in this book outlining oratorical principles that oratory calls for great knowledge, command of language, an exact memory, good delivery, wit, and insight. With numerous objections from among the orators young and old, the view is brought forth that the orator must be well versed in political and moral science, but especially in delivery he must borrow the methods of the poet with a power of expression and range of subject matter. The argument then turns on eloquence, which one disclaims as beyond mortal scope. Later, in Book II, the need for a liberal education is argued, again with the assumption that every good orator will not only quote poetry to his point but will also practice the writing of it. Although "poetic license" has come to mean doing whatever one wishes with the subject matter in order to elevate the art, such is not the intention in this oration:

> . . . The truth is that the poet is a very near kinsman of the orator, rather more heavily fettered as regards rhythm, but with ampler freedom in his choice of words, while in the use of many sorts of ornament he is his ally, and almost his counterpart; in one respect at all events something like identity exists, since he sets no boundaries or limits to his claims, such as would prevent him from ranging whither he will with the same **freedom and license** as the other. . . .

Poetry = the best words in the best order

Source: SPECIMENS OF THE TABLE TALK (July 12, 1827)
Author: Samuel Taylor Coleridge (1772-1834)
First published: 1835
Type of work: Transcribed conversation

Context: A brilliant, eloquent, tireless talker was Samuel Taylor Coleridge, who rarely failed to astonish or befuddle his auditors with the reach of his mind and the rare corners of his learning. To his nephew, Henry Nelson Coleridge, it seemed criminal that "such a strain of music" should die with Coleridge, and he formed the habit of writing down after returning home what he had heard. Published the year after Coleridge's death, the specimans of table talk cover over eleven years, ending a few days before Coleridge's death with a comment that "I wish life and strength had been spared to me to complete my Philosophy" (July 10, 1834). Imbedded in the midst of comments on Luther, Puritan objections to the surplice, Bolingbroke's style, and the fathers of the church, is the famous comment on prose and poetry that, by its simplicity, stands in sharp contrast to Coleridge's other, more elaborate and formal, definitions. It seems to have been part of an otherwise lost discussion of the Italian epic poets Ariosto (1474-1533) and Tasso (1544-1595):

> Well! I am for Ariosto against Tasso; though I would rather praise Ariosto's poetry than his poem.
> I wish our clever young poets would remember my homely definitions of prose and poetry; that is, prose = words in their best order;—**poetry = the best words in the best order.**

Poetry is man's rebellion against being what he is

Source: JURGEN (Chapter 44)
Author: James Branch Cabell (1879-1958)
First published: 1919
Type of work: Novel

Context: Jurgen, a pawnbroker in the unidentified land of Poictesme and a dabbler in verse, having said a kind word for the Devil, is relieved, as a favor, of his shrewish wife. However, since shortly after her disappearance she is seen walking in Amneran Heath, Jurgen feels it is his manly duty to seek her out. His search begins in a cave, where he learns that his only recourse in order to find her is to find Koshchei the Deathless, "who made things as they are." His search leads him into a mythical world where he undergoes many strange and fantastic adventures. At last he returns to the cave and finds Koshchei. They have a revealing conversation concerning the nature of things, the follies of men, social amenities, and other matters, all of which are satirically treated. In the course of his reply to Jurgen's timid inquiries about his wife, Koshchei calls Jurgen a "fellow rebel." Quickly Jurgen replies: "But I do not know, Prince, that I have ever rebelled. Far from it, I have everywhere conformed with custom." To this Koshchei replies:

> Your lips conformed, but all the while your mind made verses, Jurgen. And **poetry is man's rebellion against being what he is.**

Poets are the unacknowledged legislators of the world

Source: A DEFENSE OF POETRY
Author: Percy Bysshe Shelley (1792-1822)
First published: 1840
Type of work: Essay

Context: In *A Defense of Poetry,* Shelley states his Platonic theory of the art. To him, poetry is imagination—an awareness of the value and meaning of the ideas produced by reason. Poetry is "the centre and circumference of knowledge," and the poet is a "law-giver" who will lead mankind to freedom. Great poetry is the "herald, companion, and follower of the awakening of a great people to work a beneficial change in opinion or institution." For during such an awakening men have the power "of communicating and receiving intense . . . conceptions regarding man and nature." The poets themselves may not be aware of (or may even be hostile to) "that spirit of good of which they are the ministers." Their words are charged with an "electric life" which astonishes even them; "for it is less their spirit than the spirit of the age":

Poets are the hierophants of an unapprehended inspiration; the mirrors of the gigantic shadows which futurity casts upon the present; the words which express what they understand not; the trumpets which sing to battle, and feel not what they inspire; the influence which is moved not, but moves. **Poets are the unacknowledged legislators of the world.**

Policy sits above conscience

Source: TIMON OF ATHENS (Act III, sc. ii, l. 94)
Author: William Shakespeare (1564-1616)
First published: 1623
Type of work: Dramatic tragedy

Context: Timon is a generous patron of the arts and an open-hearted, lavish host. He joys in giving, and will return a kindness sevenfold. His extravagance ends in bankruptcy. Before long, his creditors become alarmed and try to collect their loans. Flavius, Timon's faithful steward, convinces him he owes more than twice what he owns. He, believing his friends will succor him in his need, sends servants to request loans from them. The first, Lucullus, tries to bribe the servant to say he was out. The second, Lucius, regrets the ill chance that finds him without means to help. He uses honeyed words, but sends no money. This exchange of words is overheard by three strangers to Athens who, aware of Timon's great mind and reputation for generosity, comment on the situation.

FIRST STRANGER
For mine own part,
I never tasted Timon in my life,
Nor came any of his bounties over me,
To mark me for his friend. Yet I protest,

. . .

Had his necessity made use of me,
I would have put my wealth into donation,

. . .

But I perceive,
Men must learn now with pity to dispense,
For **policy sits above conscience.**

Politics makes strange bedfellows

Source: MY SUMMER IN A GARDEN (Fifteenth Week)
Author: Charles Dudley Warner (1829-1900)
First published: 1870
Type of work: Essay

Context: While attributed around 1830 to Charles Hammond, editor of the *Cincinnati Gazette*, the most frequent printed reference to this quotation occurs in Charles Dudley Warner's *My Summer in a Garden*. Warner, a lawyer, coauthored with Mark Twain *The Gilded Age* and coedited *Harper's Magazine*. In *My Summer in a Garden*, a series of humorous essays on the art of gardening, he observes nature and draws curious analogies. He digresses often to make a point on any given subject. In the fifteenth essay, he begins by commenting on the fact that his absence of two or three weeks has allowed his garden to run riot. The strawberry plants, even the Colfax variety, for example, have run everywhere, an allusion to Schuyler Colfax, elected Vice-president in 1868. Further, he says, the Doolittle raspberries have mixed with the strawberries, an allusion to James Rood Doolittle, U.S. Senator and strong supporter of President Johnson. He says:

. . . I may mention here, since we are on politics, that the Doolittle raspberries had sprawled all over the strawberry-beds: so true is it that **politics makes strange bedfellows.**

Poor but honest

Source: ALL'S WELL THAT ENDS WELL (Act I, sc. iii, l. 201)
Author: William Shakespeare (1564-1616)
First published: 1623
Type of work: Dramatic comedy

Context: Bertram, young Count of Rousillon, leaves home for service at the Court of France. Behind him remain his mother, the Countess of

790

Rousillon, and her ward, the lovely and talented Helena, daughter of a physician. While living in the countess' home, Helena has fallen in love with Bertram but believes their difference in rank makes her love hopeless.

As soon as Bertram departs, Helena's depressed mood arouses the countess' suspicions. She questions the girl, allays her fears, and hears her confess her love for Bertram.

HELENA
Then I confess,
Here on my knee, before high heaven and you,
That before you, and next unto high heaven,
I love your son.
My friends were **poor but honest,** so's my love.
Be not offended, for it hurts not him
That he is loved of me.

• • •

A poor, infirm, weak, and despised old man

Source: KING LEAR (Act III, sc. ii, l. 20)
Author: William Shakespeare (1564-1616)
First published: 1608
Type of work: Dramatic tragedy

Context: Lear, King of Britain, an old man, foolishly divides his kingdom between his two eldest daughters, Goneril and Regan. He retains one hundred followers, the name of King, and the right to live with each daughter on an alternating monthly basis. Very shortly, however, Goneril, with whom he first resides, peremptorily reduces his retinue and criticizes him and his men. Lear puts a frightening curse on her and hurries off to live with Regan. Before he and his knights arrive, Regan is brought a letter from Goneril relating all that has happened. Lear is refused admittance by Regan until he apologizes to Goneril. When Goneril arrives, Lear realizes his daughters are in league against him. Reduced to impotent fury, he rushes out into the stormy, wild night with his fool. Now, we find him with his fool hurling his defiance at the elements as the storm rages about them.

LEAR
Rumble thy bellyful. Spit fire, spout rain. . . .
I tax not you, you elements, with unkindness
I never gave you kingdom, called you children,
You owe me no subscription. Then let fall
Your horrible pleasure. Here I stand your slave,
A poor, infirm, weak, and despised old man. . . .

791

Poor naked wretches, wheresoe'er you are

Source: KING LEAR (Act III, sc. i, l. 28)
Author: William Shakespeare (1564-1616)
First published: 1608
Type of work: Dramatic tragedy

Context: Lear, King of Britain, rashly divides his kingdom between his two eldest daughters, Goneril and Regan, and cuts off his youngest, Cordelia, with nothing because she cannot match her sisters' glib protestations of love for their father. Kent, a faithful friend of Lear, questions the old man's decision and is exiled. Shortly, Lear is stripped of his bodyguard and refused shelter by his daughters. Alone, except for his jester, Lear wanders the heath. Reduced to impotent fury, he curses Goneril and Regan and madly hurls defiance at the elements. Cold, miserable, deserted by all but his fool, and on the edge of madness, he is found by Kent who did not leave the country. Lear, who does not recognize Kent, allows himself and the fool to be led to the shelter of a hovel. Adversity lends Lear compassion; he takes pity on the fool and bids him enter. Before sleep, he prays. It is at this moment that his redemption begins: for the first time, he thinks of others.

LEAR

. . .

Poor naked wretches, wheresoe'er you are,
That bide the pelting of this pitiless storm,
How shall your houseless heads, and unfed sides,
Your looped and windowed raggedness, defend you
From seasons such as these? O I have ta'en
Too little care of this! . . .

A poor, weak, palsy-stricken, churchyard thing

Source: THE EVE OF ST. AGNES (Stanza 18)
Author: John Keats (1795-1821)
First published: 1820
Type of work: Narrative poem

Context: This poem reveals Keats's interest in medieval legends, and it contains many romantic elements— the love of the remote and the old, the interest in far-away lands and supernatural events. As he prays, an "ancient Beadsman" hears the noise of revelry in the castle. But a pure maiden named Madeline is oblivious of the celebration, for she dreams of the legend of St. Agnes's Eve: on that night (January 20) a virgin could have a vision of her future lover. Young Porphyro, who loves Madeline but is hated by her relatives, steals into the castle, where his only friend is "one old beldame" named Angela. Old Angela warns him to leave, but he wants her to help him enter Madeline's bedroom so that he can appear to the maiden as her lover. The old lady berates Porphyro, who vows to reveal himself to his foes if she does not aid him. Old Angela answers him, and her speech foreshadows the approaching deaths of her and the "ancient Beadsman":

> "Ah! why wilt thou affright a feeble soul?
> **A poor, weak, palsy-stricken, churchyard thing,**
> Whose passing-bell may ere the midnight toll;
> Whose prayers for thee, each morn and evening,
> Were never missed." Thus plaining, doth she bring
> A gentler speech from burning Porphyro;
> So woeful, and of such deep sorrowing,
> That Angela gives promise she will do
> Whatever he shall wish, betide her weal or woe.

The pot calls the kettle black

Source: DON QUIXOTE (Part II, Book IV, chapter 43)
Author: Miguel de Cervantes Saavedra (1547-1616)
First published: 1615
Type of work: Satirical novel

Context: Don Quixote is criticizing his fat squire as an "eternal proverb-voiding swagbelly." Sancho Panza, typical of the proverb-quoting Spanish peasant, bursts forth in a whole page of them. After all, he has many from which to select, for the Spanish language probably heads all in aphorisms. In 1930 Rodríguez Marín published a collection of 12,600 of those not included in either his own previous volume of 21,000 or in the standard 40,000 compilation by Gonzalo Correas. Says Sancho in conclusion:

> . . . he that sees a mote in another man's eye, should do well to take the beam out of his own; that people mayn't say, **the pot calls the kettle blackarse;** and the dead woman's afraid of her that is flea'd. Besides, your worship knows, that a fool knows more in his own house, than a wise man in another's.

Power tends to corrupt and absolute power corrupts absolutely

Source: LETTER TO BISHOP MANDELL CREIGHTON (April 5, 1887)
Author: John Emerich Edward Dahlberg-Acton, First Lord Acton (1834-1902)
First published: 1917
Type of work: Personal letter

Context: In 1887 Bishop Creighton brought out the third and fourth volumes of his five-volume *History of the Papacy during the Reformation.* Because Lord Acton, one of England's most noted historians, had written a frank and earnest review of the first two volumes, Creighton asked him to review the second pair. This time Acton's review was extremely harsh, criticizing in particular Creighton's apparently lenient attitude toward the Inquisition which was instituted and conducted with great cruelty and power by the Popes in the thirteenth and fourteenth centuries. A correspondence between the two men ensued; and in the end Acton's final draft, while maintaining essentially his previously-made point, was much more friendly in tone. Lord Acton's remark about power and corruption echoes an earlier observation by William Pitt (1708-1778) in a speech concerning John Wilkes in 1770: "Unlimited power is apt to corrupt the minds of those who possess it." In discussing the tremendous and unquestioned authority of the Popes, Acton writes:

> . . . I cannot accept your canon that we are to judge Pope and King unlike other men, with a favourable presumption that they did no wrong. If there is any presumption it is the other way against holders of power, increasing as the power increases. Historic responsibility has to make up for the want of legal responsibility. **Power tends to corrupt and absolute power corrupts absolutely.**

Praising the lean and sallow abstinence

Source: COMUS (Line 709)
Author: John Milton (1608-1674)
First published: 1637
Type of work: Masque

Context: In the story of this masque, written for the installation of Lord Bridgewater as President of Wales and first acted by his three children, the children must pass through a "drear wood" inhabited by the enchanter Comus, son of Bacchus and Ceres. The daughter, called in the masque the Lady, is separated from her brothers and encounters Comus and his train. Comus tries to woo her from the paths of virtue. In his efforts

794

to seduce the Lady, he sneers at the professors of morality decked out in robes trimmed with budge [lamb] fur. The Stoics, who believed that happiness consists in a life of virtue, and the Cynics, characterized by Diogenes, who lived in a tub because he scorned the ordinary amenities of civilization, preach an ascetic doctrine abhorrent to Comus. They praise an uncomfortable abstinence, but he holds that all the good things of the earth—odors, fruits, flocks—exist only to be enjoyed. Silkworms produce their smooth silk to deck out human beings; the earth contains gems and precious metals to ornament them. The passage delivered by Comus says:

> O foolishness of men! that lend their ears
> To those budge doctors of the Stoic fur,
> And fetch their precepts from the Cynic tub,
> **Praising the lean and sallow abstinence.**
> Wherefore did Nature pour her bounties forth
> With such a full and unwithdrawing hand,
> Covering the earth with odors, fruits, and flocks,
> Thronging the seas with spawn innumerable,
> But all to please and sate the curious taste?

Precious bane

Source: PARADISE LOST (Book I, l. 692)
Author: John Milton (1608-1674)
First published: 1667
Type of work: Epic poem

Context: Satan and his fellow rebel angels, having been thrust into Hell by God's power, prepare to build themselves a city and a glorious center of government. They dig, at the suggestion of Mammon, into a hill which appears to have minerals within it. The spirits soon have opened "a spacious wound" in the hillside and dig out ribs of gold to use as material for building. Milton, well guessing the reaction of his readers, comments, using the original meaning of "admire": "to wonder."

> Let none admire
> That riches grow in hell; that soil may best
> Deserve the **precious bane.**

Presbyterian true blue

Source: HUDIBRAS (Part I, Canto 1, l. 191)
Author: Samuel Butler (1612-1680)
First published: First and second parts, 1673; third part, 1678
Type of work: Burlesque poem

Context: Samuel Butler satirizes the Puritans in the person of Sir Hudibras, heightening the burlesque by explaining what a tremendously subtle philosopher he is: he is as learned as Alexander Hales, Thomas Aquinas, and Duns Scotus combined, being especially well versed in Nominalism and Realism—matters of great concern to the Puritans. He knows where Paradise is, what Adam dreamed about, whether Adam and Eve had navels, whether the serpent at the fall had cloven feet or none at all. As for his religion, he is a true blue Presbyterian. The term "true blue" is subject to several interpretations. In the light of the old adage, "True blue will never stain," it can mean that Hudibras was a stanch and faithful member of his sect. The term may also refer to the actual color blue, to the wearing of which the Presbyterians were greatly addicted; the preachers frequently wore blue aprons. The general sense of the passage is that Hudibras was an excellent Presbyterian. "True blue" now has the meaning of faithful or true. The passage in which the expression occurs is:

> For his religion, it was fit
> To match his learning and his wit;
> 'Twas **Presbyterian true blue;**
> For he was of that stubborn crew
> Of errant saints, whom all men grant
> To be the true Church Militant. . . .

Present fears are less than horrible imaginings

Source: MACBETH (Act I, sc. iii, ll. 137-138)
Author: William Shakespeare (1564-1616)
First published: 1623
Type of work: Dramatic tragedy

Context: Macbeth and Banquo, generals in the army of King Duncan of Scotland, have distinguished themselves in putting down a rebellion led by the Thane of Cawdor. The king hears of their deeds and determines to give Macbeth the title of the defeated Thane. Before the emissaries reach Macbeth, however, he and Banquo are informed by three witches that not only shall Macbeth be Thane of Cawdor, but that he shall be king and that Banquo shall be the father of kings. The king's emissaries arrive

796

and confirm the witches' prophecy that Macbeth is to be invested with the title of Thane of Cawdor. If this much is true, thinks ambitious Macbeth, can the complete fulfillment of the witches' prophecy be far behind? Lost in thought, he contemplates regicide as a way to hasten his fortune.

MACBETH

[*Aside.*] This supernatural soliciting
Cannot be ill, cannot be good. If ill
Why hath it given me earnest of success,
Commencing in a truth? I am Thane of Cawdor.
If good, why do I yield to that suggestion,
Whose horrid image doth unfix my hair,
And make my seated heart knock at my ribs,
Against the use of nature? **Present fears
Are less than horrible imaginings. . . .**

The President of the Immortals

Source: TESS OF THE D'URBERVILLES, A PURE WOMAN (Chapter 59)
Author: Thomas Hardy (1840-1928)
First published: 1891
Type of work: Novel

Context: Tess Durbeyfield, a girl of low birth and innocent heart, is seduced by a wealthy young man, Alec D'Urberville, and bears him a son who lives only a short while. When later she confesses the episode to her husband, Angel Clare, on their wedding night, Clare renounces her, and leaves her to endure a series of difficult trials. When, a considerable time later, Clare manages to forgive his wife, and returns to her, she has again fallen prey to Alec D'Urberville. In desperation she kills him to obtain her freedom. Tess and Angel are united in genuine love for each other, but their belated happiness ends abruptly when she is arrested for murder. Tess, who carried the burdens of others' sins and errors, is executed, and she ceases to be tormented by Fate.

"Justice" was done, and **the President of the Immortals,** in Aeschylean phrase, had ended his sport with Tess. And the d'Urberville knights and dames slept on in their tombs unknowing . . .

Pretty is as pretty does

Source: THE CANTERBURY TALES ("The Wife of Bath's Tale," Line 1170)
Author: Geoffrey Chaucer (1343?-1400)
First transcribed: c.1393-1400
Type of work: Collection of tales

Context: A knight in King Arthur's court is required to find the answer to the question of what women love most or be executed. He is told the answer —woman desires above all else sovereignty over her husband—by an old, foul hag, on the condition that he marry her. He agrees, but on their wedding night he finds her so repulsive that he cannot touch her. "Thou art so loothly and so oold also." She then delivers him a lecture on goodness and beauty, saying that she could make herself beautiful if she wished, but beauty would not necessarily make her good also. When she is given sovereignty over her choice, she becomes both beautiful and good. The proverb "Handsome is that handsome does" was used by Oliver Goldsmith (*The Vicar of Wakefield,* chapter 1), and is common elsewhere. In Chaucer, the loathly hag reads the knight a lecture on manners.

> **That he is gentil that dooth gentile dedis.**
> And therefore, leeve housbonde, I thus conclude:
> Al were it that myne auncestres were rude,
> Yet may the hye God, and so hope I,
> Grante me grace to lyven vertuously.

The price of wisdom is above rubies

Source: JOB 28:18
Author: Unknown
First transcribed: c.900-500 B.C.
Type of work: Religious saga

Context: Job, in the land of Uz, an upright and prosperous man and the father of many children, has been tested with God's permission by Satan, who maintains that the man of God will ultimately curse the Almighty. With his wealth and children destroyed and his own body tortured by boils, Job still refuses to curse God. Bewailing his condition, he listens to his friends Eliphaz the Teman-ite, Bildad the Shuhite, and Zophar the Naamathite, who comment on the wisdom and justice of God and the ways of the wicked. Insisting on his innocence, but recalling his agony, he reproves his friends as "miserable comforters." With an intense faith in the Almighty, but a belief in his own innocence, he continues to dispute the words of his friends, who consider him a sinful creature incapable of understanding the Lord's wisdom. In a poetic passage, the unattainable nature and immeasurable value of such wisdom are noted:

> It cannot be valued with the gold of Ophir, with the precious onyx, or the sapphire.
> The gold and the crystal cannot equal it: and the exchange of it shall not be for jewels of fine gold.
> No mention shall be made of coral, or of pearls: for **the price of wisdom is above rubies.**

Pride that apes humility

Source: THE DEVIL'S THOUGHTS (Stanza 6)
Author: Samuel Taylor Coleridge (1772-1834)
First published: 1799
Type of work: Satiric poem

Context: In 1799, during one of several reconciliations following estrangements, Coleridge and his brother-in-law, Robert Southey (1774-1843), produced "The Devil's Thoughts" as a joint bit of satire, Southey dictating several stanzas to Coleridge. First published anonymously, the poem was an instant success, and there was considerable speculation about the authorship, the names not being disclosed until many years later. The poem opens with the Devil visiting "his snug little farm the earth." There follows a loosely strung series of slaps at lawyers, druggists, booksellers and other tradesmen, the prison system, the slave trade, and so on. Reminiscent of Robert Burton's (1577-1640) "They are proud in humility; proud in that they are not proud" (*The Anatomy of Melancholy*, 1621) is the sixth stanza:

> He saw a cottage with a double coach-house,
> A cottage of gentility;
> And the Devil did grin, for his darling sin
> Is **pride that apes humility.**

Pride, which out of daily fortune ever taints the happy man

Source: CORIOLANUS (Act IV, sc. vii, ll. 37-39)
Author: William Shakespeare (1564-1616)
First published: 1623
Type of work: Dramatic tragedy

Context: Caius Martius, a brilliant general, leads the Roman forces against the Volcians, ancient enemies led by Aufidius, and defeats them near their capital, Corioles. He is named Coriolanus by his troops and returns to Rome in triumph. The Senate nominates him for Consul, but his tactless scorn for the common man and hate for the rabble do not endear him to them or their tribunes. They turn on him and obtain his banishment from Rome. He curses Rome and, leaving the city defenseless, joins his old foes the Volcians led by Aufidius, who accetps him as a commander equal in rank to himself. Together, they lead the Volcians against Rome. Aufidius, however, realizes Coriolanus is overshadowing him with his troops and resents him. He discusses Coriolanus and Rome with another officer.

AUFIDIUS

• • •

First, he was
A noble servant to them, but he could not
Carry his honours even: whether 'twas **pride,**
Which out of daily fortune ever taints
The happy man; whether defect of judgement,
. . . or whether nature, . . .
. . . made him feared,
So hated, and so banished:

• • •

A primrose by a river's brim

Source: PETER BELL (Part I, stanza 12)
Author: William Wordsworth (1770-1850)
First published: 1819
Type of work: Narrative poem

Context: This much-parodied and much-abused poem, composed twenty-one years before its publication, tells the story of Peter Bell, the potter. He is immoral, cruel, unsocial, living in the open air with access to all that is beautiful and grand in nature. But for all the effect that nature's beauties have upon him, he might as well be blind and insensible. Neither heart nor head is the better. Nature "ne'er could find the way/ Into the heart of Peter Bell." His experiences make no impression on his inner mind because he gives nothing of himself and so never furnishes any materials for his mind to be transmuted into the higher forms of thought and affection. Prior to an experience in the closing part of the poem which redeems his soul, he is "the wildest far of all."

In vain, through every changeful year,
Did Nature lead him as before;
A primrose by a river's brim

A yellow primrose was to him
And it was nothing more.

The primrose way

Source: MACBETH (Act II, sc. iii, 1. 21)
Author: William Shakespeare (1564-1616)
First published: 1623
Type of work: Dramatic tragedy

Context: Macbeth, at his wife's insistence, has just murdered Duncan, and in so doing has "murdered" sleep, "the innocent sleep,/ Sleep that knits up the ravelled sleave of care, The death of each day's life, sore labour's bath." Lady Macbeth has taken the bloody daggers back, to lay them, smeared with blood, beside the sleeping grooms. As the two guilty people look down at their bloody hands, there is a knocking at the gate without. The p o r t e r, protesting against being roused at this hour, goes to open it, and to admit Macduff and Lennox. Before opening the gate, however, the Porter makes several comments, typified by the following:

PORTER
. . . Knock, knock. Never at quiet. What are you? But this place is too cold for hell. I'll devil-porter it no further. I had thought to have let in some of all professions, that go **the primrose way** to th' everlasting bonfire. . . .

A prince and a great man fallen this day in Israel

Source: II SAMUEL 3:38
Author: Unknown
First transcribed: 1100-400 B.C.
Type of work: Religious history

Context: Israel is divided by civil war after the death of her first king, Saul. The kingdom of Israel is technically ruled by Ishbosheth, the son of Saul. The separate kingdom of Judah is ruled by David, whom the prophet Samuel had secretly anointed years before when King Saul's ineffectiveness first became apparent. King Ishbosheth argues over one of Saul's concubines with Abner, who has been one of his strong supporters. Abner, in his anger, decides to give his loyalty to David; David and Abner formulate a treaty uniting Israel and Judah with David as king. David's hot-tempered nephew Joab, jealous because he has not been consulted, pursues Abner and kills him. David, realizing that the alliance between Israel and Judah

801

is very shaky, gives Abner an elaborate burial and assures everyone that Joab alone is responsible for the death of this great individual:

And the king said unto his servants, Know ye not that there is a prince and a great man fallen this day in Israel?

The prince of darkness is a gentleman

Source: KING LEAR (Act III, sc. iv, l. 148)
Author: William Shakespeare (1564-1616)
First published: 1608
Type of work: Dramatic tragedy

Context: Two old men, blind to the evil they have fathered, make fateful decisions. Lear, King of Britain, divides his kingdom between his two eldest daughters, Goneril and Regan, and cuts off his youngest, Cordelia, with nothing. The Earl of Gloucester has two sons; Edgar, who is legitimate, and Edmund, born out of wedlock. The Earl, deceived by Edmund who is scheming to deprive Edgar of his birthright, is convinced the latter is plotting to murder him for his estates. Edgar flees and goes into hiding in the wilds disguised as a madman. Lear, stripped even of the name of King by his daughters and accompanied only by his faithful jester, wanders the stormy heath, cursing his daughters and defying the raging elements. In the storm, Kent, an old follower of Lear, finds him and the fool, and they encounter Edgar in disguise. A short time later the Earl of Gloucester arrives to help Lear. Edgar frantically acts Tom, the madman, so his father will not recognize him. (In 1819, in *Peter Bell the Third,* Percy Bysshe Shelley changed this line to "The Devil is a gentleman.")

EDGAR
· · ·

But mice, and rats, and such small deer,
Have been Tom's food, for seven long year.
Beware my follower. Peace Smulkin, peace thou fiend.

GLOUCESTER
What, hath your Grace no better company?

EDGAR
The prince of darkness is a gentleman. Modo he's called, and Mahu.

Princes and lords are but the breath of kings

Source: THE COTTER'S SATURDAY NIGHT (Line 165)
Author: Robert Burns (1759-1796)
First published: 1786
Type of work: Narrative poem

Context: The family gathered on Saturday night in an humble farm cottage was a scene Burns knew well from his own childhood as the oldest son of a tenant farmer. This was their gathering time, for Sunday marked their only break in unremitting toil. The poem opens with the old father leaving his fields to join his young children by the fireside. Presently his oldest offspring come for their weekly visit from their places of work as domestics and farm laborers. While they exchange news of each other, the mother mends worn clothing, and the father injects an occasional moral admonition. The parents are flustered when a young man comes to call on the oldest daughter, but they find him acceptable, and he joins in their frugal supper. After eating, they hold family worship, then the children who are working leave. The scene closes with the prayers of the parents. In a final comment on this family occasion, Burns declares, using a quotation from Pope, that from such humble origins comes Scotland's glory, for

> From scenes like these old Scotia's grandeur springs,
> That makes her lov'd at home, rever'd abroad:
> **Princes and lords are but the breath of kings,**
> "An honest man's the noblest work of God";
> And certes, in fair virtue's heavenly road,
> The cottage leaves the palace far behind;
> What is a lordling's pomp? a cumbrous load,
> Disguising oft the wretch of human kind,
> Studied in arts of hell, in wickedness refin'd!

Prisoners of hope

Source: ZECHARIAH 9:12
Author: Unknown
First transcribed: 520-518 B.C.
Type of work: Religious prophecy

Context: At some time after Zechariah's writing of chatpers 1-8 of the book of *Zechariah,* some other prophet, whose identity is not known, added the scripture which comprises chapters 9-14 of *Zechariah.* The writer sees in the triumphant conquest of Alexander the Great hope for the Hebrew Messiah to follow with a reign of peace, which will reunite the kingdom of Israel and extend the Lord's dominion over the entire earth. Remembering that God has covenanted to protect Israel, the prophet exhorts his listeners, the Israelites still imprisoned under Babylonian rule, to have hope because of the ultimate triumph of the Lord over Greece and the entire world:

> Turn you to the stronghold, ye **prisoners of hope:** even to-day
> do I declare that I will render double unto thee;
> When I have bent Judah for me, filled the bow with Ephraim,
> and raised up thy sons, O Zion, against thy sons, O Greece, and
> made thee as the sword of a mighty man.

Procrastination is the thief of time

Source: THE COMPLAINT: OR, NIGHT THOUGHTS ("Night the First," Line 392)
Author: Edward Young (1683-1765)
First published: 1742
Type of work: Philosophical poem

Context: In the eighteenth century this poem was honored next to Milton's *Paradise Lost*. Young, a conservative Anglican clergyman, hoped to use poetry again as a vehicle of religious truth. He also wished to write a doctrine omitted, to Young's disappointment, from Pope's *An Essay on Man,* the doctrine of belief in a future existence. This doctrine is part of a poem for which there is also a biographical background in the life of the poet. Young lost to death three persons close to him, and his mourning about them is to a modern reader the most obvious aspect of the poem. It is in a romantic tradition which was almost unknown in the eighteenth century, when poets seldom wrote about themselves. In this part of the poem advice is offered Lorenzo to remember Philander, who has failed to prepare for death and the future life:

> Beware, Lorenzo! a *slow-sudden* death
> How dreadful that deliberate surprise!
> Be wise to-day; 'tis madness to defer;
> Next day the fatal precedent will plead;
> Thus on, till wisdom is push'd out of life.
> **Procrastination is the thief of time;**
> Year after year it steals, till all are fled,
> And to the mercies of a moment leaves
> The vast concerns of an eternal scene.

The proof of the pudding is in the eating

Source: DON QUIXOTE (Part I, Book IV, chapter 10)
Author: Miguel de Cervantes Saavedra (1547-1616)
First published: 1605
Type of work: Satirical novel

Context: Still arguing about enchantments, Sancho Panza assures his master that the Princess Micomicona was really a damsel named Dorothea, and that the giant and his blood were wineskins in the store room. In trying to convince Don Quixote, he uses the common Spanish proverb: "It will be seen in the frying of the eggs," because the condition of eggs is not apparent until they are broken into the pan for frying. Motteux, in his 1701 translation, uses a corresponding English proverb. As he phrased Sancho's speech:

> . . . Gadzookers sir, are not the skins all hacked and slashed within there at your bed's-head, and the wine all in a puddle in your chamber? But you'll guess at the meat presently, by the sauce; **the proof of the pudding is in the eating,** master. . . .

Propagate the best that is known and thought in the world

Source: ESSAYS IN CRITICISM, FIRST SERIES ("The Function of Criticism at the Present Time")
Author: Matthew Arnold (1822-1888)
First published: 1864
Type of work: Critical essay

Context: Matthew Arnold, critic in prose and poetry of nineteenth century society, politics, religion, and literature, establishes his criterion for any type of criticism by stating the two principal qualities to be curiosity, an attempt "to know the best that is known and thought in the world," and disinterestedness, the refusal "to lend itself to any of those ulterior, political, practical considerations about ideas . . . which criticism has nothing to do with." In defending his principles of literary criticism, he goes beyond nationalism and says:

> But stop, some one will say; . . . when we speak of critics and criticism, we mean critics and criticism of the current English literature of the day; when you offer to tell criticism its function, it is to this criticism that we expect you to address yourself. I am sorry for it, for I am afraid I must disappoint these expectations. I am bound by my own definition of criticism: *a disinterested endeavour to learn and* **propagate the best that is known**

and **thought in the world.** How much of current English literature comes into this "best that is known and thought in the world"? Not very much I fear; certainly less, at this moment, than of the current literature of France or Germany.

The proper study of mankind is Man

Source: AN ESSAY ON MAN (Epistle II, l. 2)
Author: Alexander Pope (1688-1744)
First published: 1733-1734
Type of work: Philosophical poem

Context: Like many Europeans of his time, Pope believed in a universal and unchanging order in the world. Everything has its place, for him, in a vast chain of being. The question then is not whether man is perfect, but whether man is as perfect as he ought to be for the place he occupies in the scheme of things. The business of man cannot be to pry into God's plans; man is only to study himself and his own place in the chain of being. Following this admonition, which appears at the beginning of Epistle II, Pope looks at mankind, seeing two principles, self-love and reason, which the poet examines closely:

Know then thyself; presume not God to scan,
The proper study of mankind is Man.
Placed on this isthmus of a middle state,
A being darkly wise and rudely great:
With too much knowledge for the Sceptic side,
And too much weakness for the Stoic's pride,
He hangs between; in doubt to act or rest;
In doubt to deem himself a God or Beast;
In doubt his mind or body to prefer;
Born but to die, and reas'ning but to err.
Alike in ignorance, his reason such,
Whether he thinks too little or too much.

A prophet is not without honor, save in his own country

Source: MATTHEW 13:57
Author: Unknown (traditionally Matthew the Apostle)
First transcribed: c.75-100
Type of work: Gospel

Context: Jesus, having preached the Sermon on the Mount, healed the afflicted, raised the dead, chosen His disciples and instructed them in their

806

mission, and taught the people in parables at the Sea of Galilee, returns to his own area of Nazareth. He goes to the synagogue, where he astonishes the people with His wisdom and with stories of His works. The Nazarenes are not able, however, to reconcile His wisdom with the fact that He is "the carpenter's son." And they know His mother, His brothers, and His sisters. In the light of His humble beginnings, then, how can He presume to teach with such assurance?

And they were offended in him. But Jesus said unto them, **A prophet is not without honor, save in his own country,** and in his own house.

And he did not many mighty works there because of their unbelief.

Proud man, dressed in a little brief authority

Source: MEASURE FOR MEASURE (Act II, sc. ii, ll. 117-118)
Author: William Shakespeare (1564-1616)
First published: 1623
Type of work: Tragi-comedy

Context: Claudio, a young gentleman of Vienna, is arrested on a charge of fornication under an old and long unobserved law. He faces a penalty of death for a technical violation of the law, for upon a true contract and promise of marriage, delayed only because of some formal difficulties about dowry, Claudio has got his beloved, Juliet, pregnant. Arrested, Claudio sends to his sister, Isabella, for help. She, a novice in a convent, goes to the duke's deputy, Angelo, who holds power and enforces the strict law in Duke Vincentio's absence. She pleads for Claudio's life to no avail. But, as she gains confidence, she attacks man's presumptuous exercise of authority.

ISABELLA
. . .
O, it is excellent
To have a giant's strength; but it is tyrannous
To use it like a giant.
. . .
Merciful Heaven,
Thou rather with thy sharp and sulphurous bolt
Splits the unwedgeable and gnarled oak
Than the soft myrtle. But man, **proud man,
Dressed in a little brief authority,**
Most ignorant of what he's most assured,
. . .

Plays such fantastic tricks before high heaven
As make the angels weep;

. . .

Prunes, and prism

Source: LITTLE DORRIT (Book II, chapter 5)
Author: Charles Dickens (1812-1870)
First published: 1855-1857
Type of work: Novel

Context: William Dorrit, confined to debtor's prison for twenty years, is released when it is discovered that he has become the heir to a large fortune. The sudden wealth goes to his head, and he begins to play the part of a cultured gentleman. In an attempt to wipe away the memories of the past and to attain social polish, he takes his family to Europe. In Venice he meets a widowed Englishwoman, Mrs. General, who has dedicated her life to impressing others with her dignity and aristocratic manner. When Dorrit's daughter, Amy, enters the room, Mrs. General, the "eminent varnisher," attempts to improve the girl's social gloss. She gives her a number of words which, when spoken, form the lips attractively and advises her to say them to herself at social gatherings.

. . . The word Papa . . . gives a pretty form to the lips. Papa, potatoes, poultry, **prunes, and prism,** are all very good words for the lips: especially prunes and prism. You will find it serviceable, in the formation of a demeanour, if you sometimes say to yourself in company—on entering a room, for instance—Papa, potatoes, poultry, prunes and prism, prunes and prism.

The public be damned!

Source: THE CHICAGO TRIBUNE
Author: William H. Vanderbilt (1821-1885)
First published: 1882
Type of work: Reply to a newspaper reporter

Context: William H. Vanderbilt was the irascible and shrewd son of the founder of the Vanderbilt fortune. For his often contemptuous treatment of the public, he usually received from the press not the best possible publicity. At least two versions of his famous remark to newspaperman Clarence Dresser exist. The version by Melville E. Stone of the Associated Press indicates that Dresser, insisting on an interview with Vanderbilt during his dinner and being rebuffed, pleads that he has to reach his office by a certain hour for the interview to be published. Vanderbilt shouted, "The public be d——d; you get out of here!" The Chicago *Daily News* refused to buy the story, but the Chicago *Tribune,* unaware of the wrath of Vanderbilt with Dresser, accepted the interview. A second version, by Gus-

tavus Myers in his *History of the Great American Fortunes,* simplifies the incident. A reporter is said to have asked Vanderbilt why he did not "consider public convenience in the running of his trains. . . ." Vanderbilt blurted out:

"The public be damned!"

The Puritans hated bearbaiting, not because it gave pain to the bear, but because it gave pleasure to the spectators

Source: HISTORY OF ENGLAND (Volume 1, chapter 2)
Author: Thomas Babington Macaulay (1800-1859)
First published: 1848-1861
Type of work: History

Context: To the Puritans in their seventeenth century reformation of the Anglican Church, the austere life was the goodly life. Having reformed religion, they turned to social customs and insisted that the pleasures of the flesh be denied to insure the happiness of the soul. David Hume (1711-

1776) in his *History of England during the Reign of James I and Charles I* (1754-1757), Vol. I. chap. lxii, wrote that "even bear-baiting was esteemed heathenish and unchristian; the sport of it, not the inhumanity, gave offence." Macaulay expands the idea:

> . . . But bear-baiting, then a favorite diversion of high and low, was the abomination which most strongly stirred the wrath of the austere sectaries . . . their antipathy to this sport had nothing in common with the feeling which has, in our own time, induced the legislature to interfer for the purpose of protecting beasts against the wanton cruelty of man. **The Puritans hated bearbaiting, not because it gave pain to the bear, but because it gave pleasure to the spectators. . . .**

Put himself upon his good behavior

Source: DON JUAN (Canto V, stanza 47)
Author: George Gordon, Lord Byron (1788-1824)
First published: 1821 (Cantos III-V)
Type of work: Satirical poem

Context: Don Juan is a long, digressive, and satiric poem about the ad-

ventures of a young libertine, Juan, whom readers and critics alike persist in identifying as Lord Byron. In Canto V, Juan and an Englishman named Johnson are sold as slaves to the Sultana Gulbeyaz. While they are being led by a black eunuch to the Sultan's palace, Juan suggests to his friend that they knock the slave on the head and escape. However, both are hungry, and when they smell food cooking, they decide to defer their plans for liberty. The line quoted refers to Juan's conduct when he smells food, but readers of the poem were prone to think of Byron himself and wonder if he was ever on "his good behaviour." Byron's old publisher, Murray, brought out the first five cantos of the poem anonymously, but he was so shocked by its contents that he refused to publish any more, and the remaining cantos were published by John Hunt. In context, the line reads:

> And nearer as they came, a genial savour
> Of certain stews, and roast-meats, and pilaus,
> Things which in hungry mortals' eyes find favour,
> Made Juan in his harsh intentions pause,
> **And put himself upon his good behaviour.**

Put his shoulder to the wheel

Source: ANATOMY OF MELANCHOLY (Part. II, sec. 1, memb. 2)
Author: Robert Burton (1577-1640)
First published: 1621-1651
Type of work: Essays

Context: The author, Vicar of St. Thomas's Church in Oxford, shows his religious background by many references to the Bible. However, in this case, instead of quoting Luke 9:62, about "putting his hand to the plough," as a symbol of starting to do something rather than depending entirely on outside aid, Burton goes back in Member 2, entitled "Lawful Cures, first from God," to Aesop (fl. 550 B.C.) and his fable of Hercules and the wagoner:

> . . . To pray alone, and reject ordinary means, is to do like him in Aesop, that, when his cart was stalled, lay flat on his back, and cried aloud, Help, Hercules! but that was to little purpose, except, as his friend advised him, he make an effort himself; he whipped his horses withal, and **put his shoulder to the wheel.**

Put in her oar

Source: DON QUIXOTE (Part II, Book III, chapter 6)
Author: Miguel de Cervantes Saavedra (1547-1616)
First published: 1615
Type of work: Satirical novel

Context: As preparations for Don Quixote's third sally are progressing, the Knight's housekeeper and especially his niece attempt to persuade him to become a Knight at the King's court. He objects. At court men lead a soft life, but in the field they join those noble warriors defending the kingdom, as told about in histories. The niece interrupts angrily and calls all the stories of knights-errant a pack of lies and fables.

". . . Now by the powerful sustainer of my being," cried Don Quixote, "wert thou not so nearly related to me, wert thou not my own sister's daughter, I would take such revenge for the blasphemy thou hast uttered, as would resound through the whole universe. Who ever heard of the like impudence? That a young baggage, who scarce knows her bobbins from her bodkin, should presume to **put in her oar,** and censure the histories of knights-errant!"

Put money in thy purse

Source: OTHELLO (Act I, sc. iii, ll. 341-346)
Author: William Shakespeare (1564-1616)
First published: 1622
Type of work: Dramatic tragedy

Context: Roderigo, a young gentleman of Venice, loves Desdemona, daughter of a Venetian senator. But it is hopeless because she loves her husband, Othello, a Moor in the military service of the city. Roderigo turns to his friend, Iago, for advice. Iago, Othello's ancient (or ensign) hates the Moor for not making him his lieutenant. When Roderigo speaks of drowning himself, Iago scoffs at him and advises him to employ his reason rather than be subject to his emotions. Iago stiffens Roderigo's spine and encourages him, not merely for the latter's sake, but because Iago, crafty and dissembling, intends to use Roderigo to achieve his own designs on Othello.

IAGO

. . . I have professed me thy friend, and I confess me knit to thy deserving with cables of perdurable toughness. I could never better stead thee

811

than now. **Put money in thy purse;** follow thou the wars; defeat thy favour with an usurped beard. I say, **put money in thy purse.** It cannot be that Desdemona should long continue her love to the Moor—**put money in thy purse**—nor he his to her. . . .

Put new wine into old bottles

Source: MATTHEW 9:17
Author: Unknown (traditionally Matthew the Apostle)
First transcribed: c.75-100
Type of work: Gospel

Context: Jesus, after declaring in the Sermon on the Mount that His teachings are the fulfillment of the old law, continues to teach the people and to minister to their needs. He heals them of their ills and instructs them in the life of the disciple. Further miracles are seen as He stills the waves on the Sea of Galilee, casts out devils from two possessed ones into a herd of swine, and at Capernaum, forgives the sins of a man afflicted with palsy and then heals him. After Jesus and his followers dine with tax collectors and sinners, the disciples of John the Baptist ask why His disciples are not required to fast. Jesus explains that wedding guests do not mourn while the bridegroom is at hand; and that adherence to the old way, when the new is present, may cause the loss of both:

> Neither do men **put new wine into old bottles:** else the bottles break, and the wine runneth out, and the bottles perish: but they put new wine into new bottles, and both are preserved.

Put not your trust in princes

Source: PSALMS 146:3
Author: Unknown
First transcribed: c.400-200 B.C.
Type of work: Religious poetry

Context: As long as he lives, the poet will praise God. He admonishes his audience not to trust in men, even princes, because all men must die, and with them dies their influence. Blessed is the person who puts his faith in the Lord, Who is the Creator of the universe; the source of eternal truth; and the protector of the oppressed, the poverty-stricken, the prisoners, the blind, the strangers, the orphans and the widows. God loves

the righteous and defeats the pur-
poses of the wicked; He will reign
eternally. In contrast with the eternal
power of God is the short-lived power
of man:

> **Put not your trust in princes,** nor in the son of man, in whom
> there is no help.
> His breath goeth forth, he returneth to his earth; in that very
> day his thoughts perish.

Put out the light, and then put out the light

Source: OTHELLO (Act V, sc. ii, l. 7)
Author: William Shakespeare (1564-1616)
First published: 1622
Type of work: Dramatic tragedy

Context: Iago, ancient (or ensign) to
Othello, a Moorish military governor
of Cyprus in the service of Venice,
hates him because the latter has made
Michael Cassio his lieutenant in preference to him. The ancient determines to destroy both of them. By
means of clever dissimulation, evil
machinations, and luck, he not only
convinces the gullible Othello that his
young wife Desdemona is unfaithful
with Cassio but that both must die.
Now Othello approaches Desdemona,
who is asleep in her bed, with intent to
smother her.

OTHELLO
. . .

Yet she must die, else she'll betray more men.
Put out the light, and then put out the light.
If I quench thee, thou flaming minister,
I can again thy former light restore,
Should I repent me. But once put out thy light,
Thou cunning'st pattern of excelling nature,
I know not where is that Promethean heat
That can thy light relume. . . .

Put you in this pickle

Source: DON QUIXOTE (Part I, Book I, chapter 5)
Author: Miguel de Cervantes Saavedra (1547-1616)
First published: 1605
Type of work: Satirical novel

Context: Cervantes is fond of the
"pickle" figure. In Part I, Book II,
chap. IV, Sancho, reporting to his
master his conversation with Dul-

813

cinea, says: "I told her indeed in what a sad pickle I had left you for her sake." In Book III, chapter IV, it is "a delicate pickle," and in chapter X, Sancho speaks of "a dainty pickle." Our expression is more alliterative, "a pretty pickle." The basis of them all is the brine in which cucumbers are soaked, and named from the Dutch word that gives us "piquant." If we are not "in a pickle," we are "in the soup" or "out of our element." Don Quixote, trying to make a company of merchants from Toledo acknowledge that his lady Dulcinea del Toboso is the world's fairest damsel, is beaten by their servants. A plowman of his village carts him home, where he begs his housekeeper to send for the enchantress Urganda to come and cure his wounds. She refuses, and says:

. . . Come, get you to bed, I beseech you; and, my life for yours, we'll take care to cure you without sending for that same Urganda. A hearty curse, and the curse of curses, I say it again and again a hundred times, light upon those books of chivalry that have **put you in this pickle!** . . .

Put your best foot forward

Source: RESPECTABILITY (Last line)
Author: Robert Browning (1812-1889)
First published: 1855
Type of work: Dramatic lyric

Context: A lover is talking to his love about the nature of the world. He says that had they belonged to "respectable" society, they would have wasted years before they dared to express their love freely. Then, "How much of priceless life were spent/ With men that every virtue decks,/ And women models of their sex,/ So-ciety's true ornament,—/ Ere we dared wander, nights like this,/ Through wind and rain, and watch the Seine,/ And feel the Boulevard break again/ To warmth and light and bliss!" In his concluding stanza he comments bitterly on the symbols of conventional Society, from which they have been excluded.

I know! the world proscribes not love;
  Allows my fingers to caress
  Your lips' contour and downiness,
Provided it supply a glove.
The world's good word!—the Institute!
  Guizot receives Montalembert!
Eh? Down the court three lampions flare:
Put forward your best foot!

Put your shoulder to the wheel

Source: AESOP'S FABLES ("Hercules and the Waggoner")
Author: Aesop (fl. sixth century B.C.?)
First transcribed: Fourth century B.C.
Type of work: Moral tales of animals

Context: Probably not a part of the original corpus, the Aesopica, the story of the god of strength and weak man is as follows:

A Waggoner was once driving a heavy load along a very muddy way. At last he came to a part of the road when the wheels sank halfway into the mire, and the more the horses pulled, the deeper sank the wheels. So the Waggoner threw down his whip, and knelt down and prayed to Hercules the Strong. "O Hercules, help me in my hour of distress," quoth he. But Hercules appeared to him, and said:
"Tut, man, don't sprawl there. Get up and **put your shoulder to the wheel.**"

Quaint and curious war is!

Source: THE MAN HE KILLED
Author: Thomas Hardy (1840-1928)
First published: 1909
Type of work: Lyric poem

Context: This poem, in the form of a monologue spoken by an infantryman, is a meditation on war, which makes a virtue of murdering men one does not even know, merely because their nation is a declared enemy of one's own. The speaker has just shot and killed an enemy soldier, and he speculates that if he had met that man in peacetime at an inn, they would have talked and drunk together. Perhaps the man enlisted, as he himself did, because he was without a job. The two were much alike and without quarrel, but were made mortal enemies because of their nationality.

"Yes; **quaint and curious war is!**
You shoot a fellow down
You'd treat if met where any bar is,
Or help to half-a-crown."

The quality of mercy is not strained

Source: THE MERCHANT OF VENICE (Act IV, sc. i, 1. 184)
Author: William Shakespeare (1564-1616)
First published: 1600
Type of work: Dramatic comedy

Context: In Venice, Bassanio, a nobleman, has borrowed from Shylock, a Jewish usurer, three thousand ducats with which to court the beautiful heiress, Portia. His friend Antonio is bound as surety for the payment of the debt. In pretended jest, Shylock requires that, if the debt is not paid on the right day, he will be allowed to cut a pound of flesh from Antonio's body. Antonio accepts the strange condition, not knowing that Shylock hates him for lending money at no interest, thus damaging the Jew's business. When the appointed day arrives, Antonio cannot pay the money and is brought into court to forfeit his bond. The Duke pleads for mercy from Shylock, and Bassanio offers twice the sum of the debt; but Shylock is adamant in demanding the flesh. Portia, meanwhile, has disguised herself as a lawyer and now appears in the court. First, she appeals to Shylock's sense of mercy, in the famous speech that begins:

> The quality of mercy is not strain'd,
> It droppeth as the gentle rain from heaven
> Upon the place beneath: it is twice blest;
> It blesseth him that gives, and him that takes. . . .

Quietly sweating palm to palm

Source: FRASCATI'S (Last line)
Author: Aldous Huxley (1894-1963)
First published: 1919
Type of work: Lyric poem

Context: In this deeply ironic poem the writer depicts himself as sitting with a girl in the balcony of an ornate restaurant. They are under its "bubble-breasted" dome, from which hangs a crystal chandelier that resembles a frozen water-fall. Below them, the patrons—"human bears"—are "champing with their gilded teeth." There is the further irony of an echo of Keats ("What songs? What gongs? What nameless rites?" which sardonically hints at "What pipes and timbrels? What wild ecstasy" in the "Ode on a Grecian Urn") and of the interior of a cathedral. The dome of the restaurant suggests to the poet a nave below, where, instead of church music or the "unheard" melodies of Keats, a Negro jazz-band is producing "blasts of Bantu melody." Yet, in the final irony, this vulgar spot is the poet's "spiritual home," just as a cathedral might be such for a devout person. Here is the disillusionment of the post World War I years, for from all the noise, confusion, and blaring rag-time, the tragi-comic climax is only a sensual experience:

> But when the wearied Band
> Swoons to a waltz, I take her hand,
> And there we sit, in blissful calm,
> **Quietly sweating palm to palm.**

Quoth the raven, "Nevermore"

Source: THE RAVEN (Stanza 8)
Author: Edgar Allan Poe (1809-1849)
First published: 1842
Type of work: Narrative poem

Context: "The Raven" is Poe's most famous poem. In his essay, "The Philosophy of Composition," the poet outlined what he claimed to be the process by which the work was composed. Of the refrain, he said that he needed a single word containing a long *o* and the consonant *r;* hence, the choice of Nevermore was inevitable. Poe felt that the death of a beautiful woman was the saddest of all subjects and therefore the most appropriate for his purpose. The theme of a love that can survive even death is a familiar one in his work, while the atmosphere of intense gloom, even of despair (into which the speaker is plunged by the raven's repetition of the refrain) is also characteristic. The poem ends with the speaker's conviction, implanted by the raven's repeated answer, that he can never hope to rejoin his "lost Lenore." The refrain appears in stanza 8, which reads:

> Then this ebony bird beguiling my sad fancy
>   into smiling
> By the grave and stern decorum of the coun-
>   tenance it wore,
> "Though thy crest be shorn and shaven,
>   thou," I said, "art sure no craven,
> Ghastly grim and ancient Raven wandering
>   from the Nightly shore—
> Tell me what thy lordly name is on the
>   Night's Plutonian shore!"
> **Quoth the Raven "Nevermore."**

The race is not to the swift

Source: ECCLESIASTES 9:11
Author: Unknown
First transcribed: c.250-200 B.C.
Type of work: Religious confession

Context: The writer, to whom life is "vanity of vanities," holds that man's brief existence is of complete futility. Man's search after wisdom or pleasure leads inevitably to the grave. Governed by strict laws of nature and the purposelessness of life, man becomes no more than an animal, which also ends in the grave. Although wisdom is folly, the wise man knows that he can choose between the less vain things of the world and approach a kind of peace. Failing to understand the prosperity of the wicked and the suffering of the good and realizing that he cannot know the ways of God, the writer laments the fact of the grave, accepts what enjoyment he can from food, family, and labor, and notes again the defeat of the worthy:

> I returned, and saw under the sun, that **the race is not to the swift,** nor the battle to the strong, neither yet bread to wise, nor yet riches to men of understanding, nor yet favor to men of skill; but time and chance happeneth to them all.

Rachel weeping for her children

Source: MATTHEW 2:18
Author: Unknown (traditionally Matthew the Apostle)
First transcribed: c.75-100
Type of work: Gospel

Context: At the birth of Jesus, the Magi or wise men, seeing "his star in the east," travel to Jerusalem where they ask Herod the whereabouts of the one "born King of the JEWS." Troubled by the threat to his power, Herod tells them to find the child that he too may worship the new King. After paying homage to the Christ and being warned in a dream not to return to Herod, the wise men go immediately to their own country. Joseph, told by an angel of Herod's plan to kill the child, takes his family and flees into Egypt. Furious with the Magi, Herod orders that all male children two years old or under be killed, thus causing a tragedy comparable to the exile of the tribes of the north, over whom Rachel, the mother of Joseph and Benjamin and of the northern tribes, sorrowed (Jeremiah 31:15). Her tomb is at Rama, between Jerusalem and Bethlehem:

> In Rama was there a voice heard, lamentation, and weeping, and great mourning, **Rachel weeping for her children,** and would not be comforted, because they are not.

A rag and a bone and a hank of hair

Source: THE VAMPIRE (Stanza 1)
Author: Rudyard Kipling (1865-1936)
First published: 1897
Type of work: Lyric poem

Context: This bitter poem, associated with a painting by Philip Burne-Jones, is Kipling's picture of a man who wastes his life on a worthless woman, one who "did not understand." His substance, his honor, and his faith are thrown away, until "the fool was stripped to his foolish hide"— then the woman casually discards him. Throughout the poem runs the mocking refrain "Even as you and I" —most men are like the fool of the story. It is easy to understand why the poem called forth some rather violent replies from feminine writers.

> A fool there was and he made his prayer
> (Even as you and I!)
> To **a rag and a bone and a hank of hair**
> (We called her the woman who did not care)
> But the fool he called her his lady fair—
> (Even as you and I!)

Rain cats and dogs

Source: POLITE CONVERSATIONS (Dialogue II)
Author: Jonathan Swift (1667-1745)
First published: 1738
Type of work: Dialogue

Context: Swift's dialogues are his attempt to revive what he thought to be the dying art of conversation. He collected a large number of "polite expressions" which he thought suitable for genteel and fashionable society and worked them into dialogues. He believed, like Plato, that the dialogue is "the best way of inculcating any part of knowledge." His heroine, so to speak, is Miss Notable. Her masculine counterpart is Mr. Thomas Neverout. To these two people he has given choice lines, in the hope that they will serve as examples for "all young bachelors and single ladies to copy after." The setting of this dialogue is the home of Lady Smart, at the dinner-hour. Sir John Linger, a guest who had the misfortune to be born an outsider to "the circle of politeness," is preparing to leave the group:

LADY SMART
   Well; but, Sir John, when may we hope to see you again in
   London?

SIR JOHN

Why, madam, not till the ducks have eat up the dirt; as the children say.

NEVEROUT

Come, Sir John; I foresee it will rain terribly.

LORD SMART

Come, Sir John, do nothing rashly; let us drink first.

LORD SPARKISH

I know Sir John will go, though he was sure it would **rain cats and dogs. . . .**

Raise a hue and cry

Source: DON QUIXOTE (Part I, Book III, chapter 8)
Author: Miguel de Cervantes Saavedra (1547-1616)
First published: 1605
Type of work: Satirical novel

Context: "Hue," originally an imitative word, like "hoot," is the basis of Old French *huer*. Here it makes a couplet with "cry." Ben Jonson coupled them in the title of his masque *The Hue and Cry after Cupid* (1608). At this point in his adventures, Don Quixote is convinced that the galley slaves whom he has encountered deserve freedom. He attacks and unhorses their guard with the carbine, the prisoners turn on the others, Sancho releases Ginés Passamonte from his gyves, and all the prisoners take to their heels, afraid of the religious constabulary, the Holy Brotherhood, that keeps order on the roads of Spain. Cervantes narrates what happens next:

> . . . Sancho, who was always for taking care of the main chance, was not at all pleased with this victory; for he guessed that the guards who had fled would **raise a hue and cry,** and soon be at their heels with the whole posse of the Holy Brotherhood. . . .

The rank is but the guinea's stamp

Source: FOR A' THAT (Stanza 1)
Author: Robert Burns (1759-1796)
First published: 1795
Type of work: Didactic poem

Context: Burns's last years were spent in an atmosphere of social unrest characterized by the writings of Tom Paine and by the French Revolution, unrest that caused strife and persecution in a Scotland still largely feudal. Only in 1775 was a law passed forbidding the buying and selling of men and women in the mines and salt works. Though the political position of Burns is still argued among his biographers, in "Is There, for Honest Poverty?" we can see clearly that his basic sense of the innate worth of each man has deepened into true belief in equality and frater- nity. It is well for us to remember that it was not popular then to say, "It's coming yet, for a' that/ That man to man the warld o'er/ Shall brothers be for a' that." It was not prudent to declare, "A prince can mak a belted knight,/ A marquis, duke, and a' that,/ But an honest man's aboon his might." And it was not wise to state that the gold lay in the man himself, not in his minted mark of social position:

> Is there, for honest poverty,
>   That hings his head, an' a' that?
> The coward slave, we pass him by,
>   We dare be poor for a' that!
>   For a' that, an a' that,
>   Our toils obscure, an' a' that;
> **The rank is but the guinea's stamp;**
> The man's the gowd for a' that.

The rare few, who early in life, have rid themselves of the friendship of the many

Source: THE GENTLE ART OF MAKING ENEMIES ("Dedication")
Author: James McNeill Whistler (1834-1903)
First published: 1890
Type of work: Literary record

Context: Whistler had made a name for himself not only as an artist, but as a most independent person to whom customs, conventions, and status were meaningless. He developed, partly as a result of his quarrel with the world in general, a rough and irascible exterior, and delighted in bitter feuds and vigorous disputes, many of them with art critics; they, like most of humanity, struck him as intellectually incompetent. Whistler compiled records, edited and sometimes changed by himself, of some of his battles with art critics, and saw the material published under the title *The Gentle Art of Making Enemies.* Fittingly, the book is dedicated to the independent minority who follow their own lights rather than troop along with the crowd, for Whistler felt that the mind of the masses is inconsiderable and hopeless of improvement.

DEDICATION
**To the rare Few, who early in Life,
have rid Themselves of the Friendship
of the Many,** these pathetic Papers are inscribed.

821

Rather than be less, cared not to be at all

Source: PARADISE LOST (Book II, ll. 47-48)
Author: John Milton (1608-1674)
First published: 1667
Type of work: Epic poem

Context: Upon building their capital, Pandemonium, in Hell, the leaders of the rebel angels hold a solemn council. Satan, the leader of all, opens the debate, saying that war must continue against God. The only question for debate in the council is to be whether the recently defeated rebels should continue open warfare against God's hosts or whether they should try to regain Heaven by guile. Moloch, one of Satan's lieutenants, who is described as a sceptered king among the warrior spirits, rises first to speak in the great discussion. He is "the strongest and the fiercest spirit/ That fought in Heaven." He has no fear "of God, or Hell, or worse." Milton says of Moloch:

> His trust was with the Eternal to be deemed
> Equal in strength, and **rather than be less**
> **Cared not to be at all.**

Read, mark, learn and inwardly digest

Source: THE BOOK OF COMMON PRAYER (Page 92)
Author: Traditional; translated and arranged by Archbishop Cranmer (1489-1560)
First published: 1549
Type of work: Prayer

Context: The prayer in which this quotation appears is in the form of a collect. The word collect, meaning "gathered to-gether," originally referred to the congregation assembled, but gradually has become to mean the gathering to-gether of the prayers of the people. Its form, which comes from the Roman liturgy, consists of four parts: 1. an opening address to God; 2. a single petition with a statement of the result hoped for by its granting; 3. a pleading in Christ's name; and, 4. a concluding doxology (often omitted in the Prayer Book collects). This form may easily be traced in the beautiful Collect for the Second Sunday in Advent from the Book of Common Prayer, in which the petitioner prays for the wisdom to understand God's Word in Holy Scriptures, to the attainment of everlasting life:

> Blessed Lord, who has caused all holy Scriptures to be written
> for our learning; Grant that we may in such wise hear them,

read, mark, learn, and inwardly digest them, that by patience and comfort of thy Holy Word, we may embrace, and ever hold fast, the blessed hope of everlasting life, which thou hast given us in our Saviour Jesus Christ. *Amen.*

The real simon-pure

Source: A BOLD STROKE FOR A WIFE (Act V, sc. i)
Author: Susannah Centlivre (1667?-1723)
First published: 1718
Type of work: Dramatic comedy

Context: This sprightly, sophisticated eighteenth century comedy is full of wit, charm, and thoroughgoing good humor. It is doubtless one of the reasons why comedies of the period gained a reputation for daring. For example, one of the characters remarks that "Women, like some poisonous animals, carry their Antidote about 'em"; and she who speaks the Epilogue entertains the hope that she will find her spouse "a Man of War in Bed." The plot is frightfully complex. Colonel Fainwell is enamored of Mrs. Lovely, "a Fortune of Thirty Thousand Pounds"; but her father, who hated posterity, left her the fortune on condition she marry with the consent of four guardians he had selected for their inability to agree on anything. The plot thickens when one of the guardians, a fundamentalist, produces a candidate named Simon Pure. The Colonel, in disguise, arrives first and passes himself off as Pure. When the real Simon appears, one of the Colonel's friends provides him with a letter warning of an impostor; love triumphs eventually, the guardians are confounded, and Colonel Fainwell and Mrs. (Miss) Lovely are wed. In the letter which served to dispatch Simon Pure to his place of origin, Fainwell's friend had stated in tones of alarm that he

. . . did not doubt but he should impose so far upon you, as to make you turn out **the real Simon Pure.** . . .

The real war will never get in the books

Source: SPECIMEN DAYS ("The Real War Will Never Get in the Books")
Author: Walt Whitman (1819-1892)
First published: 1882-1883
Type of work: Personal chronicle

Context: Whitman, middle-aged at the outbreak of the Civil War, contributed his services as attendant to the wounded and diseased in some of the military hospitals. In this position he saw, as few civilians did, the

823

sufferings, and often the deaths, of many soldiers from both sides, and listened to accounts of their terrible experiences. To Whitman, the scenes in the hospitals presented the true essence of war, and he knew that very little of this would ever find representation in histories, which deal with generalities: campaigns, strategies, and issues.

> Future years will never know the seething hell and the black infernal backgrounds of countless minor scenes and interiors, (not the official surface-courteousness of the Generals, not the few great battles) of the Secession war; and it is best they should not —**the real war will never get in the books.** In the mushy influences of current times, too, the fervid atmosphere and typical events of those years are in danger of being totally forgotten . . .

Reason lies between the spur and the bridle

Source: JACULA PRUDENTUM (Number 711)
Author: George Herbert (1593-1633)
First published: 1640
Type of work: Proverbial sayings

Context: George Herbert in *Jacula Prudentum,* No. 711, says that reason lies between the spur and the bridle, that is, between being urged forward and being restrained. Although only one other person has recorded this idea in somewhat similar language— Richard Brathwaite in *Art Asleep, Husband?* (1640): "But as virtue receives her proper station in the mean, so all extremes decline from that mark"—the general idea has been popular for well over two thousand years. The most famous treatment is that by Aristotle (384-322 B.C.), in the *Nichomachean Ethics,* where he treats the golden mean. The mean, he says, is a great virtue; it always, however, lies between two extremes, both of which are undesirable in themselves and may be absolute vices; thus courage lies between fear and foolhardiness. Aristotle is careful to note that the mean is never midway between the extremes, but is always nearer one than the other, as courage is nearer to foolhardiness than to fear. Temperance is a mean between abstemiousness and licentiousness, being closer to abstemiousness. Herbert, however, has given the idea a good homely turn:

Reason lies between the spur and the bridle.

Reigned the sceptered monarch of the dead

Source: THE ODYSSEY (Book XI, 1. 597, as translated by Alexander Pope)
Author: Homer (c.850 B.C.)
First transcribed: Sixth century B.C.
Type of work: Epic poem

Context: Odysseus, the wily one, wandering nearly ten years since the ten-year seige of Troy, is finally to discover his fate. Circe, the sorceress, has directed him to the land of the Cimmerians, so that he can summon from Hades Teiresias, the blind soothsayer of great fame. While there the hero speaks to his dead mother, and to his friends, among them the great warrior Achilles. Trying to comfort the slain hero, Odysseus pays him a compliment: "Alive we hail'd thee with our guardian gods,/ And dead thou rulest a king in these abodes." Achilles replies with the oft-quoted passage celebrating life:

> "Talk not of ruling in this dolorous gloom,
>   Nor think vain words (he cried) can ease my doom.
>   Rather I'd choose laboriously to bear
>   A weight of woes, and breathe the vital air
>   A slave to some poor hind that toils for bread,
>   Than **reign the sceptred monarch of the dead!"**

Reluctant dragons

Source: THE RING AND THE BOOK ("The Pope," Line 1190)
Author: Robert Browning (1812-1889)
First published: 1868-1869
Type of work: Dramatic monologue

Context: In a long series of twelve dramatic monologues, Browning examined, from various points of view, the complicated story of a murder that occurred in Rome in 1698. Each character involved in the intricate plot is allowed to analyze the situation and his part in it. One speaker, Pope Innocent XII, must pass final judgment, for he must determine whether Count Guido Franceschini, who committed the murder, is to be executed or pardoned. The Pope, therefore, reviews the story in an attempt to assess the motives and actions of each participant. In considering the problem of temptation, the Pontiff concludes that it is sent so that man can meet and master it. Using the figure of speech of St. George conquering the dragon, the Pope asks God to send temptation so that man's strength may be tested and rewarded:

> Yea, but, O Thou whose servants are the bold,
> Lead such temptations by the head and hair,

Reluctant dragons, up to who dares fight,
That so he may do battle and have praise!

Remember the Alamo!

Source: BATTLE CRY AT SAN JACINTO, TEXAS
Author: Colonel Sidney Sherman (1805-1873)
First spoken: April 21, 1836
Type of work: Battle slogan

Context: A chapel in San Antonio, Texas, named El Alamo from the cotton wood used in its construction, was fortified by a handful of Texas revolutionists in December, 1835. They defended it against several thousand Mexican soldiers under General Antonio López de Santa Ana (1795-1876) until their ammunition gave out. Then all 184 of the defenders, including Davy Crockett, James Bowie, and William Travis, were killed in hand-to-hand fighting on March 6. Indignation at their death brought help from many parts of the United States, including a company of volunteers from Cincinnati, Ohio, under Col. Sidney Sherman, which formed Company 2 of General Sam Houston's army when it met the Mexicans at San Jacinto on April 21, 1836. Colonel Sherman provided their rallying cry when he shouted:

Remember the Alamo!

Remembered joys are never past

Source: THE LITTLE CLOUD
Author: James Montgomery (1771-1854)
First published: 1835
Type of work: Lyric poem

Context: James Montgomery, called by his early editor R. W. Griswold the "head of the religious poets of the present age," expresses the fervor of his devotion in this lyric poem describing the beauty of a cloud and its effect upon the soul of the observer. Gazing over the countryside during an excursion among the woods and rocks of Wharncliffe in 1818, the poet feels the presence of God in the beauty of nature. In particular his eye is caught by a fleecy, gold-lined cloud gleaming in the sun—for a moment he almost expects Raphael to step from the "splendid mystery." But with dusk the cloud recedes into the darkness and leaves only its image in the mind of the poet. Much like Wordsworth, who recollects "emotion in tranquillity" by imaginatively recreating "spots of time," Montgomery asserts that the beauty of this moment "lives within me; this shall be/ A part of my eternity." The poem closes:

> Bliss in possession will not last;
> **Remember'd joys are never past;**
> At once the fountain, stream, and sea,
> They were,—they are,—they yet shall be.

Remembrance of things past

Source: SONNET 30 (Line 2)
Author: William Shakespeare (1564-1616)
First published: 1609
Type of work: Lyric poem

Context: In this sonnet the poet dwells on the lamentable waste of time in his past, and this idea leads him to thoughts of his dead friends for whom he freshly grieves. But if, in the midst of these melancholy thoughts on death and loss, he can think of the friend addressed in the poem, his sorrows end and losses are as naught. The entire sonnet follows:

> When to the sessions of sweet silent thought
> I summon up **remembrance of things past,**
> I sigh the lack of many a thing I sought,
> And with old woes new wail my dear times' waste.
> Then can I drown an eye, unus'd to flow,
> For precious friends hid in deaths dateless night,
> And weep afresh loves' long since cancell'd woe,
> And moan th' expense of many a vanish'd sight.
> Then can I grieve at grievances foregone,
> And heavily from woe to woe tell o'er
> The sad account of fore-bemoaned moan,
> Which I new pay as if not paid before.
> > But if the while I think on thee, dear friend,
> > All losses are restor'd, and sorrows end.

Render therefore unto Caesar the things which are Caesar's

Source: MATTHEW 22:21
Author: Unknown (traditionally Matthew the Apostle)
First transcribed: c.75-100
Type of work: Gospel

Context: Jesus, having entered Jerusalem, is confronted by the chief priests and Pharisees, who question His authority as the prophet that the

827

people hold Him to be. When He teaches of the Kingdom of Heaven in a number of pointed parables, the Pharisees set out to trap Him by posing a question, the answer to which could involve Him in political difficulty. Asked whether or not it is lawful to pay taxes to Caesar, Jesus tells them to bring Him a coin, and then explains man's duty to the earthly kingdom of Caesar and to the spiritual kingdom of God. In no sense, however, does He mean them to be equal, for even Caesar is beneath God:

> And he saith unto them, Whose is this image and superscription?
> They say unto him, Caesar's. Then saith he unto them, **Render therefore unto Caesar the things which are Caesar's;** and unto God the things that are God's.
> When they had heard these words, they marveled, and left him, and went their way.

Resolved to ruin or to rule the State

Source: ABSALOM AND ACHITOPHEL (Part I, l. 174)
Author: John Dryden (1631-1700)
First published: 1681
Type of work: Satiric poem

Context: John Dryden, who later himself became a Roman Catholic, was bitter in his denunciation of the plot to substitute the Duke of Monmouth for the Duke of York as the heir to the British throne, to succeed Charles II. The conservative Tories, and Dryden was one, felt that the danger of having the Duke of York, a Catholic, succeed to the throne, was much less a danger than that of setting aside the constitutional succession. As a result of Dryden's view, the Earl of Shaftesbury, who aided by the Duke of Buckingham led the plot, is harshly treated as Achitophel in the poem, as this quotation shows:

> In Friendship False, Implacable in Hate:
> **Resolv'd to Ruine or to Rule the State.**
> To Compass this the Triple Bond he broke;
> The Pillars of the publick Safety shook:
> And fitted Israel for a foreign Yoke.
> Then, seiz'd with Fear, yet still affecting Fame,
> Usurp'd a Patriott's All-attoning Name.

Retired to their tea and scandal

Source: THE DOUBLE-DEALER (Act I, sc. i)
Author: William Congreve (1670-1729)
First published: 1694
Type of work: Dramatic comedy

Context: The scene of this play is a gallery in the house of Lord Touchwood, at about five o'clock in the evening. Dinner has been served and eaten. The ladies have left the dining-room, giving the gentlemen time and place for drinking, as was the custom. Careless has left the dining-room and his fellow drinkers because they have become noisy and nonsensical. Following after Careless is Mellefont, Lord Touchwood's nephew and the hero of the play, who will save Cynthia, his beloved, from the evil machinations of Maskwell and Lady Touchwood. Mellefont asks Careless if he has "turn'd flincher." Careless replies in the negative, adding that women's voices are more musical than men's, so that their nonsense is at least a little more bearable. When he inquires the whereabouts of the ladies of the dinner-party, he receives the following reply:

MELLEFONT
Why, they are at the end of the Gallery; **retired to their Tea and Scandal,** according to their Ancient Custome, after Dinner.—But I made a pretence to follow you, because I had something to say to you in private, and I am not like to have many opportunities this Evening.

The Retort Courteous

Source: AS YOU LIKE IT (Act V, sc. iv, l. 75)
Author: William Shakespeare (1564-1616)
First published: 1623
Type of work: Dramatic comedy

Context: As the play nears its end, Duke Senior, Jaques, and all the other friends of the Duke are met in the forest. Rosalind is about to make everybody happy by having all lovers marry whom they love. Touchstone, the "motley-gentleman" as Jaques calls him, enters, and to prove that he has been a courtier, says that he has "trod a measure," has "flattered a lady," been "politic" with his friend, "smooth" with his enemy, has "undone three tailors," has had "four quarrels, and like to have fought one." This man, whom the Duke calls "swift and sententious," explains how he found "the quarrel on the seventh cause":

TOUCHSTONE
Upon a lie seven times removed. . . . I did dislike the cut of a certain courtier's beard. He sent me word, if I said his beard was

829

not cut well, he was in the mind it was. This is called **the Retort Courteous.** If I sent him word again, it was not well cut, he would send me word he cut it to please himself. This is called the Quip Modest. If again, it was not well cut, he disabled my judgment. This is called the Reply Churlish. If again, it was not well cut, he would answer I spake not true. This is called the Reproof Valiant. If again, it was not well cut, he would say I lie. This is called the Countercheck Quarrelsome; and so to the Lie Circumstantial and Lie Direct.

Rich in saving common sense

Source: ODE ON THE DEATH OF THE DUKE OF WELLINGTON (Line 32)
Author: Alfred, Lord Tennyson (1809-1892)
First published: 1852
Type of work: Elegiac ode

Context: This funeral ode to Wellington, the great English soldier whose armies defeated Napoleon I near Waterloo, attempts to portray the man as well as the leader. Tennyson calls him "The last great Englishman," for he had the noblest qualities of mind and of heart and gave all of his great abilities to the service of his country. His passing is a national tragedy: "our chief state-oracle is mute"; his was "the voice from which their omens all men drew. . . ." But for those who knew him, the loss is of a rare man who never let position and power overcome his perspective or sense of values. He was

> of amplest influence,
> Yet clearest of ambitious crime,
> Our greatest yet with least pretence,
> Great in council and great in war,
> Foremost captain of his time,
> **Rich in saving common-sense,**
> And, as the greatest only are,
> In his simplicity sublime.

Rich, not gaudy

Source: HAMLET (Act I, sc. iii, l. 71)
Author: William Shakespeare (1564-1616)
First published: 1603
Type of work: Dramatic tragedy

Context: This pithy saying is usually heard as "rich but not gaudy" and implies the person or thing referred to has or reflects good taste and quiet

830

costliness, or an avoidance of the ear-marks of a *parvenu*. In a letter to his friend William Wordsworth in 1806, Charles Lamb coined the phrase, "neat, not gaudy" which conveys the same sense of discrimination but in a slightly modified form. It does not imply wealth or riches in the connota-tion. In *Hamlet,* Polonius, the chief councilor to King Claudius of Den-mark, bids his son Laertes farewell just before the young man embarks from Elsinore for France. The father continues at length, with much ad-vice:

POLONIUS
. . .

Beware
Of entrance to a quarrel, but being in,
Bear't that th' opposed may beware of thee.
Give every man thy ear, but few thy voice;
Take each man's censure, but reserve thy judgement.
Costly thy habit as thy purse can buy,
But not expressed in fancy; **rich, not gaudy,**
For the apparel oft proclaims the man;
. . .

Riches have wings

Source: THE TASK (Book III, l. 263)
Author: William Cowper (1731-1800)
First published: 1785
Type of work: Meditative poem in blank verse

Context: In addition to being reli-gious to the point of madness, Cowper was strongly influenced by the Evangelical Movement of his day. Consequently, there is much moral-izing and sermonizing in his poetry (see "Variety's the very spice of life"). The line quoted above follows a passage on the vanity of earthly wisdom—"God never meant that man should scale the heav'ns/ By strides of human wisdom" (ll. 221-222). We must make no attempt to learn about the world by our own effort, but must look to God alone for wisdom. The "philosophic tube,/ That brings the planets home into the eye" (ll. 229-230) will not discover God. The more we learn for our-selves, the more prone we are to over-look God. It is the function of philos-ophy, "baptiz'd/ In the pure fountain of eternal love . . . to indicate a God to man" (ll. 243-246). Men like Newton, Milton, and Hale are "friends of science and true pray'r" (l. 250). The apparent source of Cowper's line on riches is Proverbs 23:5—"Wilt thou set thine eyes upon that which is not? for riches certainly make themselves wings; they fly away as an eagle toward heaven." In context, Cowper's lines read:

831

All flesh is grass, and all its glory fades
Like the fair flow'r dishevell'd in the wind;
Riches have wings, and grandeur is a dream:
The man we celebrate must find a tomb,
And we that worship him ignoble graves.

Rides in the whirlwind and directs the storm

Source: THE CAMPAIGN (Last stanza)
Author: Joseph Addison (1672-1719)
First published: 1705
Type of work: Patriotic poem

Context: After some time abroad (1699-1703) on a grand tour of Europe, Joseph Addison returned to England to resume his career—already having gained some fame as a man of letters and possessing a reputation at Oxford as a writer of verse in Latin. Following the printing of a poem called "Letter from Italy," dedicated to his patron, the Earl of Halifax, came his greatest success up to that time, a patriotic tribute to the victories of the Duke of Marlborough, called "The Campaign." The poem, which in the main celebrated the victory of Marlborough at the Battle of Blenheim, is thought to have won for Addison the post of Undersecretary of State. The poem builds to a dramatic end, conjures up the excitement of battle, and lauds the heroic spirit of Marlborough:

. . . great Marlbro's mighty soul was prov'd,
That, in the shock of charging hosts unmov'd,
Amidst confusion, horror, and despair,
Examin'd all the dreadful scenes of war;
In peaceful thought the field of death survey'd,
To fainting squadrons sent the timely aid,
Inspir'd repuls'd battalions to engage,

• • •

Calm and serene he drives the furious blast;
And pleas'd th' Almighty's orders to perform,
Rides in the whirlwind, and directs the storm.

The right divine of Kings to govern wrong

Source: THE DUNCIAD (Book IV, l. 188)
Author: Alexander Pope (1688-1744)
First published: 1728-1743
Type of work: Satirical poem

Context: In Book IV of the poem, Pope shows the Goddess of Dulness coming, as he puts it, "to destroy Order and Science, and to substitute the

Kingdom of the Dull upon earth." About the goddess cluster many persons, who are vain, tasteless half-wits and pretenders to wit and wisdom. Representatives of the schools come forward to tell the goddess they help her cause by never permitting the door of learning to stand open very wide. They say, "We ply the memory, we load the Brain,/ Bind rebel wit, and double chain on chain." Dulness is quite pleased and says she wishes some pedant might rule the nation as well as his fellows rule the schools. She wishes for "Some gentle James, to bless the land again," the satire being aimed at the pedantry of James I. The goddess continues:

> "For sure if Dulness sees a grateful day,
> 'Tis in the shade of arbitrary sway.
> O! if my sons may learn one earthly thing,
> Teach but that one, sufficient for a King;
> That which my priests, and mine alone, maintain,
> Which, as it dies, or lives, we fall, or reign":
>
> • • •
>
> **"The right divine of Kings to govern wrong."**

Right makes might

Source: ADDRESS AT COOPER UNION, NEW YORK CITY
Author: Abraham Lincoln (1809-1865)
First published: 1860
Type of work: Political speech

Context: Lincoln refutes the Southern charges against the Republican Party. He denies that his party is sectional: "you will probably soon find that we have ceased to be sectional, for we shall get votes in your section this very year." The Southerners constantly refer to George Washington and Constitutional principles; but Lincoln points out that the Constitution did not condone slavery and that Washington himself condemned it. Thus Lincoln's Republicans are the real conservatives. Lincoln denies the charge that the Republicans "stir up insurrections" among the slaves. The federal government does not have the right to emancipate the slaves, but it does have "the power of restraining the extension of the institution." The nation is turning against slavery, and the Southerners cannot crush this trend by destroying the Republican Party. Refuting a Supreme Court decision, Lincoln says that the Constitution does not provide for the right to hold slaves as property. He castigates the South for threatening to destroy the Union. Then he counsels the Republicans to maintain peace and harmony. But he says the South would not be satisfied unless the Republicans condoned slavery. Republicans must fight the spread of slavery:

. . . Neither let us be slandered from our duty by false accusations against us, nor frightened from it by menaces of destruction to the government, nor of dungeons to ourselves. Let us have faith that **right makes might,** and in that faith let us to the end dare to do our duty as we understand it.

The right of conquest

Source: THE SOCIAL CONTRACT (Book I, chapter 4)
Author: Jean Jacques Rousseau (1712-1778)
First published: 1762
Type of work: Political treatise

Context: Rousseau's *Social Contract* attempts to establish that the authority of the people is absolute. To begin, he endeavors to prove that free-born men have fallen into slavery because of misconceptions of what constitutes right. In political societies strength is the basis for right; and strength leads to the use of force and to war and conquest. Conquest, then, also becomes a basis for right, but, writes Rousseau,

> With regard to **the right of conquest,** it has no foundation other than the law of the strongest. If war does not confer on the victor the right of slaying the vanquished, this right, which he does not possess, cannot be the foundation of a right to enslave them. If we have a right to slay an enemy only when it is impossible to enslave him, the right to enslave him is not derived from the right to kill him; it is, therefore, an iniquitous bargain to make him purchase his life, over which the victor has no right, at the cost of his liberty. In establishing the right of life and death upon the right of slavery, and the right of slavery upon the right of life and death, is it not manifest that one falls into a vicious circle?

Ring out, wild bells

Source: IN MEMORIAM (Part CVI, stanza 1)
Author: Alfred, Lord Tennyson (1809-1892)
First published: 1850
Type of work: Elegy

Context: It is New Year's eve, and the poet cries to the pealing bells to proclaim the coming of a new year. He looks at the year that is ending, and at all the errors, confusions, griefs, sins, and evils it contained, and hopes that all of this injury and wrong will die with the year, and disappear from human society. His vision of the future is of extreme idealism as he considers all the potentiality for good that the human spirit contains and all its possibilities to ascend, through faith in God, to exalted planes of being.

834

Ring out, wild bells, to the wild sky,
   The flying cloud, the frosty light:
   The year is dying in the night;
Ring out, wild bells, and let him die.

                •   •   •

Ring in the valiant man and free,
   The larger heart, the kindlier hand;
   Ring out the darkness of the land,
Ring in the Christ that is to be.

Ripeness is all

Source: KING LEAR (Act V, sc. ii, l. 11)
Author: William Shakespeare (1564-1616)
First published: 1608
Type of work: Dramatic tragedy

Context: The Earl of Gloucester has two sons. One, Edgar, is legitimate, the other, Edmund, was born out of wedlock. Edumnd schemes to turn the father against Edgar and deprive him of his birthright. Edgar, alarmed, flees into hiding disguised as Tom, the madman. Meanwhile, the King of Britain, Lear, has foolishly given his kingdom to two of his daughters, Goneril and Regan. They, conspiring against him, strip him of his followers, abuse him, and turn him out of doors. Accompanied only by his jester, King Lear curses his daughters, wanders the heath in a storm, and hurls defiance at the elements. Cold, miserable, enraged, and near the edge of madness, Lear and his fool are rescued by the Earl of Gloucester, who befriends him despite an injunction by Goneril and Regan not to do so. Regan and her husband discover his defection and brutally blind him. Turned loose to wander where he will, Gloucester encounters his son, Edgar. Now, near Dover, in a field between two armies, Edgar urges his father on. But Gloucester is tired of fleeing: if he is to die he is content to die here. Edgar rallies him.

                EDGAR
What, in ill thoughts again? Men must endure
Their going hence, even as their coming hither;
Ripeness is all. Come on.

                GLOUCESTER
                        And that's true too.

835

The ripest peach is highest on the tree

Source: THE RIPEST PEACH (Stanza 1)
Author: James Whitcomb Riley (1849-1916)
First published: 1881
Type of work: Lyric poem

Context: In the poem "The Ripest Peach," James Whitcomb Riley, a poet of American nature, compares his beloved to the ripest peach, which, he says, is highest on the tree. Through his metaphor the poet expresses the innate urge of man to strive to attain the things that are beyond his grasp. The poet says that from his position in the orchard "Such fruitage as her love I know, alas!/ I may not reach. . . ." Yet he can "drink the sunshine showered past her lips/ As roses drain the dewdrop as it drips." Continuing his metaphor, the poet asks why he does not choose some heart hanging in his path since "Love's lower boughs bend with them— . . ." The answer is the line that opens the poem and appears in each stanza:

> **The ripest peach is highest on the tree—**
> And so her love, beyond the reach of me,
> Is dearest in my sight. Sweet breezes, bow
> Her heart down to me where I worship now!

Rob Peter to pay Paul

Source: GARGANTUA AND PANTAGRUEL (Book I, chapter 11)
Author: François Rabelais (1495-1553)
First published: (1532-1564)
Type of work: Mock heroic chronicle

Context: Gargantua, the gigantic son of Grangosier and Gargamelle, was physically precocious as a youth, although his actions differed more in degree than kind from those of other youngsters. Rabelais has him engage in almost every kind of activity. He experiments with and apparently believes in all the superstitions of his day. Also, he breathes the cliches and commonplaces. The proverb about robbing Peter to pay Paul was widespread. It was used by John Heywood in *Proverbes* (1546), Part I, chapter 11, by Robert Burton in *Anatomy of Melancholy* (1621-1561), *Democritus to the Reader,* and by many other writers. The expression apparently got its origin in the reign of Edward VI, when the lands of St. Peter at Westminster were taken in order that money might be raised for the repair of St. Paul's in London. Rabelais uses the expression thus, speaking about Gargantua:

By **robbing Peter he paid Paul,** he kept the moon from the wolves, and hoped to catch larks if ever the heavens should fall. He did make of necessity virtue, of such bread such pottage, and cared as little for the peeled as for the shaven.

The robbed that smiles, steals something from the thief

Source: OTHELLO (Act I, sc. iii, 1. 208)
Author: William Shakespeare (1564-1616)
First published: 1622
Type of work: Dramatic tragedy

Context: Othello, a Moor and a military commander in the service of Venice, elopes with Desdemona, daughter of a Venetian senator, Brabantio. Brought before the duke by the irate father, and accused of using witchcraft to win the girl, Othello denies the charge, sends for his bride, and relates how he courted Desdemona. She comes to the duke's council chamber. Brabantio immediately puts her to a test of affection—she must choose between her husband and him. She chooses Othello. To comfort the grieving father, the duke offers sage advice.

DUKE

• • •

When remedies are past, the griefs are ended
By seeing the worst, which late on hopes depended.
To mourn a mischief that is past and gone
Is the next way to draw new mischief on.
What cannot be preserved when fortune takes,
Patience her injury a mockery makes.
The robbed that smiles, steals something from the thief;
He robs himself, that spends a bootless grief.

A rolling stone gathers no moss

Source: SENTENTIAE (Maxim 524)
Author: Publilius Syrus (First century B.C.)
First transcribed: c.42 B.C.
Type of work: Moral sentences

Context: The disputed authorship of many of these copybook sentences, perhaps used as models for the education of the young, gives rise to many theories concerning these familiar quotations. They were first attributed to Seneca, but Pliny and others give evidence of a slave from Syrus who was a mime in the first century B.C., having arrived in Rome with the astronomer Manilius and the grammarian Staberius. His plays seem to have been admired during the Augustan age and survived, according to Petronius, to the time of Nero, and the writer himself may have lived into the Christian era. In the Middle Ages the texts were bowdlerized and misplaced, and it is certain that the accretion of maxims under this name is not definitely Publius', as he is popularly called. The proverb is current today, having come to us from many sources, among which are John Heywood's *"The rolling stone never gathereth mosse"* (1546) and Tusser's *"The stone that is rolling can gather no moss."* (1557) The meaning remains constant: it is not a good thing to be always on the move, for stability gives repose and wealth. The popular version of the saying is:

A rolling stone gathers no moss.

Rome was not built in a day

Source: THE PROVERBS OF JOHN HEYWOOD (Part I, chapter 11)
Author: John Heywood (1497?-1580?)
First published: 1546
Type of work: Gnomic poetry

Context: The author is telling about a young couple who married in haste against the wishes of their aunts and uncles. He is quoting every proverb he can think of to prove his point that those who marry early usually have a long time in which to repent. In the story, the young husband is telling about returning to the home of his aunt and uncle and being coolly received. The uncle tells him that he is just like his parents; they too married for love when they did not have a penny to live on. Finally, exasperated, the uncle turns the young fellow out. Filled with dismay, he stalks away, being comforted by an old friend, who reassures him that everything will come out right in the long run. "After clouds black," he says, "we shall have weather clear," and, "All this wind shakes no corn!" The young husband responds in the widespread proverb:

> I thank you, (quoth I), but great boast and small roast
> Maketh unsavoury mouths, wherever men host.
> And this boast very unfavourly serveth;
> For while the grass groweth the horse sterveth;
> Better one bird in hand than ten in the wood.
> **Rome was not build in one day,** (quoth he), and yet stood
> Till it was finished, as some say, full fair.

838

Roses red and violets blue

Source: THE FAERIE QUEENE (Book III, Canto 6, stanza 6)
Author: Edmund Spenser (c.1552-1599)
First published: 1590
Type of work: Allegorical poem

Context: In this section of the allegory, Chrysogonee is the mother of Belphoebe, the chaste maiden who represents Queen Elizabeth I in Book III of *The Faerie Queene*. Belphoebe and her twin, Amoretta, are conceived in an immaculate manner, after Chrysogonee bathes in the forest, then lies on the grass "all naked bare" and falls asleep. The sunbeams play on her body, enter her womb and make her pregnant. As she is bathing, Spenser says:

> In a fresh fountaine, far from all mens vew,
> She bath'd her brest the boyling heat t'allay;
> She bath'd with **roses red and violets blew,**
> And all the sweetest flowres that in the forrest grew.

Rouse the lion from his lair

Source: THE TALISMAN (Chapter 6)
Author: Sir Walter Scott (1771-1832)
First published: 1825
Type of work: Novel

Context: A Scottish knight, Sir Kenneth, has gone with the forces of Richard the Lion-Hearted on the Third Crusade to the Holy Land. During a truce, while Richard lies ill in his tent amid restive allies, Sir Kenneth is sent across the desert on a mission to the cave of the Christian recluse Theodorick. After speaking to the hermit, Sir Kenneth attends a secret mass during which the king's cousin, the knight's hopeless love, drops rosebuds at his feet. An abrupt change of scene brings the next chapter back to Richard's tent. To prepare the change, Scott, who often followed the custom of including chapter mottoes, opened with lines he probably wrote himself, though he assigned them to an "Old Play":

> Now change the scene—and let the trumpets sound,
> For we must **rouse the lion from his lair.**

Rulers of the Queen's Navee!

Source: H.M.S. PINAFORE (Act I)
Author: W. S. Gilbert (1836-1911)
First published: 1878
Type of work: Light opera

Context: Sir Joseph Porter, First Lord of the Admiralty, arrives aboard the warship *Pinafore,* surrounded by the glory of his position and the adulation of many female relatives. In a song he reveals the course of his progress to his high office, and the secrets of success in the Royal Navy. He began as office boy for an attorney, and, by doing his tasks well, and always with an attention-getting flair, became an attorney himself, and, in time, a member of Parliament. His fundamental qualification as administrator of the navy was that he had never been to sea, and knew nothing of naval science.

SIR JOSEPH
Now, landsmen all, whoever you may be,
If you want to rise to the top of the tree,
If your soul isn't fettered to an office stool,
Be careful to be guided by this golden rule—
Stick close to your desks and never go to sea,
And you all may be **Rulers of the Queen's Navee!**

The Ruling Passion conquers Reason still

Source: MORAL ESSAYS, EPISTLE III (Line 154)
Author: Alexander Pope (1688-1744)
First published: 1731-1735
Type of work: Satirical poem

Context: This epistle, addressed to Lord Bathurst, is in the form of a dialogue between the poet and the nobleman to whom the poem is addressed. The general topic of the dialogue is the use of riches, whether some good line of conduct regarding them, between avarice and prodigality, can be discovered. Pope suggests that some people are motivated in their search for wealth by more than mere desire for gain, that "Some war, some plague or famine, they foresee." He adds that the desire for personal security is often the motivating force behind the drive for wealth. He goes on to say that the desire for money and other forms of wealth can become a force that leads many persons, even entire nations, into cheating one another. Such folly, he concludes, is uncontrolled, even irrational:

P[OPE]
"All this is madness," cries a sober sage: .
But who, my friend, has reason in his rage?

"The Ruling Passion, be it what it will,
The Ruling Passion conquers Reason still."

Ruling passion strong in death

Source: MORAL ESSAYS, EPISTLE I (Line 262)
Author: Alexander Pope (1688-1744)
First published: 1733
Type of work: Satire

Context: Pope's first epistle in this series is a satire "of the knowledge and the character of men," addressed to Sir Richard Temple, Viscount Cobham, an active opponent of Sir Robert Walpole in the eighteenth century. In the third section of this epistle Pope says that we learn the truth about men by finding each one's ruling passion. In their ruling passions, he states, "The wild are constant, and the cunning known;/ The fool consistent, and the false sincere." Even at the point of death, the poet maintains, everyone keeps to his ruling passion: the glutton seeks to eat at his last moment, the miser to save a mite, the vain woman to order her shroud fashionably. Not everyone is selfish in his ruling passion, nor foolish. Pope is certain that Lord Cobham will be a patriot to the very end, as he has been in life.

And you! brave Cobham, to the latest breath
Shall feel your **ruling passion strong in death:**
Such in those moments as in all the past,
"O, save my country, Heav'n!" shall be your last.

The sabbath was made for man

Source: MARK 2:27
Author: Unknown (traditionally Mark the Apostle)
First transcribed: c.60-75
Type of work: Gospel

Context: Jesus, baptized by John and tempted in the wilderness, begins His ministry in the countryside around the Sea of Galilee. One sabbath, as Jesus and His disciples pass through a field, the disciples pluck some grain to eat. The Pharisees ask Jesus why His disciples break the Jewish law by working on the sabbath. Jesus reminds them that David, being hungry, took bread from the altar for himself and his companions (1 Samuel 21:1-6); this act also was a transgression of the Jewish law. Christ then corrects the Pharisees' understanding of the purpose of the sabbath:

And he said unto them, **The sabbath was made for man,** and
not man for the sabbath:
Therefore the Son of man is Lord also of the sabbath.

841

Sabrina fair

Source: COMUS (Line 859)
Author: John Milton (1608-1674)
First published: 1637
Type of work: Masque

Context: Milton wrote this masque to celebrate the installation of the Earl of Bridgewater as President of Wales. The parts were taken by Bridgewater's three children, and the plot deals with their efforts to pass through a "drear wood" to reach their father's castle of Ludlow. The Lady (Lady Alice Egerton, the Earl's daughter) encounters the wicked enchanter Comus, son of Bacchus and Ceres, who tries to seduce her from the path of virtue. He deceives her into accompanying him to his palace where she is seated in an enchanted chair from which she cannot rise. Her brothers, led by a good attendant spirit who takes the name and form of Thyrsis, a follower of the house to which the Lady and her brothers belong, attempt to liberate her by breaking Comus's magic glass, but Comus escapes with his enchanting rod, without which the Lady cannot be freed. The only hope, according to the attendant spirit, is to invoke the aid of the nymph Sabrina, the goddess of the River Severn. Sabrina, who loves maidenhood, will be swift to aid a virgin; the attendant spirit thereupon sings a charming invocation to the nymph, of which this is the first stanza:

> **Sabrina fair,**
> Listen where thou are sitting
> Under the glassy, cool, translucent wave,
> In twisted braids of lilies knitting
> The loose train of thy amber-dropping hair;
> Listen for dear honor's sake,
> Goddess of the silver lake,
> Listen and save.

A sadder and a wiser man, he rose the morrow morn

Source: THE RIME OF THE ANCIENT MARINER (Part VII, stanza 25)
Author: Samuel Taylor Coleridge (1772-1834)
First published: 1798
Type of work: Narrative poem

Context: The two lines of this quotation are the last lines of Coleridge's poem, perhaps the most famous he wrote. It is one of the four poems which appeared in *Lyrical Ballads* as his contributions to that volume written by William Wordsworth and himself. The story of the ancient mariner who is killing an albatross brought a curse upon himself is told within a frame story. At the beginning of the poem the old sailor, under a compulsion to tell his story of curse and salvation, stops a wedding-guest just as the latter is about to attend, with two companions, a kinsman's wedding-feast, the din of which can be heard in the background. After the mariner has told his harrowing tale, the wedding-guest turns away from the nuptial festivities; the symbolic tale has taken for a time from the unwilling hearer any wish to be joyous. Coleridge describes the wedding-guest as he turns "from the bridegroom's door."

> He went like one hath been stunned,
> And is of sense forlorn:
> **A sadder and a wiser man,**
> **He rose the morrow morn.**

The saddest of all kings

Source: BY THE STATUE OF KING CHARLES AT CHARING CROSS (Stanza 2)
Author: Lionel Johnson (1867-1902)
First published: 1892
Type of work: Lyric poem

Context: The poet stands beneath the equestrian statue of King Charles I, who was beheaded by the Puritans in 1649. It is late, and the city has grown quiet beneath a clear star-filled sky, and the poet meditates upon the fine, noble soul of Charles and its destruction by an unfeeling, unappreciative mob. "His soul was of the saints; / And art to him was joy." The mass of humanity are of grosser natures, and do not understand men like Charles, but envy the nobility they can perceive in them. Charles' sadness arose not only from his being overthrown and sentenced to death, but also from the realization that he and his people existed on different planes, and that their judgments of him were hopelessly in error.

> The splendid silence clings
> Around me: and around
> **The saddest of all kings,**
> Crown'd, and again discrown'd.
>
> Comely and calm, he rides
> Hard by his own Whitehall:
> Only the night wind glides:
> No crowds, nor rebels, brawl.

Safety lies midway

Source: THE METAMORPHOSES (Book II, 137, as translated by A. E. Watts)
Author: Ovid (43 B.C.-A.D. 18)
First published: Before A.D. 8
Type of work: Mythological tales in verse

Context: Phaëthon, son of Clymene and Phoebus, the sun-god, is taunted by a friend and wants to prove that Pheobus is his father. He goes to the sun-god's palace and begs him to grant a wish to which Phoebus gladly consents. Phaëthon then tells his father that he wants to drive the sun chariot across the sky. Phoebus immediately regrets his promise, telling his son that there are many dangers, that the steeds are difficult for even him to handle. But Phaëthon insists. With a sad heart Phoebus agrees, and gives his son this advice:

> Five zones there are: your course, confined to three;
> The farthest north and south must never see.
> Next, share your heat between the earth and sky;
> Press not too low, nor set your course too high.
> Heaven's halls will kindle if too high you stray;
> Too low, the earth: your **safety lies midway.**

Sail on, O Ship of State!

Source: THE BUILDING OF THE SHIP (Line 377)
Author: Henry Wadsworth Longfellow (1807-1882)
First published: 1849
Type of work: Patriotic poem

Context: Longfellow describes in detail the building and launching of a ship and then makes the ship a symbol of the United States. The poem had great influence in awakening Americans to the importance of the Union. An old Master vows to build a strong ship that "should laugh at all disaster,/ And with wave and whirlwind wrestle!" Helping the old builder is a youth who will soon marry the Master's daughter. The vessel, symbolically named the *Union,* is built of "only what is sound and strong." At night, the young man and the maiden sit and listen to the old Master's tales of life at sea. The ship is finally completed, and the carving on the bow is "modelled from the Master's daughter! . . . And at the mast-head,/ White, blue, and red,/ A flag unrolls the stripes and stars." On "the bridal day/ Of beauty and of strength," the boy marries the girl, and the ship is wedded to "the gray old sea." Describing the launching, the poet blesses the ship, the newlyweds ("Sail forth into the sea of life . . ."), and a symbolic ship:

Thou, too, **sail on, O Ship of State!**
Sail on, O UNION, strong and great!
Humanity with all its fears,
With all the hopes of future years,
Is hanging breathless on thy fate!
We know what Master laid thy keel,
What Workmen wrought thy ribs of steel,
Who made each mast, and sail, and rope,
What anvils rang, what hammers beat,
In what a forge and what a heat
Were shaped the anchors of thy hope!

Satan finds some mischief still for idle hands to do

Source: DIVINE SONGS ("Against Idleness and Mischief," Stanza 3)
Author: Isaac Watts (1674-1748)
First published: 1720
Type of work: Didactic poem

Context: The famous Protestant writer of hymns and poems, Isaac Watts, a dignified dissenter in essentially the same tradition as the Wesleys and the earlier John Milton, sometimes wrote slight verses of a didactic nature. It would seem well that we usually recall his more awesome lines (as in "Our God, Our Help in Ages Past"), rather than his less intellectual, less deeply moving, qualitatively cruder lyrics. The latter, however, have proven highly quotable over the years—and highly adaptable to parody. Of his serious purpose in the craft of writing there can be no doubt. Watts, writing on writing, once remarked that "It degrades the excellency of the best versification when the lines run on by couplets . . . unmanly softness of the numbers, and the perpetual chime of even cadences." Watts' almost-childish simplicity, combined with his keen intellect and insight, produce an appeal somewhat like Blake's, though they sometimes cloy because of preachiness, as in his poem "Against Idleness and Mischief":

In Works of Labour or of Skill
I would be busy too:
For **Satan finds some mischief still**
For idle hands to do.

845

Say now Shibboleth

Source: JUDGES 12:6
Author: Unknown
First transcribed: c.750-400 B.C.
Type of work: Religious history

Context: In Canaan, in the time of the judges, Jephthah, a Gileadite and the appointed deliverer of the children of Israel, and the men of Gilead have conquered the hostile Ammonites. The Ephraimites, jealous of the victory, reprimand Jephthah for having moved against the Ammonites without asking for help. Jephthah replies that his call for assistance had gone unanswered and that the Lord had delivered his enemies to him. When civil war ensues between the Gileadites and the Ephraimites, Jephthah defeats the rival tribe, captures the fords of the Jordan, and sets up a linguistic method for detecting any fugitive Ephraimite who tries to cross the river:

> Then said they unto him, **Say now Shibboleth:** and he said Sibboleth: for he could not frame to pronounce it right. Then they took him, and slew him at the passages of Jordan. . . .

Saying, Peace, peace; when there is no peace

Source: JEREMIAH 6:14
Author: Jeremiah
First transcribed: c.605-500 B.C.
Type of work: Religious prophecy and exhortation

Context: Jeremiah, a prophet of the Lord sanctified before conception, foretells the coming destruction of Jerusalem by a force from the north. Reminding the Israelites of their faithfulness to the Almighty during the harsh times before the entrance into the land of Canaan, he reproves them for their present wickedness and pleads for their return to God. Appointed by God to find in Jerusalem one man of justice and truth, for whose presence He would deliver the city, the prophet fails in his search. Although the wealthy are sinful, the prophets are false, and the priests are covetous, the people do not object. Warning them to flee Jerusalem, Jeremiah again searches for one good man. In words also used by a later writer concerning false wise men (Jeremiah 8:11), the Lord, through Jeremiah, speaks of the iniquity and false hopes of the people of Jerusalem ("the daughter of my people"):

> For from the least of them even unto the greatest of them every one is given to covetousness; and from the prophet even unto the priest every one dealeth falsely.

They have healed also the hurt of the daughter of my people slightly, **saying, Peace, peace; when there is no peace.**

A scapegoat into the wilderness

Source: LEVITICUS 16:10
Author: Unknown
First transcribed: c.600-400 B.C.
Type of work: Religious history and law

Context: Moses, on Mount Sinai, receives from God the covenant, the Ten Commandments, and the civil, moral, and cultic laws for the Israelites. He instructs the people in the manner of worship and Aaron and his sons in their duties as the consecrated priests of the Israelites. Aaron, for the ritual of atonement, is ordered to sacrifice in the tabernacle a young bullock and a ram as his atonement, and to take two goats from the people as their atonement. He is to cast lots on the goats, one lot for the Lord and the other for the scapegoat or, in the Hebrew, the goat of Azezel, possibly an evil spirit. The first goat is to be sacrificed, and the second is to have all the sins of the Israelites placed on it and then released in the wilderness:

But the goat, on which the lot fell to be the scapegoat, shall be presented alive before the Lord, to make an atonement with him, and to let him go for **a scapegoat into the wilderness.**

Scared out of his wits

Source: GARGANTUA AND PANTAGRUEL (Book V, chapter 15)
Author: François Rabelais (1495-1553)
First published: 1532-1564
Type of work: Mock heroic chronicle

Context: In this bitter but funny satire on the law courts, Panurge, thinking himself lucky in having escaped from the land of the Furred-Law-cats with the loss of only a purse of gold, does not wish to return under any circumstances. Just as he and his friends are leaving in their boat, a storm comes up which drives them back toward the island. The proverb about being so frightened was later used by Joseph Addison (*The Spectator,* November 5, 1714) and by Walter Scott in Rob Roy (1817), Chapter 34. Rabelais says as the friends are about to return to the island:

. . . Panurge, **frightened almost out of his wits,** roared out, "Dear master, in spite of the wind and waves, change your course, and turn the ship's head about."

Screw your courage to the sticking-place

Source: MACBETH (Act I, sc. vii, l. 60)
Author: William Shakespeare (1564-1616)
First published: 1623
Type of work: Dramatic tragedy

Context: Ambitious Macbeth, already Thane of Cawdor, aspires to be king. He can thus fulfill his destiny, foretold him by three witches. His opportunity to hurry the future is at hand, since King Duncan of Scotland is an overnight guest in his castle. Lady Macbeth, even more ambitious, ruthless, and remorseless than her husband, has no scruples about regicide, but Macbeth has some second thoughts and misgivings. He decides against murder. Lady Macbeth comes to find him while the king and court are banqueting because the king asks for him. He tells her his decision. Immediately she upbraids him for his lack of purpose, his cowardice, and finally, his last lingering doubts.

MACBETH
If we should fail?

LADY MACBETH
We fail?
But **screw your courage to the sticking-place,**
And we'll not fail. . . .

The Sea of Faith was once, too, at the full

Source: DOVER BEACH (Stanza 4)
Author: Matthew Arnold (1822-1888)
First published: 1867
Type of work: Lyric poem

Context: Arnold, critic of nineteenth century life, could not accept the old religious faith with its worn conventions and could find no solid basis for a new faith that he struggled toward. In "Dover Beach" he describes the ebb and flow of the sea, which brings in an "eternal note of sadness." His mind bridges the centuries to Sophocles, who heard the same note on the Aegaean. Arnold then compares the full tide of the sea at Dover Beach with the "Sea of Faith." He says:

The Sea of Faith
Was once, too, at the full, and round earth's shore
Lay like the folds of a bright girdle furled.
But now I only hear

Its melancholy, long, withdrawing roar,
Retreating, to the breath
Of the night-wind, down the vast edges drear
And naked shingles of the world.

Sea of upturned faces

Source: ROB ROY (Chapter 20)
Author: Sir Walter Scott (1771-1832)
First published: 1818
Type of work: Novel

Context: Francis Obaldistone quarrels with his father, a prosperous London merchant, and goes to visit cousins in Scotland. There he meets a scoundrelly cousin, Rashleigh, who departs to take Frank's place in the London firm, and another cousin, Diana Vernon, with whom he falls in love. However, he leaves her when he learns that Rashleigh is ruining his father's business. Hastening to Glasgow to find his father's chief clerk, Frank attends a worship service where he searches with his eyes for the clerk among the congregation:

> . . . I next strained my eyes, with equally bad success, to see if, among the **sea of up-turned faces** which bent their eyes on the pulpit as a common centre, I could discover the sober and business-like physiognomy of Owen.

The sear, the yellow leaf

Source: MACBETH (Act V, sc. iii, l. 23)
Author: William Shakespeare (1564-1616)
First published: 1623
Type of work: Dramatic tragedy

Context: Now heard more familiarly as "sere and yellow leaf time of life," the sense is quite the same as Macbeth means it: fast-approaching age. In the play, Macbeth, Thane of Cawdor, usurps the throne of Scotland by murdering the lawful King Duncan and fixing the blame on others. But his has been a fitful, bloody reign. Lady Macbeth, who aided him in murder, has a sick conscience, and Macbeth sees enemies on every side. King Duncan's son, Malcolm, who fled to England when his father was assassinated, is now returning with loyal Scotsmen and English forces to wrest the throne from Macbeth. Macbeth, assured by three witches that he has a charmed life, that no one born of woman can kill him, and that he is safe until Great Birnam wood walks to his stronghold, is nevertheless sick at heart, and, awaiting attack by Malcolm, he faces the emptiness of his life.

MACBETH

* * *

I have lived long enough. My way of life
Is fallen into **the sear, the yellow leaf,**
And that which should accompany old age,
As honour, love, obedience, troops of friends,
I must not look to have; but in their stead
Curses, not loud but deep,

* * *

Seated one day at the organ, I was weary and ill at ease

Source: THE LOST CHORD (Stanza 1)
Author: Adelaide Anne Proctor (1825-1864)
First published: 1858
Type of work: Lyric poem

Context: The poetess sits before the organ in a state of restless dejection and thoughtlessly plays whatever whim dictates. Suddenly she is startled from her melancholy reverie by a chord so potently expressive that it seems to her a very sound from Heaven, a divine call which makes all her doubts and perplexities vanish. She has tried many times to remember the chord, but she cannot reproduce it and wonders if she will have to wait until her arrival in Heaven to hear it again.

Seated one day at the Organ,
 I was weary and ill at ease,
And my fingers wandered idly
 Over the noisy keys.

I do not know what I was playing,
 Or what I was dreaming then;
But I struck one chord of music,
 Like the sound of a great Amen.

Secret, and self-contained, and solitary as an oyster

Source: A CHRISTMAS CAROL (Stave One)
Author: Charles Dickens (1812-1870)
First published: 1843
Type of work: Narrative

Context: A Christmas Carol is the story of the moral awakening of a bitter, unfeeling old man, Ebenezer Scrooge. With the enlightenment he receives from a series of ghosts, Scrooge is led to repent of all his inhumanity and to become filled with love. The tale opens with a description of Scrooge as he has been for years, a man without friends and without interests beyond his bankbook and the business he runs so parsimoniously. He is a thorough miser whose soul has shriveled through negligence as its owner abandons everything in life except gold. He has no interest in anyone, but lives only for himself and his blind dedication to accumulating wealth.

> Oh! But he was a tight-fisted hand at the grindstone, Scrooge! a squeezing, wrenching, grasping, scraping, clutching, covetous old sinner! Hard and sharp as flint, from which no steel had ever struck out generous fire; **secret, and self-contained, and solitary as an oyster.**

See eye to eye

Source: ISAIAH 52:8
Author: Isaiah
First transcribed: c.800-200 B.C.
Type of work: Religious prophecy and exhortation

Context: Isaiah declares, as a prophet of the Lord, his vision of "Judah and Jerusalem in the days of Uzziah, Jotham, Ahaz, and Hezekiah, kings of Judah." Warning the people of their sins and urging them to obedience of the Lord, he foretells the coming of a messiah, the eventual fall of God's enemies, and the final greatness of His people. Another prophet, often termed "Second Isaiah," carries on the prophecy during the Babylonian exile. He prophesies the coming of the Lord, proclaims His magnificence and the joy at the arrival, and announces that the people will see vividly their Creator:

> Now therefore, what have I here, saith the LORD, that my people is taken away for nought? they that rule over them make them to howl, saith the LORD; and my name continually every day is blasphemed
> Therefore my people shall know my name: therefore they shall know in that day that I am he that doth speak: behold, it is I.
> How beautiful upon the mountains are the feet of him that bringeth good tidings, that publisheth peace; that bringeth good tidings of good, that publisheth salvation, that saith unto Zion, Thy God reigneth!
> Thy watchmen shall lift up the voice; with the voice together shall they sing: for they shall **see eye to eye,** when the LORD shall bring again Zion.

See how the generations pass

Source: SHANTUNG (Part 3)
Author: Vachel Lindsay (1879-1931)
First published: 1920
Type of work: Lyric poem

Context: The line "See how the generations pass" is used with variation throughout this fanciful, highly symbolic poem to support and add intensity to the theme—the inexplainable stability of China in ironic contrast to the fall of "stronger" empires. The roles of Confucius and the Spirit of Asia act as overtones partly explaining the intrinsic strength of the nation. With internal evidence of decay, the empire of China is reviewed in its relation to seemingly imperishable empires. The empires of Alexander, the Caesars, King Arthur, and Napoleon foresee the destruction of China before they themselves fall. Yet the fact becomes clear that while nation after nation predicts the fall of China, China alone endures. The Sphinx of the old empire of Egypt "sees all western nations spent/ Or on the rock," but "Eastward she sees one land she knew/ When from the stone/ Priests of the sunrise carved her out/ And left her lone." At last "Laughing Asia," the fanciful sea-child who co-ordinates the roles of the many empires in the story, hears from the courteous, deathless sea the prophecy that China will crumble down when the Alps and Andes, the sun and moon, crumble. The choral line introducing many of the verses begins typically:

See how the generations pass—
Like sand through Heaven's blue hour-glass.

Self-reverence, self-knowledge, self-control

Source: OENONE (Line 142)
Author: Alfred, Lord Tennyson (1809-1892)
First published: 1842
Type of work: Narrative poem

Context: Tennyson recounts the classical story of Oenone, the nymph of Mount Ida, who was the wife of Paris of Troy. Mourning the unfaithfulness of her lover, Oenone prays to the mountain: " 'O mother Ida, many-fountained Ida,/ Dear mother Ida, harken ere I die.' " She tells how she lost Paris. He came to her one day carrying an apple marked "For the most fair." He was to judge which of three goddesses—Heré (queen of heaven), Pallas (wisdom), and Aphrodite (love)—was most worthy of receiving the apple. Heré offered Paris "royal power," "ample rule,"

852

and "overflowing revenue" if he would choose her. Pallas offered wisdom. But Aphrodite offered Paris a beautiful wife (Helen). Paris chose Helen, thus bringing heartbreak to Oenone and destruction to his country. Oenone feels that he should have chosen Pallas's gift of wisdom. She quotes Pallas's speech, which epitomizes Tennyson's philosophy of life:

> " 'Self-reverence, self-knowledge, self-control,
> These three alone lead life to sovereign power.
> Yet not for power (power of herself
> Would come uncalled for) but to live by law,
> Acting the law we live by without fear;
> And, because right is right, to follow right
> Were wisdom in the scorn of consequence.' . . ."

Serpent of old Nile

Source: ANTONY AND CLEOPATRA (Act I, sc. v, l. 25)
Author: William Shakespeare (1564-1616)
First published: 1623
Type of work: Dramatic tragedy

Context: Mark Antony, one of the three rulers of Rome, whiles away his time and his cares of state in the arms of the enchanting Cleopatra, Queen of Egypt. Messages arrive from Rome which, because of their grave importance, force him, reluctantly, to take his leave of her and return home. Now, in his absence, Cleopatra cannot get Antony out of her thoughts as she speaks to her attendant, Charmian.

CLEOPATRA

. . .

O Charmian.
Where think'st thou he is now? Stands he, or sits he?
Or does he walk? Or is he on his horse?
O happy horse to bear the weight of Antony!
Do bravely horse, for wot'st thou whom thou mov'st,
The demi-Atlas of this earth, the arm
And burgonet of men? He's speaking now,
Or murmuring, where's my **serpent of old Nile**—
For so he calls me.

. . .

Set me where I bear a little more than I can bear

Source: ONE PERSON (Sonnet XVI, Lines 13-14)
Author: Elinor Hoyt Wylie (1885-1928)
First published: 1929
Type of work: Sonnet

Context: In this series of sonnets the poetess expresses in heart-rending and moving terms her love for her husband. In Sonnet XVI she vows her dedication and devotion by declaring through several exaggerated and symbolic metaphors her unfaltering ambition to uphold his "house." The first responsibility which she is willing to accept is that of transforming herself into the "timber" necessary for her role in the edifice of her husband's life. She would gladly turn her flesh into "timber for all time." She would "lop off the boughs/ Of that perpetual ecstasy that grows/ From the heart's core" in order to adjust the scope and height of her soul to him. She confesses that she is not the center or the cornerstone of his house, but as a supporting element she is willing to bear even more than she is able to bear. Her sonnet closes with the sestet:

> I am not the hearthstone nor the cornerstone
> Within this noble fabric you have builded;
> Not by my beauty was its cornice gilded;
> Not on my courage were its arches thrown:
> My lord, adjudge my strength, and **set me where
> I bear a little more than I can bear.**

Set thine house in order

Source: II KINGS 20:1
Author: Unknown
First transcribed: c.600 B.C.
Type of work: Religious history

Context: Hezekiah stands out as one of the best kings of Judah: he destroys the groves on the hilltops, the centers for pagan worship; he breaks the bronze serpent made by Moses, to which the Israelites have burned incense for centuries; and he follows all the commandments of Moses. During the early successful years of his reign, Hezekiah defies Assyria, refusing to pay the customary tribute, and drives back the Philistines. Hezekiah, still a young man, becomes seriously ill. The prophet Isaiah of Amoz comes to him with the message:

> . . . Thus saith the Lord, **Set thine house in order;** for thou shalt die, and not live.

Then he turned his face to the wall, and prayed unto the Lord, saying,

I beseech thee, O Lord, remember now how I have walked before thee in truth and with a perfect heart, and have done that which is good in thy sight. And Hezekiah wept sore.

. . . afore Isaiah was gone . . . the word of the Lord came to him, saying,

. . . tell Hezekiah . . . I have heard thy prayer, I have seen thy tears: behold, I will heal thee. . . .

Seventy times seven

Source: MATTHEW 18:22
Author: Unknown (traditionally Matthew the Apostle)
First transcribed: c.75-100
Type of work: Gospel

Context: In the town of Capernaum along the Sea of Galilee, Jesus teaches His disciples the principles by which His followers are to live in the church. They shall have the humility of a little child and forgiveness for one another. The Master has finished His discourse to His disciples, but:

Then came Peter to him, and said, Lord, how oft shall my brother sin against me, and I forgive him? till seven times?

Jesus saith unto him, I say not unto thee, Until seven times: but, Until **seventy times seven.**

The shadow of night comes on

Source: YOU, ANDREW MARVELL (Stanza 9)
Author: Archibald MacLeish (1892-   )
First published: 1930
Type of work: Lyric poem

Context: The poem is developed from the viewpoint of one lying face down upon the earth contemplating the passing of time. The poet's thoughts are structured by his strong sense of the manifestations of time, the westward movement of the sun and the flow of history. The title appropriately alludes to lines written by Andrew Marvell (1621-1678) in "To His Coy Mistress:" "But at my back I always hear/ Times winged chariot hurrying near." As the sun, at noonday when the poem opens, goes down, night seems to be approaching from the east, overtaking and destroying various civilizations on its way to the point of reference. The theme is somber; the darkness that has overtaken great places of the past moves toward another, probably America. It moves westward from Ecbatana (in Persia) to Kermanshah, Bagdad, Palmyra, Sicily, Spain, and still westward. As the sun begins its decline, the poet feels the night with all its symbolic significance almost upon him:

> And here face downward in the sun
> To feel how swift how secretly
> **The shadow of the night comes on. . . .**

The shadowed livery of the burnished sun

Source: THE MERCHANT OF VENICE (Act II, sc. i, l. 2)
Author: William Shakespeare (1564-1616)
First published: 1600
Type of work: Dramatic comedy

Context: Portia, wealthy Venetian heiress, is bound by her late father's will to be chosen for wife by lottery. All suitors will choose among three caskets—one golden, one silver, and one lead. The lead is the correct one, for it contains her portrait. Among her suitors, Portia has no choice. The Prince of Morocco comes to woo her. He tells her:

PRINCE OF MOROCCO
Mislike me not for my complexion,
The shadowed livery of the burnished sun,
To whom I am a neighbor, and near bred.
. . .

PORTIA
. . . if my father had not scanted me,
And hedged me by his will to yield myself
His wife who wins me by that means I told you,
Yourself, renowned Prince, then stood as fair
As any comer I have looked on yet
For my affection.

Shall I compare thee to a summer's day

Source: SONNET 18 (Line 1)
Author: William Shakespeare (1564-1616)
First published: 1609
Type of work: Lyric poetry

Context: This sonnet is a conscious promise on the part of the poet that beauty, whether in man, woman, or poetry itself, will live as long as men

856

have eyes to read his verse. The line quoted initiates a series of comparisons between the subject addressed and nature itself, with the subject victorious over nature's shortcomings. The poet then pays tribute to his skill of expression by promising the subject of his poem immortality through the fascination of his deathless lines. The first quatrain and the closing couplet read:

> **Shall I compare thee to a summer's day?**
> Thou art more lovely and more temperate.
> Rough winds do shake the darling buds of May,
> And summer's lease hath all too short a date.
>
> . . .
>
> So long as men can breathe or eyes can see,
> So long lives this, and this gives life to thee.

Shallow men believe in luck

Source: WORSHIP
Author: Ralph Waldo Emerson (1803-1882)
First published: 1860
Type of work: Moral essay

Context: Analyzing religion, Emerson says that he does not fear skepticism, for honest doubt can lead to the discovery of truth. The "stern old faiths" are dying, and yet "God builds his temple in the heart on the ruins of churches and religions." Religion is a highly personal matter: "Heaven deals with us on no representative system. Souls are not saved in bundles." The "moral" and the "spiritual" are eternal. "Simple and terrible laws . . . pervade and govern . . . every atom in Nature." We must have faith in the "almightiness," for "all the great ages have been ages of belief," and faith develops our highest powers and talents. "The nature of things works for truth and right forever," and eternal laws govern all happenings: "This is he men miscall Fate,/ Threading dark ways, arriving late,/ But ever coming in time to crown/ The truth, and hurl wrongdoers down . . . This is Jove, who, deaf to prayers,/ Floods with blessings unawares." Man lives in "necessitated freedom":

> **Shallow men believe in luck,** believe in circumstances: It was somebody's name, or he happened to be there at the time, or, it was so then, and another day it would have been otherwise. Strong men believe in cause and effect. The man was born to do it, and his father was born to be the father of him and of this deed, and, by looking narrowly, you shall see there was no luck in the matter, but it was all a problem in arithmetic, or an experiment in chemistry. The curve of the flight of the moth is preordained, and all things go by number, rule, and weight.
> Skepticism is unbelief in cause and effect . . .

857

A sharp tongue is the only edged tool that grows keener with constant use

Source: RIP VAN WINKLE (Paragraph 9)
Author: Washington Irving (1783-1859)
First published: 1819
Type of work: Short story

Context: One of the stories in *The Sketch Book,* "Rip Van Winkle," relates how a Dutch colonist of New York in pre-Revolutionary days meets with a strange man in a ravine of the Catskill Mountains Rip, helping him carry a heavy keg, comes upon the quaint Dutch crew of Hendrick Hudson mutely playing nine-pins. Seizing the first opportunity to sip from the keg, Rip falls into a stupor and sleeps for twenty years. On waking, he finds that he is a tottering old man, and later that his wife is dead and buried, his daughter is married, his native vil-lage has been remodeled, and America has become independent. Before his strange adventure Rip is pictured as a man averse to any sort of profit-able labor. With his dog Wolf he sits "in the shade through a long lazy summer's day, talking listlessly over village gossip, or telling endless sleepy stories about nothing." Dame Van Winkle, a termagant, has for years railed at her shiftless husband and has constantly forced Rip to suffer in "the fiery furnace of domes-tic tribulation." Irving writes:

> . . . Times grew worse and worse with Rip Van Winkle as years of matrimony rolled on; a tart temper never mellows with age, and **a sharp tongue is the only edged tool that grows keener with constant use.**

She dwelt among the untrodden ways

Source: SHE DWELT AMONG THE UNTRODDEN WAYS
Author: William Wordsworth (1770-1850)
First published: 1800
Type of work: Elegiac poem

Context: Wordsworth's five so-called "Lucy Poems" describe the effect upon the soul of the death of a beau-tiful maiden. Although there have been numerous attempts to identify Lucy, she probably refers to no spe-cific person. A letter from William and his sister Dorothy to Coleridge, in which the poet says he has no books and must write in self-defense and in which two of the poems ap-pear in longhand, suggests that they are an exercise of the creative imagi-nation. In the poem which follows the author describes his grief at Lucy's death.

858

She dwelt among the untrodden ways
  Beside the springs of Dove,
A Maid whom there were none to praise
  And very few to love:

A violet by a mossy stone
  Half hidden from the eye!
—Fair as a star, when only one
  Is shining in the sky.

She lived unknown, and few could know
  When Lucy ceased to be;
But she is in her grave, and, oh,
  The difference to me!

Hartley Coleridge (1796-1849) later wrote a parody of the poem in which he quipped: "He lived among the untrodden ways/ To Rydal Lake that lead;/ A bard whom there were none to praise,/ And very few to read."

She gave me of the tree, and I did eat

Source: PARADISE LOST (Book X, l. 143)
Author: John Milton (1608-1674)
First published: 1667
Type of work: Epic poem

Context: This is one of the saddest lines of poetry in Christian literature; the utter finality of the statement, with all the implications it has when spoken by Adam, symbol of all mankind, is forceful to the point of brutality: the deed of disobedience, bringing death, disaster, and dreadful woe, is done. And yet there is more in the statement, as Adam is immediately shown by his judge, the Messiah. Adam says that Eve, "whom thou madest to be my help,/ And gavest me as thy perfect gift, so good,/ So fit, so acceptable, so divine," gave him from her own hand the fruit to eat, the hand from which he "could suspect no ill." The implication of Adam's statement is that the fault is not really his own, that blame rests on Eve, perhaps even on God Himself. The Messiah tells Adam, however, that the blame must be Adam's alone, that Adam had a choice to make and of his own free will made that choice. And so the line rings in the reader's ear with the pathetic tones of the guilty one who would, if he could, deny the reality of his deed:

". . . from her hand I could suspect no ill,
  And what she did, whatever in itself,
  Her doing seemed to justify the deed;
  She gave me of the tree, and I did eat."

She hangs upon the cheek of night as a rich jewel

Source: ROMEO AND JULIET (Act I, sc. v, ll. 47-48)
Author: William Shakespeare (1564-1616)
First published: 1597
Type of work: Dramatic tragedy

Context: Romeo, a Montague who is love sick over "fair Rosaline," attends with his family friends a masked ball at the home of his enemies, the Capulets. There he sees the masked Juliet, a Capulet. He immediately falls completely in love with this daughter of his family's enemy. The ardor with which he expresses his love reveals Romeo's immaturity, his former inconstancy in love, and the high and rich poetic tone of the play, as he tells how Juliet's beauty is superior to all earthly surroundings and beyond compare:

ROMEO
O she doth teach the torches to burn bright.
It seems **she hangs upon the cheek of night**
As a rich jewel in an Ethiop's ear;
Beauty too rich for use, for earth too dear.
So shows a snowy dove trooping with crows,
As yonder lady o'er her fellows shows.
The measure done, I'll watch her place of stand,
And touching hers make blessed my rude hand.
Did my heart love till now? Forswear it sight,
For I ne'er saw true beauty till this night.

She is a woman, therefore to be won

Source: KING HENRY THE SIXTH: PART ONE (Act V, sc. iii, l. 79)
Author: William Shakespeare (1564-1616)
First published: 1623
Type of work: Historical drama

Context: The setting is before the French city of Angiers. After an alarum, the Earl of Suffolk enters, holding by the hand Margaret, daughter of Reignier and afterwards King Henry's queen. Suffolk calls her "nature's miracle" and tries to scheme how he, a married man, can play suitor to her. While she talks of ransom, he talks to himself about his desire for her, though he is afraid she will repulse his advances. He reassures himself, however, by saying, in a passage almost identical to one in *Titus Andronicus* (Act II, sc. i, l. 82) that, after all, she is only a woman.

MARGARET
Why speak'st thou not? What ransom must I pay?

SUFFOLK [*aside*]
She's beautiful, and therefore to be wooed.
She is a woman, therefore to be won.

MARGARET
Wilt thou accept of ransom, yea or no?

SUFFOLK [*aside*]
Fond man, remember that thou hast a wife,
Then how can Margaret be thy paramour?

She moves a goddess, and she looks a queen!

Source: THE ILIAD (Book III, l. 208, as translated by Alexander Pope)
Author: Homer (c.850 B.C.)
First transcribed: Sixth century B.C.
Type of work: Epic poem

Context: In the tenth year of the Trojan War, a truce is declared while Paris and Menelaus prepare for a duel. The winner of this single combat will claim Helen, and a peace treaty will follow, after which the Greeks will sail for home. In the meantime, King Priam and his council of elders, men too old to fight "but wise through time," view the battlefield. To them comes Helen, lonesome for her home and her husband.

These, when the Spartan queen approach'd the tower,
In secret own'd resistless beauty's power:
They cried, "No wonder such celestial charms
For nine long years have set the world in arms;
What winning graces! what majestic mien!
She moves a goddess, and she looks a queen!
Yet hence, O Heaven, convey that fatal face,
And from destruction save the Trojan race.

She must be seen to be appreciated

Source: OLD ST. PAUL'S, (Book I, chapter 3)
Author: William Harrison Ainsworth (1805-1882)
First published: 1841
Type of work: Novel

Context: Old St. Paul's is considered one of the best as well as the most popular of William Harrison Ainsworth's historical novels. It is a romance set in London at the time of the great plague and the disastrous

861

fire of 1666. Captain Disbrowe, young and impulsive, has been playing dice with Sir Paul Parravicin and Major Pillichody, an insolent bully. Since Disbrowe has lost all his money, Parravicin offers to stake double his winnings against Disbrowe's wife, a very beautiful woman according to the major, who claims to have seen and spoken to her. They roll the dice; Sir Paul wins; and Disbrowe, in desperation, draws his sword and attacks the knight. The young captain is disarmed and rushes out in a rage. The knight then turns to Pillichody:

> "Is his wife really as beautiful as you represent her?"
> "Words are too feeble to paint her charms," replied the Major.
> **"Shafts of Cupid! she must be seen to be appreciated."**

She stood in tears amid the alien corn

Source: ODE TO A NIGHTINGALE (Stanza 7)
Author: John Keats (1795-1821)
First published: 1819
Type of work: Ode

Context: Keats wrote this melancholy poem when his short life was nearing its end. Savoring the "pleasurable pain" of his bitter-sweet final days on earth, the poet is temporarily uplifted by the healthily happy song of the mysterious nightingale. Keats wants to join the bird and fly away from this real world, "Where youth grows pale, and specter-thin, and dies." The song of the nightingale represents the world of unattainable beauty, health, and peace which all humans (especially poets) desire. Keats shuns wine, and vows to reach the nightingale by flying "on the viewless wings of Poesy." The bird's song suggests images of bright, healthy summer flowers. The dying poet admits that he has often "been half in love with easeful Death." Since he cannot live long, he feels that it would be "rich to die" painlessly while listening to the nightingale's ecstatic song. But the thought of death causes Keats to feel self-pity, for he painfully realizes that the bird's melody (in contrast to the poet) lives forever. This jolting realization brings Keats back to painful reality, but not before he has evoked the mystical power of the bird's song in a stanza which many critics have called "the essence of romanticism":

> The voice I hear this passing night was heard
> In ancient days by emperor and clown:
> Perhaps the self-same song that found a path
> Through the sad heart of Ruth, when, sick for home,
> **She stood in tears amid the alien corn;**
> The same that oft-times hath
> Charmed magic casements, opening on the foam
> Of perilous seas, in faery lands forlorn.

862

She watches him as a cat would watch a mouse

Source: POLITE CONVERSATIONS (Dialogue III)
Author: Jonathan Swift (1667-1745)
First published: 1738
Type of work: Dialogue

Context: Believing himself more than adequate for the task, Swift set about in his dialogues to restore the art of conversation to a healthy state in eighteenth century England. He considered his dialogues admirable examples for young men and women to follow, declaring that properly used they could become an "infallible remedy" for the poor conversation he judged he heard. In this dialogue we find a group of upper-class persons in an after-dinner situation. The men are at their wine, the ladies, having left the gentlemen, are discussing the absent wife of Sir John Spendall:

LADY ANSWERALL
They say, she's quite a stranger to all his gallantries.

LADY SMART
Not at all; but, you know, there's none so blind as they that won't see.

MISS NOTABLE
O madam, I am told, **she watches him, as a cat would watch a mouse.**

She's no chicken

Source: POLITE CONVERSATIONS (Dialogue I)
Author: Jonathan Swift (1667-1745)
First published: 1738
Type of work: Dialogue

Context: Taking it upon himself to give new life to what he deemed the dying art of conversation, Jonathan Swift collected, with "incredible diligence," what he termed "at least a thousand shining questions, answers, repartees, replies, and rejoinders, fitted to adorn every kind of discourse. . . ." These he presented to the public in dialogue form with the above title, *Polite Conversations*. In this collection one finds many familiar sayings, sometimes in a somewhat different form. The above, for example, is more often heard today in such a form as "She's no spring chicken!" The quotation from Swift is put into the mouth of a Miss Notable. The speaker and some other people of rank are discussing one Lady Snuff:

NEVEROUT
She may pass muster well enough.

LADY ANSWERALL
Pray, how old do you take her to be?

COLONEL ATWIT
Why, about five or six-and-twenty.

MISS NOTABLE
I swear **she's no chicken;** she's on the wrong side of thirty, **if**
she be a day.

She's the Fighting Téméraire

Source: THE FIGHTING TÉMÉRAIRE (Stanza 6)
Author: Sir Henry Newbolt (1862-1938)
First published: 1897
Type of work: Patriotic poem

Context: In this poem "The Fighting *Téméraire*" Sir Henry Newbolt pays tribute to a ship that played a great part in the battle of Trafalgar. The ship, originally French, had been captured earlier by Nelson and remained in the service of the British navy. It was finally destroyed in 1838. The artist J. M. W. Turner saw the *Téméraire* as it was being towed up the Thames to be broken up, and the scene inspired him to paint the picture entitled "The Fighting *Téméraire* Towed to Her Last Berth." Newbolt's poem gives a spirited description of the ship in three phases of its life: in the morning, when the ship is fresh and the crew singing; at noon, as the ship is preparing to go into battle; and in the evening, when "There's a far bell ringing/ At the setting of the sun, . . ." and the ship is no longer serviceable. Still the renown of its days of glory lives on. The poem closes with the following lines, which are reminiscent of the scene in Turner's painting:

Now, the sunset breezes shiver,
Téméraire! Téméraire!
And she's fading down the river,
Téméraire! Téméraire!
Now the sunset breezes shiver,
And she's fading down the river,
But in England's song for ever
She's the Fighting Téméraire.

The ship of State

Source: ANTIGONE (Line 162, As translated by R. C. Jebb)
Author: Sophocles (496-405 B.C.)
First transcribed: Fourth century B.C.
Type of work: Dramatic tragedy

Context: The Theban plays of Sophocles chronicle the events in the reign of Oedipus and Creon, reigns fraught with incest and fratricide. After Oedipus abdicates the throne to remove a pestilence from his kingdom, he wanders abroad with his daughters Antigone and Ismene, who return to Thebes only after his death. They thereupon observe the tragic deaths of their two brothers, one who fights for Creon to preserve the kingdom, the other who kills his brother and whose body must perforce remain unburied. Antigone makes a ceremonial burial on pain of death and in spite of all Creon's precautions to prevent her from doing so. The Victorian translators of the classics imposed a common phrase "the ship of state" which is not present in the original, and which is variously translated as Creon's ironic speech that insurrection has now been put down and all is well: "My friends, for what concerns our commonwealth,/ The Gods who vexed it with the billowing storms/ Have righted it again," or "My friends, the very gods who shook the state/with mighty surge have set it straight again."

CREON
Sirs, **the vessel of our State,** after being tossed on wild waves,
hath once more been safely steadied by the gods . . .

Shoot, if you must, this old gray head

Source: BARBARA FRIETCHIE (Stanza 18)
Author: John Greenleaf Whittier (1807-1892)
First published: 1863
Type of work: Patriotic poem

Context: The patriotic poet Whittier praises the Union by telling the story of Barbara Frietchie, the old Maryland woman ("Bowed with her fourscore years and ten") who bravely raised the United States flag in defiance of the approaching Southern forces, under Stonewall Jackson. Jackson's men shot the flag down, but she picked it up and offered her life as a sacrifice for the Union. Her bravery impressed Jackson so strongly that he spared both the flag and Barbara:

"Shoot if you must, this old gray head,
But spare your country's flag," she said.

865

A shade of sadness, a blush of shame,
Over the face of the leader came;

The nobler nature within him stirred
To life at that woman's deed and word;

"Who touches a hair of yon gray head
Dies like a dog! March on!" he said.

All day long through Frederick street
Sounded the tread of marching feet:

All day long that free flag tost
Over the heads of the rebel host.

The short and simple flannels of the poor

Source: ELEGY WRITTEN IN A COUNTRY COAL-BIN (Stanza 2)
Author: Christopher Morley (1890-1957)
First published: 1917
Type of work: Parody

Context: Typical of many of Morley's poems picturing the simple vicissitudes of home life, this poem playfully treats one of its uncomfortable aspects. However, the grave matter of this poem, a parody on Gray's "Elegy Written in a Country Church-yard," is nothing more serious than the problems caused by an empty coal-bin. The line, "The short and simple flannels of the poor," is a parody on one of the better-known lines of Gray's poem, "The short and simple annals of the poor." Though the calamity of an empty coal-bin will not rob the world of "some mute inglorious Milton" or prove the fate of all men, it causes its discomforts. "The furnace tolls the knell of falling steam," the coal is almost depleted, and another ton cannot be afforded. The house is getting cold, and, worst of all, there will be no fire for cooking again "till coal is cheap." "Though in the icebox, fresh and newly laid,/ The rude forefathers of the omelet sleep,/ No eggs for breakfast till the bill is paid." Furthermore, as the room gets colder, no attempt to stay warm avails:

Now fades the glossy, cherished anthracite;
The radiators lose their temperature:
How ill avail, on such a frosty night,
The "short and simple flannels of the poor."

866

The short and the long of it

Source: THE MERRY WIVES OF WINDSOR (Act II, sc. ii, l. 61)
Author: William Shakespeare (1564-1616)
First published: 1602
Type of work: Dramatic comedy

Context: Sometimes heard as "the long and short of it" this saying means "in sum" or "briefly." In the play, Sir John Falstaff, an old, fat lecher, imagines that two merry married women, Mistress Ford and Mistress Page, have given him the "leer of invitation," as he says. He sends duplicate love-letters to them. The merry wives compare letters, enjoy a good laugh, and determine to be re- venged upon him. They enlist the aid of Mistress Quickly, a professional match-maker and go-between, who conveys from each of them tokens of encouragement to Sir John. Mistress Quickly comes to Falstaff at the Garter Inn, and, after a preliminary chat designed to sharpen Sir John's impatience, she speaks of Mistress Ford.

FALSTAFF
Well; Mistress Ford—what of her?

MISTRESS QUICKLY
Why, sir; she's a good creature. Lord, lord,
your worship's a wanton. Well—heaven forgive
you, and all of us, I pray—

FALSTAFF
Mistress Ford; come, Mistress Ford.

MISTRESS QUICKLY
Marry, this is **the short and the long of it.** . . .

Short arm needs man to reach Heaven

Source: GRACE OF THE WAY (Stanza 6)
Author: Francis Thompson (1859-1907)
First published: 1897
Type of work: Lyric poem

Context: Because of the profound religious themes of many of his poems, Catholic poet Francis Thompson has been compared to the metaphysical poets of the seventeenth century. In the poem "Grace of the Way" Thompson relates a vision he had, a pictorial representation of heaven and God's grace: a woman encompassing the universe. He says, "The kindred

867

kisses of the stars/ Were hers; her feet were set upon/ The moon." The woman then flows from her form, and the poet is "translated and enskied/ Into the heavenly-regioned She." The meaning of the vision, the poet says, is clear: Heaven is so near man that man needs only a "short arm" to reach it; the meeting place is "no alien Tree"; and one can read the direction "in his Lady's face." Yet daily the crowd passes by this hidden Paradise because "some have eyes, and will not see;/ . . . And fail the tryst, yet find the Tree. . . ." Upon having his vision, the poet says:

> Now of that vision I bereaven
> This knowledge keep, that may not dim:—
> **Short arm needs man to reach to Heaven,**
> So ready is Heaven to stoop to him; . . .

A short life in the saddle

Source: THE KNIGHT ERRANT (*Donatello's Saint George*) (Stanza 2)
Author: Louise Imogen Guiney (1861-1920)
First published: 1893
Type of work: Lyric poem

Context: Louise Imogen Guiney's deep religious devotion, which was strengthened by the noble character of the poet's father, is reflected in the poem "The Knight Errant" (*Donatello's Saint George*). The obvious inspiration for the poem is the marble statue of "St. George" by the Italian sculptor Donatello (c.1386-1466). The poet admits the pitfalls that are waiting for mankind, even for men who have risen to great heights. Considering the weaknesses and the failings of man in his attempt to carry out his dreams, the poet asks that the "Spirits of old . . . / . . . help me wear with every scar/ Honour at eventide." The poet sees not only the outer foes but also the "awful other foeman/ Impowered in my breast." The outer foes will be fought in the sun, but the "inner beneath the moon; . . ." The poet then asks that "Our Lady lend to me/ Sight of the Dragon soon!" The poem suggests the need of immediate action on the part of each one. The second stanza reads as follows:

> Let claws of lightning clutch me
> From summer's groaning cloud,
> Or ever malice touch me,
> And glory make me proud.
> Oh, give my youth, my faith, my sword,
> Choice of the heart's desire:
> **A short life in the saddle, Lord!**
> Not long life by the fire.

868

Shoulder the sky, my lad, and drink your ale

Source: LAST POEMS (IX, stanza 7)
Author: A(lfred) E(dward) Housman (1895-1936)
First published: 1922
Type of work: Lyric poem

Context: In his poem beginning "The chestnut casts his flambeaux," A. E. Housman develops one of his principal themes—the burden and uselessness of life, a burden that stretches from generation to generation and from century to century. The poet questions the reason for existence in a world that seems to be hostile to man and man's pursuit of happiness. In the poem, two young men have taken refuge in a tavern to escape the wrath of the storm raging outside. Their plans have been spoiled, and they can only sip their ale while the storm wears itself out. The lad speaking blames their lot on "iniquity on high" which wants to "cheat our sentenced souls of aught they crave." Just as the two of them are sitting there now drowning their sorrow and cursing "Whatever brute and blackguard made the world," so will others sit in their place tomorrow. The poem ends with the following stanza:

> The troubles of our proud and angry dust
> Are from eternity, and shall not fail.
> Bear them we can, and if we can we must.
> **Shoulder the sky, my lad, and drink your ale.**

The sight of you is good for sore eyes

Source: POLITE CONVERSATIONS (Dialogue I)
Author: Jonathan Swift (1667-1745)
First published: 1738
Type of work: Dialogue

Context: Noting with some alarm that the art of conversation seemed to be declining in his time, Jonathan Swift took it upon himself to provide an "infallible remedy" for the ills of polite discourse in eighteenth-century England. Written in dialogue form, his *Polite Conversations* include ". . . at least a thousand shining questions, answers, repartees, replies, and rejoinders, fitted to adorn every kind of discourse. . . ." The situation here is that Lord Sparkish and Colonel Atwit meet in St. James' Park, where they are joined by Mr. Neverout. The three men make their way to Lady Smart's home for breakfast. During the visit, they are joined by Miss Notable, apparently a favorite of the men. There is a brisk exchange of pseudo-witty remarks. In the course of the conversation, Lady Smart tells Lord Sparkish that the sight of him is good for sore eyes. William Hazlitt

(1778-1830) uses a similar expression, but puts it more in the form well-known today: "What a sight for sore eyes that would be." Lady Smart addresses Lord Sparkish:

LADY SMART

My lord, methinks **the sight of you is good for sore eyes;** if we had known of your coming, we would have strewn rushes for you.

Silence gives consent

Source: THE GOOD NATUR'D MAN (Act II)
Author: Oliver Goldsmith (1728-1774)
First published: 1768
Type of work: Dramatic comedy

Context: One of Goldsmith's memorable characters is Mr. Croaker, guardian to a wealthy Miss Richland, whose money he would very much like to put into his own pockets. In an effort to do so, he tries to push his son, Leontine, into marriage with the young lady. Leontine has other plans, for he has fallen in love with a girl named Olivia whom he has brought home from Paris under the pretense that she is his long-lost sister. In Act II, Croaker tries to make Leontine propose to Miss Richland. She knows Croaker's intentions and plans "to accept their proposal with seeming pleasure, to mortify them by compliance, and so throw the refusal at last upon them." Leontine, seeking to avoid the proposal, suggests that he and Croaker may be forcing her against her inclinations and says he will leave her at liberty to refuse.

CROAKER

But I tell you, Sir, the lady is not at liberty. It's a match. You see she says nothing. **Silence gives consent.**

LEONTINE

But, Sir, she talked of force. Consider, Sir, the cruelty of constraining her inclinations.

CROAKER

But I say there's no cruelty. Don't you know, blockhead, that girls have always a round-about way of saying yes before company?

870

Silent, upon a peak in Darien

Source: ON FIRST LOOKING INTO CHAPMAN'S HOMER (Last line)
Author: John Keats (1795-1821)
First published: 1816
Type of work: Sonnet

Context: In this Italian sonnet, Keats describes the rapture with which he read George Chapman's translation of Homer's poetry. Through books, Keats had explored "the realms of gold" of the ancient pagan civilizations. He had been told of the glories of "deep-browed" Homer's poetry, but he had never really felt the serene power of Homer until he read the translation by Chapman, an Elizabethan translator and dramatist. Keats and Charles Cowden Clarke stayed up an entire night reading Chapman's "loud and bold" translation. This aesthetic experience inspired Keats to feel the thrill of an explorer discovering a new planet or an unknown ocean. The poet compares himself to Cortez' first sighting of the Pacific from Darien (in the Isthmus of Panama). Perhaps the only real flaw in the poem is a historical error: the Pacific Ocean was discovered not by Cortez but by Balboa. This mistake does not spoil the poem's typically romantic mood of wonder and discovery:

> Then felt I like some watcher of the skies
> When a new planet swims into his ken;
> Or like stout Cortez when with eagle eyes
> He stared at the Pacific—and all his men
> Looked at each other with a wild surmise—
> **Silent, upon a peak in Darien.**

Simple and faithless as a smile

Source: LA FIGLIA CHE PIANGE (Stanza 2)
Author: T(homas) S(tearns) Eliot (1888-1965)
First published: 1917
Type of work: Lyric poem

Context: The poem represents various moods aroused in the poet by the Dido myth but expressing his own deep longings and frustrations. Tension between romantic cravings and a cynical nature is apparent. The epigraph of the poem, Aeneas' words to Venus (*Aeneid* I. 327), "O Maiden how may I name thee?" reflects the vague, uncertain, restless emotions of the poet. He sees in his mental image of Dido symbols of the romance of beauty and pain related with her story. "Weave, weave the sunlight in your hair—/ Clasp your flowers to you with a pained surprise," he petitions this image of his imagination. In contrast to the romantic vision of Di-

871

do's experience is the picture of Aeneas' cold, insensitive farewell. He departs "as the soul leaves the body torn and bruised." Though the poet would preserve the romance in Dido's gestures as he is able to visualize them, he finds himself unavoidably disillusioned by the commonplace of human relationships. Painfully haunted by his sympathies for the tragic figure of Dido, yet putting himself in Aeneas' place, he presents the way he would leave the lovesick maiden:

> I should find
> Some way incomparably light and deft,
> Some way we both should understand,
> **Simple and faithless as a smile** and shake of the hand.

A simple maiden in her flower

Source: LADY CLARA VERE DE VERE (Stanza 2)
Author: Alfred, Lord Tennyson (1809-1892)
First published: 1842
Type of work: Lyric poem

Context: Tennyson excoriates a high-born woman who sadistically plays with the affections of lower-class men. The speaker himself has been fortunate enough to see through her wiles: "You thought to break a country heart/ For pastime, ere you went to town./ At me you smiled, but unbeguiled/ I saw the snare, and I retired:/ The daughter of a hundred Earls,/ You are not one to be desired." The speaker rejoices in his immunity to her charms. High rank does not ensure good character, for a wise man knows that a pure soul may bear a humble name:

> Lady Clara Vere de Vere,
> I know you proud to bear your name,
> Your pride is yet no mate for mine,
> Too proud to care from whence I came.
> Nor would I break for your sweet sake
> A heart that dotes on truer charms.
> **A simple maiden in her flower**
> Is worth a hundred coats-of-arms.

The sin they do by two and two they must pay for one by one

Source: TOMLINSON (Line 129)
Author: Rudyard Kipling (1865-1936)
First published: 1891
Type of work: Narrative poem

Context: In *Tomlinson* Kipling relates the story of a man who dies and is confronted by St. Peter, who asks what good he did for the sake of man.

Unable to tell of any good, Tomlinson is sent to Hell, where the Devil asks him what harm he did to men while he lived. But Tomlinson is unable to tell of any positive evil that he has done. He is, therefore, returned to life again in order that he can determine what path he wishes to take, for he has never yet followed any positive road, either for good or for evil. His only ideas, good or bad, he has gotten from books.

"Go back to Earth with a lip unsealed—go back with an open eye,
"And carry my work to the Sons of Men or ever ye come to die:
"That **the sin they do by two and two they must pay for one by one,**
"And . . . the God that you took from a printed book be with you, Tomlinson!"

Single blessedness

Source: A MIDSUMMER NIGHT'S DREAM (Act I, sc. i. l. 77)
Author: William Shakespeare (1564-1616)
First published: 1600
Type of work: Dramatic comedy

Context: Hermia, daughter of Egeus, Duke of Athens, is ordered by her father to marry Demetrius. But she refuses because she loves Lysander. Furthermore, Demetrius is loved by Helena, Hermia's friend. Under the Athenian law, however, a daughter must obey her father's orders. Theseus tells Hermia "To you your father should be as a god." Hermia asks what the punishment will be if she disobeys her father, and the duke says that she must die or join a nunnery. He comments on her alternatives:

THESEUS
Thrice-blessed they that master so their blood,
To undergo such maiden pilgrimage.
But earthlier-happy is the rose distilled
Than that which withering on the virgin thorn,
Grows, lives, and dies, in **single blessedness.**

Sink or swim

Source: DISCOURSE IN COMMEMORATION OF ADAMS AND JEFFERSON
Author: Daniel Webster (1782-1852)
First spoken: August 2, 1826
Type of work: Commemorative address

Context: The sensibility of the entire nation was touched beyond comparison when, on July 4, 1826, both John Adams and Thomas Jefferson

873

died. The various circumstances of their association which marked the characters and careers of these great men were dwelt upon with melancholy but untiring interest. Solemn rites of commemoration were observed throughout the country; the city council of Boston appointed August 2, 1826, for such an event, and in the presence of an immense audience Daniel Webster, the famous American politician and orator, delivered the major eulogy. During the address, Webster imagines John Adams's characteristic reply to John Hancock's suggestion that the Colonies refrain from open war with Great Britain. Adams had described a conversation with Jonathan Sewell in 1774 in this manner: "I answered that the die was now cast; I had passed the Rubicon. **Swim or sink,** live or die, survive or perish with my country was my unalterable determination."

"**Sink or swim,** live or die, survive or perish, I give my hand and my heart to this vote. It is true, indeed, that in the beginning we aimed not at independence. But there's a Divinity which shapes our ends. The injustice of England has driven us to arms; and, blinded to her own interest for our good, she has obstinately persisted, till independence is now within our grasp. We have but to reach forth to it, and it is ours. . . ."

Sisters under the skin

Source: THE LADIES (Stanza 8)
Author: Rudyard Kipling (1865-1936)
First published: 1902
Type of work: Dramatic monologue

Context: The man in Kipling's "The Ladies" tells of his four "outstanding" sweethearts. The first is older and experienced. The second is a Burmese girl, "Funny an' yellow an' faithful—". The third is a Negress who stabs him because he wishes she were white. The last one is a girl from a convent who falls in love with him at first sight. He laments so many sweethearts because, "For the more you 'ave known o' the others/ The less will you settle to one." But what did the Sergeant's wife think of all this? Well, men are "like as a row of pins." The speaker has learned from his sweethearts that the same is true of women!

I've taken my fun where I've found it;
   I've rogued an' I've ranged in my time;
I've 'ad my pickin' o' sweethearts,
   An' four o' the lot was prime.
       • • •
What did the Colonel's Lady think?

874

Nobody never knew.
Somebody asked the Sergeant's Wife
An' she told 'em true!
When you get to a man in the case,
They're like as a row of pins—
For the Colonel's Lady and Judy O'Grady
Are **sisters under their skins!**

The skin of my teeth

Source: JOB 19:20
Author: Unknown
First transcribed: c.900-500 B.C.
Type of work: Religious saga

Context: Job, from the land of Uz, righteous in heart and blessed by God with many possessions and seven sons and three daughters, is tested by Satan, who has predicted that Job, under different circumstances, will turn against the Almighty and curse Him. When, however, Satan, with God's permission, takes away the wealth and children of Job and afflicts him with boils, the good man remains strong in his refusal to curse God. Visited by his friends Eliphaz the Temanite, Bildad the Shuhite, and Zophar the Naamathite, Job laments his day of birth and his life of misery and insists on his innocence. His friends argue that God does not punish the innocent, that God's wisdom cannot be understood, and that the calamities of the wicked are many. Job reproves the three men, lists his agonies caused by God, and notes his wretched physical condition.

My bone cleaveth to my skin and to my flesh, and I am escaped with **the skin of my teeth.**

The skyline is a promise, not a bound

Source: THE WANDERER OF LIVERPOOL ("The Ending," Stanza 10)
Author: John Masefield (1878-   )
First published: 1930
Type of work: Narrative

Context: The Wanderer of Liverpool is an account, in prose and poetry alternately of the *Wanderer,* a magnificent sailing ship, which became something of a legend to the seafarers of her time because of her ill-fated voyages and her captivating beauty. The poet describes in detail the circumstances of the ship's creation, her beauty and her attributes. He then gives a poetic, ballad-like rendering of the first disastrous voyage. A prose

875

treatment follows, dealing with the plight of the ship on its several other voyages before it was finally rammed an destroyed by a steamer, the *Gertrud Woermann*. A commemoration in verse, entitled "The Ending," treating the fate of the *Wanderer,* follows.

As she moved out to sea, says the poet, the "watchers of ships/ Sang from their places a song of the outgoing spirit," a commission and a blessing for the ship adventuring forth. In their song are the words:

> Go forth to seek: the quarry never found
> Is still a fever to the questing hound,
> **The skyline is a promise, not a bound.**

Sleep in Abraham's bosom

Source: KING RICHARD THE THIRD (Act IV, sc. iii, l. 42)
Author: William Shakespeare (1564-1616)
First published: 1597
Type of work: Historical drama

Context: Richard, Duke of Gloucester, has been crowned King Richard III. He realizes, however, that this crown is not secure. He knows the necessary course of his actions. He must have his nephews, the sons of Edward IV, murdered, must marry their sister, and must dispose of the two children of his other brother, Clarence. Tyrrel agrees to kill the young Princes Edward and Richard in the Tower. He and Dighton, another professional murderer, "smothered/ The most replenished sweet work of nature." When Richard is told of the death of the princes, he pauses to take stock of himself and to chart his further moves. Ironically he paraphrases the Bible (Luke XVI, 22: "The beggar died, and was carried by the angels into Abraham's bosom") in discussing the princes whom he has had slain:

> RICHARD
> The son of Clarence have I pent up close,
> His daughter meanly have I matched in marriage,
> The sons of Edward **sleep in Abraham's bosom,**
> And Anne my wife hath bid this world good night.
> • • •

Sleep in peace

Source: TITUS ANDRONICUS (Act I, sc. iii, l. 91)
Author: William Shakespeare (1564-1616)
First published: 1594
Type of work: Historical drama

Context: Titus, a noble Roman, has just returned to Rome from war, in the midst of discussion about who will succeed the late Emperor. Titus bears with him a coffin containing the remains of some of his sons, "These that I bring unto their latest home / With burial amongst their ancestors." He pours out his grief on the coffin as it is lowered into the opened tomb:

TITUS
. . .

There greet in silence, as the dead are wont,
And **sleep in peace,** slain in your country's wars.
A sacred receptacle of my joys,
Sweet cell of virtue and nobility,
How many sons hast thou of mine in store,
That thou wilt never render to me more.

Sleep softly, eagle forgotten

Source: THE EAGLE THAT IS FORGOTTEN (Stanzas 1 and 4)
Author: Vachel Lindsay (1879-1931)
First published: 1913
Type of work: Elegy

Context: "The Eagle That Is Forgotten" is an elegy addressing the deceased liberal politician, John Altgeld of Illinois (1847-1902). Making reference to the effect of his death upon others and ending on a note of consolation, the poem furnishes a picture of the man's virtues and of his peculiar but inimitable immortality. He is pictured as an eagle among men because of his service to others, and as a man who, though his name was too easily and too soon forgotten, lives on in the lives of his "eagle" progeny. Neither his enemies nor his loved ones remember him, says the poet. The enemies rejoiced at his death and the widow, the children, and "the mocked and the scorned and the wounded, the lame and the poor,/ That should have remembered forever . . . remember no more." Nevertheless, "a hundred white eagles have risen, the sons of your sons," says the poet. You are reflected and live in their zeal and valor, the same zeal and valor "that wore out your soul in the service of man." And "to live in mankind" is far better, the poet concludes, than "to live in a name." The last verse of his poem reads:

Sleep softly . . . **eagle forgotten** . . . under the stone,
Time has its way with you there, and the clay has its own.
Sleep on, O brave-hearted, O wise man, that kindled the flame—
To live in mankind is far more than to live in a name,
To live in mankind, far, far more . . . than to live in a name.

Sleep that knits up the raveled sleave of care

Source: MACBETH (Act II, sc. ii, l. 37)
Author: William Shakespeare (1564-1616)
First published: 1623
Type of work: Dramatic tragedy

Context: Macbeth, ambitious Thane of Cawdor, aspires to be King of Scotland and thus fulfill his destiny prophesied by three witches. After successfully subduing a rebellion, King Duncan stays the night at Inverness, Macbeth's castle, and so opportunity is at hand to hasten the future by assassination. Macbeth contemplates regicide but decides against it. Lady Macbeth, even more ambitious and ruthless than her husband, by means of cajolery, encouragement, and scorn, restores his purpose. In the dead of night, with all abed, Macbeth murders Duncan in his sleep. Now, frightened, remorseful, heavy with foreboding, Macbeth, as in a trance, tells his Lady that he thought he heard someone cry out as he was doing murder.

MACBETH

Methought I heard a voice cry, sleep no more.
Macbeth does murder sleep, the innocent sleep,
Sleep that knits up the ravelled sleave of care.
The death of each day's life, sore labour's bath,
Balm of hurt minds, great nature's second course,
Chief nourisher in life's feast.

Small choice in rotten apples

Source: THE TAMING OF THE SHREW (Act I, sc. i, ll. 135-136)
Author: William Shakespeare (1564-1616)
First published: 1623
Type of work: Dramatic comedy

Context: Gremio and Hortensio are suitors to Bianca, sister of Katharine and daughter of Baptista. Baptista tells these two would-be lovers that someone must marry Katharine, the older sister, before any one can be suitor to Bianca. Although they are rivals for Bianca's love, these two men vow that they will try to find a husband for the shrew Katharine even if they do despair of success. Hortensio hopes he will succeed because Katharine's father is rich. But Gremio asks Hortensio if he thinks "any man is so very a fool to be married to hell?" The following conversation ensues:

GREMIO
. . . I had as lief take her dowry with this condition—to be whipped at the high-cross every morning.

HORTENSIO
Faith, as you say, there's **small choice in rotten apples.** . . .

Small Latin and less Greek

Source: TO THE MEMORY OF SHAKESPEARE (Line 31)
Author: Ben Jonson (1573?-1637)
First published: 1623
Type of work: Poetic panegyric

Context: The quoted lines are largely responsible for the common belief that Shakespeare was not well educated, the basis for the Baconians' refusal to believe he wrote the plays attributed to him. But it must be remembered that Jonson, who wrote the poem that appeared in the first folio edition of Shakespeare's plays, was a noted Classical scholar. Thomas Fuller (1608-1661), in his *History of the Worthies of England* (1662), compares the wit-combats in the Mermaid Tavern between Jonson and Shakespeare to clashes between a Spanish great galleon and an English man of war. "Jonson, (like the former), was built far higher in learning." Actually Shakespeare did attend a "Latin School" in Stratford before going to London. Jonson, in his verses means, only that though Shakespeare was less grounded in the Classics than many of his contemporaries, the best of the Classical dramatists would admire his plays.

. . . Though thou hadst **small Latin and less Greek,**
From thence to honour thee I will not seek
For names, but call forth thund'ring Aeschylus,
Euripides and Sophocles to us . . .

Smell a rat

Source: DON QUIXOTE (Part I, Book IV, chapter 10)
Author: Miguel de Cervantes Saavedra (1547-1616)
First published: 1605
Type of work: Satirical novel

Context: Though the expression "I smell a rat," to indicate suspicion, has been traced back in English to *Image of Hypocrisy* (1550) (I, 51)

879

by John Skelton (1460?-1529), no one has ventured an opinion about its origin. Perhaps someone, sniffing a foul odor, suspected a dead rat in the house. Said the poet laureate of both Oxford and Cambridge: "If they smell a rat / They grisely chide and chant." Sancho uses the expression while discussing with his master how he has been tossed in a blanket and the Knight has slashed the wine skins. He rejects his master's explanation that in the inn "all things are ruled by enchantment."

> . . . "I believe it," quoth Sancho, "had my tossing in a blanket been of that kind; but sure 'twas the likest the tossing in a blanket of anything I ever knew in my life. And this same innkeeper, I remember very well, was one of those that tossed me into the air . . . ; so that after all I begin to **smell a rat,** and do perilously suspect that all our enchantment will end in nothing but bruises and broken bones."

Smiling the boy fell dead

Source: INCIDENT AT THE FRENCH CAMP (Stanza 5)
Author: Robert Browning (1812-1889)
First published: 1842
Type of work: Narrative poem

Context: This brief poem exemplifies military heroism and the zeal with which Napoleon's soldiers served him. Supposedly based upon a historical incident at the battle of Ratisbon, Bavaria, in 1809, the poem shows a boy riding up to the hill where Napoleon stands wondering whether his attack will be successful. The boy tells his general that victory is his, and Napoleon exults, then notices that the young soldier is wounded. The boy, proud that he has been able to offer his life for his leader, corrects him, saying that he has been more than wounded; he has been given his death-stroke.

> "You're wounded!" "Nay," the soldier's pride
> Touched to the quick, he said:
> "I'm killed, Sire!" And his chief beside,
> **Smiling the boy fell dead.**

So buxom, blithe, and debonair

Source: L'ALLEGRO (Line 24)
Author: John Milton (1608-1674)
First published: 1645
Type of work: Lyric poem

Context: After telling Melancholy to depart, John Milton calls upon Mirth, called Euphrosyne in heaven, to come to him. As Euphrosyne, she is one of the three Graces, Aglaia, or festive beauty, and Thalia, or festive joy, being the other two. Milton first speculates whether Mirth is the daughter of Venus and Bacchus, as some contend, or of the west wind, Zephyr, and Aurora, the dawn, conceived in May among violets and roses; Milton himself invents this parentage. The poet says that she is buxom, or lively and merry; blithe, or lighthearted and joyous; and debonair, or affable, courteous, and pleasant. He invokes her to hasten to him with a wide assortment of merry characters:

> Or whether (as some sager sing)
> The frolic wind that breathes the spring,
> Zephyr with Aurora playing,
> As he met her once a-Maying,
> There on beds of violets blue,
> And fresh-blown roses washed in dew,
> Filled her with thee, a daughter fair,
> **So buxom, blithe, and debonair.**

So careful of the type she seems, so careless of the single life

Source: IN MEMORIAM (Part LV, stanza 2)
Author: Alfred, Lord Tennyson (1809-1892)
First published: 1850
Type of work: Elegy

Context: Tennyson started writing *In Memoriam* upon the death of his closest friend, Arthur Henry Hallam, in 1833. The death of Hallam caused the poet to begin a complete readjustment of his life. In the poem the author gropes to recover religious faith. He expresses the hope that "nothing walks with aimless feet"; yet he knows that with this dream of his he is "An infant crying in the night." Part LV is an attempt to reconcile science and religious faith. Already in the mind of the poet was the doctrine of natural selection, which Darwin later explained in his *On the Origin of Species,* published in 1859. The poet, considering Nature's way of eliminating many of a species and often bringing only "one to bear" out of fifty seeds, falters and stretches "lame hands of faith." He can now only "faintly trust the larger hope." Opening the subject of the doctrine of selection, the poet says:

> Are God and Nature then at strife,
> That Nature lends such evil dreams?
> **So careful of the type she seems,**
> **So careless of the single life,** . . .

881

So free we seem, so fettered fast we are!

Source: ANDREA DEL SARTO (Line 51)
Author: Robert Browning (1812-1889)
First published: 1855
Type of work: Dramatic monologue

Context: Andrea del Sarto (1486-1531), called "the Faultless Painter," sits on the balcony of his house in Florence with his faithless, mercenary wife, Lucrezia. His blind love for this woman who is incapable of understanding his work has ruined him both as a man and as an artist; he has taken money given him by Francis I of France for the purchase of paintings and used it to buy this house. He knows that, as an artist, he cannot "leave the ground;" that he has perfection of technique and nothing else. He knows also that his wife is unfaithful, yet he cannot break her hold on him. Like all weak men, he blames his failure on destiny: we have, he says, only the illusion of freedom of choice; in reality, we are helpless to shape our lives and must accept what comes to us.

> Love, we are in God's hand.
> How strange now looks the life he makes us lead;
> **So free we seem, so fettered fast we are!**
> I feel he laid the fetter; let it lie!

So may he rest; his faults lie gently on him

Source: KING HENRY THE EIGHTH (Act IV, sc. ii, l. 31)
Author: William Shakespeare (1564-1616)
First published: 1623
Type of work: Historical drama

Context: Cardinal Wolsey, ambitious and unscrupulous adviser to King Henry the Eighth of England, urges the king to divorce Katharine of Aragon, his queen for twenty years. Wolsey hopes the king will then marry a French princess, and thus cement a hoped-for alliance between France and England. The king, however, falls in love with Anne Bullen, a Protestant. His plan having failed, Wolsey requests the pope to delay the divorce. A copy of this letter together with an inventory of Wolsey's wealth falls into Henry's hands. An angry king forces Wolsey to relinquish his possessions to the crown and to retire from the court. Full of repentance, and under a charge of treason, Wolsey dies. Now, word of his death is brought to Katharine, living in retirement. She finds it difficult to forgive the dead cardinal.

> KATHARINE
> **So may he rest; his faults lie gently on him.**
> Yet thus far Griffith, give me leave to speak him,

And yet with charity. He was a man
Of an unbounded stomach, ever ranking
Himself with princes; one that by suggestion
Tied all the kingdom. Simony was fair play;
His own opinion was his law.

. . .

So mayest thou live, till like ripe fruit, thou drop into thy mother's lap

Source: PARADISE LOST (Book XI, ll. 535-536)
Author: John Milton (1608-1674)
First published: 1667
Type of work: Epic poem

Context: Adam is given a series of visions by the archangel Michael before being expelled from Paradise. In the visions Adam sees the death of Abel at the hand of Cain, his brother. In this vision Adam also first sees the many ways death can come to mankind. Michael shows him the cave of death filled with people dying from all kinds and sorts of diseases. Such a description, as Milton well knew, had been a commonplace in medieval poetry. After seeing the vision of the cave of death, Adam asks Michael if there is no way to avoid the pains of illness before death. Michael replies to Adam:

> "There is . . . if thou well observe
> The rule of not too much, by temperance taught
> In what thou eatest and drinkest, seeking from thence
> Due nourishment, not gluttonous delight,
> Till many years over thy head return:
> **So mayest thou live, till like ripe fruit, thou drop**
> **Into thy mother's lap,** or be with ease
> Gathered, not harshly plucked, for death mature:
> This is old age."

So red the rose

Source: THE RUBÁIYÁT OF OMAR KHAYYÁM (Stanza 19)
Author: Omar Khayyám (died c. 1123)
Translator and adapter: Edward FitzGerald (1809-1883)
First published: 1859
Type of work: Translation and poetic adaptation of Persian poetry

Context: Omar Khayyám searches the past and develops a kind of pantheism. Past generations have merged into nature: throughout the "battered

883

Caravanserai" of history. ". . . Sultan after Sultan with his Pomp/ Abode his destined Hour, and went his way." Lions and lizards now rule where ancient cities once stood. The bodies of dead heroes fertilize the lovely flowers which ironically symbolize the essence of life. This fact teaches us to eschew "past Regrets and future Fears" by drinking from the Cup of present pleasure. Omar expresses his rather grim pantheism:

> I sometimes think that never blows **so red**
> **The Rose** as where some buried Caesar bled;
> That every Hyacinth the Garden wears
> Dropped in her Lap from some once lovely Head.
>
> And this reviving Herb whose tender Green
> Fledges the River-Lip on which we lean—
> Ah, lean upon it lightly! for who knows
> From what once lovely Lip it springs unseen!

So Tiberius might have sat, had Tiberius been a cat

Source: POOR MATTHIAS
Author: Matthew Arnold (1882-1888)
First published: 1882
Type of work: Elegy

Context: Matthew Arnold, for all his serious criticism of nineteenth-century society and politics, had a comic vein in his nature. For example, in *Poor Matthias,* which approaches the mock elegy, Arnold begins by announcing the death of Matthias, the family canary, but soon finds himself objecting to writing memorial verse to the bird, since other animal members of the Arnold household have not been likewise honored. At the end of the poem, a serious note regarding his own approaching death is in contrast to the earlier portion of the poem, where he writes of the family pets. In speaking to the corpse of Matthias, he describes Atossa the cat:

> Down she sank amid her fur;
> Eyed thee with a soul resign'd—
> And thou deemedst cats were kind!
> —Cruel, but composed and bland,
> Dumb, inscrutable and grand,
> **So Tiberius might have sat,**
> **Had Tiberius been a cat.**

So wide arms hath goodness infinite that it receives all who turn to it

Source: THE DIVINE COMEDY, PURGATORIO (Canto III, ll. 188-120, as translated by H. F. Cary)
Author: Dante Alighieri (1265-1321)
First transcribed: c.1320
Type of work: Christian allegory

Context: Moving among the shadows of those who will be saved, but who have a time to pass in Purgatory before entering Paradise, Dante casts his shadow before him. The spirits about to enter Purgatory are alarmed at the sight, but Dante reassures them: "Unask'd of you, yet freely I confess,/ This is a human body which ye see." Their fears overcome, one addresses the poet and asks if he is recognized. It is the King of Naples, Manfred, who fell defeated by Charles of Anjou in battle in 1266. He died without receiving last rites, but as he says, he hopes for eternal life:

> . . . When by two mortal blows
> My frame was shatter'd, I betook myself
> Weeping to Him, who of free will forgives.
> My sins were horrible: but **so wide arms**
> **Hath goodness infinite, that it receives**
> **All who turn to it** . . .
>   .   .   .

So wise, so young, they say do never live long

Source: KING RICHARD THE THIRD (Act III, sc. i, l. 79)
Author: William Shakespeare (1564-1616)
First published: 1597
Type of work: Historical drama

Context: After the death of King Edward IV, the Prince of Wales, later to be Edward V, is summoned to London. There he talks with his uncle, Richard, Duke of Gloucester. Edward asks about his other uncles. Richard, whose evil is so deceptive that he can lie about others and be speaking the truth about himself, tells the young Prince that he "can no more distinguish of a man / Than of his outward show, which. . . / Seldom or never jumpeth with the heart." The prince, however, continues to ask the wrong questions, wrong because they seek the truth. Richard, advancing his own course toward the throne, advises Edward to stay in the Tower until the coronation. Edward says that truth is eternal. A variant of Shakespeare's words is to be found in a play of his contemporary Thomas Middleton

(1580-1627), *The Phoenix,* Act I, sc. i: "A little too wise, they say, do ne'er live long." The dramatic irony of the speech lies in our knowledge that Edward will be murdered in the Tower.

EDWARD

But say, my lord, it were not registered,
Methinks the truth should live from age to age,
As 'twere retailed to all posterity,
Even to the general all-ending day.

RICHARD [*aside*]
So wise, so young, they say do never live long.

Sober, steadfast, and demure

Source: IL PENSEROSO (Line 32)
Author: John Milton (1608-1674)
First published: 1645
Type of work: Lyric poem

Context: Milton invokes thoughtfulness to come to him; his calling her "nun" indicates his high regard for her purity and serenity. She is sober, that is, not given to prankishness; steadfast, or firm in her pursuit of her thoughtful course; and demure, or not given to coyness and flirtation. She wears a long and flowing robe of a dark, color, probably purple, a hue associated with solemnity. Over her shoulders is a stole of fine black cloth worn in a decent and comely manner. He tells her to come, but to maintain her accustomed fashion of keeping a moderate pace such as that used by one who is engrossed in thought. His summons is:

Come, pensive Nun, devout and pure,
Sober, steadfast, and demure,
All in a robe of darkest grain,
Flowing with majestic train,
And sable stole of cypress lawn,
Over thy decent shoulders drawn.
Come, but keep thy wonted state,
With even step and musing gait . . .

Sold my reputation for a song

Source: THE RUBÁIYÁT OF OMAR KHAYYÁM (Stanza 93)
Author: Omar Khayyám (died c.1123)
Translator and adapter: Edward FitzGerald (1809-1883)
First published: 1859
Type of work: Translation and poetic adaptation of Persian poetry

Context: The Rubáiyát of Omar Khayyám expresses an epicurean view of life. The poet is primarily concerned with the brevity of life and the attempt to accomplish as much as possible during a short existence. He extols wine and rationalizes the drinking of wine: "A Blessing, we should use it, should we not?/ And if a Curse—why, then, Who set it there?" The Creator and the world of man are then depicted as the Potter and the Potter's house, where many vessels are discussing the meaning of existence. The vessels raise questions about the purpose of life, the Potter's error in making an imperfect vessel, and the possibility of a pot's being tossed "to Hell" for being "marred in making— . . ." The vessels rejoice, though, when the prospect of being filled with wine is near. The poet then says that even when he dies he wants to be buried near the garden so that his ashes "such a snare/ Of Vintage shall fling up into the Air" that any passer-by will "be overtaken unaware." Calling wine and wine-poetry his idols, the poet sadly admits:

> Indeed the Idols I have loved so long
> Have done my credit in this World much wrong,
> Have drowned my Glory in a shallow Cup,
> And **sold my Reputation for a Song.**

Some have greatness thrust upon them

Source: TWELFTH NIGHT (Act II, sc. v, l. 158)
Author: William Shakespeare (1564-1616)
First published: 1623
Type of work: Dramatic comedy

Context: Malvolio is a self-loving, pompous steward in Countess Olivia's household. He nurses ridiculous aspirations for Olivia's affections, and is disliked by Sir Toby Belch, Olivia's bibulous uncle, and Maria, Olivia's waiting woman. They, together with Sir Andrew Aguecheek, Sir Toby's friend and hopeless suitor for the countess' hand, seek revenge on Malvolio because he has officiously interfered with their drinking and merrymaking late one night. Maria prepares, in imitation of Olivia's handwriting and style, a love note to drop in Malvolio's way. He, walking in the garden, finds the note, recognizes the handwriting, breaks the seal, reads the contents and becomes convinced that the epistle is from Olivia and is meant for him. Thus he is completely gulled, and the revenge of the tricksters is well in train. The letter proper begins:

MALVOLIO [*reads*]
If this falls into thy hand, revolve. In my stars I am above thee, but be not afraid of greatness. Some are born great, some achieve greatness, and **some have greatness thrust upon 'em.** Thy fates open their hands, . . .

Some of the trouble out of King Charles' head into my head

Source: DAVID COPPERFIELD (Chapter 17)
Author: Charles Dickens (1812-1870)
First published: 1849-1850
Type of work: Novel

Context: David Copperfield, at the age of ten, is placed by his stepfather in an intolerable job, and he runs away to the only source of help, his father's maiden aunt, Betsy Trotwood. She allows to stay in her house a relative of hers, Mr. Dick, who is mentally weak, but kindly; and after David is sent to a boys' school, Mr. Dick comes to visit him each week. During one of these visits, Mr. Dick attempts to remember the year when he first saw what he regards as a mysterious figure hanging about his house. His poor brain cannot cope with dates, and the only one he can recall is 1649, the year of the execution of Charles I. It was a mistake, he says, to make him study history, which, it seemed to him, set his own mind to grappling with the problems Charles was facing. To Mr. Dick, the study of history meant personal involvement with living people.

". . . it was very soon after the mistake was made of putting **some of the trouble out of King Charles's head into my head,** that the man first came."

Some praise at morning what they blame at night

Source: AN ESSAY ON CRITICISM (Part II, l. 230)
Author: Alexander Pope (1688-1744)
First published: 1711
Type of work: Satire

Context: In this portion of *An Essay on Criticism,* Alexander Pope satirizes the would-be literary critics who vacillate in their judgments or who take on the judgments of the people about them. Pope says that those who judge a work by its author's name are bad enough, but worse are those who simply echo an opinion, however ill-grounded, heard from the lips of a nobleman. Of these, Pope exclaims, "The vulgar thus thro' imitation err,/ As oft the learn'd by being singular." But the worst of all would-be critics, according to Pope's view, are those who, while wide readers, simply change their minds about what is worthwhile for no adequate reason:

> Some praise at morning what they blame at night,
> But always think the last opinion right.
> A Muse by these is like a mistress used,
> This hour she's idolized, the next abused;
> While their weak heads, like towns unfortified,
> 'Twixt sense and nonsense daily change their side.
> Ask them the cause; they're wiser still they say;
> And still tomorrow's wiser than to-day.

Something attempted, something done

Source: THE VILLAGE BLACKSMITH (Stanza 7)
Author: Henry Wadsworth Longfellow (1807-1882)
First published: 1840
Type of work: Lyric poem

Context: In the first half of the poem we see the strength, independence, and honesty of the blacksmith; in the last half we see his tenderness and family devotion. "He goes on Sunday to the church,/ And sits among his boys." As "the village choir" sings, the sound of his daughter's voice fills him with joy and with sadness, for "It sounds to him like her mother's voice,/ Singing in Paradise." As he thinks of his deceased wife, the strong man "wipes/ A tear out of his eyes." Longfellow draws a Victorian moral in the last two stanzas. We must go through life with an awareness of our duties, and we should finish each task we begin. The blacksmith becomes a symbol for the highest ideals of the human race:

> Toiling,—rejoicing,—sorrowing,
>   Onward through life he goes;
> Each morning sees some task begin,
>   Each evening sees it close;
> **Something attempted, something done,**
>   Has earned a night's repose.
>
> Thanks, thanks to thee, my worthy friend,
>   For the lesson thou hast taught!
> Thus at the flaming forge of life
>   Our fortunes must be wrought;
> Thus on its sounding anvil shaped
>   Each burning deed and thought.

Something is rotten in Denmark

Source: HAMLET (Act I, sc. iv, l. 90)
Author: William Shakespeare (1564-1616)
First published: 1603
Type of work: Dramatic tragedy

Context: This famous saying is universally known in the English-speaking world. It connotes the suspicion that all is not as it appears in a given situation; that something, indefinite and vague, is disturbingly amiss. The colloquialisms "something smells," "it stinks," and the like are probably logical derivations from Shakespeare's line. In the play, the ghost of Denmark's late King Hamlet has been seen three successive nights on the battlements of Elsinore Castle. The most recent visitation, the night before, was witnessed by Horatio, good friend of the late king's son, Prince Hamlet. Now, late the following night, Hamlet is on the ramparts with his friend and an officer, Marcellus, when the ghost materializes. The ghost refuses to speak but beckons Hamlet to follow it. Despite the strenuous objections of his friends, Hamlet does so.

HORATIO
Have after. To what issue will this come?

MARCELLUS
Something is rotten in the state of **Denmark.**

HORATIO
Heaven will direct it.

MARCELLUS
Nay let's follow him.

Something lost behind the Ranges

Source: THE EXPLORER (Stanza 2)
Author: Rudyard Kipling (1865-1936)
First published: 1898
Type of work: Allegory

Context: Wanderlust is a part of the nature of man. In "The Explorer" Kipling paints a graphic picture of the homing instinct of man overpowered and in dialectic interplay with his desire to search for the unknown. The explorer goes from one "outpost of cultivation" to another, and with each one his eternal restlessness drives him ever onward to new quests for adventure. There is no end to the Explorer's path, for satisfaction only raises his curiosity to a higher pitch, even though he knows that other men will get the credit for what he has accomplished.

> Till a voice, as bad as Conscience, rang interminable
>   changes
>   On one everlasting Whisper day and night repeated
>   ——so:
> " 'Something hidden. Go and find it. Go and look behind
>   the Ranges——
> **"Something lost behind the Ranges.** Lost and waiting
>   for you. Go!"

Something was dead in each of us

Source: THE BALLAD OF READING GAOL (Part III, stanza 31)
Author: Oscar Wilde (1856-1900)
First published: 1898
Type of work: Ballad

Context: Oscar Wilde, convicted of sexual perversion, served two years at hard labor in Reading Gaol. The bitterness of the experience and the hopelessness of men isolated from society are reflected in *The Ballad of Reading Gaol.* The poet, speaking as an inmate, tells of a new prisoner jailed for murdering the woman he loved. The prisoner is to be hanged for his crime, whereas other men who have killed in worse ways walk free. The prisoners go about their work, trying to forget the fate of the condemned man. One evening, however, they see an open grave and know that the execution will take place the next day. All night they keep vigil and pray while phantoms seem to writhe through the prison. When morning arrives, the prisoners know that Death has entered the prison to do his deed. The prisoners lose all hope for the doomed man:

> We were as men who through a fen
>   Of filthy darkness grope:
> We did not dare to breathe a prayer,
>   Or to give our anguish scope:
> **Something was dead in each of us,**
>   And what was dead was Hope.

Sometimes I've believed as many as six impossible things before breakfast

Source: THROUGH THE LOOKING-GLASS (Chapter 5)
Author: Lewis Carroll (Charles Lutwidge Dodgson, 1832-1898)
First published: 1871
Type of work: Imaginative tale for children

Context: The distinguished Oxford mathematician, Charles Lutwidge Dodgson, is remembered mainly by his pen name, Lewis Carroll and for his beloved children's classics, *Alice's Adventures in Wonderland* and *Through the Looking-Glass* with his young friend, Alice Liddell, as heroine. In *Through the Looking-Glass,* Alice looks into a mirror and imagines that she enters the queer, reflected image of Looking-Glass House, which she discovers, is inhabited by live chessmen and which has grounds marked off in giant squares. Alice finds it impossible to believe that the White Queen is "one hundred and one, five months and a day," but the Queen, assuring her that she needs only to practice believing the impossible, boasts:

> . . . "When I was your age, I always did it for half-an-hour a day. Why, **sometimes I've believed as many as six impossible things before breakfast. . . .**"

Son of man, can these bones live?

Source: EZEKIEL 37:3
Author: Ezekiel
First transcribed: c.600-550 B.C.
Type of work: Religious prophecy

Context: The despairing Israelites receive the prophecy of Ezekiel that they shall be freed from Babylonian bondage and shall have their nation restored. Ezekiel, having been transported by God to a valley filled with dry bones, is ordered to prophesy that the bones will again become joined, and that the flesh and skin will appear on them. As Ezekiel prophesies, the bones begin to shake and return to a life-like form. Again Ezekiel is commanded to prophesy that the winds will breathe life into the bones; as he speaks the miracle happens. The Lord says that, though Israel appears as wasted as the dry bones, the life of the nation shall return, even as life has returned to the bones in the valley. Ezekiel, in relating his vision, tells of his conversation with God:

> And he said unto me, **Son of man, can these bones live?** And I answered, O Lord God, thou knowest.

892

And again he said unto me, Prophesy upon these bones, and
say unto them, O ye dry bones, hear the word of the Lord.

The sons of Belial, flown with insolence and wine

Source: PARADISE LOST (Book I, ll. 501-502)
Author: John Milton (1608-1674)
First published: 1667
Type of work: Epic poem

Context: The reader finds that one of
the characteristics of epic poetry is
lists of persons and supernatural beings; Milton's epic is no exception. In
the opening book he lists many of the
followers of Satan. They are the
fallen angels who rebelled against
God with Satan and were cast out of
Heaven. Tradition says they later became the false gods of paganism.
Among these is Belial, a generic term
from the Old Testament which Milton personifies. Belial stands for utter
profligacy and worthlessness. Milton
uses Belial and Sons of Belial inter-
changeably. In listing the false gods
he writes:

> And when night
> Darkens the street, then wander forth **the sons
> Of Belial, flown with insolence and wine.**
> Witness the streets of Sodom, and that night
> In Gibeah, when the hospitable door
> Exposed a matron to avoid worse rape.

Sorrow, not mine, but man's

Source: MORE POEMS (Prefatory poem)
Author: A(lfred) E(dward) Housman (1859-1936)
First published: 1936
Type of work: Lyric poem

Context: This poem—short, as are all
of Housman's—is the author's answer
to criticism of his work. Many critics,
while acknowledging Housman's con-
summate skill in compressing so
much into so few lines and his felicity in language, had pointed out the
narrowness of his range. He seemed
to have but one theme: the brevity of
life, the passing of all youth and
beauty. Further, the critics suggested
that his intense pessimism was delib-
erately cultivated; that his own experience could not possibly have been
as grim as his poems depicted it.
Housman's reply is that he is writing
of the human condition, not his own;
that life is essentially tragic, and we
must resign ourselves to that stark
fact of existence.

893

They say my verse is sad: no wonder;
   Its narrow measure spans
Tears of eternity, and **sorrow,**
   Not mine, but man's.

This is for all ill-treated fellows
   Unborn and unbegot,
For them to read when they're in trouble
   And I am not.

The soul can split the sky in two

Source: RENASCENCE (Last section)
Author: Edna St. Vincent Millay (1892-1950)
First published: 1917
Type of work: Lyric poem

Context: Realizing the limitations of her physical faculties, the poetess, lying on her back gazing at the sky, eager to relate with the outermost boundaries of objective reality and with the essential nature of things, transforms herself, through universal sympathy and sensitivity, into an omniscient, ubiquitous spirit. Infinity, settles upon her, brings to her ears "the gossiping of friendly spheres,/ The creaking of the tented sky,/ The ticking of Eternity." The weight of the whole universe is too much for her soul, however, and at last crushes her into the ground where, relieved of her burden, she lies in a conscious death. Her renascence is effected when, accepting the world within the realm of her humanity, she prays for a new birth. She realizes after her renascence that the world is as vast as the human heart and soul can expand. It is up to man to fill his void and to experience the essential nature of things. His capacity to live fully lies in the fact that

The heart can push the sea and land
Farther away on either hand;
The soul can split the sky in two,
And let the face of God shine through.

The soul selects her own society

Source: THE SOUL SELECTS HER OWN SOCIETY
Author: Emily Dickinson (1830-1886)
First published: 1890
Type of work: Lyric poem

Context: The retiring Emily Dickinson, noted for the simplicity and economy of her poetic style, the sharpness of images, and the asson-

894

ance and "off-rhyme" of her brief poems, often comments on the ways and nature of man. In "The Soul selects her own Society—," she notes that the soul of man sometimes chooses one companion and then rejects all others. Typically, she counters her majestic images, "chariots" and "emperor kneeling," with homey ones, "low gate" and "upon her mat." The complete poem reads:

The Soul selects her own Society—
Then—shuts the Door—
To her divine Majority—
Present no more—

Unmoved—she notes the Chariots—pausing—
At her low Gate—
Unmoved—an Emperor be kneeling
Upon her Mat—

I've known her—from an ample nation—
Choose One—
Then—close the Valves of her attention—
Like Stone—

The souls of emperors and cobblers are cast in the same mould

Source: APOLOGY FOR RAIMOND DE SEBONDE (*Essays,* Book II, chapter 12, as translated by Charles Cotton)
Author: Michel de Montaigne (1533-1592)
First published: 1580
Type of work: Philosophical essay

Context: At his father's request, Michel de Montaigne had translated the *Theologia Naturalis* of Raimond of Sebonde. Those who read his translation of the Spanish scholar's work felt that it reproached Christians for interpreting their religion to suit "human reasons" rather than relying on faith and divine guidance in their beliefs. They also objected that Sebonde's arguments were "weak and unfit" to convince the reader. Montaigne undertakes to answer these complaints, calling upon the Bible, ancient Greek and Roman philosophers, and history to support his defense. In upholding Sebonde, Montaigne points out that humans depend too much upon mortal strength and wisdom. They foolishly put their faith in kings and princes who in reality are no more wise or free from human frailties than they:

. . . **The souls of emperors and cobblers are cast in the same mould;** the weight and importance of the actions of princes considered, we persuade ourselves that they must be produced by

895

some as weighty and important causes: but we are deceived; for they are pushed on and pulled back . . . by the same springs that we are. . . . They are as prompt and as easily moved as we. . . .

Soup of the evening, beautiful soup!

Source: ALICE'S ADVENTURES IN WONDERLAND (Chapter 10, "Turtle Soup," stanza 1)
Author: Lewis Carroll (Charles Lutwidge Dodgson, 1832-1898)
First published: 1865
Type of work: Imaginative tale for children

Context: Charles Lutwidge Dodgson, a professor of mathematics at Oxford University, is remembered mainly as Lewis Carroll, the author of fantasies for children revolving around his young friend, Alice Liddell. In *Alice's Adventures in Wonderland,* the little heroine, becoming bored while her sister reads a book, chases a White Rabbit and trips, falling into the rabbit hole, which leads her to a magical land in which she has many strange adventures. Alice, after joining in the big social event of the land, a croquet match with the company at the palace of the Queen of Hearts, is advised by the Queen to hear the history of the sad Mock Turtle. The Mock Turtle and the Gryphon tell Alice of the tutelary practices of the sea and of the dances that are popular. Finally Alice and the Gryphon prevail upon the Mock Turtle to sing the song "Turtle Soup." Choked with sobs, the Mock Turtle sings:

"Beautiful Soup, so rich and green,
Waiting in a hot tureen!
Who for such dainties would not stoop?
Soup of the evening, beautiful Soup!
Soup of the evening, beautiful Soup!

Sour grapes

Source: AESOP'S FABLES ("The Fox and the Grapes")
Author: Aesop (fl. sixth century B.C.?)
First transcribed: Fourth century B.C.
Type of work: Moral tales of animals

Context: "Sour grapes" is the shortened form of the proverbial saying for which everyone knows the source. The moral tacked onto the story is usually "It is easy to despise something you cannot get." George Herbert in 1640 said "The fox, when he cannot reach the grapes, says *they are*

896

not ripe." LaFontaine in his famous *Fables* retold the story as "They are too green . . . and only good for fools." In the most recently translated version from the most accurate original, the fable is as follows:

A hungry fox saw some grapes hanging from a vine in a tree and, although he was eager to reach them, was unable to do so. As he went away, he said to himself, "They're **sour grapes.**" So it is with men, too. Some who can't do what they want because of their own inability blame it on circumstances.

Speak low if you speak love

Source: MUCH ADO ABOUT NOTHING (Act II, sc. i, l. 101)
Author: William Shakespeare (1564-1616)
First published: 1600
Type of work: Dramatic comedy

Context: Don Pedro, Prince of Arragon, promises to woo Hero, daughter of Leonato, Governor of Messina, for Claudio, a young lord of Florence, who is in Don Pedro's suite. At a masked ball, Don Pedro asks Hero if she will walk with him. Banteringly Don Pedro brings the subject around to love, and as they step away from the others, he tries to bring the conversation to his real subject.

DON PEDRO
Lady, will you walk about with your friend?

HERO
So you walk softly, and look sweetly, and say nothing,
I am yours for the walk, and especially when I walk away.

DON PEDRO
With me in your company?

HERO
I may say so when I please.

DON PEDRO
And when please you to say so?

HERO
When I like your favour, for God defend the lute should be like the case.

DON PEDRO
My visor is Philemon's roof, within the house is love.

897

Why then your visor should be thatched.

DON PEDRO
Speak low if you speak love.

Speak softly and carry a big stick

Source: A NATION OF PIONEERS (Speech at Minnesota State Fair)
Author: Theodore Roosevelt (1858-1919)
First spoken: 1901
Type of work: Speech

Context: In his address delivered at the state fair at Minneapolis, on September 2, 1901, Theodore Roosevelt, then Vice-President of the United States, first describes man's duty to his country. Proceeding from that point, he says, too, that each great nation has a duty in world leadership. He then strongly emphasizes the position of the United States in the international picture, saying that this country must be on cordial relations with others but at the same time have the force necessary to see that justice is done. This country's position in upholding the Monroe Doctrine must be maintained, he says, but maintained without prejudicing the sovereignty or the commercial interests of the countries involved. Broaching the subject of the relations of the United States with other powers, Roosevelt says:

. . . A good many of you are probably acquainted with the old proverb: **"Speak softly and carry a big stick**—you will go far."** If a man continually blusters, if he lacks civility, a big stick will not save him from trouble; and neither will speaking softly avail, if back of the softness there does not lie strength, power . . .

Speak the truth and shame the devil

Source: GARGANTUA AND PANTAGRUEL (Book V, Author's Prologue)
Author: François Rabelais (1495-1553)
First published: 1532-1564
Type of work: Mock heroic chronicle

Context: In the Prologue to the Fifth Book, the author asks the question, "Pray, why is it that people say that men are not such sots nowadays as they were in the days of yore?" He then goes on to ask a series of related rhetorical questions and finally says to the reader in a proverb which is widespread in usage:

. . . Now answer me, an't please you. . . . Come, pluck up a good heart, **Speak the truth and shame the devil,** that enemy to Paradise, that enemy to truth . . .

The spirit is willing, but the flesh is weak

Source: MATTHEW 26:41
Author: Unknown (traditionally Matthew the Apostle)
First transcribed: c.75-100
Type of work: Gospel

Context: In Jerusalem, the holy city, Christ, His ministry completed and the Lord's Supper instituted, briefly retreats from the threats of Jewish religious leaders. Taking with Him Peter, James, and John, the Master goes to the Mount of Olives in the Garden of Gethsemane. Heavy with sorrow as He awaits death, He tells the men to wait while He prays. Jesus, knowing that His disciples will be tempted to deny Him when He faces death, returns to the place where He left the chosen followers:

> And he cometh unto the disciples, and findeth them asleep, and saith unto Peter, What, could ye not watch with me one hour?
> Watch and pray, that ye enter not into temptation: **the spirit indeed is willing, but the flesh is weak.**

Spirit of Beauty, that dost consecrate with thine own hues all thou dost shine upon

Source: HYMN TO INTELLECTUAL BEAUTY (Stanza 2)
Author: Percy Bysshe Shelley (1792-1822)
First published: 1817
Type of work: Lyric poem

Context: Shelley speaks of immortal spiritual beauty, in contrast to mortal physical beauty. From Plato Shelley got the concept of "Eternal Beauty," which is "virtue itself." This pure beauty pervades the whole universe: "The awful shadow of some unseen Power/ Floats though unseen among us . . . Dear, and yet dearer for its mystery." This Spirit of Beauty "alone . . . Gives grace and truth to life's unique dream." Spiritual beauty is nourishment to human thought. "While yet a boy" the poet saw the shadow of true beauty: "I shrieked, and clasped my hands in ecstasy!" He vowed that he would dedicate his powers to beauty, and he has always hoped that beauty "wouldst free/ This world from its dark slavery,/ That thou—O awful Loveliness,/ Wouldst give whate'er these words cannot express." Thanking Beauty for blessing his early years, Shelley asks it to "sup-

899

ply/ lts calm" to his future life. The "Spirit fair" has stimulated the poet to "love all human kind." The poet wonders why "intellectual" (spiritual) beauty seems so ephemeral:

> **Spirit of Beauty, that dost consecrate**
> **With thine own hues all thou dost shine upon**
> Of human thought or form—where art thou gone?
> Why dost thou pass away and leave our state,
> This dim vast vale of tears, vacant and desolate?
> Ask why the sunlight not forever
> Weaves rainbows o'er yon mountain-river,
> Why aught should fail and fade that once is shown,
> Why fear and dream and death and birth
> Cast on the daylight of this earth
> Such gloom—why man has such a scope
> For love and hate, despondency and hope?

Split his sides with laughing

Source: DON QUIXOTE (Part I, Book III, chapter 13)
Author: Miguel de Cervantes Saavedra (1547-1616)
First published: 1605
Type of work: Satirical novel

Context: On his journey to Lady Dulcinea with the message from Don Quixote (which in reality he had forgotten to pick up), Sancho comes upon the curate and the barber from his master's village, looking for him. When they learn of the knight's proposed penance, they devise a scheme to end it. The barber will be the gentleman usher of the curate, who, dressed as a lady in distress, comes begging help from the Knight. The innkeeper's wife supplies costumes. For disguise, the barber puts on an ox's tale as a long beard. Then, as Cervantes reports:

> . . . Sancho came up with 'em just upon their demur, and was ready to **split his sides with laughing** at the sight of these strange masqueraders.

Spoken under the rose

Source: PSEUDODOXIA EPIDEMICA (Chapter 23, section 7)
Author: Sir Thomas Browne (1605-1682)
First published: 1645
Type of work: Philosophy

Context: Pseudodoxia Epidemica is an encyclopedic work, treating not only errors, but a wide variety of other matters such as natural history, su-

900

perstitions, geography, geology, and physiology. One saying explained by the author is "spoken under the rose," although today we consider the English translation as somewhat affected and are likely to use the Latin form "sub rosa." One explanation of its origin is that those attending ancient symphosiac meetings, held in secret, wore chaplets of roses. In another suggestion, a host hung a rose over the table to indicate that matters discussed during the meal were not to be repeated outside. Carved roses in ceiling decorations are still found in European council chambers. A third and more fanciful theory is that Cupid consecrated the rose to Harpocrates, the god of silence, as indication that lovers were not to kiss and tell. As Browne explains it:

> When we desire to confine our words, we commonly say they are **spoken under the rose;** which expression is commendable, if the rose from any natural property may be the symbol of silence. . . .

Spotless reputation

Source: KING RICHARD II (Act I, sc. i, l. 178)
Author: William Shakespeare (1564-1616)
First published: 1597
Type of work: Historical drama

Context: King Richard II has summoned before him Henry Bolingbroke, Duke of Hereford, and Thomas Mowbray, Duke of Norfolk, both of whom accuse each other of treachery to the king. Richard listens to the charges of each against the other, and then, because both are empassioned, Richard suggests, "Wrath-kindled gentlemen be ruled by me,/ Let's purge this choler without letting blood." But each of the antagonists is determined to defend his honor against the charges of the other. Mowbray speaks to the king about his reputation:

MOWBRAY
My dear dear lord,
The purest treasure mortal times afford
Is **spotless reputation;** that away,
Men are but gilded loam, or painted clay.
A jewel in a ten times barred-up chest
Is a bold spirit in a loyal breast.
Mine honour is my life, both grow in one,
Take honour from me, and my life is done.

901

A square person has squeezed himself into the round hole

Source: ELEMENTARY SKETCHES OF MORAL PHILOSOPHY (Lecture IX)
Author: Sydney Smith (1771-1845)
First published: 1850
Type of work: Public lecture

Context: Sydney Smith, English writer and clergyman, first achieved fame in Edinburgh with his work for the *Edinburgh Review* in 1802. Two years later the London world crowded to Albemarle Street to hear him deliver a series of lectures at the Royal Institution on moral philosophy. For three seasons, 1804-1806, he spoke on such topics as the history of moral philosophy, the powers of external perception, reason and judgment, the conduct of the understanding, taste, wit and humor, and the beautiful and the sublime. Smith himself did not take his performance very seriously as evidenced by his tossing his manuscripts into the fire as soon as the lectures were delivered. Mrs. Smith, however, rescued the manuscripts, a great deal damaged, from the flames and, after her husband's death, published the three courses in one volume under the title *Elementary Sketches of Moral Philosophy*. In Lecture IX, "On the Conduct of the Understanding," Smith stresses the importance of self-knowledge if one is to achieve happiness and success in life; all too often people find their roles miscast. (Smith's remark below is generally accepted as the origin of the phrase "a square peg in a round hole.") He continues:

> . . . If you choose to represent the various parts in life by holes upon a table, of different shapes,—some circular, some triangular, some square, some oblong,—and the persons acting these parts by bits of wood of similar shapes, we shall generally find that the triangular person has got into the square hole, the oblong into the triangular, and **a square person has squeezed himself into the round hole.**

The stag at eve had drunk his fill

Source: THE LADY OF THE LAKE (Canto I, stanza 1)
Author: Sir Walter Scott (1771-1832)
First published: 1810
Type of work: Narrative poem

Context: Sir Walter Scott seems to have felt, like Robert Louis Stevenson (1850-1894) later, that certain places cry out for appropriate actions. Scott felt this mood very strongly in the wild countryside around Loch Katrine which inspired him to write *The Lady of the Lake*. Often in this poem the

902

action is secondary to descriptions of majestic nature. Canto I opens by setting a mood of peace with a description of the evening ritual of the great red deer which will be driven in the coming dawn in a frantic hunt through the wild Trossachs valley:

> **The stag at eve had drunk his fill,**
> Where danced the moon on Monan's rill,
> And deep his midnight lair had made
> In lone Glenartney's hazel shade.

Stand not upon the order of your going

Source: MACBETH (Act III, sc. iv, l. 119)
Author: William Shakespeare (1564-1616)
First published: 1623
Type of work: Dramatic tragedy

Context: Macbeth, an ambitious general in King Duncan of Scotland's army, is to be king, and his fellow general, Banquo, is to be the father of kings, according to three witches' prophecy. Macbeth hurries fortune by murdering the king, fastening blame on others, and then being elected and crowned king. But he proves to be a bloody tyrant, and, because he has no heir, he fears Banquo. Banquo may kill him to seat his progeny on the throne in accordance with the prophecy. Macbeth has Banquo murdered, but Fleance, Banquo's son, escapes. Now, at a banquet, Banquo's ghost appears twice to Macbeth. The second time, Macbeth causes such an uproar that the feast is hopelessly ruined. Lady Macbeth takes charge when guests question her husband.

> LADY MACBETH
> I pray you speak not; he grows worse and worse.
> Question enrages him. At once, good night.
> **Stand not upon the order of your going,**
> But go at once.

Standing with reluctant feet, where the brook and river meet

Source: MAIDENHOOD (Stanza 3)
Author: Henry Wadsworth Longfellow (1807-1882)
First published: 1842
Type of work: Lyric poem

Context: Longfellow addresses a young girl on the verge of womanhood. He gives her advice about the mysterious world she is about to

903

enter: "Then why pause with indecision,/ When bright angels in thy vision/ Beckon thee to fields Elysian?" But "Life hath quicksands,—Life hath snares!/ Care and age come unawares!" But a pure and joyous heart ("the dew of youth") can overcome life's "sorrow, wrong, and ruth." The girl shall have a happy life, for she is "a smile of God." The poet evokes the girl's situation:

Maiden! with the meek, brown eyes,
In whose orbs a shadow lies
Like the dusk in evening skies!

Thou whose locks outshine the sun,
Golden tresses, wreathed in one,
As the braided streamlets run!

Standing, with reluctant feet,
Where the brook and river meet,
Womanhood and childhood fleet!

Star-crossed lovers

Source: ROMEO AND JULIET (Prologue, 1.6)
Author: William Shakespeare (1564-1616)
First published: 1597
Type of work: Dramatic tragedy

Context: For this greatest of all love stories, Shakespeare uses Arthur Brooke's *Tragicall History of Romeus and Juliet* (1562), which derives from earlier versions in Italian and French. This story of young love doomed to end in frustration and catastrophe has always been one of Shakespeare's most beloved works. Set in Italy during the hot summer, the play covers only a week in the lives of the enemy families, the Montagues and Capulets, and their two children. In the Prologue that opens the play, a Chorus— like the choruses in Classical drama— sets the scene, the tragic action, and the consequence of the folly of the lovers' parents.

CHORUS
Two households both alike in dignity,
In fair Verona where we lay our scene,
From ancient grudge break to new mutiny,
Where civil blood makes civil hands unclean.
From forth the fatal loins of these two foes,
A pair of **star-crossed lovers** take their life;
Whose misadventured piteous overthrows
Doth with their death bury their parents' strife.

904

The fearful passage of their death-marked love,
And the continuance of their parents' rage,
Which, but their children's end, naught could remove,
Is now the two hours' traffic of our stage;
The which if you with patient ears attend,
What here shall miss, our toil shall strive to mend.

The stars above us govern our conditions

Source: KING LEAR (Act IV, sc. iii, l. 35)
Author: William Shakespeare (1564-1616)
First published: 1608
Type of work: Dramatic tragedy

Context: Lear, King of Britain, announces that he will divide his kingdom among his three daughters. Foolishly, he makes his gifts dependent upon each daugther's declaration of love for him. The two eldest, Goneril and Regan, make flattering and deceptive protestations of love and are richly rewarded. Cordelia, the youngest, states simply and honestly that she loves him as a father. Angered, he cuts her off with nothing and divides her share between the other sisters. Kent, a faithful liegeman, questions the king's decision and is exiled for his pains. The King of France is impressed by Cordelia's honesty and offers marriage. She accepts and goes to France. Soon, however, discord erupts in Britain. The old king is abused, stripped of followers, and turned out to wander the heath in a storm. Enraged, humbled, nearly mad, he is rescued by Kent, his faithful follower, who, at peril of his life, did not leave Britain, and the Earl of Gloucester. Gloucester sends letters to Cordelia at Dover. She is bringing a rescuing army to England from France. Now, Cordelia has received her father, and read the letters. A Gentleman is describing her reactions to Kent.

GENTLEMAN
Faith once or twice she heaved the name of father
Pantingly forth, as if it pressed her heart;
Cried, sisters, sisters, shame of ladies, sisters!
Kent! Father! Sisters! What, i' th' storm? I' th' night? . . .

KENT
                                It is the stars,
The stars above us govern our conditions,
Else one self mate and make could not beget
Such different issues. . . .

905

The stars in their courses fought against Sisera

Source: JUDGES 5:20
Author: Unknown
First transcribed: c.750-400 B.C.
Type of work: Religious history

Context: After the death of Joshua, the Israelites, in their attempt to conquer Canaan, alternately forsake the Lord and are delivered by Him from their enemies by a series of judges. Deborah, a prophetess and judge, and Barak, the battle leader of the Israelites, are chosen to lead the people from the oppression of Jabin, king of Canaan, and his captain, Sisera. With the help of the Lord, the Canaanite army is routed, and Sisera is forced to flee and hide in the tent of Jael, who, because of her sympathy for the Israelites, offers him hospitality and then drives a nail or peg into his head. Deborah, rejoicing and praising the people and the Lord for His help in the victory, recounts in a poetically vivid description the battle scene and the natural forces at work:

> They fought from heaven; **the stars in their courses fought against Sisera.**
> The river of Kishon swept them away, that ancient river, the river Kishon. O my soul, thou hast trodden down strength.

The stately homes of England!

Source: THE HOMES OF ENGLAND (Stanza 1)
Author: Felicia Dorothea Hemans (1793-1835)
First published: 1826
Type of work: Lyric poem

Context: Mrs. Hermans sees England's homes as the foundation of a great nation. The homes are "stately," "merry," "blessed," "free," and "fair." They are filled with familial love and quiet piety, and they are surrounded by the loveliness of the English countryside. The poet hopes that "hearts of native proof" will always preserve these beautiful, hallowed homes, "Where first the child's glad spirit loves/ Its country and its God!" The first stanza paints a picture of the homes:

> **The stately homes of England!**
> How beautiful they stand
> Amidst their tall ancestral trees,
> O'er all the pleasant land!
> The deer across their greensward bound
> Through shade and sunny gleam;
> And the swan glides past them with the sound
> Of some rejoicing stream.

States, as great engines, move slowly

Source: THE ADVANCEMENT OF LEARNING (Book II, chapter 23, 1)
Author: Sir Francis Bacon (1561-1626)
First published: 1605
Type of work: Philosophy

Context: In *The Advancement of Learning* Bacon gives a synopsis of the state of learning, in all its branches, in his time. The second part is prefaced by an epistle to King James I, and in that prefatory essay Bacon presents a case for the study of all branches of knowledge, in particular stressing what in our time is termed the liberal arts and sciences. Bacon emphasizes that it is not professional training, but general learning in all subjects that will profitably increase human knowledge. The quotation cited here comes from the section on Civil Knowledge, of which Bacon wrote, "Civil Knowledge is conversant about a subject which of all others is most immersed in matter, and hardliest reduced to axiom." The context of the short quotation is as follows,

> . . . Again, **States, as great engines, move slowly,** and are not so soon put out of frame: for as in Egypt the seven good years sustained the seven bad, so governments for a time well grounded do bear out errors following: but the resolutions of particular persons is more suddenly subverted. . . .

Stay for me there

Source: EXEQUY ON THE DEATH OF A BELOVED WIFE (Line 89)
Author: Henry King (1592-1669)
First published: 1657
Type of work: Lyric poem

Context: The author of "Exequy" drags out a weary existence since the death of his beloved wife; she, who was his day, has left him in eternal night. He could put up with being exiled from her for a month, a year, ten years, if only there would be an eventual reunion; but, alas, he will never more see her until death allows him to join her. He conjures the earth to keep her carefully, saying that it will have to account to God for every grain and atom of her dust. He then tells her to sleep on, as she will not awaken until he joins her in the tomb. Until that time comes, every moment that passes is for him a step nearer to meeting her. Of his rejoining her in the tomb he says:

> . . . Thou wilt not awake
> Till I thy fate shall overtake;
> Till age, or grief, or sickness must
> Marry my body to that dust

It so much loves, and fill the room
My heart keeps empty in thy tomb.
Stay for me there; I will not fail
To meet thee in that hollow vale.

Stay me with flagons

Source: THE SONG OF SOLOMON 2:5
Author: Unknown
First transcribed: c.300-200 B.C.
Type of work: Lyric poetry

Context: A youth and maiden, ecstatic with the thrill of young love, carry on a dialogue of lyric endearments. The girl is described as very fair, the loveliest of women. Speaking of her lover, who has earlier been described as a shepherd, dark from exposure to the sun, the maiden says:

> As the apple tree among the trees of the wood, so is my beloved among the sons. I sat down under his shadow with great delight, and his fruit was sweet to my taste.
> He brought me to the banqueting house, and his banner over me was love.
> **Stay me with flagons,** comfort me with apples: for I am sick of love.
> His left hand is under my head, and his right hand doth embrace me.
> I charge you, O ye daughters of Jerusalem, by the roses, and by the hinds of the field, that ye stir not up, nor awake my love till he please.

Stay with the procession or you will never catch up

Source: FORTY MODERN FABLES IN SLANG (No. 32, "The Old-Time Pedagogue")
Author: George Ade (1866-1944)
First published: 1901
Type of work: Satire

Context: Ade, an Indiana humorist, began contributing his "Fables in Slang" to the Chicago *Record,* using satirical humor to poke fun at his countrymen's foibles. He used his own system of capitalization. "The Fable of the Old-Time Pedagogue who Came Down From the Shelf and Was Sufficiently Bumped" tells of a former school teacher in the era when "Spare the Rod and Spoil the Child" was a respected adage. He now has a daughter, who is also a teacher. When she becomes ill, he offers to substitute for her in order, as the author states, "to give the Rising Generation a slight Boost toward Useful Citizenship." However, he discovers that in the schoolroom, wall paper designing and Entomology have replaced spelling and arithmetic. When, to maintain discipline, he tries to take the rod to one of the big boys, he is floored. Thereupon he confesses: "I am a Has-Been of the First Water. And I give in. School is dismissed." Then the author adds:

MORAL: **Stay with the Procession or you will Never Catch up.**

Steal my thunder!

Source: SPOKEN COMMENT
Author: John Dennis (1657-1734)
First spoken: 1709?
Type of work: Attributed comment

Context: John Dennis, an English critic and dramatist, was famous for his ill nature. Although he was highly respected by many as a critic, he was unsuccessful as a dramatist. One of his nine tragedies, *Appius and Virginia* (1709), was harshly satirized by Alexander Pope for its bombast. In his *Essay on Criticism* Pope wrote: "But Appius reddens at each word you speak,/ And stares, tremendous, with a threat'ning eye,/ Like some fierce Tyrant in old tapestry. . . ." Pope's use of the word "tremendous" was probably intentional, for Dennis was often ridiculed for his use of the word. Open hostility developed between the two men, with the eccentric calling Pope "a stupid and impudent hunch-backed toad," an indignity for which Pope later punished him by comments private and public. For *Appius and Virginia* Dennis created a new technique for producing stage thunder. Although the play itself was unsuccessful and closed after but a few performances, the technique for producing thunder was adopted. Some time later, Dennis found his thunder-making technique used for a presentation of *Macbeth*. He jumped to his feet during the presentation and exclaimed:

See how these rascals use me; they will not let my play run, and yet they **steal my thunder!**

And stealing will continue stealing

Source: INTERNATIONAL COPYRIGHT
Author: James Russell Lowell (1819-1891)
First published: 1885
Type of work: Occasional poem

Context: James Russell Lowell, like all Americans of the nineteenth century and earlier, who had to make their living by their pens, as he often

909

complained he had to do, protested against the injustice of there not being an international copyright which would protect American authors in this country by forcing American publishers to pay for foreign material they published here and would protect them abroad by forcing foreign publishers to pay for the American material they pirated. In a typically bold, and witty way, he wrote this quatrain:

> In vain we call old notions fudge,
>> And bend our conscience to our dealing;
> The Ten commandments will not budge,
>> **And stealing will continue stealing.**

Still are the thoughts to memory dear

Source: ROKEBY (Canto I, stanza 33)
Author: Sir Walter Scott (1771-1832)
First published: 1815
Type of work: Song in a narrative poem

Context: Oswald Wycliffe has hired a murderer to kill a kinsman during the battle of Marston Moor in 1644 so that he may inherit his wealth. When he wishes to send his only surviving son with the killer to claim part of the treasure, the dreamy stripling is in his tower singing a song to the moon during which he recalls a moonlit meeting with the girl he loves, heiress of the enemy family of Rokeby. He thinks of how he chided each little cloud that hid Mathilda's beauty, but admits that he recalls them fondly since they also masked his own blushes:

> Fair Queen! I will not blame thee now,
>> As once by Greta's fairy side;
> Each little cloud that dimm'd thy brow
>> Did then an angel's beauty hide.
> And of the shade's I then could chide,
>> **Still are the thoughts to memory dear,**
> For, while a softer strain I tried,
>> They hid my blush, and calm'd my fear.

Still clutching the inviolable shade

Source: THE SCHOLAR-GYPSY (Stanza 22)
Author: Matthew Arnold (1822-1888)
First published: 1853
Type of work: Philosophical poem

Context: Matthew Arnold, who took as his task the instruction of his age, criticized in poetry and prose the narrowness of nineteenth-century thinking and called upon his fellowmen to broaden themselves in the manner of the Greek ideal of the total man. Using Joseph Glanvil's story of the poor Oxford Student who was forced to give up his studies and join a roving gypsy band whose learning he absorbed, Arnold tells the story of the scholar-gypsy who still roams the country after two hundred years. Arnold pleads with the scholar to flee the "strange disease of modern life" and to continue his search for "the spark from heaven":

> Still nursing the unconquerable hope,
> **Still clutching the inviolable shade,**
> With a free, onward impulse brushing through,
> By night, the silvered branches of the glade—

The still, sad music of humanity

Source: LINES COMPOSED A FEW MILES ABOVE TINTERN ABBEY (Line 91)
Author: William Wordsworth (1770-1850)
First published: 1798
Type of work: Lyric poem

Context: William Wordsworth, with Samuel Taylor Coleridge, initiated the Romantic movement in literature in 1798 with the publication of *Lyrical Ballads,* of which "Tintern Abbey" was the last entry. The poem, which records his emotional response to viewing the ruins of Tintern Abbey on the river Wye, is the earliest comprehensive statement of his poetic credo. As he views the "pastoral farms" and the peaceful landscape, the poet's mind is thrown back into the past, and he recollects previous visits to this beautiful valley. Realizing what he was then as contrasted with what he is now, he contemplates the strange ways by which the forces of this "unintelligible world" have formed his mind. Finally, he raises a hymn of thanks and praise for the maturity of thought which affords a deeper, more profound, and more humanitarian outlook on life. He has learned:

> To look on nature, not as in the hour
> Of thoughtless youth; but hearing oftentimes
> **The still, sad music of humanity,**
> Nor harsh nor grating, though of ample power
> To chasten and subdue. And I have felt
> A presence that disturbs me with the joy
> Of elevated thoughts.

The still small voice of gratitude

Source: THE INSTALLATION ODE (Line 64)
Author: Thomas Gray (1716-1771)
First published: 1769
Type of work: Ode to be set to music

Context: Thomas Gray spent most of his life adding constantly to his store of knowledge, for he was primarily a scholar, rather than a poet. He had a deep and continuing interest in literature and language, ancient and modern history, art and architecture, botany and zoölogy; in all these areas he was a learned man. Much of his life he spent as a recluse, living in rooms in one of the colleges at Cambridge, reading and studying. In 1768 Gray was offered a professorship in modern history at Cambridge by the Duke of Grafton, a personal friend. A year later the Duke was elected to the Chancellorship of the University. It was for his installation ceremony that Gray wrote "The Installation Ode." Gray did not particularly want to compose the "Ode," but he felt an obligation to the Duke for his kindness. The poem consists of airs, choruses, recitatives; the music was composed by a Doctor Randall, at that time Professor of Music at Cambridge. The general theme of the piece is an invocation of the blessing of the long-departed founders of the university on the occasion of the installation. Near the middle of the 94-line poem, a quartet asks and answers several questions:

> What is grandeur, what is power?
> Heavier toil, superior pain.
> What the bright reward we gain?
> The grateful memory of the good.
> Sweet is the breath of vernal shower,
> The bee's collected treasures sweet,
> Sweet music's melting fall, but sweeter yet
> **The still small voice of gratitude.**

Still they gazed, and still the wonder grew

Source: THE DESERTED VILLAGE (Line 215)
Author: Oliver Goldsmith (1728-1774)
First published: 1770
Type of work: Didactic and descriptive poem

Context: In this poem, Goldsmith gives, in his imaginary village of Auburn, an idealized picture of the simple and happy life of rural England before the Enclosure Act and the beginnings of the Industrial Revolution had driven the peasantry either to the cities or to America. In describing the village worthies, Goldsmith, like Gray, in his "Elegy in a Country Churchyard" (1751), lays stress upon the virtues of simple people, and thus he foreshadows the ideas of the Romantic poets of a generation later. One of these worthies is the village schoolmaster, who could write and cipher, measure land; furthermore:

> In arguing too, the parson own'd his skill,
> For e'en though vanguish'd, he could argue still;
> While words of learned length and thund'ring sound,
> Amazed the gazing rustics rang'd around,
> And **still they gaz'd, and still the wonder grew,**
> That one small head could carry all he knew.

Stolen sweets are best

Source: THE RIVAL FOOLS (ACT I, sc. i)
Author: Colley Cibber (1671-1757)
First published: 1709
Type of work: Dramatic comedy

Context: In the opening scene of Cibber's play we meet Sir Oliver Outwit and his son, who has "been at age this half-year." Sir Oliver is extremely proud that he is a self-made man and grumbles because his son wants an allowance on which to live. Sir Oliver says the son should live by his wits, to which advice his son replies that such persons have but ill reputation, ". . . men of honour and fortune call 'em sharpers and scoundrels." Sir Oliver brushes aside such views as nonsense and proceeds to tell how he built up his fortune, beginning as a pimp while still a youngster and progressing to being a gambling sharp while still a youth. Having built up a fortune by his wits, he is unsympathetic to the notion of giving his fortune, or even a part of it, to his son, till Young Outwit proves himself. As the father says later in the play, "Let me first have a proof, that if I shou'd give thee land, thou hast Wit enough to keep it." In answer to his son's reference to his early career as a cheat, Sir Oliver retorts:

SIR OLIVER OUTWIT
Turning a penny, sirrah! I liv'd! I liv'd! did not I live, Fool? I bustled, I stirred, I was as busy as a bee, had all the world to rove in, and cull'd a maintenance from every flower. Traverse, make honey, sirrah! and when you've tasted it, confess with me, that **stolen sweets are best.**

913

Stone walls do not a prison make

Source: TO ALTHEA, FROM PRISON (Stanza 4)
Author: Richard Lovelace (1618-1657)
First published: 1649
Type of work: Song

Context: A man of action who was also a poet, Colonel Richard Lovelace was known for his graceful bearing, dashing appearance, and gallantry. He was a Cavalier of aristocratic family who served in the Royal Army during the English Civil War, and was twice imprisoned because of his Royalist convictions. He was a man of noble character and a free spirit whose loyalties could not be shaken. In his song "To Althea, From Prison," Lovelace joyfully proclaims that so long as a man knows love and can glorify his king—in short, so long as he does not surrender his spirit— that man is free in the deepest and truest sense of the term. He concludes:

> **Stone walls do not a prison make,**
> Nor iron bars a cage;
> Minds innocent and quiet take
> That for an hermitage;
> If I have freedom in my love,
> And in my soul am free;
> Angels alone that soar above,
> Enjoy such liberty.

Strain at a gnat and swallow a camel

Source: MATTHEW 23:24
Author: Unknown (traditionally Matthew the Apostle)
First transcribed: c.75-100
Type of work: Gospel

Context: During the final stage of His ministry, Jesus preaches in Jerusalem. Speaking to a large group of people, He condemns many of the practices of the Pharisees, the most dedicated Jewish religious leaders. Though the Pharisees represent the authority of the Mosaic law, which Christ commends, they are guilty of hypocrisy, appearing very religious outwardly, but actually being of a less consecrated spirit than many lay Jews. The Master, noting that the Pharisees carefully tithe every trifle, but ignore the more important moral laws, humorously likens them to blind leaders who carefully strain out a gnat, which is unclean in the Jewish law, but ignore a camel, which is also unclean and much larger:

> Woe unto you, scribes and Pharisees, hypocrites! for ye pay tithe of mint and anise and cummin, and have omitted the

weightier matters of the law, judgment, mercy, and faith: these ought ye to have done, and not to leave the other undone.

Ye blind guides, which **strain at a gnat, and swallow a camel.**

Strait is the gate

Source: MATTHEW 7:14
Author: Unknown (traditionally Matthew the Apostle)
First transcribed: c.75-100
Type of work: Gospel

Context: Jesus, in the Sermon on the Mount, teaches the way to God and explains His own mission on earth as the fulfillment of the old law rather than the destruction of it. He guides the people in almsgiving, prayer, judgment of one's fellows, and examination of one's self, and declares the Golden Rule to be the law. Asserting that destruction or damnation is found by those who take the easy way, He says that the eternal life or the Kingdom of Heaven is gained by the few who are willing to discipline themselves to a restricted (strait) and hard earthly existence:

Enter ye in at the strait gate: for wide is the gate, and broad is the way, that leadeth to destruction, and many there be which go in thereat:

Because **strait is the gate,** and narrow is the way, which leadeth unto life, and few there be that find it.

A stranger in a strange land

Source: EXODUS 2:22
Author: Unknown
First transcribed: c.1000-300 B.C.
Type of work: Religious history and law

Context: During a great famine, Jacob led his people up from Canaan into Egypt, and settled in Goshen, a frontier-land on its eastern border. When the Hebrews entered that land, they were royally received because Joseph, a son of Jacob, was Viceroy of Egypt. In time, however, "there arose a new king over Egypt, which knew not Joseph." The Egyptians, fearing the Hebrews because of their prosperity and growth, set taskmasters over them, thereby forcing them to servitude in order to suppress and control them. Because they continued to increase in numbers, Pharaoh decreed that all Hebrew male babies should be killed. When the infant Moses could be hid no longer, his mother placed him an an ark upon the river, where he was found by Pharaoh's daughter and reared as her own. Moses grew and became learned in Egyptian wisdom and "mighty in words and deeds" (Acts 7:22). His heart was with his own people, however, and, having slain an Egyptian in defending a fellow countryman, he was forced to flee for his life. He went southeast from Egypt into the land of Midian. There he married a Midianite and settled with his father-in-law, Jethro. He appropriately names his first son Gershom (stranger). The Biblical account reads:

> And she bare him a son, and he called his name Gershom: for he said, I have been **a stranger in a strange land.**

Straw to make brick

Source: EXODUS 5:7
Author: Unknown
First transcribed: c.1000-300 B.C.
Type of work: Religious history and law

Context: God, hearing the cry of the oppressed Hebrews in Egypt, commissioned Moses to deliver them from bondage. Fearfully anticipating several problems involved in this task, Moses was assured by God in respect to each of them. To convince his own people that he was their divinely appointed deliverer, he was assured the power to perform three specific miracles as signs. Because Moses was not eloquent and feared a confrontation with Pharaoh, he was assured divine assistance and given Aaron to be his spokesman. In regard to his greatest apprehension, that Pharaoh would ignore his request that the Hebrews be granted their freedom, God assured him of divine intervention. Moses specifically was commanded to ask of Pharaoh that his people be allowed to worship their God for a period of three days, during which time they were to be released from their duties. This request only angered Pharaoh, however, and, thinking it to be an attempt by the Hebrews to shirk their duties, responded by increasing their labor. To the taskmasters went his command:

> Ye shall no more give the people **straw to make brick,** as heretofore: let them go and gather straw for themselves.
> And the tale of the bricks, which they did make heretofore, ye shall lay upon them: ye shall not diminish ought thereof: for they be idle; therefore they cry, saying, Let us go and sacrifice to our God.

916

A straw vote only shows which way the hot air blows

Source: ROLLING STONES ("A Ruler of Men")
Author: O. Henry (William Sydney Porter, 1862-1910)
First published: 1912
Type of work: Short story

Context: An Irishman, Barney O'Connor, wants to be a ruler of men, so he decides to take over a country in Latin America. He hires Bill Bowers as his army and cabinet, and the two sail to the chosen country, where they set up their headquarters in an adobe house in the port town. From time to time a native visitor spends hours talking privately with O'Connor in the back office of the house. One day Bill asks O'Connor to explain how he plans to take over the country. O'Connor tells him that agents of his revolutionary movement are already at work throughout the republic and that they are already on their way toward the overthrow of the tyrant Calderas. Later, while Bill is explaining the whole situation to a friend, he relates the experience as O'Connor had explained it:

"... The Liberal party is bound to win. On our secret lists we have the names of enough sympathizers to crush the administration forces at a single blow."
" 'A straw vote,' says I, 'only shows which way the hot air blows.' "

The strength of twenty men

Source: ROMEO AND JULIET (Act V, sc. i, ll. 78-79)
Author: William Shakespeare (1564-1616)
First published: 1597
Type of work: Dramatic tragedy

Context: Romeo has been banished from Verona after the death of Tybalt. At Mantua, where he waits for news of Juliet which Friar Laurence was to send, Balthasar, Romeo's servant, brings word that Juliet "sleeps in Capels' monument,/ And her immortal part with angels lives." Romeo then swears that he will be with Juliet that night. Calling on an apothecary, he seeks means by which he can join Juliet's "immortal part." The apothecary says that he has death-dealing drugs but protests that it is against the law to sell them. Romeo points out the apothecary's poverty and offers riches for the "mortal drugs." The apothecary says, "My poverty, but not my will consents." He then hands over the drug and the following conversation ensues:

APOTHECARY

Put this in any liquid thing you will
And drink it off, and if you had **the strength
Of twenty men,** it would dispatch you straight.

ROMEO

There is thy gold, worse poison to men's souls,
Doing more murder in this loathsome world,
Than these poor compounds that thou mayest not sell.
I sell thee poison, thou hast sold me none.
Farewell, buy food, and get thyself in flesh.

. . .

Strike while the iron is hot

Source: DON QUIXOTE (Part II, Book IV, chapter 71)
Author: Miguel de Cervantes Saavedra (1547-1616)
First published: 1615
Type of work: Satirical romance

Context: Don Quixote de la Mancha, disordered in mind, is out with his squire, Sancho Panza, in search of adventures to perform for the honor of his lady, Dulcinea del Toboso. Despairing of his sanity, one of his friends, Samson Carrasco, disguised as a knight, defeats Don Quixote and demands that he discontinue his adventures for a year. On their way home, Don Quixote and Sancho discuss the recent defeat. Sancho is disgusted because "Altisidora had bilk'd him of the Smocks she promised him." Feeling that he should do penance with 3300 lashes delivered by himself upon his own back, Don Quixote promises to pay Sancho for this self-imposed contrition. Because he needs the money, Sancho accedes. He hides among the trees, and after beating himself for a while, starts pounding the trees and groaning. Don Quixote finally makes Sancho stop for a time. But Sancho wants to finish his job while he has trees to hide among. So he pleads with his master. The proverbial advice used by Cervantes was also used by Publilius Syrus (*Maxim* 262), by John Heywood in *Proverbes* (1546), Part I, chapter 2, by Rabelais in Book II (1534), chapter 31, and by numerous other writers. Sancho says:

There's **nothing like striking while the Iron is hot,** for Delay
breeds Danger: 'Tis best Grinding at the Mill before the Water
is past: Ever take while you may have it: A Bird in Hand is worth
two in the Bush.

918

Striving to better, oft we mar what's well

Source: KING LEAR (Act I, sc. iv, l. 369)
Author: William Shakespeare (1564-1616)
First published: 1608
Type of work: Dramatic tragedy

Context: Lear, old King of Britain, has foolishly tested the love of his three daughters—Goneril, Regan and Cordelia—for him and has exiled Cordelia because she replied, truthfully, "I love your Majesty/ According to my bond, no more nor less." Lear has divided his kingdom between the other two daughters and has come to live with Goneril. But he finds her reception frosty. She tries to strip her father of his retainers and dignity. Lear rages out in protest and goes to visit his other daughter. Goneril is afraid that her father might work her harm unless Regan abuses him as she has done, so she sends a messenger to her sister informing her. Albany, Goneril's husband, who claims not to be aware of his wife's intentions, protests her treatment of her father. The following conversation ensues, in which Shakespeare uses an early version of our present-day proverb, "Let well enough alone."

> GONERIL
> . . . No, no, my lord,
> This milky gentleness and course of yours,
> Though I condemn not, yet under pardon,
> You are much more ataxed for want of wisdom,
> Than praised for harmful mildness.

> ALBANY
> How far your eyes may pierce I cannot tell;
> **Striving to better, oft we mar what's well.**

Strong Son of God, immortal Love

Source: IN MEMORIAM (Prologue, stanza 1)
Author: Alfred, Lord Tennyson (1809-1892)
First published: 1850
Type of work: Elegy

Context: This long poem is in tribute to Tennyson's close friend, Arthur Henry Hallam, who died in 1833 at the age of twenty-two. Tennyson wrote for the poem a prologue, addressed to Christ, in which he confesses that he, like all men, is often foolishly irresponsible and irreverent. He asks forgiveness for the confusions, doubts, and lack of faith he has been guilty of, and for the excess grief he has felt at the loss of his friend;

this grief, he implies, is the sin of revering the creature more than the Creator. He asks for the blessing of stronger faith, confident that in God there is for man an ever-abundant fund of grace and forgiveness and love which was manifested in the person of Christ.

> **Strong Son of God, immortal Love,**
> Whom we, that have not seen thy face,
> By faith, and faith alone, embrace,
> Believing where we cannot prove . . .

Subdue your appetites, my dears, and you've conquered human nature

Source: NICHOLAS NICKLEBY (Chapter 5)
Author: Charles Dickens (1812-1870)
First published: 1838-1839
Type of work: Novel

Context: Part of Dickens' purpose in this novel was to expose the harshness and cruelty with which some boys' schools in England were managed. In the name of discipline these inhumane masters not only beat, but starved, their boys and pocketed their food allowances. Wackford Squeers represents such a schoolmaster, and in one scene is sitting at breakfast with five small boys. While he feasts on bread, beef, and coffee, he forces the ravenous boys to wait, and at last allows them a little milk, which he has diluted, and a bit of bread and butter. Squeers justifies his actions by telling them that victory over the passions—especially hunger—is the key to self-discipline.

> "That's right," said Squeers, calmly getting on with his breakfast; "keep ready till I tell you to begin. **Subdue your appetites, my dears, and you've conquered human natur.** This is the way we inculcate strength of mind, Mr. Nickleby," said the schoolmaster, turning to Nicholas, and speaking with his mouth very full of beef and toast.

Such an excess of stupidity, Sir, is not in Nature

Source: THE LIFE OF SAMUEL JOHNSON, LL.D.
Author: James Boswell (1740-1795)
First published: 1791
Type of work: Biography

Context: Late in 1762 Boswell learned that "an irreconcileable difference had taken place between" Dr. Johnson and Thomas Sheridan (1719-1788),

920

the father of the playwright Richard Brinsley Sheridan (1751-1816). Sheridan had received a pension of two hundred pounds a year; Johnson had received nothing. Enraged, and not knowing that Sheridan's pension had resulted from political activities in an earlier year, Johnson from then on had little good to say for Sheridan. In addition, Sheridan was a popular lecturer on the English language and on public speaking, and Johnson was disturbed at the thought that such a man could influence the public in its attitudes toward language. On a later occasion, Boswell and Johnson are discussing Jonathan Swift (1667-1745) and James Thomson (1700-1748) and Boswell inquires whether Johnson does not think that Sheridan had "a great deal of wit." Johnson thinks not: "He is, indeed, continually attempting wit, but he fails." Boswell remembers a remark by Johnson about Sheridan which has been widely circulated among their acquaintances:

"Why, Sir, Sherry is dull, naturally dull, but it must have taken him a great deal of pains to become what we now see him. **Such an excess of stupidity, Sir, is not in Nature."**—"So (said he,) I allowed him all his own merit."

Such sights as youthful poets dream

Source: L'ALLEGRO (Line 129)
Author: John Milton (1608-1674)
First published: 1645
Type of work: Lyric poem

Context: John Milton says that after we experience the joys of the simple villages we turn to city pleasures: crowds of people; men of fashion who at festivals contend for the favors of fair ladies whose eyes, like stars, shed rays of influence; splendid wedding feasts featuring the god of matrimony, Hymen; beautiful masques and other entertainments—all the things that young, romantic poets dream about as they brood beside country streams:

> Towered cities please us then,
> And the busy hum of men,
> Where throngs of knights and barons bold
> In weeds of peace high triumphs hold,
> With store of ladies, whose bright eyes
> Rain influence, and judge the prize
> Of wit, or arms, while both contend
> To win her grace whom all commend.
> There let Hymen oft appear
> In saffron robe, with taper clear,

921

And pomp, and feast, and revelry,
With masque and antique pageantry;
Such sights as youthful poets dream
On summer eves by haunted stream.

Suffer a sea-change

Source: THE TEMPEST (Act I, sc. ii, l. 400)
Author: William Shakespeare (1564-1616)
First published: 1623
Type of work: Tragi-comedy

Context: Prospero, Duke of Milan, preoccupied with learning, delegates to his unscrupulous and ambitious brother Antonio many of the affairs of state. Antonio, working with Alonso, King of Naples, usurps the dukedom and puts Prospero and his daughter Miranda adrift on the sea. Luckily, the boat, equipped with his magical accoutrements, brings them to an island inhabited only by a monster Caliban, offspring of the witch, Sycorax. Prospero, perfecting his art of sorcery, has ruled the island for twelve years, commanding spirits of the air, including Ariel, and enslaving brutish Caliban. Prospero knows his brother and Alonso are on a ship near the island and causes a tempest which drives the ship ashore. He causes the travelers to be separated and bewitched. The first ship-wrecked passenger we meet is Ferdinand, son of King Alonso, led to Prospero's cave by Ariel's magic singing. (The last three lines quoted below are inscribed on the poet Percy Bysshe Shelley's gravestone.)

ARIEL [*sings*]
Full fathom five thy father lies,
Of his bones are coral made.
Those are pearls that were his eyes,
Nothing of him that doth fade
But doth **suffer a sea-change**
Into something rich and strange.

• • •

Suffer fools gladly

Source: II CORINTHIANS 11:19
Author: Paul
First transcribed: c.55-57
Type of work: Religious epistle

Context: Paul writes a vehement letter to the church at Corinth, which is guilty of rejecting him in favor of false prophets. The Corinthian Chris-

922

tians have easily been made fools of by the false leaders; so Paul tries, with irony, also to reach them on the basis of foolishness. In boasting of his missionary accomplishments, Paul explains the manner with which he has chosen to treat the erring church:

I say again, Let no man think me a fool; if otherwise, yet as a fool receive me, that I may boast myself a little.

. . .

For ye **suffer fools gladly,** seeing ye yourselves are wise.

Suffer the little children to come unto me

Source: MARK 10:14
Author: Unknown (traditionally Mark the Apostle)
First transcribed: c.60-75
Type of work: Gospel

Context: The writer of Mark records a poignant incident in Christ's ministry. People bring children to Jesus that He may touch them, even as He touches and heals those with physical disabilities. The disciples, feeling that the Master should not be bothered with such trivialities, rebuke the parents. Jesus, however, makes the disciples understand that children are not insignificant to Him and takes advantage of the opportunity to teach a spiritual truth:

But when Jesus saw it, he was much displeased, and said unto them, **Suffer the little children to come unto me,** and forbid them not; for of such is the kingdom of God.
Verily I say unto you, Whosoever shall not receive the kingdom of God as a little child, he shall not enter therein.
And he took them up in his arms, put his hands upon them, and blessed them.

Suit the action to the word

Source: HAMLET (Act III, sc. ii, l. 18)
Author: William Shakespeare (1564-1616)
First published: 1603
Type of work: Dramatic tragedy

Context: Prince Hamlet of Denmark learns that his father was murdered by Claudius, his father's brother, who is now king. Hamlet, horrified and distracted by this news, swears to avenge his father's murder. But before he does so, he must confirm the new king's guilt. When a band of players comes to Elsinore Castle, he arranges for the actors to play before his uncle a scene like the murder of his father. The king's reactions will indicate his guilt or innocence. Now, he gives the players last-minute instructions:

HAMLET

Speak the speech I pray you as I pronounced it to you, trippingly on the tongue; . . .

FIRST PLAYER

I warrant your honour.

HAMLET

Be not too tame neither, but let your own discretion be your tutor. **Suit the action to the word,** the word to the action, . . . For anything . . . o'erdone is from the purpose of playing, whose end both at the first, and now, was and is, to hold, as 'twere the mirror up to nature; to show virtue her own feature, scorn her own image, and the very age and body of the time his form and pressure. . . .

Th' supreme coort follows th' illiction returns

Source: MR. DOOLEY'S OPINIONS ("The Supreme Court's Decisions")
Author: Finley Peter Dunne (1867-1936)
First published: 1900
Type of work: Humorous dialogue

Context: Mr. Dooley, an Irish saloon-keeper, talks to his friend, Mr. Hennessey, about the Supreme Court and its decision that "th' constitution don't follow the flag." Mr. Dooley, considering the constitution as an old man, feels that it should stay at home and not endanger its health following the American flag wherever it is carried into foreign countries. He then delivers his opinions on the court's method of procedure, saying that it is disorganized and requires months to reach an agreement. Mr. Dooley is unable to decide whether the court's verdict is disadvantageous to the constitution or to the flag, but he is certain that the members of the court closely watch election outcomes.

". . . Some say it laves th' flag up in th' air an' some say that's where it laves th' constitution. Annyhow, somethin's in th' air. But there's wan thing I'm sure about."

"What's that?" asked Mr. Hennessey.

"That is," said Mr. Dooley, "no matther whether th' constitution follows th' flag or not, **th' supreme coort follows th' illiction returns.**"

924

Surely nothing dies but something mourns

Source: DON JUAN (Canto III, stanza 108)
Author: George Gordon, Lord Byron (1788-1824)
First published: 1821 (Cantos III-V)
Type of work: Satirical poem

Context: Don Juan is a long narrative poem with more digressions than narrative (see "All comedies are ended by a marriage"). The quoted line is part of one of these digressions. Here, Byron, speaking in his own person and forgetting the libertine Juan, devotes five stanzas to praising the "Sweet hour of twilight." He describes his evening rides through the pine forests of Ravenna— "haunted ground" (105), where the strident voices of the cicadas and the tolling of the vesper bell "Were the sole echoes, save my steed's and mine" (106). He apostrophizes Hesperus (Venus, the Evening Star) as bringing "all good things" to birds, beasts, and human beings (107). In Stanza 108, he describes twilight as "Soft hour! which wakes the wish and melts the heart/ Of those who sail the seas. . . ." or which "fills with love the pilgrim on his way. . . ." The vesper bell seems to mourn the dying day. The stanza ends with the lines:

> Is this a fancy which our reason scorns?
> Ah! **surely nothing dies but something mourns!**

The surge and thunder of the Odyssey

Source: THE ODYSSEY (Last line)
Author: Andrew Lang (1844-1912)
First published: 1879
Type of work: Sonnet

Context: Andrew Lang's sonnet appeared as the prefatory poem to a prose translation of Homer's *Odyssey* by Lang and S. H. Butcher. The sonnet expresses Lang's immense admiration for the Greek epic. The poet compares men of today to Ulysses and his sailors who were entertained so hospitably by Circe on her Aegean island that Ulysses seemed finally to have forgotten his original aim to return to his homeland. The enticements of Circe's island were many; it was a place where "only the low lutes of love complain,/ And only shadows of wan lovers pine . . ." Ulysses' followers finally succeeded in persuading their leader to pursue the original course. Like these men who were tired of idleness and wanted to go to sea again, modern man sees beyond the petty poetry and music of today and feels the intense power of a composition like the Greek epic. The sonnet ends with the following sestet:

925

So gladly, from the songs of modern speech
 Men turn, and see the stars, and feel the free
 Shrill wind beyond the close of heavy flowers,
 And through the music of the languid hours,
They hear like ocean on a western beach
 The surge and thunder of the Odyssey.

Survival of the fittest

Source: THE PRINCIPLES OF BIOLOGY (Part III, chapter 12)
Author: Herbert Spencer (1820-1903)
First published: 1864
Type of work: Scientific treatise

Context: Herbert Spencer, English philosopher, undertook to systematize all knowledge on the basis of science with special attention to the theory of evolution. Influenced by such men as Charles Lyell and Jean de Monet, he produced his masterwork, *A System of Synthetic Philosophy.* In the second phase of his study, *The Principles of Biology,* he argues the theory of evolution as he finds it in that science. Explaining the impact of environmental forces on living creatures, he says:

> . . . it cannot but happen that those individuals whose functions are most out of equilibrium with the modified aggregate of external forces, will be those to die; and that those will survive whose functions happen to be most nearly in equilibrium with the modified aggregate of external forces.
> But this **survival of the fittest,** implies multiplication of the fittest. Out of the fittest thus multiplied, there will, as before, be an overthrowing of the moving equilibrium wherever it presents the least opposing force to the new incident force. And by the continual destruction of the individuals that are the least capable of maintaining their equilibria in presence of this new incident force, there must eventually be arrived at an altered type completely in equilibrium with the altered conditions.

A swan-like end

Source: THE MERCHANT OF VENICE (Act III, sc. ii, l. 44)
Author: William Shakespeare (1564-1616)
First published: 1600
Type of work: Dramatic comedy

Context: The belief that the swan, which is otherwise voiceless, recognizes its coming death and sings before it occurs is at least as old as Soc-

926

rates. The expression "swan song" is firmly entrenched in our language and the idea is used in Chaucer's *The Parlement of Foules* (1372-1386), and elsewhere in Shakespeare— *Othello* (1604), Act V, sc. 2, l. 245. It was also used by Byron in *Don Juan* (Canto III, stanza 86, l. 16). In *The Merchant of Venice,* Bassanio, who is in love with the rich heiress Portia, but is unable to marry her unless, according to her father's will, he choose the casket among the three —golden, silver and lead—which contains her portrait, wants to try his luck, because, he confesses, in his uncertainty he lives "upon the rack." Portia, however, wishes him to delay making the choice because she likes his company and is afraid she will lose him because he will select the wrong casket. Portia consents, however, and cautions him:

PORTIA
Away, then, I am locked in one of them,
If you do love me, you will find me out.
. . .
Let music sound while he doth make his choice:
Then if he lose he makes a **swan-like end,**
Fading in music.
. . .

Swear not by the moon

Source: ROMEO AND JULIET (Act II, sc. ii, l. 109)
Author: William Shakespeare (1564-1616)
First published: 1597
Type of work: Dramatic tragedy

Context: In the first face-to-face meeting when the two lovers are alone, Romeo and Juliet have declared their love. Juliet, however, with maidenly hesitation and restraint, fears that she has declared her love too easily and too soon. She is afraid that though Romeo protest his love, he may not love her as ardently or as long as she loves him. At this point in their relationship, she fears, perhaps wisely, that Romeo is likely to swear more on the spur of the infatuated moment than he will care to fulfill in the sane daylight. It is natural for Romeo to swear by the moon because the moon is already on his mind, as it always is on the minds of lovers, and because, when he first saw Juliet standing in the window, he called her "the sun," and said that in her "rising" she would "kill the envious moon, / Who is already sick and pale with grief, / That thou her maid art far more fair than she." Juliet, however, knows that lovers always swear on the moon, and she wants Romeo to swear on something more constant. She would rather Romeo would "swear by thy gracious self, / Which is the god of my idolatry," or better yet that he "not swear at all."

927

O **swear not by the moon,** th' inconstant moon,
That monthly changes in her circled orb,
Lest that thy love prove likewise variable.

Sweet are the uses of adversity

Source: AS YOU LIKE IT (Act II, sc. i, l. 12)
Author: William Shakespeare (1564-1616)
First published: 1623
Type of work: Dramatic comedy

Context: In this play, which has been called Shakespeare's "most perfect comedy," Duke Senior has had his dukedom usurped by his brother, Duke Frederick. Duke Senior, banished from the dukedom, has gone into exile in the Forest of Arden, and there he and his followers "live like the old Robin Hood of England." We meet Duke Senior and his fellow lords in exile in Arden, where the duke is putting the best possible face on his misfortune. He asks his followers, "Hath not old custome made this life more sweet / Than that of painted pomp? / Are not these woods / More free from peril than the envious court?" He then further comments on the therapeutic effect of adversity and of the country life:

DUKE SENIOR
Sweet are the uses of adversity,
Which, like the toad ugly and venomous,
Wears yet a precious jewel in his head.
And this our life, exempt from public haunt,
Finds tongues in trees, books in the running brooks,
Sermons in stones, and good in every thing.

A sweet disorder in the dress kindles in clothes a wantonness

Source: HESPERIDES ("Delight in Disorder")
Author: Robert Herrick (1591-1674)
First published: 1648
Type of work: Lyric poem

Context: Although Herrick lived well into the Restoration period, and although he was the vicar of a remote Devonshire parish from 1629 to 1648, his poetry remained unchanged: he wrote either descriptions of simple country life in his parish or the gay, light-hearted love poetry characteristic of what has been called "the Cavalier" school. This little poem, scarcely more than a sketch, presents the idea that a certain carelessness in feminine

928

attire is to the poet more attractive than too much precision. The pleasure of the poem lies in the neat observation of the details that create the charming disorder that appeals to Herrick.

> **A sweet disorder in the dress**
> **Kindles in clothes a wantonness.**
> A lawn about the shoulders thrown
> Into a fine distraction;
> An erring lace, which here and there
> Enthralls the crimson stomacher:
> . . .
> A winning wave, deserving note,
> In the tempestuous petticoat
> . . .
> Do more bewitch me than when art
> Is more precise in every part.

Sweet girl-graduates

Source: THE PRINCESS (Prologue, l. 142)
Author: Alfred, Lord Tennyson (1809-1892)
First published: 1847
Type of work: Narrative poem

Context: Tennyson, poet laureate and spokesman of his time, concerned himself from his early years with the problems confronting the Englishman of the nineteenth century. In *The Princess,* he presents, half jestingly and half seriously, the issue of the education of women, by having a group of college-age men and the sister of one relate the story of Princess Ida, who founds an institution, completely devoid of males, for the education of her own sex. Her heart, however, overrules her intellect, and she learns to love the Prince to whom she has been betrothed from childhood. In the Prologue, the poet and his friends talk with Lilia, who resents woman's childish position in society and declares that if she were a princess she would construct "Far off from men a college like a man's." One of the young men replies:

> "Pretty were the sight
> If our old halls could change their sex, and flaunt
> With prudes for proctors, dowagers for deans,
> And **sweet girl-graduates** in their golden hair.
> I think they should not wear our rusty gowns,
> But move as rich as Emperor-moths, or Ralph
> Who shines so in the corner; yet I fear,
> If there were many Lilias in the brood,
> However deep you might embower the nest,
> Some boy would spy it."

Sweet is revenge—especially to women

Source: DON JUAN (Canto I, stanza 124)
Author: George Gordon, Lord Byron (1788-1824)
First published: 1819
Type of work: Narrative poem

Context: This quotation is similar to our common saying, "Revenge is sweet." It is also similar to Satan's comment, enviously thinking of Adam and Eve, "Revenge, at first though sweet,/ Bitter ere long back on itself recoils," in Book IX of Milton's *Paradise Lost.* In *Don Juan* the quotation in question is part of a series of statements, taking up several stanzas, about things that one can consider "sweet": a miser's gold to him, the hum of bees, the voices of young girls, the birth of one's first son, the taste of new vintage wine, and many more. None be so sweet, however, concludes the poet, as "first and passionate love—it stands alone,/ Like Adam's recollection of his fall." Such love is worth the sum of all the other "sweets," says Lord Byron, that he can name. The lines about the sweetness of revenge appear in the following context:

> Sweet is the vintage, when the shower'ng grapes
> In Bacchanal profusion reel to earth,
> Purple and gushing; sweet are our escapes
> From civic revelry to rural mirth;
> Sweet to the miser are his glittering heaps,
> Sweet to the father is his first-born's birth,
> **Sweet is revenge—especially to women,**
> Pillage to soldiers, prize-money to seamen.

Sweet is true love tho' given in vain

Source: IDYLLS OF THE KING ("Lancelot and Elaine," Line 1000)
Author: Alfred, Lord Tennyson (1809-1892)
First published: 1859
Type of work: Song

Context: Elaine, young daughter of the Lord of Astolot, has led a life of unblemished innocence in the isolation of her father's castle, having for companions only her father and brothers. When Sir Lancelot one day chances to visit the castle, Elaine becomes immediately and hopelessly enamored of him; and when he leaves, after only a day, to enter the court tournament, she can think of nothing but him. In the combats he is critically wounded and is taken to the cave of a hermit. Throughout a long period of recovery Elaine nurses him; and in gratitude, Lancelot asks her to name her reward. Only one thing will content her, to become his wife, but the knight is bound to his guilty love for Guenevere, and denies and abandons her. Elaine soon dies from frustrated passion and shortly before her death composes a song called "The Song of Love and Death."

> **Sweet is true love tho' given in vain,** in vain;
> And sweet is death who puts an end to pain.
> I know not which is sweeter, no, not I.

Sweeter also than honey and the honeycomb

Source: PSALMS 19:10
Author: Unknown
First transcribed: c.400-200 B.C.
Type of work: Religious poetry

Context: Just as God is glorified by the ordered universe He created, so also is His excellence exemplified by the justice of His commandments. The psalmist states that the testimony or precepts of God are constant, that the statutes or established rules of God are correct, that the commandment of God is untainted, that the reverence for God is sinless and everlasting, and that the decrees of God are reliable and ethical. God's moral codes sustain the soul and give wisdom, joy, and enlightenment to the believer. Speaking of God's moral codes, the poet argues that:

> More to be desired are they than gold, yea, than much fine gold: **sweeter also than honey and the honeycomb.**
> Moreover by them is thy servant warned: and in keeping of them there is great reward.

Sweetest love, I do not go for weariness of thee

Source: POEMS ("Song," stanza 1)
Author: John Donne (c.1572-1631)
First published: 1633
Type of work: Metaphysical poem

Context: In this song, Donne, by the use of metaphysical "wit," plays with the idea of parting from his love whom he calls "the best of me." Though parting from her will be like death, he can promise to return even more speedily than the sun. In the meanwhile, she must not sigh or weep, for, in doing so, she will sigh and weep away his soul and his life's blood, so much a part of him has she become. Therefore, it is best to consider their temporary separation as if they had, for a short while, merely "turned aside to sleep." The first stanza of the poem follows:

931

Sweetest love I do not go
For weariness of thee,
Nor in hope the world can show
A fitter Love for me;
But since that I
Must die at last, 'tis best
To use myself in jest,
Thus by feigned deaths to die.

The sweetest song ear ever heard

Source: THE PRISONER OF CHILLON (Line 254)
Author: George Gordon, Lord Byron (1788-1824)
First published: 1816
Type of work: Narrative poem

Context: Byron wrote this poem in two days while he and Shelley were touring Lake Geneva, 1816. It is introduced by a sonnet on liberty beginning "Eternal Spirit of the chainless Mind!" and is written as a monologue. The historical prisoner was François de Bonnivard (1493-1570), prior of a small monastery outside Geneva. Bonnivard was imprisoned for six years because he tried to free Geneva from the control of the Duke of Savoy so that it could become a republic. His last four years were spent in a dungeon in the Castle of Chillon beside Lake Geneva ("Leman" in the poem). He was freed by the Bernese in 1536 and returned to his home, where he lived a long and useful life. The brothers described in the poem are Byron's own inventions. The line quoted refers to the song of a bird perched on the barred window of the cell. The prisoner's youngest brother has just died, and he is completely stunned—"I had no thought, no feeling—none—/ Among the stones I stood a stone" (ll. 235-6). The bird's song restores his senses, bringing life and hope. In context the lines read:

A light broke in upon my brain,—
It was the carol of a bird;
It ceased, and then it came again,
The sweetest song ear ever heard.

Sweetness and light

Source: CULTURE AND ANARCHY ("Preface")
Author: Matthew Arnold (1822-1888)
First published: 1867-1868
Type of work: Social and moral essay

Context: In his *Culture and Anarchy,* Arnold argues against the narrowness of Hebraism with its emphasis on the development only of the religious side of man and for Hellenism with its emphasis on the development of the total man. Pointing out that the Nonconformists need the culture that is the "pursuit of our total perfection by means of getting to know, on all the matters which most concern us, the best which has been thought and said in the world . . . ," he describes this perfection with a phrase taken from Jonathan Swift's *The Battle of the Books,* wherein a self-sufficient, but restricted spider is compared with a bee, the gatherer of honey and the producer of wax for candles:

> . . . So, while we praise and esteem the zeal of the Noncon- formists in walking staunchly by the best light they have, and desire to take no whit from it, we seek to add to this what we call **sweetness and light,** and to develop their full humanity more perfectly. To seek this is certainly not to be the enemy of the Noncomformists.

Sweets to the sweet

Source: HAMLET (Act V, sc. i, l. 266)
Author: William Shakespeare (1564-1616)
First published: 1603
Type of work: Dramatic tragedy

Context: Ophelia, daughter of Polonius, the late chief councilor of King Claudius of Denmark, and who was once the beloved of Prince Hamlet, lost her senses after her father was killed. Shortly, she drowned accidentally, and now is being buried in a churchyard near Elsinore Castle. Her body is laid in the grave, and Queen Gertrude comes to the graveside to say farewell.

> GERTRUDE
> **Sweets to the sweet.** Farewell. [*Scatters flowers.*]
> I hoped thou shouldst have been my Hamlet's wife.
> I thought thy bride-bed to have decked, sweet maid,
> And not have strewed thy grave.

Take care of the pence; for the pounds will take care of themselves

Source: LETTERS TO HIS SON (Letter 19)
Author: Philip Dormer Stanhope, Lord Chesterfield (1694-1773)
First published: 1774
Type of work: Personal letters

Context: Lord Chesterfield, in a letter to his son, dated November 6, 1747, complains at the boy's tendency to be tardy in answering his earlier missives. Lord Chesterfield chides the boy by quoting from Jonathan Swift's account of Laputan philosophers who were ". . . so wrapped up and absorbed in their abstruse speculations that they would have forgotten all the common and necessary duties of life, if they had not been reminded of them by persons who flapped them. . . ." In typical fatherly fashion, but with incisive wit and in his most attractive manner, Lord Chesterfield notes: "I do not indeed suspect you of being absorbed in abstruse speculations; but, with great submission to you, may I not suspect that levity, inattention, and too little thinking, require a flapper. . . . If my letters should happen to get to you when you are . . . doing nothing, or when you are gaping by the window, may they not be very proper flaps, to put you in mind that you might employ your time much better?" Then, adds Lord Chesterfield:

I knew once a very covetous fellow, who used frequently to say **"Take care of the pence; for the pounds will take care of themselves."** . . . I recommend to you to take care of the minutes; for the hours will take care of themselves.

Take the cash and let the credit go

Source: THE RUBÁIYÁT OF OMAR KHAYYÁM (Stanza 13)
Author: Omar Khayyám (died c. 1123)
Translator and adapter: Edward FitzGerald (1809-1883)
First published: 1859
Type of work: Translation and poetic adaptation of Persian poetry

Context: Unlike most Victorian writers, FitzGerald does not moralize, and he does not extol duty and toil in his adaption of the Persian poem. He glorifies wine, which symbolizes love, sensual pleasure, revolt against restrictions, and life itself. Life is now here in all its glory: ". . . still a Ruby kindles in the Vine,/ And many a Garden by the Water blows." But life will soon be gone: "Come, fill the Cup, and in the fire of Spring/ Your Winter-garment of Repentance fling. . . . The Wine of Life keeps oozing drop by drop,/ The Leaves of Life keep falling one by one." The heroes of the past are dead, and the future is uncertain. Only the here-and-now matters:

Some for the Glories of This World; and some
Sigh for the Prophet's Paradise to come;
    Ah, **take the Cash, and let the Credit go,**
Nor heed the rumble of a distant Drum!

Take the tone of the company that you are in

Source: LETTERS TO HIS SON (Letter 17)
Author: Philip Dormer Stanhope, Lord Chesterfield (1694-1773)
First published: 1774
Type of work: Personal letters

Context: Upon his son Philip's travelling to Leipsig, the urbane Lord Chesterfield writes to him from London on October 9, 1747, urging him to choose his friends and companions prudently and not to reveal confidences to new acquaintances, lest the friendships cool and consequent glib repetition prove harmful to the confider (in this case, Philip, of course). The English nobleman advises his illegitimate, but well-beloved, son not to yield to the sudden youthful assumption that exciting companionship or youthful rapport is real friendship. It is in his next letter (XVII), also written from London, on October 16, 1747, that he discusses the necessity of pleasing one's associates in the hope of preferment and social acceptance. The cold and calculating approach to social matters may surprise those of us more used to a democratic approach to human relations—even in society, but the time was not a democratic one, and station and social reputation loomed large. So it is that Lord Chesterfield tells Philip:

> . . . **Take the tone of the company that you are in,** and do not pretend to give it; be serious, be gay, or even trifling, as you find the present humor of the company; this is an attention due from every individual to the majority. Do not tell stories in company; there is nothing more tedious and disagreeable . . .

Tale of a tub

Source: GARGANTUA AND PANTAGRUEL (Book IV, chapter 38)
Author: François Rabelais (1495-1553)
First published: 1532-1564
Type of work: Mock heroic chronicle

Context: Panurge convinces his friends Pantagruel and Friar John to voyage with him to consult with the Oracle of the Holy Bottle about whether or not he should marry. On their way they have many strange adventures, including a visit to Wild Island, which is inhabited by Chitterlings. It is here that Shrovetide, or Lent, wages constant war against the Chitterlings, who are helped by Carnival, or Mardi-gras. After describing Pantagruel's adventures with the Chitterlings, the author quotes the phrase which was used later by Jonathan Swift in one of his famous satires:

> . . . You shake your empty noodles now, jolly topers, and do not believe what I tell you here, any more than if it were some

935

tale of a tub. Well, well, I cannot help it. Believe it if you will; if you will not, let it alone.

A tale told by an idiot, full of sound and fury signifying nothing

Source: MACBETH (Act V, sc. v, ll. 26-28)
Author: William Shakespeare (1564-1616)
First published: 1623
Type of work: Dramatic tragedy

Context: Macbeth, King of Scotland, is a usurper who murders the lawful King Duncan and, when the latter's sons, Malcolm and Donalbain, flee for their lives, fastens the blame on them. Macbeth's reign is fitful and bloody. As the years pass, he gains more enemies, and many nobles desert Scotland to join Malcolm in England. Lady Macbeth, her husband's partner in assassination, suffers from a guilt-ridden conscience that will not let her sleep. There is no remedy for her illness, and she dies just as Malcolm's forces, come from England to restore the throne to its rightful claimant, attack Macbeth's stronghold. Word is brought to Macbeth of his wife's death. He bitterly philosophizes on the event, in a passage which, perhaps, contains more famous lines than any other in Shakespeare.

MACBETH
. . .
To-morrow, and to-morrow, and to-morrow,
Creeps in this petty pace from day to day,
To the last syllable of recorded time;
And all our yesterdays have lighted fools
The way to dusty death. Out, out, brief candle!
Life's but a walking shadow, a poor player,
That struts and frets his hour upon the stage,
And then is heard no more. It is **a tale**
Told by an idiot, full of sound and fury
Signifying nothing.
. . .

Talk of Shakespeare, and the musical glasses

Source: THE VICAR OF WAKEFIELD (Chapter 9)
Author: Oliver Goldsmith (1728-1774)
First published: 1766
Type of work: Novel

Context: One of the delightful incidents in *The Vicar of Wakefield* is an evening of country dancing, occasioned by the arrival of Squire Thorn-

936

hill along with "two young ladies, richly drest, whom he introduced as women of very great distinction and fashion from town." These two tried mightily to participate in the dancing, but found doing so difficult and finally, being "apprehensive of catching cold, moved to break up the ball." One of them, says Dr. Primrose, "expressed her sentiments upon this occasion in a very coarse manner, when she observed, that by the *living jingo, she was all of a muck of sweat.*" At supper the conversation was more re-served, Primrose says, but the two ladies continued their supercilious treatment of the country folk, particularly the two Primrose daughters. It is obviously this passage that Everard Webley is referring to in Aldous Huxley's (1894-1963) *Point Counterpoint* (1928) when, angered at Elinor Quarles's dallying with him, he asks sarcastically: "Shall we talk about Shakespeare? Or the musical glasses?" Primrose describes their conversation:

> . . . The two ladies threw my girls into the shade; for they would **talk of** nothing but high life, and high-lived company; with other fashionable topics, such as pictures, taste, **Shakespeare, and the musical glasses.** 'Tis true they once or twice mortified us sensibly by slipping out an oath; but that appeared to me as the surest symptom of their distinction (though I am since informed that swearing is perfectly unfashionable).

Talk of the devil, and his horns appear

Source: BIOGRAPHIA LITERARIA (Chapter 23)
Author: Samuel Taylor Coleridge (1772-1834)
First published: 1817
Type of work: Critical and philosophic essays

Context: In his philosophical-critical treatise, *Biographia Literaria,* Coleridge reprinted a series of letters he had contributed to *The Courier* in 1816, attacking the tragedy *Bertram, or the Castle of St. Aldobrand,* by Charles Robert Maturin (1782-1824). Coleridge derides the play as a compound of immorality, rant, and contrivance, ending, as it began, "in a superfetation of blasphemy upon nonsense." In the play, the Lady Imogine is married to Lord St. Aldobrand, but is still in love with St. Aldobrand's banished enemy, Count Bertram, now leader of a robber band. By the fourth act, Bertram makes himself known to Imogine and, together with his band, lies in wait for St. Aldobrand at the Lord's own castle. St. Aldobrand returns from a journey but leaves immediately to attend a religious festival. "But do not be distressed, reader," Coleridge notes, "on account of St. Aldobrand's absence! As the author has contrived to send him out of the house, when a husband would be in his, and the lover's way, so he will doubtless not be at a loss to bring him

937

back again as soon as he is wanted."
After the transaction of some further
melodramatic business, we are ready
for Aldobrand's death. Coleridge has
varied the proverb, "Talk of the devil
and he is sure to appear." In America
speak is usually substituted for *talk*.

> **Talk of the devil, and his horns appear,** says the proverb: and
> sure enough, within ten lines of the exit of the messenger sent to
> stop him, the arrival of Lord St. Aldobrand is announced. Ber-
> tram's ruffiian band now enter, and range themselves across the
> stage. . . .

Tar-Baby ain't sayin' nuthin', en Brer Fox, he lay low

Source: THE WONDERFUL TAR-BABY STORY
Author: Joel Chandler Harris (1848-1908)
First published: 1880 in *Uncle Remus: His Songs and His Sayings*
Type of work: Short story

Context: "The Wonderful Tar-Baby
Story" is one of the many tales that
Joel Chandler Harris put into the
mouth of his story-teller, Uncle
Remus. In this story the little boy
wants to know if the fox ever caught
the rabbit. In answer, Uncle Remus
tells of the fox one day getting together some tar and making a tar-
baby. The fox puts the tar-baby in a
road that the rabbit usually uses, then
hides in the bushes to see the results
of his scheme. Soon Brer Rabbit appears, spies the tar-baby, and is surprised to find the silent object in the
road. The rabbit tries unsuccessfully
to engage the tar-baby in conversation. Each time the tar-baby does not
answer, the rabbit strikes it, finally
getting his fists, his feet, and his head
stuck in the tar. On first finding the
tar-baby in the road, the rabbit tries
to open the conversation with a comment on the weather:

> " 'Mawnin'!' " sez Brer Rabbit, sezee—" 'nice wedder dis
> mawnin',' sezee."
> **"Tar-Baby ain't sayin' nothin', en Brer Fox, he lay low."**

Teach us to sit still

Source: ASH WEDNESDAY (Part I, stanza 5)
Author: T(homas) S(tearns) Eliot (1888-1965)
First published: 1930
Type of work: Religious poem

Context: The poet's spiritual experience, actually a developing faith in a
redemptive experience, takes him
through several mental and emotional

steps, each disclosing a significant state of mind, each in its order imperative to the total experience. The first step essentially involves a recognition of the nature of things as they exist. The second step is, in facing the fact of physical death and its consequence, the establishment of a faith in something beyond the flesh. Finally the poet must acknowledge the medium through which to effectuate and nourish his faith. In the first section of the poem the poet recognizes the limitations of his own powers and accepts the fact that life is prescribed by the commonplace laws of time and space. Although in this section he rejects the ideal altogether, as the poem progresses he is to convert his former yearnings and aspirations into a secure, though unverifiable, faith based upon traditional Christianity. In this first section he prays for mercy and deliverance from the critical, ineffective restlessness of his spirit. His prayer includes the request:

> Because these wings are no longer wings to fly
> But merely vans to beat the air
> The air which is now thoroughly small and dry
> Smaller and dryer than the will
> Teach us to care and not to care
> **Teach us to sit still.**

Tears, idle tears

Source: THE PRINCESS (Part IV, Line 21)
Author: Alfred, Lord Tennyson (1809-1892)
First published: 1847
Type of work: Song

Context: The princess, Ida, accompanied by the prince who seeks her hand in marriage and by a group of her fellow-members of the all-female, anti-masculine academy, walks in the fields and hills of the academy lands just as the sun is setting. One of the maids sings the emotional song of regret for the loss of happy days in the past. Ida retorts, when the song has been finished, that it is futile and wasteful to mourn past losses; one must forget or, at least, accept them and turn his attention to the future. All things are transitory, she says, and are given only a fixed span of life. The sad song of the maiden begins

> **Tears, idle tears,** I know not what they mean,
> Tears from the depth of some divine despair
> Rise in the heart, and gather to the eyes,
> In looking on the happy autumn-fields,
> And thinking of the days that are no more.

939

The tears of the crocodile

Source: EASTWARD HO! (Act V, sc. iv. l. 41)
Author: George Chapman (1559-1634), Ben Jonson (1573?-1637), John Marston (1576-1634)
First published: 1605
Type of work: Dramatic comedy

Context: Quicksilver, Touchstone's profligate apprentice, Sir Petronel, the prodigal knight who is married to Touchstone's daughter Gertrude, and Security, the usurer, are imprisoned for conspiring to get Gertrude's inheritance. Touchstone at first turns a deaf ear to the pleadings of his own wife, of their two daughters, Gertrude and Mildred, who is the mistress of Quicksilver, of Winifred, the wife of Security, and of the officer Wolf. In other works, references to crocodile tears are made by Robert Burton in the *Anatomy of Melancholy* (621-1651), Part III, Section 2, Member 2, Subsection 4, by John Suckling in *The Sad One,* Act IV, scene 5 and by many others.

TOUCHSTONE

I am deaf still, I say. I will neither yield to the song of the siren nor the voice of the hyena, **the tears of the crocodile** nor the howling o' the Wolf: avoid my habitations, monsters!

Tears, such as angels weep

Source: PARADISE LOST (Book I, l. 620)
Author: John Milton (1608-1674)
First published: 1667
Type of work: Epic poem

Context: When Satan prepares to address the rebel angels, then newly plunged into Hell, he appears straight and proud before them. The fallen angels bend their ranks to make a half circle about their leader and stand quietly to hear his words. But though he be proud and courageous, Satan cannot entirely control his emotions; three times he tries to speak, and three times he fails because his emotions get the best of him:

Thrice he assayed, and thrice in spite of scorn,
Tears, such as angels weep, burst forth: at last
Words interwove with sighs found out their way.

Tedious as a twice-told tale

Source: KING JOHN (Act III, sc. iv, l. 108)
Author: William Shakespeare (1564-1616)
First published: 1623
Type of work: Historical drama

Context: Philip, King of France, has been bested by John, King of England, who has fortified his French conquests and sailed for England. Constance, mother of Arthur, complaining to Philip about the loss of her son, is going mad with grief over her tragedy. She curses peace and wishes that her feeble hand were strong enough to shake the very earth. When she leaves, beside herself with anguish, Philip, fearing some "outrage," follows her. Lewis, the dauphin, summarizes his own opinion as well as that of Constance in these lines (cf. Homer *Odyssey* Bk. XII):

LEWIS
There's nothing in this world can make me joy.
Life is as **tedious as a twice-told tale,**
Vexing the dull ear of a drowsy man;
And bitter shame hath spoiled the sweet world's taste
That it yields naught but shame and bitterness.

Tell 'em Queen Anne's dead

Source: THE HEIR-AT-LAW (Act I, sc. i)
Author: George Colman the Younger (1762-1836)
First published: 1800
Type of work: Dramatic comedy

Context: A dramatist of the late 18th and early 19th century, George Colman the Younger succeeded his father as manager of the Haymarket Theatre in 1789. Of his numerous comedies, melodramas, and musical comedies, one of the most successful was *The Heir-at-Law*. In the opening scene of this play, Lord Duberly, the former "plain Daniel Dowlas of Gosport," has unexpectedly inherited the estate of the old Lord Duberly. His wife, acutely conscious of her *nouveau riche* status and determined that her husband shall now develop the proper habits of a gentleman, berates him for drinking his tea from a saucer, for employing the locutions of a commoner such as "hand over the milk" for "pass the milk" and "rot you" for "be damned to you." As she remarks, "Why, an oath, now and then, may slip in, to garnish genteel conversation: but, then, it should be done with an air to one's equals, and with a kind of careless condescension to menials." Above all, he must not speak further of his former days as a merchant or of his having obtained the inheritance as a result of his lawyer's having seen a newspaper advertisement. At Lady Duberly's incensed assertion that the servants might hear, he becomes exasperated:

LORD DUBERLY
Hear, and what will they hear but what they know? our story a secret!—Lord help you!—**Tell 'em Queen Anne's dead,** my lady.

Tell it not in Gath

Source: II SAMUEL 1:20
Author: Unknown
First transcribed: 1100-400 B.C.
Type of work: Religious history

Context: At his encampment as Ziklag, the young warrior, David, awaits news of the encounter of King Saul and his sons against the Philistines. On the third day a disheveled Amalekite messenger presents himself to David and discloses that the Israelite forces have been routed at Gilboa and that King Saul and his son Jonathon are among the many soldiers who have been slain. The courier, presenting Saul's crown and bracelet to David, swears that, at the command of the wounded king, he himself delivered the death-blow to Saul. Having ordered the Amalekite messenger killed, David leads the Israelites in mourning for their dead king:

The beauty of Israel is slain upon thy high places: how are the mighty fallen!
Tell it not in Gath, publish it not in the streets or Askelon; lest the daughters of the Philistines rejoice, lest the daughters of the uncircumcised triumph.
Ye mountains of Gilboa, let there be no dew, neither let there be rain, upon you, nor fields of offerings: for there the shield of the mighty is vilely cast away, the shield of Saul, as though he had not been anointed with oil.

Tell me not, in mournful numbers, life is but an empty dream

Source: A PSALM OF LIFE (Stanza 1)
Author: Henry Wadsworth Longfellow (1807-1882)
First published: 1838
Type of work: Lyric poem

Context: Two of our most quotable poems are "A Psalm of Life" and Kipling's "If," both of which have been vastly popular. As late as 1929, when Longfellow's reputation was perhaps at its lowest, a poll showed

"A Psalm of Life" to be, by all odds, America's favorite poem. Its point of view is that of Goethe's *Wilhelm Meister,* and Longfellow felt that the poem was so much a part of himself that he kept it "some time" in manuscript. It was a rallying cry against his own despondence, which he refuted in his verses. Almost every line is quotable, the first stanza being:

> Tell me not, in mournful numbers,
> Life is but an empty dream!—
> For the soul is dead that slumbers,
> And things are not what they seem.

Tell sad stories of the death of kings

Source: KING RICHARD THE SECOND (Act III, sc. ii, 1. 157)
Author: William Shakespeare (1564-1616)
First published: 1597
Type of work: Historical drama

Context: Richard II comes back from Ireland to find his cousin, the banished Bolingbroke, back in the land and gaining power every minute. At first Richard's hopes are high in opposing Bolingbroke, but every messenger brings the report of the strength of Richard's opponent. One by one the king names his former adherents, only to have each name written off as dead or his forces dispersed. He has returned too late to save his kingdom. Finally realizing the extent of his helplessness, Richard, the victim of his own mercurial nature, sinks into despair.

RICHARD
. . .

> Let's talk of graves, of worms, and epitaphs,
> Make dust our paper, and with rainy eyes,
> Write sorrow on the bosom of the earth.
> Let's choose executors and talk of wills.
> . . .
> And that a small model of the barren earth,
> Which serves as paste, and cover to our bones.
> For God's sake let us sit upon the ground,
> And **tell sad stories of the death of kings,**
> . . .

Tell that to the marines

Source: REDGAUNTLET (Chapter 13)
Author: Sir Walter Scott (1771-1832)
First published: 1824
Type of work: Novel

Context: This expression is a form of an old saying, "That will do for the marines, but the sailors won't believe it," which grew up out of the jealousy between the two British services. Byron (1788-1824) made use of a form of this saying at the end of Canto II of *The Island* (1823), in which a sailor expresses doubt of a mate's declaration of faithful love to an island girl by saying "Right . . . that will do for the marines." Scott uses the phrase thus: On a Journey into Scotland in 1763 young Darsie Latimer meets by accident and is kidnaped by a man who proves to be his uncle, High Redgauntlet. In the course of trying to rescue Darsie, his friend Alan Fairford sails aboard a smuggling boat carrying with him a letter from a priest to the stanch Stuart sympathizer Redgauntlet. Alan has naïvely failed to recognize the "priest" as the Pretender. When the smuggler captain twits him upon his being a Jacobite, Alan says he does not understand the innuendo. Exclaiming upon his claiming innocence while carrying such correspondence, the captain retorts:

"Tell that to the marines—the sailors won't believe it."

Temper justice with mercy

Source: PARADISE LOST (Book X, ll. 77-78)
Author: John Milton (1608-1674)
First published: 1667
Type of work: Epic poem

Context: When Eve, and later Adam, eat of the fruit of the tree of knowledge, the guard of angels leaves Paradise and reports the transgression to God, Who relieves them of all blame, saying that they could not prevent Satan's success in seducing mankind to disobedience, but He declares that judgment must be passed upon Adam and Eve. God's Son is declared the one to pass the judgment; God says that justice is to be colleague with mercy, that this is the reason for His choice of judge. The Messiah, who has already accepted His role as man's redeemer by suffering for man's transgressions, says to God:

"Father eternal, thine is to decree,
Mine both in heaven and earth to do thy will
Supreme, that thou in me thy son beloved
Mayest ever rest well pleased. I go to judge

On earth these thy transgressors, but thou knowest,
Whoever judged, the worst on me must light,
When time shall be, for so I undertook
Before thee; and not repenting, this obtain
Of right, that I may mitigate their doom
On me derived, yet I shall **temper** so
Justice with mercy, as may illustrate most
Them fully satisfied, and thee appease."

Ten thousand fleets sweep over thee in vain

Source: CHILDE HAROLD'S PILGRIMAGE (Canto IV, stanza 179)
Author: George Gordon, Lord Byron (1788-1824)
First published: 1818 (Canto IV)
Type of work: Narrative poem in Spenserian stanzas

Context: Throughout *Childe Harold,* Byron alternately curses and woos mankind, but his attitude toward Nature remains unchanged. He regards Nature as powerful, timeless, and immutable—an inexhaustible source of strength and inspiration. Compared with Nature, man is cruel, selfish, mean, and destructive. The quotation is from one of six stanzas in which Byron apostrophizes the ocean—the one part of Nature which man is unable to control or ruin. "His steps are not upon thy paths." His mightiest ships "are thy toys . . ./ Alike the Armada's pride or spoils of Trafalgar". The ocean remains "Unchangeable . . ./ Time writes no wrinkle on thy azure brow". In context, the quotation from Stanza 179 reads:

Roll on, thou deep and dark blue Ocean—roll!
Ten thousand fleets sweep over thee in vain;
Man marks the earth with ruin—his control
Stops with the shore . . .

Tender is the night

Source: ODE TO A NIGHTINGALE (Stanza 4, l. 5)
Author: John Keats (1795-1821)
First published: 1820
Type of work: Lyric poem

Context: In this famous ode the poet sings of leaving the harsh realities of the world, in which he is not happy. He asks that he might drink from some vintage that would take him to the nightingale "away in the forest dim," where there is no weariness, no fretting, no old age, no death come too soon. This thought is one that comes to him when, as he says, "My heart aches, and a drowsy numbness pains/ My sense, as though of hem-

945

lock I had drunk,/ Or emptied some dull opiate to the drains one minute past. . . ." In the fourth stanza of the poem the poet refutes the idea of some potion to bring happiness, regardless of its vintage. Instead, he says, he will fly away "on the viewless wings of Poesy" to the world of the nightingale and its beauty and happiness. The quotation is also famous, of course, as the title of an F. Scott Fitzgerald novel.

> Away! away! for I will fly to thee,
>> Not charioted by Bacchus and his pards,
> But on the viewless wings of Poesy
>> Though the dull brain perplexes and retards:
> Already with thee! **tender is the night.**
>> And haply the Queen-Moon is on her throne,
>>> Clustered around by all her starry Fays;
>>> But here there is no light,
> Save what from heaven is with the breezes blown
>> Through verdurous glooms and winding mossy ways.

Terrible as an army with banners

Source: THE SONG OF SOLOMON 6:10
Author: Unknown
First transcribed: c.300-200 B.C.
Type of work: Lyric poetry

Context: The poet, describing his beautiful beloved, compares her hair with a flock of goats, her teeth with a flock of freshly washed sheep, and her forehead with the pomegranate. The only daughter of her mother, she combines the freshness of the morning, the unblemished beauty of the moon, and the vigor and brightness of an army on parade:

> My dove, my undefiled is but one; she is . . . the choice one
> of her that bare her. The daughters saw her, and blessed her; yea,
> the queens and the concubines, and they praised her.
>> Who is she that looketh forth as the morning, fair as the moon,
> clear as the sun, and **terrible as an army with banners?**

A terrible beauty is born

Source: EASTER 1916 (Line 16)
Author: William Butler Yeats (1865-1939)
First published: 1916
Type of work: Lyric poem

Context: On Easter Sunday of 1916, while England was at war with Germany, the Irish Nationalists attempted an insurrection against British rule.

946

The insurrection was put down after bitter street fighting, and many of the Irish were later executed because the movement for their independence was secretly supported by Germany. Yeats knew many of these men, and this poem is a description of and a kind of requiem for them. The quotation above—which appears in slightly varying form throughout the poem—refers to the change that came over these patriots when they gave themselves to their cause. The first stanza reads:

> I have met them at close of day
> Coming with vivid faces
> From counter or desk among grey
> Eighteenth-century houses.
> I have passed with a nod of the head
> Or polite meaningless words
>
>   •   •   •
>
> Being certain that they and I
> But lived where motley is worn:
> All changed, changed utterly:
> **A terrible beauty is born.**

Thank you for nothing

Source: DON QUIXOTE (Part I, Book III, chapter 1)
Author: Miguel de Cervantes Saavedra (1547-1616)
First published: 1605
Type of work: Satirical novel

Context: Don Quixote is resting for the night. His horse, Rozinante, strays into the camp of some Yanguesian carriers from Galicia, and their mares kick at him. So do the teamsters. Calling on his squire for help, Don Quixote goes to the aid of his horse, but with the odds twenty against "one and a half fighting men," in cowardly Sancho's words, the Yanguesians beat them so badly that they flee, thinking they have killed the pair. Don Quixote tries to console his squire with tales of other knights, illtreated without suffering disgrace. He concludes:

> ". . . there is no remembrance which time will not efface, nor no pain to which death will not put a period." **"Thank you for nothing!"** quoth Sancho; "what worse can befall us, than to have only death to trust to? Were our afflictions to be cured with a plaister or two, a man might have some patience, but for aught I see, all the salves in an hospital won't set us on our best legs again."

That chastity of honor which felt a stain like a wound

Source: REFLECTIONS ON THE REVOLUTION IN FRANCE
Author: Edmund Burke (1729-1797)
First published: 1790
Type of work: Political treatise

Context: Burke has been called, Bacon alone excepted, "the greatest political thinker who has ever devoted himself to the practice of English politics." Though he never attained a political office in any degree proportioned to his ability and services, he succeeded in affecting profoundly the opinion of his times. Serving in Parliament, he was roused to action by the sympathy expressed in England for the French Revolution. The result was *Reflections,* a "letter intended to have been sent to a gentleman in Paris." In the debates which followed, Burke became separated from his friends Sheridan and Fox, and from his party. The immediate quotation reveals him deriding an age which will perpetrate the macabre butcheries of the Royal Family, an age without glory and honor:

. . . The unbought grace of life, the cheap defence of nations, the nurse of manly sentiment and heroic enterprise, is gone! It is gone, that sensibility of principle, **that chastity of honor, which felt a stain like a wound,** which inspired courage whilst it mitigated ferocity, which ennobled whatever it touched, and under which vice itself lost half of its evil by losing all its grossness!

That inward eye which is the bliss of solitude

Source: I WANDERED LONELY AS A CLOUD (Stanza 4)
Author: William Wordsworth (1770-1850)
First published: 1807
Type of work: Lyric poem

Context: Wordsworth believed that the mind functions as a storehouse for the assembly of pleasant moments. Thus, the inspirational moments which one experiences in the presence of nature's beauty, furnish not only material for present delight but also food for future thought. A poet, who by his nature is more immediately responsive to the beauty of nature, is dependent upon this faculty of "emotion recollected in tranquillity" for his creative process. Wordsworth comments, concerning this poem, that it treats more "an elementary feeling and simple impression (approaching the nature of an ocular spectrum) upon the imaginative faculty, than the exertion of it." After describing his walk among a "crowd," a "host of golden daffodils . . ./ Tossing their heads in sprightly dance," he avers, "A poet could not but be gay,/ In such a jocund company." And the wealth is greater than the immediate pleasure:

For oft when on my couch I lie
In vacant or in pensive mood,
They flash upon **that inward eye**
Which is the bliss of solitude;
And then my heart with pleasure fills,
And dances with the daffodils.

That old sweetheart of mine

Source: AN OLD SWEETHEART OF MINE (Stanza 2)
Author: James Whitcomb Riley (1849-1916)
First published: 1877
Type of work: Lyric poem

Context: The narrator in the poem allows his thoughts to turn to the past and to the times of his youth and his old sweetheart. Though he hears the voices of his children and the singing of his wife, he does not feel a "twinge of conscience" at thinking of his past happy days, because "it adds a charm/ To spice the good a trifle with a little dust of harm. . . ." His thoughts take him back to his class-room days when he used to smile behind his "lesson" at his sweetheart. In their youth they had made plans for the future, promising each other that they would live happily together until death. The narrator's dream is broken when his wife enters the room. He turns to her "To greet the *living* presence of that old sweetheart of mine." In his dream, the narrator describes their early love:

I can see the pink sunbonnet and the little checkered dress
She wore when first I kissed her and she answered the caress
With the written declaration that, "as surely as the vine
Grew 'round the stump," she loved me—**that old sweetheart of mine.**

That which is not in the interests of the hive cannot be in the interests of the bee

Source: MEDITATIONES (Book VI, 54)
Author: Marcus Aurelius Antoninus (121-180)
First transcribed: Second century
Type of work: Private meditations

Context: In this private meditation Marcus Aurelius says, "The lover of glory conceives his own good to consist in another's action, the lover of pleasure in his own feelings, but the possessor of understanding in his own actions." Again, he urges: "Train thyself to pay careful attention to

949

what is being said by another and as far as possible enter into his soul." He then gives us our proverbial saying and follows it with an illustration:

That which is not in the interests of the hive cannot be in the interests of the bee.

If the sailors spoke ill of a steersman or the sick of a physician, what else would they have in mind but how the man should best effect the safety of the crew or the health of his patients?

That willing suspension of disbelief

Source: BIOGRAPHIA LITERARIA (Chapter 14)
Author: Samuel Taylor Coleridge (1772-1834)
First published: 1817
Type of work: Critical and philosophical essay

Context: In the second edition of *Lyrical Ballads,* one of the cornerstones of the Romantic Movement in England, William Wordsworth provided a theory of poetic diction, asserting that poets ought to use the language of real life, preferably of rustic or low life. Since Coleridge collaborated in the poetry of *Lyrical Ballads,* he was identified with the preface, and he now attempted to set the record straight. Thus a large part of his *Biographia Literaria* is devoted to an attack on Wordsworth's theory, Coleridge claiming that it was wrong in principle, and that even Wordsworth did not follow it in practice. Coleridge introduces his argument by providing the background of the *Lyrical Ballads,* noting that Wordsworth, as his share of the volume, was to include poems that would "give the charm of novelty to things of every day." As for Coleridge,

. . . it was agreed, that my endeavors should be directed to persons and characters supernatural, or at least romantic; yet so as to transfer from our inward nature a human interest and a semblance of truth sufficient to procure for these shadows of imagination **that willing suspension of disbelief** for the moment, which constitutes poetic faith.

That's another story

Source: THE LIFE AND OPINIONS OF TRISTRAM SHANDY, GENT. (Book II, chapter 17)
Author: Laurence Sterne (1713-1768)
First published: 1759-1767
Type of work: Novel

Context: One of the memorable characters in *Tristram Shandy* is Corporal Trim, who served in the wars under Uncle Toby and later became his body servant. Like Uncle Toby, he is kindly and warm-hearted; also like Uncle Toby, he is deeply interested in matters military. Tristram tells of an occasion when Corporal Trim read a sermon on conscience to Mr. Shandy, Uncle Toby, and Dr. Slop. Throughout the reading, the three kept interrupting Trim to argue about the validity of the theology in the sermon, with Uncle Toby interjecting observations about battle strategy and tactics. Moreover, as the sermon proceeded, Trim was reminded, through a reference to the Inquisition, of his brother, who was at the time a prisoner in Portugal. So upset did he become that he began interrupting himself; and so distraught was he, as he approached the end, that Mr. Shandy had to complete the reading:

"——I tell thee, Trim, again," quoth my father, " 'tis not an historical account—'tis a description."—" 'Tis only a description, honest man," quoth Slop, "there's not a word of truth in it."— **"That's another story,"** replied my father.—"However, as Trim reads it with so much concern,—'tis cruelty to force him to go on with it.—Give me hold of the sermon, Trim,—I'll finish it for thee, and thou may'st go."

That's the wise thrush; he sings each song twice over

Source: HOME-THOUGHTS, FROM ABROAD (Line 14)
Author: Robert Browning (1812-1889)
First published: 1845
Type of work: Lyric poem

Context: Browning, having spent several years in Italy, expresses his longing for his homeland ("Oh, to be in England. . . .") in the spring of the year. In this two-stanza poem, the poet remembers lovingly the tiny leaves, the chaffinch, and the orchards of April. And he knows that in the coming May the whitethroats and swallows will build their nests, and the pear trees will drop their blossoms. The thrush, bursting with the first joy of spring, will repeat his song for the listener:

That's the wise thrush; he sings each song
     twice over,
Lest you should think he never could recapture
The first fine careless rapture!

951

Their strength is to sit still

Source: ISAIAH 30:7
Author: Isaiah
First transcribed: c.800-200 B.C.
Type of work: Religious prophecy and exhortation

Context: Isaiah, as prophet of the Almighty, announces his vision of "Judah and Jerusalem in the days of Uzziah, Jotham, Ahaz, and Hezekiah, kings of Judah." He declares the Lord's displeasure with the wickedness of His chosen people and urges obedience to the will of the Lord. Prophesying the destruction and ultimate deliverance of Jerusalem, Isaiah condemns the people for attempting to form an alliance with Egypt against the invading Assyrians. Such an alliance, according to the prophet, does not fit into God's plan and will fail because the people trust the Egyptians and not God:

> Woe to the rebellious children, saith the Lord, . . .
> That walk to go down into Egypt, and have not asked at my mouth; to strengthen themselves in the strength of Pharaoh, and to trust in the shadow of Egypt!
> Therefore shall the strength of Pharaoh be your shame, and the trust in the shadow of Egypt your confusion.
> For the Egyptians shall help in vain, and to no purpose: therefore have I cried concerning this, **Their strength is to sit still.**

Theirs not to reason why

Source: THE CHARGE OF THE LIGHT BRIGADE (Stanza 2)
Author: Alfred, Lord Tennyson (1809-1892)
First published: 1854
Type of work: Patriotic poem

Context: When at the Battle of Balaklava (1854) the order was given for the charge into the valley where almost inescapable death awaited, the men of the Light Brigade responded at once, displaying the perfect discipline that had been fundamental to the British military tradition. "Was there a man dismay'd?/ Not tho' the soldier knew/ Some one had blunder'd." The soldier's place is never to argue against an order, never to hesitate in obeying it, or even to attempt to judge its wrongness or rightness.

> Theirs not to make reply,
> **Theirs not to reason why,**
> Theirs but to do and die.
> Into the valley of Death
> Rode the six hundred.

Them that has china plates themsel's is the maist careful no to break the china plates of others

Source: THE LITTLE MINISTER (Chapter 26)
Author: James M. Barrie (1860-1937)
First published: 1891
Type of work: Novel

Context: Lord Rintoul, who has only recently bought a castle near the village of Thrums in Scotland, plans to marry Babbie, his ward. Babbie, however, in the dress of a gipsy has met the new minister in the town, Gavin Dishart, and the two have fallen in love. On the day before the wedding of Lord Rintoul to Babbie, preparations are being made, during which Babbie insists that a piper play "The Bonny House o' Airlie," a tune used by the Ogilvys who had once feuded with the Campbells. The tune insults Lauchlan Campbell, who is present, and he counters with "The Campbells are Coming," then stalks out. Waster Lunny, a farmer who is relating the incident, tells of his discussion with his wife Elspeth concerning the marriage of Lord Rintoul and Babbie:

". . . All I can say is that if the earl was saft enough to do sic a thing out of fondness for her, it's time he was married on her, so that he may come to his senses again. That's what I say; but Elspeth counters me, of course, and says she, 'If the young leddy was so careless o' insulting other folks' ancestors, it prove she has nane o' her ain; for **them that has china plates themsel's is the maist careful no to break the china plates of others.'** "

Them that has gits

Source: DAVID HARUM (Chapter 35)
Author: Edward Noyes Westcott (1846-1898)
First published: 1898
Type of work: Novel

Context: On his father's death John Lenox gives up his position with a New York law firm and goes to work as a bank assistant in Homeville, New York. The owner of the bank, David Harum, is quickly impressed with John's work and his character, and he soon has John move into his home where he resides with his widowed sister, Polly Bixbee. John gradually becomes a part of the community. One Sunday, after taking part in the singing at church, he meets the Verjoos sisters, who are in town for the summer. Later, at the dinner table, after John has gone to his room, David tells his sister that he saw John with Clara Verjoos and says, "I couldn't help thinkin' what a nice hitch up they'd make." Polly Bixbee then gives her reasons for the improbability of such a marriage:

953

"He hain't got anythin' to speak of, I s'pose, an' though I reckon she'll hev prop'ty some day, all that set o' folks seems to marry money, an' some one's alwus dyin' an' leavin' some on 'em some more. The' ain't nothin' truer in the Bible," declared Mrs. Bixbee with conviction, " 'n that sayin' thet **them that has gits.**"

Then farewell, Horace; whom I hated so, not for thy faults, but mine

Source: CHILDE HAROLD'S PILGRIMAGE (Canto IV, stanza 77)
Author: George Gordon, Lord Byron (1788-1824)
First published: 1818 (Canto IV)
Type of work: Narrative poem in Spenserian stanzas

Context: The Apennines, described in Canto IV, did not impress Byron because he had seen loftier mountains in Switzerland. The peak, Soracte, however, because it had been described by Horace, reminded him of his classical studies at Harrow. The passage quoted, the two preceding stanzas, and Byron's own notes are a comment on the English school system of that day. Young school boys were forced to learn the classics by rote—"The drill'd dull lesson, forced down word by word . . ." (Stanza 75). Entirely too immature to feel the power and beauty in these passages, the young scholars felt only aversion for what they might have admired as adults. This unimaginative mode of teaching had colored Byron's attitude toward Horace. In the quotation he does not exonerate himself, and in his note to Stanza 75 he confesses that he was "not a slow, though an idle boy." The first four lines of Stanza 77 follow:

> **Then farewell, Horace; whom I hated so,**
> **Not for thy faults, but mine;** it is a curse
> To understand, not feel thy lyric flow,
> To comprehend, but never love thy verse. . . .

Then to the spicy nut-brown ale

Source: L'ALLEGRO (Line 100)
Author: John Milton (1608-1674)
First published: 1645
Type of work: Lyric poem

Context: John Milton gives a picture of the joys of village life, with bells ringing and rebecks—three-stringed fiddles—summoning the youths and maidens to dance in the shade. Both young and old come forth on sunny holidays and play until evening falls. Then they go indoors and drink well-

954

seasoned ale as they tell stories of re-markable matters. A girl tells about how Mab, queen of the fairies, does the housework in return for something to eat. The teller admits having been pinched and jostled by Mab as punishment for her bad housekeeping but also tells how the queen rewards tidy housekeepers by putting a penny in their shoe. A youth who had once been led astray by a will-of-the-wisp, or fairy lantern, tells how Robin Goodfellow, or Hobgoblin, in one night threshes the grain and receives a bowl of cream as reward for his labors. The account is as follows:

> And young and old come forth to play
> On a sunshine holiday,
> Till the livelong daylight fail;
> **Then to the spicy nut-brown ale,**
> With stories told of many a feat,
> How fairy Mab the junkets eat;
> She was pinched and pulled, she said,
> And he by Friar's lantern led
> Tells how the drudging goblin sweat . . .

Thence issuing we again beheld the stars

Source: THE DIVINE COMEDY, INFERNO (Canto XXXIV, l. 139, as translated by H. F. Cary)
Author: Dante Alighieri (1265-1321)
First transcribed: c.1314
Type of work: Christian allegory

Context: In the fourth and last round of the ninth circle of Hell Dante sees a sight which is indescribable: "How frozen and how faint I then became,/ Ask me not, reader, for I write it not; . . . I was not dead nor living." The sight is Lucifer with his three weeping-eyed faces, who champs away at three sinners, flaying them alive: Judas, Brutus, and Cassius—betrayors of benefactors. "All is seen," says Virgil as he leads the way out of Hell. "Arise . . . upon thy feet./ The way is long, and much uncouth the road." When the younger poet asks how they managed to traverse the inner globe, the pre-Copernican theory of the earth is described. "By that hidden way/ My guide and I did enter, to return/ to the fair world . . ." So ends Dante's "Inferno:"

> We climb'd, he first, I following his steps,
> Till on our view the beautiful lights of Heaven
> Dawn'd through a circular opening in the cave:
> **Thence issuing we again beheld the stars.**

955

There are no dead

Source: THE BLUE BIRD (Act V, sc. ii) (The 1910 version of the play contains six acts, with a newly written Act IV. The original Act IV therefore becomes Act V.)
Author: Maurice Maeterlinck (1862-1949)
First published: 1908
Type of work: Fairy play

Context: Tyltyl and Mytyl, children of a wood-cutter, are sent in search of the Blue Bird by the Fairy Bérylune. They are given a magic diamond to help them, and are accompanied by the Dog, the Cat, Bread, Fire, Sugar, Water, Milk, and Light, who guide them. At one point Light receives a note from the Fairy Bérylune that one of the dead is hiding the Blue Bird in its tomb. They go to the graveyard, and there Tyltyl and Mytyl are directed to go inside the walls to wait alone until midnight to pass the dead under review. All of the children's companions remain at the gate of the graveyard. As they wait within the walls, Mytyl becomes frightened and questions her brother about the dead. At midnight, following instructions, Tyltyl turns the magic diamond, and the children see the mounds open and the slabs rise. An efflorescence fills the graveyard and transforms it into a sort of fairy-like garden. Searching among the flowers, Mytyl asks of Tyltyl, who is also searching, "Where are the dead?"

TYLTYL
"There are no dead."

There are two sides to every question

Source: LIVES AND OPINIONS OF EMINENT PHILOSOPHERS (Book IX, chapter 8)
Author: Diogenes Laertius (fl. 200)
First transcribed: Third century
Type of work: Biographical essays, apocryphal anecdotes

Context: Laertius evidently admired the early philosopher Protagoras, who lived in the fifth century B.C. and who studied under Democritus. The most famous saying of Protagoras, "Man is the measure of all things," Laertius subscribes to and credits Protagoras with being the originator. Here is Diogenes Laertius' concise summary of the teachings of Protagoras:

> Protagoras was the first to maintain **there are two sides to every question,** opposed to each other, and he even argued in this fashion, being the first to do so. Furthermore, he began a work thus: "Man is the measure of all things, of things that are that they are, and things that are not that they are not." He used to say that soul was nothing apart from the senses. . . .

There does not exist a vacuum in nature

Source: ETHICS (Part I, Proposition XV, note)
Author: Benedictus de Spinoza (1632-1677)
First published: 1677
Type of work: Philosophic essay

Context: The common saying, "Nature abhors a vacuum" seems to be a modification, or distortion, of the statement which Spinoza makes while he is discussing the nature of God in his *Ethics*. Some writers attempt to prove that God, being infinite, has no body, that corporeal or extended substance has no relation to the divine nature; yet they say it was created by God. Spinoza proves to his own satisfaction that no substance can be granted or conceived apart from the Deity. He refutes the argument that extended substance is finite and composed of parts that are capable of being multiplied and divided. It is absurd, he believes, to maintin that extended substance is made up of parts, for if this were possible, and a part were destroyed, the remaining parts would continue unchanged:

> Surely in the case of things, which are really distinct one from the other, one can exist without the other, and can remain in its original condition. As then, **there does not exist a vacuum in nature** . . . but all parts are bound to come together to prevent it, it follows from this also that the parts cannot be really distinguished, and that extended substance . . . cannot be divided.

There is a garden in her face

Source: THE THIRD AND FOURTH BOOK OF AIRS ("Cherry-ripe," Stanza 1)
Author: Thomas Campion (1567?-1620)
First published: c.1617
Type of work: Song

Context: This three-stanza song employs the type of "conceit" that was coming into fashion during the late Elizabethan and early Jacobean times —that is, an elaborate metaphor stretched out as far as the poet's originality would permit. The device was carried to much greater lengths by the "metaphysical" poets, but it is a feature of even this simple little song. "Cherry-ripe!" was the traditional cry of the London fruit-vendors as they walked the streets. The girl's face is compared to a garden in which grow the cherries; her lips enclose the "orient pearls" of her teeth. Yet, unlike real cherries, these cannot be bought until the girl herself calls "Cherry-ripe!" and gives permission for a kiss. The first stanza follows:

There is a garden in her face
Where roses and white lilies grow,

A heavenly paradise is that place,
Where all pleasant fruits do flow;
 There cherries grow that none can buy
 Till "Cherry-ripe" themselves do cry.

There is a method in man's wickedness

Source: A KING AND NO KING (Act V, sc. iv, l. 50)
Authors: Francis Beaumont (1585?-1616) and John Fletcher (1579-1625)
First published: 1619
Type of work: Dramatic comedy

Context: Arbaces, King of Iberia, enters the stage in Act V, sc. iv, with his sword drawn, breathing threats of the dire deeds he is about to perform. They include the murder of his friend, Gobrias, the lord protector of the realm; the incestuous ravishing of Panthea, who he believes is his sister, but for whom he has a great and apparently unnatural love; and his own suicide. When the captain Mardonius enters, Arbaces asks him if Gobrias has been summoned. Mardonius says that he has and then comments on Arbaces' wild appearance, saying that he fears the king will take his own life. Arbaces assures him that suicide is not his immediate intention. He says that he will come to it in time, and when he does he will inform Mardonius what he is going to do; he will, he says, have lived such a wicked life and will have committed so many sins that Mardonius will raise no objection. Arbaces thus sums up the situation:

> ARBACES
> **There is a method in man's wickedness,—**
> It grows up by degrees: I am not come
> So high as killing of myself; there are
> A hundred thousand sins 'twixt me and it,
> Which I must do.

There is a natural aristocracy among men

Source: LETTER TO JOHN ADAMS
Author: Thomas Jefferson (1743-1826)
Written: October 28, 1813
Type of work: Personal letter

Context: Belonging to the famous Adams-Jefferson correspondence, this letter contains Jefferson's defense of the American congressional system. He presents his concept, "not with a view to controversy, for we are too old to change opinions which are the result of a long life of inquiry and

958

reflection; but on the suggestions of a former letter of yours, that we ought not to die before we have explained ourselves to each other." It was Adams's contention that one legislative body should be composed of the wealthy, who "may be hindered from doing mischief by their co-ordinate branches, and . . . , also, they may be a protection to wealth against the Agrarian and plundering enterprises of the majority of the people." Jeffer-son, however, asserts that to "give them power in order to prevent them from doing mischief, is arming them for it." He prefers the established system, by which members of Congress will continue to be chosen from every condition and level of life. The citizens will separate "the aristoi from the pseudo-aristoi" and will usually elect "the really good and wise." Jefferson writes:

> . . . For I agree with you that **there is a natural aristocracy among men.** The grounds of this are virtue and talents. . . . The natural aristocracy I consider as the most precious gift of nature, for the instruction, the trusts, and government of society.

There is a tide in the affairs of men

Source: NEW ENGLAND TWO CENTURIES AGO
Author: James Russell Lowell (1819-1891)
First published: 1865
Type of work: Essay

Context: In writing of the New England Puritans, Lowell declares that they were not "gloomy narrow-minded fanatics" because they had political power from the beginning. The English Puritans were fanatics until they achieved power, then "they could not renew the fiery gush of enthusiasm when once the molten metal had begun to stiffen in the mould of policy and precedent." The Commonwealth therefore crumbled with the death of its leader, Oliver Cromwell. In commenting on man's career in history, Lowell quotes Shakespeare (*Julius Caesar,* Act IV, sc. 3, 1. 217):

> Truly **there is a tide in the affairs of men,** but there is no gulf-stream setting forever in one direction; and those waves of enthusiasm on whose crumbling crests we sometimes see nations lifted for a gleaming moment are wont to have a gloomy trough before and behind.

There is a tide in the affairs of men

Source: JULIUS CAESAR (Act IV, sc. iii, l. 218)
Author: William Shakespeare (1564-1616)
First published: 1623
Type of work: Dramatic tragedy

Context: Brutus and Cassius and two of their commanders discuss military strategy. They are engaged in a civil war following the assassination of Julius Caesar, an event in which they were conspirators. Against them is arrayed the army of Mark Antony, Octavius, and Lepidus. Cassius believes it is better to let the enemy seek them, but Brutus argues that it is wiser to march to Philippi and fight there. He is persuasive.

BRUTUS

• • •
You must note beside,
That we have tried the utmost of our friends;
Our legions are brim-full, our cause is ripe.
The enemy increaseth every day;
We, at the height, are ready to decline.
There is a tide in the affairs of men,
Which taken at the flood leads on to fortune;
Omitted, all the voyage of their life
Is bound in shallows and in miseries.
On such a full sea are we now afloat,
And we must take the current when it serves,
Or lose our ventures.

There is an endless merit in a man's knowing when to have done

Source: DR. FRANCIA
Author: Thomas Carlyle (1795-1881)
First published: 1843
Type of work: Essay

Context: Carlyle expressed an interest in several of the dictators in Mexico and South America, but he was especially attracted to Dr. Jose Francia, whom he called the Dionysius of Paraguay. Francia was an extremely colorful tyrant, and Carlyle deplored the fact that no Paraguayan had written an accurate account of his life. The chief source of information about the "Doctor Despot" was a book written by two Swiss surgeons, the Messrs. Rengger and Lonchamp. Detained in Paraguay for six years, they were finally released and permitted to return to Europe, where they

960

wrote their book about Dr. Francia. Carlyle does not give the book unqualified praise. Although he considers it "moderately accurate" and "not unreadable," he says it is not a good book and is "lean and dry." He says that the book's most oustanding and redeeming feature is

> . . . undisputable *brevity;* the fact that it can be read sooner by several hours than any other *Dr. Francia.* . . .
> After all, brevity is the soul of wit! **There is an endless merit in a man's knowing when to have done.**

There is death in the pot

Source: II KINGS 4:40
Author: Unknown
First transcribed: c.600 B.C.
Type of work: Religious history

Context: Of Elisha, the outstanding prophet of the Lord during the reign of Jehoram (852-843 B.C.) in Israel (the northern country resulting from the division of the Hebrew kingdom), many miraculous stories are recorded: resurrecting a dead lad, healing King Naaman of leprosy, and numerous other superhuman deeds. It is told that Elisha goes to Gilgal during a famine and orders his servant to prepare pottage for those assembled. The stew, which inadvertantly contains poisonous gourds, is ready:

> So they poured out for the men to eat. And it came to pass, as they were eating of the pottage, that they cried out, and said, O thou man of God, **there is death in the pot.** And they could not eat thereof.
> But he said, Then bring meal. And he cast it into the pot; and he said, Pour out for the people, that they may eat. And there was no harm in the pot.

There is no fire without some smoke

Source: THE PROVERBS OF JOHN HEYWOOD (Part II, chapter 5)
Author: John Heywood (1497?-1580?)
First published: 1546
Type of work: Gnomic poetry

Context: The author is telling a story which illustrates the dangers of a young man marrying a rich widow for her money. In this instance, husband and wife soon begin to have arguments, and the husband starts to develop new interests. The wife complains to the author that her husband is squandering their money, and wants advice about how to stop his doing so. This proverb about smoke and fire is widely used today in a slightly different form, "Where there's smoke there's fire." In the following quote, the author is advising the old wife to be moderate, not to nag her husband:

> Well, (quoth I), your part
> Is to suffer (I say); for ye shall preeve
> Taunts appease not things; they rather agrieve.
> But for ill company, or expense extreme,
> I here no man doubt, so far as ye deem;
> But **there is no fire without some smoke,** we see.
> Well, well! make no fire, raise no smoke, (said she);
> What cloak for the rain soever ye bring me,
> Myself can tell best where my shoe doth wring me.

There is no frigate like a book

Source: THERE IS NO FRIGATE LIKE A BOOK
Author: Emily Dickinson (1830-1886)
First published: 1894
Type of work: Lyric poem

Context: Emily Dickinson is noted chiefly for the economy of her poetic style, the vividness of her images, and the "off-rhyme" of her brief poems. Retiring by nature and private in her writing, she found a complete world in her narrow circle of friends and in her daily household chores. Her mind or a book could carry her to any land, any enchantment. Thus, in "There is no Frigate like a Book," to her a book is like a frigate, coursers, or a chariot, three romantic means of transportation, of which, through reading, even the poor can avail themselves with ease. The complete poem reads:

> **There is no Frigate like a Book**
> To take us Lands away
> Nor any Coursers like a Page
> Of prancing Poetry—
> This Travel may the poorest take
> Without offence of Toll—
> How frugal is the Chariot
> That bears the Human soul.

962

There is no god found stronger than death

Source: HYMN TO PROSERPINE (After the Proclamation in Rome of the Christian Faith, Last line)
Author: Algernon Charles Swinburne (1837-1909)
First published: 1866
Type of work: Lyric poem

Context: These lines are being spoken by a dying Roman pagan of the fourth century, to Proserpine, goddess of death and the underworld. His mood is one of ennui, and longing for release from life, from its pleasures and pains alike. He rejects everything in life, including the young Christian faith and its message of life extended for eternity. Of all the old gods he salutes only Proserpine, for while the others may bring joy, their ways are uncertain, and often their influence brings strife to earth; Proserpine offers permanent peace, respite from struggles and memories of struggles.

I know
I shall die as my fathers died, and sleep as they sleep; even so.
For the glass of the years is brittle wherein we gaze for a span;
A little soul for a little bears up this corpse which is man.
So long I endure, no longer; and laugh not again, neither weep.
For **there is no God found stronger than death;** and death is a
sleep.

There is no joy in Mudville

Source: CASEY AT THE BAT (Stanza 13)
Author: Ernest Lawrence Thayer (1863-1940)
First published: 1888
Type of work: Ballad

Context: The Mudville baseball team, trailing its opponents by a score of six to four, is up for its last inning. Some fans have already left because defeat seems certain: two players have struck out, and two others who are poor risks are up to bat before the batting turn of the crowd's hero, Casey. By a stroke of fortune, the two poor players manage to hit the ball, one getting to third base, the other to second. The crowd cheers wildly as Casey now comes up to bat, because it seems the day is saved. Two strikes are called on Casey as he lets the first two balls go by without even swinging at them. The crowd wants to kill the umpire, but Casey raises his hand and stops them. On the third ball the idol winds up and "the air is shattered by the force of Casey's blow." The last stanza gives the outcome of the game:

963

Oh! somewhere in this favored land the sun is shining bright,
The band is playing somewhere, and somewhere hearts are light.
And somewhere men are laughing, and somewhere children shout;
But **there is no joy in Mudville**—mighty Casey has "Struck Out."

There is no living with thee, nor without thee

Source: THE SPECTATOR (Volume I, No. 68)
Author: Joseph Addison (1672-1719)
First published: May 18, 1711
Type of work: Essay

Context: In one of his finest moral essays, Addison speaks on the subject of friendship. And in his May 18 meditation we see a superb economy, as well as the essentially moral tone that, though less pragmatic and less ambitious than Lord Chesterfield's, is both disciplined and warmly human. Addison, one of the arbiters of gentility and social morality in his time, moved Pope to say "No whiter page than Addison remains,/ He from the taste obscene reclaims our youth,/ And sets the passions on the side of truth;/ Forms the soft bosom with the gentlest art,/ And pours each human virtue thro' the heart." And it is largely through his magazine, *The Spectator,* that the public knew and knows his ideas and influence. In this essay Addison advises of the joys and consolations of real friendship. He advises that the length of intimacy is important to real friendship; that one should have many acquaintances, but few friends; that friendship multiplies joys and divides griefs. And while discussing variable personalities, he advances a translation from Martial:

. . . A man often contracts a friendship with one whom perhaps he does not find out 'till after a year's conversation; when on a sudden some latent ill humor breaks out upon him, which he never discovered or suspected at his first entering into an intimacy with him. There are several persons who in some certain periods of their lives are inexpressibly agreeable, and in others as odious and detestable. Martial has given us a very pretty picture . . . 'In all thy humours, whether grave or mellow/ Thou'rt such a touchy, testy, pleasant fellow;/ Hast as much wit, and mirth, and spleen about thee,/ **There is no living with thee, nor without thee.'**

There is no love lost

Source: DON QUIXOTE (Part II, Book II, chapter 22)
Author: Miguel de Cervantes Saavedra (1547-1616)
First published: 1615
Type of work: Satirical novel

Context: The idea of wasted love occurs in the title of Shakespeare's *Love's Labour's Lost.* In a negative sense, *The Witch* (Act IV, sc. iii) of

Thomas Middleton (1570-1627) declares: "There is no hate lost between us." In *Don Quixote,* Sancho, hearing his master discuss women with Basil and Quiteria, whose marriage was due to the Knight's intercession, says he wished he had heard his master discuss compatibility and incompatibility before he got married. When Don Quixote asks if Sancho's wife Teresa, is so bad, the squire evaluates her:

". . . Not so very bad, neither," answered Sancho, "nor yet so good as I would have her." "Fie, Sancho," said Don Quixote, "thou dost not do well to speak ill of thy wife, who is a good mother to thy children." **"There is no love lost,** sir," quoth Sancho, "for she speaks as ill of me, when the fit takes her. . . ."

There is no new thing under the sun

Source: ECCLESIASTES 1:9
Author: Unknown
First transcribed: c.250-200 B.C.
Type of work: Religious confession

Context: "The preacher," as the writer of Ecclesiastes terms himself, bases his philosophy upon the futility of life, "vanity of vanities; all is vanity." In spite of man's labor, he dies, a new generation arises, and nothing is accomplished. There is futility in the blowing of the wind, which only turns and blows the other way. The rivers flow to the sea, but the sea is not filled, and the moisture eventually returns to the source of the rivers from which it first sprang. Even as the author finds monotony in the workings of nature, so he also finds monotony in the activities of men:

The thing that hath been, it is that which shall be; and that which is done is that which shall be done: and **there is no new thing under the sun.**
Is there any thing whereof it may be said, See, this is new? it hath been already of old time, which was before us.

There is no primrose path which leads to glory

Source: FABLES (Book X, Fable 14)
Author: Jean de La Fontaine (1621-1695)
First published: 1673-1679
Type of work: Beast fable

Context: This fable, entitled "The Two Adventurers and the Talisman," tells about two men who read an inscription upon a wayside sign. To see something no other knight has ever seen, they are instructed to swim a nearby river, pick up a stone elephant, and carry it to the top of a certain mountain. One of the two men believes that the tasks are too dangerous to try and impossible to carry out. The other man ignores the danger, plunging into the river and swimming to the other side. He fulfills the instructions, carrying the stone elephant to the top of the designated mountain. His success results in his seeing a beautiful city appear; and, as a reward for his labors, the hero is hailed as the ruler of the city by its inhabitants. The story opens with this statement, actually the moral of the tale:

There is no primrose path which leads to glory.
Hercules with his Tasks of endless fame
Has had few rivals worth the name
Even in myth, still less in truthful story.

There is no royal road to geometry

Source: PROCLUS' COMMENTARIES ON EUCLID (Book 2, chapter 4)
Author: Euclid (fl. c.300 B.C.)
First transcribed: A.D. 400
Type of work: Apocryphal biographical anecdote

Context: Although little is known of Euclid, he is thought to have lived before Archimedes at the time of the Egyptian King Ptolemy (c.367-285 B.C.), the one who is the questioner of the great mathematician. Proclus, more than seven hundred years later, reports the incident as follows (often misquoted as "there is no royal road to learning):

But Euclid . . . constructed many of those things which were invented by Eudoxus. . . . Besides, he reduced to invincible demonstrations, such things as were exhibited by others with a weaker arm. . . . Archimedes mentions Euclid in his first book, and also in others. Besides, they relate that Euclid was asked by Ptolemy, whether there was any shorter way to the attainment of geometry than by his elementary institutions, and he answered, **there was no other royal path which led to geometry. . . .**

There is no substitute for talent

Source: POINT COUNTER POINT (Chapter 13)
Author: Aldous Huxley (1894-1963)
First published: 1928
Type of work: Novel

Context: The conflict in *Point Counter Point,* principally experienced on the emotional and mental levels, is expressed through witty and philo-

966

sophical conversation and through sophisticated social predicaments. Walter Bidlake, a sensitive writer working for a newspaper, represents the self-conscious, passive, stifled personality, selfishly, romantically, and obsessively intent upon finding something to fill his emptiness. We first meet him preparing to leave his possessive mistress, now pregnant, to attend a party for celebrities and dilettantes, given at the home of Lucy Tantamount, whom Walter, driven by his inconstant passions, finds irresistible. The weakness of his personality is further revealed in his submissive, impotent responses to Lucy's dominant spirit. However, the morning after the party, having been humiliated by Lucy's inconsiderate, almost cruel, disrespect, he goes to work resolved to control his own destiny henceforth. Although this resolution will come to nought, on paper Walter is the person he would like to be. Here he asserts himself. His book reviews are merciless and devastating. "Walter ferociously commented on lack of talent":

> . . . A bad book is as much of a labour to write as a good one; it comes as sincerely from the author's soul. But the bad author's soul being, artistically at any rate, of inferior quality, its sincerities will be, if not always intrinsically uninteresting, at any rate uninterestingly expressed. . . . **There is no substitute for talent.**

There is no such word as "fail"

Source: RICHELIEU (Act I, sc. ii)
Author: Edward Bulwer-Lytton (1803-1873)
First published: 1839
Type of work: Historical drama

Context: Cardinal Richelieu is talking to his spy, Marion de Lorme, the mistress of his enemy, the Duke of Orleans. She reports that the Duke has arranged to have her brother carry messages to Italy. But the Cardinal commands her to turn them over to his own representative, and nominates his page François. The young man hesitates.

FRANÇOIS
If I fail?

RICHELIEU
Fail—Fail?
In the lexicon of youth, which Fate reserves
For a bright manhood, **there is no such word as "fail."**
. . . Farewell, boy! Never say "Fail" again.

967

There is no vice so simple, but assumes some mark of virtue

Source: THE MERCHANT OF VENICE (Act III, sc. ii, ll. 81-82)
Author: William Shakespeare (1564-1616)
First published: 1600
Type of work: Dramatic comedy

Context: Bassanio, in love with the heiress Portia, can marry her only if, according to her father's will, he choose from among three caskets—golden, silver and lead—the one which contains her portrait. Now he stands before the three, trying to choose correctly and debating which one he shoud select. He argues with himself, knowing that the world "is still deceived with ornament." He then broods on the lesson taught in his statement. He debates further, and finally chooses:

> BASSANIO
> **There is no vice so simple, but assumes some mark of virtue** on his outward parts.
>
> • • •
>
> . . . Therefore thou gaudy gold,
> Hard food for Midas, I will none of thee.
> Nor none of thee thou pale and common drudge
> 'Tween man and man. But thou, thou meagre lead
> Which rather threatenest than dost promise aught,
> *Thy* paleness moves me more than eloquence,
> And here chose I, joy be the consequence.
>
> • • •
>
> What find I here? [*Opens the leaden casket*]
>
> Fair Portia's counterfeit.
>
> • • •

There is nothing either good or bad but thinking makes it so

Source: HAMLET (Act II, sc. ii, ll. 254-255)
Author: William Shakespeare (1564-1616)
First published: 1603
Type of work: Dramatic tragedy

Context: Prince Hamlet swears revenge for his father's murder. The murderer is Hamlet's uncle Claudius, his father's brother and present King of Denmark. To disarm his well-guarded uncle and to screen his own thoughts and actions, Hamlet pretends to be crazy. Polonius, the king's chief councilor, believes the prince to be mad and so reports to the king. The king is not convinced, however, and sets two young courtiers, Rosencrantz and Guildenstern, erstwhile friends of Hamlet, to spy upon him and learn the truth.

968

HAMLET

. . . What have you, my good friends, deserved at the hands of Fortune, that she sends you to prison hither? . . . Denmark's a prison.

ROSENCRANTZ

Then is the world one.

HAMLET

A goodly one, in which there are many confines, wards, and dungeons, Denmark being one o' th' worst.

ROSENCRANTZ

We think not so my lord.

HAMLET

Why then 'tis none to you; for **there is nothing either good or bad but thinking makes it so.** To me it is a prison.

There is nothing permanent except change

Source: FRAGMENTS OF HERACLITUS
Author: Heraclitus of Ephesus (c.540-480 B.C.)
First transcribed: Early fifth century B.C.
Type of work: Metaphysics

Context: Sometimes called the weeping philosopher, sometimes obscure, Heraclitus' 150 sentences still extant are clear and not tearful. His *logos,* as he called it, consists of a rationale, a centrality in all things which appear often as opposites because of the *flux quo* rather than the *status quo.* His basic symbol is fire: "All things are exchanged for fire, and fire for all things," which demonstrates the always changing, always the same nature of our world. The two most common proverbial statements attributed to Heraclitus are "Everything flows" and "You cannot step into the same river twice," but both come from Platonic paraphrases and are somewhat oversimplified and distorted. His is, however, the first clear statement of Relativism, which along with Existentialism, most affects modern metaphysics. Ironically, this following statement is a sophistical one, not a quotation from Heraclitus but a summary of what is thought he believed. Probably he would deny this statement (for change itself is not at all permanent but changing):

There is nothing permanent except change.

969

There is something in the wind

Source: THE COMEDY OF ERRORS (Act III, sc. i, l. 69)
Author: William Shakespeare (1564-1616)
First published: 1623
Type of work: Dramatic comedy

Context: This is one of Shakespeare's most bizarre and incredible comedies. Egeon, an old merchant from Syracuse, and his wife Aemilia had twin sons, both named Antipholus and provided with twin slaves, both named Dromio. Because of a shipwreck, the members are separated, Egeon taking with him to Syracuse a son (Antipholus of Syracuse) and one Dromio, Aemilia taking with her to Ephesus one Antipholus (Antipholus of Ephesus) and one Dromio. The comedy of errors results when the Syracusan son is summoned home by Dromio of Ephesus. He is assumed by his brother's wife to be her husband. When the real husband reaches home, he is denied admittance because presumably he is already inside. After repeatedly explaining his identity and repeatedly being denied admittance, Antipholus of Ephesus observes that there is something wrong which prevents their getting into the house:

> ANTIPHOLUS OF EPHESUS
> **There is something in the wind,** that we cannot get in.

> DROMIO OF EPHESUS
> You would say so master, if your garments were thin.
> Your cake there is warm within; you stand here in the cold.
> It would make a man mad as a buck to be so bought and sold.

There is sweet music here

Source: THE LOTOS-EATERS (Choric Song, stanza 1)
Author: Alfred, Lord Tennyson (1809-1892)
First published: 1842
Type of work: Lyric poem

Context: Tennyson adapts the story of the Lotos-Eaters from Book IX of the *Odyssey*. The poem is famous for its sensuous richness. Ulysses and his followers come upon "a land/ In which it seeméd always afternoon./ All round the coast the languid air did swoon,/ Breathing like one that hath a weary dream . . . A land of streams! . . . A land where all things always seemed the same!" "The mild-eyed melancholy Lotoseaters" come and give the sailors the "enchanted stem." The bewitched sailors sit on the beach and sing. It is sweet to dream of home and family, but "Most weary seemed the sea, weary the oar . . . Then someone

said, 'We will return no more';/ And
all at once they sang, 'Our island
home/ Is far beyond the wave; we
will no longer roam.' " They sing a
Choric Song, expressing their desire
to rest forever:

> **There is sweet music here** that softer falls
> Than petals from blown roses on the grass,
> Or night-dews on still waters between walls
> Of shadowy granite, in a gleaming pass;
> Music that gentlier on the spirit lies,
> Than tired eyelids upon tired eyes;
> Music that brings sweet sleep down from the blissful skies.
> Here are cool mosses deep,
> And through the moss the ivies creep,
> And in the stream the long-leaved flowers weep,
> And from the craggy ledge the poppy hangs in sleep.

There! little girl; don't cry!

Source: A LIFE-LESSON (Refrain)
Author: James Whitcomb Riley (1849-1916)
First published: 1880
Type of work: Lyric poem

Context: James Whitcomb Riley's
"A Life-Lesson" has been set to music a number of times. In the poem
the poet consoles the little girl at each
of three stages of her life. First he encounters her when she is a small child
and tells her not to cry over the
broken doll because "childish troubles will soon pass by.—" In her
school days, the little girl is again
consoled when she cries over her
broken slate. "But life and love will
soon come by," the poet tells her.
Then after life and love have come
by, the poet finds her with a broken
heart and can only say, "Heaven
holds all for which you sigh." Each of
the three stanzas of the poem begins
and ends with the line "There! little
girl; don't cry!"

> **There! little girl; don't cry!**
> They have broken your heart, I know;
> And the rainbow gleams
> Of your youthful dreams
> Are things of the long ago;
> But Heaven holds all for which you sigh.—
> **There! little girl;, don't cry!**

971

There lives more faith in honest doubt than in half the creeds

Source: IN MEMORIAM (Part XCVI, stanza 3)
Author: Alfred, Lord Tennyson (1809-1892)
First published: 1850
Type of work: Elegy

Context: Tennyson, grieving over the death of his friend, Arthur Hallam, imagines himself talking with a woman of uncomplicated faith. The woman, "Sweet-hearted" and compassionate, gently reprimands the poet for all the fears he has had that man's soul dies with him or perhaps succumbs to evil after death. She tells him that "doubt is Devil-born," that lack of faith is a sin produced by the influence of the Powers of Evil. But the poet is uncertain about this statement, and offers the example of Hallam, who accepted no creed blindly, but challenged all beliefs for their validity. This unflinching honesty, in the end, left him with a faith more deep rooted and genuine than he could ever have found by merely accepting a formal system.

> Perplext in faith, but pure in deeds,
>   At last he beat his music out.
>   **There lives more faith in honest doubt,**
> Believe me, **than in half the creeds.**

There never was a good war or a bad peace

Source: LETTER TO JOSIAH QUINCY
Author: Benjamin Franklin (1706-1790)
Written: Sept. 11, 1783
Type of work: Personal letter

Context: Benjamin Franklin, as the American minister to France, drew up the agreement between France and the new American nation at the end of the American Revolution. Although many of his best and closest friends were in Europe, Franklin did not hesitate over a sharp break between the New World and Europe. In his opinion, it was better to "let commerce and knowledge bind the continents naturally together," rather than the artificiality of political bonds. But he believed an imperfect peace was preferable to war; he echoed the sentiments of Cicero a milennium and a half earlier. In *Epistolae ad Atticum,* Cicero said, peace "even though unjust . . . is better than the most just war." Using similar words, Samuel Butler told the Rump Parliament in 1659 ". . . an unjust peace is to be preferred before a just war." When on September 3, 1783, the treaty between France and England was signed at Versailles, the treaty between France and America was signed in Paris. Franklin wrote a week later:

We are now friends with England and with all mankind. May we never see another war! For in my opinion **there never was a good war or a bad peace.**

There never was knight like the young Lochinvar

Source: MARMION (Canto V, stanza 1)
Author: Sir Walter Scott (1771-1832)
First published: 1808
Type of work: Narrative poem

Context: Marmion, a brave but dissolute knight of the 16th century, is sent as ambassador from King Henry VIII of England to James IV of Scotland. When Marmion waits upon the Scottish King at Holy-Rood Castle, he hears sung for the royal pleasure a song usually known as the poem "Lochinvar." This romantic short tale tells of a young knight who rides boldly to the hall where his beloved is being wed to "a laggard in love and a dastard in war." Pretending to care nothing for his loss, Lochinvar debonairly quaffs a goblet of wine and leads his "fair Ellen" in a dance, only to sweep suddenly the willing girl upon his charger and gallop away with her. The opening lines of this charming piece are:

> Oh! young Lochinvar is come out of the west,
> Through all the wide Border his steed was the best;
> And save his good broadsword he weapons had none.
> He rode all unarmed, and he rode all alone.
> So faithful in love, and so dauntless in war,
> **There never was knight like the young Lochinvar.**

There sits a judge that no king can corrupt

Source: KING HENRY THE EIGHTH (Act III, sc. i, ll. 100-101)
Author: William Shakespeare (1564-1616)
First published: 1623
Type of work: Historical drama

Context: King Henry the Eighth of England has been married to Katharine of Aragon for twenty years. Cardinal Wolsey, who has great power and influence with the king, is working secretly for an alliance with France, and wants the king to divorce Katharine and marry the Duchess of Alencon. But the king falls in love with Katharine's Maid of Honor, Anne Bullen. The king acquiesces in the divorce, and a hearing is held. But Katharine fights. She declares her devotion and fidelity to the king, refuses to be judged by Wolsey, whom she accuses of instigating the divorce, and appeals directly to the pope. Now, upset and unhappy that the king's love is going to a Protestant, Anne, the cardinal sends a message to Rome to delay the divorce, and secretly sides with Katharine. When he and another cardinal, Campeius, offer her their aid, she, angrily, misunderstands their intent.

CAMPEIUS
Put your main cause into the King's protection;

.   .   .

For if the trial of the law o'ertake ye,
You'll part away disgraced.

WOLSEY
He tells you rightly.

KATHARINE
Ye tell me what ye wish for both, my ruin.
Is this your Christian counsel? Out upon ye!
Heaven is above all yet; **there sits a Judge,
That no king can corrupt.**

CAMPEIUS
Your rage mistakes us.

There the wicked cease from troubling

Source: JOB 3:17
Author: Unknown
First transcribed: c.900-500 B.C.
Type of work: Religious saga

Context: Job, in the land of Uz, a good man in the eyes of the Lord, is blessed with seven sons and three daughters and much wealth. Satan, in a challenge to the Creator, declares that Job will curse God if he experiences adversity. God, taking up the challenge, grants Satan permission to test the righteous man. When Job loses his wealth and children but does not curse God, Satan is allowed to inflict him with boils. In agony and with his wife urging him to curse God and die and his friends weeping for his condition, Job raises not a word against the Almighty. Instead, he laments the day of his birth and ponders the state of death:

Why died I not from the womb? . . .
   For now should I have lain still and been quiet, I should have slept: then had I been at rest,
   With kings and counselors of the earth, which built desolate places for themselves; . . .

974

Or as a hidden untimely birth I had not been; as infants which never saw light.

There the wicked cease from troubling; and there the weary be at rest.

There was a sound of revelry by night

Source: CHILDE HAROLD'S PILGRIMAGE (Canto III, stanza 21)
Author: George Gordon, Lord Byron (1788-1824)
First published: 1816 (Canto III)
Type of work: Narrative poem in Spenserian stanzas

Context: In 1816, Byron's travels brought him to the field of Waterloo, where, just the year before, Napoleon had met his defeat. In Stanza 21, Byron begins a dramatic description of the famous ball held in Brussels on the eve of the battle. According to tradition, the Duke of Wellington had authorized the ball in hope of keeping the citizens of Brussels in ignorance of his plans. His officers were in attendance, but left quietly at ten o'clock to join their regiments. In the popular mind, Byron's well-known description of the eve of Waterloo is rivaled only by Thackeray's long prose description in *Vanity Fair*. The first four lines of Byron's stanza are as follows:

There was a sound of revelry by night,
And Belgium's capital had gather'd then
Her Beauty and her Chivalry, and bright
The lamps shone o'er fair women and brave men. . . .

There were giants in the earth

Source: GENESIS 6:4
Author: Unknown
First transcribed: c.1000-300 B.C.
Type of work: Religious history and law

Context: After Adam and Eve, the first of mankind, had been driven from Eden because of their disobedience to God, they established their home under the hard conditions imposed by God and began to rear children, as they had been commanded. In time the world was heavily populated with several clans and cultures of people. Cain, after having been exiled to the region of Nod for killing his brother, became the ancestor of numerous descendants, distinguished for their worldliness. From another son of Adam, Seth, developed a line distinguished for its pastoral simplicity and religiosity. By and large men were becoming more and more evil,

975

however. "The sons of God," probably referring to those who had not forgotten the tradition of their fathers, were taking the fair daughters of men as wives, from which union came children who grew into mighty men, "which were of old, men of renown." Whether these are the giants of the earth or whether the giants refer to another people the theologians cannot agree. The verse reads:

> **There were giants in the earth** in those days; and also after that, when the sons of God come in unto the daughters of men, and they bare children to them, the same became mighty men which were of old, men of renown.

Thereby hangs a tale

Source: AS YOU LIKE IT (Act II, sc. vii, l. 28)
Author: William Shakespeare (1564-1616)
First published: 1623
Type of work: Dramatic comedy

Context: Duke Senior, Amiens, and other lords are seeking Jaques in the Forest of Arden. Jaques is now reported to be "merry" since hearing Amiens sing the song "Under the Greenwood Tree." Duke Senior urges someone to seek out Jaques. At this moment Jaques enters and comments that he met "a motley fool" "Who laid him down and basked him in the sun, / And railed on Lady Fortune in good terms." Jaques then reports that the fool looked at his watch and "Says very wisely, it is ten o'clock." Then he continues the fool's speech:

JAQUES
Thus we may see, quoth he, how the world wags
'Tis but an hour ago since it was nine,
And after one hour more, 'twill be eleven;
And so from hour to hour we ripe, and ripe,

. . .

And **thereby hangs a tale.** When I did hear
The motley fool thus moral on the time,
My lungs began to crow like chanticleer,
That fools should be so deep contemplative.

Therefore is the name of it called Babel

Source: GENESIS 11:9
Author: Unknown
First transcribed: 1000-300 B.C.
Type of work: Religious history and law

Context: God, the Creator, is constantly disappointed by the sinfulness of man: because of man's sin, God drove the first people from the Gar-

976

den of Eden; because of sin, God sent a flood to destroy all mankind, except a righteous remnant, Noah and his family. After the flood, Noah's descendants multiply so rapidly that they, afraid that they will be dispersed on the earth, decide to unite by building a city with a tower reaching to Heaven and by giving themselves a name. God, seeing that the men are united and that they all speak one language and fearing that nothing will restrain them, confuses their language so that they can no longer understand one another and scatters them over all the earth. To the unfinished city and tower, God gives the name Babel, or Babylon, meaning "to confuse" or "to mix":

> **Therefore is the name of it called Babel;** because the Lord did
> there confound the language of all the earth: and from thence did
> the Lord scatter them abroad upon the face of all the earth.

Therein the patient must minister to himself

Source: MACBETH (Act V, sc. iii, ll. 45-46)
Author: William Shakespeare (1564-1616)
First published: 1623
Type of work: Dramatic tragedy

Context: Macbeth obtains the throne of Scotland by assassinating the lawful King Duncan while the latter is a guest in his castle, and fastening the blame on the king's two sons, Malcolm and Donalbain, who flee. The ursurper and his wife Lady Macbeth, who aided him in his murderous act, have an unquiet, tyrannous reign. No one is safe from Macbeth, who sees enemies on every side. More and more nobles flee to join Malcolm. Now Lady Macbeth, whose sick conscience will not let her sleep, is near death, and Malcolm's forces from England, swelled by loyal Scotsmen, approach to attack the tyrant's stronghold. As Macbeth awaits the onslaught, he and Lady Macbeth's doctor discuss her treatment.

MACBETH
• • •

Canst thou not minister to a mind diseased,
Pluck from the memory a rooted sorrow,
Raze out the written troubles of the brain,
And with some sweet oblivious antidote
Cleanse the stuffed bosom of that perilous stuff
Which weighs upon the heart?

DOCTOR
Therein the patient
Must minister to himself.

977

There's a certain slant of light

Source: THERE'S A CERTAIN SLANT OF LIGHT (Stanza 1)
Author: Emily Dickinson (1830-1886)
First published: 1890
Type of work: Lyric poem

Context: This short poem, expressed in the extremely compact metaphors which are characteristic of Emily Dickinson and which make her akin to the "metaphysical" poets of the seventeenth century, deals with first the physical and then the emotional effects of sunlight on an afternoon in winter. Physically, the light seems to have weight that "oppresses" like the deep tones of a cathedral organ. Yet the sensation leaves no outward scar on us, only an inward one "Where the Meanings, are—" This peculiar slant of light seems to hold the landscape in suspension—silent, listening. The soul of the beholder receives its "internal difference" through the foreshadowing of the "look of death" that this "certain Slant of light" produces. The poem begins

> There's a certain Slant of light,
> Winter Afternoons—
> That oppresses, like the Heft
> Of Cathedral Tunes—
>
> Heavenly Hurt, it gives us—
> We can find no scar,
> But internal difference
> Where the Meanings, are—

There's a divinity that shapes our ends

Source: HAMLET (Act V, sc. ii, l. 10)
Author: William Shakespeare (1564-1616)
First published: 1603
Type of work: Dramatic tragedy

Context: Prince Hamlet of Denmark accidentally kills Polonius, the chief councilor of King Claudius, thinking him to be the king. The latter, alarmed, sends Hamlet to England, and plans to have him summarily executed upon his arrival. Now Hamlet, returned to Denmark, tells his friend, Horatio, of the premonition he experienced on board ship that allowed him to thwart this plot on his life.

> HAMLET
> Sir, in my heart there was a kind of fighting
> That would not let me sleep;
> • • •

Rashly—
And praised be rashness for it; let us know,
Our indiscretion sometime serves us well
When our deep plots do pall, and that should learn us
There's a divinity that shapes our ends,
Rough-hew them how we will—

HORATIO
That is most certain.

There's life in the old dame yet

Source: ARCHYS LIFE OF MEHITABEL ("the retreat from hollywood," Line 34)
Author: Don Marquis (1878-1937)
First published: 1933
Type of work: Humorous poem

Context: Mehitabel the cat, accompanied by archy, the cockroach, who types poetry in lower case by leaping onto the keys, are on their way back from Hollywood, where mehitabel's attempt to enter pictures has been humiliatingly unsuccessful. Mehitabel is followed eastward by her latest brood of kittens; the third one has just died from scorpion bite, and although she is grieved at the death, she says that as an artist—she is currently infatuated with her ability in the modern dance—she must conquer her pains and carry on. Although time is passing, she believes that she has enough of youth in her to allow her a career on the stage.

> The loss of that kitten is a terrible grief
> but an aristocrat and an artist
> must bear up toujours gai
> is my motto toujours gai
>
> **theres life in the old dame yet**

There's millions in the job

Source: THE GILDED AGE (Vol. I, chapter 13)
Authors: Mark Twain (1835-1910) and Charles Dudley Warner (1829-1900)
First published: 1873
Type of work: Novel

Context: The post-Civil War era of seemingly unlimited economic expansion provides the background for this satirical analysis of dishonest large-scale enterprisers. Some operate with the help of bribes distributed in Congress; some use secret arrangements of other kinds, but all are fired with unbounded rapacity. A number of the characters in the novel are tragic-comic ones, men with inflated visions of wealth and of their own importance, but without the business ability or resources really to enter the world of high finance. Among these is Harry Brierly, a young would-be engineer whose attributes are elegance and ignorance. In his usual grandiose terms he boasts to his friend, Philip Sterling, of the profits to be made from the railroad construction scheme in which he is involved.

". . . Brown and Schaik have, or will have, the control for the whole line of the Salt Lick Pacific Extension, forty thousand dollars a mile over the prairie, with extra for hardpan—and it'll be pretty much all hardpan, I can tell you; besides every alternate section of land of this line. **There's millions in the job.** I'm to have the subcontract for the first fifty miles, and you can bet it's a soft thing."

There's no god dare wrong a worm

Source: COMPENSATION
Author: Ralph Waldo Emerson (1803-1882)
First published: 1841
Type of work: Lyric poem

Context: This poem appears at the beginning of the essay entitled "Compensation." Compensation, says Emerson, is a universal law. All nature keeps a "trembling balance." Night and day, mountain and ocean, the tides—all balance out "the feud of Want and Have." In this intricately patterned universe, "the lonely Earth" must serve some sort of necessary function; it is a 'Supplemental asteroid,/ Or compensatory spark." Frail mankind also has a place in the universe. If he finds his proper function in the eternal balance, man can acquire infinite powers:

Man's the elm, and Wealth the vine,
Stanch and strong the tendrils twine:
Though the frail ringlets thee deceive,
None from its stock that vine can reave.
Fear not, then, thou child infirm,
There's no god dare wrong a worm.
Laurel crowns cleave to deserts,
And power to him who power exerts;
Hast not thy share? On winged feet,
Lo! it rushes thee to meet;
And all that Nature made thy own,
Floating in air or pent in stone,
Will rive the hills and swim the sea,
And, like thy shadow, follow thee.

There's not a man that lives who hath not
known his god-like hours

Source: THE PRELUDE (Book III, ll. 190-191)
Author: William Wordsworth (1770-1850)
First published: 1850
Type of work: Autobiographical poem

Context: Written between 1798-1805, this poem in fourteen books describes the "growth of a poet's mind"—the formative years, his dedication to poetry, the crisis of his beliefs in association with the French Revolution, and the painstaking reestablishment of faith in himself and his poetic powers. The third book recounts his experiences at Cambridge as a college student and his uneasiness with the restraint of the classroom and the rigors of examination. Often "did I quit my comrades" and pace "alone the level fields." Here the power and beauty of nature spoke "perpetual logic to my soul." And such moments of inspirational bliss are common, he says, to the hearts of all men. He writes:

> Points have we all of us within our souls
> Where all stand single; this I feel, and make
> Breathings for incommunicable powers;
> But is not each a memory to himself,
> And, therefore, now that we must quit this theme,
> I am not heartless, for **there's not a man**
> **That lives who hath not known his god-like hours,**
> And feels not what an empire we inherit
> As natural beings in the strength of Nature.

There's nothing like being used to a thing

Source: THE RIVALS (Act V)
Author: Richard Brinsley Sheridan (1751-1816)
First published: 1775
Type of work: Dramatic comedy

Context: Captain Absolute is courting Lydia Languish under the assumed name of Ensign Beverley (see "Caparisons don't become a young woman"). Bob Acres, another suitor of Lydia's, believes that he has been insulted by Beverley, whom he has never seen and does not know to be his old friend Captain Absolute. He is finally prodded by the fire-eating Sir Lucius O'Trigger into challenging Beverley to a duel. The quoted line is spoken by Sir Lucius on King's-Mead-Fields, where he is acting as second to the reluctant Acres, who is losing his courage fast. When Sir Lucius asks Bob if he would be satisfied to lie in the Abbey, the challenger shows great alarm. The quoted line occurs in the following dialogue:

SIR LUCIUS

I suppose, Mr. Acres, you never were engaged in an affair of this kind before?

ACRES

No, Sir Lucius, never before.

SIR LUCIUS

Ah! that's a pity! **there's nothing like being used to a thing.** Pray now, how would you receive the gentleman's shot?

There's rosemary, that's for remembrance

Source: HAMLET (Act IV, sc. v, l. 175)
Author: William Shakespeare (1564-1616)
First published: 1603
Type of work: Dramatic tragedy

Context: Ophelia is the daughter of Polonius, chief councilor of King Claudius of Denmark. Prince Hamlet, the king's nephew, has been behaving erratically. To determine if he is indeed mad, she allows herself to be used by her father and the king as a decoy. Hamlet sees through the device and turns on her. She, who believed he loved her, is unsettled. Shortly afterwards, her father is killed accidentally by Hamlet, who is then sent to England. This event proves too great a blow, and she loses her mind. Later, her brother, who has had news of his father's death, returns to Elsinore Castle from France. He, Queen Gertrude, and the king witness Ophelia's mad behavior. She speaks to Laertes without recognizing him and gives him a sprig of flowers from her hair.

OPHELIA [*to Laertes*]

There's rosemary, that's for remembrance—pray you love, remember—and there is pansies, that's for thoughts.

LAERTES

A document in madness, thoughts and remembrance fitted.

OPHELIA

[*To Claudius.*] There's fennel for you, and columbines.
[*To Gertrude.*] There's rue for you, and here's some for me; . . .

982

There's some corner of a foreign field that is forever England

Source: THE SOLDIER (Lines 2-3)
Author: Rupert Brooke (1887-1915)
First published: 1915
Type of work: Sonnet

Context: "The Soldier" was included among a collection of poems expressing the poet's sentiments concerning the war. It is a solemn, tranquil poem, an expression of the poet's personal consolation in a world darkened by the threat of violent, sudden death. It proclaims a kind of inner peace, even at the prospects of violent death, based on idealistic, patriotic sentiments. Having been born and reared an Englishman, the poet thinks of himself as a part of England. Therefore, if he should be buried in a foreign field, his dust in a sense would be a part of England, "a dust whom England bore, shaped, made aware, . . . a body of England's." His consolation, then, is his identity with England. If he should die, he wishes only to be thought of as an eternal part of his native land:

> If I should die, think only this of me:
>   That **there's some corner of a foreign field**
> **That is for ever England.** There shall be
>   In that rich earth a richer dust concealed. . . .

There's such a charm in melancholy, I would not, if I could, be gay

Source: TO——— (Stanza 1)
Author: Samuel Rogers (1763-1855)
First published: 1814
Type of work: Lyric poem

Context: An English banker, poet, and patron of the arts, Samuel Rogers was born in Stoke Newington, London. His tastes, formed by extensive travel and reading, were first reflected in his poem *The Pleasures of Memory,* published in 1792. His chief poem, *Italy* (1822), did not succeed until in 1830 he spent more than £7000 on an edition illustrated by Turner and others. Rogers' fame as a conversationalist equals his fame as a poet. A friend of many of the famous persons of his day—including Fox, Sheridan, Mrs. Siddons, Scott, Wordsworth, Byron, Wellington, and Talleyrand—he was noted for his table talk and his lavish hospitality. On the death of Wordsworth in 1850 he was offered the laureateship of England but modestly declined the honor later to be conferred upon Tennyson. Of his lyric power, an early editor commented: "He is remarkable principally for the elegance and grace of his compositions, which he polishes up and smooths off as if he valued only their brilliancy and finish, and forgot that strength and force are essential to poetic harmony and the perfection of the metrical style."

One of his most memorable verses is a brief lyric in which the poet describes the exquisite pleasure of the melancholy mood. He writes:

Go—you may call it madness, folly;
You shall not chase my gloom away.
There's such a charm in melancholy,
I would not, if I could, be gay.

These are the times that try men's souls

Source: THE AMERICAN CRISIS (Number I)
Author: Thomas Paine (1737-1809)
First published: 1776
Type of work: Political pamphlet

Context: Thomas Paine arrived bankrupt in Philadelphia in November, 1774, having left England for America at the suggestion of Benjamin Franklin. In a short time he was to become the ablest propagandist for the cause of the Revolution. In a series of pamphlets, *Common Sense* and *The American Crisis,* he advocated independence and urged armed resistance to the British. Living again in England from 1787 to 1792, he incurred the wrath of the British with *The Rights of Man,* his reply to Burke's *Reflections on the Revolution in France.* Outlawed in England, he fled to Paris, only to be imprisoned for protesting against the execution of Louis XVI. When his release was obtained by James Monroe in 1794, Paine returned to America, but the deistic views expressed in *The Age of Reason* (he was falsely accused of being an atheist) brought him scorn and condemnation. In poverty and ill health he lived on until 1809. In the first of sixteen pamphlets now known as *The American Crisis,* Paine challenges the true American patriot:

These are the times that try men's souls: The summer soldier and the sunshine patriot will, in this crisis, shrink from the service of his country; but he that stands it NOW, deserves the love and thanks of man and woman. Tyranny, like hell, is not easily conquered; yet we have this consolation with us, that the harder the conflict, the more glorious the triumph.

These wretches, who never lived

Source: THE DIVINE COMEDY, INFERNO (Canto III, l. 60, as translated by H. F. Cary)
Author: Dante Alighieri (1265-1321)
First transcribed: c.1314
Type of work: Christian allegory

Context: Having entered the portals of Hell with his mentor and master Virgil, Dante hears the moans of those who lived without praise or blame but lived only for themselves. They pass on from them to a train of spirits being whirled about after a flag, "such a long train . . . I should ne'er have thought that death so many despoil'd." Dante recognizes one of these as Celestine V, who had abdicated the Papacy in 1294, thus making way for Boniface VIII, the poet's special detestation. This is the circle of the Futile.

> . . . Forthwith
> I understood, for certain, this the tribe
> Of those ill spirits both to God displeasing
> And to His foes. **These wretches, who ne'er lived,**
> Went on in nakedness, and sorely stung
> By wasps and hornets, which bedew'd their cheeks
> With blood, that, mix'd with tears, dropp'd to their feet,
> And by disgustful worms was gather'd there.

• • •

They also serve who only stand and wait

Source: SONNET XIX ("On His Blindness," Last line)
Author: John Milton (1608-1674)
First published: 1673
Type of work: Sonnet

Context: In this poem, probably written in 1655, Milton first questions the infirmity which has been visited upon him. His blindness, coming at a time when he was Latin Secretary for the Commonwealth, was both a personal and a political burden, inasmuch as his enemies used it to embarrass both Milton and the government he served. In the poem Milton asks whether God can expect much of him, sight being denied. He answers his "fond," or foolish, question by saying that the Deity does not need a man or his work; that God in His greatness is served by those who bear their burdens with patience. Milton is seeking the answer to a problem strikingly similar to that of Job, the good man beset by afflictions. At the end of the sonnet Milton states one answer to the problem of how to bear his blindness and reconcile it with his ambitions:

Thousands at his bidding speed
And post o'er land and ocean without rest:
They also serve who only stand and wait.

They are all gone into the world of light!

Source: THEY ARE ALL GONE (Stanza 1)
Author: Henry Vaughan (1622-1695)
First published: 1655
Type of work: Lyric poem

Context: Henry Vaughan was one of the "metaphysical poets" of the seventeenth century. The term was applied by Samuel Johnson in the following century to a group of lyrists who expressed their religious and emotional experiences through the medium of sacred poetry. In Vaughan's case, we find the poet combining mysticism with an ardent love of external nature. This particular poem, characterized by strong overtones of religious mysticism and references to external nature, is probably the best-known and most popular of Vaughan's works. As the poet sits alone the memories of departed friends come to him; memory "glows and glitters." The poet believes the visions of his departed friends are revealed to him by God and are intended to inspire divine love in his cold heart. Death comes to seem beautiful, though mysterious, and the poet strives to probe the unknown. He calls upon God either to clear the gloom from the vision or permit him to join in death those who have departed and now have the clear vision he seeks. The poem begins with these lines:

> **They are all gone into the world of light!**
> And I alone sit lingering here;
> Their very memory is fair and bright,
> And my sad thoughts doth clear.

They augur misgovernment at a distance

Source: SPEECH ON MOVING HIS RESOLUTIONS FOR RECONCILIATION WITH THE COLONIES
Author: Edmund Burke (1729-1797)
First published: 1775
Type of work: Political speech

Context: America had no stronger and more able friend in the English Parliament than Burke, who foresaw the potential disaster in England's stern repression of the Colonies. Moving for conciliation, Burke pointed out that any victory by force is temporary, that it does not remove the necessity of subduing again, and that "a nation is not governed, which is perpetually to be conquered." Moreover, he believed the form of government which had evolved in the Colonies to be a commendable one and the nation, with her limitless potential for growth, to be "a noble object," well worth fighting for. The Colonists were honed to a sharp degree of liberty, many of their leaders trained in the legal profession. As Burke writes:

> . . . In no country, perhaps, in the world is the law so general a study. The profession itself is numerous and powerful, and in most provinces it takes the lead. . . . This study renders men acute, inquisitive, dexterous, prompt in attack, ready in defence, full of resources. . . . they anticipate the evil and judge of the pressure of the grievance by the badness of principle. **They augur misgovernment at a distance,** and snuff the approach of tyranny in every tainted breeze.

They could not only enjoy their own religion, but prevent everybody else from enjoying his

Source: THE LONDON PUNCH LETTERS (Number 5, "Is Introduced at the Club")
Author: Artemus Ward (Charles Farrar Browne, 1834-1867)
First published: 1866
Type of work: Humorous letter

Context: In 1866 Charles Farrar Browne went to England, where he became so popular that he was eagerly sought after by the London comic papers. The editor of *Punch* was successful in engaging the humorist to write a series of articles for the magazine. The articles appeared under the title "Artemus Ward in London." In Letter No. V, which appeared in the issue of October 6, 1866, the humorist speaks first of commerce between the United States and Great Britain, reducing the subject to one case of mutual fraud with which he was acquainted. He then turns his remarks to his own family and says that except for his Uncle Wilyim, whose actions caused him to be denounced by the humorist's father, "the escutchin of my fam'ly has never been stained by Games." Emphasizing the fact that he comes from a clever family, he writes:

> The Wards is a very clever fam'ly indeed.
> I believe we are descendid from the Puritins, who nobly fled a land of despitism to a land of freedim, where **they could not only enjoy their own religion, but prevent everybody else from enjoyin his.**

They do not love that do not show their love

Source: THE TWO GENTLEMEN OF VERONA (Act I, sc. ii, l. 31)
Author: William Shakespeare (1564-1616)
First published: 1623
Type of work: Dramatic comedy

Context: Proteus, one of the two gentlemen of Verona, is in love with Julia. To further his suit, he sends a letter to her by Valentine's servant, Speed. Being deceived by Lucetta, Julia's waiting woman into thinking that she is her mistress, Speed delivers the letter to her, and reports to Proteus that the lady did not say anything about loving him. Julia, a maid ready and willing to fall in love with somebody, discusses her would-be suitors with Lucetta. Lucetta says that Proteus loves Julia best of all her suitors, but Julia does not believe the statement because Proteus does not show his love. Both females disagree on how much love a lover displays.

LUCETTA
Fire that's closest kept burns most of all.

JULIA
They do not love that do not show their love.

LUCETTA
O, they love least that let men know their love.

They have ears, but they hear not

Source: PSALMS 115:6
Author: Unknown
First transcribed: c.400-200 B.C.
Type of work: Religious poetry

Context: The Gentiles, who worship idols, have chided the Israelites, asking them where is the God that they worship? The poet responds that the God of Israel is in the heavens, and that He is able to do whatever He wishes. The gods of the Gentiles, however, are idols fashioned by men, mere statues in the form of men, incapable of sensation or movement. Those who make idols or who place their faith in them are as dead as the pagan gods themselves. The poet vividly derides the heathen images:

> Their idols are silver and gold, the work of men's hands.
> They have mouths, but they speak not: eyes have they, but they see not:

They have ears, but they hear not: noses have they, but they smell not:

They have hands, but they handle not: feet have they, but they walk not: neither speak they through their throat.

They have sown the wind, and they shall reap the whirlwind

Source: HOSEA 8:7
Author: Hosea
First transcribed: 800-700 B.C.
Type of work: Religious prophecy

Context: Israel, the divided kingdom made up of ten of the tribes of Jacob, has followed a course of degeneracy. Hosea begins to prophesy during this dark period, pronouncing the doom of the nation, which has broken faith with God. In an hour of utter dejection Israel will cry to Him, God says, but since the good has been rejected, the enemy will pursue the chosen race. Hosea discloses the words of the Lord spoken to him of the sinfulness of the Israelites and of the futility of their wicked ways:

They have set up kings, but not by me: they have made princes, and I knew it not: of their silver and their gold have they made them idols, that they may be cut off.

. . .

For **they have sown the wind, and they shall reap the whirlwind:** it hath no stalk: the bud shall yield no meal: if so be it yield, the strangers shall swallow it up.

"They love th' eagle," he says, "on th' back iv a dollar"

Source: MR. DOOLEY IN PEACE AND IN WAR ("On Oratory in Politics")
Author: Finley Peter Dunne (1867-1936)
First published: 1898
Type of work: Humorous monologue

Context: Mr. Dooley expresses his opinion on the effect of political oratory by relating the story of a ward campaign he remembers in which Smith O'Brien Dorgan, "the boy orator of Healey's slough," ran against William J. O'Brien, who never said anything in public. Dorgan's thunderous speeches at first spellbound the voters, but as weeks passed, they began to consider him a nuisance who would break up social gatherings with his impromptu tirades. When the day came, Dorgan was miserably defeated. O'Brien, who had been quietly gaining votes by buying services for the voters and by granting them small loans, explained to Dorgan that the public's love of money is stronger than their patriotism.

989

"... Th' American nation in th' Sixth Ward is a fine people,"
he says. **"They love th' eagle,"** he says, **"on th' back iv a dollar,"**
he says.

They order this matter better in France

Source: A SENTIMENTAL JOURNEY THROUGH FRANCE AND ITALY (Opening line)
Author: Laurence Sterne (1713-1768)
First published: 1768
Type of work: Travel miscellany

Context: Sterne perhaps explained the meaning of *sentimental* in his title in a letter to a friend: "I told you my design in it was to teach us to love the world and our fellow creatures better than we do—so it runs most upon those gentler passions and affections." In the book itself, he observes, "'Tis a quiet journey of the heart in pursuit of NATURE, and those affections which arise out of her." The memoir tells of countless trivial incidents which caught his interest; his descriptions of his travels and minor adventures especially reveal in great detail his sensitivity to the misfortunes of others. The account begins abruptly, and after his fashion Sterne leaves the reader to decide for himself what the opening sentence refers to:

> **They order,** said I, **this matter better in France.**— You have been in France? said my gentleman, turning quick upon me with the most civil triumph in the world.— Strange! quoth I, debating the matter with myself, That one-and-twenty miles sailing, for 'tis absolutely no further from Dover to Calais, should give a man these rights. . . . I went straight to my lodgings, put up half a dozen shirts . . . took a place in the Dover stage; and . . . by three I had got sat down to my dinner . . . incontestably in France.

They shall make thee to eat grass as oxen

Source: DANIEL 4:32
Author: Unknown
First transcribed: c.300-150 B.C.
Type of work: Religious prophecy or apocalyptic writing

Context: King Nebuchadnezzar of Babylonia, after his sages have failed to explain a dream for him, calls in Daniel, an exile of Judah who is famed for his ability to interpret dreams. Daniel propounds that the fine tree that Nebuchadnezzar saw represents the powerful king himself. The hewing down of the tree by a holy one portrays the approaching

990

madness of Nebuchadnezzar, which will last until the king shall recognize the sovereignty of God, at which time both his reason and his kingdom shall be restored to him. Nebuchadnezzar, ignoring the warning of the dream, continues in his haughty, self-sufficient way until a voice from Heaven speaks, delivering his doom:

> . . . The kingdom is departed from thee.
> And they shall drive thee from men, and thy dwelling shall be with the beasts of the field: **they shall make thee to eat grass as oxen,** and seven times shall pass over thee, until thou know that the Most High ruleth in the kingdom of men, and giveth it to whomsoever he will.
> The same hour was the thing fulfilled upon Nebuchadnezzar: and he was driven from men, and did eat grass as oxen, and his body was wet with the dew of heaven, till his hairs were grown like eagle's feathers, and his nails like bird's claws.

They should take, who have the power, and they should keep who can

Source: ROB ROY'S GRAVE (Stanza 9, ll. 39-40)
Author: William Wordsworth (1770-1850)
First published: 1807
Type of work: Literary ballad

Context: Rob Roy, the "wild chieftain of a savage clan," typifies to Wordsworth a life undistorted by "man's inhumanity to man," by "rents and factors, rights of chase,/ Sheriffs, and lairds and their domains." Rob, a Scottish Robin Hood, was lord below as the eagle was lord above, yet he was not cruel and tyrannical. Ever the "poor man's stay,/ The poor man's heart, the poor man's hand," he championed "the oppressed, who wanted strength." He represents, to Wordsworth, man's natural moral creed, the "rule of right," by which " 'Tis God's appointment who must sway,/ And who is to submit." In this hierarchy of nature, no enmity can prevail:

> The creatures see of flood and field,
> And those that travel on the wind!
> With them no strife can last; they live
> In peace, and peace of mind.

> For why?—because the good old rule
> Sufficeth them, the simple plan,
> That **they should take, who have the power,**
> **And they should keep who can.**

They that go down to the sea in ships

Source: PSALMS 107:23
Author: Unknown
First transcribed: c.400-200 B.C.
Type of work: Religious poetry

Context: The Lord is to be praised, proclaims the psalmist, because He has led the redeemed from the privation of their desert wanderings to live in a city; because He has delivered the prisoners, who had rebelled against Him, from the bondage of their gloom; because He has healed those who called to Him when they were beset with illness and fear of death; and because He has calmed the stormy waters that imperil the seamen. The stanza describing the sea illustrates the strength of this poem of praise:

> **They that go down to the sea in ships,** that do business in great waters;
> These see the works of the Lord, and his wonders in the deep.
> For he commandeth, and raiseth the stormy wind, which lifteth up and the waves thereof.
> They mount up to the heaven, they go down again to the depths: their soul is melted because of trouble.
> They reel to and fro, and stagger like a drunken man, and are at their wit's end.
> Then they cry unto the Lord in their trouble, and he bringeth them out of their distresses.
> He maketh the storm a calm, so that the waves thereof are still.

They that touch pitch will be defiled

Source: MUCH ADO ABOUT NOTHING (Act III, sc. iii, ll. 56-57)
Author: William Shakespeare (1564-1616)
First published: 1600
Type of work: Dramatic comedy

Context: Dogberry, a constable, and Verges, a headborough, and the watch are on the street and are talking nonsense about what kind of man would make the most deserving constable, and then commenting on the duty of the watch. The directions are obvious contradictions. The watch must challenge every unknown man, but if the stranger refuses to halt, the watch is to consider itself lucky to be "rid of a knave." Drunken men are to be left alone "till they are sober." The flavor of this talk is revealed in the following dialogue, including the quotation, which is close to one in *Ecclesiasticus,* 13:1. ("He that toucheth pitch shall be defiled therewith"):

DOGBERRY

If you meet a thief, you may suspect him, by virtue of your office, to be no true man; and for such kind of men, the less you meddle or make with them, why, the more is for your honesty.

SECOND WATCHMAN

If we know him to be a thief, shall we not lay hands on him?

DOGBERRY

Truly by your office you may, but I think **they that touch pitch will be defiled.** The most peaceable way for you, if you do take a thief, is to let him show himself what he is, and steal out of your company.

The thing I most fear is fear

Source: ESSAYS ("Of Fear," Book I)
Author: Michel de Montaigne (1533-1592)
First published: 1580
Type of work: Moral essay

Context: In this essay, Montaigne tells us that "doctors say that there is none which carries our judgment away sooner from its proper seat" than fear. He goes on to discuss the effect of fear on various historical characters, especially those engaged in battle. He ends with a discussion of mass fear, which he calls "panic ter- rors." In a variation of Montaigne's famous passage, Henry D. Thoreau said (in his *Journal*), "Nothing is so much to be feared as fear," and Franklin D. Roosevelt in his 1933 In- augural Address, in an effort to bol- ster the spirits of the American peo- ple, said, "The only thing we have to fear is fear itself." Montaigne says:

> **The thing I most fear is fear. . . .** Those who have been well drubbed in some battle, and who are still wounded and bloody, you can perfectly well bring them back to the charge the next day. But those who have conceived a healthy fear of the enemy, you would never get them to look him in the face. . . . And so many people who, unable to endure the pangs of fear, have hanged themselves . . . have taught us well that fear is even more unwelcome and unbearable than death itself.

993

A thing of beauty is a joy forever

Source: ENDYMION (Book I, l. 1)
Author: John Keats (1795-1821)
First published: 1818
Type of work: Narrative poem

Context: In his first major poem, Keats gives a romantic treatment of the ancient Greek myth of Endymion, the beautiful boy loved by Diana. Keats shows a typically romantic interest in classical literature, and he embellishes the old myth with luxuriant language. Our souls, the poet says, are continually uplifted by "Some shape of beauty"—the sun, daffodils, a forest. Beauty also suffuses "the grandeur of the dooms/ We have imagined for the mighty dead;/ All lovely tales that we have heard or read:/ An endless fountain of immortal drink,/ Pouring unto us from the heaven's brink." These things of beauty "Haunt us till they become a cheering light/ Unto our souls," a light we cannot live without. The poet is happy to be beginning the story of Endymion in the country in the springtime, and he hopes to finish by autumn. The opening lines reveal Keats's conception of the Greek ideal of beauty:

> **A thing of beauty is a joy forever:**
> Its loveliness increases; it will never
> Pass into nothingness; but still will keep
> A bower quiet for us, and a sleep
> Full of sweet dreams, and health, and quiet breathing.
> Therefore, on every morrow, are we wreathing
> A flowery band to bind us to the earth,
> Spite of despondence, of the inhuman dearth
> Of noble natures, of the gloomy days,
> Of all the unhealthy and o'er-darkened ways
> Made for our searching: yes, in spite of all,
> Some shape of beauty moves away the pall
> From our dark spirits.

Things are in the saddle, and ride mankind

Source: ODE INSCRIBED TO W. H. CHANNING (Lines 50-51)
Author: Ralph Waldo Emerson (1803-1882)
First published: 1847
Type of work: Ode

Context: Emerson addressed this didactic ode to William Henry Channing, a Unitarian minister and social reformer and nephew of William Ellery Channing. Emerson says that attempts at social reform and humanitarian projects will be useless until man himself is reformed, for the reformers themselves are corrupt. The American talks glibly of culture and freedom but still attacks Mexico and holds Negro slaves. "Lofty New Hampshire" is filled with "little men." Freedom is "praised, but hid." America will see real progress and re-form only when men serve other men rather than things. If we live for love, friendship, truth, and harmony, then "The state may follow how it can, As Olympus follows Jove." But men have forgotten the "law for man" while law for thing . . . runs wild":

> The horseman serves the horse,
> The neatherd serves the neat,
> The merchant serves the purse,
> The eater serves his meat;
> 'Tis the day of the chattel,
> Web to weave, and corn to grind;
> **Things are in the saddle,**
> **And ride mankind.**

Things are not always what they seem

Source: FABLES ("The Weasel and the Mice," Book IV, Fable II)
Author: Phaedrus (fl. first century)
First transcribed: First century
Type of work: Moral tales of animals

Context: Often confused and included with Aesop, the fables of Phaedrus have a different form and content. In this moral story, an old weasel is no longer able to catch lively mice. He therefore rolls himself in flour and lies on his back outside their nest. The first mouse looks at him out of curiosity only to be eaten. So with mouse two, three, and four—but finally an "old, brindled fellow" stops at the doorway and says, "Fare you well, if you are flour, which you are not. . . ." The moral is that appearances are deceiving, but Phaedrus gives the lesson before he tells the story, as follows:

> This way of writing seems to you facetious; and no doubt, while we have nothing of more importance, we do sport with the pen. But examine these Fables with attention, and what useful lessons you will find concealed under them. **Things are not always what they seem;** first appearances deceive many: few minds understand what skill has hidden in an inmost corner. . . .

Things are seldom what they seem

Source: H.M.S. PINAFORE (Act II)
Author: W. S. Gilbert (1836-1911)
First published: 1878
Type of work: Light opera

Context: Little Buttercup, a woman who lives by selling food and supplies to ships anchoring at Portsmouth harbor, has come aboard the recently anchored *Pinafore,* where there is being debated the issue of social station —is it proper for Ralph Rackstraw, a common seaman, to try to win the hand of the Captain's daughter? Little Buttercup (Mrs. Cripps) is about to reveal that many years ago she nursed both Ralph and the Captain when they were infants, and reversed the positions of the two: according to their births, Ralph should be a captain, and Captain Corcoran a seaman. As a prelude to her revelation, she sings a duet with the Captain, warning him that appearances in life are often deceiving.

> BUTTERCUP
> **Things are seldom what they seem,**
> Skim milk masquerades as cream;
> Highlows pass as patent leathers;
> Jackdaws strut in peacock's feathers.

This best of all possible worlds

Source: CANDIDE (Chapter I)
Author: François-Marie Arouet de Voltaire (1694-1778)
First published: 1759
Type of work: Satirical fiction

Context: The underlying problem of *Candide* is the problem of Job: How can evil, particularly when it afflicts the innocent, occur in a world created by an omniscient and beneficent deity? In the eighteenth century, many people, taking their cue from Leibnitz, accepted the belief that this is not simply a good world, but that it is the best of all possible worlds. They did not try to deny the existence of evil, but they claimed that evil was a necessary ingredient in a universe that is, taken as a whole, good. From such a start, they concluded that man has to accept his lot, that what seems evil to the individual is really essential in the total harmony of goodness in the world. Voltaire could not sympathize with such a theory; after the disastrous Lisbon earthquake in 1755 he decided to speak out, as he did in "Poem on the Lisbon Disaster" and in *Candide,* against philosophical optimism. In *Candide,* Dr. Pangloss (All-tongue) is a fool—and the exponent of optimism:

Pangloss taught metaphysico-theologo-cosmolonigology. He proved admirably that there is no effect without a cause and that in **this best of all possible worlds,** My Lord the Baron's castle was the best of castles and his wife the best of all possible Baronesses.

" 'Tis demonstrated," said he, "that things cannot be otherwise; for, since everything is made for an end, everything is necessarily for the best end."

This business will never hold water

Source: SHE WOU'D AND SHE WOU'D NOT; OR, THE KIND IMPOSTOR (Act IV)
Author: Colley Cibber (1671-1757)
First published: 1703
Type of work: Dramatic comedy

Context: This is the story of a woman, Hypolita, who masquerades as a man to prevent a marriage between the man she loves, Don Philip, and another woman. The romantic plot is somewhat complicated, as is often true in a Cibber comedy. Hypolita, in her pride, sends Don Philip off to marry a woman he has never seen, the marriage being arranged by his father. The girl whom Don Philip is to marry is, unknown to him, in love with his good friend Octavio, who is Hypolita's brother. Taking a desperate course, Hypolita disguises herself as a man, as Don Philip himself, to marry Rosara, Don Philip's proposed wife, who is let in on the secret. Hypolita plans to "marry" Rosara, so that Don Philip cannot. She will step aside then so Rosara can marry Octavio, leaving Don Philip free to marry Hypolita. Amid much confusion and some hilarity the plan works, in great part because of the help given the disguised Hypolita by Trappanti, a roguish servant once in Don Philip's employ. He lies and lies, to help Hypolita. At one point he swears before a magistrate that the real Don Philip tried to bribe him and force him to bear false witness against the disguised Hypolita:

TRAPPANTI

Upon this, sir, I began to demur: sir, says I, **this business will never hold water;** don't let me undertake it, I must beg your pardon; gave him the negative shrug, and was for sneaking off with the fees in my pocket.

This Government cannot endure permanently half slave and half free

Source: SPEECH AT THE REPUBLICAN STATE CONVENTION AT SPRINGFIELD, ILLINOIS
Author: Abraham Lincoln (1809-1865)
First published: 1858
Type of work: Political speech

Context: Lincoln made this speech at the close of the convention, which had just chosen him as candidate for the United States Senate. In it he is concerned about the bitter slavery debate, which is destroying the nation. He is also concerned about the spread of slavery, which had recently been sanctioned by the Nebraska Bill and the Dred Scott decision. The "dynasty" of the Supreme Court must be overthrown. If Republicans unite for the Union and against slavery, "the victory is sure to come." "Slavery agitation" has greatly increased in the last five years:

> . . . In my opinion, it will not cease until a crisis shall have been reached and passed. "A house divided against itself cannot stand." I believe **this Government cannot endure permanently half slave and half free.** I do not expect the Union to be dissolved, —I do not expect the house to fall,—but I do expect it will cease to be divided. It will become all one thing or all the other. Either the opponents of slavery will arrest the further spread of it, and place it where the public mind shall rest in the belief that it is in the course of ultimate extinction; or its advocates will push it forward, till it shall become alike lawful in all the States, old as well as new—North as well as South.
>
> Have we no tendency to the latter condition?

This is Liberty Hall

Source: SHE STOOPS TO CONQUER (Act II, sc. i)
Author: Oliver Goldsmith (1728-1774)
First published: 1774
Type of work: Dramatic comedy

Context: Tony Lumpkin and his stepfather, Mr. Hardcastle, have no great affection for each other; and Tony takes any opportunity to play tricks on the old man. His chance occurs when Mr. Marlow and Mr. Hastings, having lost their way en route to the Hardcastle country home, enter a tavern where Tony has been drinking with some companions. He directs them to the Hardcastles', but tells them the house is an inn. When the two men arrive and before they have been greeted by Mr. Hardcastle, they talk about the two girls, Miss Hardcastle and Miss Neville, whom they have come to court. Hardcastle enters and greets them warmly, but Marlow continues chatting with Hastings and ignores Hardcastle almost completely. Marlow suggests that he and Hastings on the morrow should change their attire to something more stylish than their traveling clothes.

HASTINGS [aside]
I fancy, Charles, you're right: the first blow is half the battle.
I intend opening the campaign with the white and gold.

HARDCASTLE
Mr. Marlow—Mr. Hastings—gentlemen—pray be under no constraint in this house. **This is Liberty Hall,** gentlemen. You may do just as you please here.

This is my own, my native land!

Source: THE LAY OF THE LAST MINSTREL (Canto VI, stanza 1)
Author: Sir Walter Scott (1771-1832)
First published: 1805
Type of work: Narrative poem

Context: An aged minstrel, last of the harpers, recites a tale of the love and the final union of lovers from rival families in sixteenth century Scotland. The love story is all but lost in the trappings of chivalry and enchantment. Each canto is set within a frame of lines in which the old minstrel speaks with those about him and often laments the more genial past. Particularly moving are the lines with which he begins the last canto. (Some of the language is reminiscent of Luke 24:32, in a passage discussing the appearance of Christ at Emmaus: "Did not our heart burn within us, while he talked with us by the way, and while he opened to us the scriptures?")

> Breathes there the man, with soul so dead,
> Who never to himself hath said,
> **This is my own, my native land!**
> Whose heart hath ne'er within him burn'd,
> As home his footsteps he hath turn'd,
> From wandering on a foreign strand?
> If such there breathe, go, mark him well;
> For him no Minstrel raptures swell.

This is the end of every man's desire

Source: A BALLAD OF BURDENS (Refrain)
Author: Algernon Charles Swinburne (1837-1909)
First published: 1866
Type of work: Lyric poem

Context: This grim poem, mainly an address to a woman who sells her love, is a warning that while lust is universal, and the gratifying of it often an intoxication, the fruits of love only for the sake of pleasure are bitter. Even when the woman is in her prime, there is an emptiness and sterility in her love, and her actions are a travesty of love. And when her youth begins to fade, she will be desolate, left with nothing but regrets. The poem concludes with an "Envoy," addressed to all men who take pleasure in light love:

> Princes, and ye whom pleasure quickeneth,
>   Heed well this rhyme before your pleasure tire;
> For life is sweet, but after life is death.
>   **This is the end of every man's desire.**

This is the forest primeval

Source: EVANGELINE (Prelude, stanza 1)
Author: Henry Wadsworth Longfellow (1807-1882)
First published: 1847
Type of work: Narrative poem

Context: This "Tale of Acadie" is based on a historical event—the deportation in 1755 of the French inhabitants of Nova Scotia by the British authorities. In the poem, Evangeline, an Acadian girl, is separated from her fiancé during the deportation. The lovers search for each other all their lives. Finally, when they are old, she finds him dying in a hospital. Evangeline dies from shock. In the prelude Longfellow foreshadows the approaching tragedy. The forest remains, but the Acadian inhabitants are gone, the "Men whose lives glided on like rivers that water the woodlands . . . reflecting an image of heaven." The farmers have "forever departed." "Naught but tradition remains of the beautiful village of Grand-Pré." The poet asks his readers to listen to this tale "of woman's devotion." In the first stanza, the woods seem saddened by the tragic scene they have witnessed:

> **This is the forest primeval.** The murmuring pines and the hemlocks,
>   Bearded with moss, and in garments green, indistinct in the twilight,

1000

Stand like Druids of eld, with voices sad and prophetic,
Stand like harpers hoar, with beards that rest on their bosoms.
Loud from its rocky caverns, the deep-voiced neighboring ocean
Speaks, and in accents disconsolate answers the wail of the forest.

This is the way the world ends, not with a bang but a whimper

Source: THE HOLLOW MEN (V, conclusion)
Author: T(homas) S(tearns) Eliot (1888-1965)
First published: 1925
Type of work: Metaphysical poem

Context: This quotation comes from the closing lines of a poem which, according to one of the commentaries upon Eliot, deals with "the emptiness of life without belief." The "hollow men" of the poem are those who have led empty and meaningless lives: they have been only "paralyzed force, gesture without motion." They have accomplished nothing; they are the product of the dry intellectuality of modern life. In the poem's first section they are contrasted with those who have crossed over into the world of Death with "direct eyes;" that is, with those who have had the strength to accomplish what they had planned. The "hollow men" are reminiscent of the vast throng that Dante saw on the dark plain, the souls of those who lived "without blame, and without praise." They are not "lost violent souls" but only hollow men. The last lines of the poem describe the way in which, for them and for so many of our desiccated generation, the end of life comes:

This is the way the world ends
This is the way the world ends
This is the way the world ends
Not with a bang but a whimper.

This night, before the cock crow, thou shalt deny me thrice

Source: MATTHEW 26:34
Author: Unknown (traditionally Matthew the Apostle)
First transcribed: c.75-100
Type of work: Gospel

Context: In Jerusalem, Jesus partakes of the Last Supper, at which time He says that one of the twelve will betray Him, and then goes to the Mount of Olives. There He predicts that His disciples will fall away from Him, but that after His resurrection He will go before them into Galilee. When Peter declares that, even though all other men fall by the way, he will never forsake his Lord, Jesus says to him:

. . . Verily I say unto thee, That **this night, before the cock crow, thou shalt deny me thrice.**

Peter said unto him, Though I should die with thee, yet will I not deny thee. Likewise also said all the disciplines.

This party comes from the grass roots

Source: ADDRESS AS TEMPORARY CHAIRMAN OF THE BULL MOOSE CONVENTION, CHICAGO
Author: Albert Jeremiah Beveridge (1862-1927)
First spoken: 1912
Type of work: Speech

Context: Albert Jeremiah Beveridge accepted with some hesitation the offer to make the keynote speech at the national convention of the newly formed Progressive Party, popularly called the "Bull Moose" Party, in 1912. The party had been organized as a reform movement to clear out the unhealthy elements in power and to free the government of graft. Beveridge's speech was a fighting one. His opening words made the convention delegates aware of his convictions: "We stand for a broader liberty, a fuller justice. We stand for social brotherhood as against savage individualism." Then turning his attention more specifically to the formation of the party, he says:

> We found a party through which all who believe with us can work with us; or rather, we declare our allegiance to a party which the people themselves have founded.
>
> For **this party comes from the grass roots.** It has grown from the soil of the people's hard necessities. It has the vitality of the people's strong convictions. The people have work to be done, and our party is here to do that work.

This rock shall fly from its firm base as soon as I!

Source: THE LADY OF THE LAKE (Canto V, stanza 10)
Author: Sir Walter Scott (1771-1832)
First published: 1810
Type of work: Narrative poem

Context: A lost hunter, after being sheltered by friendly strangers of a Highland clan, leaves a Loch Katrine island. Afterward, the clan chieftain, Roderick Dhu, who has been guard- ing the young Ellen Douglas and her exiled father against the King's anger, returns from a bloody raid and asks for her hand. In his fury at her re- fusal, he calls his clan to arms against

1002

the King. The hunter, Fitz-James, steals back to the island to propose to Ellen, but is also refused. He leaves, but slays his guide who had planned to betray this Lowland warrior into ambush. Lost again, Fitz-James finds a sentry who treats him overnight with the hospitality the Highland code demanded even for enemies. As the sentry leads him on his way the next morning, Fitz-James speaks against Roderick Dhu and wishes he could confront him and his men. His angered guide whistles, and an armed soldier springs up from behind every bush and rock. The guide is Roderick Dhu! Startled but brave, Fitz-James places his back against a rock and prepares to fight his foes, crying:

> "Come one, come all! **this rock shall fly**
> **From its firm base as soon as I!"**
> Sir Roderick mark'd—and in his eyes
> Respect was mingled with surprise,
> And the stern joy which warriors feel
> In foemen worthy of their steel.

This royal throne of kings, this sceptered isle

Source: KING RICHARD THE SECOND (Act II, sc. i, l. 40)
Author: William Shakespeare (1564-1616)
First published: 1597
Type of work: Historical drama

Context: Richard II is approached by his uncle, John of Gaunt, and his uncle's son, Henry Bolingbroke, later King Henry IV, with accusations against Mowbray, Duke of Norfolk. Rather than have the accuser and the accused test the accusation by resort to trial by combat, Richard banishes both Bolingbroke and Mowbray from England. John of Gaunt protests the long banishment of his son, saying that by the time Bolingbroke returns he, John, will be dead; however, Richard will not revoke his decree. Gaunt later is carried in a chair to see Richard, and "a prophet new inspired / And thus expiring do foretell of him, / His rash fierce blaze of riot cannot last." Gaunt then comments on the nobility and greatness of England and prophesies its decline:

GAUNT
. . .

> **This royal throne of kings, this sceptred isle,**
> This earth of majesty, this seat of Mars,
> This other Eden, demi-Paradise,
> . . .
> This blessed plot, this earth, this realm, this England,
> . . .

1003

That England that was wont to conquer others,
Hath made a shameful conquest of itself.

. . .

This strange disease of modern life

Source: THE SCHOLAR-GYPSY (Stanza 21)
Author: Matthew Arnold (1822-1888)
First published: 1853
Type of work: Philosophical poem

Context: Matthew Arnold, critic of his time in poetry and prose, attempted to teach his contemporaries the futility of a narrow mind and the value of an enlightened life. Choosing from Joseph Glanvil's *Vanity of Dogmatizing,* written in 1661, the story of an Oxford student, who, because of poverty, was forced to leave the university and join a band of gypsies, whose lore he acquainted himself with, Arnold transforms the scholar-gypsy into an ideal, one who rejects his own time and seeks a higher goal. Declaring that the young man, after two hundred years, still wanders about in his search, Arnold, condemns the sickness and confusion of modern life, praises the scholar for his steadfastness, and urges him to flee the turmoil of the age:

> O born in days when wits were fresh and clear,
> And life ran gayly as the sparkling Thames;
> Before **this strange disease of modern life,**
> With its sick hurry, its divided aims,
> Its head o'ertaxed, its palsied hearts, was rife—
> Fly hence, our contact fear!

This was a man

Source: JULIUS CAESAR (Act V, sc. v, l. 75)
Author: William Shakespeare (1564-1616)
First published: 1623
Type of work: Dramatic tragedy

Context: Marcus Brutus, an honorable Roman, leads the conspirators who assassinate Caesar. He does so from no selfish motive but to save Rome from the dictatorial power of Caesar and to preserve ancient Roman freedoms. But the murder results in civil war which sweeps Italy. The army led by Brutus and his fellow conspirator, Cassius, is defeated by the forces of Mark Antony and Octavius at Philippi, and, rather than be captured, Brutus runs upon his sword and dies. Now Antony pays him tribute.

ANTONY

• • •

His life was gentle, and the elements
So mixed in him, that Nature might stand up,
And say to all the world, **this was a man.**

OCTAVIUS

According to his virtue let us use him,
With all respect, and rites of burial.
Within my tent his bones to-night shall lie,
Most like a soldier, ordered honourably.
So call the field to rest, and let's away,
To part the glories of this happy day.

This was the most unkindest cut of all

Source: JULIUS CAESAR (Act III, sc. ii, l. 188)
Author: William Shakespeare (1564-1616)
First published: 1623
Type of work: Dramatic tragedy

Context: This quotation has been changed by usage and in today's speech is usually heard as "that's the unkindest cut of all," and means the cruelest remark or insult possible because of intimate knowledge or the intimate relationship of the parties involved. In its original sense the line refers to the wound made by Brutus in the body of Caesar which was totally unlooked for on Caesar's part. It was the blow that completely disillusioned Caesar regarding Brutus' professed friendship for him, the thrust that killed Caesar's spirit as well as his body. Now, during his funeral oration, Mark Antony, friend, protégé, and vowed avenger of his murdered mentor, points to the wound and employs masterful imagery and irony as he says:

ANTONY

Look, in this place ran Cassius' dagger through.
See what a rent the envious Casca made.
Through this, the well-beloved Brutus stabbed,
And as he plucked his cursed steel away,
Mark how the blood of Caesar followed it,
As rushing out of doors, to be resolved
If Brutus so unkindly knocked, or no;
For Brutus, as you know, was Caesar's angel.
Judge, o you gods, how dearly Caesar loved him.
This was the most unkindest cut of all;
For when the noble Caesar saw him stab,
Ingratitude, more strong than traitor's arms,
Quite vanquished him. Then burst his mighty heart,

• • •

This was the noblest Roman of them all

Source: JULIUS CAESAR (Act V, sc. v, l. 68)
Author: William Shakespeare (1564-1616)
First published: 1623
Type of work: Dramatic tragedy

Context: Two contending armies tear Italy apart following the assassination of Julius Caesar. The army led by Mark Antony and Octavius meets and destroys the forces of Brutus and Cassius at Philippi. Brutus, who led the conspirators in the assassination of Caesar, did so for no selfish reason but to save Rome from Caesar's dictatorial powers and to preserve ancient Roman freedoms. Rather than be taken, when he faces certain defeat, he runs upon his sword and dies. Now his enemy, Mark Antony, pays him tribute.

ANTONY

This was the noblest Roman of them all.
All the conspirators save only he
Did that they did, in envy of great Caesar;
He only, in a general honest thought,
And common good to all, made one of them.

• • •

This was their finest hour

Source: THEIR FINEST HOUR (Last line)
Author: Sir Winston Spencer Churchill (1874-1965)
First spoken: British House of Commons, June 18, 1940
Type of work: Political oratory

Context: A speech delivered first to the House of Commons and then broadcast, June 18, 1940, was entitled "Their Finest Hour." After acknowledging the military disaster to the French High Command at Dunkirk, Churchill describes the increasing size of the British army and its navy as means of deterring the German invasion of England. He sees the Battle of France concluded and the Battle of Britain about to begin, but he hopes England can stand up to the might of Hitler. His address concludes:

. . . But if we fail, then the whole world, including the United States, including all that we have known and cared for, will sink into the abyss of a new Dark Age made more sinister, and perhaps more protracted, by the lights of perverted science. Let us therefore brace ourselves to our duties, and so bear ourselves that, if the British Empire and its Commonwealth last for a thousand years, men will still say: **"This was their finest hour."**

This world surely is wide enough to hold both thee and me

Source: THE LIFE AND OPINIONS OF TRISTRAM SHANDY, GENT. (Book II, chapter 12)
Author: Laurence Sterne (1713-1768)
First published: 1759-1767
Type of work: Novel

Context: When Sterne began to write *Tristram Shandy,* he intended to continue it in annual installments for the rest of his life. This plan perhaps accounts partially for the casual, digressive narrative technique in the book. The author seems to take a great deal of time to arrive nowhere at all. This very rambling quality is, however, one of the delights of the novel. It enables Sterne to treat in detail the characters and events he has created. One of the most vivid personalities is Uncle Toby, a retired army officer who talks incessantly of battles and fortifications. For all his warlike talk, Uncle Toby is, however, "of a peaceful, placid nature—no jarring element in it—all was mixed up so kindly within; my Uncle Toby had scarce a heart to retaliate upon a fly." To illustrate this quality, Sterne describes how Uncle Toby once, after many attempts, caught a fly which had been buzzing about his head all through dinner:

". . . I'll not hurt thee," says my Uncle Toby rising from his chair, and going across the room with the fly in his hand . . . "Go," says he, lifting up the sash, and opening his hand as he spoke, to let it escape;—"go, poor devil, get thee gone; why should I hurt thee?—**This world surely is wide enough to hold both thee and me.**"

A thorn in the flesh

Source: II CORINTHIANS 12:7
Author: Paul
First transcribed: c.55-57
Type of work: Religious epistle

Context: Paul, disheartened because the church at Corinth is following false leaders instead of him, its founder and the true apostle of Christ, seeks to reveal the folly of its actions. Paul says that if the Corinthians must trust fools, then he will speak to them as a fool, but he must boast to them of his accomplishments as a missionary of the gospel. However, lest Paul should feel too exalted, he confesses, he has been given "a thorn in the flesh," a constant discomfort (probably an offensive physical illness of some kind) that keeps him humble; thus, in his discomfort he is better able to serve the Lord:

And lest I should be exalted above measure through the abundance of the revelations, there was given to me **a thorn in the flesh,** the messenger of Satan to buffet me, lest I should be exalted above measure.

For this thing I besought the Lord thrice, that it might depart from me.

And he said unto me, My grace is sufficient for thee: for my strength is made perfect in weakness. Most gladly therefore will I rather glory in my infirmities, that the power of Christ may rest upon me.

Those who lived without praise or blame

Source: THE DIVINE COMEDY, INFERNO (Canto III, ll. 34-35, as translated by H. F. Cary)
Author: Dante Alighieri (1265-1321)
First transcribed: c.1314
Type of work: Christian allegory

Context: Dante, having agreed to accompany Virgil throughout the Inferno, immediately hears "various tongues, horrible languages, outcries of woe, accents of anger," and asks the origin. Virgil answers that these are the trimmers who have no hope of death and can only envy those who have been consigned through death to a punishment. He suggests that Dante "speak not of them, but look, and pass them by."

> He thus to me: "This miserable fate
> Suffer the wretched souls of **those, who lived**
> **Without or praise or blame,** with that ill band
> Of angels mix'd, who nor rebellious proved,
> Nor yet were true to God, but for themselves
> Were only. From his bounds Heaven drove them forth
> Not to impair his lustre; nor the depth
> Of Hell receives them, lest the accursed tribe
> Should glory thence with exultation vain."

Those who think must govern those that toil

Source: THE TRAVELLER (Line 372)
Author: Oliver Goldsmith (1728-1774)
First published: 1764
Type of work: Descriptive and meditative poem

Context. In his evaluations of the merits and defects of several different European nations, the traveller has begun to consider his own homeland,

1008

England. Its great virtue, he says, is the Englishman's love of independence; but this very sense of personal freedom has led the British into error. One major consequence has been a turning away from nature toward materialism. "As nature's ties decay,/ As duty, love, and honour fail to sway,/ Fictitious bonds, the bonds of wealth and law,/ Still gather strength, and force unwilling awe." At the same time, writes the poet, in complaining of freedom's ills he does not "mean to flatter kings, or court the great." He is aware of the problems that freedom brings:

> For just experience tells, in every soil,
> That **those who think must govern those that toil;**
> And all that freedom's highest aims can reach,
> Is but to lay proportion'd loads on each.
> Hence, should one order disproportion'd grow,
> Its double weight must ruin all below.

Thou art a monument without a tomb

Source: TO THE MEMORY OF SHAKESPEARE (Line 22)
Author: Ben Jonson (1573?-1637)
First published: 1623
Type of work: Poetic panegyric

Context: A tomb is the resting place of a dead body. A monument need have no relationship with anything dead. So Jonson, in his dedicatory poem in the First Folio of Shakespeare's collected plays, declares that perhaps Geoffrey Chaucer (1340?-1400), the poet Edmund Spenser (1552?-1599) famous for his *Fairie Queene* (1590-1596), and the dramatist Francis Beaumont (1584-1616) lie dead in their graves, but Shakespeare will live on forever in his plays. Jonson writes:

> My Shakespeare, rise; I will not lodge thee by
> Chaucer, or Spenser, or bid Beaumont lie
> A little further, to make thee a roome:
> **Thou art a moniment, without a tombe,**
> And art alive still, while thy Booke doth live,
> And we have wits to read, and praise to give . . .

Thou art the man

Source: II SAMUEL 12:7
Author: Unknown
First transcribed: 1100-400 B.C.
Type of work: Religious history

Context: Having an adulterous relationship which leads to the pregnancy of Bathsheba, King David commands that Uriah, the husband of the beautiful woman, be placed in the front line of battle. The prophet of the Lord, Nathan, enraged when the king causes the death of the husband and marries Bathsheba, convinces David of his guilt by telling him a parable of a rich man who confiscates the only lamb of a poor man:

> And David's anger was greatly kindled against the man; and he said to Nathan. As the LORD liveth, the man that hath done this thing shall surely die:
> And he shall restore the lamb fourfold, because he did this thing, and because he had no pity.
> And Nathan said to David, **Thou art the man. . . .**

Thou canst not stir a flower without troubling of a star

Source: THE MISTRESS OF VISION (Stanza 22)
Author: Francis Thompson (1859-1907)
First published: 1897
Type of work: Mystical poem

Context: Francis Thompson's mystical poem *The Mistress of Vision* seems to have a deep religious meaning that is expressed allegorically. The garden is possibly Heaven; the Lady, Mary; and the sun, Divinity. The poet first has a vision of the Lady singing in the garden. Upon coming back to earth after the vision of the heavenly garden, the poet retains only "dim snatches" of the Lady's song. The poet then asks where his destined "land of Luthany," or land of song, is, and he receives the answer that he will enter it when he leaves the way of mortals. He is further told that all things in the universe are bound together so that moving a flower will cause a disturbance in the heavens. Further the poet learns that his song of suffering in life can give him the strength of the Greek hero Perseus so that he can kill the Medusa-like monster Pain. Stanza 22 of the poem is as follows:

> "When to the new eyes of thee
> All things by immortal power,
> Near or far,
> Hiddenly
> To each other linkèd are,
> That **thou canst not stir a flower**
> **Without troubling of a star;**
> When thy song is shield and mirror
> To the fair snake-curlèd Pain,
> Where thou dar'st affront her terror
> That on her thou may'st attain
> Perséan conquest; seek no more,
> O seek no more!
> Pass the gates of Luthany, tread the region Elenore."

1010

Thou hast seen nothing yet

Source: DON QUIXOTE (Part I, Book III, chapter 11)
Author: Miguel de Cervantes Saavedra (1547-1616)
First published: 1605
Type of work: Satirical novel

Context: Amadis of Gaul, disdained by the Lady Oriana, left civilization to do penance on the Poor Rock. Don Quixote decides to follow his example, as well as that of Orlando Furioso when Angelica found another love. He orders Sancho to watch him for three days and then go to Dulcinea del Toboso to report to her to what extremes of madness her disdain has driven Don Quixote. Sancho protests. "Bless my eyesight, what can I see more than I have seen already?" In his reply, the Knight of the Sorrowful Countenance expresses more grammatically our slangy term, "You ain't seen nothing yet!"

Thou hast seen nothing yet . . . thou must see me throw away my armor, tear my clothes, knock my head against the rocks, and do a thousand other things of that kind, that will fill thee with astonishment.

Thou liar of the first magnitude

Source: LOVE FOR LOVE (Act II, sc. i)
Author: William Congreve (1670-1729)
First published: 1695
Type of work: Dramatic comedy

Context: One of the characters in the play is Foresight, an "illiterate Old Fellow" who is peevish and who is very superstitious, believing in astrology, dreams, omens, and all such supernatural lore. He is also bedevilled by his second wife, a younger woman who will, he fears, make him a cuckold. Also a trial for him is his niece, Angelica, financially and psychologically extremely independent. By an earlier marriage, Foresight has a daughter named Prue, a hoyden who is expected to marry Ben, the younger son of Sir Sampson Legend. On this morning Sir Sampson comes to see Foresight about the approaching marriage; the knight is arranging for Ben to inherit his fortune, even though Ben is the younger of two sons. Sir Sampson twits Foresight about his superstitions and about the possibility of becoming a cuckold, angering the devotee of astrology:

FORESIGHT
Capricorn in your Teeth, thou Modern Mandevil; Ferdinand Mendez Pinto was but a type of thee, **thou Lyar of the first Mag-**

1011

nitude. Take back your Paper of Inheritance; send your Son to Sea again. I'll marry my Daughter to an Egyptian mummy, ere she shall Incorporate with a Contemner of Sciences and a Defamer of Vertue.

Thou Paradise of exiles, Italy!

Source: JULIAN AND MADDALO (Line 57)
Author: Percy Bysshe Shelley (1792-1822)
First published: 1824
Type of work: Narrative poem

Context: Shelley describes the situation in his Preface: "Count Maddalo is a Venetian nobleman of ancient family and of great fortune. . . ." He is too proud to take an interest in civil affairs, and his powerful intellect gives him "an intense apprehension of the nothingness of human life." Julian, "an Englishman of good family," is an atheist who believes in "the power of man over his own mind" and the perfectibility of human society. The story also involves a lovelorn maniac and Maddalo's daughter. One evening Maddalo rides with Julian (the narrator) "Upon the bank of land which breaks the flow/ Of Adria towards Venice." As usual, they argue about "God, freewill and destiny," for "Maddalo takes a wicked pleasure in drawing out [Julian's] taunts against religion." But they pause to enjoy the beauties of the Italian sunset:

> Meanwhile the sun paused ere it should alight,
> Over the horizon of the mountains.—Oh,
> How beautiful is sunset, when the glow
> Of Heaven descends upon a land like thee,
> **Thou Paradise of exiles, Italy!**
> Thy mountains, seas and vineyards, and the towers
> Of cities they encircle! . . .

Thou setter up and plucker down of kings

Source: KING HENRY THE SIXTH: PART THREE (Act II, sc. iii, l. 37)
Author: William Shakespeare (1564-1616)
First published: 1623
Type of work: Historical drama

Context: The Earl of Warwick and the children of the Duke of York, in rebellion against King Henry, are winded and sit down to rest and to talk over their loss on the battlefield. Richard (later King Richard III) enters and tries to breathe strength and resolution into their weary bones and muscles. He reports to Warwick that his brother has been killed. Warwick thereupon declares new determination to continue the war. Edward, Earl of March and afterwards King Edward IV, declares his will to fight on with Warwick.

EDWARD

O Warwick, I do bend my knee with thine,
And in this vow do chain my soul to thine;
And ere my knee rise from the earth's cold face,
I throw my hands, mine eyes, my heart to thee,
Thou setter up and plucker down of kings:
Beseeching thee, if with thy will it stands
That to my foes this body must be prey,
Yet that thy brazen gates of heaven may ope,
And give sweet passage to my sinful soul.

• • •

Thou trustest in the staff of this broken reed

Source: ISAIAH 36:6
Author: Isaiah
First transcribed: c.800-200 B.C.
Type of work: Religious prophecy and exhortation

Context: Isaiah, prophet of the Lord, declares his vision of "Judah and Jerusalem in the days of Uzziah, Jotham, Ahaz, and Hezekiah, kings of Judah." Denouncing the sins of the people and urging obedience to the will of the Lord, Isaiah prophesies the coming of a messiah, the future greatness of Jerusalem and Judah, and the destruction of the enemies of the Lord. Other prophets also foretell God's wrath, His vengeance on His foes, and His deliverance of His people. In a biographical passage, a later writer recounts the movement of Sennacherib, king of Assyria, against Hezekiah, king of Judah, and the prophesy by Isaiah of the defeat of the Assyrians. With Jerusalem surrounded, Sennacherib's envoy presents himself, demands surrender, and asks in whom Hezekiah places his trust in a time of peril:

. . . on whom dost thou trust, that thou rebellest against me?
Lo, **thou trustest in the staff of this broken reed,** on Egypt;
whereon if a man lean, it will go into his hand, and pierce it: so is
Pharaoh king of Egypt to all that trust in him.

1013

Though last, not least

Source: JULIUS CAESAR (Act III, sc. i, l. 189)
Author: William Shakespeare (1564-1616)
First published: 1623
Type of work: Dramatic tragedy

Context: This famous saying is now usually heard as "last but not least," and connotes, in a positive sense, that though a person or thing is last in enumeration, this position in no way reduces his or its importance. Originally, Antony's words subtly convey "though last, not least" in *guilt* although the complete quotation is "Though last, not least in *love.*" It is vital, however, to understand Antony's true thoughts and ultimate intentions toward the men with whom he is speaking. When Caesar is assassinated in the Senate, Antony flees in fear. Now he returns with a safe-conduct from Brutus (one of the assassins). The conspirators assure him that they acted out of love for Rome itself. Antony takes the hand of each assassin as a sign that he believes him. He really does not, but he is stalling for time to right this monstrous wrong against Caesar. Shortly before Shakespeare wrote *Julius Caesar* (1598-1600), Edmund Spenser used the same phrase, "Though last not least" in *Colin Clouts Come Home Again* (1595) as later did Pope "the last, not least . . ." in *The Dunciad* (1728).

ANTONY

· · ·

Let each man render me his bloody hand.
First Marcus Brutus, will I shake with you;
Next Caius Cassius do I take your hand;
Now Decius Brutus yours; now yours Metellus;
Yours Cinna; and my valiant Casca, yours;
Though last, not least in love, yours good Trebonius.

· · ·

Though your sins be as scarlet

Source: ISAIAH 1:18
Author: Isaiah
First transcribed: c.800-200 B.C.
Type of work: Religious prophecy and exhortation

Context: Isaiah, son of Amoz and prophet of the Almighty, declares His message "concerning Judah and Jerusalem in the days of Uzziah, Jotham, Ahaz, and Hezekiah, kings of Judah." Isaiah says that the Lord notes the rebelliousness of the Israelites and the iniquity of the nation.

The people are pressed down, and the country is destroyed. Through His prophet, the Lord stresses His weariness with burnt offerings and His love of righteousness. Acting as a judge, the Lord says that man must confront Him so that both He and man, may present arguments for their cases. If men are obedient, the Almighty says, their scarlet sins shall be made white, for obedience alone shall know the face of God:

> Come now, and let us reason together, saith the Lord: **though your sins be as scarlet,** they shall be as white as snow; though they be red like crimson, they shall be as wool.
> If ye be willing and obedient, ye shall eat the good of the land:
> But if ye refuse and rebel, ye shall be devoured with the sword: for the mouth of the Lord hath spoken it.

Thoughts that do often lie too deep for tears

Source: ODE. INTIMATIONS OF IMMORTALITY FROM RECOLLECTIONS OF EARLY CHILDHOOD (Stanza 11)
Author: William Wordsworth (1770-1850)
First published: 1807
Type of work: Philosophic poem

Context: The complex train of thought in this major Wordsworthian poem passes through three phases: (1) the perception that in youth there is a vigor and intuitive reaction to the beauty of nature which later fades; (2) a suggestion that the visionary quality of childhood is attributable to the pre-existence of the soul; (3) the reconciliation of faith with the assertion that there is a compensating gift for the loss of childhood perception. The "immortality" in this poem is not the theological term which signifies endlessness of life, but the infiniteness of human consciousness. This development of the "compensating gift" is the intellectual maturity which responds to the beauty and force of nature through a "primal sympathy" with "human suffering," which lives "In the faith that looks through death,/ In years that bring the philosophic mind." Hence, the poet grieves not the loss of the "splendour in the grass," but rejoices in the contemplative view of nature's grandeur:

> Thanks to the human heart by which we live,
> Thanks to its tenderness, its joys, and fears,
> To me the meanest flower that blows can give
> **Thoughts that do often lie too deep for tears.**

A thousand times good night

Source: ROMEO AND JULIET (Act II, sc. ii, l. 155)
Author: William Shakespeare (1564-1616)
First published: 1597
Type of work: Dramatic tragedy

Context: Romeo and Juliet have for some minutes been declaring their love for each other. She is standing in the window; he is in the orchard below. Juliet cannot fully understand why Romeo came to see her. She wonders if he loves her, and if his "bent of love be honorable," and his "purpose marriage." Juliet's nurse, standing inside the room, becomes increasingly alarmed at how long Juliet is talking and at the prospect of their being discovered. She calls for Juliet to come back into the rooms. Juliet is torn between fear for Romeo and her desire to drag out the last bitter-sweet moment of being with him. She speaks first to the nurse and then to Romeo, trying to quiet the former and to be sure that the latter fully understands her love and will send for her tomorrow: "Where and what time thou wilt perform the rite: / And all my fortunes at thy foot I'll lay. / And follow thee my lord throughout the world." Then the following words pass between them:

JULIET
To cease thy strife, and leave me to my grief.
To-morrow will I send.

ROMEO
So strive my soul—

JULIET
A thousand times good night. [*Exit above.*]

ROMEO
A thousand times the worse, to want thy light.
Love goes toward love as schoolboys from their books,
But love from love, toward school with heavy looks.

A thousand years in thy sight are but as yesterday

Source: PSALMS 90:4
Author: Unknown
First transcribed: c.400-200 B.C.
Type of work: Religious poetry

Context: The psalmist declares that all generations of man have identified themselves with the Lord. God, he says, is eternal, immortal, living before the creation of the mountains or the universe. A thousand years would be, in the eyes of God, as "a watch in the night" (the time between sunset and sunrise consisted of three watches). Man's life is, in comparison, very brief, as a sleep or as the grass that quickly grows and quickly withers. Man's sinful nature, admits the psalmist, stands constantly exposed to the pure countenance of God; his years are few. The poet then petitions the Lord to help men live their brief lives judiciously. In speaking of man's mortality and God's immortality, the psalmist says:

> Before the mountains were brought forth, or ever thou hadst formed the earth and the world, even from everlasting to everlasting, thou art God.
> Thou turnest man to destruction; and sayest, Return, ye children of men.
> For **a thousand years in thy sight are but as yesterday** when it is past, and as a watch in the night.
>
> •   •   •
>
> For all our days are passed away in thy wrath: we spend our years as a tale that is told.

Thrice is he armed that hath his quarrel just

Source: KING HENRY THE SIXTH: PART TWO (Act III, sc. ii, l. 233)
Author: William Shakespeare (1564-1616)
First published: 1594
Type of work: Historical drama

Context: The Duke of Suffolk, who has had Humphrey, Duke of Gloucester, in his keeping, has ordered two murderers to kill Humphrey. The Earl of Warwick has reported that the "commons," wanting their leader, Humphrey, are ready to revolt. Humphrey is slain. King Henry is almost maddened by this unjust homicide. Warwick accuses Suffolk of the murder. These two step outside to fight. Henry believes that victory will come to the innocent one—a belief underlying the Medieval and Renaissance practice of trial by combat, and with us today in our conviction that God aids the innocent.

HENRY
What stronger breastplate than a heart untainted!
Thrice is he armed that hath his quarrel just;
And he but naked, though locked up in steel,
Whose conscience with injustice is corrupted.

1017

Through Eden took their solitary way

Source: PARADISE LOST (Book XII, Line 649)
Author: John Milton (1608-1674)
First published: 1667
Type of work: Epic poem

Context: These are the final lines of *Paradise Lost,* leaving Adam and Eve to find their way in the world after Michael expels them from Paradise. Looking backward, Adam and Eve see the sword of God blazing over the eastern gate of Paradise, with the "dreadful faces" of heavenly guards seen below the sword. The two lonely human beings shed some tears for the loss of their first earthly home; but, comforted by the vision and Michael's narrative of Biblical history, they turn, having wiped their eyes, to face the unknown world before them. Milton's lines, in their very cadence and diction, suggest the slow steps and serious mien of Adam and Eve as they leave Eden. Yet there is peace, too, for their way is quiet, and they go hand in hand, signifying that they have for a time, come to accept one another, as well as the world, the way they are. They face the great adventure of man and his history:

> The world was all before them, where to choose
> Their place of rest, and providence their guide:
> They hand in hand with wandering steps and slow,
> **Through Eden took their solitary way.**

Through thick and thin

Source: THE CANTERBURY TALES ("The Reeve's Tale," Line 4066)
Author: Geoffrey Chaucer (1343?-1400)
First transcribed: c.1387-1392
Type of work: Collection of tales

Context: The Reeve's tale is told in response to the Miller's tale, which was about a carpenter, and the Reeve once was a carpenter. The Reeve's tale is therefore about a thieving miller. One day two lads—scholars— come to the miller's to have their wheat ground. Having been warned about how the miller steals, they determine to watch his actions closely. One, named John, says that he will stand "right by the hopper" "and see how the corn goes in." Allen, the other, says that he will be beneath "an see how the meal falls down into the trough." For the moment frustrated, the miller still thinks "The greatest clerks are not the wisest men," and knows he can outwit them. To do so, he turns their horse loose and chases it toward the fens. The phrase Chaucer uses was later used by Du Bartas (*Divine Weeks and Works* (1578), *Second Week, Fourth Day*), and has been widespread since.

The Reeve thus tells of the Miller's actions.

He strepeth of the brydel right anon.
And when the hors was loos, he gynneth gon
Toward the fen, ther wilde mares renne,
And forth with "wehee," **thurgh thikke and thurgh thenne.**

Throw fear to the winds

Source: THE WASPS
Author: Aristophanes (448-385 B.C.)
First transcribed: Fourth century B.C.
Type of work: Social satire

Context: The quotation is alien to the Greeks and is instead the result of translation, being as it is an English proverb usually given as "throw cares to the wind." Another proverb of late Elizabethan times is embodied in an anonymous quotation, "He throw'd to th' wind all regard for whats lawfull." This latter is in the spirit of the comedy by Aristophanes, who is rebuking the demagogues of Athens, especially the jurors who feather their nests with vindictive judgments. An old man Philocleon (a satiric attack on Cleon) has been imprisoned in his own house by his son to prevent the old juror from joining the other dicasts, the villainous lawyers, and the judges at court. A mock trial is held to show the old fellow the ridiculousness of the legal life and how much better it would be to enjoy life, "to throw fears to the wind," or indulge in one continuous round of pleasures, if everyone threw off the tyranny of the dishonest politicians. The play ends on a hilarious note of the old man's stealing a flute girl and dancing licentiously in the street, where he, indeed, and the barristers,

throw fear to the winds.

Tiger! Tiger! burning bright

Source: SONGS OF EXPERIENCE ("The Tiger," stanzas 1 and 6)
Author: William Blake (1757-1827)
First published: 1794
Type of work: Religious lyric poem

Context: Having written his "Songs of Innocence," a collection of clear, simple songs to and about children, Blake composed his "Songs of Experience," which deal with what the poet called "the contrary state of the hu-

1019

man soul." These latter poems are concerned with the evil in the world and employ Blake's characteristic technique of tightly-woven metaphors and symbols that are intended to convey a multiplicity of meaning. The poem from which this quotation comes is to be regarded as a companion-piece to "The Lamb" in the "Songs of Innocence." In the first poem the question is asked, "Little Lamb, who made thee?" and the reply is "He is callèd by thy name,/ For He calls Himself a Lamb." By contrasting the innocent lamb with the fearful tiger, the poet draws together both good and evil and raises the seemingly unanswerable question of whether the same Creator could have fashioned both: "Did He who made the Lamb make thee?" The poet concludes by repeating, with a slight change, the first stanza, expressing his wonder at such a terrifying creation as the tiger:

> Tiger! Tiger! burning bright
> In the forests of the night,
> What immortal hand or eye,
> Dare frame thy fearful symmetry?

Till the cows come home

Source: THE SCORNFUL LADY (Act II, sc. ii, l. 3)
Authors: Francis Beaumont (1585-1616) and John Fletcher (1579-1625)
First published: 1616
Type of work: Dramatic comedy

Context: The Elder Loveless, in love with a capricious creature known in the play only as The Lady, is commanded by that character to go on extensive travels. Before he departs from home he makes provision for his brother, the Younger Loveless, who has wasted away his estate in riotous living with a crew of worthless associates, the Captain, the Traveler, the Poet, and the Tobacco-man. The Elder Loveless leaves his steward, the frugal and careful Savil, in charge of his home, but the Elder Loveless is hardly out of sight on his travels before the Younger Loveless has moved in with his companions, a crew of loose women, and a pair of fiddlers. They are determined to spend the three hundred pounds a year at their disposal for nothing but drink, and do no eating at all. When Younger Loveless tells his companions to enjoy themselves, he tells them to kiss till the cow come home; in modern usage "cow" has been changed to "cows." As cows show great reluctance to come home of their own volition, the expression has come to mean the indefinite future, or perhaps never at all. Younger Loveless's complete passage is:

> Come, my brave man of war, trace out thy darling;
> And you, my learned council, set and turn, boys;
> Kiss **till the cow come home;** kiss close, kiss close, knaves;
> My modern poet, thou shalt kiss in couplets.

1020

Time and tide wait for no man

Source: THE PROVERBS OF JOHN HEYWOOD (Part I, chapter 3)
Author: John Heywood (1497?-1580?)
First published: 1546
Type of work: Gnomic poem

Context: A young friend has asked the author if he should marry "a maid of flowering age, a goodly one," or "a widow, who so many years bears,/ That all her whiteness lieth in her white hairs." The author has answered by bringing to mind all the "plain pithy proverbs" which have served "both old and young" as warnings to approach marriage slowly and cautiously. The friend admits the wisdom of these proverbs, but he urges that against them he can advance "other parables, of like weighty weight,/ Which haste me to wedding, as ye shall hear straight." He then rattles off some examples, including the one about time and tide, which is rather widely used in literature: Chaucer in *The Clerk's Tale,* line 118, Robert Greene in *Disputations* (1592), Robert Southwell in *St. Peter's Complaint* (1595), and Robert Burns in *Tam O'Shanter* (1787) —"Nae man can tether time or tide."

> . . . one good lesson to this purpose I pike
> From the smith's forge, when th'iron is hot, strike!
> The sure seaman seeth, **the tide tarrieth no man;**
> And long delays or absence somewhat to scan,
> Since that, that one will not another will—
> Delays in wooers must needs their speed spill.

Time for a little something

Source: WINNIE-THE-POOH (Chapter 6)
Author: A(lan) A(lexander) Milne (1882-1956)
First published: 1926
Type of work: Story for children

Context: Winnie-the-Pooh, a stuffed bear, is the hero of this cleverly told, episodic story of the little creatures of a child's fanciful world. Presumably an adult is "reviving" Pooh's adventures for a child, Christopher Robin, who figures largely in all the adventures of Pooh, his own little bear. After all, though Christopher can remember all of these episodes, he and Pooh like having them told, "because then it's a real story and not just a remembering." Throughout all of Pooh's experiences the one trait most apparent about this little bear is his enormous appetite for honey, a weakness which repeatedly gets him in trouble. There is the story of his various attempts to rob a honey tree, and of his several mishaps therefrom. The

1021

story of his gluttony when he visits his rabbit friend is also a tale of woe for this little bear "of No Brain at All." Then comes the story concerning Eeyore's birthday. Eeyore the donkey is miserable because he has "no presents and no cake and no candles, and no proper notice taken of . . . [him] at all." Therefore, Pooh takes his last jar of honey as a gift and starts for Eeyore's home. He temporarily forgets the purpose of his journey, however, when a hunger spell begins to come over him:

> . . . He hadn't gone more than half-way when a sort of funny feeling began to creep all over him. It began at the tip of his nose and trickled all through him and out at the soles of his feet. It was just as if somebody inside him were saying, "Now then, Pooh, **time for a little something.**"

Time is a kind friend, he will make us old

Source: LET IT BE FORGOTTEN (Stanza 1)
Author: Sara Teasdale (1884-1933)
First published: 1919
Type of work: Lyric poem

Context: "Let It Be Forgotten" exemplifies the author's skill in blending simplicity of phrase and style with deep, complex emotion. This short poem is a variation on a popular theme: the transiency of time and the loss of particular experiences of the past. Ironically in the very act of growing old is the balm that cures the heart broken because of loss. In conjunction with the passing of joys comes the consoling, healing anesthesia of forgetfulness. The past is to be forgotten as a flower, a fire, a hushed footfall. The implication here is that as the beauty, enchantment and delight of these things are only momentary joys that leave ineradicable impressions and then give way to new experiences, so *it,* the significant moment and experience of the past, leaves its impression then passes on almost imperceptibly. Only a vague memory is left, like a seasonal beauty "in a long forgotten snow." Presumably if life is to be bearable and meaningful the unredeemable moment must be forgotten. The first stanza reads:

> Let it be forgotten, as a flower is forgotten,
>   Forgotten as a fire that once was singing gold,
> Let it be forgotten for ever and ever,
>   **Time is a kind friend, he will make us old.**

The time is out of joint

Source: HAMLET (Act I, sc. v, l. 189)
Author: William Shakespeare (1564-1616)
First published: 1603
Type of work: Dramatic tragedy

Context: On the battlements of the Castle of Elsinore, young Hamlet, Prince of Denmark, has just encountered the ghost of his father, the late King, who has told him the terrible story of his murder by his brother, Claudius. Furthermore, the murderer has usurped the crown of Denmark and has married the widowed Queen Gertrude, Hamlet's mother. The marriage was not only performed with unseemly haste but was incestuous. These crimes young Hamlet has promised to avenge. Quickly forming his plans, he tells his friends, who also have seen the ghost, that he will pretend madness in order to hide from Claudius his real intentions. He then demands that his friends swear on his sword to keep his pretense a secret. They swear and all prepare to leave the battlements. His final remark refers to his grief at having the terrible duty of revenge thrust upon him.

> Rest, rest perturbed spirit! So, gentlemen,
> With all my love I do commend me to you.
>
> . . .
>
> . . . Let us go in together;
> And still your fingers on your lips, I pray.
> **The time is out of joint:** O cursed spite,
> That ever I was born to set it right!

A time to be born, and a time to die

Source: ECCLESIASTES 3:2
Author: Unknown
First transcribed: c.250-200 B.C.
Type of work: Religious confession

Context: The author, calling himself "the Preacher," presents his view of life with the opening words "vanity of vanities; all is vanity." Seeking wisdom, he discovers that man and nature are victims of monotony. One generation follows another, and the sun sets only to rise again. Since wisdom shows him only the folly of life, he turns to the pleasures of the world, but finds again that life is a vain striving after the wind, that the wise man and the fool both must die. Only with God can man enjoy life and labor, for God gives wisdom, knowledge, and joy to those who are good. Citing the inexorable laws of life ("To everything there is a season. . . ."), the author begins a series of opposite statements:

1023

A time to be born, and a time to die; . . .
A time to weep, and a time to laugh; . . .
A time to rend, and a time to sew; a time to keep silence, and
a time to speak. . . .

Time, you old gipsy man, will you not stay

Source: TIME, YOU OLD GIPSY MAN (Lines 1-2)
Author: Ralph Hodgson (1871-1962)
First published: 1911
Type of work: Lyric poem

Context: "Time, You Old Gipsy Man" is a poem concerned with the familiar theme of the passing of time. The poet tells Time that if he will rest or stop, he will be given silver bells for his jennet and a fine gold ring for his hand. But Time, refusing to be bribed, tightens his reins to continue his endless journey, during which he has moved from Babylon to Rome and now to London.

Time, you old gipsy man,
Will you not stay,
Put up your caravan
Just for one day?

'Tis a long road knows no turning

Source: AJAX (Line 715)
Author: Sophocles (496-406 B.C.)
First transcript: Fourth century B.C.
Type of work: Dramatic tragedy

Context: Ajax, ruler of Salamis, presumably second only to Achilles in bravery among those warriors who besieged Troy, had no real reason for joining the Greeks against the Trojans. Consequently, when Achilles had been killed and his arms given not to Ajax but to Ulysses, Ajax goes mad and slays a flock of sheep, mistaking them for the sons of Atreus who awarded the arms to Ulysses. Then in contrition Ajax calls his son to him and tells him, "The happiest life consists in ignorance." The Chorus hear Ajax planning his own demise and comment: "And Ajax, deaf to all relief,/ A frenzy-haunted man,/ Stands by to renovate my grief." "Now he broods in heart, alone,/ A deep affliction to his own." Ajax then enters with drawn sword and says: ". . . I am going thither, where I must go;/ But do ye as I bid you, and perchance/ Ye may soon hear that I have gained, in spite/ Of present evil, safe deliverance." The Chorus then comments:

Now that Ajax, his distresses
Anew laid by,
All worship to the God addresses,
Honouring them, as is most meet.
'Tis a long road knows no turning,
And there's nothing may not be,
Now, from choler and heart-burning
Huge, against the Atreidae,
Ajax relents so unexpectedly.

'Tis a rare bird in the land

Source: TABLE TALK (156)
Author: Martin Luther (1483-1546)
First published: 1566
Type of work: Conversation and anecdote

Context: During Luther's later years, various friends and disciples, particularly Antony Lauterbach and John Aurifaber, made an effort to stay with him constantly and to record verbatim his various comments on everything. As William Hazlitt said, "Did he aspirate a thought above breath, it was caught by the intent ear of one or other of the listeners, and committed to paper." The result is a discontinuous but very revealing account of Luther's thoughts and feelings. The full anecdote about the comment on the rarity of good servants is this:

> Dr. Luther's wife complaining to him of the indocility and untrustworthiness of servants, he said: A faithful and good servant is a real God-send, but, truly, **'tis a rare bird in the land.** We find every one complaining of the idleness and profligacy of this class of people; we must govern them, Turkey fashion, so much work, so much victuals as Pharaoh dealt with the Israelites in Egypt.

'Tis always morning somewhere in the world

Source: ORION (Book III, Canto III)
Author: Richard Henry ("Hengist") Horne (1803-1884)
First published: 1843
Type of work: Allegorical epic poem

Context: Horne, an adventurer and traveler who lived for awhile in Australia (where he took the name "Hengist") and who fought in the Mexican War against the United States, eventually settled in London and began writing poetry and plays in an almost Elizabethan style. In the canto to Eos, goddess of the morning, part of his epic *Orion,* Orion's "humbled

1025

and still mortal feet" take him to the Palace of the Morning. Eos bids him enter quickly, for she must soon be gone, and adds:

> " 'Tis always morning somewhere in the world,
> And Eos rises, circling constantly
> The varied regions of mankind. No pause
> Of renovation and of freshening rays
> She knows, but evermore her love breathes forth
> On field and forest, as on human hope,
> Health, beauty, power, thought, action, and advance.
> All this Orion witnessed, and rejoiced.

'T is better to have loved and lost than never to have loved at all

Source: IN MEMORIAM (Part XXVII, stanza 4)
Author: Alfred, Lord Tennyson (1809-1892)
First published: 1850
Type of work: Elegy

Context: The poet is experiencing deep pain after the death of the friend Arthur Hallam, whom he had loved. It is a pain which paralyzes him and seemingly destroys any possibility of his ever again enjoying life. "The very source and fount of day/ Is dash'd with wandering isles of night." But even at this time, he says that he would rather be a person who was able to feel love for someone, even though that love might bring him enduring grief, than to be incapable of knowing love at all. He does not envy

> The heart that never plighted troth
> But stagnates in the weeds of sloth.
>
> • • •
>
> I hold it true, whate'er befall;
> I feel it, when I sorrow most;
> 'T is better to have loved and lost
> Than never to have loved at all.

'Tis chastity, my brother, chastity

Source: COMUS (Line 420)
Author: John Milton (1608-1647)
First published: 1637
Type of work: Masque

Context: The story of this masque, written in the Elizabethan tradition for the installation of the Earl of Bridgewater as President of Wales

1026

and acted by his children, is built around the fanciful efforts of these children to reach Ludlow Castle. They must pass through a "drear wood," which is under the power of the enchanter Comus, son of Bacchus and Ceres and the symbol of unbridled license. The sister becomes separated from her two brothers, and the Younger Brother fears that she may come to harm at the hands of some ravisher. But the Elder Brother replies that her virtue is her protection; that, like the virgin goddess Diana, she can roam the hills and valleys unafraid and unmolested. His speech begins:

> . . . but yet a hidden strength
> Which if heaven gave it, may be termed her own:
> **'Tis chastity, my brother, chastity:**
> She that has that, is clad in complete steel,
> And like a quivered nymph with arrows keen,
> May trace huge forests and unharbored heaths . . .

'Tis good to keep a nest egg

Source: DON QUIXOTE (Part II, Book III, chapter 7)
Author: Miguel de Cervantes Saavedra (1547-1616)
First published: 1615
Type of work: Satirical novel

Context: The original nest egg was, of course, an artificial one put into the nest to encourage the hen to lay more. Sancho has persuaded his wife to let him accompany Don Quixote on his third sally, but tells his master of her demand that he receive a regular wage and not merely the anticipation of a share in the knight's successful conquests, a stipulation in which Sancho concurs:

> . . . For I'll trust no longer to rewards, that mayhaps may come late, and mayhaps not at all. I'd be glad to know what I get, be't more or less. A little in one's own pocket is better than much in another man's purse. **'Tis good to keep a nest egg.** Every little makes a mickle; while a man gets, he can never lose.

'Tis mad idolatry to make the service greater than the god

Source: TROILUS AND CRESSIDA (Act II, sc. ii, ll. 56-57)
Author: William Shakespeare (1564-1616)
First published: 1609
Type of work: Dramatic tragedy

Context: The Greeks offer to end the Trojan War. King Priam of Troy and his sons Hector, Troilus, Paris, and Helenus discuss the Greek condition

1027

of peace, which is, namely, the return of Helen. Formerly the wife of Menelaus, a Greek king, Helen fell in love with Prince Paris of Troy and fled with him, abandoning her husband and thus precipitating the war. Now Hector urges his father and brothers to accept the Greek offer. He argues that Troy's armies have been decimated, and that the cause of it all is not worth the cost of her keeping.

TROILUS
What's aught but as 'tis valued?

HECTOR
But value dwells not in particular will;
It holds his estimate and dignity
As well wherein 'tis precious of itself
As in the prizer. **'Tis mad idolatry**
To make the service greater than the god,
• • •

'Tis not the balm, the scepter, and the ball

Source: KING HENRY THE FIFTH (Act IV, sc. i, l. 276)
Author: William Shakespeare (1564-1616)
First published: 1600
Type of work: Historical drama

Context: The scene is the darkness before the battle of Agincourt. King Henry's troops are surrounded by superior French forces. In walking among his soldiers, Henry is not recognized, and he argues with Williams, a common soldier, about who must bear the responsibility for war. The argument becomes heated, and Williams and Henry promise to have an accounting after the battle if they survive. The two then separate, and Henry muses on the difference in station between Williams and himself. Henry says that the main difference is in ceremony and homage given him. But for this homage he must in return give up peace of mind and easy sleep.

HENRY
. . . I know,
'Tis not the balm, the sceptre, and the ball,
The sword, the mace, the crown imperial,
The intertissued robe of gold and pearl,
The farced title running 'fore the king,
The throne he sits on; nor the tide of pomp
That beats upon the high shore of this world—
No, not all these, thrice-gorgeous ceremony,
Not all these, laid in bed majestical,
Can sleep so soundly as the wretched slave,
• • •

'Tis our true policy to steer clear of permanent alliances, with any portion of the foreign world

Source: THE FAREWELL ADDRESS
Author: George Washington (1732-1799)
First spoken: September 17, 1796
Type of work: Presidential address

Context: In his final presidential address Washington describes various problems facing the new democratic government. In domestic affairs, he warns against the possible despotism of a militant two-party system; he warns against the insidious tendency of one governmental department to encroach upon another and thereby exceed its rightful sphere; he calls governmental support of religion and morality indispensable to political prosperity; he states the necessity of supporting institutions for the general diffusion of knowledge; he cautions against the accumulation of an excessive national debt. In foreign affairs, he advises: "Observe good faith and justice toward all Nations. Cultivate peace and harmony with all." To this end America must not invoke sympathy for some favorite nation; "the great rule of conduct" is to cultivate commercial relations but to shun political connections. He cautions:

> Europe has a set of primary interests, which to us have none, or a very remote, relation.—Hence she must be engaged in frequent controversies, the causes of which are essentially foreign to our concerns. . . . **'Tis our true policy to steer clear of permanent alliances, with any portion of the foreign world.** . . . Taking care always to keep ourselves, by suitable establishments, on a respectably defensive posture, we may safely trust to temporary alliances for extraordinary emergencies.

'Tis the eye of childhood that fears a painted devil

Source: MACBETH (Act II, sc. ii, ll. 54-55)
Author: William Shakespeare (1564-1616)
First published: 1623
Type of work: Dramatic tragedy

Context: Macbeth, Thane of Cawdor, has ambitions to be King of Scotland and thus fulfill his destiny prophesied by three witches. He helps King Duncan subdue a rebellion near his demesne, and that night the king is Macbeth's guest. Opportunity to hasten his future by means of regicide is given him; he considers murder, but decides against it. Lady Macbeth, even more ambitious and less scrupulous than her husband, urges, encourages, and scorns him into undertaking the deed. Macbeth murders Duncan

1029

in his sleep. Now, vision-ridden, remorseful, heavy with foreboding,
Macbeth refuses to return to Duncan's bed chamber to smear the sleeping grooms with blood and leave the
daggers with them to point blame in
their direction. Lady Macbeth upbraids him.

MACBETH
I'll go no more.
I am afraid, to think what I have done.
Look on't again I dare not.

LADY MACBETH
Infirm of purpose!
Give me the daggers. The sleeping, and the dead
Are but as pictures. **'Tis the eye of childhood**
That fears a painted devil. If he do bleed,
I'll gild the faces of the grooms withal,
For it must seem their guilt.

'Tis well an Old Age is out

Source: SECULAR MASQUE from THE PILGRIM (Line 90)
Author: John Dryden (1631-1700)
First published: 1700
Type of work: Masque

Context: In this little masque Dryden
has several of the ancient pagan deities appear: Chronos, the elderly god
of time, carrying his scythe appears
as the Grim Reaper; Janus, the Roman god of the new year, who looks
both forward and backward with his
two faces; Diana, the chaste goddess
of the hunt and the moon; Mars, the
god of war, vaunting of arms and
honor; Venus, the goddess of love;
and Momus, a god of pleasure. Each
of the deities speaks, admitting fa-
tigue and defeat. Then Momus speaks
to the gods and goddesses, concluding
with the following lines:

MOMUS
All, all, of a piece throughout;
Thy Chase had a Beast in View;
Thy Wars brought nothing about:
Thy Lovers were all untrue.
'Tis well an Old Age is out,
And time to begin a New.

To be great is to be misunderstood

Source: SELF-RELIANCE
Author: Ralph Waldo Emerson (1803-1882)
First published: 1841
Type of work: Moral essay

Context: The individual, Emerson says, must be self-reliant and self-sufficient: "To believe your own thought, to believe that what is true for you in your private heart is true for all men,—that is genius . . . imitation is suicide . . . Accept the place the divine providence has found for you. . . ." A true man is a self-trusting nonconformist, for "Nothing is at last sacred but the integrity of your own mind." Emerson rejects religious dogma and traditional morality: "the only right is what is after my constitution; the only wrong what is against it . . . I shun father and mother and wife and brother when my genius calls me . . . The great man is he who in the midst of the crowd keeps with perfect sweetness the independence of solitude." Conformity makes us false, but "For nonconformity the world whips you with its displeasure." The other enemy of self-trust "is our own consistency; a reverence for our past act or word. . . ." Self-contradiction is unimportant, for we must "bring the past for judgment into the thousand-eyed present, and live ever in a new day." The great man must realize that people will resent his preference of truth over consistency:

> . . . Speak what you think now in hard words and tomorrow speak what tomorrow thinks in hard words again, though it contradict everything you said today.—"Ah, so you shall be sure to be misunderstood."—Is it so bad then to be misunderstood? Pythagoras was misunderstood, and Socrates, and Jesus, and Luther, and Copernious, and Galileo, and Newton, and every pure and wise spirit that ever took flesh. **To be great is to be misunderstood.**

To be, or not to be: that is the question

Source: HAMLET (Act III, sc. i, l. 56)
Author: William Shakespeare (1564-1616)
First published: 1603
Type of work: Dramatic tragedy

Context: Hamlet, Prince of Denmark, has learned from the Ghost of his father the terrible story of the latter's murder by his brother, Claudius, who has usurped the crown and married the murdered King's widow, Hamlet's mother. The Ghost has made Hamlet swear to avenge the crime, and Hamlet has undertaken to assassinate Claudius. But now, conscious of the terrible duty that he, a scholar rather than a man of action, has taken upon himself, he muses on the possibility of suicide as an escape from his task. Is it better to endure quietly what fortune brings or to contend against it? Or is it better still to end one's life and thus to evade the problem altogether? The famous soliloquy begins:

> **To be, or not to be:** that is the question:
> Whether 'tis nobler in the mind to suffer
> The slings and arrows of outrageous fortune,
> Or to take arms against a sea of troubles,
> And by opposing end them? To die: to sleep. . . .

To be prepared for war is one of the most effectual means of preserving peace

Source: FIRST ANNUAL ADDRESS TO CONGRESS
Author: George Washington (1732-1799)
First spoken: January 8, 1790
Type of work: Presidential address

Context: First President of the United States (1789-1797) and "Father of his Country." George Washington has been the subject, as Professor Saul K. Padover comments, of "idolatry, hagiography, iconolatry, myth-making, and breathless patriotic oratory." His very appearance was impressive. Jefferson wrote of him: "His person . . . was fine, his stature exactly what one would wish, his deportment easy, erect, and noble; the best horseman of his age, and the most graceful figure that could be seen on horseback." Playing a commanding role in the Revolution and accepting the challenge to be the first leader of the new democracy, Washington in his initial address to the joint session of Congress sounded the call to national strength as the best means of avoiding further war. The basic idea here expressed is proverbial. Horace (65-8 B.C.), for instance, writes: "In peace, as a wise man, he should make suitable preparation for war" (*Satires,* Bk. II, line 70); and Robert Burton (1577-1640) notes: "The commonwealth of Venice in their armoury have this inscription: 'Happy is that city which in time of peace thinks of war'" (*The Anatomy of Melancholy,* Pt. II, sect. 2, memb. 6). Washington says:

> . . . **To be prepared for war is one of the most effectual means of preserving peace.**
> A free people ought not only to be armed, but disciplined; to which end a uniform and well-digested plan is requisite; and their safety and interest require that they should promote such manufactories as tend to render them independent of others for essential, particularly military, supplies.

To do a great right, do a little wrong

Source: THE MERCHANT OF VENICE (Act IV, sc. i, l. 216)
Author: William Shakespeare (1564-1616)
First published: 1600
Type of work: Dramatic comedy

Context: Antonio is in danger of having to forfeit a pound of flesh because he is unable to repay three thousand ducats to Shylock, the Venetian usurer, which he borrowed to lend to his friend Bassanio. Bassanio has prospered both in marrying Portia and in becoming wealthy. At the trial of Antonio, Bassanio says that he will gladly pay the sum of Antonio's debt ten times over if Shylock will allow Antonio to go free. Portia, unknown to her husband, has come to defend Antonio. Shylock remains obdurate in demanding forfeit of a pound of flesh. Bassanio, after being frustrated in getting Shylock to relent, requests that Balthazar, who is Portia in disguise, bend the law to achieve justice. His request and her refusal go thus:

BASSANIO
. . . And I beseech you
Wrest once the law to your authority,
To do a great right, do a little wrong,
And curb this cruel devil of his will.

PORTIA
It must not be, there is no power in Venice
Can alter a decree established.
'Twill be recorded for a precedent
And many an error by the same example
Will rush into the state.

. . .

To eat, and to drink, and to be merry

Source: ECCLESIASTES 8:15
Author: Unknown
First transcribed: c.250-200 B.C.
Type of work: Religious confession

Context: The writer, using as his theme the words "vanity of vanities; all is vanity," argues that wealth, pleasure, desires, hopes, and life in general represent only futility. Neither wisdom nor pleasure gives satisfaction, for all men end alike in the grave. The wise man, however, chooses from the vanities of the world the less vain things and knows when and how to act arbitrarily. Attempting and failing to understand the reason for the fact that the wicked often prosper and that the righteous often suffer, he turns once again to his life of pleasure:

Then I commended mirth, because a man hath no better thing under the sun, than **to eat, and to drink, and to be merry:** for that shall abide with him of his labor the days of his life, which God giveth him under the sun.

To err is human, to forgive divine

Source: AN ESSAY ON CRITICISM (Part II, l. 325)
Author: Alexander Pope (1688-1744)
First published: 1711
Type of work: Satire

Context: This is one of the most famous quotations from Alexander Pope's poetry, but the idea was not new with him. The first part of the thought is found in Sophocles' *Antigone,* "To err/ From the right path is common to mankind." And Plutarch wrote, "For to err in opinion, though it be not the part of wise men, is at least human." More than seventy years after Pope, Robert Burns, the Scottish poet, was to write similarly, in his poem entitled "Address to the Unco Guid." Pope, in his lines, is of course speaking not of human judgment generally, but of critical judgment in literary matters:

And while self-love each jealous writer rules,
Contending wits become the sport of fools;
But still the worst with most regret commend,
For each ill author is as bad a friend.
To what base ends, and by what abject ways,
Are mortals urged thro' sacred lust of praise!
Ah, ne'er so dire a thirst of glory boast,
Nor in the critic let the man be lost!
Good nature and good sense must ever join;
To err is human, to forgive divine.

To fish in troubled waters

Source: AN EXPOSITION OF THE OLD TESTAMENT (Psalm 60:11)
Author: Matthew Henry (1662-1714)
First published: 1708-1710
Type of work: Biblical commentary

Context: Following the many psalms David had written in times of trouble, Psalm 60 was intended for a day of triumph. As Henry puts it, the song ". . . was penned after he was set-tled in the throne, upon occasion of an illustrious victory which God blessed his forces with over the Syrians and Edomites: It was when David was in the zenith of his prosperity, and the affairs of his kingdom seem to have been in a better posture than ever they were either before or after." David rejoices, but does not fail to pray, "Give us help from trouble; for vain is the help of man." Henry's comment on the verse is this memorable statement:

. . . Even in the day of their triumph, they see themselves in trouble, because still in war, which is troublesome even to the prevailing side: None therefore can delight in war, but those that love **to fish in troubled waters.** . . .

To fly from, need not be to hate, mankind

Source: CHILDE HAROLD'S PILGRIMAGE (Canto III, stanza 69)
Author: George Gordon, Lord Byron (1788-1824)
First published: 1816 (Canto III)
Type of work: Narrative poem in Spenserian stanzas

Context: In the Swiss Alps, where he is traveling in 1816, Byron feels an almost Wordsworthian kinship with Nature. However, to him Nature is a means of escape from people who have misunderstood and persecuted him. There have been dark rumors about his relations with his half-sister, Augusta; he is separated from his wife; and he has exiled himself from his native land. Here, he admires the beauty of Lake Leman, but adds, "There is too much of man here . . ." In the stanza quoted, he observes that a man does not necessarily hate people because he prefers to be alone. By keeping to himself, he avoids the bitterness and contentions that are a part of human society.

> **To fly from, need not be to hate, mankind:**
> All are not fit with them to stir and toil,
> Nor is it discontent to keep the mind
> Deep in its fountain, lest it overboil
> In the hot throng, where we become the spoil
> Of our infection. . . .

To gild refined gold, to paint the lily

Source: KING JOHN (Act IV, sc. ii, l. 11)
Author: William Shakespeare (1564-1616)
First published: 1623
Type of work: Historical drama

Context: John, at his own insistence, has been crowned King of England a second time. The Earl of Pembroke reminds the king that this second coronation was "superfluous." The Earl of Salisbury then points out just how "superfluous" this second crowning really was:

PEMBROKE

This once again, but that your Highness pleased,
Was once superfluous; you were crowned before,
And that high royalty was ne'er plucked off;

. . .

SALISBURY

Therefore, to be possessed with double pomp,
To guard a title that was rich before,
To gild refined gold, to paint the lily,
To throw a perfume on the violet,
To smooth the ice, or add another hue
Unto the rainbow, or with taper-light
To seek the beauteous eye of heaven to garnish,
Is wasteful, and ridiculous excess.

To have and to hold

Source: THE BOOK OF COMMON PRAYER (Pages 301-302)
Author: Traditional; translated and arranged by Archbishop Cranmer (1489-1560)
First published: 1549
Type of work: Solemnization of Matrimony

Context: The Form of Solemnization of Matrimony as provided by The Book of Common Prayer begins with a solemn exhortation to "this company" and to the man and woman about to be joined together, in which is stated the dignity and sacredness of marriage, and the fact that the union must be a lawful one according to the law of the state and "as God's word doth allow." If there then be shown no impediment to their marriage, the couple proceed to the exchange of their vows. The father or guardian of the bride gives her into the care of the groom, and each pledges to the other a lifelong fidelity. (The words "to have and to hold" will also be recognized as supplying the title for the once popular novel by Mary Johnston published in 1900.)

I *N*. take thee *N*. to my wedded Wife [Husband], **to have and to hold** from this day forward, for better for worse, for richer for poorer, in sickness and in health, to love and to cherish, till death us do part, according to God's holy ordinance; and thereto I plight [give] thee my troth.

1036

To know that which before us lies in daily life
is the prime wisdom

Source: PARADISE LOST (Book VIII, ll. 192-194)
Author: John Milton (1608-1674)
First published: 1667
Type of work: Epic poem

Context: In Book VIII of *Paradise Lost* Adam asks the archangel Raphael about the motions of the heavenly bodies; he is answered, but Raphael exhorts Adam to seek knowledge more worthy of mankind's place in the scheme of creation. Adam thanks Raphael for the information about the heavenly bodies and for the advice, accepting the angel's admonitions. Adam's comments about what constitutes wisdom seem at first restrictive; one might, seeing the lines alone, be tempted to interpret them as a refutation by Milton of science or, as it was known in his day, natural philosophy. One should, rather, see the lines as a protest against barren speculation, not against science:

". . . apt the mind or fancy is to rove
Unchecked, and of her roving is no end;
Till warned, or by experience taught, she learn,
That not to know at large of things remote
From use, obscure and subtle, but **to know**
That which before us lies in daily life
Is the prime wisdom, what is more, is fume,
Or emptiness, or fond impertinence,
And renders us in things that most concern
Unpracticed, unprepared, and still to seek."

To love her is a liberal education

Source: THE TATLER (Volume I, number 49)
Author: Sir Richard Steele (1672-1729)
First published: August 2, 1709
Type of work: Essay

Context: The witty, prolific journalist, essayist, and social arbiter, Sir Richard Steele—whose work, along with that of Joseph Addison—is preserved in the influential eighteenth-century magazines, *The Spectator* and *The Tatler*—sets about discussing considerations of love and lust in the August 2 issue of *The Tatler,* for 1709. Steele, writing as Isaac Bickerstaff, proposes that the discussion begin with types of love symbolized by the figure of the Satyr on the one hand and the figure of Cupid, on the other. After some discussion, Bickerstaff proposes to rank various followers of the two figures and, first, speaks of one Aspasia:

. . . though her mein carries much more invitation than command, to behold her is an immediate check to loose behaviour; and **to love her is a liberal education;** for, it being the nature of all love to create an imitation of the beloved person, in the lover, a regard for Aspasia naturally produces a decency of manners, and good conduct of life in her admirers . . .

As charity is esteemed a conjunction of the good qualities necessary to a virtuous man, so love is the happy composition of all the accomplishments that make a fine Gentleman. The motive of a man's life is seen in all his actions . . .

To point a moral, or adorn a tale

Source: THE VANITY OF HUMAN WISHES (Line 221)
Author: Samuel Johnson (1709-1784)
First published: 1749
Type of work: Didactic poem in imitation of the tenth satire of Juvenal

Context: In this 368-line poem Johnson develops the theme that "All is vanity" by describing the fortunes and fates of men in general and of contemporary kings, statesmen, politicians, and soldiers in particular. Lines 191-221 depict the career of Charles X (1682-1718) of Sweden, who sought through military conquest to control most of northern continental Europe. He defeated the Danes, the Poles, and the Saxons, but was himself defeated by the Russians under Peter the Great in 1709. After five years of exile in Turkey he finally died during a minor military campaign in Norway. Johnson begins the section by inquiring, "On what foundation stands the warrior's pride,/ How just his hopes let Swedish Charles decide. . . ." He then recounts the monarch's exploits and concludes:

> But did not Chance at length her error mend?
> Did no subverted empire mark his end?
> Did rival monarchs give the fatal wound?
> Or hostile millions press him to the ground?
> His fall was destin'd to a barren strand,
> A petty fortress, and a dubious hand;
> He left the name, at which the world grew pale,
> **To point a moral, or adorn a tale.**

To put an antic disposition on

Source: HAMLET (Act I, sc. v, l. 173)
Author: William Shakespeare (1564-1616)
First published: 1603
Type of work: Dramatic tragedy

Context: Claudius, Denmark's new king, is a usurper, for the throne should have been Hamlet's by right of succession. Recently, the latter has seen and talked to the ghost of his dead father on the battlements of Elsinore Castle. The ghost tells him that Claudius murdered him, his father, in his sleep, and that his mother was adulterous with the murderer. As a result, Hamlet swears vengeance on Claudius. After his initial shock, Hamlet realizes he must swear his companions to silence, and he also must establish some ready-made excuse for any future peculiar behavior on his part. He fears he may truly go mad, or, if not, he may well feign madness to accomplish his pledge of revenge against the well-guarded Claudius.

HAMLET

. . .

But come—
Here as before, never, so help you mercy,
How strange or odd some'er I bear myself—
As perchance hereafter shall think meet
To put an antic disposition on—
That you at such times seeing me never shall,
With arms encumbered thus, or this head-shake,
Or by pronouncing of some doubtful phrase,

. . .

Or such ambiguous giving out, to note
That you know aught of me—this do swear,

. . .

To resist him that is set in authority is evil

Source: THE INSTRUCTION OF PTAHHOTEP (Number 31)
Author: Ptahhotep, vizier to King Issi (fl. 2675 B.C.)
First transcribed: c.2670 or 2675 B.C. and later re-edited
Type of work: Admonition

Context: This is one of many instructions in wisdom given by a *sbōyet* or sage to his own son or to schoolboys in wise conduct and good manners. These sayings also serve as models of expression, diction, and polite speech. Although the tomb of this instructor is still preserved, the confu-

1039

sion of dates concerns the king he served. The later editions persist into the Middle Kingdom and as late as the Eighteenth Dynasty of Egypt. This instruction includes thirty-seven separate admonitions and suggestions, as well as a prologue and an epilogue—ranging from the view that something can be learned from anyone to the belief that a good wife who is well nutured, cheerful, and well known should be cherished and made even fatter. Number 31, a central theme among early writings, has the heading "Respect for Superiors";

> Bend thy back to him that is over thee, thy superior of the king's administration. So will thine house endure with its substance, and thy pay be duly awarded. **To resist him that is set in authority is evil.** One liveth so long as he is indulgent.

To spy out the land

Source: NUMBERS 13:16
Author: Unknown
First transcribed: 1000-300 B.C.
Type of work: Religious history and law

Context: Moses, who delivered the Israelites from Egyptian persecution and who imparted the Ten Commandments and other precepts of the Lord to the Chosen People, prepares the Israelites for their journey from Mt. Sinai through the Wilderness of Paran to the Promised Land, Canaan. At the Lord's command, Moses selects a representative of each of the twelve Israelite tribes to spy out the land of Canaan. The spies are named, and the narrative continues:

> These are the names of the men which Moses sent **to spy out the land**
>
> . . .
>
> And see the land, what it is; and the people that dwelleth therein, whether they be strong or weak, few or many;
>
> . . .
>
> And what the land is, whether it be fat or lean, whether there be wood therein, or not. And be ye of good courage, and bring of the fruit of the land. . . .

To strive, to seek, to find, and not to yield

Source: ULYSSES (Line 70)
Author: Alfred, Lord Tennyson (1809-1892)
First published: 1842
Type of work: Lyric poem

Context: Ulysses bequeaths the rule of his island to his son Telemachus, who will use "slow prudence to make mild/ A rugged people. . . ." Ulysses admires his son's mild domesticity, and he accepts their difference in character: "He works his work, I mine." Ulysses calls on his old companions to join him in new travels: "Old age hath yet his honor and his toil . . . Some work of noble note, may yet be done,/ Not unbecoming men that strove with gods." The will, Tennyson says, is unconquerable, and an adventurous life is its own reward:

> Come, my friends.
> 'Tis not too late to seek a newer world.
> Push off, and sitting well in order smite
> The sounding furrows; for my purpose holds
> To sail beyond the sunset, and the baths
> Of all the western stars, until I die.
> It may be that the gulfs will wash us down;
> It may be we shall touch the Happy Isles,
> And see the great Achilles, whom we knew.
> Though much is taken, much abides; and though
> We are not now that strength which in old days
> Moved earth and heaven, that which we are, we are—
> One equal temper of heroic hearts,
> Made weak by time and fate, but strong in will
> **To strive, to seek, to find, and not to yield.**

To tell tales out of school

Source: THE PROVERBS OF JOHN HEYWOOD (Part I, chapter 10)
Author: John Heywood (1497?-1580?)
First published: 1546
Type of work: Gnomic poetry

Context: The author is recounting to a young friend some of his observations about marriage. Now he is giving an account of a husband and wife who asked his advice, which was that each go his own way. The wife took the advice and went. Now she is returned to report her experiences. Her uncle and aunt bade her Godspeed but not welcome. Taking their cue from the uncle and aunt, her other relations treated her coldly. A kinswoman took her to table, and this woman the wife hardly approves of, as the following quote demonstrates:

> A false flatt'ring filth; and if that be good,
> None better to bear two faces in one hood.
> She speaketh as she would creep into your bosom;
> And, when the meal-mouth hath won the bottom
> Of your stomach, then will the pickthank it tell
> To your most enemies, you to buy and sell.
> **To tell tales out of school,** that is her great lust;
> Look what she knoweth, blab it wist, and out it must.

1041

To tend the homely slighted shepherd's trade

Source: LYCIDAS (Line 65)
Author: John Milton (1608-1674)
First published: 1638
Type of work: Elegiac pastoral poem

Context: Milton, in the pastoral vein, rebukes the nymphs for allowing Lycidas—or Edward King (1612-1637)—to drown, but then says that they were not present when his death occurred. He admits that in addressing the nymphs he is but idly dreaming, as the Muse Calliope could not save the life of her son Orpheus; Milton thus ties Lycidas, a maker of music, to Orpheus, one of the greatest musicians of mythical times. He then turns his attention to himself and wonders what profit there is in his ceaseless efforts to write serious poetry—"to tend the homely slighted shepherd's trade"—since his efforts seem fruitless. Would it not be better, he asks, to abandon sterner tasks for the easier work of writing erotic poetry, as others do? He would sport with the nymphs Amaryllis and Neaera; that is, enjoy himself by writing love poetry. He says:

> Alas! what boots it with incessant care
> **To tend the homely slighted shepherd's trade,**
> And strictly meditate the thankless Muse?
> Were it not better done as others use,
> To sport with Amaryllis in the shade
> Or with the tangles of Neaera's hair?

To the last man

Source: HENRY IV, PART II (Act IV, sc. ii, l. 44)
Author: William Shakespeare (1564-1616)
First published: 1600
Type of work: Historical drama

Context: During a temporary cessation of hostilities between King Henry IV and the rebels, John of Lancaster, the king's son, and Westmorland have met the rebels Mowbray, the Archbishop of York, Hastings, and others. John reproaches them for rising against the king. He singles out the Archbishop, saying, "O who shall believe,/ But you misuse the reverence of your place,/ Employ the countenance and grace of heaven, / As a false favourite doth his prince's name,/ In deeds dishonourable?" The Archbishop answers that he and his fellows have just cause for complaint. He says that all he and they want is their just desires, and his statements are seconded and enlarged upon by Mowbray, as the following dialogue shows.

ARCHBISHOP OF YORK
Good my Lord of Lancaster,
I am not here against your father's peace,
But as I told my Lord of Westmorland,
The time misordered doth, in common sense,
Crowd us and crush us to this monstrous form,
To hold our safety up. I sent your Grace
The parcels and particulars of our grief,
The which hath been with scorn shoved from the Court,
Whereon this Hydra son of war is born,
Whose dangerous eyes may well be charmed asleep,
With grant of our most just and right desires,
And true obedience, of this madness cured,
Stoop tamely to the foot of majesty.

MOBRAY
If not, we ready are to try our fortunes,
To the last man.

To the manner born

Source: HAMLET (Act I, sc. iv, l. 15)
Author: William Shakespeare (1564-1616)
First published: 1603
Type of work: Dramatic tragedy

Context: This saying has, by usage, become associated with good society, and is used to explain any distinction or striking discrimination in behavior. Although here "manner" means "custom" or "behavior," the saying is sometimes given as "to the *manor* born," which implies definite association with wealth, class distinction, or gentility. The difference is not readily discernible in speech, since the two words sound identical and the context probably has a double sense—a play on the two words, as Shakespeare was fond of doing. In *Hamlet,* the prince and Horatio, while waiting late at night for the ghost of Hamlet's father to appear on the battlements, hear trumpet flourishes and peels of cannon. Hamlet explains to Horatio that, the new king, Claudius, is indulging in a drinking bout, and each toast the king proposes is celebrated thus noisily. Horatio asks:

HORATIO
Is it a custom?

HAMLET
Ay marry is't,
But to my mind, though I am native here,
And **to the manner born,** it is a custom
More honoured in the breach than the observance.
• • •

1043

To the unknown God

Source: ACTS 17:23
Author: Unknown (traditionally Luke)
First transcribed: 60-150 (probably c.80-90)
Type of work: Religious history and tradition

Context: Paul, confronted by Christ on the Damascus Road, is converted to Christianity; just as he has ardently persecuted the Christians before his conversion, he now preaches the gospel of Jesus with equal fervor, principally in the Gentile lands. His missionary efforts are frequently met with strong opposition: some Jews of Thessalonica are not content with driving him from that city, but also stir up the people of Berea, so that Paul has to flee to Athens. In Athens Paul waits for Silas and Timothy to join him, and in the meantime, he preaches to the Athenians, who are so open-minded about religion that the city is filled with idolatry of all sorts, as well as with a number of schools of philosophy. Speaking to a highly educated audience at Mars' Hill, Paul begins:

> . . . Ye men of Athens, I perceive that in all things ye are too superstitious.
>
> For as I passed by, and beheld your devotions, I found an altar with this inscription, **TO THE UNKNOWN GOD.** Whom therefore ye ignorantly worship, him declare I unto you.

To thine own self be true

Source: HAMLET (Act I, sc. iii, l. 78)
Author: William Shakespeare (1564-1616)
First published: 1603
Type of work: Dramatic tragedy

Context: Of all the lines in a great and famous speech from *Hamlet,* the line beginning "This above all" is perhaps the most commonly recalled and used. The opening phrase is employed widely in itself, to convey the sense of "this is most important" or "be sure to remember (or) do this" and is also contracted to simply "above all." It is, in addition, quoted widely with the remainder of the line of which it is a part—"This above all, to thine own self be true," which has entered the English language as a proverb. In *Hamlet,* Polonius, chief councilor of Denmark's King Claudius, gives his son Laertes much sage advice as the latter patiently waits for his father's farewell and blessing before he embarks from Elsinore for France.

POLONIUS
. . .

This above all, **to thine own self be true,**
And it must follow, as the night the day,

1044

Thou canst not then be false to any man.
Farewell, my blessing season this in thee.

LAERTES
Most humbly do I take my leave my lord.

POLONIUS
The time invites you; go, your servants tend.

To where beyond these voices there is peace

Source: IDYLLS OF THE KING ("Guinevere," Line 692)
Author: Alfred, Lord Tennyson (1809-1892)
First published: 1859
Type of work: Narrative poem

Context: The guilty love between Sir Lancelot and Queen Guinevere had been a corrupting influence at Arthur's court. To try to avert an open scandal, Guinevere orders Lancelot to leave the court. He obeys and returns to his own lands, where he becomes the center of a rebellion against Arthur. While Arthur is away subduing this revolt, Guinevere flees to a convent, and it is there that Arthur finds her upon his return. Having learned of her guilt, he renounces her forever and leaves, although, true to his ideal, he forgives her. Guinevere spends the rest of her days in the convent and is appointed abbess three years before death removes her from human strife to the land beyond. She

Was chosen abbess, there, an abbess, lived
For three brief years, and there, an abbess, past
To where beyond these voices there is peace.

To your tents, O Israel

Source: I KINGS 12:16
Author: Unknown
First transcribed: c.600 B.C.
Type of work: Religious history

Context: After the death of King Solomon, his son Rehoboam is crowned king of Israel at Schechem. In the meantime, the people notify Jeroboam, who had fled to Egypt when Solomon discovered that the prophet Ahijah had disclosed to Jeroboam that he should govern ten of the tribes of Israel and that Solomon's son should reign over only one tribe. Jeroboam heads a large delegation of Israelites in petitioning Rehoboam to improve their condition and in pledging that they, in return, will support him as king. Solomon's sages advise Rehoboam to promise to be the servant of the people, but he, choosing to follow the advice of his young friends, replies to the delegation that he will be much more oppressive than Solomon was. At these words the division of Israel commences:

> So when all Israel saw that the king hearkened not unto them, the people answered the king, saying, What portion have we in David? neither have we inheritance in the son of Jesse: **to your tents, O Israel:** now see to thine own house, David. So Israel departed to their tents.

Toll for the brave

Source: ON THE LOSS OF THE ROYAL GEORGE
Author: William Cowper (1731-1800)
First published: 1803
Type of work: Elegy

Context: "On the Loss of the Royal George" is one of a collection of short poems published after Cowper's death. According to the subtitle of the poem, it was "Written When the News Arrived, by desire of Lady Austen, who wanted words to the march in Scipio." Lady Austen was the friend who had inspired Cowper to write *The Task*. The *Royal George* was a 108-gun British man-of-war which capsized while being refitted at Spithead, August 29, 1782. The commander, Admiral Kempenfelt, and 800 sailors, marines, and visitors were lost. The poem begins:

> Toll for the brave—
> The brave! that are no more:
> All sunk beneath the wave,
> Fast by this native shore.

A Tom Fool's errand

Source: THE LIFE AND OPINIONS OF TRISTRAM SHANDY, GENT. (Book I, chapter 16)
Author: Laurence Sterne (1713-1768)
First published: 1759-1767
Type of work: Novel

Context: According to the marriage settlement between his mother, Elizabeth Mollineux, and his father, Walter Shandy, we are informed by Tristram Shandy, the wife was to have the privilege, paid for by the husband out

1046

of his own money, of having her children born wherever she chose. The wife was allotted the sum of £120 for each lying-in. In September, 1717, Mrs. Shandy, believing herself to be pregnant, insisted upon her right and was taken by Walter Shandy to London for the birth of a child. To her chagrin, and her husband's vexation, the pregnancy proved false. On the way back home to Shandy Hall,

Walter Shandy fretted about the needless trip his wife had imposed upon him, with its inconvenience and expense. What mattered most to the irritated husband was that his "wallfruit and green gages" were ripe in September and required his personal attention at their picking. To indicate his extreme irritation, he said to his wife, while riding home in the coach:

. . . Had he been whistled up to London, upon **a Tom Fool's errand,** in any other month of the whole year, he should not have said three words about it.

Tomorrow to fresh woods and pastures new

Source: LYCIDAS (Line 193)
Author: John Milton (1608-1674)
First published: 1637
Type of work: Elegiac pastoral poem

Context: At the end of *Lycidas,* John Milton tells the woeful shepherds to weep no more, because Lycidas—Edward King—is not dead, but is, through the might of Him who walked upon the waves, alive on high. There he is happy with troops of saints for company, and because he is happy, the shepherds have no real cause to beweep his death on earth. Milton also develops the idea that Lycidas has become the genius or local god of the Irish Sea in which he drowned; as the genius he will be the protector of all who travel on that perilous flood. The poet says that he

has been singing all the day through, but at last he arises, adjusts his cloak about him, and looks forward to fresh woods and new pastures in days to come. This statement is subject to three interpretations; it may mean that Milton is merely saying farewell to his poem and that tomorrow he will be occupied with something else; it may mean that he is formally abandoning the composition of pastoral poetry; or it may mean that he is looking forward to leaving England, the scene of the death of Lycidas, for a trip to Italy. He concludes the poem by saying

At last he rose, and twitched his mantle blue:
Tomorrow to fresh woods and pastures new.

Tongue; well, that's a wery good thing when it an't a woman's

Source: THE PICKWICK PAPERS (Chapter 19)
Author: Charles Dickens (1812-1870)
First published: 1836-1837
Type of work: Novel

Context: Mr. Wardle, the congenial country gentleman, has taken Mr. Pickwick and his companions into the fields for a day of hunting partridges. They are accompanied by Sam Weller, Mr. Pickwick's servant, who, in the course of the morning, reveals that despite his lack of education and his cockney dialect, he is a penetrating observer of people and possesses considerable native wisdom. When they pause at midday to take their lunch, Sam unpacks the food and makes knowing observations on its quality and suitability. The first item he finds is some beef tongue, which prompts him to make one of his pronouncements upon women: the female tongue must be regarded as a disadvantage, since women have never learned to control it and make men suffer from their interminable verbosity. Mr. Pickwick had just been told of a pie-maker who used cat-flesh in his pies:

> "He must have been a very ingenious young man, that, Sam," said Mr. Pickwick, with a slight shudder.
> "Just was, Sir," replied Mr. Weller, continuing his occupation of emptying the basket, "and the pies was beautiful. **Tongue; well, that's a wery good thing when it an't a woman's.** Bread—knuckle o' ham, reglar picter—cold beef in slices, wery good."

Too black for heaven, and yet too white for hell

Source: THE HIND AND THE PANTHER (Part I, l. 343)
Author: John Dryden (1631-1700)
First published: 1687
Type of work: Religious allegory

Context: Somewhat earlier, in *Religio Laici,* Dryden had expressed his religious views at the time. In this poem he continues his writing on religion, having been converted in the meantime to Roman Catholicism. The hind in this poem is the Roman Catholic Church; the panther is the Anglican Church, called by Dryden, ". . . sure the noblest, next the *Hind,/* and fairest creature of the spotted kind." In this poem Dryden takes a moderate view. Like other English Catholics of his time, he seems to have been fearful of the future consequences of the actions of James II, a converted Catholic, who had ascended the throne upon the death of his brother, Charles II, in 1685. In describing the panther, Dryden writes:

If, as our dreaming *Platonists* report,
There could be spirits of a middle sort,
Too black for heav'n, and yet too white for hell,
Who just dropt half way down, nor lower fell;
So pois'd, so gently she descends from high,
It seems a soft dismission from the sky.

Too low for envy, for contempt too high

Source: A VOTE (Stanza 9)
Author: Abraham Cowley (1618-1667)
First published: 1636
Type of work: Ode

Context: "A Vote" is the poetic statement of a youth who feels that books and a simple life are preferable to the world and its various activities. It is significant to note, however, that Cowley was not allowed to enjoy an uncomplicated introspective life; serving the Royal Family during England's Civil War and Restoration, he found himself in and out of favor, arrested, exiled, and a victim of intrigues. In addition, fame had been thrust upon him, for his poetry was hailed as a model of perfection in style and form. Nearing the end of an active and public life, Cowley recalls "A Vote" in the essay "Of My Selfe" as "an Ode, which I made when I was but thirteen years old." In spite of the world's glories, the natural bent of his soul has been away from them, and he reaffirms his youthful ideal:

This only grant me, that my means may lye
Too low for Envy, for Contempt too high.
    Some Honor I would have
Not from great deeds, but good alone.
The unknown are better than ill known.
    Rumour can ope' the Grave,
Acquaintance I would have, but when't depends
Not on the number, but the choice of Friends.

Too low they build, who build beneath the stars

Source: THE COMPLAINT; OR NIGHT THOUGHTS (Night VIII, l. 215)
Author: Edward Young (1683-1765)
First published: 1745
Type of work: Philosophical poem

Context: Although modern readers focus their interest on the biographical and romantic aspects of this poem, the poet intended it as a great religious work designed to combat deism and to remind mankind of the need to remember God and the life after death. The poem was originally accepted and praised highly for the success it achieved in reaching the poet's goals. Unlike many passages, this one illustrates the poet's intent. He comments on the sanguinity of youth, which regards all the world as its friend, not its foe. He goes on to point out that on the sea of life the young hopefuls meet many storms, that the storms ruin even some of the strongest. He concludes that despite worldly victory, with its attendant fame and fortune, man still cannot be secure in life on this planet:

> . . . when is man secure?
> As fatal time, as storm! the rush of years
> Beats down their strength; their numberless escapes
> In ruin end: and, now, their proud success
> But plants new terrors on the victor's brow:
> What pain to quit the world, just made their own,
> Their nest so deeply down'd, and built so high!
> **Too low they build, who build beneath the stars.**

Too proud to fight

Source: ADDRESS TO FOREIGN-BORN CITIZENS
Author: Woodrow Wilson (1856-1924)
First spoken: 1915
Type of work: Speech

Context: On May 7, 1915, the Germans sank the British steamship *Lusitania,* and many American passengers aboard lost their lives. President Wilson had been an ardent supporter of neutrality, to such a point that now severe criticism from allied nations was imminent if the United States did not change its stand and enter the war against Germany. Wilson had promised to speak in Philadelphia on May 10 before a large group of recently naturalized citizens, and, in spite of the crisis of the moment, he fulfilled the engagement. It was expected that he would make some comment on the events of the past few days. In his address, Wilson explains that now each new citizen must consider himself an American first. Then alluding to the recent disaster and his own decision in the matter, he says:

> ". . . The example of America must be a special example. The example of America must be the example not merely of peace because it will not fight, but of peace because peace is the healing and elevating influence of the world and strife is not. There is such a thing as a man being **too proud to fight.** There is such a thing as a nation being so right that it does not need to convince others by force that it is right."

1050

Toujours gai toujours gai

Source: ARCHY AND MEHITABEL ("the song of mehitabel," Line 36)
Author: Don Marquis (1878-1937)
First published: 1927
Type of work: Humorous poem

Context: The author explains that one morning he found his typewriter being used by an oversized cockroach, which, he learns, contains the soul of a free-verse poet. The roach, archy, writes poetry in small letters, since he cannot use the shift key; and from this poetry one learns of his dislike for a rat named freddy and his admiration for the alley cat, mehitabel. One of archy's first poems is his "song of mehitabel," in which he summarizes the cat's philosophy as she told it to him. "i have had my ups and downs," she says, "but wotthehell wotthehell." Mehitabel believes that her soul is that of Cleopatra, and, despite the distance she has fallen and despite the wretchedness of life, she is determined to remain young in heart and to enjoy her existence as much as she can. Mehitabel assembles her motto from French words: "toujours gai toujours gai"— always happy, always happy.

> my youth i shall never forget
> but there s nothing i really regret
> wotthehell wotthehell
> there s a dance in the old dame yet
> **toujours gai toujours gai**

A tower of strength

Source: KING RICHARD THE THIRD (Act V, sc. iii, l. 12)
Author: William Shakespeare (1564-1616)
First published: 1597
Type of work: Historical drama

Context: King Richard and his army are on Bosworth field. The opposing army is led by Henry, Earl of Richmond, afterwards King Henry VII. Richmond's follower, Blunt, says about Richard: "He hath no friends, but what are friends for fear, which in his dearest need will fly from him." Richard is told that his enemies number only six or seven thousand. He then reassures his men and himself in his next speech.

RICHARD
Why our battalion trebles that account,
Besides, the King's name is **a tower of strength,**
Which they upon the adverse faction want.

• • •

Let's lack no discipline, make no delay,
For lords, to-morrow is a busy day.

The tree is known by its fruit

Source: MATTHEW 12:33
Author: Unknown (traditionally Matthew the Apostle)
First transcribed: c.75-100
Type of work: Gospel

Context: Jesus, after delivering the Sermon on the Mount, healing the afflicted, and choosing and instructing his twelve disciples, continues His travels about the country. When He condemns the towns of Galilee for not repenting their sins, He begins to arouse the Pharisees. He defends His disciples' plucking corn on the Sabbath and His healing of a man's withered hand on the Sabbath as blameless. Accused of casting out a devil in the name of Beelzebub, He argues that Satan would not logically war against his own kind, states the fact of two opposing forces, and compares the passive man with a scatterer of flocks. Further, He asserts that each force or tree will produce according to its own kind.

> Either make the tree good, and his fruit good; or else make the tree corrupt, and his fruit corrupt: for **the tree is known by his fruit.**

Trifles light as air are to the jealous confirmations

Source: OTHELLO (Act III, sc. iii, ll. 322-323)
Author: William Shakespeare (1564-1616)
First published: 1622
Type of work: Dramatic tragedy

Context: Iago, an evil and dissembling ancient (or ensign) to Othello, Moorish military governor of Cyprus in the service of Venice, hates him because the Moor has made Michael Cassio his lieutenant in preference to him. Iago determines to destroy both Othello and Cassio, and plants in Othello's mind the thought that Desdemona, Othello's bride, is having an affair with Cassio. Diabolically, Iago pretends solicitude for Othello's sensitivities, but is really nurturing the jealous seed in his soul. Desdemona comes, sees Othello distraught, and offers him her handkerchief, a special gift from Othello. He discards it, and it falls to the floor forgotten. After they leave the room, Emilia, wife of Iago, finds it, but Iago snatches it away from her. She wishes to return the handkerchief to Desdemona, but he dismisses her. He has use for it.

• • •

I will in Cassio's lodging lose this napkin,
And let him find it. **Trifles light as air**
Are to the jealous confirmations strong
As proofs of holy writ. This may do something.
The Moor already changes with my poison.
Dangerous conceits are in their natures poisons,
Which at the first are scarce found to distaste,
But with a little, act upon the blood,
Burn like the mines of sulphur. . . .

Trip the light fantastic

Source: L'ALLEGRO (Lines 33-34)
Author: John Milton (1608-1674)
First published: 1645
Type of work: Lyric poem

Context: John Milton tells Mirth to come dancing to him, making grotesque or whimsical patterns with her feet in contrast to the stately measures of court dances. And in her right hand she is to lead Liberty, which Milton associates with the Oreads, or mountain nymphs of Greek mythology. The poet says that if he pays the honor due her, she is to admit him to her band of revelers so that he can lead a life of innocent gaiety. He wants to hear the lark begin to sing in the dark of early morning and then come to greet him in his window, while the barnyard cock scatters the last darkness of night with his crowing. The passage is as follows:

Come, and **trip** it as we go,
On **the light fantastic** toe,
And in thy right hand lead with thee,
The mountain nymph, sweet Liberty:
And if I give thee honor due,
Mirth, admit me to thy crew,
To live with her, and live with thee,
In unreproved pleasures free . . .

Trod upon eggs

Source: ANATOMY OF MELANCHOLY (Part III, sec. 2, memb. 3)
Author: Robert Burton (1577-1640)
First published: 1621-1651
Type of work: Essays

Context: Love-melancholy, according to Burton, may be exhibited in mind or in body. He speaks of the anguish of great lovers of the past who scarcely heeded the appearance of their Beloved, yet must make themselves attractive by visits to the barber and to the baths, by seeking any beautifying to make themselves more attractive, and by "walking on eggs," for fear of alienating the Lady.

'T is the common humour of all suitors to trick up themselves, to be prodigal in apparel, faultless as a lotus, neat, combed and curled, with powdered hairs, with a long Love-lock, a flower in his ear, perfumed gloves, rings, scarfs, feathers, points, etc., as if he were a prince's Ganymede, with every day new suits, as the fashion varies; going as if he **trod upon eggs.** . . .

True as steel

Source: TROILUS AND CRISEYDE (Book V, l. 831)
Author: Geoffrey Chaucer (c.1343-1400)
First transcribed: 1380-1386
Type of work: Narrative poem

Context: One of the young sons of King Priam, Troilus, observing the rites of spring during the Trojan war, is smitten by love for a young widow, Criseyde. She in turn is taken by his handsome and manly appearance, and responds to her uncle Pandarus' overtures on the young prince's behalf. He, in the meantime, thinking his love in vain, becomes a doughty warrior in the attempt to break the siege of Troy. Finally he wins the young lady's favor after she sees him ride past the castle and recognizes that he is perfection itself, as true as steel:

And Troilus wel waxen was in highte,
And complet formed by proporcioun
So wel, that kinde it not amenden mighte;
Young, fresshe, stroung and hardie as a lyoun;
Trewe as stiel in each condicioun
. . .

True love never did run smooth

Source: A MIDSUMMER NIGHT'S DREAM (Act I, sc. i, l. 134)
Author: William Shakespeare (1564-1616)
First published: 1600
Type of work: Dramatic comedy

Context: Hermia, daughter of Egeus, insists that regardless of her father's command that she marry Demetrius she will instead marry Lysander, whom she loves. Theseus, Duke of Athens, insists that the choice either to obey her father or to be put to death or forced into a nunnery cannot be softened. After delivering himself of this announcement according to Athenian law, the duke and all his attendants exit, leaving Hermia and her love Lysander together. Lysander then foolishly asks Hermia, "Why is your cheek so pale? / How chance the roses there do fade so fast?" Then Lysander assures her that love has always traveled a rough road.

LYSANDER
Ay me! For ought that I could ever read,
Could ever hear by tale or history,
The course of **true love never did run smooth.**

• • •

True nobility is exempt from fear

Source: KING HENRY THE SIXTH: PART TWO (Act IV, sc. i, l. 129)
Author: William Shakespeare (1564-1616)
First published: 1594
Type of work: Historical drama

Context: The Duke of Suffolk has been banished from England because of his murder of Humphrey, Duke of Gloucester. At the suggestion of Queen Margaret, who loves him, he has gone to France. He and two gentlemen are captured off the coast of Kent. Suffolk says that he is charged with a message from the Queen of France. The English lieutenant and others say that they are going to kill him nevertheless. Suffolk is proud and imperious. When asked by the First Gentlemen, also a prisoner, to entreat mercy, Suffolk answers haughtily, and is subsequently beheaded.

SUFFOLK
. . . No, rather let my head
Stoop to the block, than these knees bow to any,
Save to the God of heaven and to my King;

And sooner dance upon a bloody pole
Than stand uncovered to the vulgar groom.
True nobility is exempt from fear.
More can I bear than you dare execute.

The true test of civilization

Source: CIVILIZATION
Author: Ralph Waldo Emerson (1803-1882)
First published: 1870
Type of work: Moral essay

Context: Emerson has been summarizing the components of a civilization. He has already said that civilization "implies the evolution of a highly organized man, brought to supreme delicacy of sentiment, as in practical power, religion, liberty, sense of honor and taste." America is a great nation not because of her government and her large cities but because of the independence and self-reliance of her families and individuals, the "habitual hospitality," the "refining influence of women." The "vital refinements" of a civilization "are the moral and intellectual steps" which are brought about by extraordinary individuals—Moses, Buddha, Socrates, Jesus, Luther. A "purer morality . . . kindles genius, civilizes civilization":

> These are traits and measures and modes; and **the true test of civilization** is, not the census, nor the size of cities, nor the crops, —no, but the kind of man the country turns out. . . .

The true university of these days is a collection of books

Source: HEROES AND HERO-WORSHIP ("The Hero as Man of Letters")
Author: Thomas Carlyle (1795-1881)
First published: 1841
Type of work: Moral essay

Context: Prophets and poets were the heroes of the past, but the "hero as *Man of Letters* . . . is altogether a product of these new ages," and he is "our most important modern person." Carlyle explores the careers of three of these modern heroes—Johnson, Rousseau, and Burns. Unlike the gloriously victorious Goethe, these three "were not heroic bringers of the light, but heroic seekers of it." The writer is a preacher, a prophet; and his books speak "to all men in all times and places." "Books are now our actual University, our Church, our Parliament." The first universities had no books, but the invention of printing revolutionized education:

1056

. . . If we think of it, all that a university, or final highest school can do for us, is still but what the first school began doing, —teach us to *read*. We learn to *read*, in various languages, in various sciences; we learn the alphabet and letters of all manner of books. But the place where we are to get knowledge, even theoretic knowledge, is the books themselves! It depends on what we read, after all manner of professors have done their best for us. **The true university of these days is a collection of books.**

True wit is nature to advantage dressed

Source: AN ESSAY ON CRITICISM (Part II, l. 297)
Author: Alexander Pope (1688-1744)
First published: 1711
Type of work: Satire

Context: In this verse paragraph of his essay Pope takes to task those writers who think that good work consists of an unorganized heap of "glittering thoughts." He says that many poets use "a wild heap of wit" to cover up a lack of thought in their poetry, thus hiding "with ornaments their want of art." Good poetry, Pope goes on to exclaim, shows us truth in such a way that we recognize the ideas as a reflection of what we have known ourselves but could not put into words. Having delivered his opinion on false wit, Pope goes on to explain what true wit is:

> **True wit is nature to advantage dress'd,**
> What oft was thought, but ne'er so well express'd;
> Something, whose truth convinc'd at sight we find,
> That gives us back the image of our mind.
> As shades more sweetly recommend the light,
> So modest plainness sets off sprightly wit.
> For works may have more wit than does 'em good,
> As bodies perish through excess of blood.

Truth, crushed to earth, shall rise again

Source: THE BATTLEFIELD (Stanza 9)
Author: William Cullen Bryant (1794-1878)
First published: 1837
Type of work: Lyric poem

Context: This poem begins as a controlled diatribe against war. The poet describes a peaceful landscape across which soldiers once marched to battle. Ironically, the blood of these heroes was spilled, "warm with hope and valor yet,/ Upon the soil they fought to save." Now, the poet tells us, this battlefield is "calm, and fresh, and still." He hopes that the battle-cry may never be heard again. Then he addresses another "soldier," one who fights to bring new truths to mankind, "truths which men receive not now." The battle on the field was soon ended, but the prophet must struggle all his life in his "friendless warfare" for truth. And yet the lonely fighter must "nerve [his] spirit" and "blench not." For there is hope; even if the lonely individual is destroyed in the struggle ("Like those who fell in battle" on the field), truth shall finally triumph:

> Nor heed the shaft too surely cast,
> The foul and hissing bolt of scorn;
> For with thy side shall dwell, at last,
> The victory of endurance born,
>
> **Truth, crushed to earth, shall rise again;**
> Th' eternal years of God are hers;
> But Error, wounded, writhes in pain,
> And dies among his worshipers.

Truth forever on the scaffold, wrong forever on the throne

Source: THE PRESENT CRISIS (Stanza 8)
Author: James Russell Lowell (1819-1891)
First published: 1845
Type of work: Lyric poem

Context: Lowell asserts in this poem that, despite all the crimes and evils of the earth, God and law are absolute, and that one should not be influenced by the past but should look toward the future and work to make it better. Right and wrong, truth and error, are often confused in the affairs of the world, but there come times of crisis when issues are laid bare, and each must decide on which side he stands. It seems, as one considers the past, that there is little profit in dedicating oneself to truth, for the powers of evil are much of the time supreme, and crimes are often unpunished. But virtue, though crucified, helps to improve the future, and Heaven never abandons the righteous.

> Careless seems the great Avenger; history's
>   pages but record
> One death—grapple in the darkness 'twixt
>   old systems and the word;
> **Truth forever on the scaffold, Wrong forever**
>   **on the throne,—**
> Yet that scaffold sways the future, and behind
>   the dim unknown,
> Standeth God within the shadow, keeping
>   watch above his own.

1058

Truth is stranger than fiction

Source: DON JUAN (Canto XIV, stanza 101)
Author: George Gordon, Lord Byron (1788-1824)
First published: 1823-1824 (Cantos XII-XIV)
Type of work: Satiric poem

Context: In Canto XIV, Byron's hero is a guest at a house party in England (see "Cervantes smil'd Spain's chivalry away"). Juan's hostess, Lady Adeline, attempts to rescue him from an intrigue. Byron hints, however, that something may develop between Adeline and Juan: "It is not clear that Adeline and Juan/ Will fall; but if they do, 'twill be their ruin" (Stanza 99). In the next stanza he observes that a "sentimental situation" can bring "man and woman to the brink/ Of ruin." It is evidently this "truth" that is referred to in the quotation. Byron's persistent linking of love and ruin doubtless stems from his own disastrous experience with marriage. Other authors have voiced similar opinions about truth: "Truth may sometimes be improbable."— Boileau (1636-1711): *The Art of Poetry,* III, 50; "There is nothing so powerful as truth, and often nothing so strange."—Daniel Webster (1782-1852): "Argument on the Murder of Captain White" (April 6, 1830); "Truth is stranger than fiction, but not so popular."—Author unknown. Stanza 101 of *Don Juan* begins:

'Tis strange,—but true; for **truth is** always strange;
  Stranger than fiction: if it could be told,
How much would novels gain by the exchange!
How differently the world would men behold!

The truth shall make you free

Source: JOHN 8:32
Author: Unknown (traditionally John the Apostle)
First transcribed: by 130
Type of work: Gospel

Context: The Pharisees, who see Jesus in the temple, question Him mercilessly, hoping to trap Him and make Him condemn Himself. Jesus never wavers in His testimony that He is sent from God to proclaim the Gospel of truth, the source of freedom from the sinfulness with which men are fettered:

Then said Jesus to those Jews which believed on him, If ye continue in my word, then are ye my disciples indeed;
And ye shall know the truth, and **the truth shall make you free.**

Truth sits upon the lips of dying men

Source: SOHRAB AND RUSTUM (Line 656)
Author: Matthew Arnold (1822-1888)
First published: 1853
Type of work: Narrative poem

Context: Arnold, using an episode from the Persian epic *Shah Namah,* composed by the poet Firdausi around 1000 A.D., retells the story of the fight between Sohrab, a courageous warrior with the Tartars about 600 B.C., and Rustum, his father and an equally famous warrior with the Persians. When the Tartars and Persians confront each other, Sohrab, seeking his father, who does not know that he has a son, gains permission from his commander to challenge the greatest of the Persian warriors, hoping that that warrior will be his beloved father. Rustum accepts the challenge, but conceals his identity in plain armor. The two men fight savagely, and the nimble Sohrab seems on the point of winning the battle when the furious father blurts out, "Rustum!" Sohrab falls back, and Rustum plants his spear in the boy's side. When Sohrab says that his father will avenge his death, Rustum declares that no son was born to Rustum, only "a puny girl." When Sohrab proves his identity by showing a pricked seal on his shoulder, Rustum, overwhelmed by sorrow, admits his name and claims his son. Sohrab's last request is that he be buried in the land of his father and grandfather. In attempting to convince his father that a son was born to Rustum, Sohrab says:

> "Man, who are thou who dost deny my words?
> **Truth sits upon the lips of dying men,**
> And falsehood, while I lived, was far from mine."

Truth will conquer

Source: A SHORT HISTORY OF THE ENGLISH PEOPLE, J. R. Green (Chapter 5, sec. 3)
Author: John Wycliffe (c.1320-1384)
First transcribed: 1381
Type of work: Historical anecdote

Context: John Wycliffe, who at first tried only to reform what he felt were abuses within the Roman Catholic Church, later became a protester against one of its cardinal beliefs, Transubstantiation. "With the formal denial of the doctrine of Transubstantiation," Green says, "began the great movement of revolt which ended more than a century after, in the establishment of religious freedom, by severing the mass of the Teutonic peoples from the general body of the Catholic Church." When Wycliffe was condemned by Oxford University, where he taught, his friends enjoined him to silence.

. . . The prohibition of the Duke of Lancaster he met by an open avowal of his teaching, a confession which closes proudly with the quiet words, "I believe that in the end the **truth will conquer.**" For the moment his courage dispelled the panic around him. . . .

The tumult and the shouting dies

Source: RECESSIONAL (Stanza 2)
Author: Rudyard Kipling (1865-1936)
First published: 1897
Type of work: Commemorative poem

Context: The sixtieth anniversary of Queen Victoria brought government officials and troops from all the colonies of the Empire together, with nearly two hundred vessels of the Royal Navy for great celebration and ceremony. Kipling sounds a warning to those who were overcome by the great pomp and ceremony of the event, a warning that all empires pass away, and that the mood proper to such an occasion should be one of contrition, rather than of pride.

> **The tumult and the shouting dies;**
>   The Captains and the Kings depart:
> Still stands Thine ancient sacrifice,
>   An humble and a contrite heart.
>   •   •   •
> Far-called, our navies melt away;
>   On dune and headland sinks the fire:
> Lo, all our pomp of yesterday
>   Is one with Nineveh and Tyre!
> Judge of the Nations, spare us yet,
> Lest we forget—lest we forget.

'Twas for the good of my country that I should be abroad

Source: THE BEAUX' STRATAGEM (Act III, sc. ii)
Author: George Farquhar (1677?-1707)
First published: 1707
Type of work: Dramatic comedy

Context: In this play we find a change from earlier comedies. Love here is a romantic passion, rather than merely an excuse for amorous

1061

intrigue, as it was in earlier drama of the Restoration period. Here, for example, we find a gentleman of broken fortune, Aimwell, who sets out to recoup his wealth by marriage to a beautiful and wealthy young woman, only to find himself in love with her. Instead of imposing on her, he even offers to give her up, saying, "I feel myself unequal to the task of villain; she has gained my soul and made it honest like her own." There is, however, a real villain, a highwayman named Gibbet, who carries an apt name indeed. Gibbet pretends to be an army officer and tries to pass himself off to Aimwell, who appears rich, as an officer in an old marching regiment. When Aimwell asks if he has served abroad, Gibbet gives the following reply, similar to a sentiment written for a prologue by George Barrington, a pickpocket sent to Botany Bay, at the opening of the first theater in New South Wales:

GIBBET

Yes, sir, in the plantations; 'twas my lot to be sent into the worst service. I would have quitted it indeed, but a man of honor, you know—Besides, **'twas for the good of my country that I should be abroad:**—anything for the good of one's country—I'm a Roman for that.

'Twas I that beat the bush, the bird to others flew

Source: A LOVE SONNET (Stanza 11)
Author: George Wither (1588-1667)
First published: 1620
Type of work: Lyric poem

Context: Unlike most of the Cavalier poets, Wither favored the Puritans, and much of his writing pleaded their cause. He was even a captain in Cromwell's army. He is remembered today, however, for his earlier pastorals, satires, and light verse included in his *Juvenilia* (1622). His two most memorable songs are "Shall I, wasting in despair," and this one also miscalled a sonnet, that begins "I loved a lass, a fair one." In it, the poet complains without very deep feelings, about a fair maid who deserted him. Though he does not call himself a cat's paw, he tells how others profited from his courting of her, and decides that all women are frail, faithless, and unappreciative, for as he reports:

'T was I that paid for all things,
'T was others drank the wine;
I cannot now recall things,
Live but a fool to pine.
'T was I that beat the bush,
The bird to others flew;
For she, Alas! hath left me.
Falero, lero, loo.

1062

'Twere well it were done quickly

Source: MACBETH (Act I, sc. vii, ll. 1-2)
Author: William Shakespeare (1564-1616)
First published: 1623
Type of work: Dramatic tragedy

Context: Macbeth, general in King Duncan of Scotland's army, is told by three witches that he shall be Thane of Cawdor and afterward king. Immediately following the disappearance of the apparitions, he is told the king has made him Thane of Cawdor as reward for outstanding service. Therefore, if the first part of the prophecy came true, so will the second; and if so, why not hurry it along with the assistance of a murder? But Macbeth puts the thought from his mind. He writes to his wife, who, more ambitious than her lord, immediately thinks of murder as the way to the throne, and as if to aid her cause, the king comes to Macbeth's castle to spend a night. Before he arrives, Macbeth comes home, and Lady Macbeth tells him to leave the bloody business to her. Now King Duncan arrives and Macbeth, alone, speaks his thoughts. He is apprehensive of the consequences of assassination.

> MACBETH
> If it were done, when 'tis done, then **'twere well
> It were done quickly.** If th' assassination
> Could trammel up the consequence, and catch
> With his surcease, success; that but this blow
> Might be the be-all and the end-all—here,
> But here, upon this bank and shoal of time,
> We'd jump the life to come. But in these cases,
> We still have judgment here, that we but teach
> Bloody instructions, which being taught return
> To plague th' inventor. . . .

A twice-told tale

Source: THE ODYSSEY (Book XII, l. 538, as translated by Alexander Pope)
Author: Homer (c. 850 B.C.)
First transcribed: Sixth century B.C.
Type of work: Epic poem

Context: On the eve of his departure for Ithaca, after nearly ten years of wandering, Odysseus finishes telling his hosts, King Alcinous and Queen Arete, his many adventures. He recalls that he visited Hades in order to discover what lay ahead for him, that he escaped both Scylla and Charybdis, that his men ate of the forbidden cattle of the Sun and then perished at sea, that he finally stayed with Calypso who then helped him get to the land of the seafaring Phaeacians. Perhaps Homer, thought to be a minstrel himself, intrudes here by suggesting that sometimes retold stories bore the listener. Hawthorne felt otherwise in naming a book so, although Shakespeare agreed in *King John:* "Life is as tedious as a twice-told tale,/ Vexing the dull ear of a drowsy man."

> "My following fates to thee, O king, are known,
> And the bright partner of thy royal throne.
> Enough: in misery can words avail?
> And what so tedious as **a twice-told tale?**"

Twinkle, twinkle, little star

Source: RHYMES FOR THE NURSERY ("The Star," Stanza I)
Author: Jane Taylor (1783-1824)
First published: 1806
Type of work: Children's verse

Context: Jane Taylor, daughter of Isaac Taylor, an engraver, a nonconformist pastor, and an author of books for children, is herself best known for children's verse. With her sister Ann (1782-1866) she composed numerous poems which have delighted children for more than a century. Their first publication was the immensely popular *Original Poems for Infant Minds* in two volumes (1804-1805). A second venture, *Rhymes for the Nursery* (1806), includes Jane's "The Star," perhaps the most memorable single entry. In this delightful poem the author attempts to capture the voice of a child's curiosity as he gazes at the mystery of the night sky pierced by the twinkling rays of the countless stars. Lewis Carroll (1832-1898) attests the popularity of the verse by parodying it in his children's classic some fifty years later. He writes: "Twinkle, twinkle, little bat!/ How I wonder what you're at!/ Up above the world you fly,/ Like a tea-tray in the sky" (*Alice's Adventures in Wonderland,* 1865). Miss Taylor's poem begins:

> **Twinkle, twinkle, little star,**
> How I wonder what you are,
> Up above the world so high
> Like a diamond in the sky.

Two heads are better than one

Source: THE PROVERBS OF JOHN HEYWOOD (Part I, chapter 9)
Author: John Heywood (1497?-1580?)
First published: 1546
Type of work: Gnomic poetry

Context: The author is discussing with a young man the questions concerning marriage, among them the important one of whether a man should marry for love or money, a young maid or an old widow. The author is determined to illustrate his point by quoting all the "plain pithy proverbs" on his side. The young man answers with "other parables of like weighty weight." The author illustrates with some of his own experiences. This little tale is about a man and his wife who cannot make up their minds about how to act; therefore, they seek the author's advice. He advises the husband to go "to his uncle," and the lady to go to her aunt. Although the husband had already arrived at this conclusion, he had not wanted to act without consultation.

> For he, ere this, thought this the best way to be.
> But of these two things he would determine none
> Without aid: for **two heads are better than one.**

Two peas in a pod

Source: GARGANTUA AND PANTAGRUEL (Book V, chapter 2)
Author: François Rabelais (1495-1553)
First published: (1532-1564)
Type of work: Mock heroic chronicle

Context: Pantagruel, Panurge, and Friar John, on their voyage to consult the Oracle of the Holy Bottle, stop at Ringing Island. Here they learn that the inhabitants, the Citicines, have been changed into birds and are kept in cages. They are not surprised at this event, remembering other such metamorphoses in literature. The comparison to peas in a pod was used by John Lyly in *Euphues, the Anatomy of Wit* (1579), by Shakespeare in *The Winter's Tale,* Act I, sc. ii, l. 130, and by Cervantes in *Don Quixote,* Part II (1615), Book III, chapter 14, as well as by many other writers. Pantagruel and his friends when they view the caged creatures, are startled to see them:

> **looking** as like the men in my country **as one pea does like another;** for they ate and drank like men . . . , in short, had you seen and examined 'em from top to toe, you would have laid your head to a turnip that they had been mere men.

Two worlds, one dead, the other powerless to be born

Source: STANZAS FROM THE GRANDE CHARTREUSE (Stanza 15)
Author: Matthew Arnold (1822-1888)
First published: 1855
Type of work: Religious poem

Context: Matthew Arnold, critic of his age in poetry and prose, lamented the religious confusion and doubt of the time and sought, like the young man in his "The Scholar-Gypsy," the higher life, "the spark from heaven." In 1852, Arnold visited the Grande Chartreuse, a monastary of the Order of the Carthusians in the French Alps. Describing the monastary and its inhabitants as of another time, he pleads that he be accepted until he can possess his own soul again. He examines his faith and declares that he is between the old age of faith with its useless conventions and the new age whose faith will be built on some new basis, "Which without hardness will be sage,/ And gay without frivolity." He writes:

Wandering between **two worlds, one dead,**
The other powerless to be born,
With nowhere yet to rest my head,
Like these, on earth I wait forlorn.
Their faith, my tears, the world deride—
I come to shed them at their side.

'Twould be as much as my life was worth

Source: THE LIFE AND OPINIONS OF TRISTRAM SHANDY, GENT. (Book III, chapter 20)
Author: Laurence Sterne (1713-1768)
First published: 1759-1767
Type of work: Novel

Context: Laurence Sterne's whimsical nature is nowhere better displayed than in the numerous tricks of typography and format in *Tristram Shandy*. He uses countless dots, dashes, and asterisks, blank pages, black pages, pointing fingers, and even one-sentence chapters. Another oddity is that the preface to the novel, instead of appearing at the outset, occurs as Chapter 20 of Book III. Sterne announces first that all his characters are adequately occupied elsewhere at the moment. Therefore, he observes, "—'tis the first time I have had a moment to spare,—and I'll make use of it, and write my Preface." The preface concerns itself with the problem of the general lack of wit and judgment in the world. Sterne selects various particular groups and castigates them—the politicians, the educators, the physicians, and others. But when he comes to the clergy he pulls up short:

As for the Clergy,—No;—if I say a word against them, I'll be shot. . . . with such weak nerves and spirits, and in the condition I am in at present, **'twould be as much as my life was worth,** to deject and contrist myself with so bad and melancholy an account—and therefore, 'tis safer to draw a curtain across, and hasten . . . to the main . . . point I have undertaken to clear up; . . . How it comes to pass, that your men of least *wit* are reported to be men of most *judgment?*

Unarm, Eros, the long day's task is done, and we must sleep

Source: ANTONY AND CLEOPATRA (Act IV, sc. xiv, ll. 35-36)
Author: William Shakespeare (1564-1616)
First published: 1623
Type of work: Dramatic tragedy

Context: Mark Antony, a co-ruler of Rome, is so smitten with love for Cleopatra, beautiful and voluptuous Queen of Egypt, that he uses poor judgment in his decisions and acts on impulse, rather than on cool deliberation, where she is concerned. Now, dishonored by his actions and defeated by Octavius Caesar at Actium —a sea battle to decide who will rule the world—deserted by his forces, and informed that Cleopatra is dead, he feels his heart break. He asks his servant, Eros, with words that have double meaning, to remove his armor.

ANTONY
Dead then?

MARDIAN
Dead.

ANTONY
Unarm, Eros, the long day's task is done,
And we must sleep.
. . .

Unbidden guests are often welcomest when they are gone

Source: HENRY VI, PART I (Act II, sc. ii, ll. 55-56)
Author: William Shakespeare (1564-1616)
First published: 1623
Type of work: Historical drama

Context: Lord Talbot, afterwards Earl of Shrewsbury, called a "fiend of hell" or "if not of hell, the heavens sure favour him," has stormed the

1067

French city of Orleans, and routed the French out of their beds half dressed. An English soldier has discovered that he needs no arms since "The cry of Talbot serves me as a sword." After having taken Orleans, Talbot, Bedford and Burgundy, with soldiers, while in the city are approached by a messenger from the Countess of Auvergne who says that she should like to talk to Talbot, so "That she may boast she hath beheld the man,/ Whose glory fills the world with loud report." Talbot agrees to visit the Countess, but asks the other nobles to go with him. Burgundy and Bedford comment as follows:

BURGUNDY
Nay, then I see our wars
Will turn unto a peaceful comic sport,
When ladies crave to be encountered with.

BEDFORD
No, truly, it is more than manners will;
And I have heard it said, **unbidden guests
Are often welcomest when they are gone.**

An un-birthday present

Source: THROUGH THE LOOKING-GLASS (Chapter 6)
Author: Lewis Carroll (Charles Lutwidge Dodgson, 1832-1898)
First published: 1871
Type of work: Imaginative tale for children

Context: The Oxford mathematician Charles Lutwidge Dodgson is better known by his pen name, Lewis Carroll, and for his children's classics, *Alice's Adventures in Wonderland* and *Through the Looking-Glass,* whose heroine is his young friend Alice Liddell. In *Through the Looking-Glass,* Alice peers through a mirror and, by imagining herself in the reflected image, begins her adventures in Looking-Glass House, where chessmen live in a kingdom marked off as a giant chessboard. Alice meets the large legendary egg, Humpty Dumpty; and when she compliments his cravat, he is pleased and states that it is a gift of the White King and Queen:

"They gave it me," Humpty Dumpty continued thoughtfully as he crossed one knee over the other and clasped his hands round it, "they gave it me—for **an un-birthday present.**"

The uncertain glory of an April day

Source: THE TWO GENTLEMEN OF VERONA (Act I, sc. iii, l. 84)
Author: William Shakespeare (1564-1616)
First published: 1623
Type of work: Dramatic comedy

Context: Panthino, servant of Antonio of Verona, is talking with his master, Proteus' father, about the need to send Proteus on a trip because he has spent all his youth at home. Antonio readily agrees to the wisdom of the suggestion. At this point Proteus enters reading a letter from his love Julia. When asked about its contents, however, he lies, saying the letter is from his friend Valentine who urges him to come to the Emperor's palace in Milan. Antonio then doubly insists that Proteus go, decreeing, in fact, that he must leave the next morning. Proteus now realizes what a situation he has got himself into.

> PROTEUS
> Thus have I shunned the fire for fear of burning,
> And drenched me in the sea, where I am drowned.
> I feared to show my father Julia's letter,
> Lest he should take exceptions to my love,
> And with the vantage of mine own excuse
> Hath he excepted most against my love.
> O, how this spring of love resembleth
> **The uncertain glory of an April day,**
> Which now shows all the beauty of the sun,
> And by and by a cloud takes all away.

Under a spreading chestnut tree

Source: THE VILLAGE BLACKSMITH (Stanza 1)
Author: Henry Wadsworth Longfellow (1807-1882)
First published: 1840
Type of work: Lyric poem

Context: Longfellow wrote "The Village Blacksmith" as a tribute to his ancestor Stephen Longfellow, a Cambridge blacksmith. The setting for the poem was a smithy beneath a chestnut tree close to the poet's home in Cambridge. The smith is glorified as a strong, honest, industrious, self-reliant, and tender-hearted man who works "Week in, week out, from morn till night." The "measured beat" of "his heavy sledge" sounds like "the village bell" rung by the sexton. Children returning from school love to stop at the smithy in order "to see the flaming forge,/ And hear the bellows roar,/ And catch the burning sparks that fly/ Like chaff from a threshing-floor." In the first two stanzas we see the smith as the epitome of the honest laborer, the man whose pristine integrity makes him the spiritual equal of any man:

> **Under a spreading chestnut-tree**
>   The village smithy stands;
> The smith, a mighty man is he,
>   With large and sinewy hands;
> And the muscles of his brawny arms
>   Are strong as iron bands.
>
> His hair is crisp, and black, and long,
>   His face is like the tan;
> His brow is wet with honest sweat,
>   He earns whate'er he can,
> And looks the whole world in the face,
>   For he owes not any man.

Under her solemn fillet saw the scorn

Source: DAYS (Last line)
Author: Ralph Waldo Emerson (1803-1882)
First published: 1857
Type of work: Lyric poem

Context: This short philosophical poem is notable for its compression, its symbolism, and its expression of Emerson's belief in taking practical advantage of all of one's opportunities. "Hypocritic Days," who are the "daughters of Time," come to us in single file, offering us whatever gifts we choose to take from them. In other words, we can do with Time whatever we wish, and we are free to take what we want from each day: "Bread, kingdoms, stars, and sky that holds them all." Man, Emerson says, is free to accomplish whatever his heart desires. But mankind is not *aware* of this freedom. The Day (symbolizing a lifetime) comes and offers the poet infinite gifts. The poet, forgetting his early desire for glorious achievements in his life, snatches a few insignificant gifts from Time. When the Day turns away with contempt, he realizes that he has passed up glorious opportunities:

> I, in my pleachèd garden, watched the pomp,
> Forgot my morning wishes, hastily
> Took a few herbs and apples, and the Day
> Turned and departed silent. I, too late,
> **Under her solemn fillet saw the scorn.**

Under his vine and under his fig tree

Source: MICAH 4:4
Author: Unknown
First transcribed: c.750-700 B.C.
Type of work: Religious prophecy

Context: Though the prophet Micah is credited with writing most of the book of Micah, scholars assert that certain passages, including the section from which this quotation is taken, are from the hand of another writer, who presents a note of optimism, in contrast with the gloom which dominates Micah's prophecy. The writer states that, at the end of Israel's period of exile, Zion, the holy hill of Jerusalem on which is located the temple, will be glorified above all mountains. The people of many nations will pour forth to worship the Lord and will be instructed in His ways and commandments. An idealistic dream of universal peace is presented:

> And he shall judge among many people, and rebuke strong nations afar off; and they shall beat their swords into plowshares, and their spears into pruning hooks: nation shall not lift up a sword against nation, neither shall they learn war any more.
> But they shall sit every man **under his vine and under his fig tree;** and none shall make them afraid: for the mouth of the Lord of hosts hath spoken it.

Under the greenwood tree

Source: AS YOU LIKE IT (Act II, sc. v, l. 1)
Author: William Shakespeare (1564-1616)
First published: 1623
Type of work: Dramatic comedy

Context: The scene is the forest of Arden. The First Lord tells Duke Senior, who has been banished by his brother Duke Frederick and has gone to the forest, that Jaques, a lord attending on Duke Senior, is "melancholy." Now we see Jaques with Amiens, another lord attending Duke Senior. Amiens sings a stanza of a beautiful song. Jaques calls for more, but Amiens insists that the song will make him "melancholy." Jaques responds, "More, I prithee more. I can suck melancholy out of a song, as a weasel sucks eggs." This is the first stanza of Amiens' song:

AMIENS
Under the greenwood tree,
Who loves to lie with me,

1071

And turn his merry note
Unto the sweet bird's throat,
Come hither, come hither, come hither.
Here shall he see
No enemy,
But winter and rough weather.

The undoctored incident that actually occurred

Source: THE BENEFACTORS (Stanza 1)
Author: Rudyard Kipling (1865-1936)
First published: 1890
Type of work: Didactic poem

Context: With his customary worldly-wise cynicism, Kipling maintains that it is "not learning, grace nor gear" that drives Man to think and thus to advance from his primitive state; it is, rather, the "bitter pinch of pain and fear." Each weapon invented by Man demands the invention of a better one, thus testing Man's ingenuity; therefore, history is a long succession of wars. Yet the very horror of the destruction brought by war will end war, for Man learns only through suffering. Hence, all power—be it that of a tyrant or that of a mob—eventually destroys itself. This is the lesson that Man, as a realist, must learn.

Ah! What avails the classic bent
And what the cultured word,
Against **the undoctored incident**
That actually occurred?

Uneasy lies the head that wears a crown

Source: KING HENRY THE FOURTH: PART TWO (Act III, sc. i, l. 31)
Author: William Shakespeare (1564-1616)
First published: 1600
Type of work: Historical drama

Context: Despite King Henry's victory at Shrewsbury, at which battle Henry Percy (Hotspur) was slain, the rebellion continues. Henry IV's son, Prince Hal, and his sometime friends Falstaff and his partners in skullduggery, have been very much involved. In the chaotic times, King Henry finds that the affairs of the world have exiled sleep. His regrets over its loss sound not unlike those of Macbeth. Henry says: "O sleep, o gentle sleep. / Nature's soft nurse." *Macbeth* (Act II, sc. ii, l. 36) says: "Sleep that knits up the ravelled sleave of care." Again, Henry says:

"... How have I frighted thee, / That thou no more wilt weigh my eyelids down ...?" And *Macbeth* (Act II, sc. ii, 1. 35): "Macbeth does murder sleep." King Henry, brooding on the fact that all the world except himself lies asleep, can only conclude:

KING HENRY

• • •

Canst thou, o partial sleep, give thy repose
To the wet sea's son in an hour so rude,
And in the calmest and most stillest night,
With all appliances and means to boot,
Deny it to a king? Then, happy low, lie down,
Uneasy lies the head that wears a crown.

The unexamined life is not worth living

Source: THE APOLOGY (37D-38A, as translated by Benjamin Jowett)
Author: Plato (427-347 B.C.)
First transcribed: Probably one of the early dialogues
Type of work: Socratic dialogue

Context: This quotation is from the speech made by Socrates when on trial for his life on the charge of having corrupted the young men of Athens through his supposedly atheistic teaching. It is Socrates' contention that to harm his neighbors (i.e., to corrupt the youth of Athens) would be to harm himself, an act which no man would intentionally commit. As to his alleged atheism, he points out that no one can believe, as he does, in divine agencies without believing in the Gods. The parents of the young men whom he is supposed to have corrupted have brought no testimony against him; therefore, the knowledge of his innocence gives him courage. It has been suggested that he go to a foreign city and, once there, hold his tongue. But he rejects this advice, for it is his duty to probe into those very subjects which so irritate the Athenians:

... if I tell you that to do as you say would be a disobedience to the God, and therefore that I cannot hold my tongue, you will not believe that I am serious; and if I say again that daily to discourse about virtue, and of those other things about which you hear me examining myself and others, is the greatest good of man, and that **the unexamined life is not worth living,** you are still less likely to believe me. Yet I say what is true. ...

The unheroic dead who fed the guns

Source: ON PASSING THE NEW MENIN GATE (Stanza 1)
Author: Siegfried Sassoon (1886-   )
First published: 1927
Type of work: Lyric poem

Context: The town of Menin, in Belgium near the French border, was occupied by the Germans during World War I in 1914 and again in 1918. Located at an important crossing of the Lys, it was the scene of much heavy fighting. The sentiments of this poem are concentrated around the implications of one aspect of this particular battleground. On the road into the town stands a memorial gateway, commemorating the dead. On the gateway are the words: "Their name liveth forever." Apparently a list of names is included. The poet is provoked by the bitter irony of these words when he thinks of the senseless, unheroic tragedy which they commemorate. This gate cannot even guarantee that the "unheroic Dead" will be remembered. It far from compensates or answers for the crimes done against those who died. "Here was the world's worst wound," he says. Now the gateway seems to proclaim the honor of the dead with pride! "Well might the Dead who struggled in the slime/ Rise and deride this sepulchre of crime," he concludes. The first stanza begins:

> Who will remember, passing through this Gate,
> **The unheroic Dead who fed the guns?**
> Who shall absolve the foulness of their fate,—
> These doomed, conscripted, unvictorious ones?

Union gives strength

Source: AESOP'S FABLES ("The Bundle of Sticks")
Author: Aesop (fl. sixth century B.C.?)
First transcribed: Fourth century B.C.
Type of work: Moral tales of animals

Context: This story comes from world folklore rather than the fable associated with Aesop. Aesop's is quite different and involves the famous last words of wisdom to the sons, for in the original an old man carries his bundle of sticks until he is weary and then calls for Death. When Death asks why he is called, the old fellow replies, "To get you to take up my burden," meaning that man hangs on to life even when he is troubled. The popular and sentimental fable, however, describes the dying father calling in his sons, handing them a bundle of sticks, and asking each in turn to break it. When they cannot, he hands each one a stick to break, and they do so with ease.

"You see my meaning," said their father.
"Union Gives Strength."

United we stand, divided we fall

Source: AESOP'S FABLES ("The Four Oxen and the Lion")
Author: Aesop (fl. sixth century B.C.?)
First transcribed: Fourth century B.C.
Type of work: Moral tales of animals

Context: The idea that in union is strength is implicit in the American way of life, our motto, our patriotic utterances. George Pope Morris writes in 1840, "A song for our banner! The watchword recall/ Which gave the Republic her station:/ 'United we stand, divided we fall!'/ Is made and preserves us a nation." In 1768 John Dickinson's *The Liberty Song* puts it "Then join hand in hand, brave Americans all!/ By uniting we stand, by dividing we fall." Lincoln's paraphrase of Mark 3:25, "A house divided against itself cannot stand" shows the consequences of ignoring the Aesop precept, for had the oxen in the fable stood firm and together they would not have been eaten separately:

> A Lion used to prowl about a field in which Four Oxen used to dwell . . . Whenever he came near they turned their tails to one another . . . [and] he was met by the horns of one of them. At last, however, they fell quarrelling among themselves, and each went off to pasture alone. . . . Then the Lion attacked them one by one and soon made an end of all four.
> **"United We Stand, Divided We Fall."**

Universal darkness buries all

Source: THE DUNCIAD (Book IV, 1. 656)
Author: Alexander Pope (1688-1744)
First published: 1728-1743
Type of work: Satirical poem

Context: At the end of this poem, the poet shows all England delivered over to the Goddess Dulness, who says, ". . . *make one mighty Dunciad of the land.*" At her word, churches, chapels, and schools lose their sense, the people yawn and sleep. Army, navy, and diplomatic corps all sleep, too. With the muse's help the poet shows primeval night and chaos creeping across the land to take possession. Art after art leaves the scene; truth flies to a cavern; philosophy and morality expire. Nothing is left in the world once Dulness establishes her empire:

For public flame, nor private, dares to shine;
Nor human spark is left, nor glimpse divine!
Lo! thy dread empire, Chaos! is restor'd;
Light dies before thy uncreating word:
Thy hand, great Anarch! lets the curtain fall;
And universal Darkness buries all.

The unlit lamp and the ungirt loin

Source: THE STATUE AND THE BUST (Stanza 83)
Author: Robert Browning (1812-1889)
First published: 1855
Type of work: Narrative poem

Context: Robert Browning chose as his primary interest in his poetry the Renaissance, its people, and its customs. In "The Statue and the Bust," he relates the story of a futile love in Renaissance Florence. Duke Ferdinand falls in love with the new bride of the head of the Riccardi family, and she with him. As he rides below her window, he admires her. She, from the security of her window, watches for him as he rides through the town square. Time passes, and the lady grows older. To prevent the aging process, she has an unaging bust made for the window from which she has watched. The duke has a bronze equestrian statue cast of himself and placed in the town square where he has ridden. At the end of the poem, the poet delivers his preachment—in this case, an indictment of the lovers for not having striven for their love, for having accepted a passive, an inactive love:

If you choose to play!—is my principle.
Let a man contend to the uttermost
For his life's set prize, be it what it will!

The counter our lovers staked was lost
As surely as if it were lawful coin;
And the sin I impute to each frustrate ghost

Is—**the unlit lamp and the ungirt loin,**
Though the end in sight was a vice, I say.
You of the virtue (we issue join)
How strive you? *De te fabula!*

Unrespited, unpitied, unreprieved

Source: PARADISE LOST (Book II, l. 185)
Author: John Milton (1608-1674)
First published: 1667
Type of work: Epic poem

Context: In the grand council of the rebel angels held in Hell, Belial answers Moloch's suggestion that the rebels continue the warfare against God. Unlike Moloch, Belial does not believe the rebels can successfully fight against the Divine hosts and will. To persuade his audience of his point, Belial waxes rhetorical, painting verbal pictures of what God could do to the rebels, even in Hell. He suggests that Hell could explode with them, that each could be fixed to a rock in the burning lake, that the fires of Hell could be increased seven-fold, or that each spirit could be wrapped in chains and confined in the fiery lake. His conclusion is beautiful in its effective meter and accent:

> There to converse with everlasting groans,
> **Unrespited, unpitied, unreprieved,**
> Ages of hopeless end; this would be worse.

Unspotted from the world

Source: JAMES 1:27
Author: James
First transcribed: c.80-100
Type of work: Religious epistle

Context: James, variously identified as the apostle James, son of Zebedee, the second apostle James, often called "James the less," and James, the brother of Jesus, speaking as head of the Church in Jerusalem and writing to give moral instruction to the twelve tribes of Israel, proclaims tribulation as a cause of joy and patience, the efficacy of prayer, the danger of riches, the impossibility of temptation by God, and the good that comes from Him. Urging the control of self but also the importance of an active rather than a passive nature, he gives as the two qualities of pure religion compassion and unworldliness:

> Pure religion ưnd undefiled before God and the Father is this, To visit the fatherless and widows in their affliction, and to keep himself **unspotted from the world.**

Untie the Gordian knot

Source: LIVES ("Alexander the Great," as translated by Sir Thomas North, 1579)
Author: Plutarch (c.46-120)
First transcribed: 105-115
Type of work: Biography

Context: Alexander quells the Greeks who are restive after his father, Philip, dies. He then crosses the Hellespont to fight Darius, ruler of Persia. He conquers some of the cities; others willingly surrender. He meets success wherever he goes, and none can withstand him. After conquering cities along the seacoast, as far as Phoenicia,

> . . . he overcame also the Pisidians, who thought to have resisted him, and conquered all Phrygia besides.
> There in the city of Gordius, which is said to be the ancient seat of King Midas: he saw the Charret that is so much spoken of, which is bound with the bark of a cornel tree, and it was told him for a truth, of the barbarous people, that they believed it as a prophecy: that whosoever could undo the band off that bark, was certainly ordained to be king of the world. It is commonly reported, that Alexander proving to undo that band, and finding no ends to undo it by, they were so many folds wreathed one within the other: he drew out his sword, and cut the knot in the middest. So that then many ends appeared. But Aristobulus writeth, that he had quickly **undone the knot** by taking the bolt out of the ax-tree, which holdeth the beam and body of the Charret, and so severed them asunder.

Unto the pure all things are pure

Source: TITUS 1:15
Author: Unknown
First transcribed: 61-180
Type of work: Pastoral epistle

Context: The writer, calling himself Paul, but generally conceded to be a high church official, writes to one whom he calls Titus, thought to be a lower member of the governing body of the Church. Opening his pastoral letter with instructions on the proper appointment of blameless elders and bishops, he describes the good bishop as one who preaches sound doctrine and contrasts him with the false teacher, who preaches only for money. With a strong rejection of the ritual commandments and a reliance on faith, the writer says that to the spiritually clean all things are pure, that the man-made rules are of no consequence. To the false teacher or non-believer in Christ, however, all things are impure, because the false teacher is corrupt in his mind:

> **Unto the pure all things are pure:** but unto them that are defiled and unbelieving is nothing pure; but even their mind and conscience is defiled.

Unto us a child is born

Source: ISAIAH 9:6
Author: Isaiah
First transcribed: c.800-200 B.C.
Type of work: Religious prophecy and exhortation

Context: Isaiah, prophet of the Almighty, proclaims his vision of "Judah and Jerusalem in the days of Uzziah, Jotham, Ahaz, and Hezekiah, kings of Judah." He exhorts the Israelites to turn from their sinful and idolatrous ways and warns them that the Lord is prepared to destroy Jerusalem and Judah. Relating his vision of God and reproving Ahaz for his unwillingness to trust the Almighty, Isaiah finally withdraws and declares that he will wait for the proof of his prophecies. In a shift from a note of death and destruction to one of joy, he delivers his prophecy of a messiah:

> For **unto us a child is born,** unto us a son is given: and the government shall be upon his shoulder: and his name shall be called Wonderful, Counsellor, The mighty God, The everlasting Father, The Prince of Peace.
> Of the increase of his government and peace there shall be no end, upon the throne of David, and upon his kingdom, to order it, and to establish it with judgment and with justice from henceforth even for ever. The zeal of the LORD of hosts will perform this.

Unvarnished tale

Source: OTHELLO (Act I, sc. iii, l. 90)
Author: William Shakespeare (1564-1616)
First published: 1622
Type of work: Dramatic tragedy

Context: This saying means the bare, unelaborated facts of a matter—"the unvarnished truth." The original from which it is derived, however, does not convey such a stark image, but includes some truthful elaboration or

1079

interpretation. In the play, Desdemona, daughter of Brabantio, a Venetian senator, elopes with Othello, Moorish military commander in the service of Venice. Her father, aroused in the dead of night and informed of the hasty marriage, is incensed. He gathers some armed followers and starts to search out Othello. The latter, independently summoned by the duke on an affair of state, encounters the irate father and accompanies him and his followers to the council chamber where the duke is holding a late session. Othello is accused by Brabantio of bewitching his daughter, and stealing her. Witchcraft would be necessary, says he, "for nature so preposterously to err." Called upon to speak, Othello denies the charge of witchcraft, admits to the marriage, and asks pardon for his rude speech. He continues:

OTHELO
. . .
      Yet, by your gracious patience,
I will a round **unvarnished tale** deliver
Of my whole course of love, what drugs, what charms
What conjuration, and what mighty magic—
For such proceeding I am charged withal—
I won his daughter.

Unwept, unhonoured, uninterred he lies!

Source: THE ILIAD (Book XXII, l. 484, as translated by Alexander Pope)
Author: Homer (c. 850 B.C.)
First transcribed: Sixth century B.C.
Type of work: Epic poem

Context: The turning point in the Trojan War is Achilles' rejoining the battle, after Agamemnon has given back his slave girl, Briseis. Achilles slays the Trojan hero, Hector; and the Greeks run up to the corpse and "behold with wondering eyes/ His manly beauty and superior size;/ While some, ignobler, the great dead deface/ with wounds ungenerous, or with taunts disgrace. . . ." Achilles, having stripped off Hector's armor, addresses the assembled soldiers in a tribute to his friend Patroclus and in a prophecy of the fall of Troy:

"Princes and leaders! countrymen and friends!
Since now at length the powerful will of heaven
The dire destroyer to our arm has given,
Is not Troy fallen already? Haste, ye powers!
See, if already their deserted towers
Are left unmann'd; or if they yet retain
The souls of heroes, their great Hector slain.
But what is Troy, or glory what to me?

1080

Or why reflects my mind on aught but thee,
Divine Patroclus! Death has seal'd his eyes;
Unwept, unhonour'd, uninterr'd he lies!
Can his dear image from my soul depart,
Long as the vital spirit moves my heart?"

Up! mind thine own aim, and God speed the mark!

Source: TO J. W. (Stanza 5)
Author: Ralph Waldo Emerson (1803-1882)
First published: 1846
Type of work: Lyric poem

Context: Emerson berates vindictive literary critics. "Set not thy foot on graves," he admonishes John Weiss, who had written a scathing criticism of Coleridge's work. Emerson says it is unfair for a critic to try to tear apart the reputations of artists of the past. Such ghoul-like critics should let the dead rest and should immerse themselves in life: "Hear what wine and roses say." A critic commits a blasphemous sin by seeking "to unwind the shroud/ Which charitable Time/ And Nature have allowed/ To wrap the errors of a sage sublime." Instead of robbing "the dead/ Of his sad ornament," the critic should try to earn equal fame and glory:

Go, get them where he earned them when alive;
As resolutely dig or dive.

Life is too short to waste
In critic peep or cynic bark,
Quarrel or reprimand:
'T will soon be dark;
**Up! mind thine own aim, and
God speed the mark!**

Upon what meat doth this our Caesar feed, that he is grown so great?

Source: JULIUS CAESAR (Act I, sc. ii, ll. 149-150)
Author: William Shakespeare (1564-1616)
First published: 1623
Type of work: Dramatic tragedy

Context: Cassius, jealous of the fame, success, and greatness of Caesar, pours his dislike into the ears of Brutus, whom he is sounding out as a possible co-conspirator against Caesar. Brutus is a highly respected Ro-

1081

man. Although a friend of Caesar, he fears his dictatorial power and its effects on the ancient freedoms of Roman citizens. As they talk, shouts in the distance proclaim Caesar's hold on the Roman populace, who practically deify him on this day designated to celebrate his victory over Pompey, a political and military rival. Cassius reminds Brutus that Caesar, like Brutus, is a man, a Roman, and not a god; that Brutus' name is as valuable as Caesar's; that the idolizing of Caesar portends misfortunes for Rome.

CASSIUS

. . .

Why should that name be sounded more than yours?
Write them together, yours is as fair a name.
Sound them, it doth become the mouth as well.
Weigh them, it is as heavy. Conjure with 'em,
Brutus will start a spirit as soon as Caesar.
Now in the names of all the gods at once,
Upon what meat doth this our Caesar feed,
That he is grown so great? Age, thou art shamed.
Rome, thou hast lost the breed of noble bloods.

. . .

The Valley of Humiliation

Source: THE PILGRIM'S PROGRESS (Part I)
Author: John Bunyan (1628-1688)
First published: 1678
Type of work: Religious allegory

Context: The full and complete name of Bunyan's work is *The Pilgrim's Progress from This World to That Which Is to Come*. This long-titled work describes how Christian leaves his home, wife, and children to undertake the long, arduous journey from the City of Destruction to the City of Zion. During the course of the journey he encounters many temptations, in the forms of men, beasts, hideous monsters—but he overcomes them all. After struggling through the Slough of Despond, Christian reaches the Hill of Difficulty. He labors up the hill, beset by temptations still. At the top he finds a shelter, where he meets Prudence, Piety, and Charity, who prepare him for the next leg of his journey, into the Valley of Humiliation. The three accompany Christian to the base of the hill:

Then said Christian, "As it was difficult coming up, so, so far as I can see, it is dangerous going down." "Yes," said Prudence, "so it is, for it is a hard matter for a man to go down into **the Valley of Humiliation,** as thou art now, and to catch no slip by the way. . . ."

1082

The valley of the shadow of death

Source: PSALMS 23:4
Author: Unknown
First transcribed: c.400-200 B.C.
Type of work: Religious poetry

Context: The relationship between God and the individual is described metaphorically as that of the sheep and its shepherd. The poet says that since his shepherd is the Lord, his needs will be met. God guides him to lush grazing grounds and to quiet streams, so that he has peace and contentment. The Lord leads him in the right paths to uphold His name, or His reputation as a shepherd. Even though the path leads through a dark, perilous valley, where there may be thieves or dangerous beasts, the sheep, or the believer, is not afraid because his shepherd is ready to protect him with His rod and staff:

> The Lord is my shepherd; I shall not want.
> He maketh me to lie down in green pastures: he leadeth me beside the still waters.
> He restoreth my soul: he leadeth me in the paths of rigtheousness for his name's sake.
> Yea, though I walk through **the valley of the shadow of death,** I will fear no evil: for thou art with me; thy rod and thy staff they comfort me.

Vanity Fair

Source: THE PILGRIM'S PROGRESS (Part I)
Author: John Bunyan (1628-1688)
First published: 1678
Type of work: Religious allegory

Context: This is Bunyan's allegorical account of Christian's progress from sin and evil to glory and redemption, told as an account of a journey from the City of Despond to the City of Zion. The phrase "Vanity Fair" is also known, of course, through its appearance as the title of William Makepeace Thackeray's novel in the nineteenth century. In Bunyan's narrative, Christian travels through the Slough of Despond, up the Hill of Difficulty, through the Valley of Humiliation, across the Valley of the Shadow of Death, and past the very mouth of Hell. Christian meets Faithful and Evangelist, the latter being a guide for many pilgrims. Evangelist warns Christian and Faithful that they must go through the town of Vanity, where Beelzebub, Apollyon, and Legion have erected a huge fair. At the fair, warns Evangelist the travelers will be tempted by every kind of vain and worldly merchandise:

. . . They presently saw a town before them, and the name of that town is Vanity; and at the town there is kept a fair, called Vanity Fair; it is kept all the year long; it beareth the name of **Vanity Fair,** because the town where it is kept is lighter than vanity; and also because all that is there sold, or that cometh thither, is vanity.

Variety's the spice of life

Source: THE TASK (Book II, line 606)
Author: William Cowper (1731-1800)
First published: 1785
Type of work: Meditative poem in blank verse

Context: Entitled "The Time-Piece," Book II of *The Task* is full of the religiosity and moralizing beloved by followers of the Evangelical Movement, which exerted so powerful an influence on Cowper. Therefore, in writing his oft-quoted line on variety and life, Cowper is not sanctioning a healthful and welcome change in one's activity or environment—the meaning generally attributed to it by present-day quoters. On the contrary, he is expressing his scorn for the kind of people who are slaves to fashion in dress and personal adornment— "monstrous novelty and strange disguise." The popular interpretation of Cowper's line is akin to a view of Publilius Syrus (c. 42 B.C.), who said, "No pleasure endures unseasoned by variety." In context, Cowper's line reads:

> **Variety's the very spice of life,**
> That gives it all its flavour. We have run
> Through ev'ry change that fancy at the loom,
> Exhausted, has had genius to supply;
> And, studious of mutation still, discard
> A real elegance, a little us'd,
> For monstrous novelty and strange disguise.

Vaulting ambition, which o'er leaps itself

Source: MACBETH (Act I, sc. vii, l. 27)
Author: William Shakespeare (1564-1616)
First published: 1623
Type of work: Dramatic tragedy

Context: Informed by three witches that he is to be Thane of Cawdor and later king, Macbeth, valiant general of King Duncan of Scotland's army, is soon brought word that he indeed has been made Thane of Cawdor for meritorious military service, and thus the first part of the prophecy is fulfilled. Macbeth brings King Duncan home with him to spend the night. His wife, Lady Macbeth, immediately plans regicide as a means of hurrying the second half of the witches' prophecy. Ambitious, ruthless, cruel, she anticipates no remorse, but Macbeth, "too full o' th' milk of human kindness," has second thoughts and misgivings about murdering Duncan. He ruefully concludes he can find no excuse for regicide save his own ambition.

> MACBETH
> He's here in double trust;
> First, as I am his kinsman, and his subject,
> Strong both against the deed; then, as his host,
> Who should against his murderer shut the door,
> Not bear the knife myself. Besides, this Duncan
> Hath born his faculties so meek, hath been
> So clear in his great office, . . .
> I have no spur
> To prick the sides of my intent, but only
> **Vaulting ambition, which o'er leaps itself,**
> And falls on th' other—

Venture all his eggs in one basket

Source: DON QUIXOTE (Part I, Book III, chapter 9)
Author: Miguel de Cervantes Saavedra (1547-1616)
First published: 1605
Type of work: Satirical novel

Context: Having freed a group of galley slaves, Don Quixote orders them to proceed to Toboso and tell his lady Dulcinea about the feats of her Knight. Sancho begs his master to leave that part of the country before the Holy Brotherhood, the rural constabulary, comes after them. He uses sophistry to persuade the warrior knight:

> . . . to withdraw is not to run away, and to stay is no wise action, when there is more reason to fear than to hope; 'tis the part of a wise man to keep himself today for tomorrow, and not **venture all his eggs in one basket.** And for all I'm but a clown, or a bumpkin, as you may say, yet I'd have you to know I know what's what, and have always taken care of the main chance; therefore don't be ashamed of being ruled by me. . . .

Verray, parfit gentil knyght

Source: THE CANTERBURY TALES (Prologue, l. 72)
Author: Geoffrey Chaucer (1343?-1400)
First transcribed: c.1387-1392
Type of work: Collection of tales

Context: A group of people, planning a pilgrimage to Canterbury to the shrine of Thomas à Becket, have met by chance at the Tabard Inn in Southwark. They decide to travel together and to pass the time telling two stories each on the way to Canterbury and two on the way back. In the Prologue Chaucer describes each of the pilgrims in great and striking detail. The first to be described, because of his rank, is the knight, who fills his role to perfection. He "loved chivalrie,/ Trouthe and honour, fredom and curteisie." He was a good Christian and brave in battle. Chaucer in his description clearly approves of this man:

> And though that he were worthy, he was wys,
> And of his port as meke as is a mayde.
> He never yet no vileynye ne sayde
> In all his lyf unto no maner wight.
> He was a **verray, parfit gentil knyght.**

The very flower of youth

Source: THE EUNUCH (Act II, sc. iii, l. 315)
Author: Terence (Publius Terentius Afer, c.190-159 B.C.)
First transcribed: Second century B.C.
Type of work: Dramatic comedy

Context: Parmeno, the sly servant of the title, has just discovered that his young master is in love with a slave girl. Chaerea asks his servant to be "useful to him" as promised, for "this girl isn't like other girls . . . a trifle plump, they say that she's a prizefighter." But he does not care what they say about her, to him she is beautiful.

PARMENO
And what's this girl of yours like?

CHAEREA
Oh, quite a new style of face.

PARMENO
Amazing!

CHAEREA

Natural complexion, strong and healthy.

PARMENO

What age?

CHAEREA

Age? Sixteen.

PARMENO

The very flower of youth.

CHAEREA

Now you must either by force or fraud or entreaty make her mine; I don't care a straw how, so long as I have her.

The very hairs of your head are all numbered

Source: MATTHEW 10:30
Author: Unknown (traditionally Matthew the Apostle)
First transcribed: c.75-100
Type of work: Gospel

Context: Jesus, after the Sermon on the Mount, goes about the country teaching the people, healing the ill, lame, blind, dumb, and crazed, and raising the dead. Finally choosing his twelve disciples, he instructs them in their mission and warns them of their difficult life. They may expect, He says, even torture and death. Declaring that the death of the body is unimportant when compared with the death of the body and soul, He reminds them of God's concern for the small sparrow and, therefore, of God's greater concern for them:

Are not two sparrows sold for a farthing? and one of them shall not fall on the ground without your Father.
But **the very hairs of your head are all numbered.**
Fear ye not therefore, ye are of more value than many sparrows.

The very pink of perfection

Source: SHE STOOPS TO CONQUER (Act I, sc. i)
Author: Oliver Goldsmith (1728-1774)
First published: 1774
Type of work: Dramatic comedy

Context: Goldsmith's rollicking comedy-farce introduced to the stage some of the most memorable comic characters in English literature One

1087

of these is Tony Lumpkin, the son of Mrs. Hardcastle by her first marriage. She is anxious to have him marry her niece, Miss Neville, who lives with the Hardcastles in their rambling mansion in the country. Miss Neville has no intention of marrying Tony and is waiting for the arrival of her own sweetheart, who is en route from London with his friend Mr. Marlow. It is Mr. Hardcastle's hope that Marlow will be attracted to his daughter, Miss Hardcastle. Hardcastle has told his daughter of his plan, and she in turn tells Miss Neville. After discussing Marlow's qualifications for a few moments, Miss Hardcastle changes the subject.

MISS HARDCASTLE
. . . But how goes on your own affair, my dear? has my mother been courting you for my brother Tony, as usual?

MISS NEVILLE
I have just come from one of our agreeable *tête-à-têtes*. She has been saying a hundred tender things, and setting off her pretty monster as **the very pink of perfection.**

MISS HARDCASTLE
And her partiality is such, that she actually thinks him so . . .

Vice itself lost half its evil by losing all its grossness

Source: REFLECTIONS ON THE REVOLUTION IN FRANCE
Author: Edmund Burke (1729-1797)
First published: 1790
Type of work: Political treatise

Context: The characteristic passion of Burke's life was his love of order and *noblesse oblige*. In spite of the varying attitudes he held toward the different parties in England during his political career, one may easily find the key to his consistency in this central principle. When the King's party sought to increase the royal prerogative, he resisted; when the sympathizers with the Revolution sought, as Burke thought, to abolish government, he resisted. In both instances he believed he discerned an attack on either liberty or order. He had a profound respect for the accumulated wisdom and traditions of centuries of experience, and held that the bounds of liberty should be enlarged with great caution and circumspection. That a political system had lasted a long time argued that it must to a large extent fulfill its purpose and that, therefore, it should not be rashly changed. To him the sudden destruction of the political structure signaled a heinous alteration in the nature of man and his ethical code:

. . . It is gone, that sensibility of principle, . . . which ennobled whatever it touched, and under which **vice itself lost half its evil by losing all its grossness.**

1088

Village Virus

Source: MAIN STREET (Chapter 13)
Author: Sinclair Lewis (1885-1951)
First published: 1920
Type of work: Novel

Context: Main Street is a satire on the narrowness, sterility, and inadequacies of the small village. Carol Kennicott, an idealist, having married Dr. Will Kennicott of Gopher Prairie with the enthusiastic intention of beautifying and vitalizing his dreary hometown, finds to her dismay that the town has no will for improvement. Her ideas are met unsympathetically, and her efforts at reform serve only to separate her from the townspeople. Alternating between despair and hope, she grasps at every opportunity to rebuild Gopher Prairie. She tries to organize clubs, to initiate movements, and to interest the right people in her schemes. Each person to whom she appeals discloses in some way his indifference to reforms. Guy Pollock, a conservative lawyer, tells her that Gopher Prairie is not particularly bad; it is like all villages. Some day the village will be obsolete, he says. Charming cities will take its place. When asked why he stays in the dull village, Pollock replies:

> I have the **Village Virus**. . . . The Village Virus is the germ which . . . infects ambitious people who stay too long in the provinces.

The villain still pursued her

Source: THE PHOENIX (Act I, sc. iii)
Author: Milton Nobles (1847-1924)
First published: 1890
Type of work: Melodrama

Context: Carroll Graves has lost all his money and is reduced to living in an old garret that he shares with Dionysius O'Gall. To earn his living, Graves writes a continued story for the *Weekly Chambermaid's Own,* but circumstances have caused him to neglect his writing for several weeks, with the result that his editor and his readers are anxious to know what has happened to the heroine. One evening, after several interruptions, the author begins another installment of his serial. In Graves' story the heroine, Anastasia Sophronisbia, has received an anonymous letter telling her to meet her lover, Charles Arthur Algernon Swinburne Augustus, under an old oak tree near her father's castle. Upon arriving at the spot, Anastasia is greeted by the countenance of the villain, Count de Jerkmikoff. The villain tries to seize her, but Anastasia flees, calling out for her lover. The villain in pursuit mutters that the girl shall be his.

While the maiden, with profound originality and unique heroism, replied, Back! back, base violin!—back, base villain! Villain of the deepest dye! thy hellish machinations I defy! me life you may gain in this wild endeavor, but me spotless honor, hardly ev—never! never! And **the villain still pursued her.**

Villainy is no bad weapon against villainy

Source: MORALIA ("On Shyness," Chapter 13)
Author: Plutarch (c.45-c.125)
First transcribed: 90-110
Type of work: Ethical essay

Context: In this essay Plutarch is talking about the various evils of shyness, which is "an excess of modesty." He says, "We must avoid too much timidity and fear of censure, since many have played the coward, and abandoned noble ventures, more from fear of a bad name than of the dangers to be undergone, not being able to bear a bad reputation." "We must contrive a harmonious blending of the two, that shall remove the shamelessness of pertinacity, and the weakness of excessive modesty." Turning the coin over, Plutarch says, "All seemly and modest requests we ought to comply with, not bashfully but heartily," and should reject injurious or unreasonable ones. Zeno demonstrated this truth by his statement when he met a young man trying to avoid a friend who desired him to perjure himself on his behalf, "And dare not you stand up boldly against him for what is right?" Plutarch continues:

. . . For he that said **"villainy is no bad weapon against villainy"** taught people the bad practice of standing on one's defence against vice by imitating it; but to get rid of those who shamelessly and unblushingly importune us by their own effrontery, and not to gratify the immodest in their disgraceful desires through false modesty, is the right and proper conduct of sensible people.

Virtue could see to do what Virtue would

Source: COMUS (Line 373)
Author: John Milton (1608-1674)
First published: 1637
Type of work: Masque

Context: The story of the masque, which was written to celebrate the installation of the Earl of Bridgewater as President of Wales and in which his three children acted, deals with the imaginary attempt of the young people to reach Ludlow Castle, the Earl's seat. They must pass through a dark wood, inhabited by the enchanter, Comus, son of Bacchus and Ceres, and his attendant evil spirits. The sister becomes separated from her brothers, the younger of whom fears for her safety. The Elder Brother, however, is unperturbed; wise people, he claims, often seek solitude for contemplation; in addition, her innate virtue will be her protection.

> **Virtue could see to do what Virtue would**
> By her own radiant light, though sun and moon
> Were in the flat sea sunk. And Wisdom's self
> Oft seeks to sweet retired Solitude,
> Where with her best nurse Contemplation
> She plumes her feathers, and lets grow her wings. . . .

Virtue is like a rich stone, best plain set

Source: ESSAYS OR COUNSELS, CIVIL AND MORAL ("Of Beauty")
Author: Francis Bacon (1561-1626)
First published: 1612
Type of work: Moral essay

Context: In this essay, Bacon maintains that dignity and "gracious motion" and "great spirit" are more important than "delicate features," accomplishment or studied behavior. He also claims that since youth does not usually have these qualities, "no youth can be comely but by pardon." He begins his essay and sets his theme with this statement:

> **Virtue is like a rich stone, best plain set:** and surely virtue is best in a body that is comely, though not of delicate features; and that hath rather dignity of presence, than beauty of aspect.

Visit the sins of the fathers upon the children

Source: EXODUS 20:5
Author: Unknown
First transcribed: 1000-300 B.C.
Type of work: Religious history

Context: Although parts of the book of Exodus go back to the twelfth century B.C., the recording of the Mosaic law comes at about the same time as Euripides wrote a similar theme into one of his plays, *Phrixus,* of which only a few fragments are extant: "The gods visit the sins of the fathers upon the children." Some two millennia later Shakespeare comments in *The Merchant of Venice,* appropriate to the Judaic background of the play, "The sins of the father are to be laid upon the children." The most famous occurrence, however, is that of Jehovah calling upon Moses to transcribe the Commandments:

> And God spoke all these words, saying, I am the Lord thy God, which have brought thee out of the land of Egypt, out of the house of bondage.
> Thou shalt have no other gods before me.
> Thou shalt not make unto thee any graven image, or any likeness of any thing that is in heaven above, or that is the earth beneath, or that is in the water under the earth:
> Thou shalt not bow down thyself to them, nor serve them: for I the Lord thy God am a jealous God, **visiting the iniquity of the fathers upon the children** unto the third and fourth generation of them that hate me;
> And showing mercy unto thousands of them that love me, and keep my commandments.

The voice of one crying in the wilderness

Source: MATTHEW 3:3
Author: Unknown (traditionally Matthew the Apostle)
First transcribed: c.75-100
Type of work: Gospel

Context: Following the death of Herod, Joseph, having fled with his family to Egypt before the slaying of the innocents, is told by the Lord in a dream that he might return safely to Israel. Fearing, however, the new king of Judea, Archelaus, Joseph goes instead to the city of Nazareth in Galilee. Several years later, John the Baptist, wearing a camel's hair garment and eating locusts and wild honey, is found preaching in the wilderness of Judea. He calls upon the people to repent, likens his voice in the desert and his message of preparation for the coming of the Lord to those of Isaiah (Isaiah 40:3), and exhorts his hearers to smooth the road for the Lord as for a mighty king:

> For this is he that was spoken of by the Prophet Esaias, saying, **The voice of one crying in the wilderness,** Prepare ye the way of the Lord, make his paths straight.

1092

The voice of the people

Source: LETTER TO CHARLEMAGNE
Author: Alcuin (732-804)
First transcribed: c.797
Type of work: Letter of advice

Context: Alcuin of York, a British cleric who left his school in England to establish a center of learning for Charles, is remembered as the most brilliant member of Charlemagne's entourage. His accomplishments are many: educator, statesman, administrator, priest, poet, and scholar. While he suggested humanity as a keynote to ruling, he is more nearly associated with the theory of terror and antedates the teachings of Machiavelli. *"Vox populi, vox Dei,"* is Ciceronian and meant to suggest the beginnings of democratic sentiments in government, something the sage of York did not intend:

> Great as your power as King, so greatly do you excel all in fervour of holy religion. Happy the people who rejoice in such a Prince. . . . the people, by divine ruling, is to be led, not to be followed, and for witness persons of high standing are to be preferred. The saying, **"The voice of the people** is the voice of God," is not to be listened to, since the seething of the crowd is always near to madness. . . .

The voice of the turtle

Source: THE SONG OF SOLOMON 2:12
Author: Unknown
First transcribed: c.300-200 B.C.
Type of work: Lyric poetry

Context: The exuberance of youth in the springtime, the joyous infatuation of tender love, enhanced by the re-awakening of the flora and fauna, in the spring's dewy freshness flow elatedly through the verses of this song:

> The flowers appear on the earth; the time of the singing of birds is come, and **the voice of the turtle** is heard in our land;
> The fig tree putteth forth her green figs, and the vines with the tender grape give a good smell. Arise, my love, my fair one, and come away.
> O my dove, that art in the clefts of the rock, in the secret places of the stairs, let me see thy countenance, let me hear thy voice; for sweet is thy voice, and thy countenance is comely.
> Take us the foxes, the little foxes, that spoil the vines: for our vines have tender grapes.

A vote on the tallysheet is worth two in the box

Source: MR. DOOLEY'S PHILOSOPHY ("Casual Observations")
Author: Finley Peter Dunne (1867-1936)
First published: 1900
Type of work: Humorous dialogue

Context: At the end of this collection of conversations between Mr. Dooley, the saloon-keeper, and his friend, Hennessy, appear some of Mr. Dooley's aphoristic utterances. Dooley, a wordly-wise Irishman, considers himself an expert on many subjects, including politics, which he analyzes with a tolerant cynicism. This obser-vation of his on the ballot-box is typical, proceeding from his conviction that everything connected with public office is dishonestly or deceptively manipualted. Many a vote, he implies, that is placed in the voting box, disappears before the votes are counted and recorded on the tally-sheets.

A vote on th' tallysheet is worth two in the box.

The wages of sin is death

Source: ROMANS 6:23
Author: Paul
First transcribed: c.50-60
Type of work: Religious epistle

Context: The apostle Paul, who is al-most universally credited with writing this letter addressed to the Roman Christians, declares that all people are in need of the grace of God, sal-vation from sin. The Jews, though they have received the laws given by God, are unable to obey the laws completely and to save themselves; hence, both Jews and Gentiles are un-able to attain eternal life without Christ's intervention. When Jesus died, He carried the sinfulness of mankind to the grave with Him. Sin, dead, had no newness of life. Christ, then, freed from the sinfulness of mankind through His death, rose from the dead in the purity of resur-rected eternal life. Those who follow Jesus in baptism also bury their sin-fulness in death as they are baptized; thus, they too share with the Master the purity of the resurrected eternal life. Followers of Christ, having ac-cepted the pardoning grace of God, are in bondage to righteousness; those who serve sin are enslaved by death. Paul concludes:

But now being made free from sin, and become servants to God, ye have your fruit unto holiness, and the end everlasting life.
For **the wages of sin is death;** but the gift of God is eternal life through Jesus Christ our Lord.

Walk with the Gods

Source: MEDITATIONS (Book V, 27, as translated by C. R. Haines)
Author: Marcus Aurelius Antoninus (121-180)
First transcribed: c.171-173
Type of work: Philosophical essay

Context: Marcus Aurelius, the Roman emperor who wrote his meditations in Greek, was a Stoic philosopher. He believed that man should rely on the divine reason within himself and that external pleasures and sufferings should be matters of indifference. In order to walk or live with the gods, man should use their gift of reason.

> **Walk with the Gods!** And he does walk with the Gods, who lets them see his soul invariably satisfied with its lot and carrying out the will of that "genius," a particle of himself, which Zeus has given to every man as his Captain and guide—and this is none other than each man's intelligence and reason.

War is hell

Source: OHIO STATE JOURNAL
Author: William Tecumseh Sherman (1820-1891)
First published: 1880
Type of work: Extempore speech

Context: William Tecumseh Sherman, general in the Union army and participant in most of the major battles of the Civil War, is noted chiefly for his devastating march from Atlanta to Savannah. Before his death, the saying "War is hell" came to be ascribed to him, but a search of newspapers and speeches produces no such memorable remark. Attributed to speeches at various occasions, the exact remark may not have been uttered, but on August 11, 1880, at Columbus, Ohio, following a speech by President Hayes, Sherman spoke briefly to the Union veterans the words seemingly closest in meaning to his famous statement. The *Ohio State Journal* reported the words:

> There is many a boy here today who looks on war as all glory, but, boys, **it is all hell.** You can bear this warning voice to generations yet to come. I look upon war with horror, but if it has to come I am here.

Wars and rumors of wars

Source: MATTHEW 24:6
Author: Unknown (traditionally Matthew the Apostle)
First transcribed: c.75-100
Type of work: Gospel

Context: Jesus, after His confrontation in the temple in Jerusalem by the Pharisees and Sadducees, conservative followers of the law, denounces them and leaves the temple. Declaring to His disciples that not one stone of the temple will be left upon another, He goes to the Mount of Olives. When He is questioned about the time of the destruction of the temple and about the sign of the Second Coming and the Day of Judgment, He warns them that they must not be led astray by the many who will come in His name before the final day. The end, however, in spite of the wars that have taken place and will take place, is not yet at hand:

> And ye shall hear of **wars and rumors of wars;** see that ye be not troubled: for all these things must come to pass, but the end is not yet.
> For nation shall rise against nation, and kingdom against kingdom: and there shall be famines, and pestilences, and earthquakes, in divers places.
> All these are the beginning of sorrows.

Was ever poet so trusted before?

Source: THE LIFE OF SAMUEL JOHNSON, LL.D. (For 1774)
Author: James Boswell (1740-1795)
First published: 1791
Type of work: Biography

Context: The question in this quotation is about Oliver Goldsmith, well-known to both Samuel Johnson and his biographer, James Boswell. Obviously Dr. Johnson could scarcely believe that so poor a credit risk as a writer could slip so far into debt as Goldsmith apparently did before his death. Johnson asked the question rhetorically in a letter to Boswell written on July 4, 1774. Goldsmith died three months before, on April 4th. Although he had acquired a good literary reputation during his lifetime and had made considerable money, Goldsmith died far in debt, owing what was at that time a small fortune. In a paragraph in the letter, Johnson writes:

> Of poor dear Dr. Goldsmith there is little to be told, more than the papers have made publick. He died of a fever, made, I

am afraid, more violent by uneasiness of mind. His debts began to be heavy, and all his resources were exhausted. Sir Joshua [Reynolds] is of opinion that he owed not less than two thousand pounds. **Was ever poet so trusted before?**

Was ever woman in this humor wooed?

Source: KING RICHARD THE THIRD (Act I, sc. ii, l. 228)
Author: William Shakespeare (1564-1616)
First published: 1597
Type of work: Historical drama

Context: Richard, Duke of Gloucester, sets about working the evil he had announced in his opening speech. As the funeral cortege of Henry VI, whom Richard slew, passes, Richard halts it and begins paying suit to Lady Anne, widow of Edward, Prince of Wales, whom Richard had also slain. At first Lady Anne curses and defiles him. Richard begins his speech by denying that he killed Henry; then he admits that he did slay him. Lady Anne's anger and hatred apparently thaw. After arranging for a later meeting with her, and after her departure, Richard further reveals his villainy. He is going to woo her and use her. But he can only despise a woman who so quickly forgets her husband's murder and will be wooed by his "misshapen" murderer.

RICHARD
Was ever woman in this humour wooed?
Was ever woman in this humour won?
I'll have her, but I will not keep her long.
What, I that killed her husband, and his father,

. . .

And yet to win her? All the world to nothing.

. . .

Was everything by starts, and nothing long

Source: ABSALOM AND ACHITOPHEL (Part I, l. 548)
Author: John Dryden (1631-1700)
First published: 1681
Type of work: Satiric poem

Context: Much of the merit in Dryden's poem lies in its character sketches of persons prominent in the plot of the 1670's to place the Duke of Monmouth, Charles II's illegitimate son, in the place of the Duke of York as the lawful successor to the British throne. The plotters, led by

1097

the Earl of Shaftesbury and the Duke of Buckingham, sought to replace the Duke of York because of his Roman Catholic tendencies. Dryden himself thought the satirical characterization of the Duke of Buckingham as Zimri in this poem to be one of his best pieces of work, "The character of Zimri in my *Absalom* is . . . worth the whole poem; it is not bloody, but it is ridiculous enough; and he, for whom it was intended, was too witty to resent it as an injury. If I had railed, I might have suffered for it justly; but I managed my own work more happily, perhaps more dexterously." Dryden wrote of Buckingham:

> A man so various, that he seem'd to be
> Not one, but all Mankinds Epitome.
> Stiff in Opinions, always in the wrong;
> **Was everything by starts, and nothing long:**
> But in the course of one revolving Moon,
> Was Chymist, Fidler, States-Man, and Buffoon.
> Then all for Women, Painting, Rhiming, Drinking;
> Besides ten thousand freaks that dy'd in thinking.

Was there another Troy for her to burn?

Source: NO SECOND TROY
Author: William Butler Yeats (1865-1939)
First published: 1910
Type of work: Lyric poem

Context: The poet asks why he should blame the beautiful girl even if she did make his days miserable and incited ignorant and mean people to violence, attempting deeds too great for them. He rationalizes the futility of trying to resist her and explains her behavior in these lines:

> What could have made her peaceful with a mind
> That nobleness made simple as a fire,
> With beauty like a tightened bow, a kind
> That is not natural in an age like this,
> Being high and solitary and most stern?
> Why, what could she have done, being what she is?
> **Was there another Troy for her to burn?**

Watchman, what of the night?

Source: ISAIAH 21:11
Author: Isaiah
First transcribed: c.800-200 B.C.
Type of work: Religious prophecy and exhortation

Context: Isaiah, prophet of the Lord, pronounces his vision of "Judah and Jerusalem in the days of Uzziah, Jotham, Ahaz, and Hezekiah, kings of Judah." Proclaiming the Lord's wrath for the sins of His chosen people, Isaiah urges obedience to the will of the Almighty. Jerusalem and Judah will become the center of the law of the Lord. Having prophesied the appearance of a messiah and having received a vision of God on His throne, the naked Isaiah goes about announcing the future conquest of Egypt and Ethiopia by Assyria. A later prophet, calling himself "watchman," foresees the anxiety of Judah's neighbor, Edom (Dumah). The answer of the watchman may mean the inquirer will have to wait for further information regarding the dark times of the nation:

> The burden of Dumah. He calleth to me out of Seir, **Watchman, what of the night?** Watchman, what of the night?
> The watchman said, The morning cometh, and also the night: if ye will inquire, inquire ye: return, come.

Water, water, everywhere

Source: THE RIME OF THE ANCIENT MARINER (Part II, stanza 9)
Author: Samuel Taylor Coleridge (1772-1834)
First published: 1798
Type of work: Literary ballad

Context: "The Rime of the Ancient Mariner" appeared first in *Lyrical Ballads* (1798), published jointly by Coleridge and William Wordsworth (1770-1850). For that book, Coleridge had taken as his province "persons and characters supernatural, or at least romantic." The supernatural machinery of the poem emerges after the Mariner has killed an albatross. At first his shipmates are angered, but when the mist surrounding the boat clears, they insist it is right "such birds to slay." Now retribution begins. An elemental spirit who loved the albatross has followed the ship and becalms it:

> Day after day, day after day,
> We stuck, nor breath nor motion;
> As idle as a painted ship
> Upon a painted ocean.

> **Water, water, every where,**
> And all the boards did shrink;
> **Water, water, every where,**
> Nor any drop to drink.

The wave of the future

Source: THE WAVE OF THE FUTURE (Page 37)
Author: Anne Morrow Lindbergh (1907-   )
First published: 1940
Type of work: Essay

Context: This is a keenly reasoned, forcefully presented argument defending an American policy of neutrality in regard to the early aggression of Nazism. Aware that man can view the events of his time only in the narrow, limited confines of his conditioned perception, Mrs. Lindbergh, discarding the popular opinions of the day, seeks to evaluate the significance of the critical time around the turn of the decade in the light of a broadened perspective. She relates the revolution in Germany with World War I, the Russian revolution, and the rise of Fascism and other such movements characteristic of a restless, changing world. Though she does not defend militarism, she feels that ultimate good may come from what presently is apparent evil. Nazism, then, is actually a part, though a violent part, of the wave of the future. America's hope is not in suppressing the evils of Nazism; it is rather in making herself worthy and capable of a new future by reaffirming her own values and ideals. The forces that prompted Germany to launch an aggressive war should prompt America to a spiritual revolution. In her conclusion she restates the thesis of her essay:

> **The wave of the future** is coming and there is no fighting it. What is our course to be? Shall we leave our own troubles and crusade abroad? . . . The price of peace is to be a strong nation, not only physically but also morally and spiritually.

The way of all flesh

Source: WESTWARD HO! (Act II, sc. ii, l. 204)
Authors: John Webster (1580?-1625?), in collaboration with Thomas Dekker (1570?-1641?)
First published: 1607
Type of work: Dramatic comedy

Context: In *Westward Ho!* the expression "going the way of all flesh" is a joke. Monopoly, a nephew of the Earl, asks Mistress Birdlime, a procuress, if she has seen his uncle. She says she just saw him going the way of all flesh—into the kitchen. Although the inference here is that flesh is cooked in the kitchen, the expression usually means to die, as all flesh is mortal; for instance, Thomas Heywood in *The Golden Age* (1611) says: "If I go by land, and miscarry, then I go the way of all flesh"; in other words, he will die. So it is in Thomas Heywood's *Second Part of* the *Fair Maid of the West* (1631): "She by this is gone the way of all flesh." In his *Sketches by Boz:* "Mr. Watkins Tottle" (1835), Charles Dickens brings out the meaning in: "He . . . allowed us something to live on till he went the way of all flesh." When Samuel Butler names his novel *The Way of All Flesh,* he is referring to the frailties of humanity caused by the desires of the flesh. The passage in *Westward Ho!* is:

MONOPOLY

Saw you my uncle?

BIRDLIME

I saw him even now going **the way of all flesh,** that's to say, toward the kitchen. . . .

We are all in the gutter, but some of us are looking at the stars

Source: LADY WINDERMERE'S FAN (Act III)
Author: Oscar Wilde (1856-1900)
First published: 1893
Type of work: Dramatic comedy

Context: Lady Windermere, thinking her husband is causing a scandal with another woman, a Mrs. Erlynne, decides to accept the proposal of Lord Darlington, who loves her, and goes to Darlington's apartment. Mrs. Erlynne, who is actually the mother of Lady Windermere, learns what her daughter has done and wants to save her from committing the error that she herself committed twenty years earlier. Mrs. Erlynne finds her daughter alone in Darlington's rooms and persuades her to return to her home before Darlington gets to the apartment. When voices are heard outside, Lady Windermere hides behind the curtain, and Mrs. Erlynne leaves through a door. Darlington appears with several guests, among them Lord Windermere and Lord Augustus (Tuppy) Lorton. Lord Augustus, who secretly plans to marry Mrs. Erlynne, says that he has promised her not to play cards or drink again. One guest says women like to find men bad and leave them unattractively good. Darlington comments, "They always do find us bad!" Dumby, another guest, answers, "I don't think we are bad. I think we are all good, except Tuppy."

DARLINGTON
"No, **we are all in the gutter, but some of us are looking at the stars.**"

1101

We are here as on a darkling plain

Source: DOVER BEACH (Stanza 5)
Author: Matthew Arnold (1822-1888)
First published: 1867
Type of work: Lyric poem

Context: Arnold, critic of nineteenth-century life, saw in his contemporaries only narrowness in thought and confusion in religion. Observing with a loved one the ebb and flow of the full sea, which brings in an "eternal note of sadness," he is reminded that Sophocles heard the same sound on the Aegaean. To Arnold, the "Sea of Faith" was once full, but only a melancholy, withdrawing roar comes to the land now. He pleads with his love to remain with him to soften the harshness of the religious and political struggles. He says:

> Ah, love, let us be true
> To one another! for the world, which seems
> To lie before us like a land of dreams,
> So various, so beautiful, so new,
> Hath really neither joy, nor love, nor light,
> Nor certitude, nor peace, nor help for pain;
> And **we are here as on a darkling plain**
> Swept with confused alarms of struggle and flight,
> Where ignorant armies clash by night.

We are not sure of sorrow, and joy was never sure

Source: THE GARDEN OF PROSERPINE (Stanza 10)
Author: Algernon Charles Swinburne (1837-1909)
First published: 1866
Type of work: Lyric poem

Context: A well-known expression of weariness with life, this poem is the monologue of one who has found refuge, from all the vain activity and perpetual change of which life is composed, in the garden of Proserpine, queen of the regions of the dead. All things come at last to her: men, flowers, seasons, loves and hopes. But as the good in life withers and passes away, so does the evil; and at last all men must be grateful that all things have an end: Life even at its best is burdensome, for one must always fear unexpected change. Nothing is permanent, nothing is reliable or certain. Sorrow is often only a transient state of mind, and joys are ephemeral.

> **We are not sure of sorrow,**
> **And joy was never sure;**

To-day will die to-morrow;
Time stoops to no man's lure;
And love, grown faint and fretful,
With lips but half regretful
Sighs, and with eyes forgetful
Weeps that no loves endure.

We are such stuff as dreams are made on

Source: THE TEMPEST (Act IV, sc. i, ll. 156-157)
Author: William Shakespeare (1564-1616)
First published: 1623
Type of work: Tragi-comedy

Context: Prospero, a magician, rules a mysterious island, commanding spirits of the air, including Ariel and other sprites and wonders. He has a lovely daughter named Miranda. The magician causes a tempest which drives a ship onto shore. All on it survive, but Prospero causes a handsome young prince, Ferdinand, to be separated from the others, and has Ariel lead Ferdinand to him. Ferdinand, enchanted, sees Miranda, and falls in love with her, and she with him. Now, before his cell, Prospero presents for Prince Ferdinand, whom he has released from enchantment, and Miranda, a prenuptial pageant, enacted by spirits in the guise of Iris, Juno, Ceres, and nymphs. Suddenly, he puts an end to the masque with a famous speech.

PROSPERO
. . .
Our revels now are ended. These our actors,
As I foretold you, were all spirits, and
All melted into air, into thin air,
. . .
And like this insubstantial pageant faded
Leave not a rack behind. **We are such stuff
As dreams are made on;** and our little life
Is rounded with a sleep.
. . .

We are the hollow men

Source: THE HOLLOW MEN (I, Stanza 1)
Author: T(homas) S(tearns) Eliot (1888-1965)
First published: 1925
Type of work: Metaphysical poem

Context: The poem from which this quotation comes has been taken as an indictment of a whole generation, people whose lives are empty because

1103

they can believe nothing. Like the vast crowd of souls that Dante encountered on the dark plain in the vestibule of Hell, these men lived "without blame, and without praise." And just as Virgil said to Dante, "Let us not speak of them; but look, and pass;" so, in Eliot's poem, those who go into the realm of Death with "direct eyes," those who have lived affirmative lives, remember these people— if they remember them at all—only as figures stuffed with straw, grotesque parodies of men.

> **We are the hollow men**
> We are the stuffed men
> Leaning together
> Headpiece filled with straw. Alas!
> Our dried voices, when
> We whisper together
> Are quiet and meaningless
> As wind in dry grass . . .

We are truly heirs of all the ages

Source: FRAGMENTS OF SCIENCE (Vol. II, "Matter and Force")
Author: John Tyndall (1820-1893)
First published: 1871
Type of work: Lecture printed as essay

Context: John Tyndall, Irish physicist and teacher, who carried out original research in various branches of physics, was noted for his popular lectures in England and America on science. In his lecture called "Matter and Force," delivered to the working men of Dundee and later included in his *Fragments of Science,* he speaks informally of the properties of matter and the forces at work in it. After explaining molecular attraction and the power produced by combining certain materials, he points out that once the initial power from the combination has been used no more power comes from the attraction. Then he digresses to comment on man's position in the world:

> And here we might halt for a moment to remark on that tendency, so prevalent in the world, to regard everything as made for human use. Those who entertain this notion, hold, I think, an overweening opinion of their own importance in the system of nature. Flowers bloomed before men saw them, and the quantity of power wasted before man could utilise it is all but infinite compared with what now remains. **We are truly heirs of all the ages;** but as honest men it behoves us to learn the extent of our inheritance, and as brave ones not to whimper if it should prove less that we had supposed.

We boil at different degrees

Source: ELOQUENCE
Author: Ralph Waldo Emerson (1803-1882)
First published: 1870
Type of work: Moral essay

Context: Emerson discusses the art of oration. An audience is a "social organism," an instrument which is manipulated by the skilled orator, but it is also "a constant metre of the orator." The eloquent speaker can dishearten or uplift his listeners, and he "rules the minds of men," as Plato said. Thus the skilled orator enjoys great power. But he must have robust health and "strength of character," and his delivery must be "attractive and interesting." He must have "powers, intellect, will, sympathy, organs, and, over all, good-fortune. . . ." He must be "a substantial personality," and he "must have the fact, and know how to tell it" poetically. "Eloquence is the appropriate organ of the highest personal energy . . . the truly eloquent man is a sane man with power to communicate his sanity." "Every man is an orator," but we are not all inspired to oratory by the same stimuli:

> It is the doctrine of the popular music-masters, that whoever can speak can sing. So, probably, every man is eloquent once in his life. Our temperaments differ in capacity of heat, or **we boil at different degrees.** One man is brought to the boiling point by the excitement of conversation in the parlor. The waters, of course, are not very deep. He has a two-inch enthusiasm, a pattypan ebullition. Another requires the additional caloric of a multitude, and a public debate; a third needs an antagonist, or a hot indignation; a fourth needs a revolution; and a fifth, nothing less than the grandeur of absolute ideas, the splendors and shades of Heaven and Hell.

We cannot all be masters

Source: OTHELLO (Act I, sc. i, l. 43)
Author: William Shakespeare (1564-1616)
First published: 1622
Type of work: Dramatic tragedy

Context: Iago, ancient (or ensign) to Othello, a Moor in the military service of Venice, is angry and envious because he was not made Othello's lieutenant. He is pouring out his wrath to Roderigo, a young gentleman of Venice, who fancies himself in love with Desdemona, bride of Othello. Roderigo suggests that if Iago is so disgruntled, he should not sign on with Othello, to which suggestion Iago replies:

O sir content you.
I follow him to serve my turn upon him.
We cannot all be masters, nor all masters
Cannot be truly followed. You shall mark
Many a duteous and knee-crooking knave,
That doting on his own obsequious bondage,
Wears out his time, much like his master's ass,
For naught but provender, and when he's old cashiered.
Whip me such honest knaves. Others there are
Who trimmed in forms, and visages of duty,
Keep yet their hearts attending on themselves;

. . .

These fellows have some soul,
And such a one do I profess myself.

. . .

We don't give bread with one fish-ball

Source: ONE FISH-BALL
Author: George Martin Lane (1823-1897)
First published: 1855
Type of work: Humorous poem

Context: This ballad, according to the editor of *Harper's* magazine in 1855, was very popular among Harvard University students; it tells the story of a man who, apparently spurning his wife's cooking, goes to buy his dinner in town. Finding that he has only six cents, he chooses a cheap restaurant but discovers that the least expensive item, "two fish balls," costs twelve and a half cents. In embarrassment he orders one fish-ball, then a slice of bread, whereupon the waiter shouts, for all to hear, this famous line.

The waiter he to him doth call,
And gently whispers—*"one* Fish-ball."

The waiter roars it through the hall,
The guests they start at *"one* Fish-ball."

The guest then says, quite ill at ease,
"A piece of bread, Sir, if you please."

The waiter roars it through the hall,
"We don't give bread with one Fish-ball."

1106

We hanged our harps upon the willows

Source: PSALMS 137:2
Author: Unknown
First transcribed: c.400-200 B.C.
Type of work: Religious poetry

Context: The captive Israelites, the psalmist recalls, would sit on the Babylonian river banks and weep for Jerusalem. Sorrowful in a foreign land, they are unable to meet the demands of their captors that they entertain them with Jewish songs. Proclaiming his faithfulness to Jerusalem, the bard curses the sons of Cain, who aided the Babylonians in destroying the temple and the holy city. The poet describes the plight of the Hebrew prisoners:

> By the rivers of Babylon, there we sat down, yea we wept, when we remembered Zion.
> **We hanged our harps upon the willows** in the midst thereof.
> For there they that carried us away captive required of us a song; and they that wasted us required of us mirth, saying, Sing us one of the songs of Zion.
> How shall we sing the Lord's song in a strange land?
> If I forget thee, O Jerusalem, let my right hand forget her cunning.

We have changed all that

Source: LE MÉDECIN MALGRE LUI (Act II, sc. vi)
Author: Molière (Jean Baptiste Poquelin, 1622-1673)
First published: 1666
Type of work: Dramatic comedy

Context: The Physician in Spite of Himself has been termed Molière's loudest and funniest, perhaps bawdiest, comedy. Borrowing a little from an old French *fabliau,* a little from Rabelais, and a little from the *commedia dell' arte,* the dramatist created a farce-comedy that makes audiences laugh year after year. Molière has included beatings, mistaken identities, disguises, bawdy talk, a near-hanging, and a happy ending. Sganarelle, a poor woodcutter with a fondness for drink, is tricked by his scheming wife, Martine, into posing as a doctor. He is, as he says, "kicked into the medical profession." He is called, as a doctor, to attend Lucinde, a young woman who has apparently been struck dumb. She is only feigning inability to talk, however, to protest her father's choice of a husband for her. Sganarelle examines the girl and expounds upon her ailment in recollected school-boy Latin and double-talk. Géronte, the girl's father, is impressed—and puzzled:

GÉRONTE

There is just one thing that bothers me: the position of the liver and the heart. It seems to me that you place them wrongly; and the heart is on the left side and the liver on the right.

SGANARELLE

Yes, that is the way it used to be. But **we have changed all that;** now we use an entirely new method in medicine.

We have come into our heritage

Source: THE DEAD (Line 14)
Author: Rupert Brooke (1887-1915)
First published: 1915
Type of work: Elegiac sonnet

Context: This poem expresses sincere, sympathetic feelings emanating from personal experience in World War I. Underlying the tragedy with which the poem deals is a patriotic consolation. The poem begins with an apostrophe to the bugles: "Blow out, you bugles, over the rich Dead!" Then the meaning and consequences of their death are treated. The poet dwells first upon the sacrifice involved. In dying for a cause these men "laid the world away; poured out the red/ Sweet wine of youth," and by denying themselves a progeny they gave "their immortality." They assured for those remaining the triumph of eternal values. They brought us, the poet says, Holiness, Love, and Pain. The virtues and nobility of mankind are established and assured because of their purposeful add dedicated sacrifice. He concludes:

> Honour has come back, as a king, to earth,
> And paid his subjects with a royal wage;
> And Nobleness walks in our ways again;
> And **we have come into our heritage.**

We have kissed away kingdoms and provinces

Source: ANTONY AND CLEOPATRA (Act III, sc. x, ll. 7-8)
Author: William Shakespeare (1564-1616)
First published: 1623
Type of work: Dramatic tragedy

Context: This saying is no doubt the source for the slang phrases heard today, "Kiss it away" and "kiss it off." In the play, Mark Antony, one of three co-rulers of Rome along with Octavius Caesar and Lepidus, rules the eastern portion of the Roman world. He is hopelessly enamored of Cleopatra, beautiful and voluptuous Queen of Egypt. He remains with her until urgent affairs of state and threats to his position force him to return home. He makes alliances with Caesar, marries his sister Octavia to bind the renewed friendship, takes his new wife to Athens, but is unhappy. When word comes that Caesar has renewed their rivalry, he dispatches Octavia to Rome to smooth affairs, and then slips off to Alexandria and Cleopatra's arms. Meanwhile, Caesar removes Lepidus from power and is now Antony's only rival for control of Rome. When Antony gives Roman provinces to his twin children and their mother, Cleopatra, and proclaims them rulers, Caesar moves against him. Unwisely, Antony ignores his advantage on land and chooses to fight a sea battle at Actium. He flees with Cleopatra and loses. Two officers discuss the disaster.

SCARUS
Gods and goddesses,
All the whole synod of them!

ENOBARBUS
What's thy passion?

SCARUS
The greater cantle of the world is lost
With very ignorance, **we have kissed away
Kingdoms and provinces.**

We have medicines to make women speak; we have none to make them keep silence

Source: THE MAN WHO MARRIED A DUMB WIFE (II, iv)
Author: Anatole France (Jacques Anatole Thibault, 1844-1924)
First published: 1912
Type of work: Dramatic comedy

Context: Master Leonard Botal, a judge, has recently married a beautiful young woman of position and wealth, but finds marriage unhappy because his wife is tongue-tied and unable to speak. A friend recommends a doctor, Master Simon Colline, who may be able to cure his wife. The operation is successful, and the woman begins speaking, hardly pausing to give Botal a chance to say a word and preventing him from working. In a short while she has driven him to madness, and he hurriedly summons Dr. Colline back, begging him to make his wife silent once again. But the doctor answers that there is no power which can silence a woman's tongue.

1109

MASTER SIMON:
We have medicines to make women speak; we have none to make them keep silence.

MASTER BOTAL
You haven't? Is that your last word? You drive me to despair.

MASTER SIMON
Alas, your Honor! . . . . There is no elixir, balm, magisterium, opiate, unguent, ointment, local application, electuary, nor panacea, that can cure the excess of glottal activity in woman.

We have met the enemy and they are ours

Source: LETTER TO GENERAL WILLIAM HENRY HARRISON
Author: Oliver Hazard Perry (1785-1819)
Written: 1813
Type of work: Naval report

Context: It was in the War of 1812 that Perry won his famous victory on Lake Erie and opened the way for an invasion of Canada by General Harrison. In his letters to the War Department, Harrison had long been urging the importance of building a navy on Lake Erie to oppose the British fleet already established there. As a result, Captain Perry was sent to the scene to build and fit American ships. He succeeded, not only in establishing an American Navy on the lake, but also in meeting and completely defeating the British. This brilliant victory led to a successful invasion of Canada and American recovery of the Northwest. In context, the quoted line, from a letter datelined *U.S. Brig Niagara,* September 10, 1813, reads as follows:

Dear General:—
We have met the enemy and they are ours—two ships, two brigs, one schooner and a sloop.
Yours with great respect and esteem.

Oliver Hazard Perry

We have other fish to fry

Source: GARGANTUA AND PANTAGRUEL (Book V, chapter 12)
Author: François Rabelais (1495-1553)
First published: 1532-1564
Type of work: Mock heroic chronicle

Context: On their voyage to the Oracle of the Holy Bottle, Panurge and Friar John stop at Condemnation Island where they are imprisoned by

1110

the Furred Law-cats and their arch-duke, Gripe-men-all. In the mock trial that follows, Panurge is required to answer a riddle or be condemned. When Panurge says he cannot answer the riddle and Friar John says that Panurge is telling the truth, Gripe-men-all says, using a proverb later used by Cervantes, *Don Quixote,* Part II (1615), Chapter 35, and others:

> ". . . Dost thou think . . . thou're in the wilderness of your foolish university, wrangling and bawling among the idle wandering searchers and hunters after truth? By gold **we have** here **other fish to fry.** . . . People here must give categorical answers to what they don't know. . . . They must protest that they know what they never knew in their lives. . . ."

We have seen better days

Source: TIMON OF ATHENS (Act IV, sc. ii, l. 27)
Author: William Shakespeare (1564-1616)
First published: 1623
Type of work: Dramatic tragedy

Context: This saying is constantly used today and is part of everyday language. In the play, Timon is a lavish patron of the arts and a generous, open-handed host. He delights in giving. But his extravagance ends in bankruptcy. Soon, his creditors become alarmed and try to collect. Flavius, Timon's faithful steward, finally convinces him he owes more than twice what he owns. Timon believes his friends will repay kindness with kindness, and sends servants to request loans of them. Lucullus tries to bribe the servant to say that he was out; Lucius regrets the ill-chance that finds him temporarily unable to help; Sempronius takes offense that he was solicited last, and refuses. His eyes open at last, Timon invites them for a final banquet, which turns out to be water, and which he throws in their faces. Timon then deserts Athens, leaving his servants. Flavius, the steward, commiserates with them and shares his money with them. (This same quotation appears in *As You Like It,* Act II, sc. vii, l. 120, which was performed some five or six years before *Timon of Athens.*)

FLAVIUS
Good fellows all,
The latest of my wealth I'll share amongst you.
Wherever we shall meet, for Timon's sake,
Let's yet be fellows. Let's shake our heads, and say
As 'twere a knell unto our master's fortunes,
We have seen better days. Let each take some.
[Gives money.]

We left him alone with his glory

Source: THE BURIAL OF SIR JOHN MOORE AT CORUNNA (Line 32)
Author: Charles Wolfe (1791-1823)
First published: 1817
Type of work: Elegy

Context: Sir John Moore met his death during the Peninsular War of the Napoleonic Wars. In Spain, where he was commander of the British Army, he was able for a time to paralyze the French forces, but when Napoleon himself attacked he was forced to retreat. The retreat, however, ended in a brilliant victory for the British in the Battle of Corunna (La Coruña, on the northwest coast of Spain) January 16, 1809. Unfortunately, the brave commander was mortally wounded early in the day. By his own wish, he was buried before dawn, January 17, in the ramparts of Corunna. In the *Edinburgh Annual Register* (1808) appeared the following paragraph: "Sir John Moore had often said that if he was killed in battle he wished to be buried where he fell. The body was removed at midnight to the citadel of Corunna. A grave was dug for him on the rampart there, by a party of the 9th Regiment, the Aides-de-Camp attending by turns. No coffin could be procured, and the officers of his staff wrapped his body, dressed as it was, in a military cloak and blankets. The interment was hastened: for, about eight in the morning, some firing was heard, and the officers feared that if a serious attack was made, they should be ordered away, and not suffered to pay him their last duty. The officers of his regiment bore him to the grave; the funeral service was read by the chaplain; and the corpse was covered with earth." Wolfe's moving tribute to the lost leader closes with the lines,

> We carved not a line, and we raised not a stone—
> But **we left him alone with his glory.**

We love him for the enemies he has made

Source: SECONDING SPEECH FOR GROVER CLEVELAND
Author: Edward Stuyvesant Bragg (1827-1912)
First spoken: July 9, 1884
Type of work: Political slogan

Context: Bragg's first connections with Democratic conventions came in Charleston, in 1860, where he supported Stephen A. Douglas for the presidency. He was also a delegate to the Philadelphia Loyalist Convention of 1868. Later as a veteran politician from Wisconsin, he headed its delegates to the Democratic convention of 1884 in Chicago. Here he uttered his best-remembered words. Rather than "By their friends shall ye know them,"—an uncertain guide about politicians whose "friends" are created by all sorts of motives,—Bragg cites the enemies that Grover Cleveland (1837-1908) had created while governor of New York among the wire-pulling and ring-running politicians of Tammany Hall. Then, as he testified in the entry he prepared for *Who's Who in America* for 1902, he seconded the Hon. David Lakewood's nomination of Cleveland for president, in the name of the young voters of the west, and added the remark which, with two slight changes, became the Cleveland campaign slogan:

They love him most for the enemies he has made.

We loved with a love that was more than love

Source: ANNABEL LEE (Stanza 2)
Author: Edgar Allan Poe (1809-1849)
First published: 1849
Type of work: Narrative poem

Context: There has been a persistent tradition that this poem was written in memory of Poe's wife, Virginia, who died in 1847. Though several other ladies have been suggested as the inspiration of the poem, Virginia, because of her extreme youth (she was only fourteen when she married Poe and twenty-one when she died) seems the most likely candidate. In a highly romanticized fashion, typical of the author, the themes of the poem center around the picture of an ideal love destroyed by death. The love of the poet for the maiden was so great that it was envied by the "wingèd seraphs." Hence, with Poe's conviction that all the circumstances of life were against him, it was inevitable that a cold wind should blow out of a cloud "chilling and killing" his beloved, and that even her corpse should be taken from him to be buried in a tomb by the sea. Yet nothing, not even death, can separate him from the woman he so loved. The second stanza reads:

> *She* was a child and *I* was a child,
>> In this kingdom by the sea,
> But **we loved with a love that was more than love**—
>> I and my Annabel Lee—
> With a love that the wingèd seraphs of heaven
>> Coveted her and me.

1113

We must all hang together, or assuredly we shall all hang separately

Source: TRADITION
Author: Benjamin Franklin (1706-1790)
First spoken: July 4, 1776
Type of work: Attributed saying

Context: All the men who attended the Continental Congress must have known that if they were successful in their efforts they would become heroes, but that if they failed they would be traitors, subject to trial and probably death at the hands of British authorities. When the time came to sign the Declaration of Independence, John Hancock, as the presiding officer, signed his name first. According to the tradition, he remarked ominously, "We must be unanimous; there must be no pulling different ways; we must all hang together." Well he knew that he and the other signers could be signing a document that could be their own death warrant. It was a momentous occasion in more ways than one. Benjamin Franklin, who was a wry humorist, is said, also according to the tradition, to have then made his famous comment, with its pun on the word "hang," in response to Hancock. At the time, perhaps, the truth, rather than the humor, of the statement was more appreciated.

We must all hang together, or assuredly we shall all hang separately.

We must cultivate our garden

Source: CANDIDE
Author: Voltaire (François Marie Arouet, 1694-1778)
First published: 1759
Type of work: Philosophical satirical novel

Context: The story of *Candide* is Voltaire's bitter attack on the theory of Leibnitz that this is the "best of all possible worlds." The ingenuous Candide, illegitimate son of a noble German family, is taught this principle by his tutor, Dr. Pangloss. In the rambling series of events that ensues, Candide encounters every form of human wickedness, as he travels from Europe to Spanish America and finally to Turkey, where he finds his sweetheart, Cunegonde, from whom he had long been separated. There, reunited with her and his old tutor, Dr. Pangloss, he at last decides to give up his attempt to justify the evil in the world; instead, he buys a small farm. In vain does Dr. Pangloss, faithful to his philosophy, argue that Candide's sufferings are justified because they have led to his present comfortable existence on the farm. Candide's reply is simply:

" 'Tis well said, but **we must cultivate our garden.**"

We need greater virtues to sustain good fortune than bad

Source: MAXIMES (No. 25)
Author: François VI, Duc de La Rochefoucauld (1613-1680)
First published: 1665-1678
Type of work: Maxim

Context: La Rochefoucauld's maxims are observations on life by one who was a courtier, gentleman, soldier, lover—in short, a very sophisticated and worldly man. A strong current of disillusionment runs through them, and many are epigrammatic in nature, revealing a biting wit. His underlying philosophy is that virtues are all too often vices thinly disguised, and that when we do good deeds we do them from selfish and frequently sordid motives. He has his later echoes in the sour comments of Ambrose Bierce, Mark Twain, and H. L. Mencken. Although a maxim is seldom new wisdom, it presents wisdom in a more concise and pointed form. Tacitus records the words of Galba, spoken when he adopted Piso: "Hitherto, you have only borne adversity; prosperity tries the heart with keener temptations; for hardships may be endured, whereas we are spoiled by success." (*History*, Book 1, Chapter 15). La Rochefoucauld expresses the same idea, but reduced to its essentials:

We need greater virtues to sustain good fortune than bad.

We shall fight in the hills; we shall never surrender

Source: DUNKIRK
Author: Sir Winston Spencer Churchill (1874-1965)
First spoken: House of Commons; 4 June 1940
Type of work: Political speech

Context: In May, 1940, both the Dutch and Belgian Armies surrendered to the Germans. British forces were therefore left in a very precarious situation, and soon they had to retreat after the effort to defend Dunkirk proved futile. The defeat appeared to be a disaster for the British and it caused a serious decline of morale, but so dynamic was Churchill's appeal to the British people that they quickly began to rally behind the war effort.

. . . We shall go on to the end, we shall fight in France, we shall fight on the seas and oceans, we shall fight with growing confidence and growing strength in the air, we shall defend our Island, whatever the cost may be, we shall fight on the beaches, we shall fight on the landing grounds, we shall fight in the fields and in the streets, we shall fight in the hills; we shall never surrender, . . .

We shall this day light such a candle by God's grace in England as I trust shall never be put out

Source: A SHORT HISTORY OF THE ENGLISH PEOPLE, J. R. Green (Chapter 7, Section II, p. 366)
Author: Hugh Latimer (1485-1555)
First spoken: 1555
Type of work: Attributed comment

Context: When the Catholic Princess Mary, known as Bloody Mary, became Queen of England, she began a reign of terror for all heretics, meaning those people who opposed Roman Catholicism. In a bloody purge, reminiscent of the Spanish Inquisition, Mary tried to destroy the Protestants. Instead of quelling the Protestant movement, however, she merely emboldened her enemies, for the Protestants became more active, almost asking for martyrdom. Hugh Latimer, who was Bishop of Worcester and one of the new reformers, was imprisoned and finally burned at the stake, along with Bishop Ridley of London. As Latimer died, he maintained his belief in the justice of the Reformation. Speaking to Ridley, he paraphrased 2 Esdras XIV, 25:

"Play the man, Master Ridley," cried the old preacher of the Reformation as the flames shot up around him; **"we shall this day light such a candle by God's grace in England as I trust shall never be put out."**

We went through fire and through water

Source: PSALMS 66:12
Author: Unknown
First transcribed: c.400-200 B.C.
Type of work: Religious poetry

Context: The psalmist, in preparation for an offering, exhorts all nations to praise the Lord resoundingly. God's power is so awesome that His enemies cringe before Him, and all people worship Him, singing His praises. The poet urges his listeners to recall some of the remarkable acts of the Lord; for instance, He opened the waters of the sea for the Israelites to escape from Egyptian oppression; hence, the worshipers rejoice in Him, who eternally reigns over all the world. All nations should praise God for preserving them. The psalmist explains that one phase of the relationship between God and men is His testing or proving of them:

For thou, O God, hast proved us: thou hast tried us, as silver is tried.

Thou broughtest us into the net; thou laidst affliction upon our loins.

Thou hast caused men to ride over our heads; **we went through fire and through water:** but thou broughtest us out into a wealthy place.

The weaker vessel

Source: I PETER 3:7
Author: Peter
First transcribed: 60-70
Type of work: Religious epistle

Context: Peter, writing perhaps from Babylon what seems to be a circular letter to several churches in Asia Minor, praises God for the redeeming power of Christ and notes the fulfillment of the Old Testament prophecies. Declaring the Son to be the "living stone" of God's house and urging the people also to be "living stones" of the spiritual house, he exhorts them to obey the powers of government and to imitate the sinless Christ. In a list of instructions for domestic tranquillity and grace, he tells wives to be submissive to their husbands, but he also admonishes husbands to honor their wives that the couple may have together eternal life:

> Likewise, ye husbands, dwell with them according to knowledge, giving honour unto the wife, as unto **the weaker vessel,** and as being heirs together of the grace of life; that your prayers be not hindered.

Wear your learning, like your watch, in a private pocket

Source: LETTERS TO HIS SON (Letter 30)
Author: Philip Dormer Stanhope, Lord Chesterfield (1694-1773)
First published: 1774
Type of work: Personal letters

Context: The fourth Earl of Chesterfield, continuing a series of letters of advice to his son—whom he hopes to persuade in the ways of becoming a valuable and gentle member of the upper classes—urges the boy to exercise modesty and discretion in all things. In his letter to young Philip from Bath on February 22, 1748, Lord Chesterfield notes that "Gener- osity often runs into profusion, cour- age into rashness, caution into timid- ity. . . ." Offering further advice, Chesterfield states that "Vice, in its true light, is so deformed, that it shocks us at first sight, and would hardly ever seduce us, if it did not, at first, wear the mask of some virtue." As to modesty in comportment, Lord Chesterfield tells his son that if he

1117

. . . would avoid the accusation of pedantry on one hand, or the suspicion of ignorance on the other, abstain from learned ostentation. Speak the language of the company that you are in; speak it purely, and unlarded with any other. Never seem wiser, nor more learned, than the people you are with. **Wear your learning, like your watch, in a private pocket:** and do not pull it out and strike it; merely to show that you have one. If you are asked what o'clock it is, tell it; but do not proclaim it hourly and unasked, like the watchman.

Welcome the coming, speed the parting guest

Source: THE ODYSSEY (Book XV, line 83, as translated by Alexander Pope)
Author: Homer (c. 850 B.C.)
First transcribed: Sixth century B.C.
Type of work: Epic poem

Context: At the suggestion of Athene, disguised as Mentes and later Mentor, Telemachus goes forth from Ithaca to seek news of his father Odysseus who has been gone nearly twenty years, ten years after the Trojan War is over. He visits in the palace of Menelaus and Helen, the latter the cause of the war, albeit unwittingly since she was the tool of the gods. The youth so resembles his father that the host wishes to hear all about him, and to tell all he knows of Odysseus since the war. Yet the king knows that Telemachus wants to continue his search for his father, so he does not insist that the young man tarry. After the following speech, Menelaus sends Telemachus on his way.

"If with desire so strong thy bosom glows,
Ill (said the king) should I thy wish oppose;
For oft in others freely I reprove
The ill-timed efforts of officious love;
Who loves too much, hate in the like extreme,
And both the golden mean alike condemn.
Alike he thwarts the hospitable end,
Who drives the free, or stays the hasty friend:
True friendship's laws are by this rule express'd,
Welcome the coming, speed the parting guest."

Well done, thou good and faithful servant

Source: MATTHEW 25:21
Author: Unknown (traditionally Matthew the Apostle)
First transcribed: c.75-100
Type of work: Gospel

Context: Jesus, after leaving the temple in Jerusalem, where the Phari- sees and Sadducees, through planned questions, attempt to trap Him in he-

1118

retical or treasonous answers, goes to the Mount of Olives. There He explains to His disciples the nature of the times preceding the Day of Judgment and the signs of His own Coming. Indicating that only God knows the exact day, He teaches, in the parable of the five wise and five foolish virgins, that man must always be prepared for the coming of the Lord. In a second parable, He says that the Kingdom of Heaven will be like the man who, before a long journey, gives his three servants for safekeeping five talents, three talents, and one talent, respectively. The first two servants double the number of talents entrusted to them; the third buries his one talent. On his return, the master praises the two responsible servants and condemns the fearful one. When the first servant presents to his master the five extra talents:

> His lord said unto him, **Well done, thou good and faithful servant;** thou hast been faithful over a few things, I will make thee ruler over many things: enter thou into the joy of thy lord.

Well this side of Paradise!

Source: TIARE TAHITI (Next to Last line)
Author: Rupert Brooke (1887-1915)
First published: 1915
Type of work: Metaphysical poem

Context: The poet, speaking to his beloved, is contemplating the prospects of a life after death as conceived by the wise and as contrasted to the paradisiacal but very earthly life he is sharing now in the South Seas with his beloved. He is puzzled and dismayed by the idea that all things blend into the Absolute at the end of time. "All are one in Paradise," he reasons. "Instead of lovers, Love shall be." All lovely things will lose their uniqueness and peculiar beauty; there will be no more individuality or physical pleasures, no more dreaming under the ferns or dancing or kissing. "Oh, Heaven's Heaven!—but we'll be missing/ The palms, and sunlight, and the south," he exclaims. Then he calls on his beloved to live today in this life and to experience the earthly joys. "Hear the calling of the moon"; enjoy human love in a world of variety, contrast, and activity:

> Dive and double and follow after,
> Snare in flowers, and kiss, and call,
> With lips that fade, and human laughter
> And faces individual,
> **Well this side of Paradise!** . . .
> There's little comfort in the wise.

Westward the course of empire takes its way

Source: ON THE PROSPECT OF PLANTING ARTS AND LEARNING IN AMERICA
(Stanza 6)
Author: George Berkeley (1685-1753)
First published: 1752
Type of work: Didactic poem

Context: Berkeley's one famous poem was inspired by his project of founding a college in the Bermudas, a project he pressed because he believed the English colonists, and the natives, of those islands ought to have educational facilities. Berkeley was granted a charter by the crown, but the necessary funds could not be raised; as a result, the project never came to fruition. In his poem Berkeley envisions a new golden age in the world; he hopes a time is about to occur when men are guided by reason and virtue, when education will be free from pedantry of all sorts. In the New World he hopes to see a British empire flourish, along with a renaissance of all the arts. He hopes America will be as he thinks Europe was when it was young, that America will produce wise and noble men, as Europe supposedly had. Berkeley says that four-fifths of history have already passed, but that the last and best period is yet to come. The site will be, of course, America. Berkeley's sentiments appealed to others in early America: John Quincy Adams said, in his *Oration at Plymouth* (1802), "Westward the star of empire takes its way." The last stanza of Berkeley's poem begins with the quotation:

> **Westward the course of empire takes its way;**
> The four first acts already past,
> A fifth shall close the drama with the day;
> Time's noblest offspring is the last.

A whale ship was my Yale College and my Harvard

Source: MOBY DICK (Chapter 24)
Author: Herman Melville (1819-1891)
First published: 1851
Type of work: Novel

Context: Ishmael has signed up on the *Pequod* with his cannibal friend Queequeg for a whaling cruise. Now in a chapter called "The Advocate," he starts to set right some misapprehensions about the whaling industry: "As Queequeg and I are now fairly embarked in this business of whaling; and as this business of whaling has somehow come to be regarded among landsmen as a rather unpoetical and disreputable pursuit; therefore, I am all anxiety to convince ye, ye landsmen, of the injustice hereby done to us hunters of whales." He quotes statistics to demonstrate how much money is invested in and how much profit made from this industry. Then he answers such objections as "The whale no famous author, and whaling no famous chronicler?" "No good blood in their veins?" and "No dignity in whaling?" He concludes this chapter by saying:

> . . . if, at my death, my executors, or more properly my creditors, find any precious MSS. in my desk, then here I prospectively ascribe all the honor and the glory to whaling; for a **whale-ship was my Yale College and my Harvard.**

What a world of gammon and spinnage it is

Source: DAVID COPPERFIELD (Chapter 22)
Author: Charles Dickens (1812-1870)
First published: 1849-1850
Type of work: Novel

Context: After completing his education at the Canterbury school which he had attended by the generosity of his aunt, David Copperfield goes to London. There he meets James Steerforth, an old schoolmate, and with him returns to Yarmouth to visit Peggotty, his mother's former maid, whose kindness had meant so much to him in earlier years. In Yarmouth with Steerforth one evening, Copperfield is introduced to a strange-looking woman named Miss Mowcher, a hairdresser, who presents a fascinating appearance because of her thick, shirt-limbed body and her unaffectedly charming ways. She tells him that his face is "like a peach," and "quite tempting," to which remark Copperfield responds as graciously as he can. Miss Mowcher pretends to be embarrassed at his compliments, which she calls "gammon and spinnage" (nonsense).

> I said that I congratulated myself on having the honour to make hers, and that the happiness was mutual.
> "Oh, my goodness, how polite we are!" exclaimed Miss Mowcher, making a preposterous attempt to cover her large face with her morsel of a hand. **"What a world of gammon and spinnage it is,** though, ain't it!"

What fools these mortals be!

Source: A MIDSUMMER NIGHT'S DREAM (Act III, sc. ii, l. 115)
Author: William Shakespeare (1564-1616)
First published: 1600
Type of work: Dramatic comedy

Context: Demetrius, who is in love with Hermia, but who is loved by Helena, Hermia's good friend, is followed into the woods by Helena. He becomes angry with her for following him. Puck, fairy servant of Oberon, King of the fairies, is ordered to place on the eyelids of the sleeping Demetrius some of the juice of the magical flower love-in-idleness, so that when he awakes he will fall in love with Helena, whom he will see first. Puck, however, mistakes Lysander for Demetrius, and places the love-juice on Lysander's eyelids. When he awakes, he sees first not his real love Hermia, but Helena, to whom he professes his love. Helena thinks Lysander is making fun of her and resents his professions. Oberon discovers Puck's mistake and places some of the juice on Demetrius' eyes, then has Puck place Helena near so that she will be the first creature that Demetrius sees when he awakes. Puck is amused by all these happenings. He sums up his disdain for all concerned in his remark:

PUCK
Captain of our fairy band,
Helena is here at hand,
And the youth, mistook by me,
Pleading for a lover's fee.
Shall we their fond pageant see?
Lord, **what fools these mortals be!**

What hath night to do with sleep?

Source: COMUS (Line 122)
Author: John Milton (1608-1674)
First published: 1637
Type of work: Masque

Context: The plot of the masque, which was acted by the three children of Lord Bridgewater, just installed as President of Wales, deals with the "perplexed paths" of a forest through which the young people must pass to reach their father's castle. In the forest is Comus, son of Bacchus and Ceres, a figure symbolizing unbridled license. He enters the scene, with a band of attendants who have been transformed by his magic into creatures with the heads of beasts and the bodies of humans. Comus announces that it is now night, the time for enjoyment. The spirits, the fairies, and the elves are dancing in the forest. Night, says Comus, should not be wasted on sleep, for Venus and Cupid are awake, and it is time for love:

And on the tawny sands and shelves
Trip the pert fairies and the dapper elves;
By dimpled brook and fountain brim,
The wood-nymphs decked with daisies trim,
Their merry wakes and pastimes keep:
What hath night to do with sleep?
Night hath better sweets to prove,
Venus now wakes, and wakens Love.

What have I done unto thee?

Source: NUMBERS 22:28
Author: Unknown
First transcribed: c.1000-400 B.C.
Type of work: Religious history and law

Context: Laying waste the lands before them on the way to Canaan, the Israelites arrive at the plains of Moab. Balak, the Moabite king, fearful of the approaching Israelites, sends emissaries to the prophet Balaam of Pethor to persuade him to come and curse the invaders. Refusing to make the journey without God's approval, Balaam, at God's command, rejects the pleas of the first group and goes with a second group with the admonition to do only what God bids. Saddling his ass, Balaam begins the journey, but angers God, Who places an armed angel before the ass, which first carries Balaam into a field, then crushes his foot against a vineyard wall, and finally lies down under him. Balaam strikes the ass with a staff:

> And the Lord opened the mouth of the ass, and she said unto Balaam, **What have I done unto thee,** that thou hast smitten me these three times?
> And Balaam said unto the ass, Because thou hast mocked me:
> Then the Lord opened the eyes of Balaam and he saw the angel of the Lord standing in the way. . . .

What is a cynic?

Source: LADY WINDERMERE'S FAN (Act III)
Author: Oscar Wilde (1856-1900)
First published: 1893
Type of work: Dramatic comedy

Context: Lord Darlington, trying to save Lady Windermere from a scandal involving her husband and a Mrs. Erlynne, reveals to Lady Windermere his love for her and asks her to go away with him. She refuses. Later in the evening Darlington takes several friends, including Lord Windermere, to his apartment, not realizing that Lady Windermere is waiting there to accept his proposal. Also in the apartment is Mrs. Erlynne, who is actually Lady Windermere's mother and who has come to persuade her daughter not to make the same mistake she herself made twenty years earlier. Just as Darlington's party arrives, Lady Windermere hides behind a curtain, and Mrs. Erlynne leaves through a door. In the conversation that ensues, Darlington reveals his love for a married woman, the only good woman he feels he has ever met. Two of the guests, Dumby and Cecil

1123

Graham, jest about good women. Dumby says Darlington is lucky to love a woman who does not love him. Dumby continues that he would like women to leave him alone so that he would have some time, not to educate himself, but to forget what he has learned.

DARLINGTON

"What cynics you fellows are!"

GRAHAM

"What is a cynic?"

DARLINGTON

"A man who knows the price of everything, and the value of nothing."

What is man, that thou art mindful of him?

Source: PSALMS 8:4
Author: Unknown
First transcribed: c.400-200 B.C.
Type of work: Religious poetry

Context: The psalmist, considering God's greatness, exclaims in amazement that man should have a position of significance in the universe. So far above the comprehension of man is God's majesty that man's attempts to describe it are as the first babbling efforts at speech of the infant. God overcame the powers of resistance and deftly formed the earth and the heavens, manifestations surpassed only by the excellence of the Creator himself. Why, then, should God watch over man? Yet man is only a little lower than God and is given the right to control all of the things created by God. Thus the name of the Lord is to be praised:

When I consider thy heavens, the work of thy fingers, the moon and the stars, which thou hast ordained;
What is man, that thou art mindful of him? and the son of man, that thou visitest him?
For thou hast made him a little lower than the angels, and hast crowned him with glory and honour.

What is so rare as a day in June?

Source: THE VISION OF SIR LAUNFAL (Part I, "Prelude," Stanza 5)
Author: James Russell Lowell (1819-1891)
First published: 1848
Type of work: Narrative poem

Context: The Holy Grail, the cup out of which Jesus partook of the Last Supper, was by tradition carried to England by Joseph of Arimathea and there guarded by his descendants who were required to be chaste in thought, word, and deed. When one of them broke his vow, the cup disappeared. The Knights of King Arthur and, in Lowell's poem, even others who lived after them, devoted their lives to a search for it. Lowell invents the story of a knight, Sir Launfal, who after roaming the world to seek it, finds it in his own castle, the cup that the knight had humbly filled to quench the thirst of a leper. The poet starts with a prelude comparing his own efforts to the search by a musing organist for his theme. "Rare" has the meaning, not of uncommon, but of precious or delightful. Lowell describes the coming of Spring, the time when Sir Launfal remembers his pledge to go seeking the Grail.

> And **what is so rare as a day in June?**
>   Then, if ever, come perfect days;
> Then Heaven tries earth if it be in tune,
>   And over it softly her warm ear lays;
> Whether we look, or whether we listen,
> We hear life murmur, or see it glisten.

What is the city, but the people?

Source: CORIOLANUS (Act III, sc. i, l. 199)
Author: William Shakespeare (1564-1616)
First published: 1623
Type of work: Dramatic tragedy

Context: Ciaus Martius is a brilliant Roman general who leads the Roman forces against the Volcians and defeats them. Although he is able, Martius, now known as Coriolanus, has overweening pride of name and hates the rabble of Rome. They reciprocate. But, because of his great victory, he comes home in triumph, and is nominated by the Senate to the office of Consul. During his absence, the plebeians have been granted tribunes, two of whom, Brutus and Sicinius, hate Coriolanus, and hope to see him fall. Nominated for Consul, Coriolanus, although it is distasteful to him, bows to tradition and stands in the Forum begging votes. His contempt for the common man repels the people, but he nevertheless gains their support. As he is preparing to leave, Brutus and Sicinius turn the people against him and convince them he would deprive them of their liberties. Enraged by the ingratitude of the people, he is so outspoken that the tribunes seize upon his words as an excuse to call him traitor and demand his death. Coriolanus' old friend, Menenius, together with other senators, intervenes and helps him.

SICINIUS
[addressing throng.]
You are at point to lose your liberties
Martius would have all from you; Martius,
Whom late you have named for consul.

MENENIUS
Fie, fie, fie,
This is the way to kindle, not to quench.

FIRST SENATOR
To unbuild the city, and to lay all flat.

SICINIUS
What is the city, but the people?

What is truth?

Source: JOHN 18:38
Author: Unknown
First transcribed: By 130
Type of work: Gospel

Context: This is the famous question put by Pilate to Jesus after the Jews had led Him into the hall of judgment. Pilate has asked them what accusations they have brought, and their reply is that Jesus is a malefactor but that it is not lawful for them to put anyone to death. Pilate, with the ultimate responsibility of the judgment thrust upon him, inquires of Jesus if He considers Himself to be the King of the Jews, for on the answer depends Jesus' guilt in the eyes of the Roman Imperium. Jesus' reply is the famous "My kingdom is not of this world." He goes on to say that He was born "to bear witness unto the truth," and that "every one that is of the truth heareth my voice." Pilate's almost despairing question was used by Bacon as the opening sentence of his Essay on Truth. " 'What is truth,' asked jesting Pilate, and would not stay for an answer." In turn, Aldous Huxley used Bacon's phrase "Jesting Pilate" as the title of a volume of essays (1926). The passage from John follows:

Jesus answered, My kingdom is not of this world: if my kingdom were of this world, then would my servants fight, that I should not be delivered to the Jew: but now is my kingdom not from hence.

Pilate therefore said unto him, Art thou a king then? Jesus answered, Thou sayest that I am a king. To this end was I born, and for this cause came I into the world, that I should bear witness unto the truth. Every one that is of the truth heareth my voice.

Pilate saith unto him, **What is truth?** And when he had said this, he went out again unto the Jews, and saith unto them, I find in him no fault at all.

What makes all doctrines plain and clear?

Source: HUDIBRAS (Part III, Canto I, l. 1277)
Author: Samuel Butler (1612-1680)
First published: First and second parts, 1663; third part, 1678
Type of work: Burlesque poem

Context: Hudibras, a burlesque of the typical Puritan, having had an encounter with a magician, astrologer, and wise man named Sidrophel, whom he robs, repairs to his ladylove, a widow of some wealth. She sets upon him infernal spirits who beat him and then put him through an inquisition. When a spirit demands to know why Hudibras has wooed the lady, he readily admits that money makes all matches. He denies that he loves her and admits that if he had married her, he would have taken possession of her wealth and put her on an allowance. He admits having lied to her, having thought that she had little sense. The spirit then puts Hudibras through a catechism about why certain things are done: What makes a wretch a child of God or one of the infernal spirits, what justifies beating out others' brains and murdering them, what makes people orthodox in new sects in which they do not believe, what makes rebelling against kings a true and worthy cause? The answer in every instance is money. People believe new doctrines for money and repudiate them and believe still others for more money. The dialogue goes:

> **What makes all doctrines plain and clear?**
> About two hundred pounds a year.
> And that which was proved true before
> Prove false again?— Two hundred more.

What man dare, I dare

Source: MACBETH (Act III, sc. iv, l. 99)
Author: William Shakespeare (1564-1616)
First published: 1623
Type of work: Dramatic tragedy

Context: Macbeth and Banquo, generals in King Duncan of Scotland's army, are told by three witches that Macbeth shall be Thane of Cawdor and afterwards king, and that Banquo shall be the father of kings. Shortly, word is brought that the king has made Macbeth Thane of Cawdor for brilliant military service. Macbeth, ambitious and impatient, assassinates King Duncan in his sleep. The blame is fastened on the king's sons who, fearing for their own safety, flee, one to England, the other to Ireland. Thus, hastening his future through regicide, Macbeth is elected and crowned King of Scotland. But he is uneasy. Because he has no heir, he fears Banquo will kill him to secure his own line in accordance with the witches' prophecy. He plans a banquet and invites Banquo and his son Fleance, but arranges to have them murdered en route. Banquo is killed, but Fleance escapes. Now, informed of Banquo's death, he is about to partake of the banquet when Banquo's ghost appears at the table. Only Macbeth can see it, and is frightened. The banquet continues. The ghost appears again. Macbeth is greatly perturbed and causes a commotion as Lady Macbeth tries to calm him. He stares at the ghost.

MACBETH

What man dare, I dare.
Approach thou like the rugged Russian bear,
The armed rhinoceros, or the Hyrcan tiger,
Take any shape but that, and my firm nerves
Shall never tremble.

• • •

What, never? Hardly ever!

Source: H.M.S. PINAFORE (Act I)
Author: W. S. Gilbert (1836-1911)
First published: 1878
Type of work: Light opera

Context: Early in the first act is introduced the crew of the British warship *Pinafore* and their commander, Captain Corcoran. The feelings of the crew toward him are revealed by the boatswain's injunction to the crew: ". . . let us greet him as so brave an officer and so gallant a seaman de-

1128

serves." Captain Corcoran gives a summary of his qualities: "Though related to a peer,/ I can hand, reef, and steer,/ And ship a selvagee;/ I am never known to quail/ At the fury of a gale,/ And I'm never, never sick at sea!"

> ALL
> What, never?
>
> CAPTAIN
> No, never!
>
> ALL
> **What, never?**
>
> CAPTAIN
> **Hardly ever!**
>
> ALL
> He's hardly ever sick at sea!

What pity is it that we can die but once to serve our country!

Source: CATO (Act IV, sc. iv, ll. 81-82)
Author: Joseph Addison (1672-1719)
First published: 1713
Type of work: Dramatic tragedy

Context: Doomed to fight against the powerful Caesar for the soul of Rome, Cato leads with courage and eschews personal safety in the cause of political altruism. The moving speech of Cato upon meeting the corpse of his battle-slain son reminds us, in part, of the final words of Nathan Hale, the American patriot who expressed regret that he had only one life to give to his country. When Joseph Addison's play was first produced, in 1713, it was acclaimed by both the Tories and the Whigs. Each party insisted that the Duke of Marlborough, hero of the Battle of Blenheim, was represented in the drama. The whigs insisted that Cato represented the Duke; the Tories claimed that Addison intended that the character of Caesar be construed as a portrait of Marlborough. This controversy, however, in no way dulls Cato's magnificently courageous pronouncement:

> CATO
> (meeting the corpse) Welcome, my son! Here lay him down, my friends,

1129

Full in my sight, that I may view at leisure
The bloody corse, and count those glorious wounds.
How beautiful is death, when earn'd by virtue!
Who would not be that youth? **what pity is it
That we can die but once to serve our country!**

What should they know of England who only England know?

Source: THE ENGLISH FLAG
Author: Rudyard Kipling (1865-1936)
First published: 1891
Type of work: Patriotic poem

Context: Rudyard Kipling's nationalism and patriotism knew no bounds. The occasion for "The English Flag" was an incident recorded in the *Daily Papers.* "Above the portico a flagstaff, bearing the Union Jack, remained fluttering in the flames for some time, but ultimately when it fell the crowds rent the air with shouts, and it seemed to see significance in the incident." Kipling answers by telling what the Four Winds say about the grandeur of the British Empire. Each Wind—North, South, East, and West—extols the glory of England, their theme being that only those who are familiar with the far-flung Empire really understand the true power of England.

Winds of the Worlds, give answer! They are whimpering to and
fro—

. . .

And **what should they know of England who only England
know?**—

What small potatoes we all are

Source: MY SUMMER IN A GARDEN (Fifteenth Week)
Author: Charles Dudley Warner (1829-1900)
First published: 1870
Type of work: Essay

Context: Charles Dudley Warner, newspaper editor, co-author with Mark Twain of *The Gilded Age,* and coeditor of *Harper's Magazine,* observed nature and from his observation wove "curious analogies." In the series of light, humorous essays called *My Summer in a Garden,* he writes of his experiences as a gardner, using his experiences as starting points for discussions of various topics. In the fifteenth essay or chapter, he comments on his potato crop in a time of drought:

. . . Digging potatoes is a pleasant, soothing occupation, but not poetical. It is good for the mind, unless they are too small (as many of mine are), when it begets a want of gratitude to the bountiful earth. **What small potatoes we all are,** compared with what we might be! We don't plow deep enough, any of us, for one thing.

What the dickens

Source: THE MERRY WIVES OF WINDSOR (Act III, sc. ii, 1. 18)
Author: William Shakespeare (1564-1616)
First published: 1602
Type of work: Dramatic comedy

Context: Sir John Falstaff, an old, fat, and foolish lecher, imagines that two light-hearted married women, Mistress Ford and Mistress Page, desire him. He sends them identical love-letters. They compare notes, have a good laugh, and resolve to be revenged upon him. In the meantime, their husbands have been informed of Sir John's behavior. Master Page trusts his wife and is undisturbed, but Master Ford is upset and jealous. Now, Mistress Ford has arranged an assignation with Falstaff, but Mistress Page will be with her, and they will make a fool of the fat knight. Mistress Page is on her way to the Ford house. She, preceded by Robin, Sir John Falstaff's handsome little page, encounters Master Ford in the street. She knows he is jealous and makes sport at his expense. He asks about the lad, Robin.

FORD
Where had you this pretty weathercock?

MISTRESS PAGE
I cannot tell **what the dickens** his name is my husband had him of. What do you call your knight's name, sirrah?

ROBIN
Sir John Falstaff.

FORD
Sir John Falstaff!

MISTRESS PAGE
He, he, I can never hit on's name. . . .

What therefore God hath joined together, let not man put asunder

Source: MATTHEW 19:6
Author: Unknown (traditionally Matthew the Apostle)
First transcribed: c.75-100
Type of work: Gospel

Context: Jesus after leaving Galilee and going into Judea beyond the Jordan, is approached by the Pharisees and asked whether it is lawful for a man to put away his wife for any cause. Jesus replies that when God created them he created male and female. And because, He says, of this fact, the man leaves his father and mother and cleaves to his wife. The two then become one body; they are no longer two. With this reasoning, He proclaims the law of marriage and divorce:

> Wherefore they are no more twain, but one flesh. **What therefore God hath joined together, let not man put asunder.**

What things have we seen done at the Mermaid

Source: THE NICE VALOR ("Letter to Ben Jonson")
Author: Francis Beaumont (1585?-1616)
First published: 1647
Type of work: Epistle in verse

Context: Some innkeeper prior to 1643 put a sign with a mermaid over the door of a tavern that extended from Bread St., to Friday St., in London, south of Cheapside and east of St. Paul's Cathedral. In rooms upstairs he served food to the gentry. Here, according to tradition, Sir Walter Raleigh, after his Cadiz expedition of 1596, met with his famous friends, Donne, Spenser, and a coterie of dramatists, Beaumont and Fletcher, Marlowe, Greene, Jonson, and Shakespeare. The Mermaid Tavern probably burned in the Great Fire of 1666. Beaumont, who frequented the meetings, voices his homesickness for the place to Ben Jonson in a letter of about 1605, written from a country estate where Beaumont and Fletcher are working on a play:

> I lie and dream of your full Mermaid wine.
>
> Methinks the little wit I had is lost
> Since I saw you; for wit is like a rest
> Held up at tennis where men do the best
> With the best gamesters. **What things have we seen**

Done at the Mermaid: heard words that have been
So nimble and so full of subtle flame,
As if that everyone (from whence they came)
Had meant to put his whole wit in a jest, . . .

What will Mrs. Grundy say?

Source: SPEED THE PLOUGH (Act I, sc. i)
Author: Thomas Morton (1764-1838)
First published: 1800
Type of work: Dramatic comedy

Context: First produced at Covent Garden in 1800, this comedy is one of the best of Morton's amusing plays. An early editor, Epes Sargent, comments that Morton reveals a vivacity, an unforced pleasure, and broad, genuine humor. "His comedies were so highly prized in their day, and such was their uniform success, that he was not infrequently paid a thousand pounds for one. They still, with few exceptions, keep honourable possession of the Stage. *Speed the Plough* is perhaps the oftenest played of any in this country." As the drama opens, Farmer Ashfield welcomes home his contentious wife, who is indignant that the products of her neighbor, Mrs. Grundy, have been more favorably received at the market. She prattles that "Farmer Grundy's wheat brought five shillings a quarter more than ours did," that "the sun seems to shine on purpose for him," and that "Dame Grundy's butter was quite the crack of the market." In exasperation, Farmer Ashfield attempts to check his wife, but his attempts are futile. In later scenes, concerned for her daughter's chastity (II, iii) and perturbed by the indecorum of her husband's riding in Susan's coach (V, i), Dame Ashfield queries: *"What will Mrs. Grundy say then?"* Her name has become proverbial for conventional propriety and moral decorum.

Be quiet, woolye? aleways ding, dinging Dame Grundy into my ears—**what will Mrs. Grundy zay?** What will Mrs. Grundy think? Casn't thee be quiet, let ur alone, and behave thyself pratty?

What you don't know would make a great book

Source: A MEMOIR OF THE REVEREND SYDNEY SMITH BY HIS DAUGHTER LADY HOLLAND (Chapter 11)
Author: Sydney Smith (1771-1845)
First published: 1855
Type of work: Biographical memoir

Context: Sydney Smith, educated at Winchester and Oxford, was an English clergyman noted as the wittiest man of his time. In Edinburgh in

1133

1798 as tutor to the son of an English gentleman, he proposed the founding of the *Edinburgh Review* and, with Jeffrey, Brougham and Francis Horner, shared in its actual establishment. He superintended the first three numbers and continued to write for it for twenty-five years. After leaving Edinburgh, he lectured in London, held livings in Yorkshire and Somersetshire, and was made prebendary of Bristol and Canon of St. Paul's. No political writing of his time was more effective than his in presenting the need for toleration and reform; indeed Smith has been compared to Swift, though he lacks the bitterness and savagery of the 18th-century satirist. Lady Holland, his daughter, in writing the memoir of her famous father a decade after his death, remarks that her purpose is to depict the real man—as he can never be gaged through his own work—"the mode of life, the heart, the habit, the thoughts and feelings, the conversation, the home, the occupation." Allowing the man to speak for himself insofar as possible, she quotes freely from documents and records, both public and private. One cannot read far without being captivated by the clergyman's exuberant and spontaneous wit. Lady Holland records, for instance, this illustration of his verbal dexterity:

Some young person, answering on a subject in discussion, "I don't know that, Mr. Smith," he said, smiling, "Ah! **what you don't know would make a great book.**"

Whatever is best administered is best

Source: AN ESSAY ON MAN (Epistle III, l. 304)
Author: Alexander Pope (1688-1744)
First published: 1733-1734
Type of work: Philosophical poem

Context: The keynote of Pope's third epistle in *An Essay on Man* is that God works in many mysterious ways to achieve His ends, that diversity in human society all comes out at the divine goals. True religion and good government both originate, suggests the poet, regardless of their forms, in the principle of love, while tyranny and superstition derive from fear. He says that reason enables human beings to get along with one another and to help one another; the whole universe has an order, known to God, if not to man, Who has ordered the world for mankind's benefit. Pope's advice is then as follows:

For forms of government let fools contest;
Whate'er is best administer'd is best:
For modes of faith let graceless zealots fight;
His can't be wrong whose life is in the right.

In Faith and Hope the world will disagree,
But all mankind's concern is Charity:
All must be false that thwart this one great end,
And all of God that bless mankind or mend.

Whatever is, is right

Source: AN ESSAY ON MAN (Epistle I, l. 294)
Author: Alexander Pope (1688-1744)
First published: 1733
Type of work: Philosophical poem

Context: In *An Essay on Man* Pope argues that mankind cannot possibly know and judge the Creator and his handiwork, inasmuch as man can know only his own place in the great chain of being. Pope argues in the first epistle that man should not become embittered about his place nor complain because human beings are imperfect. As Pope puts it, ". . . say not man's imperfect, Heav'n in fault;/ Say rather, man's as perfect as he ought." Along with this statement, Pope admonishes man not to have so much conceit as to believe himself the final cause of creation. Summing up, in the last verse paragraph of the first epistle, Pope writes:

Cease then, nor Order imperfection name:
Our proper bliss depends on what we blame.
Know thy own point: this kind, this due degree
Of blindness, weakness, Heav'n bestows on thee.
Submit.—In this, or any other sphere,
Secure to be as blest as thou canst bear:
Safe in the hand of one disposing Pow'r,
Or in the natal, or the mortal hour.
All Nature is but art, unknown to thee;
All chance, direction, which thou canst not see;
All discord, harmony not understood;
All partial evil, universal good:
And, spite of pride, in erring reason's spite,
One truth is clear, **Whatever is, is right.**

Whatever is worth doing at all, is worth doing well

Source: LETTERS TO HIS SON (Letter 1)
Author: Philip Dormer Stanhope, Lord Chesterfield (1694-1773)
First published: 1774
Type of work: Personal letters

Context: In his first letter to his son (who, although illegitimate, also bore the name Philip Stanhope), Lord Chesterfield advises him on the ne-

1135

cessity of attention to detail in a gentleman's daily life and habits. Lord Chesterfield was well qualified to offer such advice, being widely travelled, and a gentleman—as well as highly regarded at court and an intimate of such literary leaders of his day as Swift, Pope, and Voltaire. A fastidious eighteenth century peer, who earlier in the letter urges his son to bear with unavoidable ". . . accidents, rubs, and difficulties . . ."

and to avoid negligence and laziness, as well as to gain the desire to excel in all things, including speech and writing, Chesterfield notes that without self-discipline one cannot make his mark in the world. Sounding a bit like Polonius, he assures his son of his belief in his intellectual and social capacity, saying ". . . you have the means in your hands . . ." and adding:

> . . . In truth, **whatever is worth doing at all, is worth doing well;** and nothing can be done well without attention; I therefore carry the necessity of attention down to the lowest things, even to dancing and dress.

What's done is done

Source: MACBETH (Act III, sc. ii, l. 12)
Author: William Shakespeare (1564-1616)
First published: 1623
Type of work: Dramatic tragedy

Context: Macbeth, Thane of Cawdor, murders King Duncan of Scotland, hoping to hasten the fulfillment of a prophecy by three witches that he shall soon be king. Impatient and ambitious, he assassinates the king in his sleep while the latter is a guest in his castle. Lady Macbeth smears the king's grooms with blood, thereby fastening blame on them. The death discovered and the house aroused, Macbeth slays the king's grooms, claiming they are instruments of murder. The king's sons, aware of treachery and afraid for their lives, flee, one to England, the other to Ireland. Because of their flight, suspicion fastens upon them as perpetrators of the crime, and Macbeth is elected King of Scotland. But he is not content, for he fears Banquo, a former fellow-general whom the witches prophesied would be the begetter of kings. Because Macbeth has no heir, the fact that Banquo's offspring shall gain the throne rankles in him, and he plans to have Banquo and his son Fleance murdered. As he plots, Lady Macbeth sends for him. He comes, brooding. She misreads his thoughts, thinking he is conscience-stricken.

LADY MACBETH
How now my lord, why do you keep alone,
Of sorriest fancies your companions making,

1136

Using those thoughts which should indeed have died
With them they think on? Things without all remedy
Should be without regard: **what's done is done.**

What's in a name?

Source: ROMEO AND JULIET (Act II, sc. ii, l. 43)
Author: William Shakespeare (1564-1616)
First published: 1597
Type of work: Dramatic tragedy

Context: Romeo stands beneath the window enraptured at the sight of his beloved Juliet above him. He feels that he should reveal his presence in the orchard but is too much bewitched. Instead of speaking to her, he debates with himself whether he should speak. While he remains silent, Juliet, completely unaware of his presence, without shame or self-consciousness, pours out her love and her awareness of the terrible plight of these "star-crossed" lovers because they are members of warring families. Her speech contains one of her more beautiful and pathetic statements, the poignant rhetorical question:

JULIET
'Tis but thy name that is my enemy.
Thou art thyself, though not a Montague.
What's Montague? It is nor hand nor foot,
Nor arm nor face, nor any other part
Belonging to a man. O be some other name.
What's in a name? That which we call a rose
By any other word would smell as sweet;
So Romeo would, were he not Romeo called,
Retain that dear perfection which he owes
Without that title. Romeo doff thy name,
And for thy name which is no part of thee,
Take all myself.

What's past help, should be past grief

Source: THE WINTER'S TALE (Act III, sc. ii, ll. 223-224)
Author: William Shakespeare (1564-1616)
First published: 1623
Type of work: Tragi-comedy

Context: Leontes, King of Sicilia, believes his wife, Queen Hermione, is guilty of adultery with his boyhood friend, Polixenes, King of Bohemia. He publicly proclaims her an adulteress, takes her small son, Mamil-

1137

lius, from her, and throws her into prison. She is pregnant and soon gives birth to a girl. Leontes disowns the child. Brought to trial, Hermione defends herself and declares her fidelity with dignity. Word is brought from the oracle of Delphi that convinces Leontes he has misjudged his wife and Polixenes. But before he can right the wrong, Mamillius, his son, dies of grief at his mother's sufferings. At the news, Hermione swoons, is removed from the court, and her waiting woman, Paulina returns with the news that she, too, is dead. She rails at Leontes with effect, but when rebuked by a lord, is contrite at her behavior.

PAULINA

I am sorry for't.
All faults I make, when I shall come to know them,
I do repent. Alas, I have showed too much
The rashness of a woman; he is touched
To the noble heart. What's gone, and **what's past help,**
Should be past grief.

• • •

What's past is prologue

Source: THE TEMPEST (Act II, sc. i, l. 253)
Author: William Shakespeare (1564-1616)
First published: 1623
Type of work: Tragi-comedy

Context: Antonio, the usurping Duke of Milan, and Alonso, the King of Naples, together with Alonso's brother, Sebastian, an aged counselor, Gonzales, and others, are at sea, and, during a tempest, their ship is driven ashore on an island. They believe themselves to be the only survivors, and that Alonso's son, Ferdinand, is dead. Weary, all fall asleep except Sebastian and Antonio. Antonio, who stole his dukedom from his brother, hints to Sebastian that he can kill his brother, Alonso, and become the new King of Naples. Sebastian demurs, asserting the heir to the throne is Claribel, the Queen of Tunis. Antonio scoffs at him and continues his insidious suggestions.

ANTONIO

• • •

She that dwells
Ten leagues beyond man's life. She that from Naples
Can have no note, unless the sun were post—
The man-i'-th'-moon's too slow—till new-born chins
Be rough and razorable. She that—from whom
We all were sea-swallowed, though some cast again,
And, by that destiny, to perform an act
Whereof **what's past is prologue;** what to come,
In yours and my discharge.

1138

What's yours is mine, and all mine is yours

Source: THE THREE PENNY DAY (Act II, sc. ii, 1. 323, as translated by George
    E. Duckworth)
Author: Titus Maccius Plautus (c.255-184 B.C.)
First transcribed: Second century B.C.
Type of work: Dramatic comedy

Context: The maxims in regard to friendship are many and ancient. Shakespeare, who certainly had some familiarity with Latin, copies this one word for word in *Measure for Measure,* an appropriate apothegm to the theme of the play. In the original, however, the young man who says it is really using his sententious father's own words to get his way. In our time, with our penchant for satirizing serious quotations, the saying in regard to the double standard in marriage is "What's yours is mine and what's mine's my own."

> LYSITELES
> There's a young man here of noble family, a friend and companion of mine, who hasn't managed his affairs with much care and caution, father; I want to do him a favor, if you have no objection.

> PHILTO *(ironically)*
> Out of your own funds, I suppose?

> LYSITELES
> Of course; for **what's yours is mine, and all mine is yours.**

Whatsoever a man soweth, that shall he also reap

Source: GALATIANS 6:7
Author: Paul
First transcribed: c.49-52
Type of work: Religious epistle

Context: Paul writes to the churches of Galatia to make explicit the relationship between faith in Christ and the law of Moses. Christ, the fulfillment of the law and prophecy, brings to believers freedom from enslavement under the law: a Gentile does not have to become first a Jew and then a Christian, Paul says. The freedom from the Jewish legalistic code does not, however, remove the obligation of the believer to live a life worthy of the spiritual gift of eternal life which he has received:

> Be not deceived; God is not mocked: for **whatsoever a man soweth, that shall he also reap.**

1139

For he that soweth to his flesh shall of the flesh reap corruption; but he that soweth to the Spirit shall of the Spirit reap life everlasting.

And let us not be weary in well doing; for in due season we shall reap, if we faint not.

The wheel is come full circle

Source: KING LEAR (Act V, sc. iii, l. 174)
Author: William Shakespeare (1564-1616)
First published: 1608
Type of work: Dramatic tragedy

Context: This saying is not infrequently heard as a synonym for "we're right back where we started," or whenever, after a passage of time or events, we are faced with a similar set of conditions or circumstances. It may also mean that the roles of two persons are reversed but in a similar set of circumstances. In the play, the sons of the Earl of Gloucester, two half-brothers, are at odds with each other. Edmund, the illegitimate son, seeks to deprive Edgar of his rightful inheritance. The father believes Edmund, and Edgar flees into hiding, disguised as Tom, the madman. Edmund, meanwhile, rises to great power and place. Ultimately, however, Edgar encounters him, brands him traitor, challenges him to combat, and defeats him. Edmund, wounded, acknowledges that Edgar is in the right.

EDMUND
Th' hast spoken right, 'tis true.
The wheel is come full circle; I am here.

When angry, count ten before you speak

Source: A DECALOGUE OF CANONS FOR OBSERVATION IN PRACTICAL LIFE
Author: Thomas Jefferson (1743-1826)
First written: February 21, 1825
Type of work: Personal letter

Context: Thomas Jefferson was one of the most enlightened men of his generation. Besides statecraft, his interests included classical learning and literature, scientific speculation and experiment, agriculture, architecture, and education. Throughout his life he was in constant communication with friends and acquaintances in all parts of the world, and his letters make fascinating reading. In an epistle written the year before his death, he conveys philosophic counsel to his namesake, Thomas Jefferson Smith. Writing at the request of the boy's father, the aged statesman remarks that the "writer will be in the grave before you can weigh its counsels." Following a poetic description of "a good man" which stresses the importance of moral stamina and sound spiritual development, Jefferson states ten maxims designed as practical advice for the problems of daily life. The tenth is concerned with the passion of wrath. The lawyer hero of *Pudd'nhead Wilson,* by Mark Twain (1835-1910), has, however, a wrier maxim, which the quick-tempered Twain himself found useful throughout life: "When angry, count four; when very angry, swear" (*Pudd'nhead Wilson,* Chapter 10). Jefferson writes:

When angry, count ten before you speak; if very angry, an hundred.

When Duty whispers low, <u>Thou must</u>, the youth replies, <u>I can</u>

Source: VOLUNTARIES (Part III)
Author: Ralph Waldo Emerson (1803-1882)
First published: 1863
Type of work: Lyric poem

Context: Emerson glorifies freedom and urges his readers to fight for the "Eternal Rights." He castigates the sin of slavery, a sin that is perpetuated by the cowardice of lawmakers: "Heart too soft and will too weak/ To front the fate that crouches near. . . ." God will fight on the side of the slaves. "Justice conquers evermore," and God will reward those who have fought bravely for justice. Emerson's ideal man is the one who recognizes his own divine potentialities and fearlessly uses them to fight for freedom and justice:

> In an age of fops and toys,
> Wanting wisdom, void of right,
> Who shall nerve heroic boys
> To hazard all in Freedom's fight,—
> Break sharply off their jolly games,
> Forsake their comrades gay
> And quit proud homes and youthful dames
> For famine, toil and fray?
> Yet on the nimble air benign
> Speed nimbler messages,
> That waft the breath of grace divine
> To hearts in sloth and ease.
> So nigh is grandeur to our dust,
> So near is God to man,
> **When Duty whispers low, <u>Thou must</u>,**
> **The youth replies, <u>I can</u>.**

1141

When Greeks joined Greeks

Source: THE RIVAL QUEENS; OR, THE DEATH OF ALEXANDER THE GREAT (Act IV, sc. ii, 1. 419)
Author: Nathaniel Lee (1655-1692)
First published: 1677
Type of work: Dramatic tragedy

Context: Lee combined a theme of passionate love with manly and war-like elements in an attempt to appeal to all ages and classes, as well as both sexes. The play was an early declamatory tragedy, of the sort which delighted the audiences of the eighteenth century. In the play, Alexander the Great returns to Babylon, where he issues orders for a great feast. All present, with one exception, shower praise upon their great commander. The one exception is proud old Clytus, who served under King Philip, the father of Alexander. Clytus, in his pride, refuses to don Persian robes; he also refuses to kiss either the earth or the hand of Alexander. When the talk turns to war, Alexander is acclaimed as the greatest of warriors. Only Clytus dissents. He believes that King Philip, was "a better general and more expert soldier." He says that Philip fought men, while Alexander fights women.

CLYTUS
. . . I have seen him march,
And fought beneath his dreadful banner where
The stoutest at this table would ha' trembled.
Nay, frown not, sir; you can not look me dead.
When Greeks joined Greeks, then was the tug of war,
The labored battle sweat, and conquest bled.

When half-gods go, the gods arrive

Source: GIVE ALL TO LOVE (Stanza 6)
Author: Ralph Waldo Emerson (1803-1882)
First published: 1846
Type of work: Lyric poem

Context: "Give all to love," Emerson says. The true lover must sacrifice everything for love—family, friends, property, reputation, "and the Muse." Love is a god, and we must "Follow it utterly." True love is "not for the mean"; if lovers have courage and valor, they will be rewarded: "They shall return/ More than they were,/ And ever ascending." And yet the lover, in spite of his sacrifices and his devotion, must keep himself forever "Free as an Arab/ Of [his] beloved." "Cling with life to the maid," Emerson advises; but if she falls in love with another, then let her go. We must sacrifice all for our lover, but we must not hold her as a prisoner of love. We cannot put moral restrictions on a beloved. Let her go if she has a "roving eye," for someone better can take her place in the lover's heart:

> Though thou loved her as thyself,
> As a self of purer clay,
> Though her parting dims the day,
> Stealing grace from all alive;
> Heartily know,
> **When half-gods go,**
> **The gods arrive.**

When I consider how my light is spent

Source: SONNET XIX ("On His Blindness," First line)
Author: John Milton (1608-1674)
First published: 1673
Type of work: Sonnet

Context: The greatest blow of John Milton's life was his blindness, which he attributed directly to the intense work he had done in preparing the reply of the Commonwealth government to Salmasius' *The Support of the King*. Milton sought to defend the execution of Charles I. The keenness with which Milton felt his blindness is reflected also in the comments of the blind Samson in *Samson Agonistes*. Eventually he was successful in accepting his affliction as one of the mysteries of God's will; and his success in overcoming his loss to become a great poet is one of the supreme human achievements of English literature. Blindness struck when Milton was aware of his gift for writing but had far from fulfilled his literary ambitions. In the opening lines of the sonnet he recognizes that his talent, like those of the parable, should not be hidden:

> **When I consider how my light is spent,**
> Ere half my days, in this dark world and wide,
> And that one talent which is death to hide,
> Lodged with me useless, though my soul more bent
> To serve therewith my Maker, and present
> My true account. . . .

When I was in love with you, then I was clean and brave

Source: A SHROPSHIRE LAD (XVIII, stanza 1)
Author: A(lfred) E(dward) Housman (1859-1936)
First published: 1896
Type of work: Lyric poem

Context: A. E. Housman, in the poems that made up the slim volume called *A Shropshire Lad,* is preoccupied with youth. Youth to him is essentially tragic, for it lasts, in its beauty, such a short while. It is also tragic because of the effects of experience on its innocence. Youth either refuses to learn or, if it learns, the lesson is one of suffering. Further, the poet has no patience with the sentimentalities traditionally associated with this period of life. In this short poem he punctures the sentimental notion that love can reform a wild young man. The little tragedy is told in eight lines:

> Oh, **when I was in love with you,**
> **Then I was clean and brave,**
> And miles around the wonder grew
> How well did I behave.
>
> And now the fancy passes by,
> And nothing will remain,
> And miles around they'll say that I
> Am quite myself again.

When lilacs last in the door-yard bloomed

Source: WHEN LILACS LAST IN THE DOOR-YARD BLOOM'D (Line 1)
Author: Walt Whitman (1819-1892)
First published: 1865
Type of work: Elegy

Context: Walt Whitman wrote four elegies to President Lincoln, appending them to the second edition of *Drum Taps* under the title "Memories of President Lincoln." The speaker mourns the death of the president in language of uncontrollable grief. He brings to the coffin a sprig of lilac that symbolizes his grief for the "powerful western fallen star," a grief that will recur each spring with the blooming of the lilacs. The hermit thrush singing in the swamp offers him comfort, but the poet delays to mediate on his grief. Finally he walks into the swamp with two companions, "the thought of death" and "the knowledge of death." He listens to the hermit thrush's ecstatic carol to death, the "Dark mother," whose embrace offers bliss rather than sorrow or terror. The poem closes with a mood of comfort and reconcilement that has replaced the anguish of the opening stanza:

When lilacs last in the door-yard bloom'd,
And the great star early droop'd in the western sky in the night,
I mourn'd—and yet shall mourn with ever-returning spring.

When lovely woman stoops to folly

Source: THE VICAR OF WAKEFIELD (Chapter 24)
Author: Oliver Goldsmith (1728-1774)
First published: 1766
Type of work: Song

Context: A major incident in this novel centers on the seduction of Olivia Primrose by Squire Thornhill, a worthless libertine who traps women into false marriages and soon abandons them. He attempts this deception with Olivia, but the marriage turns out to be perfectly legal, and he is caught in his own trap. The seduction, however, in no way lessens the love that the Primroses feel for their daughter. Shortly after the affair, the family breakfasts in the countryside at the very spot where "Olivia first met her seducer, and every object served to recall her sadness." So moved is Mrs. Primrose that she asks Olivia to sing a brief song which she calls a "melancholy air." Olivia sings so exquisitely that her father is deeply moved. T. S. Eliot (1888-1965) in *The Waste Land* (1922) uses the song's opening line in a passage of his own poem showing a modern girl's casual attitude toward sex: "When lovely woman stoops to folly and/ Paces about her room again, alone,/ She smoothes her hair with automatic hands,/ And puts a record on the gramophone."

When lovely woman stoops to folly,
    And finds too late that men betray,
What charm can soothe her melancholy,
    What art can wash her guilt away?

The only art her guilt to cover,
    To hide her shame from every eye,
To give repentance to her lover,
    And wring his bosom—is to die.

When shall I see those halcyon days?

Source: THE CLOUDS (Line 465, as translated by T. Mitchell)
Author: Aristophanes (c.448-c.385 B.C.)
First transcribed: Fourth century B.C.
Type of work: Dramatic comedy

Context: This deft and witty treatment of Socrates and the Sophists make of this play one of the most engaging for modern audiences so befuddled with relativism and existentialism. Here an old man Strepsiades tries in vain to learn the double talk from the Thoughtery in order to baffle his creditors. Unable to get his son Phidippides to attend the school —an attempt to exercise poetic justice, for it is the son whose riotous living has brought bankruptcy upon them—the old fellow goes but does not understand a single word. Hence, he queries the chorus concerning the school and what it can do for him, although in this less fanciful and more accurate translation the common expression is absent: "And what am I to gain?" "With the Clouds you will obtain/ The most happy, the most enviable life." "Is it possible for me/ Such felicity to see?" "Yes, and men shall come and wait/ In their thousands at your gate, . . ." Here, however, is the well-known translation:

STREPSIADES
What, I pray you!

CHORUS
What but to live the envy of mankind
Under our patronage?

STREPSIADES
When shall I see
Those halcyon days?

CHORUS
Then shall your doors be throng'd
With clients waiting for your coming forth, . . .

When sorrows come, they come in battalions

Source: HAMLET (Act IV, sc. v, ll. 78-79)
Author: William Shakespeare (1564-1616)
First published: 1603
Type of work: Dramatic tragedy

Context: Ophelia is the daughter of Polonius, chief councilor to King Claudius of Denmark. Her brother Laertes is abroad. To determine if Prince Hamlet, the King's nephew, who has been behaving erratically, is indeed mad, she allows herself to be used by her father and the king as a plant. Hamlet sees through the device and turns on her. She, who believed he loved her, is unsettled. Shortly after this event, her father is killed accidentally by Hamlet, who is then sent to England. This death is too much for Ophelia. With Laertes absent, and with no one to turn to for support, she loses her mind. King Claudius and Queen Gertrude witness her mad behavior; then Claudius turns to Gertrude, saying

1146

CLAUDIUS

O this is the poison of deep grief, it springs
All from her father's death. And now behold,
O Gertrude, Gertrude—
When sorrows come, they come not single spies,
But **in battalions. . . .**

When the cloud is scattered, the rainbow's glory is shed

Source: WHEN THE LAMP IS SHATTERED (Stanza 1)
Author: Percy Bysshe Shelley (1792-1822)
First published: 1824
Type of work: Lyric poem

Context: When the source dies, then the produce disappears. The destruction of the lamp and the lute extinguishes light and music; likewise, "The heart's echoes render/ No song when the spirit is mute . . . When hearts have once mingled,/ Love first leaves the well-built nest;/ The weak one is singled/ To endure what it once possessed." Love is frail and fleeting. By putting our faith in unstable emotions, we leave ourselves subject to abandonment and heartbreak: "From thy nest every rafter/ Will rot, and thine eagle home/ Leave the naked to laughter,/ When leaves fall and cold winds come." The first stanza develops the theme symbolically:

> When the lamp is shattered,
> The light in the dust lies dead;
> **When the cloud is scattered,**
> **The rainbow's glory is shed.**
> When the lute is broken,
> Sweet tones are remembered not;
> When the lips have spoken,
> Loved accents are soon forgot.

When the evening is spread out against the sky

Source: THE LOVE SONG OF J. ALFRED PRUFROCK
Author: T(homas) S(tearns) Eliot (1888-1965)
First published: 1915
Type of work: Metaphysical poem

Context: The description of the evening with which the poem opens is a "conceit," as the metaphysical poets used the term; that is, a similarity between apparently unlike objects has been perceived by the mind of the poet. By this means, the reader is startled, almost shocked, into atten-

1147

tion. The poem, ironically called a "love song," describes a timid, inhibited, ineffectual man as he goes toward a fashionable reception. He proceeds on his way hesitatingly: he knows that he will meet overwhelmingly intellectual people but that he will be too shy to talk and yet too shy to leave. So he goes through the side-streets, in a cheap part of the city, to the reception where he will be unhappy because of his awareness of his timidity and his fear of being laughed at. The poem begins:

> Let us go then, you and I,
> **When the evening is spread out against the sky**
> Like a patient etherized upon a table;
> Let us go, through certain half-deserted streets,
> The muttering retreats
> Of restless nights in one-night cheap hotels. . . .

When the frost is on the pumpkin

Source: WHEN THE FROST IS ON THE PUNKIN (Refrain)
Author: James Whitcomb Riley (1849-1916)
First published: 1882
Type of work: Dialect poem

Context: In his poem "When the Frost is on the Punkin," James Whitcomb Riley gives an animated picture of the farm in the autumn of the year. He says "it's then's the times a feller is a-feelin' at his best. . . ." Though other seasons have their merits, the late fall stands out because it is the time of completed harvest—barns are filled with corn, the cider-making is over, and "your wimmern-folks is through/ With their mince and apple-butter, and theyr souse and saussage, too! . . ." The poet is so pleased with the season and his plentiful harvest that if the Angels were "wantin' boardin', and they'd call around on *me*—/ I'd want to 'commodate 'em —all the whole-indurin' flock—. . . ." The following is the end of the second stanza with the concluding line that is repeated as a refrain:

> But the air's so appetizin'; and the landscape through the haze
> Of a crisp and sunny morning of the airly autumn days
> Is a pictur' that no painter has the colorin' to mock—
> **When the frost is on the punkin** and the fodder's in the shock.

When the steed is stolen shut the stable door

Source: THE PROVERBS OF JOHN HEYWOOD (Part I, chapter 10)
Author: John Heywood (1497?-1580?)
First published: 1546
Type of work: Gnomic poetry

Context: The author is recounting to his young friend, who seeks advice on marriage, a story which demonstrates that it is better not to marry in haste and repent in leisure. The story concerns a young couple who sought the opinion of the author about their marriage and were advised to return to their former homes. The young wife went back to her uncle and aunt but found there a cool welcome. The aunt felt that the young lady had acted in haste. Although the young wife declares that she is repentant, the aunt is not convinced. The aunt's proverb about the steed and stable is a widely quoted one.

> Too late, (quoth mine aunt), this repentance showed is:
> **When the steed is stolen shut the stable durre.**
> I took her for a rose, but she breedeth a burr;
> She cometh to stick to me now in her lack;
> Rather to rent off my clothes fro my back,
> Than to do me one farthing worth of good.

When thou art at Rome, do as they do at Rome

Source: DON QUIXOTE (Part II, Book IV, chapter 54)
Author: Miguel de Cervantes Saavedra (1547-1616)
First published: 1615
Type of work: Satirical novel

Context: Surely one of the early pilgrims who went to Rome started the practice that caused Robert Burton to set down in his *Anatomy of Melancholy* (1621) (Memb. 2, Subsec. 1): "When they are in Rome they do there as they see done." We say "When in Rome, do as the Romans do." Sancho Panza, riding his ass, Dapple, from his island to join his master, meets half a dozen pilgrims. To his surprise, one of them addresses him by name and identifies himself as a former shopkeeper from Sancho's village, Ricote the Morisco. He invites Sancho to have lunch with them. The squire watches their lusty manner of eating and the way they pour down their wine.

> Sancho admired all this extremely; he could not find the least fault with it; quite contrary, he was for making good the proverb, **When thou art at Rome, do as they do at Rome.** . . .

When you are old and gray and full of sleep

Source: WHEN YOU ARE OLD (Stanza 1)
Author: William Butler Yeats (1865-1939)
First published: 1893
Type of work: Lyric poem

Context: This poem is a loose paraphrase of the famous sonnet by Pierre de Ronsard (1524-1585) beginning "Quand vous serez bien vielle, au soir, à la chandelle . . ." Like Ronsard, Yeats describes an old woman sitting by the fire dreaming of her youth and of her beauty long since fled. Ronsard ends his sonnet with the admonition that since his beloved will one day be this old woman, with only her memories to cherish, she should not spurn his love today when it is offered. Yeats has a different ending: the beloved, when she is old, will read his poems and will understand that he alone loved her for her "pilgrim soul," that is, for the essential part of her, and she will remember ". . . how love fled." The first stanza follows:

> **When you are old and grey and full of sleep,**
> And nodding by the fire, take down this book,
> And slowly read, and dream of the soft look
> Your eyes had once, and of their shadows deep; . . .

When you call me that, smile!

Source: THE VIRGINIAN: A HORSEMAN OF THE PLAINS (Chapter 2)
Author: Owen Wister (1860-1938)
First published: 1902
Type of work: Novel

Context: The Virginian, a tall, lanky cowboy, originally from Virginia, is sent to Medicine Bow to meet a man from the East who is going to visit Sunk Creek ranch, some 263 miles from the town. As the visitor's baggage had not arrived with him, he and the Virginian must spend the night in town to wait for the baggage before making the trip to the ranch. Several times during the afternoon, Steve, a friend of the Virginian, calls the latter a son-of-a —, without the Virginian's becoming upset. That evening, however, while the Virginian is playing cards in the saloon, one of the players, Trampas, says to him: "Your bet, you son-of-a —." The Virginian's reaction follows:

> The Virginian's pistol came out, and his hand lay on the table, holding it unaimed. And with a voice as gentle as ever, the voice that sounded almost like a caress, but drawling a very little more than usual, so that there was almost a space between each word, he issued his orders to the man Trampas:—
> **"When you call me that, smile!"**

When you have eliminated the impossible, whatever remains, however improbable, must be the truth

Source: THE SIGN OF FOUR (Chapter 6)
Author: Sir Arthur Conan Doyle (1859-1930)
First published: 1890
Type of work: Short story

Context: While working on the case of the mysterious disappearance of the father of Miss Mary Morstan, Sherlock Holmes explains and demonstrates to Dr. Watson his method of observation and deduction. As the case develops, Thaddeus Sholto confesses that his father, John Sholto, a good friend to Mary's father, Captain Morstan, was involved in the disappearance and accidental death of the latter. A valuable treasure left by John Sholto on his death had just turned up and was to be shared with Mary Morstan. Thaddeus takes the interested parties to his brother's house where the treasure is supposedly being kept, but on arriving they find that the brother has been murdered. Sherlock Holmes learns that two people had been in the room with the murdered man: one had lowered a rope to allow the second to enter through the window. At this point Dr. Watson cannot understand how the first entered the room. He asks Holmes for the solution, and the detective replies:

"You will not apply my precept," he said, shaking his head. "How often have I said to you that **when you have eliminated the impossible, whatever remains, however improbable, must be the truth?**" . . .

Where are the snows of yester-year?

Source: THE BALLAD OF DEAD LADIES (Last line)
Author: François Villon (1431- ?)
First transcribed: 1461
Type of work: Ballad

Context: In this melancholy poem, Villon wonders at the passing of all beauty, exemplified by the passing of beautiful ladies of history, for example, Lady Flora, Hipparchia, Héloïse, Joan of Arc. He ends each of the four stanzas with the refrain about the passing of snow. The same lament was used by Justin H. McCarthy (1861-1936), in *A Ballad of Dead Ladies: After Villon, Envoy.* Villon's poem concludes:

Nay, never ask this week, fair lord,
Where they are gone, nor yet this year,
Except with this for an overword—
But **where are the snows of yester-year?**

Where burning Sappho loved and sung

Source: DON JUAN (Canto III)
Author: George Gordon, Lord Byron (1788-1824)
First published: 1821 (Cantos III-V)
Type of work: Lyric poem

Context: This lyric poem, a lament for the present slavery of Greece, is inserted bodily between Stanzas 86 and 87 of *Don Juan,* Canto III. It purports to be the song of a poet who is entertaining Juan and Haidée in the absence of the latter's pirate father. The poet is a clever fellow who can suit his song to any audience: "In France, for instance, he would write a chanson;/ In England a six canto quarto tale;/ In Spain he'd make a ballad or romance . . ./ In Greece, he'd sing some sort of hymn like this . . . (Stanza 86). Sappho (fl. about 600 B.C.) was a native of Lesbos, an island of Greece. Only a few fragments of her poetry survive, but these are marked by great beauty and passion, the kind of poetry that would appeal to Byron. The first stanza of the poem is as follows:

> The isles of Greece, the isles of Greece!
> **Where burning Sappho loved and sung,**
> Where grew the arts of war and peace,
>   Where Delos rose, and Phoebus sprung!
> Eternal summer gilds them yet,
> But all, except their sun, is set.

Where ignorance is bliss, 'tis folly to be wise

Source: ODE ON A DISTANT PROSPECT OF ETON COLLEGE (Lines 99-100)
Author: Thomas Gray (1716-1771)
First published: 1747
Type of work: Didactic poem

Context: In this typically neoclassical ode, his first published work, Gray describes Eton College, England's most famous preparatory school, as he sees it from a distance. The prospect of the spires and of the hills and playing fields leads him to observe that the innocent young scholars and athletes are unaware of the vicissitudes and tribulations they will face in later life: "Alas, regardless of their doom,/ The little victims play!/ No sense have they of ills to come,/ Nor care beyond today. . . ." All too soon, "the fury Passions" will beset the young men. In the last stanza the poet decides that it would perhaps be unkind to disturb them now by telling them of what later life holds. Gray's final sentence echoes the sad conclusion reached by the ancient Preacher: "He that increaseth knowledge increaseth sorrow." (Ecclesiastes 1:18)

To each his suff'rings; all are men,
   Condemn'd alike to groan,
The tender for another's pain;
   Th' unfeeling for his own.
Yet, ah! why should they know their fate?
Since sorrow never comes too late,
   And happiness too swiftly flies,
Thought would destroy their paradise.
No more, **where ignorance is bliss,**
   'Tis folly to be wise.

Where lingers late the rose

Source: ODES (Book I, Ode 38, "Away with Oriental Luxury!" l. 3, as translated by C. E. Bennett)
Author: Horace (65-8 B.C.)
First transcribed: 23-13 B.C.
Type: Ode

Context: Horace, unlike many of his contemporaries, hated the sumptuous luxury of "Persian elegance." He preferred the plainer, simpler things. Ode 38 in its entirety develops this theme of his preference for simplicity.

Persian elegance, my lad, I hate, and take no pleasure in garlands woven on linden bast. A truce to searching out the haunts **where lingers late the rose!** Strive not to add aught else to the plain myrtle! The myrtle befits both thee, the servant, and me, the master, as I drink beneath the thick-leaved vine.

Where more is meant than meets the ear

Source: IL PENSEROSO (Line 120)
Author: John Milton (1608-1674)
First published: 1645
Type of work: Lyric poem.

Context: In speaking of great poets, Milton mentions Chaucer. He refers to the *Squire's Tale,* which tells how a strange knight mounted on a horse of brass, rides into a festival given by the Tartar Khan Cambuscan, where he presents to Cambuscan's daughter, Canace, a magic mirror and ring. Chaucer tells one of Canace's adventures with the ring and then mentions what he will tell about Canace's brothers, Cambalo and Algarsife, and Canace's wedding, and at this point breaks off the tale. Milton wishes to know what else great poets can tell him, especially about enchantments that have a deeper significance than the words at first hearing convey. He writes:

Or call up him that left half told
The story of Cambuscan bold,
Of Camball, and of Algarsife,
And who had Canace to wife,
That owned the virtuous ring and glass,
And of the wondrous horse of brass,
On which the Tartar king did ride;
And if aught else great bards beside
In sage and solemn tunes have sung
Of tourneys and of trophies hung,
Of forests, and enchantments drear,
Where more is meant than meets the ear.

Where nobody gets old and bitter of tongue

Source: THE LAND OF HEART'S DESIRE
Author: William Butler Yeats (1865-1939)
First published: 1894
Type of work: Dramatic fantasy

Context: Bridget Bruin is criticizing her son Shawn's wife, Mary, for neglecting her chores and day-dreaming while reading an "old book," written by the Bruin grandfather. Father Hart defends the young: "Their hearts are wild,/ As be the hearts of birds, till children come." Father Hart then lightly admonishes Mary: "You should not fill your head with foolish dreams./ What are you reading?" Mary then replies:

MARY
How a Princess Edain,
A daughter of a King of Ireland, heard
A voice singing on a May Eve like this,
And followed, half awake and half asleep,
Until she came into the Land of Faery,
Where nobody gets old and godly and grave,
Where nobody gets old and crafty and wise,
Where nobody gets old and bitter of tongue.

Where the bee sucks, there suck I

Source: THE TEMPEST (Act V, sc. i, l. 88)
Author: William Shakespeare (1564-1616)
First published: 1623
Type of work: Tragi-comedy

Context: Prospero, formerly Duke of Milan and now a master magician, rules a mysterious, enchanted island. He commands Ariel, a spirit of the air, who does his magic bidding. Ariel looks forward eagerly to his freedom but meanwhile serves Prospero faithfully. Now, by means of a tempest and a shipwreck, he brings Prospero's old enemies and some friends before him into his magic circle. Ariel busily helps his master don his old ducal robes so that, when the magician releases the group before him from their enchantment, they will recognize him. As Ariel flits about he sings a charming song to his imminent freedom.

ARIEL

Where the bee sucks, there suck I.
In a cowslip's bell I lie.
There I couch when owls do cry.
On the bat's back I do fly
After summer merrily.
Merrily, merrily, shall I live now,
Under the blossom that hangs on the bough.

Where wealth accumulates, and men decay

Source: THE DESERTED VILLAGE (Line 52)
Author: Oliver Goldsmith (1728-1774)
First published: 1770
Type of work: Didactic and descriptive poem

Context: Goldsmith wrote this poem as a protest against the conditions in rural England brought about by the Enclosure Act and the early effects of the Industrial Revolution. The village of Auburn is an idealized picture of rustic life before these two causes had driven the country people into the cities or to America. Like Burns in the later "Cotter's Saturday Night" (1786), Goldsmith saw the peasantry as the mainstay of the nation and deplored the destruction of the simple village life of an earlier time. He moralizes thus on the situation:

Ill fares the land, to hast'ning ills a prey,
Where wealth accumulates, and men decay:
Princes and lords may flourish, or may fade;
A breath can make them, as a breath has made;
But a bold peasantry, their country's pride,
When once destroy'd, can never be supplied.

1155

Wherever Macdonald sits, there is the head of the table

Source: THE AMERICAN SCHOLAR
Author: Ralph Waldo Emerson (1803-1882)
First published: 1837
Type of work: Moral essay

Context: In this oration, delivered at Harvard in 1837, Emerson explores the nature and duties of the scholar, especially the American scholar. The true scholar is "Man Thinking," the self-trusting man who fearlessly refuses to "defer . . . to the popular cry." The scholar is influenced by Nature, the complement of the human soul, and by Books, which reflect the inspiration of the Oversoul. The scholar should read only enough of a book to see how the author has transmuted "life into truth." The American scholar should break free of Europe and develop his own soul and his own culture. Books are of value only as an inspiration. "The one thing in the world, of value, is the active soul . . . The soul active sees absolute truth and utters truth, or creates. In this action it is genius . . . genius looks forward . . . genius creates." Action is essential to the scholar; "Man Thinking must not be subdued by his instruments." Action and labor produce wisdom: "Only so much do I know, as I have lived." "Life is our dictionary." The scholar's duty is "to cheer, to raise, and to guide men by showing them facts amidst appearances." He is a free man and a fearless leader. A genius with a firm will and a strong character is always accepted as a leader, and his spiritual power is evident in any situation:

> . . . Not he is great who can alter matter, but he who can alter my state of mind. They are the kings of the world who give the color of their present thought to all nature and all art, and persuade men by the cheerful serenity of their carrying the matter that this thing which they do is the apple which the ages have desired to pluck, now at last ripe, and inviting nations to the harvest. The great man makes the great thing. **Wherever Macdonald sits, there is the head of the table.** . . . The day is always his who works in it with serenity and great aims. The unstable estimates of men crowd to him whose mind is filled with a truth. . . .

While stands the Coliseum, Rome shall stand

Source: CHILDE HAROLD'S PILGRIMAGE (Canto IV, stanza 145)
Author: George Gordon, Lord Byron (1788-1824)
First published: 1818 (Canto IV)
Type of work: Narrative Poem

Context: In this stanza Bryon is quoting from Gibbon's *The Decline* *and Fall of the Roman Empire* (1781), Chapter 71. The saying, originally reported by Bede, is attributed to the Anglo-Saxon pilgrims of the late seventh or early eighth century. In the poem, Byron describes the Coliseum by moonlight—"This long-explored but still exhaustless .mine/ Of contemplation . . ." (Stanza 128). Byron's own contemplations lead him, not only to the past grandeur of Rome and a stirring description of a dying gladiator, but also to his own wrongs, and he invokes Time and Nemesis to bring vengeance on his detractors (Stanzas 130-132). Eighteen stanzas of Canto IV are devoted to the Coliseum and Byron's reflections concerning both it and himself. In the last line of Stanza 145, he expresses his opinion of the world that has driven him into exile.

> "While stands the Coliseum, Rome shall stand;
> When falls the Coliseum, Rome shall fall;
> And when Rome falls—the World."
> . . . and these three mortal things are still
> On their foundations, and unalter'd all;
> Rome and her Ruin past Redemption's skill,
> The World, the same wide den—of thieves, or what ye will.

While there's life there's hope

Source: THE IDYLLS OF THEOKRITOS (Fourth, as translated by Barriss Mills)
Author: Theokritos (305?-250 B.C.)
First transcribed: Third century B.C.
Type of work: Pastoral poem

Context: Battos and Korydon, two countrymen, are discussing cows. They talk about the health of the cows and about various other things. Battos says that the pipe Aigon once made is mildewed. But Korydon says no, that he has the pipe and plays it sometimes. He then plays a song which ends with a comment on Amaryllis. The proverb has been widely used, for example by Cicero (*Epistolae* IX, 10), by John Gay (*The Sick Man and the Angel*), and many others. The following conversation ensues between Battos and Korydon:

BATTOS

Lovely Amaryllis, we'll never forget you, even in death. You alone were as dear to me as my goats, when you died. A bad spirit rules my fate.

KORYDON

Console youself, dear Battos. Things may be better tomorrow. **While there's life there's hope.** Only the dead have none. It's god's will, whether we have sun or rain.

Whistling to keep myself from being afraid

Source: AMPHITRYON (Act III, sc. i)
Author: John Dryden (1631-1700)
First published: 1690
Type of work: Dramatic comedy

Context: Although it was condemned for grossness and ribaldry in later and less uninhibited times, Dryden's comedy enjoyed great popularity in its own day, and continued long as a stock item in the repertoire. The line quoted above, although still an item of popular usage, has evolved considerably. For example, Robert Blair, in a long and somewhat lugubrious poem entitled *The Grave* (1743), creates this familiar image:

Oft, in the lone Church-yard at Night I've seen

By Glimpse of Moon-shine, chequering tho' the Trees,

The School-boy with his Satchel in his Hand,

Whistling aloud to bear his Courage up . . .

Whereas today, of course, we refer to such uneasy optimism quite simply as "whistling in the dark." The plot of Dryden's comedy is basically quite simple; Jupiter intends to seduce yet another mortal and beget one more minor god. In this case the object of his desire in Amphitryon's wife. One of the arrangements he makes involves the oafish servant Sosia; a junior god impersonates the latter, and the usual confusion results. The real Sosia, no matter what he does, is beaten for his pains. When Amphitryon desires a strict account from him, the unfortunate begins his story:

SOSIA

. . . In plain prose then,—I went darkling, and **whistling to keep myself from being afraid.** . . .

The white man's burden

Source: THE WHITE MAN'S BURDEN (Stanza 1)
Author: Rudyard Kipling (1865-1936)
First published: 1899
Type of work: Political poem

Context: On December 10, 1898, the United States and Spain came to peace. In "The White Man's Burden" Kipling gives vent to his vigorous nationalistic expansion attitudes. He states quite clearly his ideas about the role of the conquered in an almost Greco-pagan manner, and he gives his views about what he thinks the relationship among Cuba, the Philippines, and the United States will be. The poem is a warning to the United States, a warning of what it may expect in its new role as a colonial power.

Take up the White Man's burden—
Send forth the best ye breed—
Go bind your sons to exile
    To serve your captives' need;
To wait in heavy harness
    On fluttered folk and wild—
Your new-caught, sullen peoples,
    Half-devil and half-child.

Whited sepulchres

Source: MATTHEW 23:27
Author: Unknown (traditionally Matthew the Apostle)
First transcribed: c.75-100
Type of work: Gospel

Context: Jesus, in the temple in Jerusalem, is considered to be a prophet of God by many people, but a false teacher by the Pharisees and Sadducees, strict followers of the law. By asking various questions, His enemies hope to force Him to give heretical or treasonous answers. Provoked finally by their disbelief, their corruption, and their hindrance to the believer, He denounces them with a series of specific failures, which begin with the stern words "Woe unto you, scribes and Pharisees, hypocrites!" In the sixth denunciation, He calls attention to their outward purity, but their inward rottenness:

Woe unto you, scribes and Pharisees, hypocrites! for ye are like unto **whited sepulchres,** which indeed appear beautiful outward, but are within full of dead men's bones, and of all uncleanness.
Even so ye also outwardly appear righteous unto men, but within ye are full of hypocrisy and iniquity.

Whither thou goest, I will go

Source: RUTH 1:16
Author: Unknown
First transcribed: 450-250 B.C.
Type of work: Religious narrative

Context: Because of a famine in Palestine, Elimelech, his wife, Naomi, and their two sons, Mahlon and Chilion, leave their native Bethlehem and go to the land of Moab. After a short time, Elimelech dies. Naomi selects two Moabite maidens, Orpah and Ruth, as wives for her sons, but after

1159

ten years the sons also die. Naomi, now a widow and childless in a strange land, decides to return to Judah, the famine being over. Orpah and Ruth accompany Naomi as far as the border between Moab and Judah, intending to go to Bethlehem with her. Naomi, however, urges them to return to the homes of their families because, if they go with her, they, as strangers in Bethlehem, would have little hope of getting husbands. Orpah obediently returns to Moab, but Ruth says:

> . . . Entreat me not to leave thee, or to return from following after thee: for **whither thou goest, I will go;** and where thou lodgest, I will lodge: thy people shall be my people, and thy God my God. . . .

Who breaks a butterfly upon a wheel?

Source: EPISTLE TO DR. ARBUTHNOT (Line 308)
Author: Alexander Pope (1688-1744)
First published: 1735
Type of work: Satire

Context: This poetic epistle is cast in the form of a dialogue between the poet and his good friend, Dr. Arbuthnot. Pope uses the poem to make deadly satirical comments upon his contemporaries, with whom he found little favor himself. The "butterfly" of this quotation is John, Lord Hervey, a well-known, seemingly harmless, court favorite of the time. Pope, for some unexplained reason, conceived an antipathy for the man, who seems undeserving of the following lines the poet wrote about him:

> Let Sporus tremble—A. What? that thing of silk,
> Sporus, that mere white curd of Ass's milk?
> Satire or sense, alas! can Sporous feel?
> **Who breaks a butterfly upon a wheel?**

Who can refute a sneer?

Source: PRINCIPLES OF MORAL AND POLITICAL PHILOSOPHY (Vol. I, Book V, chapter 9)
Author: William Paley (1743-1805)
First published: 1785
Type of work: Philosophical treatise

Context: An English theologian and philosopher born in Peterborough, William Paley graduated from Cambridge in 1763 and became a fellow of his college. In 1776 he retired to the rectory at Musgrave, Westmoreland, and later held various church offices. In his voluminous work on moral and political philosophy, Paley describes "that science which teaches men their duty, and the reasons of it." In Book V, "Duties Toward God," the author speaks of the necessity of reverencing the Deity, of informing and directing those less inclined to belief by a solemnity and decorum of conduct. While a freedom of inquiry concerning spiritual matters is necessary, Christianity must never be made "a topic of raillery, a theme for the exercise of wit or eloquence, or a subject of contention for literary fame and victory." Referring to Edward Gibbon's *Decline and Fall of the Roman Empire* as an illustration (though not specifically naming it), Paley brands such a work "one continued sneer upon the cause of Christianity." He writes:

> . . . The knowledge this author possesses of the frame and conduct of the human mind, must have led him to observe, that such attacks do their execution without inquiry. **Who can refute a sneer?** Who can compute the number, much less, one by one, scrutinize the justice, of those disparaging institutions which crowd the pages of this elaborate history?

Who cannot live on twenty pounds a year cannot on forty

Source: THE TEMPLE: THE CHURCH PORCH (Stanza 30)
Author: George Herbert (1593-1633)
First published: 1633
Type of work: Political precepts

Context: The Church Porch contains seventy-seven stanzas of wholesome advice with which *The Temple* begins. Herbert warns against lust, against drinking more than two glasses of wine at a sitting, against oaths and swearing, idleness, sloth, sneaking, gluttony, and a host of other undesirable activities. He says that one should not be ashamed of living by rules, as all of nature is governed by them. One should be thrifty, but not covetous, and should live within his income. Youth can afford to spend the total income for the year, but those advancing in age must make provision for the future by saving. But in saving, one should be careful not to let accumulating become too important. Nor should one run into debt. If he cannot live on a certain sum, he will not be able to live on twice that amount, as the spendthrift's desires always exceed his income, no matter how large it may be. Herbert states the matter thus:

> By no means run in debt; take thine own measure.
> **Who cannot live on twenty pound a year**
> **Cannot on forty.**

Who ere shee bee, that not impossible shee

Source: WISHES. TO HIS (SUPPOSED) MISTRESSE (Stanza 1)
Author: Richard Crashaw (1613?-1649)
First published: 1646
Type of work: Lyric poem

Context: Crashaw's poetry is characterized by the use of rich and sensuous imagery, ornate devices, and elaborate metaphors. Deeply religious by nature and emotionally intense, he introduces one of his ideals in this poem. Taking her feature by feature, quality by quality, Crashaw sets forth his standard of womanhood until her portrait is complete. It is hardly surprising, in view of his requirements, that he never found her. After all, no human being could possess so many virtues: Crashaw is describing an angel. For all that his angel may be a dream impossible to attain, she is nonetheless that ideal all men consciously or unconsciously seek; and the poet speaks, perhaps, more universally than he intended:

> Who ere shee bee,
> That not impossible shee
> That shall command my heart and mee;
>
> . . .
>
> Till that Divine
> *Idaea,* take a shrine
> Of Chrystall flesh, through which to shine:
>
> Meet you her my wishes . . .

Who ever loved that loved not at first sight?

Source: HERO AND LEANDER (Line 176)
Author: Christopher Marlowe (1564-1593)
First published: 1598
Type of work: Narrative poem

Context: Leander, a youth who lives in Abydos, goes to the feast for Adonis held at Sestros, which is across the Hellespont from his home. At the temple there, he sees the priestess of Aphrodite, Hero. As she lifts her head from "sacrificing turtles' blood" her gaze meets that of Leander, and they instantly fall in love. The idea of instantaneous love was used by Shakespeare in *As You Like It,* Act III, sc. V, 1. 82, by George Chapman in *The Blind Beggar of Alexandria* (1598), and rather closely paralleled by Edward Gibbon in *Memoirs* (1796). Marlowe says:

> It lies not in our power to love or hate,
> For will in us is overrul'd by fate.
>
> . . .

Where both deliberate, the love is slight;
Who ever lov'd, that lov'd not at first sight?

Who is Silvia?

Source: THE TWO GENTLEMEN OF VERONA (Act IV, sc. ii, l. 38)
Author: William Shakespeare (1564-1616)
First published: 1623
Type of work: Dramatic comedy

Context: Valentine, one of the two gentlemen of Verona, has gone to Milan, where he has fallen in love with Silvia, the saucy and charming daughter of the Duke of Milan. The duke wants Silvia to marry Thurio, whom she detests. Informed by Proteus, the other gentleman of Verona, who has himself now abandoned Julia, his sweetheart of Verona, for Silvia, that Valentine means to elope with his daughter, the duke banishes Valentine from the country. Then he urges Thurio to press his suit. Thurio brings a group of musicians to the duke's palace to serenade Silvia. The song these musicians sing is one of Shakespeare's loveliest, as the first stanza demonstrates:

SONG

Who is Silvia? what is she,
That all our swains commend her?
Holy, fair, and wise is she:
The heaven such grace did lend her,
That she might admired be.

Who is to bell the cat?

Source: AESOP'S FABLES ("Belling the Cat")
Author: Aesop (fl. sixth century B.C.?)
First transcribed: Fourth century B.C.
Type of work: Moral tales of animals

Context: Although the original group of tales attributed to Aesop does not include this story, it does include a similar one in which the cat tries to outwit the mice who have retreated to their holes. The cat plays dead and hangs himself by his tail from a hook. The mice come out and say, "Very good, but I won't come near you even if they make a moneybag of you." In the popular fable, however, the mice believe they have a solution to their problem. One mouse says, "You will all agree . . . that our chief danger consists in the sly and treacherous manner in which the enemy approaches us. . . . I venture, therefore, to propose that a small bell be procured, and attached by a ribbon round the neck of the Cat. By this means we should always know when she was about, and could easily retire while she was in the neighborhood."

> This proposal met with general applause, until an old mouse got up and said: "That is all very well, but **who is to bell the Cat?**" The mice looked at one another and nobody spoke. Then the old mouse said:
> "It Is Easy To Propose Impossible Remedies."

Who saw life steadily, and saw it whole

Source: TO A FRIEND (Line 12)
Author: Matthew Arnold (1822-1888)
First published: 1849
Type of work: Sonnet

Context: Matthew Arnold, critic in poetry and prose of the nineteenth century, took upon himself the task of enlightening his contemporaries. Condemning the narrowness of the thinking of his times, he turned to the age of glory of Greece and found there the answer to the complete life, to the rounded mind and man. In his "To a Friend," he cites three of the Greeks most influential in his own life —Homer, whose adventure stirs his soul; Epictetus, whose Stoic philosophy sustains him; and Sophocles, whose plays with their serenity indicate the whole man, one who is not afraid to look straight at life and see it in its totality. Of Sophocles, he says:

> But be his
> My special thanks, whose even-balanced soul,
> From first youth tested up to extreme old age,
> Business could not make dull, nor Passion wild;
> **Who saw life steadily, and saw it whole;**
> The mellow glory of the Attic stage,
> Singer of sweet Colonus, and its child.

Who shall decide when doctors disagree?

Source: MORAL ESSAYS (Epistle III, 1. 1)
Author: Alexander Pope (1688-1744)
First published: 1731-1735
Type of work: Satirical poem

Context: This verse essay was addressed by the poet to Lord Bathurst and is cast into the form of a dialogue between the poet and the nobleman.

Pope chose as the subject of his poem the use of riches, beginning with the assumption that little is known about the subject, and that the popular views, based on mere opinion and prejudice, are wrong. The poet says that people ordinarily think of only two extremes in the use of wealth, avarice and prodigality, with no degrees between identified. Pope himself gives no final answer. In the quotation, when he uses the word "doctors" he does not mean medical men, as a twentieth century reader might assume; rather, he means learned men, or philosophers, as the word commonly meant in his time. The first question raised in the dialogue is spoken by the poet:

P[OPE]

Who shall decide when doctors disagree,
And soundest casuists doubt, like you and me?
You hold the word from Jove to Momus giv'n,
That Man was made the standing jest of Heav'n,
And gold but sent to keep the fools in play,
For some to heap, and some to throw away.

Who steals my purse steals trash

Source: OTHELLO (Act III, sc. ii, l. 157)
Author: William Shakespeare (1564-1616)
First published: 1622
Type of work: Dramatic tragedy

Context: Iago, evil and dissembling ancient (or ensign) to Othello, a Moorish military governor of Cyprus in the service of Venice, hates him because the Moor has made Michael Cassio his lieutenant in preference to himself. Iago, who has a reputation for honesty, determines to destroy both Othello and Cassio. By crafty maneuvers and luck, Iago plants in Othello's mind the thought that Cassio is having an affair with Othello's wife, Desdemona. Iago intimates that he knows more of this affair than he admits, a device calculated to lead Othello on. Othello impatiently desires to know Iago's thoughts, but Iago exquisitely stretches him upon the rack of doubt.

IAGO
• • •

It were not for your quiet nor your good,
Nor for my manhood, honesty, or wisdom,
To let you know my thoughts.

OTHELLO
What dost thou mean?

1165

IAGO

IAGO

Good name in man, and woman, dear my lord,
Is the immediate jewel of their souls.
Who steals my purse steals trash; 'tis something, nothing;   2
'Twas mine, 'tis his, and has been slave to thousands;
But he that filches from me my good name
Robs me of that which not enriches him,
And makes me poor indeed.

OTHELLO

By heaven I'll know thy thoughts.

Whoever he be that tells my faults, I hate him mortally!

Source: PARAPHRASES FROM CHAUCER ("The Wife of Bath, Her Prologue,"
Lines 351-352)
Author: Alexander Pope (1688-1744)
First published: c.1709
Type of work: Narrative poem

Context: As a young man Pope undertook to modernize portions of Chaucer's poetry to the English of the early eighteenth century. In this portion of the Wife of Bath's Prologue, that self-willed woman tells how she became intimate with her clerk and vowed if ever her husband died to take the clerk as her husband. As it turns out, the husband dies, and, after a brief month, the Wife of Bath marries the clerk, who has twenty years to her forty. The marriage is not a happy one, for the Wife is stubborn, willful, and a "rambler." Her young husband tries to preach to her, showing her faults to her and citing examples of good women. When his sermons prove unavailing he even, by the Wife's admission, strikes her on the face. His words and blows make no difference, for his spouse tells her fellow pilgrims on the way to Canterbury:

All this avail'd not, for **whoe'er he be**
That tells my faults, I hate him mortally!
And so do numbers more, I'll boldly say,
Men, women, clergy, regular and lay.

Whoever in discussion adduces authority uses not intellect but memory

Source: NOTEBOOKS (Aphorisms, Number 1)
Author: Leonardo da Vinci (1452-1519)
First transcribed: c.1500
Type of work: Notations on life and art

Context: The remarkable genius of Renaissance man was that he managed all things so well. No one, not even Michaelangelo, had so many sides to his nature as the great artist of The Last Supper and The Mona Lisa. In his notebooks, transcribed in a special shorthand, are many divisions, mostly directed to the business of drawing, of inventing, and of experimentation. These "pre-imagin- ings" or speculations are balanced with traditional wisdom, often in new and startling form. The basis of the selection is his belief that "the mutual desire of good men is knowl- edge." And while he was an icono- clast in many ways, he declares "I speak not against the sacred books, for they are the supreme truth." In a most recent translation, the following heads the division of wise sayings:

Whoever in discussion adduces authority uses not intellect but memory.
Good literature proceeds from men of natural probity, and since one ought rather to praise the inception than the result, you should give greater praise to a man of probity unskilled in let- ters than to one skilled in letters but devoid of probity. . . .

Whoever thinks a faultless piece to see, thinks what never was, nor is, nor ever shall be

Source: AN ESSAY ON CRITICISM (Part II, ll. 53-54)
Author: Alexander Pope (1688-1744)
First published: 1711
Type of work: Satire

Context: Pope admonishes the reader, "A perfect judge will read each work of wit/ With the same spirit that its author writ." He warns against seeing a work of art only as a collection of parts, recommending that we learn to look at a poem, any piece of literature, in its entirety, for little faults can al- ways be found, he maintains. He points out that discrepancies will be found "Where Nature moves, and Rapture warms the mind" of the poet. In other words, Pope is telling us not to look at the details of language, ver- sification, and thought alone, but rather to see these simply as parts of a complete work of art:

Whoever thinks a faultless piece to see,
Thinks what ne'er was, nor is, nor e'er shall be.
In every work regard the writer's end,
Since none can compass more than they intend;
And if the means be just, the conduct true,
Applause, in spite of trivial faults, is due.
As men of breeding, sometimes men of wit,
T'avoid great errors must the less commit;
Neglect the rules each verbal critic lays,
For not to know some trifles is a praise.

Whom the gods would destroy they first make mad

Source: SENTENTIAE (Maxim 911)
Author: Publilius Syrus (fl. first century B.C.)
First transcribed: c.42 B.C.
Type of work: Moral sentences

Context: While the first evidence of this ancient proverb is found in Euripides' "Those whom the Gods wish to destroy, they first deprive of their senses," the Latin proverb is the one which has come down to us: *Quos deus vult perdere, prius dementat.* In Sophocles' play *Ajax,* the giant-warrior illustrates the truth of the belief when, because of his pride, he decides to murder all the Greek leaders. Athena thereupon makes him mad so that he slaughters sheep and cattle in the belief that he is wreaking vengeance, whereupon he falls on his sword. Lycurgus four hundred years earlier comments: When falls on man the anger of the gods,/ First from his mind they banish understanding. Boswell quotes Johnson as saying this is the proverb everyone quotes but of which no one knows the source. Dryden states in a poem: For those whom God to ruin has design'd,/ He fits for fate, and first destroys their mind. Longfellow in America quotes the original almost verbatim:

Whom the Gods would destroy they first make mad.

Whom the king delighteth to honor

Source: ESTHER 6:9
Author: Unknown
First transcribed: c.400-100 B.C.
Type of work: Religious narrative

Context: Ahasuerus, reigning monarch from India to Ethiopia, unable to sleep one evening, orders his book of chronicles read to him. Hearing of

1168

the bravery of Mordecai in reporting a plot of two of the king's eunuchs against his life, Ahasuerus ascertains from his servants that Mordecai has never been honored for this service. Haman, a recently appointed court official, happens just to have entered the palace with the intention of petitioning the king to hang Mordecai, who, being a strict Jew, refuses to bow down as Haman passes. The king summons Haman, intending discreetly to seek his advice for honoring Mordecai:

> . . . What shall be done unto the man whom the king delighteth to honor? Now Haman thought in his heart, To whom would the king delight to do honour more than to myself:
> And Haman answered. . . .
> Let the royal apparel be brought which the king useth to wear, and the horse that the king rideth upon, and the crown royal which is set upon his head:
> . . . that they may array the man withal **whom the king delighteth to honour,** and bring him on horseback through the street of the city, and proclaim before him. . . .

Whom the Lord loveth he chasteneth

Source: HEBREWS 12:6
Author: Unknown
First transcribed: 60-96
Type of work: Religious argument and exhortation

Context: The writer, arguing firmly the revelation of God through Christ, shows that the new faith of Christianity goes beyond the faith of the Old Testament. Declaring the ineffectiveness of the old ritualistic practices, he warns the people of the day of judgment, but encourages them for their faithfulness. He defines "faith" ("Now faith is the substance of things hoped for, the evidence of things not seen") and illustrates it by citing from the Scriptures the sufferings experienced by men of God. Exhorting the people to persevere through Christ in the many struggles before them, he notes the suffering of Christ and says that God causes His children to suffer for reasons of discipline and love:

> For **whom the Lord loveth he chasteneth,** and scourgeth every son whom he receiveth.
> If ye endure chastening, God dealeth with you as with sons; for what son is he whom the father chasteneth not?

Whom unmerciful Disaster followed fast and followed faster

Source: THE RAVEN (Stanza 11)
Author: Edgar Allan Poe (1809-1849)
First published: 1845
Type of work: Lyric poem

Context: In this intricately structured, highly musical, and supremely melancholy poem, Poe reveals the haunted mind of a man who is tormented by the death of his beloved, "the lost Lenore." A mysterious raven appears at his window at midnight. The raven can speak only one word—"Nevermore." In the grief-crazed man's mind, the bird is a visitor from "the Night's Plutonian shore," a messenger who can bring him some news of Lenore, some hope of his seeing her again in another world. Unfortunately, the raven answers all of the man's frantically hopeful questions with that grimly final word, "Nevermore." When the bird first enters the room, the man marvels to hear it uttering such a strange word so clearly. He tries to explain the bird's one-word vocabulary in human terms, not yet daring to recognize the raven's supernatural nature. Unaware that the bird will be his eternal tormentor, the "neverflitting" reminder of his unending loneliness, the man tries to rationalize the ominous word, "Nevermore":

> Startled at the stillness broken by reply so aptly spoken,
> "Doubtless," said I, "what it utters is its only stock and store,
> Caught from some unhappy master **whom unmerciful Disaster
> Followed fast and followed faster** till his songs one burden bore—
> Till the dirges of his Hope that melancholy burden bore
>   Of 'Never—nevermore.' "

Whose house is of glass must not throw stones

Source: JACULA PRUDENTUM (Number 196)
Author: George Herbert (1593-1633)
First published: 1640
Type of work: Proverbial saying

Context: To George Herbert, English divine and poet, and the author of *The Temple,* is attributed a collection of proverbs first issued in 1640 under the title of *Outlandish Proverbs* and reissued in enlarged form in 1651 as *Jacula Prudentum.* The work contains 1184 sayings either wise or witty, or both. A large number of the sayings exist in similar forms, some in books with specific authors but many simply in the traditional speech of the folk. The most commonly heard variant of the proverb about glass houses is "People who live in glass houses should not throw stones." Both this form and Herbert's mean that people who are guilty of faults should not criticize others, lest their own faults be held up to ridicule. The "glass houses" apparently originally meant houses with glass windows instead of oiled cloth, as is seen in John Ray's A *Collection of English Proverbs* (1670): "Who hath glass windows of his own must take heed how he throw stones at his neighbor's house." A more fanciful variant is contained in Shebeare's *Matrimony* (1745): "Thou shouldst not throw stones, who have a head of glass thyself." The general idea is well expressed in Herbert:

Whose house is of glass must not throw stones at another.

Whose little body lodged a mighty mind

Source: THE ILIAD (Book V, 1. 999, as translated by Alexander Pope)
Author: Homer (c.850 B.C.)
First transcribed: Sixth century B.C.
Type of work: Epic poem

Context: In this book are related the heroic deeds of Diomedes, he who wounds Aeneas and his mother Aphrodite. Hector rallies his forces and enlists the aid of Ares, god of war, who also is wounded by Diomedes, thus putting a stop to interference in the battle on the plains of Troy. Stentor speaks out and shames the Greeks, though Athene rallies them, once more commenting on Tydeus, father of the great warrior Diomedes. (There was another small man, called Little Ajax, who threw the spear farthest and ran almost as fast as Achilles.)

> Degenerate Prince! and not of Tydeus' kind
> **Whose little body lodged a mighty mind;**
> Foremost he press'd in glorious toils to share,
> And scarce refrained when I forbade the war . . .
> Such nerves I gave him, and such force in fight,
> Thou too no less hast been my constant care;
> Thy hands I arm'd and sent thee forth to war. . . .

Whoso would be a man, must be a nonconformist

Source: SELF-RELIANCE
Author: Ralph Waldo Emerson (1803-1882)
First published: 1841
Type of work: Moral essay

Context: Emerson's essay "Self-Reliance" contains some of his most quoted epigrams (see "To be great is to be misunderstood" and "A foolish consistency is the hobgoblin of little minds"). Here Emerson argues against the tyranny of custom, of tradition, against any force that keeps a man from being himself. The first law of man should be to trust himself. The boy is nonchalant and outspoken; he spontaneously tells you exactly what he thinks. But the man, as he grows older, is forced by society into conformity, for, according to Emerson, society is in conspiracy against individualism. Yet it is only by being individuals that we can accomplish anything worth doing even though society will be displeased with us. "No law," says Emerson, "can be sacred to me but that of my nature." The seventh paragraph of the long essay begins

> **Whoso would be a man, must be a nonconformist.** He who would gather immortal palms must not be hindered by the name of goodness, but must explore if it be goodness. Nothing is at last sacred but the integrity of your own mind. . . .

Why don't you speak for yourself, John?

Source: THE COURTSHIP OF MILES STANDISH (Part III, l. 339)
Author: Henry Wadsworth Longfellow (1807-1882)
First published: 1858
Type of work: Narrative poem

Context: Longfellow writes of his Pilgrim ancestors, John and Priscilla Alden. Miles Standish, "a blunt old Captain," asks young John Alden to propose to Priscilla for him. Standish is a lonely widower, and he is afraid to propose to her himself. Alden hesitates, for he is also in love with Priscilla. But he finally consents to carry out "the lover's errand." Alden praises Standish in such a clumsy manner that Priscilla turns against the Captain. Standish loses the maiden because he has not followed his own advice: ". . . if you wish a thing to be well done,/ You must do it yourself, you must not leave it to others!" John has been praising Standish passionately:

> But as he warmed and glowed, in his simple and eloquent language,
> Quite forgetful of self, and full of the praise of his rival,
> Archly the maiden smiled, and, with eyes overrunning with laughter,
> Said, in a tremulous voice, **"Why don't you speak for yourself, John?"**

Why should life all labor be?

Source: THE LOTOS-EATERS (Choric Song, stanza 4)
Author: Alfred, Lord Tennyson (1809-1892)
First published: 1842
Type of work: Lyric poem

Context: Ulysses' sailors try to rationalize the fact that they have given up going home in order to stay on an island of numb tranquillity. They are tired of "heaviness," "distress," and "weariness": "All things have rest; why should we toil alone,/ We only toil, who are the first of things. . . ." Their "inner spirit" tells them the message they want to hear: "There is no joy but calm!" They wish to be like the flower, which "Ripens and fades, and falls, and hath no toil. . . ." They wish to bask in the sweetness of "mild-minded melancholy." After all, they would cause only disruption if they returned home after so many years. They have had "enough of action, and of motion. . . ." They will relax like gods: "slumber is more sweet than toil," and work is tiresome:

> Hateful is the dark-blue sky,
> Vaulted o'er the dark-blue sea.
> Death is the end of life; ah, **why**
> **Should life all labor be?**
> Let us alone. Time driveth onward fast,
> And in a little while our lips are dumb.
> Let us alone. What is it that will last?
> All things are taken from us, and become
> Portions and parcels of the dreadful past.
> Let us alone. What pleasure can we have
> To war with evil? Is there any peace
> In ever climbing up the climbing wave?
> All things have rest, and ripen toward the grave
> In silence—ripen, fall, and cease;
> Give us long rest or death, dark death, or dreamful ease.

Why so pale and wan, fond lover?

Source: AGLAURA ("Song," Stanza 1)
Author: Sir John Suckling (1609-1642)
First published: 1638
Type of work: Song

Context: Suckling, a dazzling, extravagant Cavalier, who committed suicide rather than live in poverty and exile, wrote in an equally gay and informal style. Much influenced by Donne, he had a light-hearted attitude towards many situations that to others would seem extremely serious.

In this short poem from his play *Aglaura* (the production of which cost him three or four hundred pounds) he jestingly points out to the young lover the folly of the traditional procedure of rejected lovers; that is, of going about pale and mute. If one's best speech and appearance can have no effect on the lady, what can be expected of all this melancholy? The first and last stanzas of the lightly cynical song are:

> **Why so pale and wan, fond lover?**
>   Prithee, why so pale?
> Will, when looking well can't move her,
>   Looking ill prevail?
>   Prithee, why so pale?
>
>   .   .   .
>
> Quit, quit, for shame! this will not move,
>   This cannot take her.
> If of herself she will not love,
>   Nothing can make her:
>   The devil take her!

The wicked man will always find an excuse for evil-doing

Source: FABLES ("The Wolf and the Lamb")
Author: Aesop (fl. sixth century B.C.?)
First transcribed: Unknown
Type of work: Moral anecdote

Context: A Wolf and a Lamb chance to meet at a stream one day while drinking, the Wolf upstream from the Lamb. The Wolf, however, wants to pick a quarrel with the Lamb, so he accuses the Lamb of muddying the water that the Wolf must drink. The Lamb protests that this is impossible since he is downstream. Next the Wolf accuses the Lamb of having used ill language about him a year ago. This time the Lamb points out the impossibility of this charge because he was not even born at that time. Aesop ends the fable thus:

. . . The Wolf, finding it to no purpose to argue any longer against the truth, fell into a great passion, snarling and foaming at the mouth, as if he had been mad; and drawing nearer to the Lamb, "Sirrah," says he, "if it was not you, it was your father, and that is all one." So he seized the poor innocent, helpless thing, tore it to pieces and made a meal of it.
MORAL: **The wicked man will always find an excuse for evil-doing.**

The wife of thy bosom

Source: DEUTERONOMY 13:6
Author: Unknown
First transcribed: 1000-300 B.C.
Type of work: Homiletic religious law and history

Context: Moses, now an aged leader, has brought the Israelites through the wilderness to the edge of the Jordan River, but, having been told by God that he cannot cross into Canaan with them, he instructs them in God's purpose through the laws given earlier. He stresses the point that an Israelite must never serve the gods worshiped by his heathen neighbors. Even if his son, daughter, friend, or the wife of his bosom tries secretly to persuade the Israelite to worship these other gods, he must not agree, and further, he must not conceal the guilt of the person in desiring to turn from God, but he must, rather, be first to stone the idolater:

> If thy brother, the son of thy mother, or thy son, or thy daughter, or **the wife of thy bosom,** or thy friend, which is as thine own soul, entice thee secretly, saying, Let us go and serve other gods, which thou has not known, thou, nor thy fathers;
>
> . . .
>
> Thou shalt not consent unto him, nor hearken unto him. . . .

Wild-goose chase

Source: ROMEO AND JULIET (Act II, sc. iv, l. 75)
Author: William Shakespeare (1564-1616)
First published: 1597
Type of work: Dramatic tragedy

Context: The morning after Romeo and Juliet have fallen desperately in love and have made their plans to meet again, Mercutio and Benvolio, Romeo's friends, are walking a street in Verona searching for Romeo, who did not come home all night. They think that the "pale hearted wench, that Rosaline,/ Torments him so, that he will sure run mad." After a little more talking, however, they come upon Romeo and accuse him of having purposely given them the slip the preceding night. All three engage in punning and verbal skirmishing. As Romeo gets the better of Mercutio for the moment, the latter protests:

MERCUTIO
Nay if our wits run the **wild-goose chase,** I am done; for thou hast more of the wild goose in one of thy wits than I am sure I have in my whole five. . . .

The will to do, the soul to dare

Source: THE LADY OF THE LAKE (Canto I, stanza 21)
Author: Sir Walter Scott (1771-1832)
First published: 1810
Type of work: Narrative poem

Context: This poetic version of a sixteenth century legend opens with a stirring account of a hunter, who calls himself Fitz-James, chasing a stag into the wild Trossachs region of Scotland. When at last his horse dies under him, the hunter is lost and far separated from all companions except his black hounds. On Loch Katrine's shore he sounds his hunting horn, wondering whether it will be answered by his friends or Highland plunderers. Amazed, he sees in response a little skiff push out from an island, guided by an enchanting girl. She calls aloud for her father, thinking it was his horn she heard, only to start and push her light boat back into the lake when the stranger steps forth. Then she pauses to gaze upon the unknown intruder, who will at the poem's end prove to be James V of Scotland:

> On his bold visage middle age
> Had lightly press'd its signet sage,
> Yet had not quench'd the open truth
> And fiery vehemence of youth;
> Forward and frolic glee was there,
> **The will to do, the soul to dare.**

Wine and women will make men of understanding to fall away

Source: ECCLESIASTICUS 19:2
Author: Jeshua, son of Sirach
First transcribed: c.200-175 B.C.
Type of work: Apocryphal literature of the Old Testament

Context: In the book of *Ecclesiasticus,* Jeshua, son of Sirach, an Israelite renowned for his wisdom, combines both his own original proverbs and many proverbs of the Hebrew tradition. He warns his readers that even the wise and bold men cannot succeed if they yield themselves to the lures of wine and women; they can expect an inheritance of only corruption and death:

> **Wine and women will make men of understanding to fall away:** and he that cleaveth to harlots will become impudent.
> Moths and worms shall have him to heritage, and a bold man shall be taken away.

The wine of life is drawn

Source: MACBETH (Act II, sc. iii, l. 100)
Author: William Shakespeare (1564-1616)
First published: 1623
Type of work: Dramatic tragedy

Context: Macbeth, Thane of Cawdor, and his wife have great and impatient ambitions. He aspires to be King of Scotland. He murders King Duncan, an overnight guest in his castle, in his sleep in order to usurp the throne and thus fulfill the prophecy of three witches who told Macbeth that he would become king. Now, the next morning, two noblemen arrive to see King Duncan. Macbeth greets them. One, Macduff, goes to the king's chamber, finds the king dead, and rouses the house. Macbeth feigns surprise and dismay at the news of the regicide.

MACBETH

Had I but died an hour before this chance,
I had lived a blessed time; for from this instant,
There's nothing serious in mortality.
All is but toys. Renown and grace is dead,
The wine of life is drawn, and the mere lees
Is left this vault to brag of.

Wine that maketh glad the heart of man

Source: PSALMS 104:15
Author: Unknown
First transcribed: c.400-200 B.C.
Type of work: Religious poetry

Context: God, whose greatness is shrouded in light, can only be partially comprehended by man. In the seas is the foundation of the dwelling place of the Lord; the clouds are his chariot. At the sound of His voice the earth takes form. And in the earth:

He causeth the grass to grow for the cattle, and herb for the service of man: that he may bring forth food out of the earth;
And **wine that maketh glad the heart of man,** and oil to make his face to shine, and bread which strengtheneth man's heart.
The trees of the Lord are full of sap; the cedars of Lebanon, which he hath planted;
Where the birds make their nests: as for the stork, the fir trees are her house.
The high hills are a refuge for the wild goats; and the rocks for the conies.

The winter of our discontent

Source: KING RICHARD THE THIRD (Act I, sc. i, l. 1)
Author: William Shakespeare (1564-1616)
First published: 1597
Type of work: Historical drama

Context: The great Samuel Johnson called this play "one of the most celebrated of our author's performances." Taken from Holinshed's *Chronicles,* this work has always been one of the theater's greatest triumphs. It picks up where *King Henry VI, Part III* left off. In that play, Richard, Duke of Gloucester, later King Richard III, stabbed King Henry, who in his dying breath predicted "more slaughter" for his murderer. With Richard's brother now installed as Edward IV, Richard opens this play with a statement of triumph and with a revelation of his already-planned villainy. The poetic and dramatic intensity of the play is immediately evident. The first lines have become a commonplace, with the play on "sun" as the badge of the House of York:

RICHARD
Now is **the winter of our discontent**
Made glorious summer by this sun of York;
    • • •
I, that am curtailed of this fair proportion,
Cheated of feature by dissembling nature,
Deformed, unfinished, sent before my time
Into this breathing world, scarce half made up,
And that so lamely and unfashionable
That dogs bark at me as I halt by them—
    • • •
I am determined to prove a villain,
    • • •

Wisdom is justified of her children

Source: MATTHEW 11:19
Author: Unknown (traditionally Matthew the Apostle)
First transcribed: c.75-100
Type of work: Gospel

Context: Jesus, beginning His ministry in His native province of Galilee, preaches in the towns around the Sea of Galilee, delivers the Sermon on the Mount, performs miraculous acts of healing, and commissions twelve disciples, warning them that they will be persecuted for professing His name. In his prison cell, John the Baptist hears of the passionate young religious leader in Galilee and sends his disciples to ask if this is the Messiah. Jesus answers the query of John' followers by telling them to judge for themselves by His deeds. He notes that neither the asceticism of John the Baptist nor His own ministry, characterized by associating with all the people has gained the approbation of the people:

> For John came neither eating nor drinking, and they say, He hath a devil.
>   The Son of man came eating and drinking, and they say, Behold a man gluttonous, and a winebibber, a friend of publicans and sinners. But **wisdom is justified of her children.**

A wise and an understanding heart

Source: I KINGS 3:12
Author: Unknown
First transcribed: c.600 B.C.
Type of work: Religious history

Context: Young King Solomon goes to Gibeon to offer sacrifices to God. While he is there, God tells him in a dream that He will grant him a request. Solomon answers humbly that he is only a little child and asks God to give him wisdom and understanding in judging the large Israelite nation, God's people. God is pleased with Solomon's petition because he has not selfishly requested long life, wealth, or the life of his enemies. God tells Solomon:

> Behold, I have done according to thy word: lo, I have given thee **a wise and an understanding heart;** so that there was none like thee before thee, neither after thee shall any arise like unto thee.
>   And I have also given thee that which thou hast not asked, both riches, and honor: so that there shall not be any among the kings like unto thee all thy days.

The wisest, brightest, meanest of mankind!

Source: AN ESSAY ON MAN (Epistle IV, l. 282)
Author: Alexander Pope (1688-1744)
First published: 1733-1734
Type of work: Philosophical poem

Context: The topic of the fourth epistle of Pope's essay is the nature of happiness. He points out that external rewards are not always conducive to contentment. He notes that riches, honors, noble birth, fame, superior talent cannot, whether singly or in combinations, insure happiness for the individual. Only virtue whose object is universal, he says, can bring happiness, and that "the perfection of Virtue and Happiness consists in a conformity to the Order Of Providence here and a resignation to it here and hereafter." To prove his points he offers a handful of examples:

> To sigh for ribands if thou art so silly,
> Mark how they grace Lord Umbra or Sir Billy.
> Is yellow dirt the passion of thy life?
> Look but on Gripus or on Gripus' wife.
> If parts allure thee, think how Bacon shined,
> **The wisest, brightest, meanest of mankind!**
> Or, ravish'd with the whistling of a name,
> See Cromwell damn'd to everlasting fame!
> If all united thy ambition call,
> From ancient story learn to scorn them all.

The wish was father to the thought

Source: KING HENRY THE FOURTH: PART TWO (Act IV, sc. v, l. 93)
Author: William Shakespeare (1564-1616)
First published: 1600
Type of work: Historical drama

Context: After the defeat of the rebellious barons, King Henry gathers his sons around him. Then he falls into a fit of apoplexy and is laid in a bed. Prince Hal, the future Henry V, next in line for the throne, comes in and sits beside his father, whom he thinks dead. Seeing the crown on the bed beside the king Hal begins to meditate on his coming reign. He promises himself that nothing will force the crown from him. He will pass "this lineal honor" on to his successor. He then steps into another room, wearing the crown. King Henry wakes and misses it. When told that Hal is wearing it, the king mistakes his son's reason for putting it on. Hal tells his father that he thought he was dead: "I never thought to hear you speak again." Like Francis Bacon in his *Essays* (1596-1625) "Of Custom and Education," who said "Men's thoughts are much according to their inclination," Henry thinks that Hal can hardly wait to ascend the throne. But being older and more experienced, he knows that the crown is a mixed blessing, as he tells his son, in words on which the current popular expression is based:

KING HENRY
Thy wish was father, Harry, to that thought.
I stay too long by thee, I weary thee.
Dost thou so hunger for mine empty chair,

1180

That thou wilt needs invest thee with my honours,
Before thy hour be ripe? O foolish youth,
Thou seek'st the greatness that will overwhelm thee.

. . .

With a grain of salt

Source: DON QUIXOTE (Part II, Book IV, chapter 37)
Author: Miguel de Cervantes Saavedra (1547-1616)
First published: 1615
Type of work: Satirical novel

Context: The Romans spoke of taking an unbelievable story "cum grano salis," (with a grain of salt), to make it easier to swallow. The druggist mentioned by Sancho did not like "old waiting women," and required a grain of salt to make them more palatable. The arrival of the Disconsolate Matron is announced. She is coming to beg Don Quixote to redress her wrongs. Sancho, taking her Spanish title of Dueña to mean a waiting woman, is sure her coming will spoil his chances to receive preferment.

> . . . I remember I once knew a Toledo pothecary, that talked like a canary bird, and used to say, wherever come old waiting-women, good luck can happen there to no man. Body of me, he knew them too well and therefore valued them accordingly. He could have eaten them all **with a grain of salt.**

With all her faults she is my country still

Source: THE FAREWELL (Line 28)
Author: Charles Churchill (1731-1764)
First published: 1764
Type of work: Satiric dialogue

Context: Charles Churchill, a dissipated clergyman who during the last four years of his life acquired notoriety and fame as a satirist, writes in this poem a dialogue between a poet and his friend. It is the poet's intention to bid farewell to England, to look somewhere else for the objects of his ridicule. The friend, amazed at this "whim" and "errour of the brain," asks why he should roam into foreign countries when there are "knaves and fools enough at home." If the object is to find material for satire, "search all round/ Nor to thy purpose can one spot be found/ Like England." Considering the corruption in the courts, both legal and regal, and the mismanagement of foreign affairs, the poet can muster only an ironically impotent reply, but William Cowper, in *The Task* (1784), through a similar expression conveys his sincere love for his native land: "England, with all thy faults I love thee still,/ My country!" (Book II, lines 206-207).

No more of this—tho' Truth (the more our shame, The more our guilt)

. . .

Declaim from morn to night, from night to morn, Take up the theme anew, when day's new-born, I hear, and hate—be England what She will, **With all her faults She is my Country still.**

With bag and baggage

Source: AS YOU LIKE IT (Act III, sc. ii,/l. 171)
Author: William Shakespeare (1564-1616)
First published: 1623
Type of work: Dramatic comedy

Context: Rosalind, daughter to Duke Senior, is banished as her father was. Celia, daughter to Duke Frederick—who has usurped his brother's throne—accompanies Rosalind to the forest of Arden. Rosalind, disguised as Ganymede, a country fellow, is loved by Orlando, who nails love poems to her on trees throughout the forest. Touchstone, a clown, and Corin, a shepherd, are walking in the woods talking nonsense when they come upon Rosalind, who is reading one of Orlando's poems which she has found. Celia, disguised as Aliena, Ganymede's sister, enters, also reading these love verses. Rosalind protests: "O most gentle Jupiter, what tedious homily of love have you wearied your parishioners withal, and never dried, have patience good people." Celia then asks Touchstone and Corin to leave them. The former replies.

TOUCHSTONE
Come shepherd, let us make an honourable retreat, though not **with bag and baggage,** yet with scrip and scrippage.

With one foot already in the grave

Source: MORALIA ("Of the Training of Children", Chapter 17)
Author: Plutarch (c.45-c.125)
First transcribed: 90-110
Type of work: Ethical essay

Context: Plutarch maintains that children should be trained in physical, military, and moral education, with great emphasis on philosophy.

1182

Special consideration should be given to the child's teacher and to the servants and friends who surround him.

The child should be kept from all base men, especially from flatterers, who:

> . . . Utterly ruin both fathers and sons, bringing sorrow to the old age of those and the youth of these, and dangling pleasure as an irresistible lure to get their advice taken. To sons who are to inherit wealth fathers commend self-restraint, flatterers profligacy; fathers frugality, flatterers extravagance; fathers industry, flatterers indolence, saying "All life is but a moment. We must live, not merely exist. Why should we give a thought to your father's threats? He's an old twaddler **with one foot already in the grave,** and before long we'll take his coffin on our shoulders and carry him out."

Within a stone's throw

Source: DON QUIXOTE (Part I, Book III, chapter 9)
Author: Miguel de Cervantes Saavedra (1547-1616)
First published: 1605
Type of work: Satirical novel

Context: Measuring distance by the flight of an arrow or the casting of a stone (we say "as far as you can throw a cat by the tail") is a common figure of speech. In Chapter IX, Ginés de Passamonte comes upon the sleeping Don Quixote and his squire. Scorning the bony nag Rozinante, he makes off with Sancho's donkey. The following morning, bewailing his loss, Sancho proceeds on foot. He comes upon a portmanteau which contains clothes, but fear of the Holy Brotherhood keeps him from touching it. He also discovers a mule that, according to a passing shepherd, has been dead a long time. The shepherd confesses he has not dared touch either the harness or the luggage. Sancho agrees:

> ". . . 'Tis just so with me, gaffer," quoth Sancho; "for I saw the portmanteau too, d'ye see, but the devil a bit would I come **within a stone's throw** of it; no, there I found it, and there I left it. . . . He that steals a bellwether shall be discovered by the bell."

Without a wink of sleep

Source: DON QUIXOTE (Part I, Book II, chapter 4)
Author: Miguel de Cervantes Saavedra (1547-1616)
First published: 1605
Type of work: Satirical novel

Context: Shutting one's eyes for a moment is a wink, and so the expression for no sleep became "without a wink of sleep." Pisanio tells Imogen

1183

in Shakespeare's *Cymbeline* (1610) (Act III, sc. iv, l. 103): "Since I received command to do this (kill her as a strumpet), I have not slept one wink." Chapter 33 of Part II of *Don Quixote* begins: "Sancho slept not a wink all that afternoon." Bucolic literature about the loves of shepherdesses for shepherds and for nobles masquerading as shepherds, was popular in Spain's Golden Age, so Cervantes had to include a sample. A goatherd explains to Don Quixote that "that fine shepherd and scholar Chrysostome," is one more victim of Marcella, the "devilish untoward daughter of rich William." Dressed in the garb of a shepherdess, she roams the countryside doing "more harm in the country than the plague would do."

. . . Here sighs one shepherd, there another whines; here is one singing doleful ditties, there another is wringing his hands and making woeful complaints. You shall have one lay him down at night at the foot of a rock, or some oak, and there lie weeping and wailing **without a wink of sleep,** and talking to himself till the sun finds him the next morning. . . .

Without sneering teach the rest to sneer

Source: EPISTLE TO DR. ARBUTHNOT (Line 202)
Author: Alexander Pope (1688-1744)
First published: 1735
Type of work: Satire

Context: This "epistle" is, in the poet's own words, "a sort of bill of complaint." Pope used it to answer those who had satirized him both before and after the publication of his *Dunciad,* in which he had slashed satirically at almost everyone on the contemporary English literary scene. Indeed, this epistle is indicative of the backbiting enmity which marred much of Pope's life and career, making the poet an unhappy man. In this section of the poem Pope says that the truly great poet should be able to bear having his brother poets about him; but if he cannot, says Pope, one notes the following signs of envy:

Should such a man, too fond to rule alone,
Bear, like the Turk, no brother near the throne;
View him with scornful, yet with jealous eyes,
And hates for arts that caus'd himself to rise;
Damn with faint praise, assent with civil leer,
And **without sneering teach the rest to sneer;**
Willing to wound, and yet afraid to strike,
Just hint a fault, and hesitate dislike;
Alike reserv'd to blame or to commend,
A tim'rous foe, and a suspicious friend;
. . .
Who but must laugh if such a man there be?

Wives are young men's mistresses, companions for middle age, and old men's nurses

Source: ESSAYS OR COUNSELS, CIVIL AND MORAL ("Of Marriage and Single Life")
Author: Francis Bacon (1561-1626)
First published: 1612
Type of work: Moral essay

Context: Bacon argues that single men are better able to do great work because they are unencumbered. They do not have as much concern for the future, because they are childless. Nor do they have as much compassion as married men. Thus Bacon argues both sides of the case, being apparently personally uncommitted. He says: "He that hath wife and children hath given hostages to fortune; for they are impediments to great enterprises, either of virtue or mischief." He goes on to say:

Wives are young men's mistresses, companions for middle age, and old men's nurses.

Wives may be merry, and yet honest too

Source: THE MERRY WIVES OF WINDSOR (Act IV, sc. ii, l. 103)
Author: William Shakespeare (1564-1616)
First published: 1602
Type of work: Dramatic comedy

Context: Sir John Falstaff, an old, fat, and foolish lecher, imagines that two light-hearted married women, Mistress Ford and Mistress Page, desire him. He sends them duplicate love letters. They compare notes, have a hearty laugh, and resolve to teach him a lesson. First, Mistress Ford arranges an assignation with him. He comes to her house. Shortly, Mistress Page arrives with news that Master Ford, accompanied by the Constabulary, is on the way home. Falstaff, alarmed, hides in a large basket of dirty laundry. Almost smothered in greasy linen, he is unceremoniously dumped in a ditch. Undaunted, he makes arrangements for another rendezvous with Mistress Ford. Again an alarm is raised. Falstaff is seeking another mode of escape. While Mistress Ford is finding a disguise for him in another room, Mistress Page talks to the audience.

MISTRESS PAGE
Hang him dishonest varlet, we cannot misuse him enough.
We'll have a proof by that which we will do,
Wives may be merry, and yet honest too.

• • •

The wolf also shall dwell with the lamb

Sovrce: ISAIAH 11:6
Author: Isaiah
First transcribed: c.800-200 B.C.
Type of work: Religious prophecy and exhortation

Context: As the prophet of the Almighty, Isaiah proclaims his vision of "Judah and Jerusalem in the days of Uzziah, Jotham, Ahaz, and Hezekiah, kings of Judah." He urges the Israelites to turn from their wickedness and prophesies the destruction of Jerusalem and Judah because of the wrath of the Lord. In a particularly vivid passage, Isaiah describes the advance on Jerusalem of the Assyrian army, in this case, the instrument of the Lord for His punishment of the Israelites. But His anger is turned on the enemy army, and Isaiah foretells the coming of a messiah, an anointed one, from the house of David:

> And the Spirit of the Lord shall rest upon him, the spirit of wisdom and understanding, the spirit of counsel and might, the spirit of knowledge and of the fear of the Lord;
>
> . . .
>
> But with righteousness shall he judge the poor, and reprove with equity for the meek of the earth: and he shall smite the earth with the rod of his mouth, and with the breath of his lips shall he slay the wicked.
>
> . . .
>
> **The wolf also shall dwell with the lamb,** and the leopard shall lie down with the kid; and the calf and the young lion and the fatling together; and a little child shall lead them.

The wolf from the door

Source: COLIN CLOUT (Line 153)
Author: John Skelton (c. 1460-1529)
First published: Original edition undated; c. 1519
Type of work: Satiric poem

Context: In this long poem pointing out the excesses and evils in the church and among the clergy, Father Skelton compares the humble with the worldly priests in a form now known as Skeltonics. John Heywood uses the proverb at about the same time, and later in America Howell says it is madness to marry "unless you have wherewith to at least keep the wolf from the door." In Skelton the poem answers the Biblical question "Who will rise up with me against evil doers? Or who will stand up with me against the workers of iniquity? No one, O Lord!"

The temporality say plain
How bishops disdain
Sermons for to make,
Or some labor to take.
And for to say troth,
A great part is sloth . . .
Howbeit some there be
(Almost two or three)
Of that dignitie,
Full worshipful clerks,
As appeareth by theeir works,
Like Aaron and Ure,
The wolfe from the door
To werrin and to keep
From their ghostly sheep. . . .

Wolf in sheep's clothing

Source: AESOP'S FABLES ("The Wolf in Sheep's Clothing")
Author: Aesop (fl. sixth century B.C.?)
First transcribed: Fourth century B.C.
Type of work: Moral tales of animals

Context: In the original cluster of Aesopic tales, those attributed to the legendary Aesop, appear numerous stories of the wolf and his problems in getting lamb chops. This, the most famous, has a very different ending in the original: "A wolf once decided to change his appearance in order to get plenty of food. He put a sheepskin around him and joined the flock as it grazed, deceiving the shepherd by his trick. As night came on, the beast was shut up in the fold along with the flock, the entrance was barred, and the whole enclosure secured. But when the shepherd was ready to eat, he killed the wolf with his knife. So it is that he who plays a role in foreign finery often loses his life and finds the stage a contributory cause of his great disaster." The moral must originally have been that appearances are *not* deceiving. In the popular version, however, the wolf used the lamb's mother's fleece.

. . . The Lamb that belonged to the sheep . . . began to follow the **Wolf in the Sheep's clothing** . . . (who) soon made a meal off her . . .

The wolf is at the door

Source: THE WOLF AT THE DOOR (Stanza 1)
Author: Charlotte Perkins Stetson Gilman (1860-1935)
First published: 1894
Type of work: Lyric poem

Context: As a child Charlotte Perkins Stetson Gilman knew poverty and debt intimately. Possibly as a result of her childhood experience, she became interested in economics, sociology and anthropology. Through her study of mankind's problems and the aid she gave to movements for the improvement of the status of women, she attempted to further her principal aim, which was to elevate society in general. "The Wolf at the Door" reflects the desire of the poet to draw mankind out of an innate indolence. "We are born to hoarded weariness," the poet says, and "Nothing the day can give/ Is half so sweet as an hour of sleep. . . ." Yet to yield to that inborn desire would lead to "A fate no man can dare—/ To be run to earth and die by the teeth/ Of the gnawing monster there!" To emphasize the dangerous consequences of inaction, the poet concludes her poem with the following stanza:

> There's a hot breath at the keyhole
> And a tearing as of teeth!
> Well do I know the bloodshot eyes
> And the dripping jaws beneath!
> There's a whining at the threshold—
> There's a scratching at the floor—
> To work! To work! In Heaven's name!
> **The wolf is at the door!**

A woman is only a woman, but a good cigar is a smoke

Source: THE BETROTHED (Line 50)
Author: Rudyard Kipling (1865-1936)
First published: 1885
Type of work: Satirical poem

Context: Kipling uses his bent for humor in "The Betrothed" when Maggie begins the poem with an ultimatum saying, "You must choose between me and your cigar." The poet muses on the permanence of a cigar that, when finished, can be replaced by another equally as good as the first. Then he points to the fact that a wife could hardly be thrown away for ". . . the talk of the town." Finally, he writes:

> A million surplus Maggies are willing to bear the yoke;
> **And a woman is only a woman, but a good Cigar is a Smoke.**

Light me another Cuba; I hold to my first-sworn vows,
If Maggie will have no rival, I'll have no Maggie for spouse!

A woman sat, in unwomanly rags, plying her needle and thread

Source: THE SONG OF THE SHIRT (Stanza 1)
Author: Thomas Hood (1799-1845)
First published: 1843
Type of work: Humanitarian poem

Context: Hood, a minor romantic poet, wrote "The Song of the Shirt" to awaken the public to the hardships of workers in England. The woman in the poem is depicted as a widow who has to support her family by sewing for seven shillings a week. The destitute woman sings a song of protest: " 'It is not linen you're wearing out/ But human creatures' lives . . . Oh, God! that bread should be so dear,/ And flesh and blood so cheap!' " The woman's heart and brain are "be- numbed" by the ceaseless labor. She longs to breathe fresh air and enjoy nature. But she cannot even find time to weep. She is becoming like the steam engine, "A mere machine of iron and wood/ That toils for Mammon's sake,/ Without a brain to ponder and craze/ Or a heart to feel— and break!" The woman is a hopeless slave who " 'has never a soul to save,' " but the poet wishes that her song "could reach the rich!" The first stanza describes the woman:

> With fingers weary and worn,
>   With eyelids heavy and red,
> **A woman sat, in unwomanly rags,**
>   **Plying her needle and thread—**
> Stitch! stitch! stitch!
>   In poverty, hunger, and dirt,
> And still with a voice of dolorous pitch
>   She sang the "Song of the Shirt."

Women and elephants never forget an injury

Source: REGINALD ("Reginald on Besetting Sins")
Author: Saki (Hector Hugh Munro, 1870-1916)
First published: 1904
Type of work: Short story

Context: The story, "Reginald on Besetting Sins," is part of Munro's sketches, *Reginald.* In this particular story he tells of a lady who becomes addicted to telling the truth, a habit which, according to Munro, is contrary to the nature of women. At first she tells only small truths, but later her habit becomes such that she will tell her age not only in years, but also in months. On one occasion she tells Miriam Klopstock *exactly* how the latter looked at a ball. Her friends, of course, attempt to dissuade her from this dangerous habit. She goes to her dressmaker and, while she is being fitted, dares to reproach Madame Draga for the fitting. When she leaves, she realizes that Madame Draga's temper will be reflected in the bill. Her ultimate downfall, however, occurs when she has the audacity to tell the cook she drinks.

. . . On a raw Wednesday morning, in a few ill-chosen words, she told the cook that she drank. She remembered the scene afterwards as vividly as though it had been painted in her mind by Abbey. The cook was a good cook, as cooks go; and as cooks go she went.

Miriam Klopstock came to lunch the next day. **Women and elephants never forget an injury.**

Women are only children of a larger growth

Source: LETTERS TO HIS SON (Letter 49)
Author: Philip Dormer Stanhope, Lord Chesterfield (1698-1773)
First published: 1774
Type of work: Personal letters

Context: Lord Chesterfield, who often seems to the modern reader a genteel, but cold-blooded, pragmatist with—like Shakespeare's Polonius—many ulterior motives and a super-abundance of advice, makes quite clear his negative attitude toward women in a letter to his son, Philip, dated London, September 5, 1748. In the passage, Lord Chesterfield seems at complete odds with John Dryden, who says, in Act IV, sc. i of *All for Love,* "Men are but children of a larger growth." Dryden's play is dated 1678.

. . . **Women, then, are only children of a larger growth;** they have an entertaining tattle, and sometimes wit; but for solid reasoning, good sense, I never knew in my life one that had it, or who reasoned or acted consequentially for four-and-twenty hours together. Some little passion for humor always breaks in upon their best resolutions. Their beauty neglected or controverted, their age increased . . . instantly kindles their little passions, and overturns any system of consequential conduct. . . . A man of sense only trifles with them, plays with them . . . as he does with a sprightly, forward child; but he neither consults them about, nor trusts them with serious matters; though he often makes them believe that he does both. . . .

The women come and go talking of Michelangelo

Source: THE LOVE SONG OF J. ALFRED PRUFROCK
Author: T(homas) S(tearns) Eliot (1888-1965)
First published: 1915
Type of work: Metaphysical poem

Context: The title of this poem is deeply ironic, because the speaker is a man far too timid ever to sing a love-song, or, indeed, ever to express what he really thinks. He is a guest at a reception at which the other guests are oppressively intellectual. He is never a part of the conversation: he is too shy and self-conscious to meet the company on equal terms. He is miserable and bored, yet his shyness prevents him from leaving, for he is afraid of being laughed at. The pretentious intellectuality and the brittle conversation of the guests at the party are summed up in the description of the women, as Prufrock hesitates between staying and summoning up enough courage to leave.

In the room **the women come and go
Talking of Michelangelo.**

And indeed there will be time
To wonder, "Do I dare?" and, "Do I dare?"
Time to turn back and descend the stair,
With a bald spot in the middle of my hair. . . .

Women wear the breeches

Source: ANATOMY OF MELANCHOLY (Democritus Junior to the Reader)
Author: Robert Burton (1577-1640)
First published: 1621-1651
Type of work: Essays

Context: As introduction to this lengthy volume comes a hundred-page "Democritus Junior to the Reader." The author describes Hippocrates (460?-377 B.C.), the "Father of Medicine," coming to see Democritus and finding him cutting up beasts in hopes of discovering the cause of madness and melancholy. The visitor laments that he has no leisure for such investigations, but Democritus chides him for esteeming so highly the unimportant things about him. Democritus himself only laughs at such things. What would he do today, Burton asks, when there is so much greater cause for laughter:

To see . . . children rule; old men go to school; **women wear the breeches,** . . . and in a word, the world turned upside downward. . . .

The wonderful one-hoss shay

Source: THE DEACON'S MASTERPIECE (Stanza 1)
Author: Oliver Wendell Holmes (1809-1894)
First published: 1858
Type of work: Satirical poem

Context: This poem, which Holmes subtitles "A Logical Story," has been read as a subtle satire on the collapse of Calvinism. The edifice of Calvinism, like the deacon's "one-hoss shay," was constructed with masterful logic, but it wore out and disintegrated. On the day of the Lisbon earthquake in 1755, "the Deacon finished the one-hoss shay." Usually "a chaise *breaks down,* but doesn't *wear out,*" for it always has *"somewhere* a weakest spot." But the Deacon builds it so "that it *couldn'* break daown" by making the weakest spot "uz strong uz the rest." Time passes; the Deacon and his children and grandchildren die. But "the stout old one-hoss shay" is still as good as new. It lasts a century. Then in 1855, on the day of the hundredth anniversary of the earthquake, "the parson takes a drive" in the shay, composing a sermon as he rides along. But in the middle of his sermon, the shay collapses at "Just the hour of the Earthquake shock!" The chaise had not broken down; it had worn out. "It went to pieces all at once," so uniformly that it looked as if it had been ground at the mill. "End of the wonderful one-hoss shay./ Logic is logic. That's all I say," Holmes quips. He describes the marvelous quality of the shay and its hundred-year decay:

Have you heard of **the wonderful one-hoss shay,**
That was built in such a logical way
It ran a hundred years to a day,
And then, of a sudden, it—ah, but stay,
I'll tell you what happened without delay,
Scaring the parson into fits,
Frightening people out of their wits,—
Have you ever heard of that, I say?

Woodman, spare that tree!

Source: WOODMAN, SPARE THAT TREE (Stanza 1)
Author: George Pope Morris (1802-1864)
First published: 1830
Type of work: Lyric poem

Context: This well-known appeal for the preservation of an oak tree was written by a Philadelphia-born journalist and poet and published in New York's *Mirror* that he founded. He also wrote a drama and an opera, besides compiling anthologies of poetry by other writers. His own verse first appeared in a complete volume in 1852. The four stanzas of this poem were probably inspired by "The Beech Tree's Petition" (1805) by Thomas Campbell (1777-1844) that cries:

"Oh, leave this barren spot to me!
Spare, woodman, spare the beechen
    tree!"

Morris appeals for the life of the tree, not only because of its glory but for the childhood connections of his sisters and himself with it. He promises that as long as he has "a hand to spare," it shall not be felled. The first stanza is the best known.

Woodman, spare that tree!
    Touch not a single bough!
In youth it sheltered me,
    And I'll protect it now.
'T was my forefather's hand
    That placed it near his cot;
There, woodman, let it stand,
    Thy axe shall harm it not.

A word to the wise is enough

Source: DON QUIXOTE (Part II, Book IV, chapter 30)
Author: Miguel de Cervantes Saavedra (1547-1616)
First published: 1615
Type of work: Satirical novel

Context: To the Romans this phrase in Latin, Verbum sat sapienti, was so common that they abbreviated it, verbum sap. Benjamin Franklin (1706-1790) declared in the Preface to *Poor Richard Improved* (1758): "A word to the wise is enough, and many words won't fill a bushel." Today we say "sufficient" for "enough." Having read the first volume of Don Quixote's adventures, the Duke and Duchess invite him and his squire to visit them, intending to provide adventures for the sequel. However, the announcement of the approach of Countess Trifaldi ("Three Skirts"), called the Disconsolate Matron, with a request for help from the Knight, poses a problem in protocol. How far should courtesy go toward a mere countess? When Sancho offers a suggestion, his master wants to know who bade him speak. The squire explains:

• • •

. . . Who bid me? . . . Why, I myself did. Han't I been squire to your worship, and thus served a 'prenticeship to good manners? And han't I had the Flower of Courtesy for my master, who has often told me, a man may as well lose at one-and-thirty with a card too much, as a card too little? Good wits jump; **a word to the wise is enough.**

1193

The Word was made flesh

Source: JOHN 1:14
Author: Unknown (traditionally John the Apostle)
First transcribed: By 130
Type of work: Gospel

Context: The atuhor, using "Word" to mean Jesus, implies by this appelation that in Jesus are found the absolute qualities of wisdom and truth. He declares that the "Word" existed before the beginning of time, with a separate identity from God, yet a part of God in a transcendent sense. In Jesus, or the "Word," rests the creative, living force of the Almighty, giving light to men, or the ability to comprehend or to reach across the chasm that separates the divine from the human. Though Christ made the world and has always permeated the very being of the universe, men have not recognized Him. But to the few who have received the "Word," He has given a spiritual rebirth which has made them heirs of the Lord in spirit. This eternal "Word" has assumed the physical form of man, Jesus, yet retains the glory of the divine; thus, He has lived among men in order to expedite man's reaching God:

And **the Word was made flesh,** and dwelt among us, (and we beheld his glory, the glory as of the only begotten of the Father,) full of grace and truth.

Words are but empty thanks

Source: WOMAN'S WIT; OR, THE LADY IN FASHION (Act V)
Author: Colley Cibber (1671-1757)
First published: 1697
Type of work: Dramatic comedy

Context: The woman's wit of this play is the wit of Leonora, a scheming young woman who wishes to have all the men her suitors. Charles Longville knows her real character and tries to expose her falsity to Lord Lovemore, his friend who wishes to marry Leonora. Longville is prompted by his sister's love for Lord Lovemore, as well as by his friendship for the man. Leonora discovers what is happening and, by using her wits, tries to bring enmity between the two friends to hide her own perfidy. She even goes to such lengths as to lie about being already married to Longville herself and to falsify letters between Longville and his fiancée, Olivia. Leonora over-reaches herself, however, and is exposed at last for the villainess she is. The misunderstanding between Longville and his fiancée is cleared up, and Lord Lovemore realizes how Leonora has fooled him. Longville assures his sister that there is hope that Lovemore will marry her:

And now, *Emilia,* there is a blooming hope for thee, which time can only ripen: mean while intrust thy heart with me, and be assur'd, thou ne'er shalt blush, when I think to part with it.

EMILIA

This is beyond a brother's love: **words are but empty thanks;** my future conduct best will speak my gratitude.

Words are wise men's counters

Source: LEVIATHAN (Part I, chapter 4)
Author: Thomas Hobbes (1588-1679)
First published: 1651
Type of work: Philosophy

Context: After treating of matters such as the senses, fancy, and memory, Hobbes takes up the subject of speech. As truth consists in the right ordering of words, a person using words must bear in mind what each one means. Similarly, one who reads books must understand how his author uses his words. Thus in the correct definition of words lies the first use of speech, the acquisition of science or knowledge. And in wrong definitions or none at all lies the first abuse of speech, for when a man does not understand what he reads, the conclusions he draws must certainly be mistaken. Men who take all their instruction from books without meditating upon what they read are actually inferior to the merely ignorant, because their minds are filled with error, whereas the minds of the ignorant are empty. Wise men use words as the instruments of thought, but fools value them for themselves, accepting the authority of Cicero or Aristotle or Thomas Aquinas without reflecting upon what these men actually said. The passage as Hobbes expresses it is:

For **words are wise men's counters,**—they do but reckon by them; but they are the money of fools. . . .

Words, sweet as honey

Source: THE ILIAD (Book I, l. 332, as translated by Alexander Pope)
Author: Homer (c.850 B.C.)
First transcribed: Sixth century B.C.
Type of work: Epic poem

Context: "The wrath do thou sing, O goddess, of Peleus' son, Achilles, that baneful wrath which brought countless woes . . ." So begins the *Iliad* with an invocation to the muse of poetry. This wrath leads nearly to the murder of the Greek general Agamemnon by the warrior Achilles, who bitterly resents his leader's suggestion that he surrender the beautiful Briseis. The goddess Athene restrains the sword of impetuous Achilles, but he swears to his king that he will no longer fight against the Trojans. The ancient and wise Nestor, who had advised three generations of Achaeans, then tries to make peace between the two:

> To calm their passion with the words of age,
> Slow from his seat arose the Pylian sage,
> Experienced Nestor, in persuasion skill'd;
> **Words, sweet as honey,** from his lips distill'd: . . .
> "What shame, what woe is this to Greece! what joy
> To Troy's proud monarch, and the friends of Troy!
> That adverse gods commit to stern debate
> The best, the bravest, of the Grecian state. . . ."

Work out your own salvation

Source: PHILIPPIANS 2:12
Author: Paul
First transcribed: c.60
Type of work: Religious epistle

Context: Paul, probably writing from Rome in a time of persecution, addresses the church at Philippi. He thanks the people for their assistance and prays that they may continue to do the work of Christ and to live the righteous life. Describing his imprisonment as effectively spreading the gospel, he notes that some of the people have renewed their activity, but that others have doubted the validity of his message. With the knowledge that all will be well for him in life or death, he says that his mission is important for the followers of Christ. Admonishing the people to a life of love and Christ-like humility, he tells them that he has in the past been able to help them, but that now with him in prison they must take on the burden of their own redemption with humility in the sight of God:

Wherefore, my beloved, as ye have always obeyed, not as in my presence only, but now much more in my absence, **work out your own salvation** with fear and trembling:

For it is God which worketh in you both to will and to do of his good pleasure.

Working men of all countries, unite!

Source: THE COMMUNIST MANIFESTO (Concluding paragraph)
Authors: Karl Marx (1818-1883) and Friedrich Engels (1820-1895)
First published: 1848
Type of work: Political document

Context: "A spectre is haunting Europe—the spectre is Communism." This document that changed world history begins with a warning and ends with a gloomy forecast—at least for capitalism. It was written to foment revolt, and it appeared at a time when social conventions were ripe for revolution. The League of the Just was organized in 1836. It held its first congress in London during the summer of 1847, at which time, under the direction of Friedrich Engels, it became known as the Communist League. The second congress came in December of the same year, and Engels and Marx were commissioned to prepare a declaration of principles and a plan of action. They lost no time and published the *Manifesto* in January, 1848. Simply stated, the *Manifesto* portends the collapse of capitalism resulting from the overthrow of the bourgeois by the proletarians. This "inevitable" overthrow was to result from the friction between the two classes—bourgeoisie and proletariat—at dialectic conflict. The *Manifesto* was written long before *Capital* —Marx's masterpiece that was the end-product of years of careful and scholarly research—but it contains the central theory of Communistic doctrine.

> The Communists disdain to conceal their views and aims. They openly declare that their ends can be attained only by the forcible overthrow of all existing social conditions. Let the ruling classes tremble at a Communistic revolution. The proletarians have nothing to lose but their chains. They have a world to win.
> **Working men of all countries, unite!**

The world is charged with the grandeur of God

Source: GOD'S GRANDEUR (Line 1)
Author: Gerard Manley Hopkins (1844-1889)
First published: 1918
Type of work: Sonnet

Context: In this well-known sonnet Hopkins expresses his strong faith in God and in the divine Being's direct interest in Earth and its inhabitants. All of nature contains signs of the might and majesty of God, but men have ignored them for generations and have so defiled the earth that it seems as base as they. Yet nature's pure essence remains and will never be exhausted, because of the ministrations of the Holy Ghost who "over the bent/ World broods with warm breast and with ah! bright wings."

1197

The world is charged with the grandeur of God.
It will flame out, like shining from shook foil;
It gathers to a greatness, like the ooze of oil
Crushed.

The world is too much with us

Source: THE WORLD IS TOO MUCH WITH US
Author: William Wordsworth (1770-1850)
First published: 1807
Type of work: Sonnet

Context: Wordsworth's poetry constantly posits a concern with the relationship between the inner life of man and the outward life of the world of nature. It is his fundamental conviction that human happiness is to be found only when the "discerning intellect of man" is "wedded to this goodly universe in love and holy passion." In effect, man must maintain a sensitivity to the beauty and power of nature for the sake of his spiritual well-being. Thus, it is understandable that the poet, on numerous occasions, condemns the materialism which, in blinding man to the splendor of his environment, makes him captive to his own avarice. In another sonnet ("London, 1802") he warns that inward happiness is inevitably forfeited to the unmitigated pursuit of material comfort, that man's greatest enemy is the temptation to sacrifice his moral values for the sake of popularity or profit. Here, asserting that he would "rather be/ A Pagan suckled in a creed outworn" than a Christian insensitive to the voice of nature, he writes:

The world is too much with us; late and soon,
Getting and spending, we lay waste our powers:
Little we see in Nature that is ours;
We have given our hearts away, a sordid boon!

The world must be made safe for democracy

Source: WE MUST ACCEPT WAR (Message to the Congress, April 2, 1917)
Author: Woodrow Wilson (1856-1924)
First spoken: 1917
Type of work: Speech

Context: President Woodrow Wilson's message to Congress on April 2, 1917, is a request for a declaration of war against Germany. The President traces the aggressive acts of German submarines against United States vessels and says that if this country continues on its path of neutrality it will still be drawn into war without the rights of belligerents. The object in going to war, he says, is to vindicate the principles of peace. He points out that the United States is not against the German people, for those people, too, have been oppressed by their tyrannical government. The President names specific acts of the German government prejudicial to the harmony of the relations of this country with its allies and neighbors. Wilson says:

> . . . We are glad, now that we see the facts with no veil of false pretense about them, to fight thus for the ultimate peace of the world and for the liberation of its peoples, the German people included; for the rights of nations great and small and the privilege of men everywhere to choose their way of life and of obedience. **The world must be made safe for democracy.** Its peace must be planted upon the trusted foundations of political liberty. . . .

A world of sighs

Source: OTHELLO (Act I, sc. iii, l. 159)
Author: William Shakespeare (1564-1616)
First published: 1622
Type of work: Dramatic tragedy

Context: Desdemona, daughter of Brabantio, a Venetian senator, elopes with a Moor, Othello, a military commander in the service of Venice. Her father, aroused in the dead of night and informed of the elopment, is incensed. He bring his grievance and Othello before the duke, who is in late council. He accuses Othello of using witchcraft in his courtship, for black magic would be necessary, he says, "for nature so preposterously to err." Othello, called upon to speak, denies the use of charms, witchcraft, magic, and drugs. He relates the story of his courtship; how he pictured for Desdemona the story of the battles, sieges, fortunes, narrow escapes, and wonders of his life. He speaks of Desdemona's reaction:

OTHELLO
. . .
My story being done,
She gave me for my pains **a world of sighs.**
She swore, in faith 'twas strange, 'twas passing strange,
'Twas pitiful, 'twas wondrous pitiful.
She wished she had not heard it, yet she wished
That heaven had made her such a man.
. . .

1199

The world, the flesh, and the devil

Source: THE BOOK OF COMMON PRAYER (Page 54)
Author: Traditional; translated and arranged by Archbishop Cranmer (1489-1560)
First published: 1549
Type of work: Litany

Context: The Litany is a form of a general type of prayer consisting of a series of biddings made by a leader, each petition being answered by a brief response from the people. Used in ancient times by pagans and Jews alike, the form was taken over and developed by the Christian Church in the fourth century. The Litany from which this quotation is taken was first issued in 1544 during the reign of King Henry VIII and is the oldest part of The Book of Common Prayer. The additions and subtractions of successive generations have not changed the matchless grace of its style and rythm, nor lessened its power as an epitome of Christian supplication. That he may be delivered from all evil, both material and spiritual, the humble petitioner prays:

> From all blindness of heart; from pride, vainglory and hypocrisy; from envy, hatred, and malice, and all uncharitableness,
> *Good Lord, deliver us.*
> From all inordinate and sinful affections; and from all the deceits of **the world, the flesh, and the devil,**
> *Good Lord, deliver us.*

The world was on thy page of victories but a comma

Source: TO NAPOLEON (Lines 12-13)
Author: John Clare (1793-1864)
First published: 1835
Type of work: Sonnet

Context: Clare eulogizes Napoleon as the greatest hero of all time. In comparison with Napoleon, all other heroes of history have been "puny, vague, and nothingness." Imprisonment on an island could not confine his brilliant mind, which "Swept space as shoreless as eternity." Napoleon continued to "strain for glory" till the end of his life:

> Thy giant powers outscript this gaudy age
> Of heroes; and, as looking at the sun,
> So gazing on thy greatness, made men blind
> To merits, that had adoration won
> In olden times. **The world was on thy page**
> **Of victories but a comma.** Fame could find
> No parallel thy greatness to presage.

1200

The worldly hope men set their hearts upon

Source: THE RUBÁIYÁT OF OMAR KHAYYÁM (Stanza 16)
Author: Omar Khayyám (died c.1123)
Translator and adapter: Edward FitzGerald (1809-1883)
First published: 1859
Type of work: Translation and poetic adaptation of Persian poetry

Context: Omar here continues to emphasize the shortness of life. We know neither whence we came nor where we shall go. We cannot unravel "the Master-knot of Human Fate." "Ah, make the most of what we yet may spend,/ Before we too into the Dust descend. . . ." We should take as our example "the blowing Rose," which merrily scatters its riches around it. Those who horde and those who squander share the same fate: we soon die, and our defeats and victories during life are meaningless. Only hedonism can give a brief meaning to life, for nothing lasts:

And those who husbanded the Golden Grain,
And those who flung it to the winds like Rain,
   Alike to no such aureate Earth are turned
As, buried once, Men want dug up again.

The Worldly Hope men set their Hearts upon
Turns Ashes—or it prospers; and anon,
   Like Snow upon the Desert's dusty Face,
Lighting a little hour or two—is gone.

The world's mine oyster

Source: THE MERRY WIVES OF WINDSOR (Act II, sc. ii, l. 3)
Author: William Shakespeare (1564-1616)
First published: 1602
Type of work: Dramatic comedy

Context: This famous saying is associated with eager, ambitious, even arrogant youth. It is usually heard today in a modified form, "the world's his oyster," about a young man who cannot wait to conquer the world. In the play, Pistol, a braggart follower of Sir John Falstaff, a self-fancied lady-killer, refuses to do Sir John a service the latter requests. Now, at the Garter Inn, Pistol asks a loan of Sir John, who indignantly refuses. Pistol, only half in jest, whips out his sword, and compares the fat, round knight to the world and his purse to an oyster.

FALSTAFF
I will not lend thee a penny.

PISTOL

Why then **the world's mine oyster,**
Which I with sword will open.

FALSTAFF

Not a penny. . . .

The worm will turn

Source: DON QUIXOTE (Part II, Author's Preface)
Author: Miguel de Cervantes Saavedra (1547-1616)
First published: 1615
Type of work: Satirical novel

Context: The original worm was not of the kind that could be crushed to death when stepped on, but the Anglo-Saxon "wyrm," a serpent. Today's pithy equivalent of Cervantes' expression is "The worm will turn." At the end of Part I of *Don Quixote* (1605), appears the promise of a sequel. Before Cervantes published his sequel, an unknown writer of Tordesillas published from Tarragona a spurious second volume. The infuriated Cervantes hurried to complete his own book, published the next year with a preface declaring:

> Bless me! reader, gentle or simple, or whatever you be, how impatiently by this time must you expect this Preface, supposing it to be nothing but revengeful invectives against the author of the *second* Don Quixote. But I must beg your pardon; for I shall say no more of him than every body says, that Tordesillas is the place where he was begotten, and Tarragona the place where he was born; and though it be universally said, that **even a worm, when trod upon, will turn again,** yet I'm resolved for once to cross that proverb. You perhaps now would have me call him coxcomb, fool, and madman; but I'm of another mind; and so let his folly be its own punishment.

The worst friend and enemy is but Death

Source: PEACE (Line 14)
Author: Rupert Brooke (1887-1915)
First published: 1915
Type of work: Sonnet

Context: Brooke, one of the War Poets, in "Peace" shows his characteristically inspired optimism in the face of very real physical dangers. The peace of which he speaks is a peace which transcends the physical oppres-

1202

sions around him. Speaking for himself and his comrades, he thanks God, "Who has matched us with His hour," for having commissioned and fortified them and for having blessed their endeavors with a vital, challenging purpose. In this demanding and purposeful endeavor, all burdens and dangers are limited to the physical ones. As long as they are engaged in a significant cause, "there's no ill, no grief, but sleep has mending,/ Nought broken save this body, lost but breath." Therefore, in spite of the physical agonies, which have an ending, an inner peace is available which is as strengthening as it is lasting. The war, then, is only an instrument of physical evil and cannot harm the inner harmony and peace of soul. In this, war is

Nothing to shake the laughing heart's long peace . . .
But only agony, and that has ending;
And the worst friend and enemy is but Death.

The worst is yet to come

Source: SEA DREAMS (Conclusion)
Author: Alfred, Lord Tennyson (1809-1892)
First published: 1860
Type of work: Narrative poem

Context: This poem is a study on the Christian doctrine of forgiveness and its application in everyday life. A poorly-paid clerk had invested all the money he had saved in twelve years in a non-existent Peruvian gold mine. When he discovered that he had been the victim of fraud, he conceived a hatred for the man who had tricked him. His wife has tried to bring him to forgive the trickster, but in vain. One day the two men meet on the street, and the clerk's resentment is brought to new heat. But he hears shortly after of the man's death and, at last, is convinced by his wife to forgive the crime. The man observes that although the criminal is forgiven, the consequences of his crimes have not yet been fully realized. He tells his wife that

'His deeds yet live, **the worst is yet to come.**
Yet let your sleep for this one night be sound;
I do forgive him!'

The worst of madmen is a saint run mad

Source: SATIRES ("The Sixth Epistle of the First Book of Horace," Line 27)
Author: Alexander Pope (1688-1744)
First published: 1738
Type of work: Satirical poem

Context: In this poetic epistle, dedicated to William Murray, later Lord Mansfield, Pope says to his friend that some people subscribe to the notion of Horace, as translated by Richard Creech, "Not to admire, is all the art I know,/ To make men happy, and to keep them so." Pope, on the other hand, suggests that one can be led by such a thought to fear either to admire or to express admiration. He admits that the pleasures of the world are vain, but that one should not let life be guided by fear of admiring or desiring them. Pope, a true son of neoclassical, eighteenth century English culture, makes a case for the middle course, for going to neither extreme in desiring or disdaining worldly vanities:

> If weak the pleasure that from these can spring,
> The fear to want them is as weak a thing:
> Whether we dread, or whether we desire,
> In either case, believe me, we admire:
> Whether we joy or grieve, the same the curse,
> Surprised at better, or surprised at worse.
> Thus good or bad, to one extreme betray
> Th' unbalanced mind, and snatch the man away;
> For Virtue's self may too much zeal be had;
> **The worst of madmen is a saint run mad.**

Ye shall be as gods, knowing good and evil

Source: GENESIS 3:5
Author: Unknown
First transcribed: c.1000-300 B.C.
Type of work: Religious history and law

Context: According to the Hebraic story of creation, after the heavens and earth had been created and the living things of the earth were growing and abounding according to the laws of their nature, God created man and placed him in a garden called Eden. Adam and Eve, the first man and woman, in the bliss of Eden were allowed the fruit of every tree with the exception of one, the tree of the knowledge of good and evil, the fruit of which they were not to eat on the penalty of death. Satan, disguised as a serpent and intent upon disgracing God and leading mankind into sin and hence to death and destruction, approached the woman, who had not

1204

heard God's command concerning the tree of good and evil directly, in order to lead her into disobedience. When questioned by the serpent about the trees from which they could eat, Eve repeated the command of God, which she had perhaps heard from Adam. The serpent's unassuming question is his first major step toward Eve's psychological defeat. His second step is his reply to her answer:

> . . . Ye shall not surely die:
> For God doth know that in the day ye eat thereof, then your eyes shall be opened, and ye **shall be as gods, knowing good and evil.**

The years like great black oxen tread the world

Source: THE COUNTESS CATHLEEN (Concluding lines)
Author: William Butler Yeats (1865-1939)
First published: 1892
Type of work: Dramatic tragedy

Context: The play is laid "in Ireland in old times," during famine. Penniless, the people sell their souls to demons in order to buy food. But Countess Cathleen, because this is her land and these her people, sells all her possessions to help the poor. The demons steal her money and prevent her from helping her peasants. Then to keep the people from the demons, she forces the demons to return the peasants' souls in exchange for hers, which she is willing to sell. After the bargain, "she has only minutes" to live, as one of the demons says. When she dies, she is forgiven in Heaven for her impiety because she tried to help the peasants. After the Angel has promised forgiveness for the Countess, Oona, her foster-mother, concludes the play with the following lines:

> OONA
> Tell them who walk upon the floor of peace
> That I would die and go to her I love;
> **The years like great black oxen tread the world,**
> And God the herdsman goads them on behind,
> And I am broken by their passing feet.

The years which certain people call a "certain age"

Source: BEPPO: A VENETIAN STORY (Stanza 22)
Author: George Gordon, Lord Byron (1788-1824)
First published: 1818
Type of work: Narrative poem in mock-heroic style

Context: Beppo was written in 1817, a year before the first canto of *Don Juan.* Both poems are in ottava rima (eight-line stanzas rhyming a b a b a b c c), both are satires written in mock-heroic style, and both are modeled on a poem by John Hookham Frere (1769-1846) published under the pseudonym "Whistlecraft" (1817-1818). The very slight plot in *Beppo* serves merely as a peg on which to hang satire. Beppo, a Venetian gentleman, returns to Venice in Carnival time, disguised as a Turk, and confronts his wife, Laura, and her "cavalier servente" (gallant or lover), the Count. The outcome is quite different from that in *Othello:* ". . . since those times was never known a/ Husband whom mere suspicion could inflame/ To suffocate a wife no more than twenty,/ Because she had a cavalier servente" (Stanza 17). Beppo and the Count are reconciled over a cup of coffee, and Laura is once more the submissive wife. The lines quoted refer to Laura. In context they read.

> She was not old, nor young, nor at **the years**
> **Which certain people call a "certain age,"**
> Which yet the most uncertain age appears.

Yeoman's service

Source: HAMLET (Act V, sc. ii, l. 36)
Author: William Shakespeare (1564-1616)
First published: 1603
Type of work: Dramatic tragedy

Context: Prince Hamlet of Denmark accidentally slays Polonius, chief councilor of King Claudius, thinking him to be the king. Claudius, alarmed, sends Hamlet to England and plots to have him executed upon his arrival. One night on board ship en route to England, Hamlet cannot sleep. He has a premonition of evil. He rises in the dark, goes to the cabin of his traveling companions who know the king's intent, and steals their royal commission to deliver him to death. Hamlet returns to his own cabin and prepares a fake commission, consigning his false companions to that death. He tells Horatio how he performed the trick.

> HAMLET
> Being thus benetted round with villainies—
> •   •   •
>   I sat me down,
> Devised a new commission, wrote it fair—
> I once did hold it as our statists do,
> A baseness to write fair, and labored much
> How to forget that learning, but sir, now
> It did me **yeoman's service**—
> •   •   •

Yet marked I where the bolt of Cupid fell

Source: A MIDSUMMER NIGHT'S DREAM (Act II, sc. i, l. 165)
Author: William Shakespeare (1564-1616)
First published: 1600
Type of work: Dramatic comedy

Context: Titania and Oberon, Queen and King of the fairies, argue because Titania will not give to Oberon a little changeling boy for his page. In order to make Titania obey him, Oberon sends Puck, also called Robin Goodfellow, on a journey to get the juice of "a little western flower" which "Before, milk-white; now purple with love's wound, / And maidens call it, love-in-idleness." The juice from this marvelous flower, when touched to the sleeping eyelids, will make the person fall madly in love with the "next live creature that it sees." Oberon's knowledge of this magical flower came when he saw Cupid, "Flying between the cold moon and the earth," fire his "love-shaft." Cupid missed his target, but Oberon watched:

OBERON

. . .

Yet marked I where the bolt of Cupid fell.
It fell upon a little western flower;
Before, milk-white; now purple with love's wound,
And maidens call it, love-in-idleness.

. . .

Yet the light of a whole life dies when love is done

Source: THE NIGHT HAS A THOUSAND EYES (Stanza 2)
Author: Francis William Bourdillon (1852-1921)
First published: 1890
Type of work: Lyric poem

Context: Francis William Bourdillon develops his short poem "The Night has a Thousand Eyes" through the use of analogy. As "the bright world dies/ With the dying sun," so "life dies/ When love is done." The poet magnifies the importance of his theme by introducing elements of the vast universe—the "thousand eyes" of the night, "the dying sun," and "the bright world." But just as the suns of other solar systems are useless in furnishing light to man's bright world, so man's reason, "the thousand eyes" of the mind, is incapable of furnishing the will to live after love has disappeared from man's heart. The short poem is as follows:

The night has a thousand eyes,
And the day but one;

1207

Yet the light of the bright world dies
With the dying sun.

The mind has a thousand eyes,
  And the heart but one;
Yet the light of a whole life dies
When love is done.

Yet this will go onward the same though dynasties pass

Source: IN TIME OF "THE BREAKING OF NATIONS" (Stanza II)
Author: Thomas Hardy (1840-1928)
First published: 1917
Type of work: Lyric poem

Context: Hardy uses several simple contrasts to make his point that nations and empires, for all their grandness and glory, are artificial things, and, like all things made by the hand of man, they will pass away. Only the common ways of everyday life are really of permanent duration. The plowman driving his horse slowly up and down the field, the smoldering of heaps of uprooted weeds, the young man walking with his lover, truly represent humanity and the activity which is fundamental to life.

Only a man harrowing clods
  In a slow silent walk
With an old horse that stumbles and nods
  Half asleep as they stalk.

Only thin smoke without flame
  From the heaps of couch-grass:
Yet this will go onward the same
  Though Dynasties pass.

Yond Cassius has a lean and hungry look

Source: JULIUS CAESAR (Act I, sc. ii, l. 194)
Author: William Shakespeare (1564-1616)
First published: 1623
Type of work: Dramatic tragedy

Context: Julius Caesar, returning from the games and festivities which mark his victory over his political rival Pompey, catches sight of Cassius conversing with Brutus. Cassius, a disgruntled man, jealous of Caesar's fame and accomplishments, is sounding out Brutus, a friend of Caesar, as a possible co-conspirator against Caesar. Although Caesar does not

1208

hear what Cassius and Brutus are discussing, he is struck by the intensity and brooding countenance of Cassius. He calls his young friend and companion, Mark Antony, to his side for consultation. (Shakespeare improved upon the original saying found in the chapter on Antony in *Plutarch's Lives:* Plutarch phrased it less aptly, thus: " 'It is not,' said Caesar, 'these well-fed, long-haired men that I fear, but the pale and the hungry-looking'; meaning Brutus and Cassius.")

CAESAR

Let me have men about me that are fat,
Sleek-headed men, and such as sleep a nights.
Yond Cassius has a lean and hungry look;
He thinks too much. Such men are dangerous.

You are old, Father William

Source: THE OLD MAN'S COMFORTS AND HOW HE GAINED THEM (Line 1)
Author: Robert Southey (1774-1843)
First published: 1799
Type of work: Didactic poem

Context: In Southey's unrelentingly moral poem a young man asks Father William why, though old, he is content, cheerful at the thought of death, and spry. Father William replies that he spent his youth thinking of his age, "abused not my health," "thought of the future, whatever I did," and "remember'd my God!" Were it not so easily parodied, the poem would long since have been forgotten. One of the parodies, Lewis Carroll's (1832-1898) in *Alice's Adventure's in Wonderland* (1865), is far better known than the original. Carroll's poem opens: " 'You are old, Father William,' the young man said,/ 'And your hair has become very white;/ And yet you incessantly stand on your head—/ Do you think, at your age, it is right?' " Southey's poem begins:

"You are old, Father William," the young man cried,
"The few locks which are left you are grey;
You are hale, Father William, a hearty old man,
Now tell me the reason, I pray."

"In the days of my youth," Father William replied,
"I remember'd that youth would fly fast,
And abused not my health and my vigour at first,
That I never might need them at last."

You can ask me for anything you like, except time

Source: THE CORSICAN (March 11, 1803)
Author: Napoleon Bonaparte (1769-1821)
First published: 1910
Type of work: Diary or journal

Context: R. M. Johnston, in *The Corsican,* has compiled from Napoleon's own words a journal-account of the French emperor's life. Rising from the ranks as an artillery officer, he in time achieved absolute dictatorial power. In August, 1802, he was made consul for life and received the right to choose his successor. Hereditary monarchy was thus on the point of being re-established, after his many solemn protestations to the contrary. In May, 1803, open hostilities resumed with England over Malta and the interpretation of the treaty of Amiens. Realizing the impending turn of events in March, Napoleon was anxious to court the friendship of Russia, lest a Russo-English alliance materialize. Consequently, he dispatched an aide, Chef de brigade Colbert, to Russia with overtures of peace. The orders read:

> . . . You will proceed to Russia. . . . In conversation you will emphasize the esteem in which Russians are held in Paris. . . . You will speak of the First Consul as very busy planning canals, starting manufactories, and working at matters of public education.
>
> Go, sir, gallop, and don't forget that the world was made in six days. **You can ask me for anything you like, except time.**

You can lead a horse to water but you can't make him drink

Source: THE PROVERBS OF JOHN HEYWOOD (Part I, chapter 11)
Author: John Heywood (1497?-1580?)
First published: 1546
Type of work: Gnomic poetry

Context: The author is quoting all the proverbs he knows to demonstrate that there is wisdom in the oft-quoted maxims against early marriage. Now he is telling a story about a young husband whom he advised to leave his wife and go back to his uncle. As soon as this young husband gets back home, he apologizes to his uncle for having disobeyed him. The uncle, however, is not so forgiving. He quotes the old proverb, "Follow pleasure, and then will pleasure flee;/ Flee pleasure, and pleasure will follow thee." Thus the young man erred in running too hotly after pleasure. In disobeying the older man's advice, the young man, the uncle says, merely proves an old proverb, one that is widely employed in folk speech, with

1210

numerous variations. In America, for example, Emerson has the variant: "One man may lead a horse to water, but ten canna gar him drink." Heywood's version is this:

A man may well bring a horse to the water,
But he cannot make him drink without he will.

You can't make a silk purse out of a sow's ear

Source: POLITE CONVERSATION, DIALOGUE II
Author: Jonathan Swift (1667-1745)
First published: 1738(?)
Type of work: Satire

Context: Jonathan Swift, Dean of St. Patrick's, Dublin, and probably the most brilliant satirist in all English literature, writes a preface and three dialogues purporting to instruct people of fashion in polite conversation. The dialogues consist of plotless chit-chat employing a staggering number of old adages and other clichés. The saying about the inability to make a silk purse out of a sow's ear is one of many in English indicating that you cannot make anything valuable from worthless materials; one parallel is in George Herbert's *Jacula Prudentum:* "Of a pig's tail you can never make a good shaft"—or arrow. Sitting at the dinner table and discussing the recently departed Sir John Linger, speakers say as follows:

COL. ATWIT

I was once with him and some other company over a bottle; and, egad, he fell asleep, and snored so hard, that we thought he was driving his hogs to market.

MR. NEVEROUT

Why what! you can have no more of a cat than her skin; **you can't make a silk purse out of a sow's ear.**

You have hit the nail on the head

Source: GARGANTUA AND PANTAGRUEL (Book III, chapter 34)
Author: François Rabelais (1495-1553)
First published: 1532-1564
Type of work: Mock heroic chronicle

Context: Panurge, the friend of Pantagruel, is seeking advice from men of various professions on whether or not he should marry. After hearing all their arguments, he is still undecided. To Rondibilis, the physician who has been giving a lengthy, allegorical discourse on cuckoldry, Panurge gives the proverb which is widespread:

> . . . Your words being translated from the Clapperdudgeons (beggars' slang) to plain English, do signify that it is not very inexpedient that I marry, and that I should not care for being a cuckold. **You have** there **hit the nail on the head.** . . .

You lie in your throat

Source: HENRY IV, PART II (Act I, sc. ii, 1. 97)
Author: William Shakespeare (1564-1616)
First published: 1600
Type of work: Historical drama

Context: Falstaff is walking down the street with his page, who carries his sword and buckler. The page has just returned from consulting a doctor about Falstaff's health and he jokes with Falstaff about the doctor's report. Falstaff blusters, as usual. The Lord Chief Justice approaches, but Falstaff, in pique, will not see him. The Justice addresses Falstaff, but Falstaff, through his page, tells the Justice that he is deaf. The Justice has his servant pull at Falstaff's elbow; whereupon Falstaff berates him for being a beggar at a time when the king needs soldiers badly. Then master and the servant bluster at each other:

FALSTAFF
Why sir, did I say you were an honest man? Setting my knighthood and my soldiership aside, I had lied in my throat if I had said so.

SERVANT
I pray you sir, then set your knighthood and your soldiership aside, and give me leave to tell you, **you lie in your throat,** if you say I am any other than an honest man.

You may fire when you are ready, Gridley

Source: AUTOBIOGRAPHY
Author: Admiral George Dewey (1837-1917)
First spoken: May 1, 1898
Type of work: Naval orders

Context: As part of America's movement against Spanish forces, Dewey, commander of the U.S. Pacific Squadron, was ordered on April 25, 1898,

1212

to capture or destroy the Spanish Pacific fleet. The Spanish-American war had begun that month, following the Spanish sinking of the U.S. battleship *Maine* in Havana harbor. Dewey's force reached Luzon, the Philippines, on April 30, and in two engagements on the following day off Cavité, near Manila, destroyed the whole Spanish fleet. As his ships approached the enemy, in the early morning, Dewey called up to Captain Charles V. Gridley, who was stationed in the flagship's conning tower as gunnery spotter, giving him the order which has since become famous.

> At 5:41 Dewey looked up at the conning tower. In a calm voice of assurance, heard throughout the ship, he said: **"You may fire when you are ready, Gridley."**

You may go whistle for the rest

Source: DON QUIXOTE (Part I, Book III, chapter VI)
Author: Miguel de Cervantes Saavedra (1547-1616)
First published: 1605
Type of work: Satirical novel

Context: Sancho, in his efforts to prevent his master from going to investigate the noise made at a fulling mill where the hammers are pounding clay into the cloth to stiffen it, tells how a goatherd tires of his courting of a shepherdess. His new coolness inflames her and he has to flee from her, with his flock. At a river, there is a small boat with capacity for an oarsman and one goat, so the goatherd takes one across, returns for another, and another. Then Sancho pauses to ask Don Quixote:

> ". . . How many goats are got over already?" "Nay, how the devil can I tell!" replied Don Quixote. "There it is!" quoth Sancho, "did I not bid you keep count? On my word, the tale is at an end, and now **you may go whistle for the rest.**"

You shall not crucify mankind upon a cross of gold

Source: THE CROSS OF GOLD (Speech at the National Democratic Convention, Chicago, 1896)
Author: William Jennings Bryan (1860-1925)
First published: 1896
Type of work: Speech

Context: William Jennings Bryan's "The Cross of Gold" speech, delivered at the National Democratic Convention of 1896 in Chicago, was possibly the cause of his winning the presidential nomination of the party.

1213

In Congress Bryan had become a supporter of the silver-purchase act. At the convention he was asked to take charge of the debate in the final discussion of the party's platform. In his speech on that occasion Bryan first traces the history of the silver movement, showing its importance to this country. He then calls on the United States to take the lead in restoring bimetallism and not to have a gold standard simply because England has it. Attacking the defenders of the gold standard, Bryan concludes:

> . . . If they dare to come out in the open field and defend the gold standard as a good thing, we will fight them to the uttermost. Having behind us the producing masses of this nation and the world, supported by the commercial interests, the laboring interests, and the toilers everywhere, we will answer their demand for a gold standard by saying to them: You shall not press down upon the brow of labor this crown of thorns, **you shall not crucify mankind upon a cross of gold.**

You take my life when you do take the means whereby I live

Source: THE MERCHANT OF VENICE (Act IV, sc. i, ll. 376-377)
Author: William Shakespeare (1564-1616)
First published: 1600
Type of work: Dramatic comedy

Context: Portia, in defending Antonio against Shylock, argues that Shylock is indeed entitled to the pound of flesh that Antonio put as bond against the 3000 ducats he borrowed for his friend Bassanio. But she says that since there is nothing in the contract about any blood, if Shylock spills one drop of Christian blood his life will be forfeited. Shylock, realizing that his evil design has been frustrated, tries to recover his 3000 ducats, saying he will be satisfied. Portia, however, invoking a law against any alien who seeks the life of a citizen, tells Shylock that half his property is forfeited to Antonio and the other half to the state. Shylock protests against the severity of this law:

SHYLOCK
Nay, take my life and all, pardon not that.
You take my house, when you do take the prop
That doth sustain my house. **You take my life
When you do take the means whereby I live.**

1214

You throw the sand against the wind, and the wind blows it back again

Source: MOCK ON, MOCK ON, VOLTAIRE, ROUSSEAU (Stanza 1)
Author: William Blake (1757-1827)
First published: 1913
Type of work: Lyric poem

Context: This poem, found among the Rossetti manuscripts and not published until modern times, might be called a contrast between the religious view and the scientific view of life. To Blake, with his deeply mystical nature, Newton was often the symbol of a narrow rationalism, the creator of a mechanical picture of the world, and, with Locke, the destroyer of the "harmony and peace" of Eden, that is, of pre-industrial England. Voltaire and Rousseau were to Blake equally repellent figures, deists from the rationalistic era of the Enlightenment. In the poem, he is saying that their mockery of religion is as futile as the act of a man who throws a handful of sand against the wind, which merely blows back into his face the grains he has vainly hurled. The first and last stanzas of the poem are:

> Mock on, mock on, Voltaire, Rousseau;
> Mock on, mock on, 'tis all in vain!
> **You throw the sand against the wind,**
> **And the wind blows it back again.**
>
> . . .
>
> The Atoms of Democritus
> And Newton's Particles of Light
> Are sands upon the Red Sea shore,
> Where Israel's tents do shine so bright.

You would pluck out the heart of my mystery

Source: HAMLET (Act III, sc. ii, ll. 380-381)
Author: William Shakespeare (1564-1616)
First published: 1603
Type of work: Dramatic tragedy

Context: Prince Hamlet learns that his father was murdered by his father's brother Claudius, who is now king, and that his mother, Queen Gertrude, was adulterous with him. Hamlet swears to avenge his father's murder. First he must confirm his uncle's guilt. Hamlet arranges to have some actors play a scene like the murder of his father before Claudius and the court. Claudius betrays his guilt when he abruptly stops the play and leaves the hall, followed by his startled and confused court. Both Claudius and Gertrude are conscience-stricken and disturbed by the play.

Now Gertrude sends two courtiers, Rosencrantz and Guildenstern, to summon Hamlet to her chamber. Hamlet has only contempt for these false friends. He snatches up a recorder from a passing musician.

HAMLET
. . . Will you play upon this pipe?
It is as easy as lying; . . . these are the stops.

GUILDENSTERN
But these cannot I command to any utterance of harmony; I have not the skill.

HAMLET
Why look you now how unworthy a thing you make of me. You would play upon me, you would seem to know my stops, **you would pluck out the heart of my mystery,** you would sound me. . . .

You'll be a man, my son!

Source: IF (Last line)
Author: Rudyard Kipling (1865-1936)
First published: 1910
Type of work: Didactic poem

Context: "If" ranks with Longfellow's "Psalm of Life" in being quotable; almost every line has become a familiar phrase. For many years graduating classes in America voted it their favorite poem. Developed through a long series of conditional clauses, the poem establishes the qualities that Kipling and his contemporaries considered essential for the type of man they admired: a man imperturbable, self-contained, and self-reliant, calm in both triumph and disaster; and, above all, capable of getting his job done. Such were the men who built the British Empire, and this was the sort of poem admired when poetry was unashamedly didactic.

If you can dream—and not make dreams your master;
    If you can think—and not make thoughts your aim;
If you can meet with Triumph and Disaster
    And treat those two impostors just the same;

. . .

If you can fill the unforgiving minute
    With sixty seconds' worth of distance run,
Yours is the Earth and everything that's in it,
    And—which is more—**you'll be a Man, my son!**

The young are slaves to dreams; the old servants
of regrets

Source: ANTHONY ADVERSE (Chapter 31)
Author: Hervey Allen (1889-1949)
First published: 1933
Type of work: Novel

Context: Anthony Adverse, an apprentice to the prominent merchant, Mr. Bonnyfeather, is sent to Cuba to collect a long-overdue debt. While in Cuba as the guest of the hospitable Signore Carlo Cibo, he meets a monk, Brother François, who has a great effect on him. Anthony sees in the monk's countenance a radiant beauty of character; he is spellbound by the story of his dedication to a life of self-denial. Later on, Signore Cibo tells Anthony that Brother François is a dangerous man. His efforts to live his religion complicate things, and his sympathies for slaves have upset the authorities. Since Cibo is a convincing pragmatist, Anthony cannot protest entirely. Yet he confesses that the monk had stirred something in him of which he had not been aware. Cibo replies that perhaps the monk is not as unique and extraordinary as Anthony thinks. Perhaps it is youth which has been affected. Then Cibo adds philosophically:

. . . The only time you really live fully is from thirty to sixty. . . . No, **the young are slaves to dreams; the old servants of regrets.** Only the middle-aged have all their five senses in the keeping of their wits. . . .

The young man who has not wept is a savage, and the old man
who will not laugh is a fool

Source: DIALOGUES IN LIMBO (Chapter III)
Author: George Santayana (1863-1952)
First published: 1906
Type of work: Philosophic dialogue

Context: Santayana develops his theme by means of a dialogue among several shades, including Democritus and Alcibiades, and the spirit of a Stranger from earth. The Greek philosopher Democritus, an exponent of atomism, argues that man's madness —the opinion that he has of things around him—is natural but that philosophy can teach him the true nature of things. Supporting Democritus' theory, the Stranger from earth tells the story of a child who had given beautiful names to flowers and plants and who then burst out crying when a botanist told him that they were only flowers and plants. The Athenian general Alcibiades, presented in the flower of his youth, says he would have cried too if he had seen his moments of crowning triumph as only clouds of atoms. The shock of seeing reality as it is, Democritus adds, is natural and man has a right to weep.

He concedes the necessity of the illusion in which man encloses reality; yet, he says, philosophy has the duty of teaching the truth. He then says to Alcibiades:

Has not my own heart been pierced? Shed your tears, my son, shed your tears. **The young man who has not wept is a savage, and the old man who will not laugh is a fool.**

Young men are fitter to invent than to judge

Source: THE ESSAYS OR COUNSELS (XLII, "Of Youth and Age")
Author: Sir Francis Bacon (1561-1626)
First published: 1625
Type of work: Moral essay

Context: Bacon, as he writes in this little essay, is neither for nor against youth. He says, for example, ". . . the invention of young men is more lively than that of old; and imaginations stream into their minds better, and as it were more divinely." He sees that there are advantages to youth, as there are advantages to age.

After commenting on different temperaments in both young and old, Bacon asserts that "the virtues of either age may correct the defects of both." While in the bare quotation under discussion it may seem that Bacon is disparaging youth, the context proves that he is not:

. . . **Young men are fitter to invent than to judge;** fitter for execution than counsel; and fitter for new projects than for settled business. For the experience of age, in things that fall within the compass of it, directeth them; but in new things, abuseth them. The errors of young men are the ruin of business; but the errors of aged men amount but to this, that more might have been done, or sooner.

Your intentions are honorable

Source: THE BARBER OF SEVILLE (Act IV, sc. vi)
Author: Pierre de Beaumarchais (1732-1799)
First published: 1775
Type of work: Dramatic comedy

Context: Count Almaviva, a Spanish grandee, in a vain effort to be with his lady love, the fair Rosine, follows her from Madrid to Seville and assumes,

1218

first, the guise of a soldier named Lindor, and then that of a music teacher named Alonzo, but the most he accomplishes is to slip her a letter. The cause of his failure is Dr. Bartholo, the crafty old guardian, who plans to marry his ward himself. Even with the able assistance of Figaro, Barber of Seville, Count Almaviva is thwarted at every turn. At last his efforts seem crowned with success when he and Figaro manage to enter the doctor's house via a window and come face to face with Rosine. However, Rosine has been poisoned against her lover by the insidious Bartholo, who has convinced her that she is to be snatched away and sold to the unknown Count Almaviva. When, therefore, the count, known to her as Lindor, makes advances, she spurns them. The crowning insult, she implies, would be to have him pretend that his intentions are honorable. The quoted line appears in the following dialogue:

COUNT

You, Rosine! the companion of an unfortunate man without fortune, without birth! . . .

ROSINE

Birth, fortune! Don't talk of things that come by chance, and if you assure me that **your intentions are honourable. . . .**

Your old men shall dream dreams

Source: JOEL 2:28
Author: Joel
First transcribed: 1000-100 B.C.
Type of work: Religious prophecy

Context: The prophet Joel, reminding his listeners that their crops have been wiped out by drought, locusts and other insects, urges them to turn to the Lord and repent. He promises that God will restore all that they have lost. After they have become reconciled with God, there will be an outpouring of the Spirit, in which all of the chosen race, not merely the prophets, will have ecstatic religious experiences:

And it shall come to pass afterward, that I will pour out my Spirit upon all flesh; and your sons and your daughters shall prophesy, **your old men shall dream dreams,** your young men shall see visions:
And also upon the servants and upon the handmaids in those days will I pour out my Spirit.

1219

You're a better man than I am, Gunga Din!

Source: GUNGA DIN (Last line)
Author: Rudyard Kipling (1865-1936)
First published: 1890
Type of work: Narrative poem

Context: In "Gunga Din" Kipling tells of the water boy who, throughout the most violent battle, is always near whoever needs him to give his precious drink. And yet, very little credit is ever given poor Gunga Din, who has, if ever there was one, a thankless task. Nevertheless, Gunga Din gives up his life in serving those who perpetually scorn him. Kipling declares that, because Din is a heathen, he will surely be giving water to the roasted souls in Hell. Yet the British soldier, who is the speaker in the poem, cannot but admire the unassuming courage of the poor water boy.

> 'E'll be squattin' on the coals
> Givin' drink to poor damned souls,
> An' I'll get a swig in hell from Gunga Din!
> Yes, Din! Din! Din!
> You Lazarrushian-leather Gunga Din!
> Though I've belted you an' flayed you,
> By the livin' Gawd that made you,
> **You're a better man than I am, Gunga Din!**

You're a poor benighted 'eathen but a first-class fightin' man

Source: FUZZY-WUZZY (Stanza 4)
Author: Rudyard Kipling (1865-1936)
First published: 1890
Type of work: Dramatic monologue

Context: Typical of Kipling is his respect for any man who can put up a good fight. In "Fuzzy-Wuzzy" he extolls the courage of the natives of the Anglo-Egyptian Soudan. In 1884 the British lost a battle against the Soudanese, and this poem is written out of respect for the fighting zeal and ability of the natives whom the British Expeditionary Force had to face.

> 'E rushes at the smoke when we let drive,
> An', before we know, 'e's 'ackin' at our 'ead;
> 'E's all 'ot sand an' ginger when alive,
> An' e''s generally shammin' when 'e's dead.
> 'E's a daisy, 'e's a ducky, 'e's a lamb!
> 'E's a injia-rubber idiot on the spree,
> 'E's the on'y thing that doesn't give a damn
> For a Regiment o' British Infantree!

So 'ere's *to* you, Fuzzy-Wuzzy, at your 'ome in the Soudan;
You're a poor benighted 'eathen but a first-class fightin'
man; . . .

You're the goods

Source: THE VOICE OF THE CITY ("From Each According to His Ability")
Author: O. Henry (William Sydney Porter, 1862-1910)
First published: 1908
Type of work: Short story

Context: Vuyning, a well-dressed man of leisure who lives on his father's money and spends his time at the club, is bored with the other club members and is disheartened at having his marriage proposals rejected by his sweetheart. While strolling down the street, he is accosted by a crook, Emerson, also known as Rowdy the Dude, who appeals to him for help. Emerson's problem is his clothes: no matter how much he pays for them, he never looks good in what he wears. He has turned to Vuyning because he considers him to be the best-dressed man he has seen. Vuyning, delighted to have a change from the boring atmosphere of his club, gives Emerson advice on men's fashions, then takes him to the tailor. Five days later, Emerson, immaculately clothed, dines at the club with Vuyning and delights the latter's colleagues with his description of the West. The next day, before leaving for the West, Emerson thanks Vuyning for his help with his clothes:

"I've been looking for some guy to put me on the right track for years," said Emerson. **"You're the goods,** duty free, and halfway to the warehouse in a red wagon."

Youth is like spring, an over-praised season

Source: THE WAY OF ALL FLESH (Chapter 6)
Author: Samuel Butler (1835-1902)
First published: 1903
Type of work: Novel

Context: Butler examines the domestic situation he considers rather typical of the nineteenth century, in which the family is dominated by a tyrannical father who sustains himself with a mixture of self-righteousness and self-pity, while keeping his children bowed beneath a calculated persecution. His example early in the novel is the family of George Pontifex, who never tires of impressing his sons with the contrast between

1221

his own merits and their worthlessness. Inasmuch as so many young people, he feels, are reared in such harsh and unhealthy emotional climates, Butler asserts that youth is not the idyllic time many believe it.

> To me it seems that **youth is like spring, an over-praised season** —delightful if it happen to be a favoured one, but in practice very rarely favoured and more remarkable, as a general rule, for biting east winds than genial breezes. Autumn is the mellower season, and what we lose in flowers we more than gain in fruits. Fontenelle at the age of ninety, being asked what was the happiest time of his life, said he did not know that he had ever been much happier than he then was, but that perhaps his best years had been those when he was between fifty-five and seventy-five, and Dr. Johnson placed the pleasures of old age far higher than those of youth.

The youth of America is their oldest tradition

Source: THE WOMAN OF NO IMPORTANCE (Act I)
Author: Oscar Wilde (1856-1900)
First published: 1894
Type of work: Dramatic comedy

Context: Lady Hunstanton has invited several guests to her country home, among them Hester Worsley, a young American woman who had entertained Lady Hunstanton's son in Boston when he was visiting there. Before the appearance of the hostess, Lady Caroline Pontefract tells Hester a little about the other guests. Hester says she has already met Gerald Arbuthnot, a bank employee, and found him charming. When Gerald arrives, he announces that he has been offered the job of secretary to Lord Illingworth. Gerald then invites Hester to take a stroll, and shortly after their departure, Lord Illingworth arrives. Illingworth makes several uncomplimentary remarks about America, finally commenting that when bad Americans die they go to America. The remark makes another guest, Kelvil, a member of Parliament, say to him: "I am afraid you don't appreciate America, Lord Illingworth. It is a very remarkable country, especially considering its youth."

LORD ILLINGWORTH
"The youth of America is their oldest tradition. It has been going on now for three hundred years. To hear them talk one would imagine they were in their first childhood. As far as civilization goes they are in their second."

Youth, that's now so bravely spending, will beg a penny by and by

Source: ALL LOVELY THINGS (Stanza 1)
Author: Conrad Aiken (1889-   )
First published: 1916
Type of work: Lyric poem

Context: This poem has a common theme: the recognition of the passing of time and the transiency of all things. Involved in this theme is a twofold concern: speculation upon fate and memory of the past. The first two verses are concerned with mutability. The poet's attention is upon the lovely aspects of life. "All lovely things will fade and die," he says. Fine ladies and the goldenrod will fade. "The sweetest flesh and flowers are rotten/ And cobwebs tent the brightest head." Youth which is so active and lively now will in time be spent. With a nostalgic pain the poet longs for the past to return. "Come back, true love! Sweet youth, return!" Yet he is painfully aware that the past can never return and that even the present beauties must die. The poem begins with a statement of its theme:

> All lovely things will have an ending,
> All lovely things will fade and die,
> And **youth, that's now so bravely spending,**
> **Will beg a penny by and by.**

Youth's a stuff will not endure

Source: TWELFTH NIGHT (Act II, sc. iii, l. 53)
Author: William Shakespeare (1564-1616)
First published: 1623
Type of work: Dramatic comedy

Context: The hand of the young, beautiful, and wealthy Countess Olivia is sought by a foolish knight, Sir Andrew Aguecheek. Sir Toby Belch, Olivia's uncle, encourages, for his own bibulous and financial ends, Sir Andrew's quite hopeless suit. Sir Andrew, recently persuaded to remain in attendance on Olivia for another month, is drinking and carousing with Sir Toby late at night. They are joined by Feste, Olivia's jester, who is prevailed upon by the two tipsters to sing a love song. This is the second stanza:

> FESTE
> What is love? 'Tis not hereafter;
> Present mirth hath present laughter,

What's to come is still unsure.
In delay there lies no plenty,
Then come kiss me sweet and twenty.
Youth's a stuff will not endure.

Acknowledgments
and Copyright Notices

Appreciative acknowledgments are made to the following publishers, authors, agents, and literary trustees for permission to reprint copyrighted material included in this book.

1225

1226

AUTHOR INDEX

I

To fish in troubled waters, 1034

HENRY, O.
Ethics of Pig, The
As Busy as a one-armed man with the nettle-rash pasting on wall-paper, 44
Octopus Marooned, The
It was beautiful and simple as all truly great swindles are, 512
Rolling Stones
Straw vote only shows which way the hot air blows, A, 917
Strictly Business
Except in street cars one should never be unnecessarily rude to a lady, 223
Voice of the City, The
You're the goods, 1221

HENRY, PATRICK
Speech in the Virginia Convention of Delegates
Give me liberty, or give me death!, 289
Speech on the Stamp Act, House of Burgesses
If this be treason, make the most of it, 469

HERACLITUS OF EPHESUS
Fragments of Heraclitus
There is nothing permanent except change, 969

HERBERT, GEORGE
Jacula Prudentum
For want of a nail, 268
Half the world knows not how the other half lives, 332
He who lies with the dogs, riseth with fleas, 364
Reason lies between the spur and the bridle, 824
Whose house is of glass must not throw stones, 1170
Temple, The
Love bade me welcome, 596
Methoughts I heard one calling, "Child"; and I replied, "My Lord.", 634
Only a sweet and virtuous soul, like seasoned timber, never gives, 747
Who cannot live on twenty pound a year cannot on forty, 1161

HERODOTUS
History of the Persian Wars
Long arm of the law, The, 588

HERRICK, ROBERT
Hesperides |
Gather ye rosebuds while ye may, 284
Here a little child I stand heaving up my either hand, 375
Liquefaction of her clothes, The, 577
Sweet disorder in the dress kindles in clothes a wantonness, A, 928

HEYWOOD, JOHN
Proverbs of John Heywood, The
All is well that ends well, 20
Beggars should not be choosers, 82
Better late than never, 90
Butter would not melt in her mouth, 121
Fat is in the fire, The, 235
Fear may force a man to cast beyond the moon, 242
Half a loaf is better than none, 331
Haste makes waste, 342
Hold their noses to the grindstone, 386
I know which side my bread is buttered on, 441
It's an ill wind that blows no good, 519
Look before you leap, 590
Love me, love my dog, 599
Make hay while the sun shines, 606
Many hands make light work, 620
More the merrier, The, 650
Neither fish nor flesh, 680
New broom sweeps clean, A, 684
One good turn deserves another, 738
Out of the frying pan into the fire, 756
Penny for your thoughts, A, 771
Rome was not built in a day, 838
There is no fire without some smoke, 961
Time and tide wait for no man, 1021
To tell tales out of school, 1041
Two heads are better than one, 1065
When the steed is stolen shut the stable door, 1148

You can lead a horse to water but you can't make him drink, 1210

HILLYER, ROBERT
Thermopylae
Men lied to them, and so they went to die, 628

HIPPOCRATES
Aphorisms
Life is short, and the art long, 567

HITLER, ADOLF
Mein Kampf
Big lie, A, 93

HOBBES, THOMAS
Leviathan
Words are wise men's counters, 1195

HODGSON, RALPH
Eve
Oh, had our simple Eve seen through the make-believe!. 727
Time, You Old Gipsy Man
Time, you old gipsy man, will you not stay, 1024

HOLMES, OLIVER WENDELL
Brahmin Caste of New England, The
Brahmin caste of New England, The, 107
Chambered Nautilus, The
Build thee more stately mansions, O my soul, 113
Deacon's Masterpiece, The
Wonderful one-hoss shay, The, 1192
Last Leaf, The
Last leaf upon the tree, The, 543
My Aunt
One sad, ungathered rose, 743
Old Ironsides
Aye, tear her tattered ensign down!, 63

HOME, JOHN
Douglas
Like Douglas conquer, or like Douglas die, 573

HOMER
Iliad, The
Achilles absent was Achilles still, 5
First in banquets, but the last in fight, The, 250
Gods! How the son degenerates from the sire!, 305
Green old age, A, 323
Noble mind disdains not to repent, A, 694
Not to be flung aside are the glorious gifts of the gods, 701
Plough the watery deep, 785
She moves a goddess, and she looks a queen!, 861
Unwept, unhonoured, uninterred he lies!, 1080
Whose little body lodged a mighty mind, 1171
Words, sweet as honey, 1195
Odyssey, The
Honest business never blush to tell, An, 390
Human form divine, The, 403
In the lap of the gods, 488
Reigned the sceptered monarch of the dead, 825
Twice-told tale, A, 1063
Welcome the coming, speed the parting guest, 1118

HOOD, THOMAS
Past and Present
I remember, I remember the house where I was born, 447
Song of the Shirt, The
Woman sat, in unwomanly rags, plying her needle and thread, A, 1189

HOPE, LAURENCE
Less Than the Dust
Less than the dust, beneath thy chariot wheel, 553

HOPKINS, GERARD MANLEY
God's Grandeur
World is charged with the grandeur of God. The. 1197
Pied Beauty
Glory be to God for dappled things, 293
Terrible Sonnets, The
Frightful, sheer, no-man-fathomed, 276

HORACE
Ars Poetica
Homer himself hath been observed to nod, 390

IX

AUTHOR INDEX

XV

XXIV